Solomon's Proof

And what rough beast, its hour come round at last,
Slouches towards Bethlehem to be born?
--William Butler Yeats, *The Second Coming*, 1920

Solomon's Proof:

A Psycho-Spiritual Journey to World Consciousness

As recorded, transcribed, and written by

Rashan Barcusé

RABBONAI PRESS
Boulder, Colorado

Copyright © 2007-8 by Rashan Barcusé

All rights reserved. Published in the United States by Rabbonai Press.

To contact the publisher, or for copies of this book use the form available at: www.SolomonsProof.com

ISBN 978-0-615-18537-8

This book is a psycho-spiritual memoir that reflects the integrative theories of C. G. Jung and the spiritual practices of the great Yoga masters. Names, characters, places, and incidents are taken from a combination of waking and dreaming states, including meditations and visions.

1st edition, December 2008

2nd edition, November 2024

Cover photography by J.B. and cover design by J.S., based on a concept by R.B.

Note: The Hebrew word השלמה (Hash'•la•mah), which appears on the cover, spine, and title page, and in the chapter headers, is translated as conciliation, integration, completion, or to make whole again, depending upon the context. It is derived from the same root word as shalom and Solomon.

Preface

To my father, a master of verbal, mathematical, and abstract reasoning and symbology. To my mother, for her nurturing and love of the theatre. To both of them, for their loving nature—until I was an adult I never knew the rarity of the love and empowerment you gave me.

This book is the result of an unusual collaboration with my friend and teacher, Michael David Solomon. I have used extensive footnotes and appendices, including Michael's own commentary, to elucidate meanings in and remove ambiguities from his teachings. While some of these annotations may seem elementary, as time passes I expect that they will take on greater significance in aiding future generations' understanding of the customs and events from this historical milieu. However, do not let the ubiquitous nature of the footnotes serve as a distraction from the flow of the story: you may find that returning to them after you have completed each chapter is the best of both worlds.

Please be aware that *many of these footnotes were added years after the events that they are designed to inform*, and often refer to either later editions of supporting documents than were available at the time these dialogues took place, or to information that Michael provided me during our many editing sessions, to frame the discussions I had captured on tape. Additionally, all quotations from the Christian *Bible* refer to the King James Version unless otherwise noted, for reasons that shall become apparent later in this book.

Passages from Michael's journals, which he gave me during the latter stages of our editing, were added after he had reviewed most of the manuscript.

It is my belief that any questions you may have concerning the veracity of any statements and/or events in this book will be answered within the next few years by events that we will witness and in which we will all participate.

Rashan Barcusé
Boulder, Colorado
December, 2008

Table of Contents

Preface	ix
Table of Contents	xi
Invocation	xiii
Prologue	xv
Chapter 1 – The Meeting	1
Chapter 2 – A Plan	31
Chapter 3 – The Charter	72
Chapter 4 – Friends	116
Chapter 5 – The Torus	149
Chapter 6 – Television	191
Chapter 7 – Yoga	228
Chapter 8 – Dreams	270
Chapter 9 – Pastels	324
Chapter 10 – Radio	355
Chapter 11 – Transcendence	386
Chapter 12 – Resurrection	421
Epilogue – Symbols of Integration	457
Appendix 1 – Excerpts from the Home Rule Charter	464
Appendix 2 – Prolegomena to Any Future Metaphysics	467
Appendix 3 – Introduction to Yoga	472
Appendix 4 – The Bard's Ghost	478
Appendix 5 – Chimera's Dream of Twelve Paintings	574
Appendix 6 – The Proof	579
Appendix 7 – Michael's Notes	609
Appendix 8 – The Anatomy of Treason	675

Invocation

[Chor.] O for a Muse of fire, that would ascend
The brightest heaven of invention,
A kingdom for a stage, princes to act,
And monarchs to behold the swelling scene!
--"William Shake-speare," Prologue to *Henry V*

A genuine first-hand religious experience ... is bound to be a heterodoxy to its witnesses, the prophet appearing as a mere lonely madman. If his doctrine prove contagious enough to spread to any others, it becomes a definite and labeled heresy. But if it then still prove contagious enough to triumph over persecution, it becomes itself an orthodoxy; and when a religion has become an orthodoxy, its day of inwardness is over: the spring is dry; the faithful live at second hand exclusively and stone prophets in their turn.
--William James, *The Varieties of Religious Experience*

We shall require a substantially new manner of thinking if mankind is to survive.
--Albert Einstein

One must start with the impossible in order to reach the possible.
--Hermann Hesse

By the roots of my hair some god got hold of me.
I sizzled in his blue volts like a desert prophet.
--Sylvia Plath, *The Hanging Man*

What a chimera then is Man! What a monster, what a chaos, what a contradiction, what a prodigy.
--Blaise Pascal, *Pensees*

If I am not for myself, then who will be for me? And if I am only for myself, then what am I? And if not now, when?
--Rabbi Hillel

Therefore you also must be ready; for the Son of Man is coming at an hour you do not expect.
--Matthew 24:44

Prologue

During the past generation, there has been much anticipation over the coming of the Millennium and the changes that this is predicted to bring. Many cultures have prophesies and myths concerning a great teacher, an avatar, the Messiah, Christ, Buddha, Imam Mahdi, et al., who is expected to appear and guide humankind through this period.

Specific individuals have also been named in this context, though at the time of this writing there appears to be no widespread movement to recognize any one of these spiritual beings as the fulfillment of such prophesies. Perhaps this is because there is little agreement as to what characteristics, signs, or powers such an individual would exhibit.

Expectations for such *siddhis*[1] range from godlike powers of omniscience, omnipotence, and omnipresence to those of a World Teacher capable of establishing the context for our present condition and framing the decisions that we must make in order to create a sustainable global society.

This book is not only an exploration of these ideas but a declaration that the Chosen One is on the planet at this time. As you shall read, it is appropriate that I use this term, "The Chosen One," since he is one of us, different only in the sense that his assignment is so singularly significant. By this I don't mean that he is a one-time event in the universe, as those who misunderstand the Christ story infer, but rather that he is the singularity of the moment in a regular (though rare) periodicity of such incarnations—what Michael terms in his proof[2] a "spiritual anomaly."

Of course, it is not my saying so that makes this true, for history shall judge this claim by its actual manifestation in space-time. Since you are one of the more than six billion people who shall make this history, I urge you to approach these pages with an open mind and compassionate heart, for in this disposition so shall you change the world.

Rashan Barcusé
Boulder, Colorado
December, 2008

---

[1] From Sanskrit: "Powers or accomplishments."
[2] See *Appendix 6 – The Proof*, or www.SolomonsProof.com.

1

The Meeting

"When the student is ready, the teacher appears."
--Ancient yogic saying

I realize that the claim I am about to make is outrageous, and one that raises questions concerning my sanity. Before this book was published in the form that you now see it, I approached a variety of agents and publishers with the manuscript, and though many found it compelling, they told me it couldn't be considered a work of non-fiction. Some even urged me to refine the story's dynamics and reposition it as fiction.

But I am not a novelist. I am simply trying to chronicle my real life relationship with a remarkable person. So, after these rebuffs, and at a loss as to how to move forward, I called a friend of mine, a writer and editor in New York City. He told me, "Look, readers are more sophisticated than they were back when Carlos Castaneda wrote *The Teachings of Don Juan*. They might have been led on for a book or two, believing that Carlos really met a Yaqui sorcerer. But sooner or later, everyone caught onto the idea that Don Juan was just a figment of Carlos' imagination, or perhaps his higher self. Readers are past that now. So, for you to go on in this day and age about some guy you claim is the Messiah, that's crazy. Nobody's going to go along with this. No matter what you claim, people will think it's fiction, some kind of delusion on your part. There's got to be some hitch. You can be ambiguous, but you've got to stay ahead of your readers and let them know that you know what they're thinking."

I mulled over his advice and wondered what kind of hitch there can be to reality? But as Castaneda described it in his series of books, to know Don Juan is to know a separate reality. And therein lies the wormhole to a different dimension: I assure you that I'm not crazy; I simply flip a switch and experience a reality different than the average couch potato, a reality even different than that experienced by the well-read or the adventurous.

2 » Solomon's Proof

So, what is this "separate reality," you ask? Is it really so different than everyone else's reality? And if so, is there any validity to it? I'll leave that for you to decide, after you've heard my story.

It starts in the spring of 1975. Given the number of people on planet Earth at that time, it was a one in four billion chance that I would meet such a person. But that was enough.

It was a Saturday, which meant forgetting about my day job as a certified public accountant at Arthur Andersen, and relaxing. Occasionally on such days, I'd smoke a small bowl of pot, let go of the countless details of my audit work from that week, and then set off to visit one of Boulder, Colorado's numerous independent bookstores. "The little smoke," as Castenada called it, allows me to quickly alter my perceptions; by "stopping the world," I momentarily leave the cause-and-effect mind-set of time and money, and take a more expansive view of life's possibilities. You might be of the opinion that this type of laissez-faire attitude towards cannabis is passé—that people should stop indulging themselves like this when they've graduated college, get a job, and start their "adult life"—but I've never been one for such artificial distinctions. I relish living in two worlds, those of commerce and art.

Nevertheless, who would have guessed, while browsing through dusty bookshelves in the psychology section of Rocky Mountain Books and Plants, that of all the people in the world I could meet, I meet this person, and here of all places? Of course, my reaction would have been the same regardless of the spot where'd we met—but of our eventual meeting, I'm now certain it was bound to happen. Honestly, we wouldn't have it any other way, would we—this sense of the miraculous? But still, our meeting is in this bookstore, in front of these musings on the mind.

It's not that I'm a stranger to this establishment either. I frequent this place, regularly scouring a few selected sections, finance and management mostly, with an occasional foray into the theatre section for inspiration. This may seem like a strange combination, but I assure you that it's perfectly normal for creative people to have boring jobs. Wasn't Einstein a patent clerk when he wrote the Special Theory of Relativity? And didn't Faulkner work for the post office and Wallace Stevens sell insurance—just to name a few? For me, living the dual life of a CPA and thespian is what I've always done. At NYU, despite the anti-materialistic nature of the times, in the late '60's and early '70's, my approach remained methodical: I studied accounting and theatre. Even as a child, though lavished with cultural events by my parents, my scholastic training remained very practical. Why would it change now?

Okay, I admit I have some eccentricities. Sometimes, on rare occasions, I come in here to order books in French, my native tongue, just to keep myself fresh. And I'm always reading a novel, no matter how much business reading I'm required to do. But on this day I'm in the psychology section, on a mission to salvage my relationship with my long-time girlfriend, Chimera.

The problem, she tells me, is that I'm insensitive, or at least not sensitive enough. At first I don't have a clue what she's talking about. Aren't Frenchmen supposed to be more sensitive than most men? Maybe she's just over-sensitive. After all, she chose to call herself Chimera. She could have kept her given name, Thalia,[1] for if ever there was a muse who could turn the mundane into art it is she. But no, she didn't feel comfortable in that skin, too dreamy and serene for our girl, she of the lingering parental storms and a painter's tempestuous instincts. So, Chimera it is—a sometimes inspired, sometimes sullen force. How shall I make peace with such an enigma? And one that I so ardently desire?

In this case, I've taken the initiative by searching for a book that she says will help me illuminate my feminine side. I begin to find my rhythm in scanning the shelves as if they were a detailed spread sheet, left to right, top to bottom, systematically contemplating each title, searching for something stimulating enough to warrant further inspection.

Then, in the midst of my hunt, I have the rarest of experiences—one that completely alters the direction and nature of my life. He approached me, for I admit, I'm not in the habit of approaching people I don't know. But, as I said, that's what long-shots are about, and on this day my number comes in.

"You seem to be searching for an appropriate volume of Jung's?"

I'm startled by the unexpected words from a stranger who has been browsing nearby.

---

[1] Thalia is the Greek muse of comedy and bucolic poetry.

4 » Solomon's Proof

"Yes," I reply, attempting to visually mark my place on a shelf just above my head, before turning and addressing the man. "My girlfriend insisted that I read a book on the feminine psyche. She said it would help me understand her—and myself ..."

"Ah, *The Way of All Women*[2] by Harding?" he says.

"How'd you know that?" I ask, incredulous at his wild guess.

"An educated guess," he says. "Simple, really. You know, Jung plus feminine studies equals M. Esther Harding. There really aren't that many other possibilities."[3]

I'm still surprised by his deduction, but quickly steady my guard, wary of his attempt to commandeer my search party. "Anyway, that's how I became aware of Jung's ideas," I say. "I started exploring his notion of the marriage of the male and female within."

"It's hard not to be impressed by his work," the stranger says. "Jung was the first to fully synthesize Eastern and Western thought. What Leonardo did for the individual, Jung did for the world—he exponentially expanded our consciousness by coaxing our brain hemispheres—left and right, West and East, male and female—to talk to one another."

"I'm just beginning to explore this," I admit, softened by his succinct description. This was, after all, the mid-70's, and such ideas were still relatively new. "Perhaps you've got a recommendation for me?"

"Of course. This one right here would be perfect for you."

I watch as he picks out a modestly-sized hardcover book, thin in comparison to other volumes in the Bollingen/Princeton series of Jung's works. It's entitled *Aion: Researches into the Phenomenology of the Self*.[4]

"Why this?"

---

[2] Harding, M. Esther, *The Way of All Women*, Longmans, Green and Co., London, 1933.
[3] Not in 1975, anyways. One might also investigate the works of Marie-Louise Von Franz for the origins of Jungian female studies or, more recently, for male-female relationship studies, John Wellwood's *Love and Awakening: Discovering the Sacred Path of Intimate Relationship* and *Journey of the Heart: The Path of Conscious Love*, reissued in 1996 and 1997 by Harper, as well as Robert A. Johnson's work, particularly *We*, published by Harper, San Francisco, 1985.
[4] Jung, Carl, *Aion: Researches into the Phenomenology of the Self*, Volume 9, Part II, The Collected Works of C.G. Jung, Bollingen Series XX, Princeton University Press, 1959.

"Simple. You're interested in improving your relationship with your partner. In order to accomplish this you must distinguish between the romantic notions of love that we project onto others from love that is accepting and unconditional, that is, *universal* love—agape, as the Greeks called it, the Messiah's or Christ's or the Avatar's love. This begins with loving your self, which requires, among other things, for you to love both the masculine and feminine parts of your self."

I'm struck by the sophistication of this utterance, as if it were a ready-made audio cassette that this odd fellow quickly retrieved and inserted into his brain's tape player. Like Aladdin with his magic lamp, I'm eager to try the genie again. I check the aisle in both directions.

"So how will this book help me to do that?" I ask, relieved that no one is watching or within earshot.

"In here you'll find an essay entitled, *Christ, a Symbol of the Self*. Start there, for Christ or Messiah or Avatar is, among other things, an archetype or anomaly within each of us that embodies what Jung calls the divine marriage,[5] a union of the male and female psyche, anima and animus."

I fail to grasp how Jesus will help me with my girlfriend, who is decidedly not a Christian, and who resembles the Princess Scheherazade more than the Prince of Peace.

"Jung uses the term Christ, meaning anointed one, not Jesus, because it's a universal state of mind, not an individual person," he begins again.

He corrects even my thoughts!

"It's Jung's belief," he continues as he moves closer to me, his eyes penetrating whatever resistance I have at this point, "that the Christ archetype, call it what you will, represents the most realized example of an integrated being, the synthesis of both sexual energies as well as our higher and lower selves. If you are to succeed in your quest, then that must be your goal: to reconcile the opposites within you; to unify all your disparate parts into one being. Otherwise, how could you love something different if you did not recognize it within yourself? As the ancients say, 'As above, so below.' Ergo, the microcosm reflects the macrocosm, and vice versa.[6]

---

[5] See Jung, *ibid.*, *The Syzygy: Anima and Animus*.
[6] As symbolized by the Star of David (✡).

When you achieve this synthesis, you are reborn into a qualitatively new state of consciousness, the higher self—your own Messiah, Christ, Buddha, or Krishna consciousness—call it what you will.

"Like most men," he continues without pause, as if he were just making colloquial conversation, "you may not understand how you confuse your subconscious yearnings, your *anima*, or feminine side, with the persona of your girlfriend. But when you learn the difference, you'll take a big step toward reconciling your masculinity and femininity, toward achieving the Divine Syzygy—your own Christhood or Messiah nature. So you see, your girlfriend is related to Christ consciousness in a very direct way."

Again, he reads my mind and answers me! I glance both ways again, wanting to keep this oracle to myself, and am relieved to find no one has noticed our conversation. Suddenly I'm anxious about pressing my luck. Maybe I'm confusing hunger with anxiety—they do share the same convolutions in our brain—but it occurs to me that I haven't eaten all day and it's almost two in the afternoon. It's not the munchies I tell myself; it's real hunger.

"I'd like to continue this," I say, suddenly aware that I had ceased a series of hypnotic nods that had followed each of his statements. "Should we go next door for some tea or a bite to eat?"

"Sure," he says, holding up a large, dusty volume with a bizarre, horned creature on the cover, a strange combination of human and glyph. "I've found what I came here for."

"*The Book of Wisdom or Folly*?"[7] I ask, noting the rather striking resemblance between my acquaintance and the cover illustration.

"Just the epistles of a crazy old man to his magical son," he replies as we make our way to the cash register.

☼ ☼ ☼

The Carnival Café is one of those old school vegetarian restaurants, founded on the principles of macrobiotics, which began to appear in the

---

[7] Aleister Crowley, *The Book of Wisdom or Folly*, Level Press, San Francisco, CA, 1972. "It shall be his child and that strangely. Let him not seek after this; for thereby alone can he fall from it." (p. viii).

early seventies. This seems to please my new friend, who smiles as he peruses the menu.

"You like it, I see." Up until now, I never thought twice about the quality of the Carnival's fare. It's the only vegetarian restaurant in Boulder, and I stop in often on my walks through town. I know it may seem odd to you, a Frenchman who doesn't eat meat, but it's just one of many changes I experienced after leaving my native land and going away to school.

"Yes, if only to know that Taoist Chemistry has more than one practitioner," he says. It strikes me that, in addition to his large vocabulary, my genie speaks a rather elevated but unidentifiable American dialect.

"You haven't been here long then? I mean in Boulder," I ask.

"No, actually. I've just returned from Chicago."

"Why was that?"

"I finished my business there."

"Which was? If you don't mind me asking, I mean," I quickly add. I can't help being interested, I'm an auditor and a playwright; it's my nature to interrogate. And after all, he initiated this intimacy.

"A combination of things," he says, apparently unfazed. "My goal was to pay off my student loans; I ended up teaching Yoga downtown. But I vowed to come back here, so, *voilà*!

I'm pleased to hear my acquaintance properly pronounce this commonly abused figure of speech, managing to combine the "v" and "w" sounds in the French *voi-* without flattening it with an English accent. "You've been here before?"

"For a few years, yes. I had some friends who went to college here. After I visited their place up in the hills, I was convinced this is where I'm supposed to be. I just had to tie up some loose ends before settling in."

"You plan to stay then?" I ask.

"Definitely! Chicago was about money and karma—but that's taken care of for now. The mountains are different. You can lose yourself here. In fact, it was an experience I had while meditating on top of a local mountain that brought me back here."

"Sounds prophetic."

"More of a vision quest," he says, "like Black Elk or Moses practicing austerities in high places.

"I see." I'm startled by my acquaintance's grandiose comparison. "Is that where you're staying now, in the high country?" I ask.

"Right. About twenty miles from here, a little above 9000 feet."

It seems like hours by the time our waitress finally appears out of the kitchen with our order. Food, of course, is a national pastime in France, and having worked in a restaurant in New York, too, I can't help but notice the laid-back approach to service I always get here and almost everywhere else in Boulder. I want to say it's just the plethora of hippies, but I have to admit that the colorful, arid landscape—the shimmering, dreamy painted desert and idyllic alpine greenery—encourages a studied indolence.

"You're gonna groove on this," our waitress assures us, sashaying up to the booth with our plates.

I've opted for the Millet Soy Loaf, with lightly steamed Brussels sprouts and herb bread hot out of the oven, along with Ch'ai tea. My friend, still nameless, ordered the Adzuki Sunflower Brown Rice stir fry seasoned with garlic and miso, some steamed asparagus shoots mixed with Daikon radishes, almonds, tamari, and sesame salt, the same herb bread, and some Ginseng tea.

"I see you've been eating this way for a while," I say, admiring his plate, secretly wanting to hijack a sample of his entrée with my fork.

"I'm not a strict vegetarian," he says, "but I love good cooking."

"Rashan Barcusé," I say, finally breaking the ice and extending my hand, sans fork. It's hard for us French to make friends, but I'm adjusting to the familiarity Americans readily express.

"Mike Solomon," he says, putting down his chopsticks and shaking my hand. "Good to meet you!"

"Rashan Barcusé, now there's an interesting name," Mike says, again with a decent accent.

"Well, my father is French, hence the Barcusé, and my mother Algerian, for the Rashan."

"How does your family balance the Catholic and Islamic thing?" Mike asks, wasting no time turning interrogator.

"That's not so easy," I admit. "My mother's family, though not fanatical, does have a profound faith in Allah."

"With Mohammed as his Last Prophet?" Mike wonders.

"I suppose," I shrug, not wanting to recall my family's sometimes pointed religious discussions.

"You suppose!" presses Mike. "The exclusivity of a faith—a key point to the reconciliation of religious differences—and you suppose?"

"Mon Dieu!" I say, taken aback by his aggressive tone.

"You don't see the value in discussing this?"

"Not really."

"I apologize then," he says. "It seems so integral to the big picture. At least to me, that is."

"Why is that?"

"Now that the U.S. has finally left Vietnam," Mike begins, "the biggest threats to world peace, other than nuclear war, are religious beliefs, and the only way to defuse them is to recognize the absurdity of their exclusive claims."

"That's always been true, hasn't it—these religious conflicts?" I remark, not wanting to debate the Vietnam War and be reminded of France's part in this colonial misadventure.

"Not necessarily," he says. "There's evidence of a time when worldwide spiritual beliefs had more in common than they do now."

"You mean the legend of Atlantis or something like that?" I ask, not knowing what kind of cosmic reference to expect from the intellectual repository of my erudite friend.

"That's another story," he promises, as if he had pre-packaged clip waiting on his mental audiocassette player, cued up and ready to roll. "But even if you don't accept the evidence that Atlantis existed, such a unity could exist in the future. Everything changes, and what is false once is later true, and vice versa. In 11th and 12th century Moorish Spain, Muslims, Christians, and Jews lived together in peace and creative prosperity, all of 'the same book' as they saw it. There's no reason to assume we're relegated forever to be at each other's throats over religious beliefs."

"Maybe so," I say.

"No, not 'maybe so.' Necessarily so!"

"What has this got to do with Catholicism and Islam?" I say, finally running out of patience. "Why should this be important to me?"

"Because unless we recognize our spiritual commonalities, we'll remain unable to *share*. That is the world's problem in a nutshell—our wants outracing what the garden can provide."

"The *garden*?" I ask.

"Yes, the Garden of Eden. Buddha's Western Paradise. Valhalla!" Mike says. "Remember, 'The kingdom of heaven is at hand.'"[8]

"Okay," I say, wilting under the onslaught. "I admit it's important that my mother and father are tolerant of each other's beliefs. Besides, now my dad is a recovering Catholic and my mom converted to Bahá'í."

"And your grandparents?" Mike presses on. "How tolerant were they of religious differences?"

"That's a different matter," I concede, instantly recalling a Sunday with my paternal grandparents in Avignon. We are entering the Sainte Claire chapel on *Rue des Teinturiers*. This is where Pétrarch met Laure for the first time and fell in love with her, and where I would, seven centuries later, fall in love with Marguerite, my childhood sweetheart.

Within these walls, I watch the devout parents of my once-Catholic father reverently perform the sacred rituals. I imitate them to ease my sense of awkwardness. My *grand-maman* dutifully explains the meaning behind each rite to me. But at seven years of age, and despite her earnest efforts, I'd rather be playing with my friends along the Rhône, making up war games in which we defend the city against the Goths or Visigoths, Franks or Saracens. There, our rules make sense and fit the circumstances; if they don't work, we change them. "Pay attention," *grand-maman* says.

Then briefly, I'm back with Mike, until another memory arises just as suddenly. This time I'm with my maternal grandparents, outside a mosque. A stern bearded man in black robes and hat is discussing current events and points of the law with my *grand-papa*. I'm ignored by the adults, and the conversation goes on much too long. My antsiness is apparent. As we are walking away I'm admonished for not showing due respect to the *imam*.

"Exactly!" Mike says, as if he were responding to my memory as well as my verbal admission of my grandparents' conservative religious character. "If so-called Christians believe that '*Only* through Jesus … ,' and Muslims believe that 'Mohammed is the *Last* Prophet,' and Jews

---

[8] Matthew 4:17

believe that 'We are the *Chosen* People,'[9] and the next group proclaims its own exclusivity, *ad infinitum*, then the wholeness, and thus the 'holiness,' of the 'One-Without-A-Name' and all that it engenders is shattered, each piece only partly true. From a marketing point of view it may be easy to understand why powerbrokers from these three religions would each attempt to paint their covenant with the Almighty as an exclusive agreement, but from a spiritual point of view, such exclusivity is nonsense, mere dogma.

"There is only one source, only one world, and while there may be many dimensions to it, and we each may describe our point-of-view differently, it remains indivisible. It's as Einstein said, by traveling faster than the speed of light you don't end up getting outside the universe, you end up back where you started. Our universe was all one substance in the nanoseconds just before the Big Bang, and those connections are still with us."[10]

"I appreciate the passion of your argument and even some of its logic"—I say, duly noting in my mind what again felt like a pre-taped homily—"including the idea that the unification of spiritual thought, whether it occurred in the past or not, could possibly occur in the future. But it's not probable. *Jamais de la vie*! To me, it's just so much utopian smoke, an unreachable goal."

"Utopian? Perhaps once," Mike says. "But now it's a necessity—if we're going to survive."

"Are you telling me that you expect all the worlds' religions—Jews, Christians, Muslims, Hindus, Buddhists, Zoroastrians … cults of Zeus even—to admit that their beliefs are only part of the whole picture, to admit that they're wrong?

"No. Not wrong," Mike assures me. "They're all partially right. They just need to be put into proper context."

---

[9] "No … apostle will come after me, and no new faith will be born." (Mohammed's last sermon, 632 C.E.) "I am the way, the truth, and the life: no man cometh unto the Father, but by me." (John 14:6) "For you are a people holy to YHVH your God. He has chosen you from all the people on the face of the whole earth to be his own chosen ones." (Deuteronomy 7:6)

[10] Little did I realize at the time that using this concept Mike would later show me his proof for the Big Bang, String Theory, and beyond. (See *Appendix 6 – The Proof* or www.SolomonsProof.com.)

"A lot of people have tried to do that," I say, once again wondering who this guy thinks he is.

"There's always great resistance to the big picture; most people are like a fish in water—they can't see their way out of the small pond that is the brief time and limited space they inhabit. But conditions have changed," he says. "There's enough information out there now to tie it all together, synthesize the entirety of human knowledge."

"And you're able to do this?" I ask.

"Yep, that's my bag."

"That's why you knew about Esther Harding?" I ask, half-mocking his earlier zinger.

"Like I said, that was simple. Unifying religions—that's more complicated."

"Yet you seem to believe you can explain that too."

"Sure," Mike says. "They're all cut from the same fabric of the one universe."

I picture Mike as a gunslinger in the old West. He's awfully fast on the draw. I'm glad we're only firing words. I try to juke him.

"So then, you're saying that my father and mother have essentially compatible beliefs, despite having been raised Catholic and Muslim, and having become apostate and Bahá'í?"

"Yes, of course," he says. "And it would be through their love for each other and for life itself that they, and others, are able to see this connection—that Jesus and Mohammed and Buddha and Abraham and Krishna and Zoroaster and Lao Tsu and Bahá'u'lláh[11] and each and every one of us are all different aspects and emanations of the same divine energy, each with our own role in revealing truth."

"Then what about the ideological conflicts between these groups—and all the religious wars that follow from this? Clearly most believers don't live by what you're saying, or place much meaning in it," I say, happy to point out the shortcomings of my friend's argument.

"That's where all of these philosophies are limited by time," Mike shoots back. "Individually, each of their truths is not the whole,[12] but only

---

[11] The central messianic figure in the Bahá'í faith.
[12] A reference to, "the truth is the whole" which, I later discover, is one of Mike's favorite sayings, in the manner of Georges Wilhelm Friedrich Hegel, *A Preface the*

a facet, like Harry Haller's experience in *Steppenwolf*,[13] when he looks in the mirror and sees the many parts of his self.[14] Only taken together do these unrelated ideas make a whole, a whole that is more than each part separately, a whole that is without limit and therefore indescribable, everything but no thing in particular, unnamable."

Mike's articulateness aside, I assure myself that all these disparate philosophies are not so easily dismissed. How could society manage without long-standing behavioral guidelines like the Ten Commandments and the Nicene Creed?[15]

"Would you like some more tea?" Mike asks.

"Sure, but after that it's time for me to get home."

"Does this bore you?"

"No, I'm just not sure what it means," I say.

"What it means is that we're approaching a critical moment in human development, and that we as a species have some serious decisions to make that will dramatically effect how, or whether, we evolve and survive."

"I'd be happy just keeping it together with my girlfriend," I say.

"You've taken a step in that direction today."

"You mean by reading this book you recommended?"

"It's a start."

At this point, I'm glad the conversation ends. My defenses are exhausted by Mike's irrepressible arguments and unflappable self-

---

Phenomenology of Mind, translated by Walter Kaufman, etc., particularly the lovely metaphor of the acorn that grows into an oak tree.

[13] Hermann Hesse, *Steppenwolf*, Atlantic Paperbacks, 1957.

[14] After Harry has met Pablo, smoked the yellow cigarette Pablo gives him, and fallen under his influence.

[15] "The Nicene Creed is the most widely accepted and used brief statement of the Christian Faith. In liturgical churches, it is said every Sunday. It is common ground to East Orthodox, Roman Catholics, Anglicans, Lutherans, Calvinists, and many other Christian groups. Many groups that do not have a tradition of using it in their services nevertheless are committed to the doctrines it teaches." (from www.iclnet.com) The Nicene Creed lists the basic "Christian" beliefs, e.g., "We believe in one Lord, Jesus Christ, the only son of God, eternally begotten of the Father …"

confidence. We exchange pleasantries. I let him go without exchanging numbers. "I'm sure we'll meet again," I say, not really thinking this likely.

☼ ☼ ☼

Okay, so maybe it was *gauche* of me not to ask for Mike's telephone number. But as I said earlier, I am *avec excentricité*. Witness the childhood recollections of Catholicism and Islam that Mike's probing had stimulated. Do they not reveal behavior lacking in *savoir-faire*? Yes, I know that children always squirm in church, or whenever they're subjected to the droning of adults. But I am no different today, decades from my youth. When I'm not at work, I remain like a child who prefers to invent his own stories to explain how things work. I make them up, as a playwright would, fashioning new ones when I tire of the old ones. I may be just like the other adults who use words and rituals, sacred or profane, to cover their discomfort with the unknown, but I'm happier with my own myths than with any of the current crop of mass delusions. So, at the time we met and this all started, however curious and well-wrought Mike's myths might have been, I was not ready to replace my own with them.

Two days later, however, for the first time in many years I begin to dream about my parents, René and Ahlam. Afterwards, I wonder about the forces that brought them together and kept them together: the serendipity of their relationship—meeting on a photo shoot for an architectural magazine; and their mutual artistic interests—my mom an interior designer and my dad an ad agency art director. It seems to me that this intersection of *haute couture* and coincidence is what defined my childhood: a series of seemingly random, but sublime, moments. Now, my encounter with Mike—in which I find his arguments both elegant and irreverent—plays right into these experiential expectations of mine, and thus into my innermost remembrances and dreams.

All this ruminating comes as a surprise to me. I thought I was done with Mike when I left him at the Carnival Café. Yet in the mornings, in the wake of these parental visitations, I'm constantly reminded that he stimulated this re-emergence of childhood memory. On top of these uncomfortable reminders, and with no second thoughts, I make time to read the essay, *Christ: a Symbol of the Self*, which he had recommended. I feel as if I'm being drawn into a relationship with Mike, despite my conscious effort to avoid it. I tell myself that there's a reason why this is happening to me, this feeling of being simultaneously pulled forward into his world and backwards into my own, but I am at a loss to know what it is.

Yet no fondness for whimsy or the avant-garde could have fully prepared me for what I would be called upon to do as a result of my acquaintance with this man. If that sounds ungrateful, I don't mean it that way. While getting to know him during these nearly three decades has been trying at times, I can now admit, despite all my denials to the contrary, that Mike intrigued me from the beginning. But this is now, and what I'm describing to you here was then.

☼ ☼ ☼

Chimera is curious about my new acquaintance. She listens carefully as I describe my meeting.

"Have you been smoking again, Rashan?" she asks, striking a tone much like my mother would, when admonishing me for eating too much candy.

"What difference would that make?" I reply. "What I heard, I heard."

"What you heard is what you heard when you heard it."

"Hey, when you have an extra piece of pie, do I treat you as if you're irrational? A little smoke doesn't make me forget what I'm doing, or what other people do or say."

"Okay, so you found what he said interesting?" she asks, backing off the confrontation without seaming to retreat.

"Yes," I admit. "It's odd though; I don't agree with most of what he said, but psychologically, he's gotten inside my head."

"Maybe he's been through it himself?" Chimera says, staring at me with her dark eyes.

Unable to break my gaze, I'm reminded how easy it is to get lost there.

"You mean a man finding his feminine side?" I ask, managing to momentarily avert my eyes.

"Yes. It would be hard for a man to understand the nature of receptivity if he hadn't experienced it for himself, within himself," she says, her eyes widening in stages for emphasis.

"He seems to know what he's talking about."

"What's his name?"

"Mike Solomon."

She looks at me curiously, cocking her head. "Hmm. Maybe you'll run into him again."

"Who knows?"

"Well, I hope you do! It's more than a coincidence you met him looking for a book on relationships."

☼ ☼ ☼

Normally, I'd wait a few weeks before returning to Rocky Mountain Books and Plants, but here it is a week to the day after I met Mike and I'm on my way back. I'm no longer confident in the memory of that conversation, which, in light of my dreams, has taken on a mystique—each of Mike's pre-fabricated sermons remaining aglow in my mind.

As an accountant, I find this disturbing. I'm trained to get the hard facts, not some touchy-feely version. But the facts, the numbers representing a transaction, are not always easy to discover; people who massage numbers are clever—they lie, and they have a head start. When I'm auditing, I can't afford to take too many wrong turns, or I'll never discover what's going on. I need to gain my client's confidence, get a feel for the integrity of their information, while remaining impervious to their guise. So when my memories of Michael's comments begin to take on surreal qualities I get suspicious. Am I softening up? What kind of charlatan have I fallen for?

I stop in at Ead's News and Smokeshop, a weathered one-story ramshackle brick building across the main drag from the bookstore, and pick up a couple French magazines that have recently come in. Then I cross the street to the bookstore and plant myself near the psychology section for awhile, sitting in a comfortable leather chair, sipping tea, leafing through my new reading material. I look up every now and then to see if Mike has walked in.

After a half hour of this, I become restless. What am I doing casing out this joint, like Sherlock Holmes on someone's trail? I'm acting compulsively over some latter-day spiritualist, I try to tell myself. There are lots of "new age" sophists in town these days. Chalk it up to "That's Boulder!" and move on, I think—but I can't.

I walk back to the counter in the front room where Eddie Ward, the gravelly-voiced poet-proprietor of the bookstore, stands. With his droopy felt cowboy hat, bushy eyebrows, and rusty moustache, Eddie always reminds me of Yosemite Sam.[16]

"Howdy," he says as I approach.

"Hey, Eddie. How's it goin'?" I try to use colloquial speech around Eddie, who has crafted his own unique Rocky Mountain patois from the quaint, to-the-point language of the miners around whom he grew up.

"It's goin'. People are still readin' books," he says.

"Yep, that's a good thing," I say. "Say, I wanted to ask you about someone I met here last week."

"Pickin' up girls in my bookstore, man?" he jokes.

"No, actually," I laugh, embarrassed at the thought, "I haven't tried to do that since college."

"Well, I wouldn't blame ya if ya did," Eddie says. "What with women are wearin', it's getting' hard for books to compete."

"True enough, but I've got all I can handle in that department. In fact, that's what I wanted to talk to you about. I was in here last week, in the psychology section, trying to patch up things with my girlfriend, when I met this odd fellow. He just started talkin' to me. One thing let to another and we ended up having lunch together."

"You mean Michael?" Eddie says. "I saw you go out together."

"You know this guy?"

"Sure. He comes in here pretty regular."

"Well, I had a strange experience with him. We talked, and for the most part it was okay, but when I got to thinkin' about it later, I found myself scratching my head, wondering if I heard him right."

"You mean Michael's raps on everything in the universe?" Eddie says with a bit of mischief in his eyes.

---

[16] A Warner Brothers' cartoon character.

"Yeah, it was almost like he had these ideas already recorded. Every time I asked him a question, all he had to do was access a track he had numbered in his head—and 'Presto!'—there was the answer."

"Right," Eddie confirms. "The ideas seem ready-made."

"Right," I reply. "Like he already has it all down."

"They change though," Eddie says. "He varies 'em accordin' to the conversation."

"You talk with him a lot?"

"A few times. I've overheard some conversations."

"This is something he does all the time then?" I ask. Maybe Mike's some kind of a spiritual stalker, I think, trying to recruit lost souls for his final crusade.

"No, I wouldn't say that," Eddie assures me. "He just seems to attract people to his self. Somebody asks him a question, and he's off to the races."

"But he asked me a question first!" I say.

"I'm not sayin' he isn't forward, just that he's an independent sort. Doesn't seem attached to whether he's changed your mind or not, but more than willin' to try."

"Yeah, I know what you mean," I said. "Well, thanks for tellin' me that. I was just thinking about my conversation with him and got to wonderin'."

"Anytime," Eddie replies. "You're not the first to ask about him."

After that, I stopped trying to hunt down Mike. He did pop up in my mind a lot, though. I figured I'd run into him soon enough.

☼ ☼ ☼

It's nearly a year before I see him, though, and a lot has changed on all fronts. In the world, the U.S. has officially left Vietnam, and the aftermath throughout Southeast Asia is a mess. The locals are all at each other's throats, especially in Cambodia and Laos, and reports of genocide are just beginning to surface. And things aren't any better here in my adopted homeland. Americans are still governed by two men they did not vote for, Gerald Ford and Nelson Rockefeller.

But it's election season, 1976. I take my responsibilities as a naturalized citizen quite seriously, and am looking forward to voting in my first presidential election. That it's happening on the 200th anniversary of the Declaration of Independence underscores to me the value of such a right. As a child in Avignon, I learned that freedom is one principle on which the French and Americans agree. France helped secure American independence during the Revolutionary War; America returned the favor in World War II. The Statue of Liberty, given as a gift somewhere in-between those two intercessions on each other's behalf, symbolizes this bond. When I lived in New York as a student at NYU, I would occasionally find myself looking out to sea at that great lady and thinking about this connection between my native country and my adopted land. Now I will get to vote and choose a new President.

At home, too, there is hope for change. Reading that book by Jung has something to do with it. I realized that all this "left brain, right brain" pop psychology that I run across constantly in the media and among my friends is a corruption of what Jung had described, far more organically, as the marriage of opposite forces. I boil this down to the idea that if I ignore the part of me which is dark, receptive, fertile, and nurturing, then there's no way that I can live up to my creative potential. If I want my plays, not to mention my relationship with Chimera, to be successful, I must commit to developing these feminine attributes, and be comfortable with them in the same way that I'm comfortable with my everyday masculine identity. For a Frenchman, this should be easy.

Chimera notices the change in me.

"Flowers! What's the occasion, Rashan?" She is quite taken when I show up with roses out of the blue, interrupting her cooking.

"No occasion. I just feel like giving you flowers."

"Okay," she says, "I'll take it for that—a beautiful thought," moving against me and planting a brief kiss on my lips.

I'm satisfied thinking that I've made a small step in finding a way out of the mercurial pattern of our relationship.

But a few days later we're at it again, arguing over whether it's time to have a baby.

"I'm not so sure we're ready for it," I reason. "We're both working hard. You know I'm in line for partner—and your work is just beginning to sell. I just think it would be better if we waited a couple of years. Things will be more established."

Talking like this always reminds me of my mother's urgings to have a profession to fall back on in case my playwriting doesn't make me rich and famous in America. She encouraged this approach after I learned to balance her checkbook while still in grammar school. "A born accountant," she said. Even my father chided me about the fickleness of career in the arts, a prospect which, at the time, I favored over mundane occupations. "I love designing theatre sets when I can, Rashan," he used to say, "but it doesn't pay the bills."

"Rashan," Chimera emphasizes, "things will never be perfect. In two years you'll have some other excuse."

"Nurturing a baby is a full-time job," I say. "There are lots of babies that don't get enough attention. I don't want ours to have that problem."

"Is that what you think we'll do? Not give our baby enough attention!" Chimera says in a huff, folding her arms across her chest.

"Look, I know that we'd always try to do our best," I say, attempting to defuse the situation. "But I'm afraid we'd be running in too many directions. I'll feel derelict."

"Like I said, Rashan, things will never be perfect. Love is what gets you through," she says and walks out of the kitchen.

☼ ☼ ☼

A week later, I'm on my way to the post office, to send off the latest rewrite of my new play to the artistic director of my favorite theatre in Denver, Le Canard, when I spot Mike coming out of the county courthouse. He's wearing what appear to be a Nepalese or Tibetan jacket and a round, flat-topped Asiatic hat to brace himself against the cool weather blowing down off the peaks.

"Mike!" I shout at him from across the lawn as I wave my hand. "How are you?"

"Rashan!"

"What are you up to?" We meet near the center of the plaza, next to the old tile fountain built twenty years before by the Lions Club.

"Just dropping in on my friends down here at the county ..."

"Your friends at the county?"

"... the Commissioners, the County Clerk, the Elections Director."

"I didn't realize that you're a politician," I say. With Mike it's one surprise after another.

"A politician? Oh, G-d help me, no!" he exclaims. "Horse-trading for commercial interests is not an occupation for which I have any time, unlike most of our 'public servants.'"

"I see," I say smiling, reminded of Mike's penchant for the grandiose. "Well, I'd love to hear about what you *are* doing then. I've got some things to tell you as well."

"You do?"

"Yes. Do you have a little while? We could catch a bite somewhere?"

"Sure! How about Fred's?" Mike asks, indicating the direction with his head. "I've got a soft spot for the place. His brother used to own a restaurant in my hometown."

As we begin to walk across the courthouse lawn to Fred's, which is right across the street, I pick up on Mike's offering of personal information. "Your hometown? Chicago, right?" I ask, remembering our first conversation.

"About a half hour north of Chicago," Mike says. "The home of Bud's Restaurant. We used to go there after school for cherry Cokes and fries."

"That doesn't sound very macrobiotic!"

"Macrobiotic!" Mike laughs. "Remember what Herman Aihura said."

"Herman Aihura!" Now I'm laughing too. "Who the hell is Herman Aihura?"

"He became president of the George Asawa Macrobiotic Foundation after Asawa died from what appeared to be his highly neurotic concern over the 'yang-ness' of every food particle he imbibed."

"Good G-d, Mike! What did Mr. Aihura say?"

"He said, 'If you're *Do O Raku Monu* anything you eat is macrobiotic.'"

"*Sacré bleu!*"

"No, really," Mike continues, brushing aside my exasperation. "It translates roughly from the Japanese as 'If you live in a state of perpetual ecstatic delight, anything you eat is macrobiotic,' or basically, with the right attitude you can transmute anything. You know, like a combination of Meher Baba's,[17] 'Don't worry. Be happy,' and the *I Ching*'s,[18] 'Everything furthers.'"

"You do seem to have an answer for everything," I say.

Mike arches his left eye brow, as if simultaneously amused and surprised, and counters, "As my father used to say, 'Man searches for reasons to support his beliefs.'"

Just then, as we stand before the front desk at Fred's, the hostess appears.

"Smoking or non-?" she inquires. This is years before Boulder became one of the first cities to adopt a non-smoking law for all public buildings.

"Non-," Mike replies.

"Evanston, Kenilworth, Winnetka, Hubbard Woods, Glencoe, and points north ...," the gray-haired guitar player on the side stage of the restaurant announces after blowing a train whistle. It's his introduction to Glenn Miller's *Chattanooga Choo-Choo*.

As the hostess shows us to a sunny seat along the brick wall opposite the performer's platform in the front room, I can't help but express my relief at Mike's preference for seating. If there's anything that bugs me about France, it's the constant cigarette smoking everywhere. "I'm happy to see that at least you don't smoke."

"Oh, not very often, anyway, and not tobacco," Mike says. As common as pot smoking is these days, and as I said, though I indulge myself, I had somehow not associated it with a macrobiotic Yoga teacher.

Our waitress appears. Mike smiles and gives a wave of recognition.

"Rashan, this is Diane Bukowski. Diane, Rashan Barcusé," Mike says. "Diane's an actress. We met at one of my Yoga classes."

"I'm a playwright myself," I said, "when I'm not a CPA."

"I know what you mean," she says. "It's the old story, most actors wait tables, or most waiters are actors. I can never remember which is which."

---

[17] An Indian holy man considered by many to be the avatar. He practiced silence for much of his life.
[18] The *I Ching,* or *Book of Changes*, Wilhelm/Baynes translation, with a forward by C.G. Jung, Bollingen Series XIX, Princeton University Press, is recommended.

In our twenties all, we laugh. We hadn't overused this one yet.

"One day, perhaps we will not be so confused," I say.

"So you'll call me then, the next time you audition?" she asks. "I've seen your stuff."

"Okay," I promise, flattered and happy to oblige this attractive, upfront redhead. "I've got a new play about to be produced in Denver."

"I'll give you my number," she says, leaving the menus with us.

The fare at Fred's is emphatically American, meaning there are few vegetarian choices available. When it comes time to order, all I can find is a grilled cheese sandwich and Boulder's own Celestial Seasonings Emperor's Choice herbal tea.

"Try a side of the coleslaw," Mike suggests as Diane notes my order. You'll like it. "We used to bring it home by the quart. It's the creamiest on the planet."

"Yes, I'll have a side order of coleslaw as well," I say, proceeding as if Mike has suggested a particularly good Pinot Noir.

"And I'll have the fish sandwich *avec pomme de frites*, and some iced tea, Diane," Mike rattles off, barely looking at the menu.

"I'll be back with your drinks in a minute," she says, smiles, and leaves. I watch her walk away.

"She got her graduate degree in theatre at the University of Colorado," Mike says. "She's as good an actress as she is good-looking."

"What's this about a Yoga class?" I ask, turning back to Mike and changing the subject, embarrassed at my obviousness.

"I was asked to give a talk by a former member of the Royal Shakespeare Company who teaches at CU. Diane was one of his grad students."

"How did you know that theatre's an interest of mine?" I remember from our previous meeting Mike's apparent ability to read my mind.

"That looks like a manuscript there, which you're about to send to Le Canard," he says, with only the faintest of ironic smiles and a raised left brow, as if he were Sherlock Holmes.

"So it is," I admit, relieved at such a simple answer. How did you get involved in teaching Yoga to acting students?"

Mike's face lights up. "I don't have any formal stage training, but my mom did musical theatre, and I've always enjoyed the whole atmosphere. The theatre inspires—with artistry and magic, and characters from other times and places speaking strange dialects, telling unheard stories—like a time machine!" he says. Then, after a beat he turns on the gravity, leaning towards me and looking directly into my eyes.

"But the greatest value of theatre," he says, "is that it ties us to rituals that serve our need for spiritual community."

"Rituals for spiritual community?" I ask.

"Sure. To paraphrase Maxwell Anderson[19] paraphrasing Aristotle, 'The theatre is a religious institution dedicated entirely to the spiritual exaltation of humankind.' It reenacts our soul-wrestling; it heals by affirming, protecting, and inspiring. In an anthropological sense, theatre is a symbolic expression of our innate culture. It's a remnant from a time when our daily rituals included music, song, dance, masks, costumes, props, fire, and the spoken word."

"The church considers that pagan." I observe.

"The church does the same thing! And pagan! It's the church that's pagan! It's the church that's turned the monotheistic mysteries into idol worship and political control! Imagine! Jesus—heir to Abraham, the man who smashed idols—seeing the graven images that populate churches in his name! They've taken icons of Jupiter and Juno and made them into Jesus and Mary!" Mike punctuates his exclamation by rapping the table with his fist, rattling the silverware and glassware.

"Whoa, Mike! Cool it!" I say.

"As if they could bottle G-d like a genie!" he nearly shouts.

I am bug-eyed by this point; we are beginning to draw looks from the other patrons. My genie is certainly out of the bottle.

"All this from the theatre," I say, trying to make light of Mike's fire and brimstone.

"Ah," he pauses, calming slightly. "Freedom of speech," he says, pointing for emphasis, "is the lifeblood of the theatre. It is the theatre, more than the Constitution, which protects our right of social criticism, especially in times of great censorship—like the present."

☼ ☼ ☼

---

[19] Early 20th Century American playwright who won the Pulitzer Prize for drama in 1933 for *Both Your Houses*.

"I'm surprised they didn't throw us out of there," I remark as we exit Fred's into a pristine spring afternoon.

Mike gazes up at the Flatirons, perfectly flat sheets of stone that sheath the foot of the Rocky Mountains, just blocks from where we stand.

"Well, it's Boulder," he says. "Everyone's a seeker here; it's a spiritual supermarket." He shrugs his shoulders. "Besides, I'll argue with anyone on these issues—the Holy See, the Caliphate, the Sanhedrin—bring 'em on!"

"Mike, you really are a bit touched, you know?"

"That's just the tip of the iceberg." He shrugs.

"I almost forgot to tell you," I say, stopping him as we approach the plaza. "That essay you picked out for me last year—Jung's *Christ, a Symbol of the Self*—it's beginning to have an impact."

"How so?" he asks.

"I used some of the ideas in my new play, but mainly it's affected my relationship with Chimera, my girlfriend."

"Chimera, you say?" Mike leans forward and stares at me.

"My girlfriend," I repeat. "It's not her real name. She took it from Greek mythology to signify her 'conflicting natures.'"

"Yes, I know what it means," says Mike. "Is she a painter?"

"How did you know that?"

"I think we've met."

"Really?" I'm quite surprised. I even feel a little violated.

"I believe we spoke at the meditation center above the Boulder Bookstore on Pearl Street."

"Hmm. That may be. She's been going there for a while," I say, afraid I've already betrayed some jealousy in my voice.

"An interesting coincidence. So, tell me how the essay helped you. What happened?" Mike asks, quickly putting his curiosity over Chimera behind him.

"His ideas are dense," I start, "and it took me a while to assimilate what he was saying. But as Chimera had said and you reiterated, it's important for me to develop my receptive nature—to get in touch with my feminine archetypes."

"How did you do that?"

"You remember when we met—you guessed that I had been reading *The Way of All Women*?"

"Yes, but it was more than a guess."

"Okay. Well, Chimera had suggested that book because she felt I had no sense of my own nurturing instincts. She said that as long as I was separated from that part of myself I would keep looking to her for nurturing—as if she were my mother. She also said this was affecting my attitude toward having children. So she wanted me to explore the nature of femininity from a woman's perspective."

"Then you read Jung?"

"Yes, and it helped me to see that the feminine nature which Harding describes is a part of me."

"Just like that?" he asks.

I realized that much as I now wanted to avoid discussing Chimera with Mike, I couldn't. Mike had suggested an essay to read, I read it, and now we are talking about the results. I've worked myself into an emotional corner from which there is no way out but to come forth with my story.

"Well, not quite that simply," I say. "Chimera seems to have more of a handle on this than I. She's done some work with a Jungian therapist, so she explained it to me."

"That's dangerous, Rashan."

"Dangerous?"

"Having your partner psychoanalyze you. Look, Chimera's probably right: most heterosexual men have the same problem you have; and because of their macho self-image or sexual insecurities or whatever else, they're unable to suffer the idea of having a feminine side, let alone develop it. Fair enough. But having her analyze you puts you on uneven footing."

"But she's very forgiving about it, Mike. I mean, what's the problem if she really puts her finger on it?"

"You seem to have accepted all this just to make peace. How often does she bring this up?" Mike asks, obviously unconvinced by my explanation.

"Whenever I fall into a typical, unfeeling male attitude."

Mike says nothing.

"Every couple of weeks or so," I add. "Maybe less."

"What are your issues with her?"

"Silly things, really."

"Your issues aren't important?"

Again, I don't know what to say. On the one hand, I'm a bit uncomfortable going through this with someone I don't know well. Besides, judging from his earlier reaction, he might have his own designs on Chimera; but on the other hand, he does seem to know a lot about this stuff, and as a man—a perspective from which I could benefit.

"Yes, they're important, because they're my issues. But in the context of a man being out of touch with his feelings, they seem less valid."

"Are you sure?"

"Not absolutely."

"If you're not sure, then how would you like some independent verification of your feelings?"

"Like what?"

"Try them out on me. I'm a third party."

What have I got to lose? I'm probably not telling him anything he doesn't already know. And as Chimera said, he seems to have been through these things. At least he's read all the books.

"Okay," I take the plunge. "I'm beginning to have some doubts about our compatibility."

"You're not sure about whether you and Chimera should be together?"

"I don't feel this way all the time. Just sometimes."

"Like when?"

"When her demons come up, for example."

"What do you mean by demons?"

"She hears voices, Mike. Or, at least that's what she calls them."

"What kind of voices?"

"Voices from her past—that tell her she's unwanted. They make her feel inadequate … undeserving. She gets depressed about this stuff and withdraws emotionally."

"It's what pop psychology calls 'self talk,'" Mike says. "To the listener it may sound as if someone else is talking to them, but it's simply their own mind repeating something that had been reinforced earlier in their life. That's how neurosis is passed down through the generations. These thought patterns, whether they're positive or negative, usually get absorbed at a time when the listener's defenses are undeveloped, and are perpetuated subconsciously and semi-consciously until some listener down the line intervenes and takes conscious control of his or her pattern."

I could count on Mike for some sort of definitive explanation. These ideas were all still new in the '70's, and he seems to be as well-versed in them as anyone else I'd met or read.

"Well, in Chimera's case," I say, "she doesn't seem to be able to shake them."

"And that's causing you to question whether you should be together?"

"I'm a happy guy, Mike. I'm twenty-seven and make it a point to enjoy life. You know—*joie de vivre*. I have a hard time believing that a relationship is about suffering."

"Then why did you get involved with Chimera?"

"It wasn't always this way. At first it was easy. I fell in love with her quickly. We were both working at the same café in the Village in New York. She was attending classes at the Art Students League and I was an accounting and drama student at NYU. She was the most beautiful woman I'd ever met, and I was impressed with her painting, too. She felt the same about me and my acting. And, while our families are very different, we both have one parent who is Arabic. So between the mutual physical attraction, artistic admiration, and a few other quirky things, our life together as students was great."

"What caused it to change?" Mike asks.

"After we graduated and moved to Boulder, things began to deteriorate, at least for me. I began to perceive imperfections in her. Her demons. She's not as concerned with housekeeping as I am. Even her interest in New Age philosophies is too much at times."

"What about your faults? You've got a list of things that you don't like about her, things that are giving you second thoughts about your relationship, because you're a 'happy guy' and 'don't need the pain.' But you admit that you're not in touch with your own feelings and that Chimera is helping you overcome this. These two statements don't jibe. As an accountant, can you see that this type of thinking—her deficits, your surpluses—is like keeping two sets of books, and then not knowing it? It seems to me you ought to be thinking about how you can help her with her issues, just like she's doing for you. Isn't that why they call it a balance statement?"

I stopped, dumbstruck by the simplicity of Mike's argument. There wasn't much I could say, but I tried.

"I'm successful at my job, and my career in the theatre is building. I live a comfortable life, and my relationship has, up until recently, been satisfying. But what you're saying is that I've been selfish."

"You're putting off the inevitable, Rashan. If you want love, then open yourself up; accept the pain with the joy. You can't hedge with love. It's got to be unconditional."

"This isn't the first time this has happened to me," I admit, feeling an old wound. My voice trails off and I see Marguerite standing before me. She's just finished telling me it's over between us. She places her hand on my cheek momentarily, then turns and walks away, out of my life. My heart feels that ache once again. Her poem comes back to me.

> I learn'd--
> The heart can bind itself alone,
> And faith may oft be unreturn'd.
> Self-sway'd our feelings ebb and swell--
> Thou lov'st no more; --Farewell! Farewell!
>
> ... Thou hast been, shalt be, art, alone.[20]

"The pain frightens me. It reminds me of my first love—when I lost her."

"This will keep repeating itself, Rashan," Mike says, "until you consciously work through it. It's a test."

"I'm embarrassed."

"Don't be," Mike says. "Men are taught to suck it up and harden themselves against life's blows, and there's certainly nothing wrong with finding a way to weather the storm, but this survival instinct often turns into a one-dimensional behavior that keeps men from getting in touch with their feelings. Sooner or later, if we want to evolve, we've got to open our hearts to love, regardless of how we've been hurt before."

---

[20] From *Isolation: To Marguerite*, Matthew Arnold (1822-1888).

"I can see your point," I say, not entirely convinced that my heart is ready for this. "I should face the facts, then, and work through it—with Chimera and with myself."

"It's not as bad as you make it out to be. You'll see. It's actually liberating. Like Jung says, it's a whole different way of perceiving and experiencing—one that puts you in touch with a force that makes you wonder why you ever held back." Mike leans my way and puts a hand on my shoulder. "Just remember, 'Ask and you shall receive ...'"[21]

"Thanks. I appreciate your help," I say, startled, yet somehow undeterred by the patriarchal tone of his pronouncement. "I'm thinking I'd like to be able to get in touch now and then—bounce some ideas off you."

"Sure. In fact, I could use your help," Mike says as he reaches into his jacket. "Here's my number. Why don't you and Chimera come up and visit me one of these days? I've got a project I'd like to talk over with you."

His card reads:

>Michael David Solomon
>Ashtanga Yoga[22]
>459-3533

---

[21] John 16:24
[22] At this time, *Ashtanga Yoga* still meant literally what it does in Sanskrit, "the eight limbs (steps or petals) of Yoga," and was not commercial branding for a particular product and manner of teaching.

2

The Plan

"Of all the systems of religion that ever were invented, there is none more derogatory to the Almighty, more unedifying to man, more repugnant to reason, and more contradictory in itself, than this thing called Christianity. Too absurd for belief, too impossible to convince, and too inconsistent for practice, it renders the heart torpid, or produces only atheists and fanatics. As an engine of power it serves the purpose of despotism; and as a means of wealth, the avarice of priests; but so far as respects the good of man in general, it leads to nothing here or hereafter."
--Thomas Paine, *The Age of Reason*, 1795

"Christianity might be a good thing if anyone ever tried it."
--George Bernard Shaw

On my way back to the car, I think about such a visit. Mike has given me an illuminating insight—that I must open up to Chimera and love her unconditionally, forgiving her idiosyncrasies just as she forgives mine. The moment he said it I realized it was true, yet seconds after he put his finger on my problem and with a sense of possibilities returning to me, the most horrid thoughts jump out of the recesses of my mind.

Why didn't Chimera mention that she knew Mike from the meditation center? I remember Chimera's odd look the first time I mentioned Mike's name to her. Is there some reason she didn't say anything? Then Mike abruptly switched the topic of our conversation when he found out who my girlfriend is. I've read enough about so-called religious and spiritual figures to know that many of them fool around, and I can't help but wonder if there's something going on here that I don't know about?

If there is, what seems like a straightforward suggestion from Mike for working things out with Chimera could be just a token to cover something insidious. If that's the case, what value would his advice be anyway? What kind of a teacher would that make him?

And what does that say about Chimera's honesty with me? Even if what Chimera and Mike have suggested to me about love is true, how can I open myself up to them: Chimera who holds back on me, or Mike whose ambitions are unclear? I may be French in my approach as a lover, but I've never understood the convention of mistresses and such. Put me down as a monogamist.

So, it seems as if I have a choice of two very different paths: open myself up to Chimera on faith and trust Mike, or keep both these relationships in limbo for the time being and see what happens. Based on my gnawing concerns about the nature of Mike and Chimera's relationship, I decide on the latter course. Before I take Mike up on his offer for us to visit, I must first discover, without arousing suspicion, what's going on between the two of them. Besides, for the next few weeks I'm intent on finishing my play, *Theatres of Love*. We're about to hold auditions and go into rehearsal at Le Canard, and I need to have a working script in hand.

☼ ☼ ☼

About a week before the auditions, I call Diane to invite her as I had promised. I've been thinking about her a lot since Mike introduced us. In fact, as I rewrite the play, I've been grooming one of the characters to resemble her. I found her not only playfully assertive, even a bit of a flirt, but alluring as well—and her coloring and features remind me of Marguerite.

I call her from my office. After a couple of tries I reach her at home late one afternoon.

"Diane, this is Rashan Barcusé calling. We met a while back at Fred's Restaurant. I was with Mike Solomon."

"Hi. Sure. I remember."

"I told you I'd call when we were going to hold auditions *et voilà*!"

"Great! I really appreciate it," she says. "Hang on a sec. Let me grab a pen."

She puts the phone down. My heart is racing. Usually, I let Le Canard's artistic director handle the details of an audition, but after dealing with the preliminaries and telling her to prepare two contrasting monologues, I push on.

"I've got a particular part I'd like you to read for," I say.

"Oh?"

"Yes, I wrote it for you. I hope it works."

"I'm flattered." She pauses. "All on the basis of our abbreviated conversation?"

"You made quite an impression on me."

"I have to admit there were some sparks," she says.

I take a deep breath.

"Well, I'm glad I wasn't imagining that," I say.

I can hardly wait for the auditions to come around. I spend extra time at the office getting ahead on a couple of audits so I'll be able to trim my work hours during rehearsals.

"How's the script?" Chimera asks me a couple of days before the audition.

"We'll see."

"I suppose you'll know more after the read through," she says.

"Yes, probably a lot more."

I am aware of the irony of this statement as I say it, and have some guilt over it, but feel justified in straddling the fence. I'm not ready to confront Chimera about her feelings toward Mike, and like I said to Mike about her and me: I have my doubts about our relationship. I tell myself it's easier to let these questions slide until after the play begins its run. My questions about Mike can wait as well. In his case, though, while I've decided to put off a visit, I don't want to ignore him. Instead, I decide to call him soon and invite him to opening night.

I never know what kind of a turnout to expect for an audition. Sometimes, even with a good script, a respected director, and a reputable theatre, the timing is wrong and the casting choices are limited, and I end up with a less than thrilling cast. This isn't New York, after all. But I only need five actors for this piece and we've got 40 people signed up to audition over two nights, with callbacks scheduled a few days after that.

After the first hour, it's clear to me that I'll have my choice of many fine actors. The Denver talent pool is certainly growing, I think. What I need to do is find the best combination of talent hidden within this evening's hopefuls, like a sculptor would discover life in a slab of marble. Sometimes even, as with Michelangelo's *David*, you can do the impossible with material that others have rejected.

For the role of Suki, the part I've now modeled after Diane, I need someone who can juggle anger and gaiety. During my theatre career, I've learned that the best actors are able to transcend the limitations of their own personality and effectively project whatever emotions are called for in their characterizations, even if these emotions are a problem for them personally. They can do this as long as they're willing to admit to their feelings around these issues. They accomplish this "transcendence of the personality" either by method acting, using what Stanislavski called "affective memory" to manifest the emotion, as Brando could do for instance, or by pure imitation to simulate the emotion, which was Olivier's talent—but, in either case, the emotions projected by good actors ring true. Those that fail at this either can't act or are stunted by their denial around unresolved emotional issues.

Diane is the third actress auditioning specifically for this role, and her two monologues show me a lot. For her darker monologue, Diane's choice of excerpts from Queen Margaret's speeches in Henry VI and Richard III is a *coup de maître*. She not only gives me a variety of shades of anger, but nobility and courage of tragic proportions—and the piece is unique, her own edit of the text. Diane's lighter monologue, as Billie Dawn from *Born Yesterday*, Judy Holliday's Broadway and Hollywood star vehicle, has everyone in the house beside themselves.

Mike was right—Diane has the chops—which makes my choice easy: she gets the part of Suki. I turn my attention to the other four characters and begin to shorten the list. During callbacks, I'm able to play Diane off against three different men before deciding on my final choice of whom to cast opposite her. Then I find three equally strong actors to fill out the rest of the cast.

Two weeks later we begin rehearsals four nights a week. I have six weeks to get the play ready. This works out to about the same amount of rehearsal time that a full-time professional theatre company gets in two weeks.

As always, there is as much going on after rehearsal as there is during rehearsal. It's much like my audit work, believe it or not—if you want to know the real story behind what you see on stage or in the books, you have to get to know the players. At the end of the first week, I ask Diane to have a drink with me. We go to a neighborhood cantina frequented by Denver police, civic center workers, bail bondsmen, and attorneys.

"So how is it that you know Mike?" I ask, hoping that a reminder about how we met would be a good ice-breaker.

"I was in my second year of acting school and he was directing a video on Shakespeare. He was co-producing it with one of my teachers, Anthony Kirk."

"Oh, right!" I say. I already knew this. "Mike told me that Anthony had been one of the founding members of the Royal Shakespeare Company."

"Yes," she said, before cutting directly to the chase. "What else did Mike tell you?"

"That behind all that beauty is a fine actress," I said.

"And?"

"That's it. But as I've already found out, he was telling the truth."

"Mike always tells the truth," Diane says.

"Really? You know him that well?"

"I've had dinner with him, and drinks a couple of times."

"I see."

"Nothing more than that," she says meeting my eyes. "He's a brilliant guy and we enjoy each other's company, but we're not going in the same direction."

"And what direction is that?" I ask.

"I'm an actress. I live a vagabond's life. I may go to New York; I may find a leading man. Who knows?" she shrugs. "Michael is a yogi. He lives by a code. He has to be truthful."

"You think so? Drinks and talk—isn't that the prescription for a whiskey priest?"

"Or Holy Communion," she replies. "I think truth is almost a constant with him." Diane pauses. "That was the first thing that struck me when he came to our movement class in grad school and talked to us about Yoga."

"That interested you, the Yoga thing?" I ask.

"*He* interested me. But he must have had something else going on. He didn't make a pass."

"You wanted him to?" I can't help feeling jealous.

"It's not often a guy doesn't with me." She takes out a cigarette and fires her lighter. "But yes, like I said, I *was* interested. Now we're friends. I see him at shows now and then, and he comes into the restaurant to eat and say hi. He has this ability to be Platonic, unlike most heterosexual guys."

"You think it's that simple with him?" I ask.

"I don't think it's simple; he's just such a brain. He's always pursuing some intellectual quest, proving this or that, or focusing on some spiritual truth. I enjoy talking with him about the theatre, but metaphysics can get a bit elusive after a few hours, at least for me. I have a hard time connecting it to real life."

"I know what you mean. But I don't think anybody can be that way all the time."

"Well, I'd be sorely disappointed to learn that he was looking for it and turned me down."

I laugh at her bluntness.

"Yeah, it would take some willpower to turn you down," I say.

"Is that what's this is about, Rashan?" she says, looking right through me.

It takes me a few seconds to catch my breath.

"In part," I admit.

"There's no 'in part' to these things, Rashan; like the man sings, it's 'All or nothing at all / If it's love, there is no in between.'[1] You know this. Your play doesn't cut any slack."

"Yes, I know, but a powerful actress is a mighty thing to behold."

"But behold is all you can do if you're already involved."

---

[1] "All Or Nothing At All," A. Altman, J. Lawrence (Leeds Music Co. ASCAP), the most famous recording of it being that sung by Frank Sinatra, May 16, 1966, Los Angeles, to Nelson Riddle's arrangement.

"I am, at this point," I say, trying to leave the question open for another day.

☼ ☼ ☼

After that, over the course of rehearsals, Diane and I have drinks with the cast and crew on a few occasions. During these get-togethers I sit next to her and pick her brain about her lines or her blocking.

We don't talk about Mike then, but what she said to me that first night over beers and platter of nachos piled high with beans, cheese, guacamole, jalapenos, and sour cream sticks with me. Diane put me in my place with surgical efficiency, yet without malice. Here I have been impugning the nature of Mike's interest in Chimera, and hers in him, and now I'm inside out over my leading lady. Sooner or later I'm going to have to deal with these issues; so, as planned, I invite Mike to opening night and the cast party afterwards—I'll wait until after that to talk with Chimera about her feelings toward him.

Le Canard is located a short walk south from downtown, about six blocks from 17th Street's canyon of skyscrapers that form the backbone of Denver's skyline, not far from where today I can look north and see Michael Graves' remodel and expansion of the public library facing Daniel Libeskind's free-standing freeform addition to the art museum. As I approach the theatre, the steeple and the inscriptions on the façade remind me that it was converted from the old Swedish Evangelical Free Church. How fitting, I think, recalling what Mike told me at our first meeting, about theatre being the taproot of religion. Since those remarks, every time I walk into this space I feel an extra layer of meaning enveloping my work.

On opening night, the intensity of the occasion is magnified because I wrote *and* directed the play. Generally, it's not recommended that a writer direct his own work—it's easy to overlook subconscious possibilities that someone else would naturally discover—but I learn so much about my writing from directing my own scripts that I've never put much stock in that theory.

Le Canard's publicist has done a great job of papering the house tonight. In addition to patrons and subscribers and my own guest list, the critics from the major dailies are in attendance. On top of that, our pre-show publicity generates enough reservations and walk-up traffic to sell out. I have a number of last minute details to take care of, but still manage to greet a few guests.

A few minutes after eight o'clock, the lights fade, then slowly come up from the blackout. My adrenaline takes over and the performance flies by. I anticipate every rough spot along the way, hoping that we've worked out the kinks, and for the most part we have: the few wrinkles are so slight, I don't know that the audience will notice.

Finally, the lights come down. I'm relieved to hear immediate applause that, thankfully, sustains itself for a respectable curtain call. Then I'm in the lobby accepting accolades from everyone. The conversation is so polite, I can't tell whether the play has succeeded or not. In the next couple of days, I'll be interested to read what the critics say—whether they understand the production or not, they can make us or break us at the box office—but tonight it's time to party.

I move through the crowd, enjoying the banter, wine, and hors d'oeuvres. Chimera joins me early on during the evening, but is sidetracked by a couple of friends, and I continue to mingle. Later, I notice that she and Mike have a prolonged *tête-à-tête*. I try to read their body language. They obviously enjoy one another's company.

Then I run into Diane.

"An enlightening performance, Diane," I say.

"For you, too!" she says excitedly.

I nod slowly, mesmerized by her fresh, enthusiastic response.

"There's a lot to work with," she says. "More than you or I thought."

"I see that now."

"I'm amazed how much of me is in Suki," she says, "as if you were privy to a part of me that I've only dreamed of."

"I think you're giving me more credit than I deserve," I say, wanting her to go on. "I thought I kept it pretty simple."

"But that's it," she says. "There was plenty of space to play and time to change. I found an awareness in Suki that I've been seeking in myself—the ability to step back from obstacles and put them into perspective. You made me take a deep breath. It's a great part."

I inhale deeply. "What you do with the silence is your talent, not mine," I say, trying to fully savor this connection.

"Flip sides of the same thing:" she says. "Writing to create the space; acting to fill it."

I hardly know where to go with this. What would Rabelais do? What was out of reach now seems so close. I look at her as if she were the reflection in my mirror, unable to speak and afraid to move for fear the illusion will be broken.

Just then Chimera comes up.

"Hi," she says.

Diane and I break away from each other's gaze at the same moment and look at Chimera who's looking at me.

"Hi," I say, blinking while trying to return to earth. Then, back to my senses, I make the introductions.

"You were something else," Chimera says to Diane.

Diane smiles. "I was just telling Rashan how easy his writing made it," she says.

"Funny how that is," Chimera says thoughtfully—"each of us is so much better at expressing our best side when we're helping someone else."

"That's exactly what I was saying," says Diane. "This role has shown me the gap between myself and my aspirations."

"A mirror," says Chimera. "Like my paintings are to me."

"You paint?" Diane says. Then turning to me, "Rashan, why didn't you tell me this?"

"I don't know. I guess we never got around to it," I say, trying to look innocently from Diane to Chimera.

"Let's get some more wine," Diane says to Chimera. "My mom is a painter," she says, taking Chimera by the arm and heading off. I'm speechless as I watch the women turn and make their way across the room. Diane turns and gives me a smile. I don't know what to think.

"Cat got your tongue?" I hear someone ask. I break out of my reverie and turn to see Michael with a bemused expression on his face.

"Cats, actually," I say.

"Women will do that to you," Michael says, "especially two as talented as that."

Michael is encouraging about the play. He says that although the main characters don't fully integrate themselves, by the end of the piece they've come to a better understanding of the choices they face as individuals, to evolve or wither. "This gives us hope," he says, "without insulting us with a pat answer."

This seems like a fair assessment to me, pretty much along the same lines as what Diane was saying. After all, why should there be closure? I don't feel particularly integrated myself, coming from a generation that is obsessed with the process of self-discovery, not the end result. Admittedly, there's a bit of French existentialism in this notion of unfinished business as well. During our conversation, Mike again invites me to visit him in the mountains and reminds me that he has a project he'd like to discuss. "And bring Chimera," he says. I promise to call, explaining that I'd been so busy with the play I hadn't had the time to follow up.

By the end of the evening, I'm feeling pretty good with what I've heard from everyone, and in the following days the reviews are mixed, but work in our favor: the younger critics say it speaks to them and their friends; the older ones question its morality. We sell about 80 percent of our house for our ten scheduled Friday and Saturday night performances and extend the production an extra three weeks, or six shows. It's a successful run—the actors get paid and the theatre takes care of its bills and salts a little away for the experiments that don't work as well.

☼ ☼ ☼

I finally get around to telling Chimera that Mike has invited us to visit.

"You seemed to enjoy chatting with Mike at the premiere." I begin.

"Yes, he's very engaging," she says, "as you've said."

"You didn't tell me you knew him already."

She pauses and looks at me, without blinking an eye. "I thought you'd be jealous," she says.

"Jealous? Why? Is there some reason I should be?"

"No. I just thought that's how you'd feel."

"Well, I do now," I say, "given that Mike changed the subject when he found out about us—and you decided not to say anything when I told you I'd met him."

"I see. It seems that either way—whether I told you or not—you'd feel the same way," she says. "It would have been better to tell you, but part of me said, 'It couldn't be the same guy I met before—that would be too much!'"

"So, you *do* have something for him?"

"I admit I find him attractive," she says, looking at me squarely, "but that doesn't mean anything."

"How am I supposed to know that?" I ask.

"Because I'm committed to you, and you know that," she says. "Besides, whatever physical stuff I felt when I first met Michael has changed."

"Michael, is it?"

"That's what he called himself when I met him, and given his behavior, that's how I see him—as a spiritual being. It's what we talked about when I first met him at the meditation center, and it's what we talked about at the cast party."

"And what makes you think Michael sees his relationship with you as spiritual?"

"He hasn't done anything that would make me think otherwise," she says. "I think you're over-reacting."

I remember that Diane, like Chimera, had similar "spiritual" things to say about Michael—and my conscience reminds me that I, on the other hand, can't characterize my interest in Diane as spiritual. I let my suspicions concerning Chimera and Michael rest for the moment.

"Did he tell you that he wants us to come visit him about a project?" I ask.

"No. What kind of project?" Chimera asks.

"I don't know. I guess we should expect it to be 'spiritual,'" I say, clearly making Michael's invitation a litmus test for Chimera's and Diane's claims.

☼ ☼ ☼

Like Chimera, I begin referring to him as Michael, rather than the familiar Mike. As she said, she finds this formal reference fits his behavior, particularly his intellectual propensities it seems to me. I try to reassure myself with the thought that 'Michael' is how he has it on the card he gave me, and attempt to ignore the nagging idea that Chimera has idealized him into some sort of guru.

By the time I get around to calling Michael after the play has closed, it's been over two months since opening night. I don't think about him much, except in the context of my jealousy surrounding Chimera. I'm aware that this association works against any appreciation for the spiritual and intellectual qualities that I've observed in him, but such is my current state. I haven't know him that long, I tell myself.

He is living in the town of Wayne, about 20 miles west of Boulder in the mountains. I make plans to drive up with Chimera and spend the following Sunday at his place.

Wayne is an old mining camp. It came to life in 1860 when Cy Deardorff discovered the Columbia vein, from which he extracted $5,000,000 in gold. Soon, the surrounding hills were quilted with claims. By 1865, six hundred people lived in the immediate vicinity. In the decades that followed, the population continued to climb, until several thousand people were within walking distance of the town, making it the largest mining camp in Boulder County. When the U.S. went off the gold standard in the 1930's, Wayne, like most mining towns, was abandoned. After World War II, when the State of Colorado decided to inventory its municipalities and de-incorporate the ghost towns, Wayne barely avoided extinction, surviving the ax by meeting two important qualifications: It had just enough adults to fill the town council, thereby being able to govern itself; and the municipality provided a service to its inhabitants—it had a water system. In fact, I'd read that Wayne is the only remaining town in the state to distribute unchlorinated water.

In the late 1960's, when the hippies began to arrive in Colorado in search of sunshine, wilderness, and cheap pot, remote and mostly vacant Wayne became a desirable spot. The hippies moved in and through the years a good number of them managed to buy or build a motley assortment of houses in town.

Motoring into the quarter section[2] hamlet of Wayne this Sunday morning, it seems that life here has changed little since I last passed through

---

[2] In surveying and homesteading, a quarter section is a square tract of land, half a mile on each side, thus ¼ square mile or 160 acres. A few years after this visit, it was discovered that Wayne originally had been deeded an additional quarter section, which had been forgotten in the aftermath of the mining collapse.

eight years before. The yellow and rust slag piles from the glory holes still dot the hillsides. Junk cars are everywhere. Disheveled children play on the hillsides, creek bed, and roads, and most of the houses have that stressed look so common to locations in extreme climates at the edge of civilization. Wayne is situated just a few miles east of the Continental Divide, at an elevation over 9200 feet. In Colorado, this still means plenty of warm days, even in the winter surrounded by snow. But despite the year-round pleasantness, the current perception of the Rocky Mountains—as inaccessible and culturally backward—keeps the number of visitors down.

"Don't you find it a non sequitur that Michael lives here?" I wonder aloud. "I mean, look at this place! In the Alps this would be considered a disaster area."

"Maybe that's Michael's point." Chimera replies.

"What is?"

"He's an iconoclast, and this place would certainly challenge the values of most people."

"That's for sure," I respond.

Following Michael's directions to his house isn't easy. None of the roads are marked, so landmarks substitute for signs. After passing the turnoff to the post office, town hall, and school, we drive by a corral next to the general store, then the original assay office and a new log firehouse. The road begins to climb again and we follow it all the way up to the Peak-to-Peak highway before realizing that we missed our turn. We turn around, head down the hill, and drive back toward the general store. We park next to the store and get out to seek directions, pausing in front of a green delivery truck. The truck is up on blocks, and it's covered by an assortment of chrome auto parts, giving it the look of a tin jewel box.

Just as we're about to turn and head for the store, a thin leathery fellow with a nearly toothless grin slides open the side door of the truck. He's holding a coffee cup in one hand and a hand-rolled cigarette in the other.

"Can I help you folks?" he asks.

"Yes," I say. "We're looking for Michael Solomon's house."

"Yogi Mike?" he asks.

"Right," Chimera says. "That would be him."

"He lives just up the hill there," he says, pointing with his cigarette hand. "I was hoping you needed some shoe repairs. This is my shop." He steps down off the truck.

"Actually, we were admiring your collage," Chimera said. "We didn't know this was a working space."

"I make and repair shoes—actually, any leather goods." He puts his cigarette in his mouth and holds out his hand. "Jim Pierre," he says.

"Do you have any of your work inside?" Chimera asks.

"Sure," he says. "C'mon in."

"Just for a couple of minutes," I say. "We've got to get up to Michael's."

The tight, smoky, sunlit quarters in the rear compartment are packed with shoes of every sort and manner of condition.

"These are great," Chimera says, picking up a pair of lace-up knee-high dark brown hiking books. I wince. Les Folies Bergere it ain't.

"I make them to order. Boots, sandals, shoes, slippers, vests, belts, wallets, even lingerie," he says, looking at Chimera, then checking her out.

"That's an intriguing thought," she says. I look at her inquisitively and she smiles back.

"Would you like some coffee or anything?" Jim says.

In the close quarters I can smell the whiskey he's been drinking with his coffee.

"We'll have to come back when we have more time," I say.

"Yes. I've got some ideas," Chimera says, looking directly at me.

Driving back up the hill, we revisit Michael's directions in light of Jim Pierre's assistance, pull off at the first hairpin turn, and follow a dirt road through a stand of evergreens. As soon as we emerge from the trees, there is a driveway diving dramatically off the road, down the hillside to our left. We park our car along the road and walk down the driveway. I can see the back of the house Michael had described, a white clapboard Victorian with aqua trim. As Chimera and I switch-back down the path, a gingerbread-trimmed eave comes into view, then a classic five-sided bay window crowned with the same decorative pattern. In front of it all, facing down the canyon and out to the plains, a white picket fence runs along the bluff, from the house to the outhouse, which sits on a precipice with a perfect view down the canyon.

Chimera and I make our way single-file down the path to the house, through a family of mature, shimmering golden aspen trees on the terrace leading to the door. As we pass the side of the house, Michael's head pops out of a trench that snakes between the front of the house and the edge of the bluff.

"Hey, guys!" he shouts. "Welcome to Wayne, home of the free!"

Michael boosts himself out of the nearly six-foot deep dugout. The fill from his digging is piled between the excavation and the edge of the bluff, giving the appearance of a World War I entrenchment. Michael brushes himself off.

"Sorry for the mess. I promised myself there'd be running water this winter, so I've got to get below frost line and run the new pipe before the weather sets in."

"That's a pretty deep trench," Chimera says stepping toward the edge, nearer Michael.

"It's got to be," he says. "Otherwise, some morning you'd wake up with no water and, come spring, a busted pipe. Kaboom!" Michael's hands and voice imitate an explosion of water in front of Chimera. She laughs.

Down the hillside from us, a couple of dogs start barking. Michael goes over the bluff and yells their names—"Chief! Shadow!"—and they quiet down.

"Dogs and traffic," he says as he walks back toward Chimera and me. "The two most common municipal complaints across the country. We have our own version up here. People move here with their dogs and think they can let them run free. Then the dogs pack, chase and hunt deer, and go through everyone's garbage."

"In the city it's mostly their barking," I say. "Sometimes it goes on for hours."

"That's the point, Rashan," Michael says. "You're getting treated like a dog by your neighbors. In the end, untrained dogs aren't much different than wolves. They'll run up to you in the woods with that wild look in their eye, while you're enjoying a meditative walk, and you're not sure whether they want to be petted or take a piece out of you."

"What do you do?" Chimera asks.

"Folks do all sorts of things," Michael says. "In the old days, if a dog attacked you in the street, you could shoot it. They never took that law off the books here."

"Really!" Chimera says.

"But I'm not worried about being attacked by dogs," Michael says. "It's the owners that are the problem."

Michael gestures that we precede him up the steps and across the enclosed front porch into the house. I lead the way.

"I'm glad you could make it," Michael says to Chimera. "It's always a pleasure."

I don't turn around, but imagine that she smiles at this bit of chivalry.

Despite the house's classical design, the exterior walls of the porch are covered with an informal array of sun-bleached barn wood streaked with warm earth tones and sprinkled with burnt orange and mustard yellow highlights, in a striking zigzag pattern.

"Nice colors," I remark to Michael.

"Methane," he says. "The fumes from the manure in the coop where the boards were taken from is what gives it that glow. Ironic, no?"

Once across the porch and through a substantial oak door with a smoked-glass window, we're in the kitchen. The ceiling is elevated—at least nine feet, I'd guess. A black, chrome-trimmed wood-burning cook stove, replete with a water jacket and a hot water tank, dominates the room. Where the stove pipe slips through the back wall, there are water stains: a sign that the house was abandoned and the stove in disuse at one time. On the interior wall, a built-in pantry with a sliding smoked-glass door showcases a hearty stock of depression era glassware and assorted jars of home-canned fruits—gifts most likely, judging from the variety of labels. The formal, floral designs on the smoked-glass are echoed in the elegant patterns of the faded wallpaper, particularly the border that circumscribes the room along the tops of the walls. On the opposite side of the kitchen, the entire southwesterly wall is lined with tall windows, filling the room with natural light. Counters made from weathered timbers run the length of this wall, with a set of sinks directly in the middle. Finally, a well-worn table, thick with the patina of countless conversations, and the four sturdy, padded, wooden chairs surrounding it, beckon to us. It's a comfortable combination of antique and function, all pleasingly softened around the edges.

"I'm so happy we're finally able to get together!" Michael says. "Please, have a seat. How was the drive? The canyon roads can be so crazy on the weekends."

"It was a breathtaking, really, with all the aspen beginning to turn," Chimera smiles. "And the light is spectacular. I'd love to paint here."

"Anytime," says Michael. "I'll show you some great spots."

"Do you paint, Michael?" I ask.

"No," he answers, "but I know these woods."

"I could use some new subjects," Chimera muses.

"Say, would you like something to nosh on," says Michael. He gets up and walks to the pantry. "How about some coffee and bagels? Cheese? Fruit?"

"Sure," I say. "We didn't get going early enough to have breakfast."

I remember this morning's lovemaking and suddenly feel less insecure.

"It's funny how we've all met so serendipitously," I say.

"That's one way to look at it," says Michael, turning from Chimera to me. "Or perhaps it's synchronicity."

"Meaning there's some reason behind it?" I say.

"Yes," says Michael, "but not in the Western sense of a measurable cause and effect. Our having been in the same place at the same time is significant unto itself: a combination of simultaneity and meaning. The fact that it happened three times, twice with you and me, at the bookstore and the courthouse, and once with Chimera and me, at the meditation center, goes beyond what even Jung would call an acausal connection. I'd say it's fate."[3]

"Oh, right," Chimera smiles. "That's how you guys met, in the psychology section."

---

[3] See *Forerunners of the Idea of Synchronicity* and *Conclusion*, from *Synchronicity* in C.G. Jung, *The Structure and Dynamic of the Psyche*, Volume 8, 2nd ed., Princeton University Press, 1969, pp. 485—519, and *The I Ching, or Book of Changes*, Richard Wilhelm and Cary F. Baynes translations, forward by C.G. Jung, Bollingen Series XIX, Princeton University Press, 27th printing, 1997, pp. xxiv-xxv.

"Yes, I admit psychology is a fascination," Michael confesses, "especially if it's connected with spiritual healing, but don't let me get started on that."

Chimera looks like she's about to ask a question and get him started on that. I decide to take a short cut.

"You know, when you first invited me up here you never told me what you were doing down at the county courthouse. Do you hold some kind of office here in town?" I ask, hoping to hear about the project he had invited me here to discuss.

"A variety of offices actually, some elective, some honorary, some 'unordained,'" Michael says, beginning to roll out his inimitable all-encompassing philosophic style. "At a certain level, public service has always interested me. In high school I held class offices; in college I organized against the Vietnam War. Vigilance about questions of governance and freedom and social justice seems to be a key part of the Jewish experience, and one that I take seriously."

Despite the obvious cultural clues in Michael's name and some physical characteristics, his ethnicity had seemed secondary to me. He seems far too erudite and cosmopolitan to be pigeonholed.

"There is that element of social reform, isn't there?" I venture, trying not to sound like the gentile that I am.

"It couldn't be any other way," Michael says. "What other people have been so besieged through the ages because of their beliefs, by so many different groups over so long a period, nearly 6,000 years. Activism becomes a necessity, not only for tribal survival, but for everyone's sake—as part of the human journey."

"So, you're saying persecution made the Jews stronger?" Chimera asks.

"Yes, specifically its psychological and spiritual effect on a portable, invisible G-d," Michael says. "The inquisitions, pogroms, and such only made their basic monotheistic beliefs more resolute, leading to the memorization of the holy books that, along with a strong dose of reverence for higher law, spawned a culture based on faith and education. The G-d of the Jews is popular indeed. So much so that the Christians and the Muslims, to propagate their new belief systems, preached that G-d had not only abandoned the Jews in their favor, but that they each in turn represented a better monopoly on the Truth.

"Yes," I say, "the Middle East conundrum."

Michael nods and continues. "The answer to this dilemma of exclusivity lies in the one option that remains unfilled—since the Christian Jesus has come and gone and most Christians act as if he's never coming back and the Islamic vision of a Imam Mahdi has been lost in a sea of totalitarian fundamentalism—which means, expect the Hebrew Messiah, yet awaited by the Jews.

"Seriously!" I say.

"Abraham, Moses, Jesus, Marx, Freud, and Einstein all developed analyses that are, like the monotheistic culture from which they sprang, dependent upon the same single principle—the interdependence of all things. This is what made each of them revolutionaries in their day and what underlies my own teachings as well."

"Thinking holistically seems so self-evident," Chimera says.

Michael continues his roll.

"Many people understand the concept of unity, without understanding its implications and the willingness to live by them. Those who feel their connectedness to all of creation strive to act against the self-centered functions that hold so much of human behavior in its sway—against the instinctive remnants of our animalistic heritage and the ego that carries out their bidding."

I sense that Michael's just getting warmed up, but he surprises me by returning to my question.

"So," he says, "when I arrived here and discovered that the town had initiated the process of creating a Home Rule Charter—a set of guidelines for the behavior of the body politic—naturally I volunteered to write it."

"A political tract?" I was intrigued that my friend had committed some of his ideas to paper.

"I'm concerned how people evolve; how they express their capacity for love and sharing; how they treat others. There's no particular 'ism' in this—and it's not that I don't constantly battle my own self-preservative instincts like everyone else—but overall, it's my desire to make this life a happier, more enlightening experience.

"Having read political science and economics at Stanford during a time when it was still possible to study without academic censorship of alternatives to imperialism, I developed very specific ideas about what I thought governance should look like. So, in the wake of the drafting this charter and its approval by the electorate, I ended up drawing the attention of county officials."

"Didn't Wayne already have laws?" Chimera asks.

"Yes, but they were statutory laws, ones that had been created by the state legislature to provide a generic structure for municipalities. In effect, the laws of all cities in the State of Colorado, from 1876 to 1910, were the same across the board. But in 1910, when the City of Denver had become so large and complex that this arrangement no longer worked, the legislature enacted an amendment to the state Constitution that allowed large cities to modify state laws within areas considered 'of local concern.' This law was further modified two more times, first for medium-sized cities, and later for all cities and counties. So, it was in this context that the Town of Wayne began the process of creating its own Home Rule Charter, sort of a Declaration of Independence on a local scale."

It was just like Michael, I thought, to take advantage of some wrinkle in constitutional law.

"And you wrote this document," Chimera asks rhetorically, as if to indicate to Michael that he should get to the point.

"For the most part, yes." Michael replies. "I wrote about two-thirds of it based on other charters I read and guidelines issued by the Colorado Municipal League. The rest I drafted based on the ideas of the Charter Commission, of which I was a part."

I begin to wonder how the Home Rule Charter differs from state law, but Michael abruptly presents me with an *quid pro quo*.

"Not many political scientists get to put their theories into practice," Michael continues. "To be twenty-five years old and to get a chance like Plato—writing his *Republic* and instituting it at Syracuse—is a gift: like being part of a Golden Age." Michael leans forward onto the table. "Quintessential moments such as these are what my life is about. That's why, as I tell you about this project, I'd like you to think about making a commitment."

I'm struck by Michael's use of the term "quintessential" to define his life compared to what I have recently come to see as the random, serendipitous nature of my own experiences. Then I'm suddenly brought back to the present as Michael's words echo in my consciousness: "A commitment, Michael?"

"Yes, as a writer."

"I'm not sure what you're asking."

"I'm happy to talk about the Home Rule Charter of the Town of Wayne. In fact, here's a copy of it"—he says, pushing a manila envelope towards me that he had left out on the table—"along with some background information. But this is just a small part of my project."

"And you want me to help?" I asked.

"Yes, I'm going to need some help keeping track of it."

"In what way?"

"Think of it like an audit," Michael says. "You've got primary receipts and working papers and the books themselves, but there needs to be an audit report that makes sense of it all. So, I'd like you to think about taking notes on our discussions."

"Well, I'm not sure how to respond. I've found our talks compelling, and I admit I'm intrigued by the nature of your political activities. But why do you want me to take notes? What's the purpose?"

"You know, Rashan, I enjoy you simply for who you are, and that really is quite enough—to be friends—but after I discovered that you're a playwright, I understood why the universe brought us together: Your ability to write about the complexities of character and action allow you to do something for me that I best not do for myself.

"On top of this, you've shown me that you have a feel for the subtleties of psychology—your recent play reveals a strength there. I'm also impressed with your range of ideas and your craft. And the fact that you're always looking for new challenges is a perfect testing ground for what I have to offer. Even the conservative nature of your auditing career works in your favor, as a skeptical counterpoint to my beliefs. So, I know you're the one to do this."

"Do what? You still haven't told me why I would take notes."

I don't understand why my friend, who has up until this time always been so utterly direct, seems to be beating around the bush.

"Pardon me for being so obtuse, but this is something that I don't discuss with very many people; it's a delicate subject. I'll get to the point here, but I don't want you to think I'm crazy."

"Michael," Chimera intervenes, "you're not any more eccentric than the rest of us. What could be so crazy?"

Michael takes a deep breath. "I've had a vision."

"Now we're talkin'! See, that's not so crazy." Chimera says. "Prophesy might not be commonplace, but it certainly happens."

"Whether it's prophetic or not remains to be seen," Michael cautions, "but I know that what I've experienced is central to my life, and that I've got about thirty years to pull it off."

"Th-thirty years!" I stutter, nearly spitting out my coffee. I swallow and try to gather myself. "You want me to make a commitment for thirty years!"

"I realize this is a lot to ask," Michael says, "but I can't write this myself. I may be dead before it gets finished."

"What are you talking about! I don't even know what any of this is about. What's this about your dying?"

"Okay," Michael starts reassuringly, "I've reached a point in my life where everything I have done, what I'm doing now, and surely everything that I will do makes perfect sense to me. I realize that anyone can experience this—all it takes is the willingness to listen to what the universe is telling you, and then be proactive about it—but, at this juncture, I've been led to believe that somebody will appear in my life to document the procession of events, and you seem like the guy. It'll be great material for your work—I guarantee it. I'm only asking you to chronicle our conversations, like a journal of sorts."

"I still don't understand what this is about," I say. "And this dying bit."

"Yes, Michael," Chimera jumps in. "We need some details."

"Okay," he says, "given the long odds on my existence in the first place, I suppose it's possible there's a chance that I won't die in the process of manifesting the avatar—that surviving the arsenal we call America is a possibility—but the odds aren't so hot! The American power elite is very efficient at blowing people away and covering it up—auto accidents, heart attacks, drug overdoses, plane crashes, suicides, and, of course, bald-faced assassinations. And if that weren't enough, there are plenty of so-called Christians armed to the teeth, ready to defend their perverted notions of Jesus—a bigoted capitalist superman with a cross on his chest, who supports obsessive consumption and the wars necessary to sustain such lifestyles, a shameless hypocrite who preaches self-righteousness, not love."

"Isn't this a bit presumptuous, this avatar business and your savage characterization of religious fanatics?" I ask in my most understanding voice, hoping to find a thread back to reality. "What is it that you think will make you a target?"

"I don't deny the possibility that this won't happen," he says, appearing to refocus. "I mean, if Jesus descends, robes fluttering, from a golden cloud some Easter morning, then more power to him, but as the Christian *Bible* says, 'the Son of Man is coming at an hour you do not expect,'[4] and I might add, in a manner you do not expect. So, in the absence of the supernatural scenario, I want you to think about what the Messiah would look like to you, a playwright. What kind of persona or role-play do you think it will take to convince masses of people that he indeed fulfills the requirements? What is it, exactly, that makes him the 'anointed one,' the world teacher, or spiritual anomaly?"

"An interesting premise given the number of people and beliefs out there," I say.

"Wasn't it Einstein that said, 'If at first the idea is not absurd, there's no hope for it'?" Michael asks.

Chimera raises her eyebrows. She is apparently as surprised at all this as I am. I try to appear calm.

"But perhaps you are just a serpent offering an apple?" I say.

"It's funny that you use that metaphor, Rashan, because in the Hebrew language the words *serpent* and *messiah* have the same numeric value.[5] I know this is a rather esoteric point, but it's important.

---

[4] Matthew 24:44

[5] In Gematria, a Talmudic and Qabalistic science, MShICh (Messiah) and NChSh (the Serpent in Eden) = 358 (from Aleister Crowley, *The Book of Thoth*, Lancer Books, New York [no date, reprint dated approximately to the 1970's], p. 100). Michael writes in 2004: Note that the serpent is perceived entirely different in the Orient, where it represents the latent power within, *Kundalini*, which, when awakened, is a regenerative and evolutionary force that bestows enlightenment, growth, and peace. The Aztecs, too, worshipped a serpent god, Quetzalcóetl. Thus, in this light, the moral of the garden of Eden parable is really "a little knowledge is dangerous," as opposed to "women are fallen because Eve took the apple," which leads us, today, to the conclusion that we have arrived at a surfeit of knowledge, enough to empirically prove that science and spirituality are cut from one and the same universe.

Remember, the Son of Man (Messiah) 'will come as a thief in the night.'[6] He will be perceived as the antithesis of what many so-called true believers expect. This is what the apocalypse is about. '... [T]he last shall be first, and the first last: for many be called, but few chosen.'[7] Those that have been the loudest about their faith will discover that their behavior is, effectively, pious claptrap. 'Many will say to me in that day, Lord, Lord, have we not prophesied in thy name? And in thy name have cast out devils? And in thy name done many wonderful works? And then I will profess unto them, I never knew you: depart from me, ye that work iniquity.'[8] ... 'Depart from me, ye cursed, into everlasting fire, prepared for the devil and his angels: For I was hungered and ye gave me no meat: I was thirsty, and ye gave me no drink: I was a stranger, and ye took me not in: naked, and ye clothed me not: sick, and in prison, and ye visited me not.'[9]

"That's why I believe that many contemporary self-styled religious persons would, much like the Romans two thousand years ago, kill someone they perceive as a snake and only later realize he is their spiritual savior. The apple of knowledge offered by the serpent-messiah (Quetzalcóatl, Lion of Judah) will be bitter to many."

"You've obviously anticipated these questions," I say in measured tones, still striving to maintain some semblance of reality in the face of this messianic onslaught, "but this does not seem possible. It sounds like a remake of *The Passover Plot.*"[10]

"What I'm proposing is no more mythological than what most people accept as truth. I'll tell you a story, Rashan, yours to do with what you will." Michael stops and raises his right hand to his chin, pondering, as if searching for a place to start. He looks toward Chimera.

"When I began my study of Yoga, shortly before I met you at that meditation center," he says, "I already knew that 'the guru is inside of me.' I know this sounds egotistical, but if you think about it, this idea has

---

[6] II Peter 3:10
[7] Matthew 20:16
[8] Matthew 7:21-23
[9] Matthew 25:31-43
[10] *The Passover Plot* is a novel published in America in the late 1950's in which Jesus and his friends knowingly arrange the details of the crucifixion so that he survives, thus perpetuating the myth of his physical immortality and cementing his martyrdom.

always been central to spiritual teachings—that each person has a spark of divinity—or what I believe science should call the 'anomaly'—inside of us." He turns to me. "It's also true that relative to most people on the planet, I've led a privileged and blessed life, not only socio-economically—which opened a whole universe of educational and vocational options to me—but in many other ways as well.

"Knowing this, it's been important to me to find some way to give back. When I discovered Yoga, I knew I had found the key to transforming the empowerment I've been given into something that would benefit others."

"So, you're saying," Chimera says, shifting forward in her chair and leaning toward Michael, looking him right in the eye in her inimitable flirtatious yet fully-cognitive manner, "that you had an altruistic purpose in mind when you started doing Yoga?"

"I thought it was altruistic, yes," he says, without blinking. "Later, I learned that my notion of altruism was elementary compared to where I had to evolve to accomplish my goals. But that's one of the great gifts of Yoga—it's a refined system for reawakening the spiritual truth inside of each of us, helping us to attain our higher selves and to fulfill our purpose here."

Chimera shifts back against her chair and leans in the other direction. "So who is your teacher—Trungpa?" she asks.[11] "I mean, from my own practice, I think a good teacher really helps."

"That day we met, I had come to the meditation center to talk with Trungpa," Michael says. "I'd never met him before; I was just looking for some enlightened conversation. In most cases, though, I'd agree with you—teachers are important, and most people need at least one to become a yogi. But even with a good teacher, there can be major obstacles to enlightenment."

"Like what?" she says.

"Like the 'guru effect,'" he says. It's parallel to the transference problem in psychology, where patients put all their trust in therapists and

---

[11] Chögyam Trungpa, Rinpoche, founder of the international Shambhala community and Naropa University in Boulder, Colorado, and author of many books including, *Cutting Through Spiritual Materialism* and *Shambhala: The Sacred Path of the Warrior*.

invest them with all the positive characteristics they seek in themselves. In Yoga, this same type of adoration occurs between *chelas* and *gurus*.[12] Both the patients and the *chelas* fail to recognize the divine or exemplary qualities within themselves that they are projecting onto the psychologists and *gurus,* thus delaying or, in many cases, preventing their own self-realization.

"But at first the patient or the *chela* isn't capable of assuming these characteristics," Chimera counters. "They need a teacher."

"That's right," Michael says, "in almost all cases."

"So you're trying to tell me you're different?" she says almost coyly.

"I believe I am different than most people in important ways, yes, starting with the empowerment I was talking about."

"Okay, I can understand about empowerment, having had so little when I was a kid. So what did you do about a teacher?" Chimera asks.

"I went it alone," Michael says. "It's not my path to have a designated Yoga or meditation teacher."

"That's not recommended," Chimera says.

"Right, I wouldn't recommend my path to anyone else," he responds, "but such a practice isn't unprecedented—there are others who have succeeded here."

"Trungpa doesn't recommend it," Chimera says. "He calls students without teachers 'unguided missiles.'"

"I've seen some, yes," Michael says, "but take Ramakrishna[13]; he knew. From an early age, certain people know who they are and what they must do. And while they're aware of the downsides of a self-directed practice, they persevere and succeed because they receive guidance in other forms.

"So," Michael smiles and continues, "I began the study of Yoga when I was 21 years of age, without a formal guru, and within a short period of time I underwent a powerful awakening."

Michael is dead serious now, no longer camouflaging himself with euphemisms. "Following this transformation, this rebirth, I became aware of the growing popular interest in the many prophesies that point to this upcoming period of time, what we call the Millennium. And I began to see

---

[12] Literally, student and teacher, from Sanskrit.
[13] Sri Ramakrishna, 19th century Indian holy man who taught the unity of all religions, and who founded no sect (See http://www.ramakrishna.org/rmk.htm).

this historical window as a tremendous opportunity to accelerate the shifts in consciousness necessary to guarantee a healthy future for life on this planet."

I am just sitting and breathing, trying hard not to judge.

"Okay, then," I respond, "the coming Millennium, still almost a quarter of a century away, is potentially a window of opportunity. Certainly there will be a lot of people wound up about it. And you feel that you have the wherewithal to take advantage of this brief state of flux?" I ask, wanting a confirmation that I've understood him correctly. Maybe, I think, if we do this a step at a time Michael will end up with a more realistic, more palatable vision of events, just as we work our way through errors and judgmental differences in an audit. As a Frenchman, this type of diplomacy comes naturally.

"Absolutely," he says. "You know, it's not as if I haven't spent time seeking out others that potentially had better answers than I. I've listened to Satchidananda, Krishnamurti, Maharishi Mahesh Yogi, Guru Maharaji, Chögyam Trungpa, Sai Baba, and the rest, studied Einstein and Heisenberg, and read all the political, economic, and social theorists, but so far I haven't found any approach that's satisfies me as being comprehensive enough to both loosen monopoly capital's stranglehold over all of human activity, that is, the worship of mammon, and to kick start the next step in human evolution.

"Look," he continues, "most people think that 'proving' you're the Messiah or Christ or spiritual anomaly means raising the dead and feeding the masses with loaves and fishes, but that's exactly what the editors of the Christian *Bible* and those who now control its legacy want you to believe, because it gives them control over you forever, since no one, Jesus included, is going to reappear and fulfill these mythological fantasies.[14] My job is to invalidate this type of thinking and supplant it with something closer to the truth."

---

[14] This point of view, which separates Jesus' teachings from the mythological elements (added to the *New Testament* to create an aura of invincibility and awe), is shared by such diverse thinkers as Thomas Jefferson and the current roster of the Jesus Seminar, as well as a variety of current scholarship, including the available testaments of the other apostles (found in the lat '40's and early '50's at Nag Hammadi [the *Gnostic Gospels*] and Qumran [the *Dead Sea Scrolls*]) that were suppressed by those who first edited and published the *New Testament*.

At the time, I found this statement completely outrageous. It goes so far beyond the scope of what I had come to accept as possible and sane that I couldn't think of anything to say.

Chimera had no such problem verbalizing her feelings. "Michael, as a woman my first reaction is that it's not unusual to find men who think this way. Most men have a lot of ego tied up in their worldview. But you've got to admit the idea of putting yourself up there with Jesus is a bit farfetched. I mean, c'mon!"

"Farfetched is okay," Michael says. "Look, I know what I'm presenting seems crazy, which is why I told you that I avoid discussing it with most people, but sooner or later I had to talk about this, and it appears that you are the right people. So hear me out. Rare events are by their nature farfetched. But 'one must start with the impossible in order to reach the possible,'[15] right? I have scientific proof for what I'm saying, and I'd like to share with you guys, what I call 'the Anomaly Principle.'"

"This is part of some theory you've developed?" I ask.

"I call it a proof, not a theory,[16] but we'll get to that if you decide to stick with this," Michael says. "For now, though, I'm going to simplify this and just say that anomalistic events, that is, rare events which don't seem to follow form, are, in the big picture, predictable. In other words, we *know* certain events are going to happen, but we can't know *when*. Conversely, based on Heisenberg's Uncertainty Principle, if we knew *when* these events were going to happen, we *wouldn't know* the nature of the event."

"That seems like a tautology," I say.

---

[15] Hermann Hesse

[16] Here was another distinction that I didn't understand the importance of at the time. Later I was to see that, indeed, Michael did have a proof that begins with his model of light and shows how science and spirituality describe an identical reality. When Grigory Perelman's solution to Poincaré's Conjecture was accepted in 2006, Michael was quick to show how me the solution served as a check for his model of light and thus his proof. It was icing on the cake when, in the same week that he made perfect use of Poincaré's and Perelman's work, Michael showed me the experimental evidence for String Theory. It seems that his model of light operates like the Philosopher's Stone, unlocking the relationship of all things, including the appearance of the World Teacher, the unifying principle of all religions, and the next step in human evolution. (See *Appendix 6 – The Proof* or www.SolomonsProof.com.)

"Not exactly," Michael says, "It's part of quantum theory, which, I might note, begins with the concept of light just like the Torah. Let me put it a different way. According to the Anomaly and the Uncertainty Principles, we *know with certainty* that a spiritual anomaly, someone like Abraham or Jesus or Buddha or Krishna, will appear. But, as I said, we *don't know when* this will happen."

"That seems like a prophesy, not a statement of fact," I say.

"No," Michael says. "When Matthew quotes Jesus as saying, 'Therefore you also must be ready; for the Son of Man is coming at an hour you do not expect,'[17] that is prophesy. When I say, 'Know that the anomaly is coming, but at a time and manner you know not,' that is a prediction based on science. The fact that they are saying the same thing is one of the key points of my proof."

"You can prove that science and religion are the same?" I ask.

"Science and spirituality," Michael corrects. "Yes, they are two ways of looking at the same thing and I can prove this, and extrapolate from it as well."

"How can you prove it," Chimera asks, "by another theory?"

"Hang on a second," Michael says to Chimera. "Don't be prejudiced against something just because it involves men and words."

"Michael, I grew up around men who used their learning to lord over their families; half of what they said was just speculation and gibberish."

"Okay, I share your view that the use of complex thought processes often indicates self-absorption and control issues, and I understand the 'lost in intellectual space' glazed-eye look that comes when someone goes off on their 'theories,'" Michael says. "But really, that phenomenon is a response to intellectuality based on ego—conceptualizations that originate from the frontal lobes of the brain."

"The ego is here to stay," Chimera says.

"That's why the experience of union, or Yoga, within each of us, the conjoining of our own masculinity and femininity, the Divine Syzygy that I've been telling you about, is so important. It's one of the keys to using words from the heart and transcending the egocentric use of symbolic forms."

"But really, Michael, what you describe is still using the ego."

---

[17] Matthew 24:44

"Not in the same way as you're accustomed, Chimera. Look, your feeling that the conscious mind can only take you so far, that it's the tip of the iceberg, is true. Words *can* be a trap, like any symbol, but they are not necessarily such. This is what *Jnana* Yoga and Qabalah are about—liberation through knowledge: finding the place within from which truth springs, and then expressing that truth using the symbolic forms of the ego as a tool.[18] It's not the only path or necessarily the best path, but it is a bona fide expression of enlightenment, and an important one given the stranglehold that various belief systems and symbolic progressions have over human populations."

"So, you're saying that you have attained a way of thinking that is from the heart?" I ask.

"Yes," Michael says, "from the heart and the higher self.

"The *Yoga Sutras*,[19] as taught for thousands of years, claim that certain cognitive events can be inspired at the moment they occur, given the proper state of the practitioner. Certainly you've experienced the rhapsody of music: a symphony, one note at a time, lasts for an hour or more; and jazz soloists trade extended improvisations. Complex mathematical formulae, another symbolic form, allow us to land on the moon. Who's to judge another's phraseology or logic? Remember in *Amadeus*[20] when the Archduke tells Mozart that his composition has 'too many notes'? Audiences understood his ignorance and laughed at it! Similarly, this is my composition, Chimera. My words stand on their own merit. Words are necessary tools in proving the unity of all things, for many have used words to distort the truth and undermine its unity."

---

[18] Michael's paraphrase of his favorite of the Yoga Sutras of Patanjali is: "*Siddhis* (powers, accomplishments) may be gained by (or through the use of) *bahkti* (Michael's principal path, Love and Compassion), *pranayama* (breath), *mantrum* (chanting), birth (astrology, he is an Aries, with seven planets and four grand trines in Fire), herbs or *ganja* (as in *The Teachings of Don Juan: A Yaqui Way of Knowledge*, the sacraments), *jnana* (knowledge coincident with attention/presence, Light), *raja* (meditation), etc." Michael indicated to me that all these paths have come into play in his life.

[19] An ancient collection of oral teachings, at least 4,000 years old but probably much older, used to train yogis, that were written down by Patanjali approximately 2,500 years ago in India. Many different translations and interpretations are extant and are referred to later in this book.

[20] A play and film about the life of the genius composer/musician Wolfgang Amadeus Mozart.

"So who's to judge whether what *you* say is truth or lies?" Chimera asks.

"Spoken words are like dreams," Michael continues. "They may represent simply our attempts to heal some mundane day-to-day annoyance; they may be our own projections; or they may give us a glimpse of the future or some universal revelation; but in any case, there is generally no conscious intention to create dreams, they simply happen, acting as authentic read-outs of our unique, inner truths. So it is with instinctive, spoken words. It's up to you to judge whether I come from a place of truth, delusion, or charlatanry."

"So it's like painting." Chimera says.

"Sure," Michael replies. "A clear mind and heart allow one to channel truth, like a Sybil."[21]

"That is not so easy," she says.

"Not so easy is right," says Michael, "but not impossible."

"So, Michael," I say, trying to bring the focus back to the conversation, "what was your vision?"

As one might expect from a student of Jung, and as he had just intimated, Michael's vision was actually a dream.

"This particular dream began like others I've had over the years," he starts. "I'm sitting in a lotus position in a quiet subdued place, an attic, meditating, when suddenly I have the sense that an evil presence is impinging on my space. Normally in this dream sequence, I begin to vocalize sounds that seem to be in some sort of ancient language, perhaps Atlantian. Simultaneously, I begin to levitate from the floor, and the vibratory combination of the sound and the levitation drives the negative force away."

Chimera clears her throat and looks at me playfully before addressing Michael. "How long has this been going on? Is this going to happen to me if I keep doing Yoga?"

Michael laughs.

"I'm sure the symbols of integration in your dreams are, and will continue to be, much different than what I've described," Michael says.

---

[21] A type of psychic, named after Sybil Leek, and thereafter a popular term in the genre of 20th Century science fiction. Sybils possess the ability to read a person's truth.

"But at the time, mine followed this pattern; I've probably had four or five dreams like this over the past five years," he says pausing. Then lowering his voice he softly resumes, "But in this particular dream something is different; for some reason the negative force feels greater and makes me feel more vulnerable. I still levitate, using the vibration of the ancient words, but the negative force refuses to be dispelled. Just when the evil seems insurmountable, a voice rises within me, and in English I say, 'I am Christ!' And the oppressive negativity is dispelled instantaneously."[22]

> *This morning, a couple of months after I have begun my rigorous practice of Yoga, I am compelled to look at my face closely in the mirror. For some time I've been aware of the aversion of Paleolithic peoples to use mirrors, or even to be photographed for that matter, and I attribute this behavior to the effect that such imaging has on triggering ego-related activities, as has been shown in chimpanzees. So, today's practice is somewhat unusual for me. What strikes me immediately, after getting over the relatively drawn look I have developed with the weight loss from my new lifestyle, is the life-long mark on my brow. In the context of my recent readings on Yoga, Buddhism, and Jungian psychology, I can't help but wonder about the significance of this dot located precisely over my third eye. What is happening to me? Am I the Buddha? The Christ? The Messiah? Where shall I be led by this transformation that I am undergoing?*[23]

---

[22] The pattern in this dream is similar to one Michael tells me about years later. (See *Chapter 9 – Pastels*) "It's like the dream I had as a child about a wolf," Michael says. "We lived for a short time with my immigrant grandfather, Jacob Solomon, in a dark apartment building in Gary, Indiana. In this recurring dream I am on the second story landing, locked out of our apartment, and a wolf walks up the stairs and eats me. Finally, after the dream has re-occurred several times, and in the midst of it again one night, I refuse to be frightened and *let* the wolf eat me. That was the key; the dream never recurred. I take it that my childhood lesson in faith and submission was a steppingstone to a receptivity that opened the door to Christ or Messiah consciousness. By solving that problem, I learned to trust my own shadow, and that made it possible for me to have my 'I am Christ' dream as an adult."

[23] As I mentioned in the Preface, shortly before publishing this work, among the papers I received from Michael were his journals. I have interspersed entries throughout this book wherever they seem appropriate. This one is dated September, 1970.

Michael pauses to look back and forth between Chimera and me. I study his face, noticing for the first time what appears to be a birthmark, a small indented circle or dot, in the middle of his brow, centered right on the location of his third eye.

"It was obvious to me that the work I had been doing for some years had finally paid off," he says, before pausing again. He seems very focused now. 'By the roots of my hair some god got hold of me. I sizzled in his blue volts like a desert prophet.'"[24]

Chimera and I are too stunned to say anything.

"You know that book I recommended to you, Rashan?" he asks.

"You mean the Jung volume with that essay—*Christ, a Symbol of the Self,*" I reply.

"Yes. With concepts from that book in mind, I made a conscious effort over the years to awaken and strengthen my *anima*, my feminine side. Between my increased receptivity from that psychoanalytic endeavor, and my Yoga practice, with its practices of purity of thought and purpose, I can only conclude that my strategy worked. I don't mean to say it was easy," he says, "but the dream indicated to me that my innermost soul had aligned itself with the anomalistic archetype I'd been seeking."

"Okay," I concede, "if that's the case, what does it mean? Isn't this a state available to anyone who comes along? Isn't that Jung's point? What makes you think that by successfully navigating these waters you aren't just another enlightened being, like so many others?"

"In one sense it's true that I am only another enlightened being like so many others. This very point was made by the person we call Jesus, when he taught the apostles to heal others just as he did.[25] So, yes, the Messiah or Christ consciousness can be taught. In a parallel sense, though, there is a specificity and personality to Messiah or Christ consciousness,

---

[24] Sylvia Plath, *The Hanging Man*.
[25] Matthew 10:1-8. "And when he had called unto him his twelve disciples, he gave them power against unclean spirits, to cast them out, and to heal all manner of sickness and all manner of disease. ... These twelve Jesus sent forth, and commanded them, saying, 'Go ... to the lost sheep of the house of Israel. And as ye go, preach, saying, "The kingdom of heaven is at hand." Heal the sick, cleanse the lepers, raise the dead, cast out devils: freely ye have received, freely give.'"

that is, a representation of it in the flesh, a spiritual anomaly, as it were, who is the world teacher, the lawgiver. Jesus was not the first and he, or Mohammed for that matter, or the present spiritual anomaly is not the last. Avatars (Magids, in Hebrew), even those of the highest order, appear with periodicity."

"So," I ask, "you're saying that above and beyond believing that your dream indicated you had attained Messiah or Christ consciousness, you also believe that you represent a singularity in this regard—the present serial embodiment of the Messiah or Christ? That's hard to swallow, Michael."

"Yes, I agree that for anyone to believe they represent this specific anomaly seems like a huge ego trip—it's the biggest statement anyone could make. And it's not that I come to this lightly; as I said, 'if some other Messiah descends, robes fluttering, from a golden cloud some glorious morning, then more power to him,' but this is how I read what's being presented to me, especially considering my proof."

"What does your proof have to do with this?" Chimera asks.

"It's not just that I prove that science and spirituality represent the same truth, or that the universe is made from light, or that the spiritual anomaly is going to appear, but that proving this is, in and of itself, a proof of the incarnation of that anomaly."

"Why would that be?" I ask.

"For a number of reasons," Michael replies. "First, no one has ever proved this before. Second, according to prophesy and science, no one but the spiritual anomaly *could* prove this, because the time of his or her appearance is known only to this being as a direct representation of the Universal Anomaly or G-d. Third, the implications of this proof on human knowledge are nothing less than the Philosopher's Stone itself—the transformation of all manner of disparate thinking into one integrated system, logical and acausal, scientific and spiritual, dimensions beyond what Einstein ever dreamed of for the Unified Theory—so who else but the philosopher-king, or rabbi-high priest, could deliver it. Fourth, as a result of seeing this holistic, universal truth, humankind will have what it needs to evolve beyond the present crossroads, to choose light over darkness, higher self over instinct and ego, to see all religions as one, as prophesized; and, if they do so, the person delivering this gift to them is by definition the spiritual anomaly, the Messiah or Christ, etc. And fifth and finally, the proof and the declaration are the same thing—the spiritual anomaly is saying, 'I am the anomaly and this is my proof; I am here at an hour and in a manner that you did not expect, combining science and prophecy.'"

"You actually think this will happen?" asks Chimera.

"Thinking this will happen is actually not much of a help," Michael says. "I have to proceed as if what I do is critical to making it happen. Whether humanity responds is not wholly within my control, except to the degree that I contribute toward this end."

"So," I say, "you admit that you don't know whether the world will change as a result of your proof."

"Correct, just as Moses', Jesus', or Marx' well-publicized prescriptions are rarely practiced, especially by those who claim to be their followers. But I do know that the spiritual anomaly will appear, and that my being this anomaly is indicated by the teachings. In the end, the proof is in the pudding: The value of my words will either be recognized and acted upon or it won't, but it is my responsibility to put forth my proof and my vision in a manner I deem to be the most effective possible for the long-term."

I felt a sense of vindication, finally, after all this grandiose metaphysical posturing. Despite his dream, or "vision," and his proof, Michael's claims, it seems, can only be borne out by history itself.

"You have to admit this is a lot to absorb all at once?" I say, trying to find the most politic means of claiming my victory.

"Of course. I understand. At times it's a bit much for me as well," Michael says.

"Yet still," I say, "this is still a cause for which you feel you may have to die."

"Oh that," Michael brushes off what is, for me, a very disturbing psychological imperative. "Think about how many people depend upon their churches to 'accommodate' the materialism of the world that surrounds them. I mean, for the most part Jews, Christians, Muslims, Hindus, Buddhists, Taoists, Zoroastrians, Bahá'ís, and the rest have all found a way to legitimize the accumulation of excess capital within their spiritual universe, legislating greed into the very fabric of religion! But I won't be enshrining money. 'Ye cannot serve G-d and mammon.'[26] So,

---

[26] Matthew 6:24, Luke 16:13.

what I'm saying, Rashan, has ramifications that in the past have been taken as a threat to the established churches and states, and will continue to be taken so in the present. The Romans murdered Jesus not because the Jews told them to kill him—that is a fabrication used to sell the story to the Holy Roman Emperor Constantine—but because Jesus did not recognize Caesar's suzerainty over the world, as his statement about G-d and mammon shows. Again, this is the same message that Moses gave the Israelites—G-d is offended by worship of the golden calf.[27]

"Imagine Jesus showing up at the Vatican today," Michael continues. "'Thanks for holding my chair for two thousand years. Now if you'll just step aside,' he says, 'I'll proceed from here.' He would never make it out of Rome alive. Contemporary Romans would excuse his murder by quoting a phrase their predecessors have consistently misread in the Christian *Bible* and by which they wrongly justify placing the state above G-d on this plane: 'Render therefore unto Caesar the things which are Caesar's; and unto G-d the things that are G-d's.'[28] Jesus was mocking the coinage with Caesar's visage.

"So, if what I say is heard by enough people and becomes a threat to those in power—the neo-Roman churches, states, economic kingmakers and shareholders, and all their minions—then they will have their choice of religious fanatics, patriotic zealots, and techno-fascists from whom to choose their assassin: The same as when organized crime, wealthy Cubans, armament manufacturers, the CIA, and LBJ all wanted JFK dead. They had a choice of assassins from whom to choose. And sloppy as their work was, they got away with it by shoving their mythology, the Warren

---

[27] Exodus 32:7-29
[28] Matthew 22:21; Mark 12:17; Luke 20:25. Michael writes in 2006: As Michael Baigent so astutely documents in *The Jesus Papers: Exposing the Greatest Cover-Up in History*, HarperSanFrancisco, 2006, Jesus' remarks were carefully couched to respond to this trick question on the part of the Pharisees. Cognizant of the slaughter the Roman's had inflicted on any Jews that refused to pay taxes to state, Jesus was at this time seeking to avoid a final confrontation over this particular issue, since he had bigger fish to fry. So his remarks toward the coin with Caesar's image upon it must be seen as contemptuous, not respectful. In support of this, Baigent perceptively points out that Jesus was crucified, a Roman punishment for sedition, not stoned, as he would have been if it were the Jews who had him executed for religious crimes.

Commission Report, down everyone's throat, just like the so-called *New Testament.*"

"Michael!" Chimera jumps in. "Radical as you talk, you honestly think that someone is going to come shoot you? I mean, you just said it remains to be seen whether what you've got to say even gets heard. Nobody even knows you exist!"

"Granted this is speculation right now," Michael calmly replies, "but when all of this is published, that will be a different matter. Look, I've spent a lot of time exploring my commission. I considered law and politics once, but felt that the commercial interests that control both professions would be an insurmountable constraint. I considered religion, but the abuses rampant throughout religious sects clearly indicate the depravity of these institutions. And science, too, like church and state, generally serves the needs of capital, not the spirit. But, art, now there's the rub. Folks say, 'it's *only* theatre,' or 'it's *only* a novel.' But under the guise of art we can speak our piece for as long as we can get away with it."[29]

"You really think it's that grim? Chimera asks."

"Machiavelli wasn't writing fiction," Michael replies. "I've got to be realistic. Look, I was trained in this stuff—my degree is in political science and economics. This isn't some nonsense I picked up from corporate-controlled newspapers, magazines, or broadcasts. Believe me, I'm interested in preserving myself as long as possible without shirking my responsibility to speak what's in my heart and mind. But if it comes down to having to die for my beliefs, I have no problem. And this is the one thing I promise you that you *will* learn from Yoga, Chimera, if you keep at it: You have eternal life. 'I lay down my life to take it up again.'[30] Because 'he that believeth on me hath everlasting life.'[31] So, I aspire to spread my message as far and wide as I can before the gig is up. And besides, we've seen that martyrdom is effective." He smiles.

---

[29] Mario Vargas Llosa, the Peruvian novelist, recently observed, "I don't think there is a great fiction that is not an essential contradiction of the world as it is. ... This is the great contribution of the novel to human progress. You know, the Inquisition forbade the novel for 300 years in Latin America. I think they understood very well the seditious consequence that fiction can have on the human psyche." (http://www.nytimes.com/2002/03/28/books/28VARG.html?)
[30] John 10:17
[31] John 6:45

"Okay," Chimera exhales, "I can understand your point-of-view. Basically, you're asking Rashan to create a record of this in case anything happens?"

"Yes, a testament, as it were. You see, my dilemma is that I don't have a lineage like the Dalai Lama. No men in robes wandered into my family's apartment in New York City, laid out a set of common objects and observed me choosing specific personal possessions and relics from my previous life that would indicate the identity of the soul who inhabits this bodily vehicle. It's only since the Chinese have perpetrated their version of the Holocaust on these people that such ancient lineages are being disrupted in Tibet. But the House of David has experienced this chaos repeatedly. David himself ascended the throne based on his skills, not his birthright. The rightful heirs of David, Solomon, and Jesus are left to their wits and the dispersed, meager remnants of their heritage to prove their legacy. So it's important that those committed to witnessing our mission not only have the wherewithal to be as objective as possible, but they must also be clever enough to get their document out to the public without it being hijacked, like Jesus' teachings were by those working for their own self-righteous purposes, and later in the interests of the Holy Roman Empire and their instruments of control, such as the Church and the Inquisition."

I can see now that what I perceived as my earlier victory in getting Michael to admit to the speculative nature of his cause did nothing to dampen his belief in it.

"Given that scenario, I see why you would expect some flack," I say.

"So you understand the importance of getting this right?" he replies.

"You believe you can prove this legacy—that you're descended from the House of David?" I ask, using Michael's own words.

"Yes," Michael replies. "This Home Rule Charter that I've given you is only a sidebar, an appendix, though an important one, Rashan. If you choose to help me with this, I'll provide you with a scientific proof that I am the manifestation of the prophesized World Teacher. We'll also develop a plan for how this proof and other teachings will be promulgated."

"You really do believe that all this actually proves you are the prophesized 'spiritual anomaly,' as you called it," Chimera says.

"As much as it is possible to prove such things. After that, it is up to other human beings to judge. If they are motivated in growing numbers by my words, then yes, that would be the final step of the proof."

Chimera and I have nothing to say. Michael pauses again and looks at each of us.

"Would you make a commitment if you thought you could significantly change the world?" he asks.

☼ ☼ ☼

The dance at the end of a conversation is as a bookend to the beginning, and thus Chimera and I slowly and politely extricate ourselves from the immediate clutches of destiny in order to step back and consider the consequences. As we walk to our car, the last vestiges of sunlight are going down behind the mountain named after the left-handed leader of the Arapahos, Chief Niwot.[32] Luminescent golds and vibrant pinks crown the Continental Divide. We don't say anything until our pride and joy, the restored 1960 Volvo PV544 is safely rolling down Left Hand Canyon past the rock-spire sentinel that is said to be Niwot's profile, a stoic stone visage which frames the approach to the mountain that bears his name and scrutinizes everyone that ventures up or down, through the Turn of Events.[33]

"That's not exactly what I was expecting," I manage to get out after a couple of minutes.

"Hah!" Chimera laughs, punctuating my understatement.

"Is he mad? I mean, can someone in their right mind believe such things about themselves?"

"It's been done before," she says.

---

[32] Chief Niwot predicted that the Boulder Valley would become over-populated by white people because it is so beautiful. At one time, the Boulder County Commissioners commissioned a bust of Niwot for the County Courthouse lawn. The plaque accompanying the bust quoted Niwot's curse. The Chamber of Commerce later influenced the removal of the bust and plaque and had it located 'elsewhere.' Eventually the bust was returned to the courthouse lawn, but with a different inscription.

[33] A famous local landmark that separates those who live in Wayne from those who live below 9000'.

"Yeah, and look what happened that time."

"Try to see this differently, Rashan, from a Jungian point of view."

"You're saying to see Michael as someone who has achieved Christ consciousness through the integration of the self?"

"Basically, yes. It's a safer way of seeing him. It makes him like you said up there, just someone who may have achieved this psychological state."

"He's asking me to chronicle his life and our relationship, something that will involve working with him quite closely over many years, and I'm questioning his sanity."

"I understand. You don't think he's achieved integration of the self," Chimera says.

"It sounds like you believe him!" I snap. Immediately my adrenaline is flowing, I'm wound up, and my imagination is off and running once again. "What do you have for him?"

"Whoa, Rashan!" Chimera demands. "Take it easy. Where's this coming from?"

"It seems like you're very chummy with Michael for having only met him twice."

"You're still jealous of him?"

"Should I be?"

"Look, I admit I feel that Michael's an intelligent and charming guy, but you're imagining something that's not going on. We had this conversation a week ago."

"Then what are all these sparks that seem to be happening between the two of you?"

"We have a spiritual connection."

"So, you trust him."

"I understand his spiritual plight."

"And what's that?"

"He's a talented guy who gets into Yoga and undergoes a transformation. Because of his personal empowerment, he's able to take the implications of his experience to the limit."

"That's exactly what Diane told me!"

"Well, then! You can see the validity of our perspective."

"That doesn't mean he's 'The One.'"

"Right, not necessarily. But the possibility exists."

"But you think it's true."

"No. I'm not sure. But I understand his premise," she says.

"Okay." I take a deep breath and try to calm down. "What do you think about my getting involved with him, as his Boswell so to speak?"

"I don't see what you have to lose. Documenting this would be interesting in itself; it could be fodder for a new play. Who knows what else might happen?"

3

The Charter

"*I tremble for my country when I reflect that God is just: that his justice cannot sleep forever: that considering numbers, nature and natural means only, a revolution of the wheel of fortune, an exchange of situation, is among possible events: that it may become probable by supernatural interference! The Almighty has no attribute which can take side with us in such a contest.*"
--Thomas Jefferson, *Notes on Virginia*, Volume XVIII, 1782.

"*There is nothing more difficult to plan, more doubtful of success, nor more dangerous to manage than the creation of a new system. For the initiator has the enmity of all who would profit by the preservation of the old system and merely lukewarm defenders in those who would gain by the new one.*"
-- Niccolo Machiavelli, *The Prince*, 1513

It's difficult not to think about Michael's enigma: Successfully integrating one's self is something I'm trying to do myself—but believing that such an accomplishment makes you an avatar or *the* Avatar, even if your dreams inform you of such, is a quantum leap. However, some of Chimera's empathy has worn off on me. I can see that because Michael believes what he told us, doesn't mean he's crazy, just as, in a contrapositive sense, believing it doesn't make it true.

I've been in situations like this with my audit work, where an executive will tell me in all sincerity that he believes his company's books are in order, and I wonder whether he's crazy, blind, or just a great liar. In Michael's case, however, my "audit" is still in progress and I don't have any facts to disprove his contentions, at least not yet.

But where does that leave our mutual project, what I, as an auditor, call the "working papers," so to speak? In my study the next morning I sit staring at the envelope he gave me. My feelings of both fascination and unease tell me our visit raised more questions than it answered. I can understand Michael's point about the danger inherent in criticizing the establishment. After all, most of the assassinations that Americans witnessed in the '60's and early '70's targeted liberal or leftist figureheads. In each case, the evidence seemed to indicate that a conspiracy at a higher level could have or surely existed, but nothing was ever proven, at least not by the committees appointed to whitewash the events—witnesses disappeared and evidence was suppressed and impounded.

Assassination, then, is simply a risk that comes with the territory of criticizing church, state, and big business. No self-respecting artists, prophets, or political figures would alter their work because of threats against their life, even if they might avoid walking down certain alleys—though such precautions are no guarantee of safety. For every Molière who dies a natural death, there is a Zola who is murdered by the authorities. And though America is a much younger country than my native France, it certainly has a growing list of comparable men and women of principle, such as Thomas Paine and the Reverend Martin Luther King.

Yet Michael seems such a long ways from recognition like this as a result what he is doing. The Home Rule Charter that he has written is hardly two years old, and other than a few lawyers from Denver requesting copies of it for their clients (older landowners who spend their summers in Wayne and who, before the hippies, ran the town as their private club), no one is taking much notice.

And some of Michael's historical claims are a bit of a stretch. During our visit he discussed early Christian history as if he is privy to information from which the rest of us are sequestered, like his claim that Jesus' teachings have been "hijacked." But where others just throw up their hands at the factionalism, divisiveness, and exclusivity of the world's religions, Michael seems to treat the problem as if it were an empirical exercise, a matter of uncovering the facts and integrating them into present-day global relationships, as if that would suddenly make everything okay.

Then there is the matter of the "attraction" between Michael and Chimera. Chimera wants me to believe that their connection is simply spiritual, and as much as I would like to believe this, I'm not so sure. Isn't this just another way of becoming interested in someone and wanting to discover more about them? And what kind of a man wouldn't be flattered by the attention of a beautiful and, in this case, talented woman? Then there's all the sex scandals involving "spiritual" leaders—Christian, Buddhist, Hindu, Judaic, and the rest—which don't make me feel any safer. Carnal desire has been hiding behind spirituality forever. Victor Hugo wrote about it in *Notre-Dame de Paris*.[1] Yet if I decline Michael's invitation to "witness" his work, what am I going to tell Chimera—that I don't trust her? She might see him anyway, or leave me. That's not what I want. And if I refuse Michael's offer and tell her I think he's crazy, she might question my judgment, with the same unsatisfactory results.

And who am I to question Chimera's honesty? Perhaps what I'm projecting onto Chimera and Michael are simply my own desires concerning Diane. And what are these desires now? I thought I had sublimated my feelings for her into our work, and yet, at the cast party, when she expressed her admiration for my writing, I felt an attraction to her that was stronger than before, something even more basic than the unexplored sexual frontier.

So what is it that I want and need? From the beginning, didn't I think Michael had some answers to questions in my life? Now, again, like that time on the courthouse plaza—when I was caught between telling him what was going on in my life and wanting to withhold information about Chimera—my fate is to continue the dialogue.

I open the envelope. Michael's notes appear in the margins and on the back of a series of mimeographed sheets that hold copies of the Prefactory Synopsis,[2] Preamble, and Home Rule Charter of the Town of Wayne. He also has given me a ream of photocopies of the clerk's minutes that begin with the first meeting of the General Assembly of the Town of Wayne, after the Charter had been approved by a statutory referendum.[3]

---

[1] Otherwise known as *The Hunchback of Notre-Dame*.
[2] In the Colorado constitution's Home Rule Charter amendment, a Prefactory Synopsis is legally required explanation of intent, like a preface.
[3] See *Appendix 1 - Excerpts from the Home Rule Charter* of the Town of Wayne, Colorado for sections of the charter relevant to our discussion. The charter was approved in May, 1975.

Some of the material is quite presumptive, especially considering that Wayne is such a small town. But overall, being a naturalized citizen of the United States and an admirer of the American Revolution, much in the manner of my French ancestors—who, I must repeat, given the present-day hysteria of Francophobia,[4] not only aided in the American colonists' success at breaking the bonds of the English monarchy, but sent them the Statue of Liberty to commemorate this remarkable feat—I am impressed with the approach taken in these documents. In fact, I believe that many of the sentiments expressed in the Charter's Preamble go further than the Declaration of Independence, the Preamble to the Constitution of the United States, or the United Nations' Universal Declaration of Human Rights.[5]

I also suppose it should be no surprise, having marveled at Michael's ability to connect any one fact to any other fact, that he would seek to tie political and legal structures to some higher truth; and from the opening phrases in the Preamble to the Charter, it's clear that this is a political manifestation of spiritual ideas, reminding me of the writings of Rousseau. But what examples do we have of nations, states, or cities that actually live up to such ideals? None that I can think of. Does Michael think his political theories, if put into practice, would somehow escape this fate?

☼ ☼ ☼

It takes me parts of ten days of reading, re-reading, and thinking about the Charter before I decide to accept Michael's offer to chronicle his activities and the development of our relationship. I tell myself that it's not much different than an audit engagement: As long as it proceeds in a reasonable manner and in consonance with Generally Accepted Accounting Principles[6]—in this case the basic precepts of journalism—then the

---

[4] Starting in 2002, when the French resisted American and British imperial designs on Iraq.
[5] Adopted on December 10, 1948
[6] GAAP usually refers to U.S. accounting standards that began in the early 1930's to regain the public's trust for investing in the markets. It has had its ups and downs since then. In the first decade of the 21st Century, the consolidation of the world financial system necessitated a transition to a new set of guidelines, International Financial Reporting Standards (IFRS).

engagement is valid. If not, I am empowered to release myself from the contract.

Given the general time constraints in my life, though, I'm hoping that Michael will make the work easier by agreeing to let me tape our conversations. Not only would this produce a more accurate rendering, but it would make it easy for me to record my observations as I travel and ruminate on what I'm experiencing. I decide to wait until the following Saturday, thirteen days from our visit, to call him.

After exchanging pleasantries, I tell Michael that I've spent some time going over the Charter and that I've decided to accept his invitation to serve as chronicler of our friendship and a witness to his efforts.

"I still have my doubts, mind you," I tell him, "but, overall, I believe the project is worthwhile."

"It's natural to have doubts, Rashan," he tells me. "You feel that you don't have enough information, because what I've described to you demands a leap of faith, which is scary. If it helps at all, I can tell you that I go through my own changes over what the universe has presented to me—much in the vein of 'Why have you forsaken me?'[7] So, I appreciate that you're skeptical—it bolsters your objectivity. As the Dalai Lama has said, we should put everything to the test and decide for ourselves whether to have faith in it."

I'm pleasantly surprised by Michael's generous point of view. It gives me breathing room to observe his "psychological integration," as Chimera puts it, without having to beat myself up over doubts and questions about any larger "spiritual mission" to which he may be called. All I have to do is ask questions and let the genie answer.

And thankfully, Michael finds no problem with my request to tape record our conversations, so the process is unfolding in as straightforward a manner as I could hope.

"Back in my student days," Michael says, "when we were planning demonstrations against Stanford University—for its involvement in the research and development of chemical, biological, and electronic warfare devices being used in Vietnam—there was a lot of paranoia going around over FBI wiretaps and such. And, in fact, there were a number of

---

[7] Psalms 22:1; Matthew 27:46; Mark 15:34. Jesus' doubts on the cross are actually an expression of faith, as evidenced by the Torah (*Old Testament*) prayer from which his words are derived.

informants within our group of protesters, which we discovered years later when we requested copies of our FBI files under the Freedom of Information Act.[8] But for myself, I never worried about such things. I figured if anybody was listening to me, they might learn something; if it were the FBI, then so much the better. I would say to my roommate and fellow anti-imperialist theoretician, 'Could you speak up for the bug. We want to make sure they thoroughly understand our reasoning here.' And the Feds are still coming around, investigating anyone they call a radical or a terrorist, often following up on actions fomented by their own agent provocateurs, like the Sacco and Vanzetti charade—a manufactured excuse to maintain our own SS.

"So the notion of you, my friend, recording our conversations as a way of creating a journal of my activities is a blessing, if nothing else. How could I have anything to hide? It is, after all, no more than what I've already been doing, with my conscience or Superego, to use Freud's term, subconsciously recording each of my actions, even the most mundane. The Great Anomaly that animates creation is omnipresent; it is both the voice and the ear. This is the great truth of hypnotism: It is all recorded within us; there is no secrecy from G-d."

"Fellow theoretician?" I ask, trying to escape the clutches of yet another copyrighted sermon.

"Yes. My compadre, Herr Offenbacher."

"Surely you're joking."

"No. His name is Paul Offenbacher. As political science majors, we worked together on an essay entitled, *The Dialectics of Matter*.[9] We were updating the basis of Dialectical Materialism in light of the paradigm shift from Newtonian physics to the Einsteinian universe, from two-dimensional Euclidean thinking to the relativistic mentality of four-dimensional space-

---

[8] Michael writes in 2004: The Act was passed in 1967 and amended in 1975 to include citizen access to investigatory files compiled for law enforcement purposes. However, according to the current DOJ website, "agencies may withhold information pursuant to nine exemptions and three exclusions contained in the statute. The FOIA applies only to federal agencies and does not create a right of access to records held by Congress, the courts, or by state or local government agencies."

[9] Michael further evolved these concepts into his final proof (see *Appendix 6 –The Proof.*) that incorporates Poincaré's Conjecture as a check and proves the Big Bang Theory, String Theory, the appearance of the World Teacher, the unity of all religions, and the next step in human evolution.

time, from cause and effect to synchronicity. The paper, an outline, really, of our theory, got us into the California Institute of the Arts without undergraduate degrees from Stanford. We used to joke that he was Engels to my Marx. Thus, 'Herr.'"

"At least it's not 'Hair,' like the musical," I joke.

"That's not so far-fetched," Michael responds. "You remember how revolution and art overlapped in the late '60's: The students played music at the barricades in Paris; at Stanford, Offenbacher and I used the same p.a. system[10] for rallies and demonstrations as we did for our ten-piece soul band."

"I see," I say, hardly flinching from this reminder of Michael's radical past and realizing, not without some alarm, that I seem to be getting acclimated to his extreme beliefs. I tell myself that it was the mention of demonstrations in Paris and, therefore, the instinctive Frenchman in me, steeped in the principles of "Liberté, Égalité, Fraternité," that made his comments go down so easy. Indeed, such a reference might have eased my resistance toward this latest glorification of social unrest if he hadn't mentioned a "fellow theoretician." But discovering that I'm not Michael's first Boswell—that I'm competing against this memory of a revolutionary comrade, Offenbacher—*now that* raises my antennae! After all, it took some soul-searching for me to agree to this assignment, with part of the attraction being its perceived uniqueness. So, this is something I'll have to investigate, I tell myself, my auditing instincts alerted to the possibility of a character witness that's already been through this process with Michael.

"I'm glad you feel so open about this," I continue matter-of-factly, hoping that my tone of voice hasn't revealed my bruised feelings or ulterior motives. "I've taken some notes from my reading, so I'll just start with them."

I engage the portable tape recorder that's coupled to my telephone and content myself with the thought that at least Michael's response to the tape-recording issue seems consistent with his talk about being open and unafraid.

"What place does this Charter have in the larger scheme of things, both politically and spiritually?" I begin.

---

[10] A public address system, minimally consisting of a microphone, an amplifier, and speakers.

"Let's begin with the political," Michael starts, "and work our way to the spiritual. Think of it this way, first you have the Constitution of the United States which, relative to other such nation-founding documents, offers the foremost opportunity, at least on paper, to provide freedom to its citizens. Then within this structure you have the State of Colorado which allows municipalities to create their own local laws. Down one more notch, you have the most liberal county in the state serving as a nourishing incubator. Finally, you have the Town of Wayne, remote from the dominant culture-business[11] and populated by somewhat like-minded representatives of the counter-culture. Put them together and you have a perfect prescription for creating a customized political subdivision."

Michael pauses for effect—"How many places do you think there are like this around the world?" he asks.

"I'd expect that there's a least a few," I offer, attempting, as always, to bring some levity to the conversation."

"Right," Michael allows, "probably only a few. And of those few, how many had the wherewithal to commit their vision to paper and outline a democratic and ecologically-sound society?"

"Fewer still," I admit, "though, just because some government or other claims to be open and responsive to its citizens, or considerate of the environment, doesn't mean that it's so."

"Granted, in practice even so-called progressive social organizations are not always as evolved as we might wish, if at all. But political evolution, like evolution itself, is a complex dialectical process that, like Yeats' 'rough beast … slouches towards Bethlehem,'[12] teetering between freedom of consciousness and the limitation of laws and governance. For example, the original U.S. Constitution counted slaves as only three-fifths of a person, but starting within that legal framework the nation has made inroads against bigotry. I'm not saying that the pace of this progress is

---

[11] Michael employs this term à la Marshall McLuhan in *Culture Is Our Business*, McGraw Hill, New York, 1970, as another way of saying how culture and life itself has been reduced to a commodity by capitalism.
[12] William Butler Yeats, *The Second Coming*, 1920.

heartening or even acceptable,[13] but again, that's why I want to take advantage of this window of opportunity on the horizon."

"And that's what this is about? A blueprint for others to follow?" I ask.

"I would never say that there is only one way to do anything, because, of course, there are infinite ways, and that is what each of us must discover for ourselves—our own unique gifts that we bring to the world. Along these lines, I hope that this particular work, the charter, will be seen as having some notable anomalistic qualities, specifically the translation of spiritual precepts into political reality. And while I grant that others have created their own versions of the next evolutionary statement of human political development as well, and I salute them, their local limitations are apparent from our present vantage point. As I said, we have a special incubator here, in the hills of Boulder County, with elements of freedom rarely experienced in history. So, if we compare this ongoing global vision-quest—this search for organizing principles that will allow humanity to live together in a sustainable manner—to a multitude of sperm seeking to fertilize an egg, we are reminded that, generally, only one gets to represent the 'father.' In the end, a certain someone is going to break through, crack the code, and get things hopping, just as there are often more than a few people or groups on the verge of a major scientific discovery, but usually only one person, or one coordinated group, finds the key. So, as I've said before, until or unless someone else shows up with better credentials, I must assume that I'm the point man here, at least for this age, and this charter is an introductory effort toward that end."

"If that were so, that you're the new Moses, so to speak, then why begin with this document?"

"Admittedly, a political document is a small, very limited start. But it's coming up first in our chronicles because it's a non-sectarian establishment of principles as well as an adaptable, open-ended institutional template. Before we get too deeply immersed in my full proof, I need to make the point that I'm not here to establish a theocracy, but stimulate a transition to a spiritualized world that depends upon free, educated, compassionate, and artistic individuals—where people have spiritual

---

[13] Michael writes in 2008: Even Obama's election does not change this fact, as the racist threats against him, fueled by the morally-depraved campaign of McCain and Palin, clearly indicate.

practices and share available resources with one another; where they vote within an *auditable* democratic framework; where we rule ourselves in the interests of the whole, and where there are no slaves, or even wage-slaves—for our current manner of organizing ourselves, around arbitrary material values, is morally repugnant to the evolution of the spirit in flesh.

"Following this charter there will be other such 'white papers'—as scientists call them, or what auditors, such as yourself, call 'working papers'—that will bear witness to our efforts at spiritualizing human relationships. So, this charter is step one in a holistic vision that includes the re-establishment of peace between the religions, even beyond the example I mentioned to you the first day we met—that of Islam, Christianity, and Judaism during the 11th and 12th centuries in Moorish Spain. Our present knowledge and technology make it possible to behave on a higher level, to evolve as human beings by integrating masculine and feminine qualities with spiritual and scientific principles in personally unique and individualistic expressions. And it's up to each of us, through our own chosen practices, to make this happen."

"Beginning with a change in the political structure of the planet?" I ask. "That hardly seems realistic."

"Think about it like this, Rashan: If you were G-d trying to come up with a plan to substantially alter the direction of the human race, what would you do? What I'm proposing is a mirror of creation: Differentiation rooted in unity. I'm *not* proposing that political change precede spiritual change, nor am I endorsing the opposite approach. We have started here simply because we have chosen to format our principles into a book that is, for the most part, presented chronologically. I would be the last one to deny that 'As a man is in his heart, so shall he be.'[14] Evolution is a dialectical process in which all elements are interacting simultaneously, and change in any one aspect is reflected throughout the hologram."

After my recent soul-searching about whether I should take on this project, and specifically my concerns over Michael's far-fetched claims, I'm immediately struck by the force with which he picks up his case. Whether or not I believe what he says, or even understand it, is secondary. It's as if by setting aside his reticence, and telling Chimera and me the specifics of his dream, he unchained something powerful within himself that allows

---

[14] Paraphrase of Proverbs 23:7.

him to switch his point of view to that of his "higher self," as he calls it. Still, I'm unable to accept his version of reality. He's too lucid to be psychotic, but too audacious to be taken seriously. Despite this, though, or perhaps because of it, I'm fascinated by the details: How does someone with Michael's intelligence maintain such an extreme set of beliefs in the face of a world so at odds with his perspective?

"And despite the revolutionary nature of such an undertaking and knowing that if your effort gathers momentum you'll run into vehement, even violent, resistance, you persist?"

"As I told you, I'm not looking to get offed,[15] but we've all got to go sometime or other and I can hardly shrink from my responsibilities. I've been given a beautiful gift and I'm happy to apply it."

I press on.

"Michael, I notice that the entire front end of your proposed preamble was eliminated from the final version. What's behind this?"

"Shallow thinking, actually," he says. "Perhaps you're familiar with a style of popular literature that so revels in colloquialism it loses its meaning after a generation or two? There is a faction among the Charter Commission members who believe that using slang is an evolved form of communication. Terminally hip, I guess you'd call them. They are unable to differentiate between pop-culture and civilization, much like religious adherents who can't distinguish between temporal and universal truths. This intellectual near-sightedness is an example of what Herbert Marcuse calls repressive desublimation,[16] that is, the belief that because we can say or do anything in any manner (such as reading pornography, for instance, or choosing between sixteen different types of hairspray), we are free. This is a simplistic and ultimately degrading concept of freedom because it ignores individual responsibility for choosing enlightened action. Dostoevsky tried to make a similar point in *The Brothers Karamazov*— because everything is permitted does not mean we can do anything we want. Having ethics and taking responsibility matters."

---

[15] A colloquial term used at the time to mean assassinated, murdered, or killed.
[16] Herbert Marcuse was, arguably, the foremost theoretician of the New Left in the late 1960's and early 1970's. A German Jew who emigrated to the U.S. to escape Nazism, Marcuse received a professorial appointment at the University of California at San Diego. The use of the term *repressive desublimation* is explored in his classic work on Marxism and Freudianism, *Eros and Civilization*.

"So, you're saying that this 'pop' type of thinking is common?"

"The attitude we experienced in Wayne over the charter is not so different from the anti-intellectualism we discussed when you and Chimera visited me. It's a defense mechanism of uneducated or undereducated people, the power elite notwithstanding, just like the Church mocking Galileo. When people dismiss elevated discussions as 'Ivory Tower nonsense' or 'male ego-constructs,' or call such things 'heresy,' they miss hearing the elegant solution when it is voiced. The corporate-owned mass media has replaced the monolithic stranglehold of the Church, but the controlling purpose behind its simplistic propaganda is the same."

"How can you compare pop-psychology with medieval superstitions?"

"What you call medieval superstitions still hold sway among the pseudo-religious. So-called fundamentalists, whose beliefs are based on translations that completely miss the point, are trying to teach creationism in schools and turn tribal admonitions against homosexuality, based on the imperatives of offspring for survival in their nomadic world, into universal truth, while simultaneously reveling in the conveniences of modern technology derived from the very scientific principles they eschew to defend their mythologies. Ultimately, anti-intellectualism, or, in the case of the Charter Commission, slang-based thinking, is intrinsically contradictory and self-defeating. What better illustrates this than so-called Muslims or Christians or Jews calling for war or demeaning gays? At best, these aspects of religious belief systems only represent ephemeral, temporal norms. What is "cool" today was "hot" yesterday. But empirical thinking is a universal evolutionary refinement of our symbolic forms. It can no more be ignored than standing erect, from which it was born, or attaining our higher selves, which it spawns. A toaster, a computer, an atomic bomb, and genetics, actually work. They are based on *operational* theories. So it is with spiritual reality. Even if the average person may not be able to tell the difference between blowing smoke and holy fire, even if science and science fiction may look the same to those whose boundaries extend no further than popular culture, in the end, there is cognition that is inspired—for example, Arthur C. Clarke's vision of geo-stationary satellites or Jules Verne's submarines—and that which is not. The *Yoga Sutras* distinguish between ordinary and extraordinary knowledge quite plainly.[17] It could be no other way, given the unity of opposites."

"So, in short, you're saying there was a debate over the style of the preamble of the charter?"

"Yes, and rather than have my work edited by those subscribing to this 'pop' school of linguistics, I withdrew those sections that were too elevated for them to understand. Again, this is the same issue we have with present-day fundamentalists: They lack historical perspective and, thus, have no frame of reference from which to evaluate the information that comes their way. They're as susceptible to 'Thou shall' and 'Thou shall not' as they are to 'Buy now' and 'Eat this,' or 'Believe this' and 'Forget that.' The significance of historical references is lost on them. It's as if human development stopped the day Bishop Irenaeus of Lyons edited and packaged Matthew, Mark, Luke, and John and tried to suppress all the other testaments.[18] So, I believed then, as I do now, that my delineation of the spiritual root of political behavior is important, even if the hipsters do not, and thus I preserved a copy of these passages for some later use—and this is the discussion that I've been waiting for."

My brain had to take a breather. In this case, it wasn't just Michael's egoism wrapping itself in "historical significance": Despite my growing familiarity with his rare ability to think and speak in paragraphs, and despite my improved recovery rate from these expostulations, my thinking had to catch up. He's not the only one I've ever met who could do this to me—a few professors come to mind—but he does seem to do this with impressive regularity, with an elevated and complex level of discourse beyond my training.

"I find it somewhat curious, Michael," I say, with a journalistic eye toward the tape recorder, "that despite your compelling arguments, the majority of the group didn't go for your phraseology."

"It's like you said earlier about resistance to change," Michael says. "People naturally defend themselves against ideas that threaten their belief systems. You and I, Rashan, live in a very rarefied conceptual atmosphere.

---

[17] Taimni, I. K., *The Science of Yoga*, The Theosophical Publishing House, Adyar, Madras, India, 1961, pp. 101-109, or more recently in Feuerstein, Georg, *The Yoga-Sutra of Patanjali*, Inner Traditions International, Rochester, Vermont, 1979, pp. 52-53.
[18] Pagels, Elaine, *The Gnostic Gospels*, Vintage Books, New York, 1989.

Most people don't have the background to appreciate the subtleties of what we discuss, and our persuasiveness is limited, after all, by the fact that on the physical plane we appear just as imperfect as any other mortal. When Jefferson wrote the Declaration of Independence, he was horrified by the hatchet job done to many of his concepts by delegates operating in their own, limited self-interest.[19] They were unable to align themselves with the vision of such a gifted person. The same thing happened to Adams after he drafted the Constitution of the Commonwealth of Massachusetts. So it has been down through the ages: locals fail to see genius in their midst. No prophet is immune to this blindness. 'Can any good come from Nazareth?'[20] they asked. 'For Jesus himself testified, that a prophet hath no honor in his own country.'[21]

"This historic resistance to significant contemporary insights—anomalies in the scientific sense—is one of the reasons I'm happy that you've consented to commit our conversations to the page. Whether they garner any comparisons to the exalted examples I cite, is irrelevant at this point; if only a few people find value in our ideas, then we will have done something significant. Of course, I hope that the effect of these dialogues goes much further, and I believe that the key to their long-term general distribution is in the compilation of their entirety. So, I'm compelled to bare my truth to you. It's not for me to question any longer whether I must do this: 'Thy will be done.'[22] I insist that it is only having the utmost humility before my creator, and the knowledge that it is not 'I' doing this, which allow me to be a vehicle for what I am presenting to you."

If I accept the idea that evolved verbal expressions can be seen, as Michael argues, not as run-of-the-mill egotistical outbursts, but as a spiritually-inspired form of the truth, Michael's perspective defies common mortality. Think about it. Have you ever met anyone who would dare make such claims! And always, no matter where I start with him, he folds

---

[19] Among other deletions, Jefferson's comments concerning the immorality of slavery were stricken from the document (for another example, see the quote at the head of this chapter). A similar axe-wielding occurred when John Adams' guarantee of freedom of speech was removed from his draft of the Constitution of the Commonwealth of Massachusetts.
[20] John 1:46
[21] John 4:44
[22] Luke 11:2.

the subject back to some earth-shattering cosmic truth. Of course, it is this oratorical gift, the silver-tongued Devil, so to speak, that stiffens my resistance.

"I understand what you're saying," I say. "I'm trying to be as objective and as thorough as possible, and I appreciate your willingness to address issues that I consider problematic, even if your answers seem to come off as egocentric. So, let me press on.

"Within the body of the Charter itself," I continue, "you invest the town with every possible power, and then turn this authority over to a General Assembly that can only operate if fully one-quarter of its qualified electors are present. This seems like such an unrealistic percentage to require, a democratic pipe dream, an encumbrance on the political and corporate body. As a CPA and consultant, I'd question the logic of any corporation structured in such an idealistic manner."

"Given the lackadaisical attitude Americans have toward their freedoms, I would agree, but at the time the Charter was written," Michael recalls, "there were about a hundred and fifty people living in the town, and of that number, only about ninety-five adults. So, in a town that commonly celebrated full moons, solstices, birthdays, holidays, and other events in a communal fashion, getting twenty-four people to show up for a town meeting was not a difficult task. Of course, there were those that resisted the Charter, primarily folks who had served on the old, autocratic town council, but there weren't enough people with this sentiment to prevent the transition to direct democracy. And this is what Wayne's charter is really about: Much like the ancient Greek city-states, the town is a *polis* in the truest sense of the word.

"But it's not only small towns in which direct democracy can be implemented. As the world's electronic communications evolve,[23] and with it the possibility of universal improvement in education, decentralization of power becomes more feasible, and democracy can assume a larger role even in big cities, states, nations, and the world itself. We live in a global village, in neighborhoods, among affinity groups, all connected to each other."

---

[23] Not long before this current conversation was taped, on February 16, 1978, the first computer bulletin board system was created (CBBS in Chicago, Illinois), and, shortly thereafter, on January 5, 1980, the first personal computer was released by Hewlett-Packard.

"Michael," I interrupt, "again, this seems like an impossible scenario, a fantasy ... a fiction."

"I'm not suggesting that representative government be done away with," he tries to assure me, "at least not at this relatively unevolved moment in human history, but that is an eventual possibility. I have no choice but to see it this way—given my intrinsic faith in the spiritual evolution of humankind—and to will such an outcome. So, yes, I recognize what you're saying, and all the possibilities for failure, but it's a waste of my time to think about those scenarios—as I've said, what was once utopian is now necessary for survival: we are at our evolutionary crossroads and this is the next progressive step. Yes, there are those who will vigorously resist any move in this direction because their position and identity are tied to the control that they exert over the governmental, media, and intelligence apparatuses in this country—through financial contributions to representatives, legal and otherwise—and the manipulation of the balloting process itself, not to mention their influence abroad through military and economic warfare.

> So here we are, in a perfect position to confront that segment of the ruling class that directly benefits from the war in Vietnam. Hewlett-Packard, General Dynamics, Lockheed, Northrup Aviation, Union Oil, Tenneco, the west coast edition of the Wall Street Journal, and, of course, the university's own Stanford Research Institute all have sites in the industrial park, which sits on school grounds, creating a synergy that not only fuels the development of the Silicon Valley, but feeds this high-technology corridor with engineers, lawyers, and MBAs. On top of that, such "luminaries" as Bill Hewlett and David Packard, both of whom have made more than $600 million from sales of weaponry for this undeclared war, sit on the Board of Trustees of the university.
> What will it take for these men to understand that there is no justification for killing 6 million people?[24] "It's

---

[24] Including the 50,000 plus American deaths, and counting North and South Vietnamese soldiers and the civilians of Vietnam and Cambodia (the secret war Nixon tried to hide that resulted in the destabilization and subsequent lawlessness of the Khmer Rouge, as documented the Oscar award-winning film, *The Killing Fields*), the figures run over six million.

> *all about stopping the spread of communism,"* they say, but history will show it's all about controlling oil, rubber, tungsten, rice, and cheap labor—just as it was for the French before them—not to mention their profits from equipping this war: the planes, the boats, the guns and the ordnance, plus the automatic procurement and replacement of these items as they are spent and destroyed.
>
> *Only serious losses of capital and domestic destabilization will stop these people from continuing their crimes against humanity. That is the intent of our protests—to cost them money, change public opinion, and mobilize the masses. Tomorrow we will shut down the Stanford Industrial Park.*[25]

"Ultimately, though," he continues, "this hegemony of capital is not just a political problem, one that could be solved, say, through real campaign finance reform—which, I might add would be a worthwhile interim step—or even a political revolution; it is a spiritual problem, one that requires replacing the cynicism and greed of the instincts and ego with the optimism and love that comes from the higher self and from the One-Without-A-Name, the Great Anomaly. To paraphrase Thomas Jefferson in the Declaration of Independence, and as I wrote in the charter preamble that I withheld, 'When a state ceases to respect the fact that it exists only by consent of an informed and educated governed, then it loses its legitimacy, and political change is aligned with spiritual necessity.' And just like Jefferson, 'I have sworn upon the altar of God, eternal hostility against every form of tyranny over the mind of man.'[26]

"So, you can see how the political model that we're offering here is more an expression of inner well-being than it is a manifestation of some organizational theory. In this way, we propose to minimize dogma and repression. And since, as I have noted, I shall found no church, this preamble and charter, then, represent the spiritualization of public policy."

"Although you support secret balloting."

"Of course—that is a fundamental principle of democracy. In Wayne's circumstance, that is why we made the General Assembly

---

[25] As noted in Chapter 2, excerpts from Michael's diary have been inserted throughout this book. This entry was dated May 15, 1969.
[26] From a letter to Dr. Benjamin Rush of September 23, 1800.

principally a vehicle for sending referendum questions, what political scientists call initiatives, to a free vote[27] of the people: Because a show of hands for or against your friends by public hand-raising in a small town or neighborhood—where everyone knows everyone else's business—would be manipulative and divisive."

"Okay," I respond, again unable to avoid noticing the compositional style in which Michael verbalizes his thoughts. It is as if, once more, his ideas had been pre-drafted in his brain, waiting to be accessed, and unnervingly, it seems that my own questions are beginning to take on some of these qualities. Thankfully, though, he has not hijacked my capacity for critical thinking, as he seems to be doing with my vocabulary and syntax.

"But," I continue, "your attempt to outline a connection between spirituality and political action seems dangerous. Didn't the loss of distinctions between religious and secular values drive millions of Europeans to seek freedom in America?"

"I agree that there is a danger in this," Michael replies, "but I am not attempting to drag religion into the secular world. I believe in the constitutional separation of church and state, and am not promoting religion whatsoever. Our goal is to increase the consistency between spiritual behavior and public behavior, one individual at a time. We may think globally, but each of us, for the most part, can only act locally, and political structure provides one means for accomplishing this. Really, what I'm calling for here is not so new. Adams and Jefferson[28] would concur

---

[27] Michael writes in 2004: I refer to the traditional "secret" ballot of democracies, by which individuals get to mark their choices in private without oversight or undue influence by anyone else, AND that the auditing of such a voting process, including the purging of the rolls, is publicly conducted by governmental, not corporate, bodies, AND that the results are publicly disseminated and subject to review by the eligible electorate and the courts, if necessary.

[28] Indeed, Jefferson made this quite clear: "[When] the [Virginia] bill for establishing religious freedom ... was finally passed ... a singular proposition proved that its protection of opinion was meant to be universal. Where the preamble declares that coercion is a departure from the plan of the holy author of our religion, an amendment was proposed, by inserting the word "Jesus Christ," so that it should read "a departure from the plan of Jesus Christ, the holy author of our religion." The insertion was rejected by a great majority, in proof that they meant to comprehend within the mantle of its protection the Jew and the Gentile, the Christian and Mahometan, the Hindoo and infidel of every denomination." -- Thomas Jefferson: Autobiography, 1821. ME 1:67

with this approach; they believed in personal responsibility and, of course, the separation of church and state. I am simply restating an old argument, one which, in this conversation, I've already used for individuals: 'As people are in their hearts, so shall they be.'"[29]

The phone line crackles. On that note, I admit I'm struck, despite my familiarity with Michael's lineage, by the reiteration of his Solomonic biblical reference[30] of only minutes before. I swallow and, steeling myself against the insidious implications of this subtext, move on to my next query. "We've talked a little about your relationship with various county officials. What's their reaction to having a political anomaly such as Wayne within their jurisdiction?"

"What makes the Town of Wayne an anomaly is more than just its Charter, Rashan. The town also has a Waiver from Disinfection from the state that took four years to secure, legally entitling it to leave its water untreated, meaning unchlorinated. And then there's the matter of the town outlawing flush toilets."

I couldn't help but laugh. "What's that about?"

"In 1896, when the town was incorporated, one of the original ordinances declared that all privies had to be sealed vaults, and that these vaults could not contaminate the ground water. This law, coupled with a constantly moving, underground fed, gravity-operated water supply, made Wayne one of the few mining camps to escape the cholera epidemics. Because the Rocky Mountains are relatively new geologic phenomena, the soil is very thin, and water naturally percolates through it quickly, as opposed to mature soil which can filter streams in about a hundred yards. In rural areas such as this, flush toilets dispose of their water through leach fields. Given the nature of the soil, the water from leach fields in Wayne reaches local creek beds before the effluents have been properly filtered by the ground. This causes unacceptably high levels of *coliform bacillus* in the area streams. By legislating against flush toilets and encouraging composting outhouses, the town is basically protecting[31] the local environment. One even can argue that the combination of unchlorinated drinking water and the lack of flush toilets make Wayne's water policy the

---

[29] A paraphrase of Proverbs 23:7.
[30] Proverbs is attributed to Solomon.
[31] Or, in some cases, even improving the environment, depending upon how the byproduct (compost) of the evolved outhouse is used.

strictest in the nation. And, since this 1896 law far antedates any federal clean water legislation, the case can be made that the Town's water policy, since it's older *and* stricter than state or federal laws, supersedes those laws.[32] This is part of the thinking behind the assumption of all those powers in the first article of the Charter.[33] While the county, the state, and the federal government may not agree with this legal interpretation, until forced otherwise Wayne, the highest town in this drainage basin in the Atlantic watershed of the North American continent, not only has the cleanest water, coming in and going out, of any city in the world, but regulates that water according to its own laws."

It strikes me in passing, with this weird example, that much of what Michael says and does involves something unique and quintessential, just as he claimed earlier when we spoke at his house. But the believer within me admitting this, the skeptic counters that such a pattern doesn't indicate necessarily that anything extraordinary will come of it, only that Michael collects interesting tidbits as any decent raconteur would.

"So part of your dialogue with the county involves this issue of clean water and waste disposal?"

"Yes, we've gone back and forth over this for quite some time, but so far, it's our building department that's issuing the permits, not the county."

"You seem to imply that there are other areas of contention involving jurisdiction?"

"There are. When hippies first arrived in Wayne, seven or eight years ago, the Boulder County Sheriffs Department was still making regular patrols through here. But recently, we secured a grant from the Colorado Law Enforcement Administration to send our Town Marshall to the State Police Academy. At first, the instructors were repelled by his long hair and beard, but they got used to it and our candidate got his certification. Now, when the county or the state has an issue, they have to go through our police officer. This obviously allows us much greater control over how we enforce our laws. It even gives us some leverage where the FBI is concerned, when they come snooping around."

---

[32] Indeed, years later the Town's policies were challenged and upheld in state court.
[33] See *Appendix 1 - Excerpts from the Home Rule Charter* of the Town of Wayne, Colorado.

I couldn't help but wonder, given the cultural differences that arose in America in the late '60's, between an older generation whose idea of a good time consisted of "wine, women, and song" and a younger generation's taste for "sex, drugs, and rock 'n' roll," what kind of clashes had been going on locally. This could be an explosive issue, I think.

"So when it comes to pot, for instance, how does Wayne handle the legal issues?"

"The federal and state governments will tell you that drugs are their jurisdiction and, of course, they have manipulated the laws to support this contention. But the fact is that Ann Arbor, Michigan legalized marijuana a few years ago.[34] Part of the corporate, and thus federal, strategy has been to classify marijuana[35] as a narcotic, which is a fabrication that belies the legitimacy of those promulgating such laws. Nixon commissioned study after study until he could find someone who would vouch for the lie that marijuana was not only worse for people than tobacco and alcohol, but that it invariably led to the use of actual narcotics—when, in fact,

---

[34] In 1974, voters in Ann Arbor, Michigan, amended the city charter to create one of the country's most liberal laws for marijuana possession. It set the fine at only $5. That was increased in 1990 to $25 for a first offense, $50 for a second offense and at least $100 for further offenses.

[35] The use of the word *marijuana*—Mexican Spanish slang, rather than the then more common *cannabis,* the Latin name for the plant—was originally adopted as part of a racist strategy by those in control of the government and the press. In the '30's, this campaign took on an economic component: to eradicate cannabis' industrial component (hemp) to create a safe monopoly for the more expensive and more toxic paper-making processes upon which Hearst, Kimberly-Clark, St. Regis, and DuPont were depending. For DuPont, prohibitions against hemp would also bolster sales for their new line of synthetic fibers. The well-orchestrated corporate-funded campaign included newspapers, film, and political rhetoric, attempting to reverse, at the least, 5,000 years of human history. There are a variety of books that deal with this subject and the whole campaign against marijuana, including: the recent best-seller, Eric Schlosser's *Reefer Madness: Sex, Drugs, and Cheap Labor in the American Black Market*, Houghton Mifflin Co., 2003; Jack Herer's *The Emperor Wears No Clothes: The Authoritative Historical Record of Cannabis and the Conspiracy Against Marijuana* (AH HA Publishing, Van Nuys, CA, 11th edition, pp. 25-44); *The Hemp Manifesto : 101 Ways That Hemp Can Save Our World* by Rowan Robinson; *Why Marijuana Should Be Legal* by Ed Rosenthal and Steve Kubby; *Marijuana Myths Marijuana Facts: A Review Of The Scientific Evidence* by Lynn Zimmer and John P. Morgan; and *Reefer Madness : The History of Marijuana in America* by Larry Ratso Sloman.

marijuana has a variety of medical applications including treatments related to glaucoma, chemotherapy, and such.³⁶

"What are so-called 'drugs,' really?" he continues. "Take wine—is it a food, medicine, sacrament, intoxicant, or drug? The answer depends entirely upon one's intent and psycho-genetic persuasion. But while corporate America does not control marijuana, it understands that—as Carlos Casteneda's *The Teachings of Don Juan* ³⁷ or Patanjali's *Yoga Sutras* ³⁸ indicate—its use can subvert the disease of materialism that supports their power. This is the real battle. The powers that be are not against drugs. They've subsidized tobacco (which is as addictive as heroin and kills by the truckload) and sugar (for which 'witches,' that is herbalists, were burned for objecting to its importation, resulting in a disastrous loss of knowledge of natural medicines) for centuries. The government also has its hands in the drug trade—and a powerful pusher it is—directing the production and distribution of heroin and cocaine, from Asia and South

---

³⁶ The sordid history of Nixon's crusade is summarized at http://www.alternet.org/story.html?StoryID=12666. The federal government, in their zeal to eliminate the counter-culture, continues to refuse to recognize these medical uses and continues to classify cannabis as a narcotic. Despite the fact that, by 2001, eight states had passed medical marijuana laws, the U.S. Drug Enforcement Administration acts otherwise, even trying to prevent citizens from voting on the matter (http://www.nytimes.com/2002/03/30/national/30DIST.html?). See "San Francisco Resists Medical Marijuana Raids," @ http://www.alternet.org/story.html?StoryID=12414 and Martha Mendoza, "S.F. officials, fed vie over medical pot," The *Associated Press*, 3/15/02, in *The Denver Post*. By the late '90's, approximately 10,000 studies had been done on marijuana, including about 4,000 in the U.S., and of the dozen that had shown negative results, none have been replicated. So overwhelming is the evidence of marijuana's natural uses that in 1983 the Reagan-Bush administration floated the idea of having all American universities and researchers destroy all research done between 1966-76 (Herer, *op. cit.*, pp. 43-44).

³⁷ Don Juan, the Sonoma Indian Medicine Man (mentioned in *Chapter 1 – The Meeting*), suggests that "the little smoke" can help one "see," "stop the world," and become "a person of knowledge," after which the sacramental herb is dispensable.

³⁸ In one of its many sutras (Section IV, verse 1), this ancient collection of yogic precepts includes "ganja" as a viable path, as equally capable as devotion, chanting, or other spiritual practices, for producing enlightened consciousness.

America to the Europe and North America.[39] So, what scares the ruling classes about marijuana and other psychotropic substances, including the ritual use of peyote by the Native American Church,[40] is that these uses potentially represent the end of their ability to play upon selfish, instinctive-based fears as a means of controlling the masses."

"Michael, don't you think you're pushing things too far? I mean, first you tie spirituality to the political process, and now you're promoting drugs."

"Look at your linguistic inferences. I represent a legitimate, though seemingly new, tribe, Rashan. One that, like Native Americans and the Native American Church, or Catholicism, for that matter, should have the right to its own sacraments, if it so wishes. As I say, it's how cannabis is used that matters. There's no legitimate scientific reason for the current prohibition—it's all about ethnocentrism and the ruthlessness by which the worshipers of the almighty dollar, the idolaters of the golden calf, the whores of Mammon, seek to control the planet."

"You think you can actually convince Joe six-pack that his government legislates against pot because it fears the values of the counter-culture?"

"This is not about Joe six-pack, but those who are manipulating him: social Neanderthals[41] whose evolutionary limits have been reached, and who now stand in the way of sustainable planetary organization. While we must have compassion for those whose hearts are knotted by ego and ignorance, the health of the biosphere of this planet is at stake and we must

---

[39] For a rundown of the CIA's involvement in drug trafficking, detailed by a former narcotics officer, see http://www.fromthewilderness.com/free/ciadrugs/index.html. The resurgence of the heroin trade following the Bush II invasion of Afghanistan is documented later in this book. The drug trade in South America, its connection to the continuing guerilla war and its use as an excuse to steal the natural resources of that continent, is analyzed at length at http://www.narconews.com/). Recently, Venezuela accused the DEA itself of being a drug cartel (Fabiola Sanchez, "Venezuela criticizes DEA as 'new cartel,'" *Associated Press*, May 7, 2007, 6:16 PM EDT).

[40] See Faye Flam, "Hallucinogens offer sobering hope," *Knight Ridder Newspapers*, 12/4/03, in the *Denver Post*.

[41] Recently, with sober vindication, Michael pointed out to me evidence that Neanderthal genes are carried by some modern humans. See http://www.nytimes.com/2002/03/07/science/07ORIG.html?.

be steadfast in defense of the life-force here. My position may be a call to arms for the fascists—'Think not that I am come to send peace on earth: I came not to send peace, but a sword'[42]—but this is only metaphorically correct, for it is the sword of righteousness that I wield."

"But these people you resist, they have all the guns and money."

"By that they admit they are weak and vulnerable. Surely you remember Giraudoux's[43] Countess Aurelia?"

"*The Madwoman of Chaillot*? That was a fantasy."

"Really? Didn't the Nazis leave and the Vichy fall?

"So you think the world can be so easily transformed?"

"Easily? No, but in the same manner: by changing hearts and minds, just as in Aurelia's Paris of the mind. And here, where we live, is such a place: one of a few islands in a sea of ignorance that allow us some room for the questioning and experimentation necessary to create a sustainable society. I say this not because I believe that marijuana is the be all and end all to any kind of new society. Don't misunderstand me, it is abused and used as an intoxicant just like alcohol and, as I said, it is by no means required or necessary for spiritual breakthroughs. But it can, as I've witnessed, open certain doors of perception that allow for spiritual experiences—experiences which can be permanently absorbed through meditation and daily practice. It *can*, I insist, be used as a sacrament. So when the Boulder County Sheriffs told us that they wouldn't hassle us as long as they didn't see it growing from the road, the legal issues concerning pot in Wayne were no longer a problem."

"But what about the federal government? Surely they can't allow this kind of behavior?" I'm aghast that someone like Michael, who purports to be a spiritual leader, would align himself with such a controversial and potentially harmful legal problem, even if what he says is true.

"You're right, Rashan, those who control the federal government are loath to allow any flexibility here, because, as I said, they understand the cultural stakes. But at this point, they are not very sophisticated in their abilities to prevent it. When DEA agents showed up wearing mod clothes, driving a glossy new van, and spying from its one-way mirror windows in the hopes of entrapping one of our residents for a small amount of hashish,

---

[42] Matthew, 10:34
[43] Jean Giraudoux, (1882-1944), French playwright.

they were too obvious and oblivious to be successful; and when they returned to investigate rumors of the whereabouts of Bernardine Dohrn and Patty Hearst,[44] again they left empty-handed. The pattern was repeated so often across the country that *Newsweek* ran a cover story on it, 'The FBI's toughest foe: The Kids.' As I said, they still come around here, taking pictures and bugging who knows what—our town meetings? There could be an informant among us. What does it matter?

"So, yes, there are many areas of contention between the free port of Wayne and the authorities, but Boulder County finds us more of a curiosity than an adversary: sometimes amusing, sometimes annoying, but not a serious threat to their psychological, emotional, or political well being. After all, to the rest of the country Boulder is considered as far out as Wayne is to Boulder. They understand us. And actually, the County Elections Department is fascinated by the workings of our referendums by mail. The lowest turnout we've had for any vote has been 55% of those *eligible,* which in Wayne means anyone over 18 who has lived in the town for more than 32 days.[45] Compare this to turnout percentages across the rest of the country, which are measured against those *registered.*"[46]

"Given the general complacency of Americans toward voting, that's not a bad turnout," I say, "but ballots by mail, wouldn't that be easy to manipulate?"

"It's become a hot topic around the country. The Cook County Clerk in Chicago, of all places, expressed concern. I guess according to The Machine's[47] definition, fraud is when the ballot box *can't* be stuffed. And

---

[44] Bernardine Dohrn was a member of the Weathermen, an underground splinter group of the Students for a Democratic Society, and was a "fugitive from justice" at this time. She is now a faculty member at Northwestern University Law School. Patty Hearst—the granddaughter of William Randolph Hearst, the newspaper magnate and father of Yellow Journalism—was kidnapped by the Simbianese Liberation Army (SLA) and was seemingly converted to their radical agenda. She later recanted her actions as part of her "plea bargaining." She was eventually pardoned by President Bill Clinton.
[45] A basic federal requirement for voting eligibility.
[46] A normal U.S. election is usually decided by the participation of one-half of the registered voters, who, themselves, represent about one-half of those eligible to vote. So, representatives are elected and laws enacted by roughly 25% of the electorate, less than half the percentage of those who vote in Wayne.
[47] In Chicago, longtime mayor (1955-76) Richard Daley's political organization was known as The Machine.

of course, Republicans are opposed to voting by mail because anything that increases turnout makes it more difficult for them to manipulate the outcome by outspending the opposition on advertising or by some other steal-the-vote scheme. But as an accountant, Rashan, you've got to believe that any kind of election is auditable if proper procedures are followed."

"You grew up in Chicago, right?" I was reminded.

"Right—about 25 miles north."

"You had just returned from there when we first met."

"I'd been teaching at the Yoga Retreat in the city."

"And having witnessed Chicago voting, you still want to encourage these experimental voting practices?"

"Absolutely. I watched Daley and his organization strong-arm everyone for years—and put JFK in the White House with stuffed ballots.[48] But it was the lack of audit procedures that made this possible. With verifiable checks and balances in place, voting by mail is not any different than absentee balloting, so it's hardly new. And despite Republican opposition to combining motor vehicle and voter registration, more jurisdictions are starting to encourage early voting.[49] Again, Wayne has

---

[48] Approximately 100,000 ghost votes from Chicago gave Illinois' electoral votes to Kennedy instead of Nixon, providing the margin of victory in the 1960 presidential election. As honor among thieves goes, Nixon didn't complain. He was, of course, later drummed from office for a burglary, one of his most minor crimes. Later, in 2000 and 2004, Al Gore and John Kerry let the Bush crime family steal two elections, one in Florida and the other in Ohio.

[49] While Michael was trying, at this time, to stimulate democratically-minded jurisdictions to encourage early voting, the actual implementation of this practice over the years has been a mixed bag of legal and illegal practices. In November, 2000, Florida Governor Jeb Bush disenfranchised 57,000 voters by purging Democrats and minorities from the rolls (claiming they were felons), setting up roadblocks in minority precincts, and rejecting recounts in order to get to get his brother appointed President by the Republican-controlled Supreme Court (all the while supporting a campaign that accused Clinton of moral decrepitude); while in November, 2001, Boulder County conducted its first county-wide election by mail. On June 2, 2002, Elizabeth Olson reported that voting over the Internet was being tested in Switzerland ("E-democracy tested in Switzerland," *The New York Times*), though we do not have the details of the auditing process. By November, 2004, in the U.S., legitimate early voting by real voters casting absentee ballots, mail-in ballots, and traditional ballots, at polling places that opened as much as a week or two early, was more than offset by pre-programmed, unauditable electronic voting machines that generated hundreds of thousands of over-votes for

served as a political incubator for the cutting edge of this change. It's the natural evolution of democracy."

It's not difficult to see that if Michael had a larger stage, his point-of-view would quickly make him controversial. Still, at this point, his ideas are just magnetic patterns on my audio cassettes. I wonder, then, about the path—from where we are today to the conditions almost 30 years in the future—that will provide him with the window of opportunity he seeks for influencing human evolution.

"Where do you see Wayne's government going from here?" I ask.

"I don't see the Charter needing a lot of changes in order to accommodate future needs. That's not the issue. The greatest challenge facing the town is for more people to take responsibility for their own governance. Despite its relatively high voting percentages, Wayne has apathy problems much like the rest of the United States. Democracy depends upon an educated public, and compassionate governance depends upon an evolved constituency.[50] So, as I stated in the beginning of this discussion, political evolution is dependent upon spiritual work. It's a tough haul, though. The powers that be aim to keep the masses uneducated and disenfranchised, and what passes as spirituality in this country is simply lip-service to political catch-phrases designed to deliver votes. That's why I teach a Yoga class at the Town Hall here—spiritual practice is at the core of the change we seek."

George W. Bush and other right-wing candidates and ballot issues. Most of this fraudulent campaign, which targeted Florida, Texas, Ohio, and California, was carried out by Five Star Trust, a complex shell of offshore corporations funded by Bush and Saudi business enterprises. (Wayne Madsen, "Votergate: More details emerge," www.onlinejournal.com, 12/1/2004, Wayne Madsen, "Texas to Florida: White House-linked clandestine operation paid for 'vote-switching software,'" www.onlinejournal.com, 12/6/2004, www.buzzflash.com, "Survey Research Center of the University of California at Berkeley indicates electronic voting machines awarded 130,000 – 260,000 excess votes to Bush in Florida," 11/18/2004, and Steven Rosenfeld, "The Perfect Election Day Crime," www.tompaine.com, 11/12/2004.) The Bush regime has also exported these techniques abroad, for use in recent elections, unsuccessfully in Venezuela, and successfully in Belgium and the Ukraine.)

[50] "Enlighten the people generally, and tyranny and oppressions of body and mind will vanish like evil spirits at the dawn of day." --Thomas Jefferson

"Are you saying that you believe Yoga should be standard practice for everyone?" I ask.

"Not standard in the sense of required. At the culmination of Hesse's *The Glass-Bead Game*,[51] the meditative arts are seen as a normal part of one's elective education. These practices, including Yoga, aren't religion, but provide access to the stuff of which religions claim to be made. There are yogis of every religious stripe and some that are of no definitive faith, but what they practice is the ultimate human science, the art of spiritual evolution. So, as we've previously discussed, there are as many paths as there are people, but I consider the practice of Yoga the most effective and coherent system for re-awakening one's soul and for discovering one's unique purpose. The manner in which one implements this practice is his or her own."

I don't know much about Yoga, but despite Michael's reassurances I am still reticent about the seeming linkage of spiritual practice and governance. I have a great deal of respect for the U.S. constitution's separation of church and state, which I consider a cornerstone of the American republic—something we did not have in writing in France until 1905. Yet, it is nice to think that spirituality, in and of itself, could exist in a political framework without dogmatic implications.

"Can you explain this re-awakening? What exactly is it that we've forgotten, and why do you connect it to statecraft?"

Michael pauses and smiles as if he had been waiting for this question.

"Living as we all do within one and the same universe and having evolved from the same primordial material, the plasma ball that was present at the Big Bang, we are all intrinsically related. This interdependence, between the multiplicities of constantly changing phenomena, is the tie that binds us each to the other. I call this anomalistic bond love (agape), for that is how we experience the Great Anomaly (or G-d principle) in human form.[52] It is the natural cohesive bond of the universe—and one which can no more be quantified than the universe itself—which it animates—as Heisenberg's Uncertainty Principle shows. It

---

[51] Hermann Hesse's final work, *Magister Ludi* or *The Glass-Bead Game* (*Das Glockenspiel*), after which he was awarded the Nobel Prize for Literature in 1946.
[52] The heart (where love dwells) is the first organ formed in the vertebrate embryo. See *Appendix 6 – The Proof*, 7.6. Individual Spiritual Practice as the Next Evolutionary Step.

is this innate acceptance and unconditional devotion—with which each of us is born—that gets buried through our exposure to an environment of superstition, negativity, and fear: what we call 'society' and 'culture.' That's why we're indebted to the vigilant Yoga practitioners, who, over the millennia, preserved these teachings until a time when they could be promulgated without suppression from church, state, industry, and other entities that feel threatened by the empowerment of the individual. By opening ourselves to love, we reawaken what we already know within ourselves—the evolutionary truth our unique and anomalistic potential—and thereby change the nature of society. So, again, spirituality is ultimately a political act."

"This sounds like the Crusades."

"The precepts of Yoga don't permit violence; it's 'the meek who shall inherit the earth.'"[53]

"I've always wondered what that means, 'the meek,'" I say, knowing that Michael would have a canned answer for this. But, hey, that's what this collaboration is about, getting his raps down on tape.

"Yoga re-engineers the mind-body-spirit to free its latent evolutionary energy, what the yogis call *kundalini*, which, when properly directed, brings about the spiritual re-birth of the practitioner. This re-birthing process is universal; everyone has the potential to experience it; it's the healing power of the soul. Just as our bodies cut, bleed, coagulate, scab, and heal without conscious guidance, so our souls have the power to heal our spiritual wounds. This basic yogic transformation is the same rebirth described by Christianity and other belief systems: Metaphorically, the Apocalypse in *The Revelation of St. John the Divine* paints a very similar cycle of psychological death and re-birth to *The Tibetan Book of the Dead*. The universality of this process means it is an organic truth innate to humans. Yoga is simply the science designed to catalyze this healing energy with a minimum of dogma surrounding its implementation. When this happens, and we tap the inner light into which we are reborn, there is no differentiation between the source of this light and the individual receiving it. We all share this undifferentiated state of purity and simplicity, this mildness and acceptance of G-d's way, the inexplicable

---

[53] Matthew 5:5

enigma at the core of existence, the anomaly. This is the meekness of love."

"So, you're saying that 'being reborn' is not a phenomenon exclusive to Christianity?"

"Correct. Being reborn 'in spirit' could just as easily be identified as the egoless state within Buddhism. The use of religious dogma to describe the meaning of this 'reborn' state, whether by Christians or anyone else, is antithetical to the transformation taking place, so anyone telling you that it only occurs in Christianity obviously hasn't been reborn in spirit, only in dogma. When I teach Yoga, one of my practices is to intersperse, within each class, the reading of passages from a broad selection of spiritual writings—to present a spectrum of inspiring experiences to my students who are in the process of tapping into their essence. My hope is that this eclectic sampling provides them with the encouragement they need to create their own unique spiritual paths. We need everyone's gift to transform the world to a better place, not inflexible religious dogma or homogenized media propaganda."

> *Who am I and why am I here, now that I no longer have formulaic answers and ready made truths? What choice do I have but to trust in the revelation of each moment and follow these steppingstones to a new self that is in the process of becoming within me? In what better way may I be assured of my path than for the universe to reveal it to me based on my most honest and informed choices?* [54]

"But even among Yoga practitioners, as you call them," I say, "aren't there various schools and points of contention as to how best to teach? How do you get around these natural conflicts?"

"A good point, Rashan. This is an important issue, similar to the infighting that goes on between different religious sects. When it comes to spiritual practice, whether it's one form of Yoga or another, or some other meditative practice, the ability to separate universal truths from temporal dogma is critical if we are truly going to evolve. This is where your expertise in theatre is invaluable for what I'm trying to do."

---

[54] September, 1971.

"Now we're on to theatre? What's this got to do with Yoga?" I say, while secretly giving thanks that I have my tape recorder to capture the message that's bound to follow, sparing me the effort of its rote conveyance, so that I can consider what he's saying.

"I told you that I've enjoyed theatre since I was a kid, and as keen observer I can think of at least four areas in which Yoga and theatre can be mutually beneficial. The first has to do with what we've just been talking about—dogmatism. Like religious texts, ancient Yoga teachings contain both universal and temporal truths, and it's these latter, transitory ideas which need to be weeded out. Most of these outdated concepts are derived from Yoga's long-established, close association with Hinduism and are really nothing more than superstitious band aids that substituted for scientific data, which was unavailable at that time.

"These beliefs are comparable, say, to the question of eating pork for Jews and Muslims. The lack of understanding of germs and, subsequently, of trichinosis, led to this prohibition. There is nothing inherently more debased about a swine than a bovine, because, of course, there's nothing debased about either. The real questions here, today, should have to do with sustainability and health issues, of meat-eating versus vegetarian proteins. The prohibition against pork is a temporal belief. It does not address eternal truths.

"Another prime example would be religious prohibitions against homosexuality. Here, the *Torah*,[55] the Christian *Bible*, and the *Koran* mix inspired spiritual guidance with the prejudices of fearful old men seeking ways to defend their vulnerable tribes through propagation. Homosexuality, which is a naturally occurring genetic variation in mammal populations, was branded taboo because its unions fail to issue warriors, and because of the sexual insecurity of its critics.

"Ignorance plays out the same way for Yoga schools that are awash in doctrine, or acting schools and theatre companies that rigidly adhere to one approach or method—in the long run inflexibility is never fruitful. So,

---

[55] The bible of Judaism, alternately called the *Pentateuch* or *The Five Books of Moses*. The Christian and Islamic references to the *Torah* as the *Old Testament* are considered derogatory by the Jews who, given the prejudicial conduct they have experienced from so many practitioners of these religions, do not believe that they have been shown any indication that their belief system has been superseded by these latter-day derivatives of Judaism.

I'd suggest that Yoga and theatre could mutually benefit from a combined practice, each checking the other's doctrinaire tendencies."

"Put that way, I can see where the combination might be useful," I say, "but I'm not entirely sure where this is going."

"This leads to the second area in which these two arts can benefit from associating with each other: What the theatre calls availability. Have you ever noticed how an actor's limitations are directly related to their own emotional issues? For example, an actor who is an angry person often has difficulty projecting anger on stage that's consonant with the character he is portraying, instead interjecting images of anger derived from his own limited experience."

Once again Michael pulls a pet subject of mine out of thin air. While his propensity for this no longer shocks me, the regularity with which it happens is hard to ignore. Life is full of coincidences, I try telling myself while involuntarily nodding in agreement with what he says.

"Right," I say. "I would agree with that. It's something I thought about during the casting of *Theatres of Love*."

"How so?"

"I was concerned about finding the right actress to play Suki. The character undergoes some subtle changes with her anger issues, so I needed someone who, herself, didn't have problems there."

"And you found that in Diane?"

"Right. She did this really interesting piece in her audition, a compilation of Queen Margaret's speeches from Henry VI and Richard III. I was impressed by the distinctions she drew in Margaret's feelings. I made the right choice in casting her. She found places in Suki I didn't know were there."

"Yes, she mentioned that afterwards," says Michael.

"She told you that?" I ask, disappointed to hear that she had shared what I thought was a private moment between us.

"Yes. You remember that during her graduate training I spoke to her class about the spiritual aspects of Yoga?"

"Right," I replied. "Both you and she have mentioned that."

"Well, a couple of months back she called me up and expressed some interest in learning Yoga. I told her I'd be happy to teach her as long as she stopped smoking tobacco."

"Really!" I tried to gather myself, remembering how Diane had spoken so admiringly of Michael. "And so she's been working with you?"

"Yes, she's a natural, it seems."

"So, you're saying that her performance in my play was, in a sense, a proof of concept for what you're proposing?" I asked with some impatience, feeling as if I have been left out of the loop, not privy to Michael and Diane's experiment.

"That's a fair assessment," Michael says. "She arrived at the rebirthing phase rather quickly."

I was dumbfounded. All I could do was nod my head.

"So, as I was saying," Michael continues, "yogic re-birthing creates greater availability in an actor—more space if you will, for his or her character's feelings and ideas, and consequently less expression of the neurotic details of the actor's personality. During the rehearsal process, this availability further enables actors, who are already being encouraged to explore the boundaries of their character's behavior."

"You're saying that during the early stages of rehearsal, when directors are encouraging risk-taking, the extra availability induced by Yoga provides that much more space for character exploration?"

"Exactly," Michael says.

"But doesn't this really deliver the same thing that method acting or other techniques promise?"

"Sure, method and technique give all artists, including yogis, a basic palette for their work. But seminal performance—performance that transforms us, that goes beyond a rearrangement or recycling of classic elements—is inspired. It's my contention that the unique nature of each of our souls, rediscovered by the re-birthing process of Yoga, combined with the exploratory nature of the arts, would increasingly generate these anomalistic, inspirational moments. I'm not saying this isn't achieved otherwise, only that its incidence would be increased."

While much of Michael's ideas about acting and directing are common wisdom, the dovetailing of these with Yoga practices strikes me as novel. He may say he's untrained in the theatre, but it seems that he has rather swiftly swept my leading lady off her feet.

"So, in other words," I ask, "you're saying that the integration of Yoga and theatre would increase availability of actors *and* combat the tendency of dogma to creep into both of these disciplines?"

"Right," he replies.

"And that would improve the quality of theatre?"

"Among other things, yes."

"So, if I might turn the tables, what do Yoga practitioners get out of acting?"

"The relativity of personality," Michael says. "The understanding that despite the lure of the ego, it is availability that is ultimately linked to that which is transcendent. It may be true, as Jung says, that humankind is in need of symbols of integration and transformation, objects to which the ego attaches itself for the good of its organic health, but we need to understand that these symbols are simply catalysts (not sacred in and of themselves) for our ongoing spiritual transformation in which we replace the darkness of fear and ignorance with the light of consciousness and pure being. This is the light that pours into availability. The process is the same in theatre and spirituality: in theatre, availability is for character; in spirituality, availability is for the G-d principle, the consciousness of Abraham, Jesus, Buddha, Krishna, etc. In both cases, availability may be activated through Yoga."

"And G-d, or the 'G-d principle' as you're calling it now, is the Great Anomaly that you've spoken of?"

"Yes."

"And you use this term because it is non-denominational, non-dogmatic?"

"Yes, as well as fundamentally unknowable."

"If it's unknowable, why do we seek it?"

"This leads us," Michael says, "to the third area where the Yoga benefits theatre—faith. Through the spiritual rebirthing process of Yoga, we unavoidably come to faith in the unseen force that animates creation. In the theatre, this can translate into faith that your next line is waiting in your subconscious and muscle memory to be 'discovered' or brought forth as thought—seemingly unrehearsed and spontaneous, as new to the speaker as to the listener. You have to admit that this state is central to the gestalt at the heart of theatre?"

"I never considered that, Michael, but I know the experience you're talking about—when acting disappears and we experience truth."

"Exactly," Michael says. "So what we call transcendental in Yoga is much the same dynamic as what we call transformation in the theatre; enlightenment and catharsis are different degrees of the same over-arching process."

"And what process is that?" I ask.

"The fourth area of mutual interest that exists between Yoga and theatre: ritual and rebirth," Michael says. "In Paleolithic times—when humans had just removed themselves from the jungle and their anthropoid past—spirituality and community were celebrated in rites that included music, dance, song, masks, costume, and the elements, such as fire and water. This goes back our earlier discussions and the Maxwell Anderson quote."

"Yes, 'The theatre is a religious institution dedicated entirely to the spiritual exaltation of humankind.'"

"Right," Michael smiles. "Because churches have become, for the most part, instruments of control, power, and exclusivity, it falls upon the arts and Yoga to exalt the human spirit in non-dogmatic ways that encourage the development of each individual's unique gift and, in turn, the evolution of humankind.[56] As I've said, it is the sum of humanity's individual treasures that will provide the answers we need to create a sustainable and loving world. This is not to say that this will be a 'perfect' world, nor that we can somehow, by evolving, avoid the pain of being incarnate on this plane, but I do believe that there is a transcendental state of being that surpasses both pain and joy—and that is grace, a state which we can achieve through this integration of Yoga and theatre, spiritual practice and ritual and rebirth, as we've just discussed."

"So how would you propose including Yoga as part of an actor's preparation?"

"Many dance academies and acting conservatories already include exercises based on the *physical* branches of Yoga. I'm suggesting that this practice be extended simply by adding some meditative practices aimed at individual and group awareness. It would be an experiment, but one that we've seen produces impressive results."

---

[56] For example, see Ali Daraghmeh, "Ex-Palestinian militant turns to theater," *Associated Press*, January 17, 2008.

"Okay, then how would your approach to teaching Yoga to actors differ from the way in which you've taught Yoga to others?"

"If we were walking into a pre-existing professional theatre company, I think our approach necessarily would be different than if we were setting up a curriculum for an acting academy. It would also depend on whether we were dealing with, say, an equity house, an existent troupe with a core ensemble, or auditioning an entirely different set of non-equity actors for each production. Setting up a group practice of a meditative art would obviously work better in a situation where the make-up of the group has some continuity from production to production and from season to season, just as such familiarity generally benefits the ensemble's artistic performance.

"But any theatre or school that uses Yoga postures and relaxation techniques should be giving the participants some background on the system they're using. For example, one of the sacred elements of theatre productions is the detailed replication of customs, mannerisms, and dialects from other cultures and times. This is how the theatre transports us to places we would otherwise never have the opportunity to visit. It's the duty of the director and dramaturge to research these details and recreate them in a factual manner, unless they're doing some kind of hybrid design or purposeful anachronism. So, then why wouldn't a theatre company feel the same responsibility to inform its actors of the deeper nature of one of the physical training methods that they're using, particularly if they're truncating it?"

"I see your point," I say, "as long as we're only talking about informing the process—because once actors have reached the point in their careers, where they're journeymen, the imposition of an external training method seems a stretch, unless it's to inform the movement or subtext of a particular play; otherwise, such practices only work if actors choose it for themselves."

"Right. Diane took that initiative. But what about your interest in experimental theatre? Haven't you always wanted to have your own troupe to stretch your boundaries? As I said there's nothing dogmatic about this. It's just a working hypothesis, an exercise used at the director's discretion. But it seems a natural fit—the rituals of our Paleolithic ancestors, the rituals of the theatre, and the rituals of Yoga—they are all centering exercises. And, of course, directors use all sorts of techniques to prepare actors."

Admittedly, I'm wary of Michael's proposal to introduce Yoga into a rehearsal process—it's hard not to feel constant subversive implications in his ideas and, despite his denials, the latent dogma in any such teachings—but he nevertheless makes a compelling case for it. Maybe my feelings of jealousy over Diane are clouding my thoughts on this? I think back on some of the experimental productions to which my father exposed me at the Avignon Festival in my youth. What would I have to lose if I took up Michael's challenge in my own work? I put this idea on the back burner, feeling a little overwhelmed with what I have on my plate right now.

Although I have more questions for Michael concerning re-awakening through Yoga, we've drifted far afield from the Wayne Home Rule Charter, and I feel mentally exhausted from so much thinking.

I tell Michael that I plan on bringing my chronicle of our conversations—from the day we met through this morning's discussion—up to date as soon as possible. He encourages me to do so for my own sake, since "it will be hard to catch up on events once things take off."

Later that day, after I've had a chance to recuperate, I recall the conversation with a healthy degree of astonishment. I began the call with the intention of debriefing Michael on the charter and I ended up discovering a whole new way of looking at actors' training. I'm eager to listen to the recording to find out exactly how we got there. I reluctantly admit to myself that when I'm not bristling at one of his political or religious comments or about his relationships with Chimera and Diane, I enjoy his interdisciplinary free-associative banter.

☼ ☼ ☼

In the weeks that follow, the demands of my accounting practice interrupt my plans to start work on the book, but, as they say, it's the day job that pays the bills.

I have always worked hard to produce exemplary work for Arthur Andersen, and it's paid off. I got my CPA license in near record time, and was recently was made partner at the Denver office—the youngest ever to do so. But my career success hasn't been without its price. The lack of time I've given to Chimera and the struggles we've had are directly related to the long hours I keep for the firm (not to mention my theatrical career). But surely one must support oneself? I may wish that the world was a better place and that artists and teachers and care-givers were paid their due, but that's not the case. It's nearly impossible to live in this society and not be part of a contradictory system in which a few thrive at the expense of the many. Besides, what are you going to replace it with? So, I apply myself, and my work grows. Ever since I made partner, just after *Theatres of Love* closed, I haven't given a thought to my next theatre project.

Then I was called to headquarters in Chicago, where I was asked to sit on the company's international task force that will monitor and lobby the European Economic Union's recently established Court of Auditors.[57]

While in Chicago, I also decide to follow up on one of the two additional pieces of Michael's personal information that I gleaned from our last conversation—that he had worked at a place called the Yoga Retreat.

I'm in the Windy City for a whole week, and on Thursday afternoon our meeting breaks up early. I turn down dinner plans with one of my associates on the pretext of visiting a long-lost relative, and go for a walk. I stroll up Michigan Avenue from my hotel in the Loop, past the heart of the upscale shopping district, to Walton Street, not far from the stretch of classy condos that line Lake Shore Drive heading north all the way to the ritzy suburbs of the North Shore.

I turn west on Walton, and about half way to Rush Street, where I plan to take in dinner and some of the Near North Side's best jazz clubs this evening, I find the sign for the Yoga Retreat. I walk into the building foyer and climb up to the second floor, which turns out to house both a restaurant and the main classroom and meditation hall.

I feel fortunate to find all-vegetarian fare on the posted menu and walk in. Beyond the front counter, there are about a dozen wooden tables with gaily-colored padded chairs and enough windows to give the feel of a country kitchen. The hostess shows me to a small table next to a window. She's an attractive brunette, perhaps ten years older than I, wearing a

---

[57] On July 22, 1975, a treaty giving the European Parliament wider budgetary powers and establishing a Court of Auditors was signed. It entered into force in June 1977.

leotard and a sari. It's about four-thirty in the afternoon, and other than one couple across the way, I'm the only customer.

I discover from reading the narrative preceding the menu that the cook is a noted macrobiotic chef and author. I think back to Michael's comments concerning "Taoist chemistry" during our meal at the Carnival Café just after we had first met. This is obviously a spot where he learned a lot about that subject.

The waitress is an attractive Nordic-looking young woman with long blonde hair and sky blue eyes. I'm not terribly hungry, so I start with the house tea, a salad, and some bread. When the waitress returns with my tea, she gives me the opportunity that I came here for.

"I don't think I've seen you here before," she says.

"No, I'm from out of town, from Denver," I say. I skip the reference to Boulder because it had not attained the notoriety that it was soon to achieve from a Newsweek article concerning its free-spirited lifestyle.

"I hear it's beautiful out there," she says. "All those mountains ..."

"Oh, yes," I assure her. "They are every bit as beautiful in person as they are in the ads. But you know, most of the people there live on the plains. You have to make a day of it to get up into the hills and enjoy them."

"I hadn't realized that," she says. "So, how did you find this place?"

"Actually a friend of mine told me about it—Michael Solomon."

"The Rabbonai?" she asks.

"I hadn't heard that one before," I reply. "He's a Yoga teacher, if that's what you mean."

"That's not exactly what that means," she says. "It's an honorific title meaning 'Master.'"

"Really?" I ask. I'm startled, thinking that Michael has a cult following back here. "People call him that here?"

"Just me," she says. She introduces herself as Cynthia. "We're close friends," she sighs. "How do you know him?"

"We met in a bookstore," I say. "We've become good friends. I'm writing a book with him."

"You're writing *the book*?" she asks, astonished. She sits down across from me.

"You know about the book?" I ask, as surprised as she is.

"Michael said that he would tell his story in a book, but that he couldn't write it."

"He told me the same thing—that he couldn't write it. Did he ask you to write it too?" I ask, now wondering if I had found another Herr Offenbacher, another Boswell.

"No!" She laughs. "We used to talk about it, but he wasn't ready to start. The book was something in the future, just like his living in the mountains. Besides, I was too attached."

A mist of melancholy suffuses her wistful recollection.

"He does seem to have plans," I say.

"Yes he does," she sighs again.

At that point, two women enter the restaurant and she excuses herself.

That evening, listening to Yousef Lateef in a smoky club a few blocks away, I think about Cynthia's remarks. Like Diane, she seems to have developed a strong attachment to Michael, although in Cynthia's case I assume the relationship had gone a bit further. I wonder whether it's Michael's detachment, and not his "spirituality," that attracts women to him. Perhaps I should have played hard-to-get with Diane?

☼ ☼ ☼

Given the new connection in my mind between Diane and Cynthia, when I get home I put off discussing with Chimera my conversation in the restaurant. However, she has no such reticence in discussing her liaisons.

"I had tea with Michael," she says during our catch-up conversation over breakfast.

As always, this gets me going.

"Couldn't stay away from him," I say.

"What are you saying?" she says.

"I mean, here I am away on business, and you've got to go see Michael."

"That's not what happened! He called for you, wondering how things were going on the project."

"And you parlayed that into a date," I say.

"A date! Look, he's my friend too! I thought he could help me with my own issues. Just because you don't find his advice of value doesn't mean other people don't."

"So, did he help you?"

"He gave me some things to think about," she says, and cuts off the conversation.

☼ ☼ ☼

Nearly six months later I find myself in San Francisco, going through the books of a branch office for one of my Denver accounts. I still haven't begun to commit my conversations with Michael to paper as I had promised. Sure, I've been incredibly busy, but it's my skepticism that seems to be encouraging this procrastination. I'm still convinced—despite the fact that everyone I've met who knows Michael thinks highly of him—that I'll find something about him which shoots a hole in the façade. So, after days filled with research into my client's operation, I spend my evenings doing the same sort of work—investigating Michael's background, following up on the other piece of personal information I picked up in our last conversation.

When I question my motives for this sleuthing, I reassure myself that I'm just doing what Michael asked me to do at the beginning: present an objective, even skeptical, account of his activities. He told me that one of the reasons he's chosen me to do this is that I'm a skilled auditor, and part of that perspective involves a healthy respect for the value of personal investigations. Just as it is not the financial books of a corporation that most often reveal the existence of corruption, but rather an indication in a conversation with an employee or some other passing incident, so it is with biographical subjects: friends and acquaintances can tell you more than you can discover from the person himself. And so it is with my research into the required character traits of the *soi-disant*[58] "Avatar."

My nocturnal investigations begin with one of my colleagues in the San Francisco office, a graduate of Stanford. Early in the week, over drinks after work, I ask him if he would call the university and see if they have any contact information for Paul Offenbacher, the fellow Michael had

---

[58] From French, meaning "so-called."

described as his "fellow theoretician" back in his school days. I tell my colleague it's a favor for a friend of mine. Later in the week he hands me a telephone number and tells me it wasn't easy to obtain. He says the university doesn't release personal information except by consent, and Offenbacher's name doesn't appear in any reunion class books, verifying my own fruitless attempts. I'm appreciative of the effort and don't ask him how he got the information, assuming, like a journalist, he has his own "unidentified sources."

I wonder how Sherlock Holmes would justify hoodwinking his friends to get the goods on his suspects? I tell myself that this subterfuge is for the greater good. What if Michael turns out to have a murky past? I could save the world a lot of trouble by exposing him before he starts bamboozling others.

I call Offenbacher's home number that evening and reach him.

"Paul, my name's Rashan Barcusé. I'm a friend of Michael Solomon's from Denver," I say.

"The Dad?" he says.

I'm at a loss as to how to respond. It seems that every friend of Michael's to whom I talk has a different name for him—Yogi Mike, Rabbonai, and now, The Dad.

"The Dad?" I ask.

"Sorry," Offenbacher says. "It's an old nickname for Michael. I think it goes back to middle school."

"I see. That's what you called him when you were college chums?"

"Yeah, a few of us called him that. It seemed to fit. You know—that authoritative, self-contained air. How do you know him?"

"We're writing a book together," I say. "Michael mentioned your name. He said you guys were political activists, and that you wrote a paper together?"

"We did some writing together," he says, offering me nothing more.

"Look, I know this is odd, getting a call out of nowhere about your past. Michael told me how you guys used to joke about being bugged and all that. In fact, that's how your name came up. I asked him if I could tape record our conversations for the book and he told me the two of you used to joke about the FBI listening to your conversations."

"Right," he says. "Michael never seemed to care who might be listening or what might go on his permanent FBI record. We still see them snooping around here every now and then."

"Who," I ask, "the FBI?"

"Yep. It's the old Stanford radical list," he says. "I wouldn't be surprised if they're still following Michael in Colorado, with their guns and licenses to kill."

Apparently, my mention of the old FBI story dispelled some of Offenbacher's reticence, but it all sounded a paranoid to me. "Their possible snooping still doesn't seem to matter to Michael," I say.

"That's what I mean about his self-confidence," Offenbacher says. "His belief in himself, no matter what he's doing—as if he can change the world through persuasion. In our political theory classes, he used to ace the essay exams. He could tie any thought to any other thought, like his mind *is* the Dialectic."

"Yeah, his raps are something else," I say, trying to insinuate myself into Offenbacher's memory by using a colloquial term from the '60's.

"But it was the same with everyday stuff. One time, we were traveling cross-country to get back to school and we ran out of money in Reno. We were both underage, but Michael decides that he'll go into a casino and see what he can scare up. He tells me to repeat this Japanese Buddhist chant we just picked up from a friend in St. Louis. You remember the old "Nam-Myoho-Renge-Kyo" chant?[59] He didn't even get carded, and he won enough money at blackjack to get us out to the coast. I thought it was hilarious, but he downplayed it, like it was just a matter of course, like he expected it, a tool someone left just for him, at the perfect time."

"I had a similar experience when we met," I say. "He came up to me in a bookstore, knew what book I had been reading, and told me what to read next. Talk about audacious!"

"Well, that's The Dad," Offenbach says. "What's he up to now?"

---

[59] This chant, very popular in the late '60's in America, is derived from the teachings of Nichiren Daishonin (1222-1282), the founder of Nichiren Shoshu, "The One and Only True Buddhism for the [sake of] eternal prosperity and happiness for all mankind."

"Well, like I said, he's got me chronicling our relationship," I say, feeling chummy. "He's teaching Yoga in a small town up in the Colorado hills and, like you said, believes he's going to change the world."

"That doesn't surprise me," Offenbach says. "Michael came out here from Colorado after he first started doing Yoga. He stopped talking for a while—claimed he was practicing some kind of Hindu austerity. I thought he was crazy and took him down to see some shrinks at Langley Porter.[60] They interviewed him and told me he was perfectly sane and that perhaps I should examine my own perceptions of reality. That was a shock! It threw a wrench in our relationship. We lost track of each other after that."

"Nothing's changed," I say. "He's still making people question their own sanity."

Offenbacher laughs. We exchanged pleasantries and hang up.

---

[60] Langley Porter Psychiatric Institute, part of the University of California School of Medicine, San Francisco.

4

Friends

"Artists are the antennae of the race but the bullet-headed many will never learn to trust their great artists."
-- Ezra Pound

"For one human being to love another human being: that is perhaps the most difficult task that has been entrusted to us, the ultimate task, the final test and proof, the work for which all other work is merely preparation."
-- Rainer Maria Rilke

Not until I return from San Francisco, some six months after I last spoke to Michael, do I begin to find the time to start typing. But the going is slowed by the demands of my accounting practice and a few infertile attempts at playwriting, and it's almost a year later before I have recreated our first three conversations, transcribed our telephone call, and summarized my investigative side trips.

I call Michael and tell him I've written a rough draft. We talk mostly about personal stuff. He has received a grant from the county to perform the duties of town manager for the Town of Wayne. He's also been finalizing his proof of the convergence of science and spirituality.

I tell him I'd like to hone the rough draft before he reads it, and he assures me that there's no rush. He's got a couple decades before he needs to read it, he says with a chuckle, but maybe we can get together soon and talk at greater length.

☼ ☼ ☼

Before I begin editing I ask Chimera to read the draft, giving her copies of the first three chapters. A few weeks later, she and I have a conversation about what I've written and the direction that the project might take.

"I've finished reading what you gave me, and ..." she begins and then hesitates.

"And what?"

"I think you've accurately portrayed your experience so far, but ..."

"What is it that's not working for you?" I ask, slipping into that suggestive state where her pronouncements take on the import of a muse.

As I mentioned earlier, she reminds me of Scheherazade, a consummate storyteller and fabulist. In Chimera's case, she blends these talents by writing stories that accompany her paintings. To many of her clients, these tales are as compelling as the paintings themselves. I'm envious of the ease at which she works in both media, compared with my own struggles at telling a story. I assume her abilities are genetic, or at least inherited character traits passed down through behaviors on both sides of her family.

Chimera's father, Jamshyd al-Din, worshipped books. He was born in Yazd, Iran, and immigrated to New York in 1945, working first for his uncle in a grocery store. Eventually he garnered enough capital to start a bookstore. His family tree includes Zoroastrian priests as well as Sa'di.[1] He is a fiery man with a wicked temper, but very literate. Even in his second language of English, he has a way with words.

Chimera's mother, Mnemosyne Zorbas, is a first generation Greek-American. Her parents came to New York in 1933 from a fishing village on Levcos, an island in the Aegean Sea. "Nemo," as she was called by her friends, studied classics at CCNY and, after her divorce from Jamshyd, taught history in the New York City public schools.

So, when Chimera questions my exposition, I listen.

"As you know, I'm impressed with Michael," she begins. "He's an extremely intelligent man and seems to have a comprehensive vision of

---

[1] Muslih al-Din (1213?-1292?), Persian poet, known as Sa'di, admired for his blend of cynical wisdom and kindness. Well educated and traveled, Sa'di wrote many popular works including the *Golestan*, a collection of rhymed prose and poetry that serves to illustrate the moral lessons of the Koran.

what it will take to make a significant change on this planet. But it's very early in the game, and I don't know enough about him to judge whether he's got the wherewithal to pull off something like this. And even if he does have the means, he still needs a few breaks. You know, the whole idea is still very far out."

"Yes," I say. "That's why it's crucial that I describe his peculiarities. He's not just some person with a delusion, like some Haight-Ashbury[2] acid head who thinks he's Jesus, or an armed cult leader on a Messianic power trip. And I admit that, as you say, he appears to have the spiritual, intellectual, and emotional resources to make a go of this, though, again, it's early and there's no telling what direction this could take. But the notion of a Messiah is complex. It's difficult to describe what would be involved such a thing. Even after some research, I'm still uncertain."

"Yes, it's difficult."

"But you feel there's something missing?" I ask, painfully aware that Chimera is holding back the *pièce de résistance*.

I know this because our relationship has changed dramatically in the last six months—mostly because I've tried to be more honest about my feelings of jealousy over Chimera and Michael's relationship and my own desires toward other women, particularly Diane. But letting Chimera read about the details of these feelings in the draft of my first three chapters is a leap of faith for me. I wait for her to take advantage of my vulnerability and lower the boom over my emotional and spiritual infidelities.

Instead, she analyzes my writing. Perhaps my relativistic French morality is wearing off on her.

"I know this is a chronicle, Rashan, not a novel, but as a reader I want to know more about Michael. Where did he grow up? He obviously did well in school, but what are the events that shaped his life and make him believe the path he's chosen is something a rational person would even consider."

"So, you're suggesting that I interview him?"

"Not anything that formal. When you met me there was no interview. Yes, you were interested in who I was, and in all the details that

---

[2] The cross-streets of a neighborhood in San Francisco where the hippie movement began, during the Summer of Love, 1967.

would, after the initial blush of our attraction, make it possible for us to spend our lives together. But you found this out through our friendship, not an interview. Since this book you're doing with Michael is a long-term project, and you're hoping to explore what makes him tick, I think you need to find some activities to do together."

"Okay," I say, still not getting the gist of what she's saying.

"You still don't know him," she continues. "You write that Michael could be just another seducer, and you're right—there are plenty of gurus out there that, in the controlled environment of their *satsangs*[3] or ashrams, appear attractive. But usually there's a gap between their public persona and their private life. If your book is going to convince anyone that Michael is the psycho-genetic combination—'the one-in-four-billion' spiritual anomaly, as you call it—who will be a major catalyst for the evolution of humankind, then you've got to show me, the reader, that he's as together in his private life as he seems to be in his work.

"Your description of Diane's and Cynthia's feelings for Michael is a start, and I agree in part with your take that my feelings play into this as well, but I want to know more. If women are often attracted to him in this way, there's bound something interesting there that we don't know. He's lived around here for a while. Maybe you should find some ex-girlfriends of his to check this out."

"Isn't that a bit like wondering how sleeping with Marilyn Monroe affected John Kennedy's presidency?"

"Not really. Look, we know that politics, as it is today, is a nasty business. Kennedy's sex life, or Nixon's for that matter, has little if anything to do with their ability to govern. But we're talking about an avatar, or perhaps *the* Avatar—someone in whom we expect a greater degree of consistency. Michael's a man who is evolving like everyone else—but how he's evolving is the question. Since you're going to chronicle his life and your experiences with him, I want to know if he's really who and what he makes himself out to be."

"That may be something easier for you to discover," I say.

"What's that supposed to mean?"

---

[3] From the Sanskrit, meaning wisdom-sessions or knowledge sharing.

"I mean, you said you wanted to know what his ex-girlfriends think of him. But as a guy, I'll never have a relationship like that with him."

"It seems odd, given the jealous feelings you've had, that you'd suggest I get to know him better. I'm not sure what kind of passive-aggressive response this is."

"Look, I'm trying accept that you're attracted to him, whether it's just spiritual or not. This shouldn't be a problem for me; it's not as if I've never had feelings for female friends, as you know. But I love you, and I get hung up on my attachment. That seems natural. So, I think it's unfair to characterize my vacillation between jealousy and detachment with some psychoanalytic verbiage. It's like Michael says, 'It's dangerous to be analyzed by your partner.'"

"Rashan, you're changing the subject," she says, surprisingly collected in light of my hyperbolic projections. "This is not about me. It's about your profile of Michael. Look, would it help if I told you that if Michael's interested in anyone it's Diane, not me."

"You're telling me they're seeing each other?"

"No. But she's hoping that things might develop."

"Seriously? Don't you think that would be a breach of professional etiquette—a yogi dating his student?"

"He's not her shrink. And besides, Diane tells me it's nothing that formal. She just asked him for some physical and mental exercises, and they get together and work on them."

"Well, he hadn't mentioned anything to me. I wonder if he's trying to keep me from writing about it?"

"That's another thing. Until I'd read what you'd written, I had no idea that you'd told him what we talk about in private."

Finally, I think, she's ready to deliver the *coup de grâce*. "It's just like I wrote," I say, attempting to defend myself, "it was unavoidable. He suggested I read the Jung essay and it affected the way I perceived my development and our relationship. That's why he suggested I read it in the first place—he knew it would change me."

"I'm just uncomfortable sharing my demons with the world."

"Well, if it's any consolation, Michael and I are doing it too. It's what writers do—just like my play, *Theatres of Love*. You were okay with that."

"Yeah, I was," she says, "but that didn't seem so personal. She pauses. "I guess it's just the intensity of our whole relationship with Michael. You're attracted to his mind; I'm attracted to his spirit. But I still think it's *you* that should pursue the friendship. It's more likely that he'll discuss his relationships with you—'shop talk,' you know, between guys. And besides, you're writing the book."

Chimera's point is well taken, and it isn't hard to come up with a way to make this work. Michael has offered to get involved in my next play as—what shall I call his role?—a "ritual advisor," teaching Yoga to my actors. If I'm going to take him up on that, I ought to spend some time at the theatre with him and make sure that we could work together in such a setting. Besides, I'm enjoying the investigative side of my "audit," pursuing my scoop on 'The Would-Be Messiah.'"

☼ ☼ ☼

The following week I call Michael and invite him to see a regional premiere that is being directed by a friend of mine at a small theatre in Boulder. I explain to him that I'm interested in his offer to work together during the rehearsal process for my next play, though I have no idea when I'm going to find the time to write another play. Regardless, I think our getting together would be a good way to explore our mutual perspectives on theatre, which seems to be the only common language we speak.

Michael picks me up in his truck, a '49 Ford flathead six, with the original wooden planks still on the bed.

"Where'd you get this thing," I ask with feigned derision.

"Thing! Did you hear that Ud-n-ud-n? This uppity theatrical dilettante called you a thing!" he thunders with glorious mock woundedness.

"My apologies, Michael," I ceremoniously reply, adopting his dramatic manner. "I guess I haven't been properly introduced," giving my best imitation of an Elizabethan bow while sitting on nearly thirty-year-old seat springs.

"This, my friend, is Ud-n-ud-n, one of the stalwart mechanical war-horses assigned to provide safe passage to the pioneers of the paleo-cybernetic age." We both break out laughing at this preposterous description that tops off the foppish drift of our conversation, but Michael is not done. "Seriously, Rashan, to be the proud owner of one of a handful of now legally antique vehicles is a badge of honor in Wayne, and Ud-n-ud-n is the only machine on the mountain that can make it up the Turn of Events in fourth gear."

"A feat worthy of Pegasus," I play along. "But why 'Ud-n-ud-n?'"

"Ah, that's the sound he makes walking in granny gear. He's the lowest geared truck in captivity."

"In captivity?" I marvel. "So there are other trucks still at large, lurking on abandoned mining trails and such that may have lower gear ratios?" I ask.

"Yes, but they're ghosts now, like Orville and Noah, shells of their former selves. Kaput."

"Well, Michael, hitch old Ud-n-ud-n to the shay[4] and head out to East Pearl Street. We got a play to catch."

The Guild Theatre complex is ensconced in an industrial park, secreted amongst the high tech start-up companies that spread eastward across the Boulder Valley, eventually joining Colorado's silicon corridor which runs north-south from Fort Collins, through Denver, to Colorado Springs.[5] A sandwich board, set out on the sidewalk each evening, is the only indication that, hidden behind the smoked-glass windows of a nondescript prefabricated steel-framed concrete and stone amalgam, lies a space for the performing arts.

There is still a glow in the western sky highlighting the Flatirons, a mountainous sheath that, like a magnetic backstop, marks Boulder's location from any vantage point along the Front Range, adding a

---

[4] A reference to the chorus of an early 20th Century popular song that goes: "…Put on your old gray bonnet/with the blue ribbon on it,/While I hitch old Dobbin to the shay,/And through the fields of clover,/We'll drive to Dover,/On our golden wedding day."

[5] By the end of the 1990's, the City of Boulder and nearby parts of Boulder County had more software jobs per capita than the Silicon Valley. Denver and Colorado Springs were also ranked in the top 15. See Andy Vuong, "Boulder-Longmont still tops," *The Denver Post*, 3/14/02.

surrealistic geologic element to the post-modern manufactured neighborhood into which we have driven.

"What do you know about this play?" Michael asks.

"I'm not familiar with the playwright, but the director is a former girlfriend of mine from college, before Chimera."

"Really? Have you seen any of her work since then?"

"Yes, actually a number of times. I even auditioned for her once."

"It always nice to be able to come back to love relationships as friends, don't you think?" he asks.

I can't believe that Michael has begun to talk about this, playing right into Chimera's suggestion of a week ago. At times like this, when her poetic license anticipates such synchronicity, I wonder why she ever changed her name from Thalia.[6]

"Yes, I'm always touched when that happens," I say. "It's as if one speaks soul to soul without desire clouding the communion."

"Not a bad description," he concurs.

"You have friends around like this, then?" I ask, trying to take advantage of my good luck.

"Sure, in Wayne, in Boulder, San Francisco, Chicago …"

"Whoa there, Michael, how much longer does the list get?"

"You mean as far as ex-lovers? Oh, I don't know. I don't think about it in that way. The whole question of intimate relationships has more to do with the evolution of souls than the seduction scenarios our society is so fond of hyping to sell magazines and movies. When we move on, there are those we lose track of, those we can't see, or those we don't want to see. Matters of the heart are difficult to explicate. That's why there's poetry … or platonic relationships."

"Platonic relationships?"

"Sure, like my relationship with Chimera."

My chest suddenly tightens and my breath shortens. I didn't expect to discuss this subject; in fact, I most certainly was trying to avoid it.

---

[6] As mentioned in Chapter 1, Thalia is the Greek muse of comedy and bucolic poetry.

"That's how you'd describe your relationship with Chimera, as platonic?" I muster.

"I think it's a good example of what I'm talking about, Rashan," he says with zest, as if oblivious to the implications this subject has for me. You know, it's not the first time in my life that I've had a spiritual connection with a woman who's already involved in a relationship with a friend."

"So, that's how you see this?"

"Sure. Look, I know that this seems like an odd situation, especially for you, since we're both guys and these things often turn competitive and all that. But given where I'm coming from and what I've got to do in this life, getting involved in a love triangle, or a *ménage à trios*, is out of the question."

"So, you're not physically attracted to Chimera?" I challenge.

"Of course I am, Rashan! But that doesn't mean I have to act on it."

"What then determines whether you *do* act on such impulses?" I ask.

"Part of a Yoga practice involves not being ruled by ones senses and instincts. That's how the higher self comes to the fore. I choose not to act on such impulses when it's inappropriate and harmful."

"And when is that?" I ask, still unconvinced by Michael's altruistic self-characterization.

"It's just like I already said. You and Chimera have an intimate relationship. As long as that's the case, it's not my karma to involve myself unless it's on the level of helping the two of you to work it out. In fact, it may be my karma not to have intimate relationships."

Associating celibacy with Michael had never even entered my mind, though I know it can be a consideration for those who lead ascetic lives.

"You're saying you're celibate? I'm shocked."

"I was once, Rashan—for eighteen months, when I first took up Yoga; it could happen again some day. Who knows? Much of what I have to do in this life involves spiritual counseling. Such practices sometimes work better when one is relatively free from desire, to transcend the cycle of attachment and pain—which brings us back to where we started: the idea of entering into a platonic relationship with someone we'd been intimate with."

After mentally noting that Michael has once again neatly dove-tailed a complex discussion, I venture further. "So why is it that we so often end up estranged from people we once loved?"

"It seems to depend on the pain that was inflicted and the inability of those involved to see the big picture, the rhyme and reason for why the relationship took place. It's an old adage, but when difficult things happen to us we must ask ourselves what we're supposed to learn from them, what's the lesson."

The asphalt parking lot surrounding the theatre is irregularly leveled as is often the case between closely constructed, yet sporadically planned, warehouse space, and, after parking Ud-n-ud-n, Michael and I make our way down a banked parking area to the double-doors and lobby. There are two working spaces inside the building, one set up with a proscenium stage and tiered scaffolding to hold the seating; the other is a black box that flexes according to the director's preference. It is this latter one, with the stage elevated and the chairs on the floor, into which we enter and find some seats.

As it turns out, the play, *Kindertransport*, written by Diane Samuels, is about Eva Schlesinger, a nine-year old Jewish girl from Hamburg, who is sent by her parents to London in the late 1930's in the hopes that she might survive the coming Holocaust. For years she steadfastly refuses to give up hope of ever seeing her parents again. But finally, unable to tolerate the disappointment any longer, Eva caves in, accepts her new mother and homeland.

I did not think about the effect of such a story on Michael. As I said, I didn't know what it was about. It's at intermission when I get the first hint that, beyond the gravity of the piece itself, Michael has been deeply touched.

"I have an aunt who survived Auschwitz," he says. "She has the number tattooed on her arm. When I was old enough to understand what this meant, around ten years of age, I was shocked by the monstrosity of it."

"Michael, I apologize for my insensitivity! I had no idea, really!"

"No need to apologize, Rashan. It's normal for me to see some cinema and theatre about the Holocaust every year. I think that's a healthy dosage—enough to be reminded of the event and the Jewish experience, yet not an obsession. It's not as if this is the only holocaust that humankind has perpetrated."

"But the scale of it, Michael!"

"Oh, yes. It was particularly efficient. But the Jews as a people survived this attempt at genocide just as they have in the past—and, as usual, with a vengeance."

"A vengeance?"

"I know that word has the connotation of violence or injury, but I don't mean it in this way, only in the manner by which the ideologies that perpetrated such hatred have been, one at a time, laid to waste.[7] Like when the Pharaoh dreams that there is to be born among the Jews one who will lead his people from their enslavement in Egypt, so he orders the death of all first born Hebrew male children. Somehow Moses escapes this fate and grows up to not only lead the slaves from bondage, but to deliver a set of laws that, theoretically, became a pillar of Judaism—and later, and only theoretically as well, of Christianity and Islam. Likewise, Herod dreams that there is to be a child born to the Israelites who will threaten the hegemony of Rome. And again, the order goes out to kill male Jewish children. Once more, a great prophet escapes this fate, and Jesus, actually Ee-ah-sh-oo-ah,[8] goes on to establish a new doctrine based on love and

---

[7] This same notion is echoed in a recent article concerning some Torahs that survived the Holocaust: "This really is an opportunity to look up to the heavens and say, he who laughs last, laughs best," Rabbi Youlus said. "The Nazis really thought they had wiped Jews off the face of the earth, and Judaism. Here we are taking the ultimate symbol of hope and of Judaism and rededicating it and using it in a synagogue. And we'll take it to Auschwitz. You can't beat that." --Rabbi Menachem Youlus, who runs the nonprofit Save a Torah foundation in Wheaton, Maryland. (James Barron, "From Auschwitz, a Torah as Strong as Its Spirit," *The New York Times*, April 30, 2008)

[8] Michael insists that so-called Christian attempts at G-d's name and Jesus' name are way off the mark. Using the Hebrew letters to say "Jehovah" or "Yaweh" is not only blasphemous, but mispronounced, and Jesus' name, derived from the Hebrew as Joshua or Yeheshuah, is also wrong. While Michael wouldn't pronounce the name of G-d for me, he did give me this phonetic pronunciation of Jesus' name. For more details on the Doctrine of the Sacred Tetragrammaton (the name of G-d), see "Jesus" in *Appendix 7 – Michael's Notes*.

compassion—and, theoretically again, a major component of Christianity and Islam. Finally, we suffer Hitler who attempts to use various occult practices, including the involuted swastika, to enforce a 'final solution' in the hopes of putting an end to the Judaic prophesies that run counter to his vision of an Aryan future. Not only does Hitler fail, like Pharaoh and Herod before him, but the Avatar for this age, like Moses and Jesus, has survived, and shall unveil a new teaching worthy of this millennium—a teaching that needs to be taken to heart, not theoretically, but practically, if we are to survive."

> *What is the difference between believing that one has Christ consciousness and believing that one is the Christ or the Messiah or the 'anointed one'? Yes, it's true that Jesus suggested we can all follow his pattern[9] and enjoy the same state of being, but doesn't this presuppose that we become one with him and what he represents, and not simply a believer whose actions appear consistent with his teaching? And if this is so, and we do the work, then isn't such consciousness reborn in us and isn't the so-called Second Coming, or coming of the Messiah, really a constant recurrence running throughout humanity? Yes, but this is only one aspect of the Avatar's periodicity: higher logic dictates that, as was the case with previous incarnations, there is an anomalistic occurrence which represents the special, not general, case of the Christ or Messiah or Avatar or Spiritual Anomaly phenomena. And in addition to my dream in which I state, "I am Christ," do not the historical and prophetic circumstances also point to this possibility? With the family names of Solomon and Boas and the dearth of genealogical records, the proof is simply in the life put forth.*

I am astonished! From what seems to be a reminder of a painful tragedy, he presents me with spiritual mission of global proportions that has survived, as far as I can tell, for almost six thousand years.

---

[9] "I have given you an example, that ye should do as I have done unto you." John 13:15

"And so you're saying that all these tragedies—the trials of Egyptian slavery, the Roman crucifixion, the Nazi Holocaust—are G-d's way of proving that his message can't be denied?" I ask.

"That's a difficult and potentially explosive thought, Rashan. It's as if by agreeing to a covenant with the Great Anomaly, the Hebrews became a human sacrifice to a force that asks the ultimate faith and price to prove its omnipotence, just like Abraham was asked to sacrifice his first born, Isaac, and G-d 'himself' sacrificed 'his son,' Jesus. It should be clear to us now, standing at this crossroads of human development, that the purpose of this 'chosen' relationship was to create the eschatological conditions which would nurture a prophet, or spiritual anomaly, at this point in time, one who could read the clues of history and discover his assignment for himself. Yes, this relationship is certainly special, but it does not follow that it is exclusive. The One True Faith is not Judaism, Christianity, Islam, Buddhism, Hinduism, Taoism, Zoroastrianism, Bahá'í, or any other specific religion or practice. Spirituality in theory and practice must move beyond the confines of 'isms' and boxes and names and ethnicities. In this dispensation, one of the principles that must be stressed is the non-exclusivity of the covenant. We are all unique expressions of a source that is without a name or face or symbol—and it is time that we encourage each other to express his or her unique facet in consonance with the Golden Rule."[10]

"It does seem, though, Michael," I say, "that there's an evil force in all those efforts that you just described—a force working against G-d's revelation to humankind—that begs for a Judeo-Christian explanation."

"Rashan, the Antichrist, as we call it, is just a metaphor for the dark side of the force, our own shadow or instinctive nature, anything that works against the Christ or higher consciousness within each of us. That's what is meant by, 'Every spirit that dissolveth Jesus ... is Antichrist ... of whom you have heard that he is cometh.'[11] One can pick out any number of historical events and persons that reflect this tendency. You name them—Pharaohs, Caesars, Fuehrers, Czars, Socialist tyrants, Chairmen of the Central Committee, Monopolists, Presidents, CEO's—the cynical,

---

[10] See "Golden Rule" in *Appendix 7 – Michael's Notes*.
[11] (I John 4:3 [DV])

greedy, and violent breed. World-wide materialism is the disease of the Antichrist."

"You're putting Presidents and capitalists in the same bag as dictators?"

"Why not? Ultimately they both enslave. Look, one of the definitions of fascism is the corporate state,[12] and what is America's so-called advanced industrial society if not a nation whose political and social system is controlled by business interests and the dictates of an oligarchy defined by large concentrations of capital?[13] What we have here is not Italian or German or Spanish fascism, but our own American brand of fascism. We may still have the trappings of democracy and republicanism, but these processes are now manipulated by money, not votes, just as Jefferson, Lincoln, Hayes, Eisenhower, and FDR warned us.[14] And the

---

[12] Sabine, George H., *A History of Political Theory*, Holt, Rinehart and Winston, New York, 1961, p. 919 and following. Also, "Fascism should more properly be called corporatism because it is the merger of state and corporate power." -- Benito Mussolini.

[13] While we Americans have been trained to keenly identify the opposite of fascism, i.e., government intrusion into and usurpation of private enterprise, we have not been trained to identify the usurpation of government by private enterprise. Our European cousins, on the other hand, having lived with Fascism in several countries during the last century, know it when they see it, and looking over here, they are ringing the alarm bells. David G. Mills, Esq., from http://www.informationclearinghouse.info/article7260.htm.

[14] In Eisenhower's famous farewell speech he warned, "In the councils of government, we must guard against the acquisition of unwarranted influence, whether sought or unsought, by the military-industrial complex. The potential for the disastrous rise of misplaced power exists and will persist." It should be noted that long before Eisenhower's remarks Jefferson declared, "I hope we shall ... crush in its birth the aristocracy of our moneyed corporations, which dare already to challenge our government to a trial of strength and bid defiance to the laws of our country (Letter to George Logan, 1816), and Lincoln more ominously warned, "Corporations have been enthroned. An era of corruption in high places will follow ... until wealth is aggregated in a few hands ... and the Republic is destroyed." President Rutherford B. Hayes followed with, "This is a government of the people, by the people and for the people no longer. It is a government of corporations, by corporations, and for corporations." FDR was blunter: "The real truth of the matter is, as you and I know, that a financial element in the large centers has owned the government ever since the days of Andrew Jackson." --

third world bears the brunt of this inequity. Under the guise of free trade and democracy, we suck them into modernization loans that allow us entry into their markets, which we then monopolize, paying local labor pennies a day to make our clothes and grow our sugar, and indebting their governments to us forever.[15] Fascism is not something that died with Mussolini, Hitler, Batista, Franco, and Somosa. It's rampant in our society, with particular support among the rich. Where else would the justification of worshiping money above all else find such fertile ground? And the churches long ago capitulated to this. Most of what is called Christianity in America and Europe is really Mammon worship, so the integration of church and state, just as the prophets of fascism foresaw, is here, now."

I am ready to launch into my defense of democracy and capitalism when the bell tolls for Act II of *Kindertransport*. Michael smiles at me as we turn to re-enter the theatre. I force a smile in return.

I am still roiling from Michael's prophetic pronouncements about the Holocaust, the coming Avatar, and American fascism when the crippling denouement of the play re-doubles my shock. In a scene that I shall never forget, Frau Schlesinger returns from Auschwitz to reunite with her daughter. The mother's haunting ghostlike remnant of her former self, a survivor of hell itself, shakes the entire theatre. Eva, who has been irreparably traumatized by the loss of her parents, rejects her mother, sending her away as if the Holocaust were her mother's fault, as if her mother had not sent her away to England out of love. Later, it is Eva, in turn, who is rejected by her own daughter.

In the truck on our way back downtown to have some tea and unwind, Michael reveals the basis of the catharsis he experienced from the play.

President Franklin D. Roosevelt, November 21, 1933. The courts, which serve the oligarchy, have ruled that corporations are persons, and thus corporate rights have eroded and superceded personal rights.

[15] Michael's comments here were later completely confirmed by Joseph Stiglitz, the 2001 Nobel Prize winner in Economics. At one time, Stiglitz was Chief Economist of the World Bank. He was fired in 1999 for disavowing their economic policies. He later came clean in an interview with noted investigative reporter Greg Palast, explaining the process whereby western banks and the U.S. Treasury seize control of nations they have drawn into borrowing relationships.

"Most Holocaust pieces concentrate on the event itself, but this play is like *The Pawnbroker* or *Sophie's Choice* [16] in that it focuses on how the Holocaust affects those who *survived* it. Beyond that, though, I think I now understand for the first time the emotional detachment I observed in my aunt and how her trauma was passed along to her oldest daughter, who lost her sanity as an adult."

"I'm not sure what you mean."

"My aunt is a loving person, but sometimes it was as if she became someone else, someone foreign to her husband and her children and her relatives, someone cold and unfeeling, as if she was revisiting the detachment that helped her survive the concentration camp."

> *At age twelve, I was deeply struck by Leon Uris' Exodus. Emblazoned in my memory is the story of Uri escaping the gas chambers by showing a Nazi guard how well he could forge the guard's signature on the spot. I work on adapting my own hand to any writing style I encounter in the hopes that, as a Jew, I will be capable of avoiding extermination just as Uri has. Even today, when I am complemented on my hand, I cannot help but think of Auschwitz.*

"Such a scar on all of us," I manage to get out. "The monstrosity of such crimes is unspeakable. How do you reconcile such evil with your vision of spiritual change? Doesn't it ever seem hopeless to you?"

"Hopeless? No, Rashan, as long as there is life, there is hope. L'chaim! Hitler's failed 'Final Solution' to 'the Jewish question' does show us, though, how thin a veneer civilization is."

"And what does this veneer cover?" I ask, not sure where he is going with this.

"Our instinctive behavior, the genetic inheritance that we carry through our evolution—survival instincts, self-preservation, fight or flight,

---

[16] *The Pawnbroker* is a movie about a holocaust survivor, for which Rod Steiger was nominated for the Oscar for Best Actor in 1965. Later, *Sophie's Choice*, for which Merle Streep won the Oscar in 1982 for Best Actress, echoed similar themes.

among other things, and our ego, much as we discussed in Wayne not long ago. These reflexive phenomena, which helped us survive in the jungle, are capable, at any time, of turning us against our fellow humans."

"So what makes you think that this kind of behavior won't always plague us? It seems that history is filled with examples like this."

"I can give you two reasons, right off, why we can overcome such behavior. First, evolution itself. The force that drives change and consciousness never stops. Before we became 'human' and for much of humanity's 'pre-historic' development, we killed to survive. There is no shame in this, no 'sin.' It is simply instinctive. Today, this type of behavior is no longer necessary to survive, except where we make it so. And we continue to make it so because we believe history teaches us that it is justified—so-called Social Darwinism—but this is a misreading of history."

"But all the history that I've ever read has been a succession of wars and tyranny," I protest. "In what way is it a 'misreading of history' to assume it will always be like this?"

"In one sense, Rashan, what you're saying makes perfect sense because it is, in fact, the story that you've been given. Ultimately, though, it's a misreading because much of the history of the peoples on this planet has been destroyed or altered. You are reaching conclusions derived without the benefit of all the evidence. We talked about this when we first met, at the Carnival Café, and in a lengthy phone conversation as well: I told you about Muslims, Christians, and Jews living in peace during the 11th and 12th centuries in Spain. I also said that there is evidence of a time when worldwide beliefs had more in common than they do now."

"Yes."

"Well, let me tell you about the two most significant events which I believe contribute to this lack of knowledge concerning these ancient civilizations: The Flood and Caesar's burning of the libraries at Alexandria."

As had been my practice since getting Michael's approval, I carry my portable tape recorder with me everywhere on the chance that I might run into him or need to record my own spontaneous thoughts. Whenever we are together, I turn it on, as a matter of course, so that its habitual use draws less attention to itself. Sometimes, as is the case while we drove to and from the theatre this evening, the background noises that get recorded make it more difficult for me, at a later time, to recreate the conversations verbatim. But, in general, I have no trouble transcribing the dialogue and recreating my own reactions and thought processes.

As we pull up to The Sceptre, which is both a café and bookstore, I remind myself how important these conversations are for the work to which I have committed. For some reason, the crazier it gets the more I think I'm on to something, whatever that might be.

"The Flood and the burning of the Library at Alexandria seem like such disparate events," I say.

"Disparate, yes, in the sense that one was an 'Act of God,' as the insurance people say, and the other an 'Act of War,' as the political and military honchos rant, but in effect these two events, more than any others, have separated us from our own history."

"How so? I mean The Flood is a mythology more than anything else."

"It's easy to feel that way, since so many biblical references are of questionable veracity or have been twisted for the Machiavellian purposes of the Church, but The Flood is an event that has been documented cross-culturally, by Scandinavians, Chinese, and many others. Each of these cultures places the occurrence of the event at the same time in history, though each ascribes a different meaning to it, just as each culture shades its perception of the G-d principle, the Great Anomaly, according to its superstitions and science. Here, in the so-called Christian West, we associate The Flood with Noah and his G-d. But elsewhere its origins are tied to other deities and causes."

"So, you're saying that The Flood actually occurred as an event independent of any particular religious interpretation?"

"Exactly. In fact, an acquaintance of Einstein, a Russian physicist by the name of Immanuel Velikovsky, wrote some books[17] on this subject based on the scientific and cultural evidence available to him at the time. While establishment science has always been loath to accept Velikovsky's theories about these cataclysms, there is plenty of evidence to indicate that the events themselves did happen. Anyway, that's a subject of another

---

[17] *Worlds in Collision, Ages in Chaos, Earth in Upheaval*, etc.

lengthy debate, but the data indicates that eighty percent of those on earth at the time perished in a flood brought about by the close proximity of a large gravitational body, say something the size of Venus, that came as close to the Earth as the Moon, perhaps closer."

"Really!"

"So, not only was much of what was written prior to this time lost in the deluge, but the shift in the earth's axis that accompanied this cataclysm disrupted the life-sustaining patterns of most of those cultures that did survive."[18]

"This is hard to believe, Michael!"

"Rashan, witness the wooly Mammoths that have been pulled frozen from the ice in Siberia with food still in their mouths, surrounded by tropical vegetation, or the Chinese *Annals* that describe a week of darkness that occurred at the same time that the *Torah* says Joshua stopped the sun in the sky for seven days."

"*C'est incroyable*! And why haven't we heard of these things before?"

"Because it's not in the interest of those who have convinced the world that, as you said, 'history is a succession of wars and tyranny' to let anyone believe otherwise, else their excuse for institutionalizing cynicism and greed and maintaining their own power would be lost. As Will Rogers said, 'I doubt if there is a thing in the world as wrong or unreliable as history. History ain't what it is. It's what some writer wanted it to be.'"

"Simply that?"

"As my father often reminded me and as I've said to you before, 'Man searches for reasons to support his beliefs.'"

"If that's so, Michael, then wouldn't you be doing the same?"

"That's correct, Rashan. I freely admit to that. However, some beliefs tie together more of the facts and have the power to change the world for the better, while others poison hearts and minds. The current accepted 'Truth' on many subjects is simply myth posing as history. What I

---

[18] According to this theory, the area least affected by climate change was the land surrounding the Himalayas. This would account for China and India having the largest present-day populations, since their survival was aided by high ground, and required little adaptation in the manner of food, clothing, and shelter.

am offering you is history appearing to be myth. That's my job here: to promulgate a vision consistent with spiritual transformation, one that unifies seemingly irreconcilable belief systems and furthers humankind's evolution toward light conscious of itself."[19]

"So, what you're saying is, when history is liberated from politics, hope is restored."

"Well put."

"But even if I accept your claim that the historical record is full of massive holes, how does this prove that there was a time when history was not 'a succession of wars and tyranny?'"

"In trying to prove that our instincts won't continually rule us I must show you that consciousness evolves. In doing this, it seems I must convince you that your reference to our past as 'a succession of wars and tyranny' is simply myth posing as history. If I can get you to accept this premise, even if only 'for the purposes of discussion', we can move on to a discussion of whether there has ever been a time or will be a time when our higher, spiritual selves have ruled or will rule society at large. To accomplish this, I posit three examples in support of my argument that such a condition has happened and will happen again.

"The first is that despite the dearth of historical data, there are still extant indications that Atlantis was, for a time, a widespread, spiritually cohesive civilization."

"Now you really are talking myth, Michael."

"Actually, Rashan, there is a specific reference to Atlantis in the writings of Plato, a variety of allusions to Atlantian philosophy in the cosmology of the Egyptians, and indications in both Africa and South America of common ancestors."

"What's that supposed to mean?"

---

[19] Michael: On October 17, 2002, while attending the opening of the Denver Center Theatre Company's production of Thornton Wilder's classic *The Skin of Our Teeth*, I ran across this quote from Wilder in the Center's study guide: "Democracy has a great duty: to create new myths, new metaphors and new images to show the new condition of dignity into which Man is entering." --Given in a speech in Germany in 1957.

"It means that we can roughly reconstruct the basis of Atlantian spiritual practice, its influence, and the transition of its history and teachings into what we generally interpret as mythology."

"This is a bit much for me to accept, Michael, but for the purposes of argument, where does this lead us?"

"My second example in support of my premise that our instincts won't continually rule us is that consciousness has proven itself to be a progressive phenomena, one that evolves over time, and that there is reason to expect this pattern to hold its own against our animal nature."

"And what proof do you have of this."

"Others have done it before us: Jesus, Gandhi, Martin Luther King, Krishna, Buddha, St. Francis, Mother Theresa, Bahá'u'lláh, The Dalai Lama, and on and on, to name only a few well-known examples. Take your choice. Each of these beings has come face-to-face with his or her own instinctive nature and learned to consciously disengage from its patterns and make decisions derived from his or her higher self, which looks to the greater good."

"And the third example that our instincts won't continually rule us?" I ask, lacking any refutation to this point.

"The third example is one I gave you when we first met."

"I don't recall that."

"You said that global spiritual practice is a utopian idea, and I asked you if you ever had experiences of unity and perfection in your own life. My point being, that if you have had spiritual experiences, then couldn't you make these the premise for your belief system as easily as some negative emotion or thought—say 'a succession of wars and tyranny'—that happened to temporarily influence your consciousness?"

"That's a good question, Michael," I had to admit. "So, you are here to teach that everyone can simply remodel their behavior based on a more productive belief system?"

"Maybe not 'simply,' Rashan, but yes, you get it. That's a profound thought, is it not? We begin each universal cycle as stardust, and we become conscious light. Within this evolutionary process—being driven by a force without a name, but nevertheless a force that has shown us that consciousness is the by-product of its being—we have moved from spirit to source quanta to inorganic matter to organic compounds to life to living tissue conscious of itself as spirit. And, finally, that this spiritual consciousness, call it what you will, can be replicated."

"Okay, Michael. That's a lot to bite off at once, but to simplify your point, you're saying that evolution shows us that there is more to history than human beings acting as an instinct-driven, fear-based species, and that this is why there is hope for the future."

"A perfectly good summary: Even evolution evolves—in humanity's case this means that our instincts (and ego), which helped us survive in the jungle and in the aggressive societies that followed, must be overcome if we are to evolve in a sustainable and peaceful manner. We're looking for the long-term solution."

"That a tall order, Michael, going from a war-torn, atrocity-laden world to one spiritually-based.[20] What makes you believe others will choose to accept this vision?"

"You mean other than those who already share it?"

"Yes, other than this minority."

"First, Rashan, I'd say that for peoples' hierarchy of needs[21] to be met, including their spiritual needs, it is becoming increasingly obvious that we must organize ourselves in an entirely different manner. Only in this way shall the planet survive and people thrive. There are simply too many people using too many resources in a non-sustainable fashion to continue our current patterns for much longer. The excuses of those who control this process,[22] that somehow science or G-d will find a way to replenish

---

[20] On the other hand, Michael's vast clipping file (which he gave to me shortly before this book was published), on subjects which he finds particularly crucial to his mission, contains two articles that support the view that both physical and emotional evolution can occur in short time-frames. See *The Denver Post,* May 4, 1997 "Lizard test in Caribbean shows evolution can be fast," page 29A, and *The Denver Post,* May 28, 1997 "Study shows children can unlearn violent behavior in 6 months," page 4A.

[21] As per Abraham Maslow's pyramidal concept that ranges from physiological needs to self-actualization.

[22] Michael: That is, the oligarchy who control the means of production and distribution of goods, services, and information, including oil and power generation, the press, the government, and consequently the intelligence and military apparatuses.

these building blocks, are simply smokescreens for their own greed. We must take responsibility for ourselves. Science and G-d are us. They are one and the same."

"You can show this to be so?"

"Yes, at this point I can. That is part of the proof I've been working on, and I'll get to that, but let me continue.

"The second reason that others will come to accept this vision is that our technology will, someday soon, put us in a position to contact and affect other beings that have already worked through many of these same questions. When this happens, we shall need to be more spiritually evolved as a planet than we are now, if we are going to take our place among other evolved beings within our known universe."

"Whoa, Michael, it's one thing to come in here like some specter out of the *New Testament* and try shaking up everyone's belief system, but now you're telling me that this involves aliens?"

"I prefer the term extra-terrestrials, which implies beings from planets other than Earth. Look, Rashan, both you and I know that to believe there *aren't* other beings out there in the universe that have been around longer than us is more outrageous than believing that the earth is flat. The odds against it are beyond astronomical."

"Okay, but do you think most people are prepared for the consequences of that fact?"

"I have compassion for those whose psychological, emotional, and social well being is disrupted by the presence of a spiritual anomaly or Messiah or Christ in the flesh on earth, and the fact that there are a multitude of beings throughout the universe that have already traveled down this same path, but nevertheless it's my assignment to deliver this news."

"And that's where I come in?"

"Right. You have accepted an assignment to be part of this, and you have the talent to be successful. I have my own assignment as well. We must both do our work, just like everyone else. We can't dwell on naysayers."

"So, let's say we accept the odds for the existence of beings other than earthlings, what do these extra-terrestrials have to do with how we evolve?"

"That's interesting question, isn't it? They serve as examples to us. Remember my axiom that individually we each have a unique gift to express in this universe?"

"Of course."

"Well, in the same way, the people of this earth have their own unique path when it comes to evolution, though, granted, we have much to learn from our neighbors and most frequent visitors from the Pleiades and Zeta-Reticuli 1 and 2."[23]

"So, you know these folks!"

"Not personally, no, but there are others who have met them, even the U.S. government has had contact."

"Seriously?"

"I have that on good authority."

"Such as whom?"

"A former Secret Service agent that I know."

"Really!"

"This should be no surprise, Rashan. Both the Balinese and the Cherokee believe they are descended from Pleiadians. But this connection to extra-terrestrial life is only important in the sense that it makes our own evolutionary choices clearer. For example, the Pleiadians chose, a long time ago, to breed themselves in such a way as to dampen their emotions and instincts. While this has helped them in their path to evolve both spiritually and technologically, it also has caused problems."

"Problems?"

"Yes, both sexually and artistically."

"That's a bit obscure."

"Think of it this way, Rashan: Imagine that you have no instinct for reproduction, that is, little testosterone and adrenaline to fuel your physical nature. How could I direct you in Romeo and Juliet's balcony scene? What would you have to give me?"

"Very little I suppose. I've had actors like that, Michael!"

"Well, maybe you know some Pleiadians and just aren't aware of it."

"Very funny."

---

[23] See "Extra-terrestrials" in *Appendix 7 – Michael's Notes*.

"Seriously, as Stanislavski[24] would say, the affective memory needed for an appropriate rendition of this scene is missing, right?"

"Yes."

"So, as a being in this solar system, at the cusp of an age in which we humans are both capable of altering our genetic structure and willing to make decisions that will further our ability not only to survive but flourish in a world of love and beauty, wouldn't you choose to find a way to both retain your biological heritage and, at the same time, create a nurturing and educational environment in which one could both spiritually evolve and innately understand the emotional basis of the art that your species has created?"

"Whew! Michael. The complexity of your thoughts is a bit much, even for a well-educated person like me. But, yes, if I've followed your premises thus far, then you're saying that we have an evolutionary choice: We can evolve differently than the Pleiadians and still get to where we need to go; we can retain our instinctive and sexual nature, and still become peaceful and artistic beings."

"That is my thesis, Rashan, that we earthlings have our own unique and wonderful path."

Michael is about half-way through his latté at this time. He apparently frequents this place, because the fellow behind the counter said hello to him when we approached, and asked him if he wanted his usual. Michael says he doesn't come in that often, but that it's a badge of honor with the owner that he remembers his customers' preferences. It may have been that I was taken in by this razzle-dazzle, for despite my penchant for herbal tea at this hour, I uncharacteristically ordered a latté. I'd like to think, though, that I simply felt that I needed to make the most of the opportunity to sit and talk with Michael.

"Okay," I said, "your arguments for why humankind can transform itself and evolve beyond its instincts and its ego are noted. So let me ask you this, earlier you said that you could show me that science and G-d were one and the same. What did you mean by that?"

---

[24] Konstantin Sergeyevich Stanislavski, 1863-1938, Russian actor, director, teacher, co-founder of The Moscow Arts Theatre and creator of "The Method," the most influential system of acting in the Western world.

"I'm glad you joined me in a latté, Rashan, because you're gonna need to be awake to follow me on this one."

"I figured," noting, as is often the case, that there is an inexplicable synchronicity between Michael's remarks and my thoughts, even concerning incidental details.

"Okay, there are three steps to understanding the convergence of science and spirituality. The first is grasping a basic principle that underlies physics, philosophy, and religion. The second is understanding my model of quanta, which explains how light is both wave and particle. And the third step is extrapolating the implications of this model on human evolution."

As Michael begins to outline yet another of his theories, I can't help but see—despite my continuing reticence over the radicalism of his ideas—that the caliber of his intellectual gifts make a plausible case for a special role in the order of things. It isn't as if I feel he knows everything, or as if I believe everything he tells me. Hardly. But I am getting the sense that he knows everything he needs to know to explain his vision of a sustainable and peaceful world. I also haven't found any chinks in his encyclopedic armor. He seems to be fully-integrated from subject to subject, and, as far as I'm able to determine, from his soul to his everyday actions—his platonic relationship with Chimera being a prime example that's fresh in my mind.

"Let's start with the parallel between Taoism and Judaism," Michael begins. "The *Tao Tê Ching*[25] begins with the line, 'The Tao that can be spoken is not the Tao.' What Lao Tsu is saying here is 'That which is eternal cannot be described in words, because it is greater than anything that can be symbolized, since it includes absolutely everything.' This teaching point is very similar to the stipulation of the Jews when it comes to representing the name of G-d. In Hebrew, the supreme name of G-d is represented by four letters, Yod, Hé, Vau, and Hé again. Among the many blasphemies of what we call Christianity—that is, not the teachings of Jesus but the hijacked Roman version of the events that many mistakenly take as the inspired Word of G-d—is that these four letters, as we have discussed

---

[25] *Tao Tê Ching* (*The Way of Life*), written by Lao Tsu in the 6th Century B.C., is the foundation of Taoism. Due to religious repression in China and other factors, there are currently only about 20 million followers remaining.

before, have been pronounced variously as Jehovah or Yahweh, neither of which would be correct if one dared to actually pronounce them. Yet, whenever a Jew comes across these letters in the process of prayer, he or she is prohibited by doctrine from pronouncing the letters as they are written, and must substitute the word 'Adonai' instead."

"Right, I've heard that," I say.

"The *de facto* lesson in this practice," Michael continues, "is that there is no name that can be given to the Deity that would not be blasphemous, because the Deity cannot be confined to such limitations as may be imposed by human speech or other symbolic forms. Therefore, both the Taoists and the Jews agree: There is a force that cannot be named which is behind all of creation. To continue this analogy, we find a philosophical parallel in Plato's Allegory of the Cave. Essentially, he is saying that what we perceive is only the shadow on the wall and not that which is casting the shadow or generating the light."

"Okay. So far I follow you. These two religions, Taoism and Judaism, and even Platonism, have the same basic premise, which is, 'the force that animates the world is unnamable and fundamentally unknowable.'"

"Exactly. And further, the fact that these ancient belief systems are fundamentally aligned on this concept points to a teaching that is far older, to tenets of a spiritual truth far more universal. But it is a truth that has been lost to us. The Flood not only disrupted historical remembrance, it disrupted the continuity of spiritual teachings as well, just as I was saying about Atlantian spiritual practices earlier. Today, the beliefs that we have inherited in modern religions are inconsistent and corrupted remnants of this universal truth."

"That statement will not make you a popular man, Michael."

"This isn't a popularity contest, Rashan. As we've already discussed, many will mistake the world teacher for a devil. This is the message in the Hebrew words for serpent and messiah having the same numerical value."

"Yes, you've explained that many saw Jesus' teachings as a threat, and this led to his death."

"Right. The Romans, starting with Herod, saw Jesus as a revolutionary capable of stirring the masses and undermining the authority and control of the state.[26] Well, the present is no different. America is the historical heir of Rome,[27] and those that rule it would do the same to true Christians today as they did to Jesus and his followers—they would do away with them in some way, and then absolve themselves of guilt by calling Christ and his followers 'assassins, radicals, drug-dealers, or terrorists.'"

"So, you don't care that your pronouncements on religion will offend Muslims, Hindus, Jews, Christians, and the rest."

"Oh, it's not that I don't *care,* but there are believers and then there are believers. There are those for whom religion is a stick which with they beat others in an attempt to convince themselves of their superiority; they will feel offended because the truth disarms them of this weapon; their behavior is not spiritual, it is political and imperial, like all fundamentalists. And then there are those who truly understand in their hearts; they will not be offended; they will rejoice at the universality of faith."

"That's the hope anyway."

"Right. So to get back to our analogy, science has come to the same conclusion as this tenet of Judaism, Taoism, and Platonism, the expression of which is epitomized in Heisenberg's Uncertainty Principle."

"You lost me there."

---

[26] "From Day 1 in Galilee, Jesus was waging a frontal assault on Roman commercialism," Crossan contends. "He opposed the dislocation of peasant life caused by the Roman building boom in Galilee. It's no surprise that he gets himself executed. He's putting the kingdom of God against Caesar, and he' going to get squashed. It's just a matter of when." John Dominic Crossan, author of *Who Killed Jesus?: Exposing the Roots of Anti-Semitism in the Gospel Story of the Death of Jesus,* Harper, San Francisco, 1996, as quoted in *Mysteries of Faith,* ed. Jeffery L. Sheler, Ed., *U.S. News & World Report,* Washington, D.C., 2001, pp. 33-34. In other words, Jesus opposed Roman imperialism. That is why he was crucified—for sedition. If he had been found guilty of blasphemy by Jewish authorities, as the Christian *Bible* infers, he would have been stoned to death.

[27] Michael writes: I refer to an article in *National Geographic* on the Romans that states, "Their story is our story." "The Power and the Glory of the Roman Empire," July and August issues, 1997.

"Werner Heisenberg, a contemporary of Einstein's, defined the limitations of scientific knowledge in a nifty piece of logic called The Uncertainty Principle. Essentially, Heisenberg showed that it is impossible to be certain of both the velocity *and* position of a sub-atomic particle. On the surface, the reason for this is simple. Quanta are the fundamental units of space-time, so we will never be able to distinguish between their wave and particle phases because the probability of both is the same."

"What you're saying is that Heisenberg defined the limits of measurement, beyond which is uncertainty."

"Correct again, Rashan. You seem to understand more about physics than you let on."

"Well, I'm picking it up from you, as difficult as it may be."

"Understanding science is not as difficult as you make it. It's one thing have the capacity to design experiments and derive formulae and quite another to be able to understand scientific discoveries after the fact. Be that as it may, though, if one universalizes the findings of Heisenberg's Uncertainty Principle, as you just have, the result is perfectly aligned to the message in the Hebrew symbols Yod, Hé, Vau, Hé or the *Tao Tê Ching*'s opening lines, or Plato's allegory, that is: There is a force at the core of the universe that we cannot name or describe with certainty. We see only the force's manifestations. In this analogous sequence, it is easy to see that science, philosophy, and spirituality are saying the same thing, and that we as human beings, products of both the unknowable force and its observable evolution, are the vehicle through which this proof is tendered."

"This is your proof of the convergence of science and spirituality?"

"As I said earlier, there are three steps, and this—grasping the basic uncertainty that underlies physics, philosophy, and religion—is the first step in that proof to the degree that, as we have just noted, proof or certainty exists.

"Michael, as you know, I have a great deal of respect for your intelligence, yet theoretical physics is a highly sophisticated subject that takes not only genius, but years of specialized study to make even the most rudimentary headway. What makes you think that you have anything to teach the sophisticated minds that comprise this very elite group?"

"You're right, Rashan, in that it does take many years of study to be able to grasp the mathematics of physics. But my opposition to this notion that the principles of the universe can only be understood by a few is what stimulated me as a youngster to study Einstein and to continue my research for the last fifteen years. Heisenberg saw this quite clearly when he said, 'Perhaps it is not too rash to hope that new spiritual forces will again bring us nearer to the unity of a scientific concept of the universe.' The fact is, higher logic supersedes math, physics, and the rest."[28]

> *Another seventh grade school day has ended and we are homeward bound on the bus. A friend of mine has taken a book out of the library entitled* The First Book of Topology, *from the same series as* The First Book of Chess *that is part of my small but growing personal library. As we are riding along, bouncing on noisy old seats, I open the book and am immediately captivated by the model of the Torus, which looks like a doughnut, except with a dotted line forming the inner circle. "What kind of an object is this?" I ask, unaware of the key role it will play in my later conceptualization of a single model that describes both the particle and wave properties of light. Almost six years later, as a senior in a high school physics class, I am presented with two separate models to explain the dualistic nature of light. "This won't do," I think, revealing my monotheistic prejudices. "There must be one model that explains both behaviors."*[29]

I contemplate this revelation for a moment and recall that my countryman, René Descartes, though a scientist and mathematician, was best remembered for his philosophical conclusions. "You've been studying Relativity Theory for fifteen years?" I ask.

---

[28] Heisenberg, Werner, *Philosophic Problems of Nuclear Science,* Fawcett Premier Books, New York, 1952, p. 28.
[29] As mentioned earlier in this book, Grigory Perelman's proof of Poincaré's Conjecture, accepted in 2006, serves as a check for Michael's proof. It's also worth repeating that the principles of Michael's model provide him with the ability to interpret existing scientific evidence and use it to prove the existence of strings, thus supplying the last piece in the puzzle for the legitimacy of String Theory and its elegant mathematical equivalencies for gravity, electromagnetism, the strong force, and the weak force. (See *Appendix 6 – The Proof.*)

"Yes, but only on what I call a 'conceptual' basis. You see, when I was in school I had a circle of friends who were very gifted. We even had discussions about the tendency of theoretical physicists to burn out at a relatively young age. One of my friends avoided a career in physics for this very reason—to avoid peaking too early in his career."

"So you're saying that you made a conscious decision when you were still in high school to avoid theoretical physics as a vocation because of this burn-out factor?"

"Yes. That's why I've kept my studies at a high-level, 'conceptual' view. I thought it would preserve my staying power and give me more time to work on my model while I continued with my broader work."

"So this 'proof' you've been working on is a long-term project?" I ask.

"I don't know why this should surprise you. Think about it: not only have I consciously been working on my mission for a number of years, but given the nature of my work, I must have been guided since time immemorial to do this, as has everyone else in their own regard."

"You lost me."

"What I'm saying is that the data necessary to show the perfection of the universe through the use of symbolic forms is a collective effort that is unfolding as a result of forces intrinsic to the universe. Not all of what I have done is conscious, and even those parts of it that I would consider conscious and a result of my free will are not necessarily so, but potentially only my perception of the process. This is the dialectic of free will and determinism: they are simultaneous, as proven by Chaos Theory."

"Again, Michael, this is pretty rarified stuff. Can we just say that your boss is always a step or two ahead of you?"

"Much like I'm a step or two ahead of you in this proof."

"Touché."

"So, getting back to steps two and three of my proof, I'm thinking we could handle this much like we did with my political model of the Home Rule Charter. I'll send you a copy of my premises, along with a few drawings, and after you've had time to mull them over you can call me and we'll talk about them. How does that sound?"

By this time we are closing down the place. The lattés are long since exhausted and their effect is beginning to subside. After Michael drives me home in Ud-n-ud-n, I am still contemplating the ramifications of what we have just discussed. The work that I am attempting to describe has taken on a greater breadth than I ever could have imagined. Michael's claims for his proof will likely attract a lot of science buffs to this material, I think, beginning to imagine the marketing campaign for my best seller.

Chimera is asleep when I get home, but stirs when I enter the bedroom.

"What time is it?" she asks.

"A little after midnight. Sorry to wake you up."

"That's fine. I tried to wait up for you. How did it go?"

"Really well. We covered at lot of ground."

"So ..."

"Well to begin with, we fell right into a discussion of former lovers. I couldn't believe it!

"And ..."

"Michael is very convincing. He seems to be beyond blaming anyone for what did or didn't work out, and he seems to be friendly with a number of women that he's had intimate relationships with."

"A number of women?"

"I didn't ask for a count. He just mentioned a few cities."

"I see," she said, seemingly disappointed.

"He didn't brag or anything. He said it was about 'evolving.'"

"That sounds more physical than spiritual."

"Oh, he said it could happen with platonic relationships as well. That's where he mentioned you."

"Me?"

"Yeah. He characterized his relationship with you as platonic."

"Well, that's what I've been telling you," she says, sounding a bit self-righteous.

"But he did say he was attracted to you."

"He did?" That seems to wake her up.

"He said attraction is only natural, part of our instincts, I think he said, but that his Yoga practice is such that he has control over his desires."

"That's it?" she said, not quite satisfied.

"He also said—How did he put it?—that he takes his role as a spiritual counselor seriously, and that he has to be careful about inappropriate relationships. Something like that."

"That does seem evolved, I guess," Chimera says somewhat wistfully.

"Well, it sounds that way," I said, "but who knows. He also said that he's practiced celibacy at different times as well."

"Really? For how long?"

"Eighteen months, he said."

"Really! That's not anything I could imagine," Chimera says with a faint smile without blushing.

"Me neither."

"Well, at least we agree about that!" she says, now wide-eyed and earnest.

This is too good of an opportunity to pass up.

"How 'bout we 'shake' on that, gorgeous?" I say, attempting my best Bogart imitation. "I can tell you about the rest of the discussion in the morning."

"Sounds like a deal." Chimera smiles and opens her arms.

5

The Torus

"All truths are easy to understand once they are discovered; the point is to discover them."
--Galileo

"Every great scientific truth goes through three stages. First people say it conflicts with the Bible. Next, they say it has been discovered before. Lastly, they say they have always believed it."
--Louis Agassiz, nineteenth-century biologist

In the glow of a more pleasant mood than we've felt in months, Chimera and I continue last evening's discussion over breakfast the following morning.

"So, what else did you guys talk about?" she asks after she sits down and has a few sips of tea.

"The play was about the Holocaust and, as it turns out, Michael has an aunt who survived Auschwitz."

"I hadn't thought about that possibility. How did he take it?"

"Just as he always does: the long view. Like I described last night—about his relationships—his feelings about the Holocaust seem to be past any notion of blame. He says he sees a couple of Holocaust pieces a year and that it's important to remember that such things are being perpetrated all the time, even now, by and on all sorts of people."

"A rather generous view for someone who's been personally affected."

"Yes," I say remembering my parents' and their friends' loathing for the Vichy Nazi collaborators. "I'm beginning to see why his politics are so radical. I mean, he's made me aware that being a Jew is like being a target: if you don't take some active role in deflecting or terminating the flack, you'll be destroyed; and that there have been a succession of belief systems that have made the elimination of the Jews central to their beliefs. Of course, the Jews seem to take this as part of some big cosmic plan. Last night Michael laid out a whole scenario in which the Holocaust was just the latest example in a succession of so-called supreme rulers' attempts to put an end to the lineage of the Hebrew avatars."

"Really!"

"He says there's a congruency between the Pharaoh seeking to kill the infant Moses, Herod trying to do the same with the infant Jesus, and finally, Hitler attempting to eliminate the next avatar, namely himself."

"Huh!" says Chimera, temporarily dumbfounded. "That's original. But it makes some sense. Heroes prove themselves by overcoming cosmic life-threatening situations. It's a theme in all great epics."

"So, you're saying that Michael's vision is just a fantasy, like King Arthur or something."

"I didn't mean to imply that it's fictitious, only that it fits in with the pattern of such tales. Even mythology and religious storytelling are derived from facts. King Arthur was probably a real person, just like Jesus—only their stories were embellished to support political and religious agendas."

"Funny, that's much what Michael was saying last night—what we think of as truth is often myth posing as history, and what he's offering is history posing as myth. But that's hard for me to buy."

"Rashan, you like to believe what you read in the *Denver Post* or *The New York Times*, but journalists are storytellers, whether they admit it or not. They pretend to be objective, while ignoring who taught them and who's paying them. They necessarily end up coloring their reports with some pre-conceived ideology."

Obviously, Chimera and I have never been on the same page politically.

"I admit Michael's got some great stories," I say, "but that's how I have to take them—as stories. Get this. As a teenager, he says he consciously set out to create a new model for light by reinterpreting the relationship between waves and particles—the basis of quantum physics."

"He doesn't lack for self-confidence," says Chimera.

"No, hardly—and, at this point, I don't have the wherewithal to dispute him. He segues from history to science to philosophy to what have you, and it's all I can do to come up with a few questions. Last night, using Heisenberg's Uncertainty Principle, he outlined what he calls a proof for the convergence of science and spirituality—his roadmap for integrating all human knowledge!"

"You seem enthralled."

I visibly start as Chimera accuses me of the very thing I have been criticizing—that she and Diane and Cynthia are in Michael's thrall, even if they each express it in their own unique way. I immediately attempt to justify my behavior and distance myself from any notion that I've been seduced by Michael's persuasiveness.

"He was forthcoming over his relationships," I argue, "and his powers of interdisciplinary synthesis are impressive, even to someone like me—it all seems genuine. But don't mistake my enthusiasm for advocacy. I'm not a cheerleader here, just a reporter and an auditor. None of this matters unless he survives the test of time. Whether Michael's private life is as principled as his public persona, and whether others will find his ideas compelling, remains to be seen. I admit, though, that I am curious how people will interpret his message—whether they will see it as spiritual and having to do with sharing, or whether they will see it as political in nature, as an attack on Western values."

"How people perceive these things will largely depend on your description."

"I'm still sorting it out. As an accountant, my predisposition is much different than Michael's, and I think most Americans, many Europeans, and affluent people everywhere have strong beliefs about preserving the system—even if it is based on self-interest and even if, as he claims, it intrinsically drives economic and military expansion. So, I don't expect Michael's message to gain acceptance—and what will that say about who he is?"

"That's like asking whether Jesus' message is any less truthful just because many people, even those who call themselves Christians, pay it no mind and worship money, not G-d, just like Michael says."

"What's so surprising about that? That's what everybody spends their time doing, working for money."

"Not everyone, Rashan. Some people work at what they like and receive money for that."

I ignore the implications of Chimera's comment regarding my own situation. "Well, like I said, I don't accept his politics. I told him that his agenda seems utopian."

"Funny you should say that," Chimera says, "you're the guy who wants everything perfect before we have a baby."

My brain's instinctive defenses try to block what she says, but to no avail. I'm too stunned to think.

"I'm going to have to give that some thought," I say. "I'm not sure what it means."

"It means everything is already perfect," she says.

"How you can say that? Things could always be better."

"That doesn't mean they're not perfect right now."

"Right now, I'm struggling to stay up-to-date with 'The Michael Chronicles' and be as objective as I can."

"Okay," she says, "do the same thing for our relationship. Since we can't be utopian, think about being present in the moment."

I feel trapped, but not ready to give up.

"I'll think about it," I promise, "or think about thinking about it. I can't decide."

She shifts in her chair. "What are you struggling with in the book?" she asks after a few moments. "Let's start there," she says, reeling me in.

"Michael said he'd send me some supporting material on his physics theories. After the glimpse I got of this last night, I'm not sure how much sense the average reader will be able to make of it, even after I've massaged it."

"I'll be happy to be your guinea pig," she says. "If you can make sense of science to me, you're a stud."

"You make intelligence sound sexy," I say, fondly recalling last night.

"It's the only way I can find out what you guys are saying about me."

☼ ☼ ☼

A few weeks later an envelope arrives. On top of a short manuscript is a note from Michael in which he apologizes for the delay in getting the packet to me. He says he's been busy and that he'll explain later.

I put the note aside and leaf through the manuscript. The first few pages are typed on onion skin paper. There are also a couple of lines of handwritten formulae. When I hold the pages up to the light, I can see a couple of spots where he corrected typos. I assume Michael doesn't have access to a copy machine in Wayne, so he had to retype these pages from his originals. The drawings, I guess, are simply traced from his sketches.

Needless to say, it takes a few days of serious thought and subconscious mulling for me to begin to assimilate Michael's take on the workings of quanta and its relevance to human behavior. As I wade into the material, I remember how Michael characterized these notes the other evening at The Sceptre Café: "… a scientific model of fundamental forces that will lead to a paradigm for right action in the sphere of human affairs."[1] Just how Michael proposes to get there, though, is not evident to me.

As I study his notes, I write down a few questions.

Later, when I'm satisfied that I've made my best effort at understanding his paper, I telephone him. Michael isn't home, so I try calling him back later. Still no answer. This goes on for days and my concern grows. This is years before the invention of fax machines, pagers, and cell phones. Even answering machines are a relatively new thing. After a couple of weeks of this, on a Saturday, I decide to go to Wayne and find him.

Going up into the mountains on the weekend, with no deadlines or appointments, is the ultimate getaway. The Denver-Boulder area has, by far, the closest government-designated wilderness areas of any metropolis in the nation, which is one of the principal reasons why so many people have moved here.

Chimera is up early and working in her studio. I skip my workaday morning routine. Instead of showering, I don a flannel shirt and a pair of jeans, smoke a bowl, let Chimera know where I'm going, and head out.

It's a gray, overcast day, a rarity in these parts. After a stop for a latte and bagel at The Sceptre, I drive north out of Boulder to Lee Hill Road, take a left, and use the shortcut to Left Hand Canyon, the gateway to Wayne.

---

[1] See *Appendix 2 – Prolegomena to Any Future Physics* for the full text of Michael's notes on physics.

As I get closer to Wayne, I begin to drive into drifting clouds, which appear to be leading a cold, sinking, northerly weather front. Winter has lingered in these parts, and during breaks in the fog, patches of snow are visible on the shoulders of the road and on the mountainsides. The drive seems much longer than I remember and it's hard to make out any landmarks. I half expect to end up on a different planet, like some Twilight Zone episode.[2]

Soon, dilapidated and broken-down cars begin to appear along the roadside and I realize that either I've made it to Wayne or have been waylaid to some heavenly junkyard. A body suddenly jumps out of the fog right next to my car and I swerve to avoid it. What the hell was that!

I pull over between a couple of heaps, and jump out. Appearing out of the fog is the figure of Jim Pierre, the gritty leather craftsman Chimera and I met a couple of years ago.

"Man, I'm sorry! I didn't see you!" I shout, still in shock.

"No problem," he says as we abruptly stop in our tracks, facing each other in the road. "You missed me by a mile."

I'm relieved that he's taken this so calmly, and begin to take a couple of deep breaths.

"Say, you're the guy I met a ways back," he says. "You were looking for Yogi Mike's pad. You had that foxy girlfriend."

"Uh, yeah, that was us," I manage. "Rashan Barcusé," I say.

"Jim Pierre," he says. "Well, good to see you. How about givin' me a ride the rest of the way up the hill?" he asks. "I've got something I want to show you."

"Sure," I say, feeling that I owe him a lot more than a lift, as if I'd been caught in a strange twist of that old adage about becoming responsible for someone after saving his life—except that this incident was, to use Michael's term, a contrapositive of that: I had nearly killed him by accident, and had to use all my powers to avoid it.

We pile into the car and begin to chug our way slowly up the steep grade in the fog, still as thick as a cloud, with only the dead cars on the side of the road to mark the way.

"What brings you up here?" he asks.

---

[2] Writer Rod Serling's award-winning television series known for its bizarre plot twists.

"I'm lookin' for Yogi Mike," I say, falling into the vernacular. "I've been tryin' to get in touch with him for a couple of weeks. I'm hopin' he's okay."

"Oh, he's okay," Pierre says.

"He's around?"

"Sometimes."

We get to Pierre's chrome-encrusted panel truck.

"Pull in right here," he says. "You look like you need to relax before going to see the Yogi."

"I really should get up there."

"Relax. C'mon in for minute," he says.

"Okay, but then I'll have to get going," I say, not having the heart to turn the guy down.

Upon entering the automotive jewel box, I find a place to sit in-between all the shoes and boots and belts and vests and such, while Pierre stirs the embers in a little potbelly stove. The fire immediately jumps to life.

"Impressive," I say.

"Coal," he says. "That's the ticket. A good chunk'll get you through the night. We lucked out and scored some anthracite this winter. Not too common in these parts. It burns hotter and cleaner than the soft stuff."

"I'll have some coffee here in a minute," he continues. "You look like you've seen a ghost."

"I thought I hit you with my car," I say, reliving the near miss.

"The fog magnifies things," he says. "It's the opposite of car mirrors. It was further than it looked."

"Well I'm glad for that!" I say, further unburdening myself. "Sure, I'd love something warm." I look around the room at the myriad of leather goods.

"As soon as the coffee's done dripping," he says, removing a metal pot of boiling water from the stove and pouring its contents into a coffee filter, "I want to show you something."

"What's that? I ask.

"Hang on a second he says." He goes over to the cabinet and pulls out a bottle of Jack Daniels.

"Whoa," I protest. "I'll pass on that."

"Really, man, you need a little juice," he insists. "It'll bring your color back."

I look at the man I nearly ran over not a half hour ago. What am I going to do, I ask myself, turn him down?

"Okay, just a small hit," I say, and watch as he pours a couple of fingers into my coffee cup.

After a couple of sips, I'm feeling no pain.

"Well, what is it that you wanted to show me?" I ask.

He goes to the back of the van and pulls down a box from the stowaway shelf that runs atop the cabinets mounted along the inside of the side panels.

"Here," he says. "I made this for your girlfriend. What was her name?"

"Chimera. She's a painter," I say.

"Well, anyone can see she's more than that," he says. "Open it."

I open the box and do a double-take.

"Take it out," he says.

I pick up the leather bustier and unfold it.

"This is quite something," I say, gazing at the provocative top.

"Not to mention what it'll look like when she's in it," he says.

"Well, I don't know," I say. "It seems a little small."

"Believe me," he says, "it'll be perfect."

I look at him questioningly.

"I've been making these things for a long time, man," he says. "There are a couple of adjustments, here in the front and in the back. It'll fit like a glove."

I hold the bustier further away and take a long look at it.

"You think she'll like this?" I ask, secretly admiring the soft black leather.

"There aren't too many women who can wear something like this," he says. "She seemed like the kind of woman who isn't shy about making a statement."

"Well, that's certainly true," I say.

By the time I gather myself together, pay Pierre his due for the bustier, and make my way to the door, I'm a little unsteady on my feet, the combination of the pot from this morning, my adrenaline from the near miss, Wayne's altitude, and Pierre's whiskey having taking a toll.

I drive very slowly up the hill. The fog has dissipated somewhat, and I'm able to find my way to Michael's house and park on the road behind it.

I pull on my stocking cap, wrap my scarf around my throat, zip up my jacket, open the door, and brave my way down the snow-drifted driveway and icy, footprint-pocked path. Though not possessed of my normal sure-footedness, I avoid falling and breaking my neck. When I reach the bottom, I find no signs of the water line excavation that had the area under siege during my first visit, which seems like a lifetime ago. The ground is frozen solid but flat, and I crunch my way to the porch door, open it, and find myself at the kitchen door. I knock.

A few moments later, I'm shocked to see Diane at the door.

"Rashan!" she says.

Bug-eyed, I manage to say, "Hi."

"What a surprise," she says. "What brings you up here?"

"I was going to ask you the same question," I say, feeling an irrepressible resurgence of feelings for her.

"I believe you have to answer my question first," she says coyly, adjusting to my obvious attentiveness.

"I've been trying to get in touch with Michael. I'm concerned about him," I say. "I tried calling, but never got an answer. You know I'm working on a book with him."

"Yes, of course. He's been busy with his new job. Can I get you something?"

"I see. I didn't realize. Water please. I just had some of Jim Pierre's coffee."

"How'd you end up there?"

"I ran into him on the road. I mean I nearly ran over him. So, I gave him a lift. Then we got to talking and he showed me a bustier he made for Chimera."

"He knows Chimera?"

"We'd been up here once before and stopped for directions. He couldn't take his eyes off her."

"Kind of like you with me?" she says.

I laugh. "Right," I say, immediately disarmed.

"Well, guys are guys," she says. "It's complimentary and troublesome, depending."

"So, what brings you here?" I ask.

"Compliments and trouble," she says, smiling.

"I see."

"I understand your confusion," she says. "Things have happened pretty fast. We're living together now."

"Really!" I say, flabbergasted, and then managing to recover, "Congratulations! I had no idea."

"Either did we," she says and laughs heartily. I follow suit.

"So, how did all this happen?" I ask, relaxing a bit, and falling into Diane's direct approach. "Last time we talked about Michael, you made it sound like 'ne'er the twain shall meet.'"[3]

"I had a change of heart."

"Michael had mentioned something about you calling him for Yoga instruction."

"Yes. I'd been thinking about that conversation you and I had, and what I told you about my attraction toward him, and what I thought stood between us."

"About you living 'a vagabond's life'?"

"You remember my exact words?" she says, surprised.

"'Guys are guys,'" I say. "Besides, I'm a playwright. I've been over that scene between us a few times. '…a powerful actress is a mighty thing to behold.'"

"'But behold is all you can do if you're already involved,'" she says, not missing a beat, as if we had been rehearsing this script all along.

"And so it seems this is our fate," I say. "Tell me about your change of heart."

"I realized that I'd painted myself intoi a corner," she says. "I had defined my life as having no center, adrift in a sea of leading roles and leading men, destined for some tragic ending, shipwrecked on the rocks."

I laugh at her melodramatic description. "What made you see that?"

"Michael."

"He explained it to you?"

"No. Like I said, I was interested in him, and motivated to find out why he showed some interest in me, yet didn't take it any further."

"What did you find out?"

---

[3] From *The Ballad of East and West*, by Rudyard Kipling.

"What I already thought—that he's in touch with the eternal and knows what is genuine and what isn't."

"And this is genuine, what you have?"

"It is now," she says, "after what I've been through."

"What's that?"

"A rebirthing."

"Really?"

"It feels that way."

"Well, *c'est admirable*! Maybe I'll experience that some day."

"You and Chimera both," she says. "You just need to be honest about what's holding you back."

"That's what Michael keeps telling me."

"Bad habits are like addictions, Rashan. Sometimes you have to be on the verge of losing what's most important to you before you're willing to make the necessary changes. What's to hide, anyways? It's all on the table, whether we admit it or not."

I'm a bit startled by the absoluteness of her comment.

"That's pretty much what Michael said to me when I asked him if I could tape record our conversations."

"Yeah, I know that rap," she says, "about the FBI and all that."

"Right," I say, suddenly realizing that all my notions about Michael's mental storehouse of cross-referenced ideas are probably correct. The guy has these things catalogued in his brain, like the Scriptorium that Murray used when building the O.E.D.[4]

"What's your take on what he's trying to do?" I ask her.

"You mean 'the man on a mission'?" she asks.

I laugh. "Yes."

"I know there are risks involved, but a life without risks isn't much of a life. Michael's living here in the wilderness because he's willing to take the risk of living a different kind of life. You know, he grew up in an upper middle-class home, well-educated, with plenty of opportunities had he wanted to follow a life of material gain. But he rejected that. Human

---

[4] In 1879, when the Philological Society of London made an agreement with Oxford University Press and James A. H. Murray to begin work on a *New English Dictionary* (later known as the *Oxford English Dictionary*), a metal warehouse, filled with pigeon-holed wooden cases, was erected to hold all the raw word citations gathered from thousands of volunteers.

activity is unsustainable at the level lived by the upper-middle and wealthy classes. So why wouldn't I fully support a guy who understands what it takes to change things in a big way?"

We seem to have cut to the chase rather quickly, but I brave on. "You think a large-scale change could happen?"

"It better happen, otherwise the planet's fried," she says. "Why bother wondering if you can change it when you don't have a choice but to try? The rest is a waste of time."

She makes it all sound so simple that I immediately lapse into wondering if Michael isn't on his way toward establishing some sort of mass dogma. Then I remember Chimera's comment when she thought that I had been enthralled by Michael's cosmology. I'm forced to admit that I didn't hear any catch phrases that sounded as if Diane was repeating something verbatim, like some mindless devotee. She senses my scrutiny.

"I've been around the block," she says. "I know a good man when I see one."

☼ ☼ ☼

Chimera is not as surprised as I am by the news. I guess her newfound friendship with Diane had given her some sense of what was happening. For me, though, it's as if I had been seeing Michael in a vacuum, where I was the only one who had a relationship with him. Sure, Chimera had told me that he was giving Yoga instruction to Diane and, yes, I had managed to dig up other people who knew him and who had provided me with some additional perspective on his multifaceted life, but somehow these connections seemed peripheral to my relationship with him and the import of our book project. My subconscious capacity for repressing such obvious things from myself surprises me.

Suddenly, I'm acutely aware that Michael has a personal life wholly separate and unknown to me.

One evening a few weeks later, after returning home late from work, Chimera informs me that Michael has returned my call.

"What's he doing?" I ask. "Did he fill you in on anything?"

"I didn't ask," Chimera responds. "I was more interested in taking advantage our platonic relationship."

Not long ago, my body would have gone into alert mode over this kind of comment from Chimera—even if she was jibing me—but the reality of Michael living with Diane had begun to set in. I take a deep breath.

"What about it?" I ask.

"After what you said about his attitude toward me, it being platonic and such," Chimera says, "I feel safer talking to him, like the air's been cleared. And I've accepted that my demons are on the table. So, when he asked me how I was doing I opened up and starting talking about it."

My reprieve from jealousy is short-lived, and once more it appears as if I am in a bind. For the purposes of the book, discussions about Chimera's and my psychological journey could serve as beneficial examples. Additionally, it seems that Chimera and I could benefit from Michael's spiritual input. But besides being a friend and collaborator, Michael is, at least subconsciously for me, still a rival, and opening up to him in this way makes me feel vulnerable. I try to fight off my instincts.

"How was it?" I ask.

"I talked to him about my Jekyll and Hyde responses to conflict—either assuming that whatever goes wrong is my fault, or projecting blame onto others."

I don't say anything for fear of ending up in the doghouse. The frailty of the ego, as it flip-flops between superiority and inferiority complexes, is so easy to see in others, and so difficult to see in ourselves. She looks at me, then away, picking up where she left off.

"He said that such behaviors are common, that most people don't recognize when they're doing these things, and that the solution involves being able to step back from one's lower self in order to see these behaviors."

"That's easier said than done," I say.

"That's where, Michael says, a spiritual practice makes the difference, like Yoga or meditation—or something like that—even as simple as taking a deep breath and counting to ten. It's an evolutionary step."

I'm filled with that same alarming feeling as when Diane and Cynthia talked about Michael—yet Chimera, too, is using her own words. Does that make her a disciple?

"So that's something you're interested in?" I ask, trying hard to ignore my concerns.

"Yes, I think so. I'd like to try something other than psychotherapy or medication."

"It sounds like a fruitful conversation then," I say, continuing to make my way carefully. "Are you okay sharing the details?"

"I can see," Chimera says, "that documenting Michael's work is important, so I'm trying to find a comfort level around being included in the book. I thought about what you said—'it's what we do as artists.'"

And to think, all this unfolded after one deep breath on my part.

☼ ☼ ☼

Later, when I finally reach Michael, he explains that he has started working on a new project.

"Sorry for not getting back to you right away. I've just hooked up with some people that are starting to build a new public television station for Denver-Boulder. It's one of the last two unused non-commercial slots in the top 20 TV markets in the United States! I've hardly slept in weeks, trying to get this off the ground."

"Wow!" I exclaim, forever unaccustomed to Michael's surprises.

"We're not sure when we're going on the air, though. KRST is opposing our application for a construction permit."

"One public station is fighting another?"

"Yes. They say it's because of the competition we would create for subscribers—but there are four smaller markets in this country with two public TV stations. More likely, we represent a cultural threat."

"A cultural threat?" Here we go again with the paranoid propaganda again.

"Sure. It's much the same as I explained before, when we were talking about Nixon's determination to find a way to keep marijuana categorized as a narcotic. He believed that those who smoked pot were a threat to the value system which perpetuated his power and the power of those like him."[5]

---

[5] "We wouldn't be here if it weren't for psychedelic drugs. In terms of the role of psilocybin in human evolution on the grasslands of Africa, people not on drugs were behind the curve. The fact is that, in terms of human evolution, people not on psychedelics are not fully human. They've fallen to a lower state, where they're

"That's basically true, isn't it?" I ask.

"It depends on how it's used. Smoking pot doesn't necessarily facilitate any political or spiritual consciousness. People abuse it as a drug just like alcohol or actual narcotics, though it hardly wreaks the damage of those killers. But it can be used as a sacrament, too, as we've discussed, like the bread and the wine.[6] Or it can be used as a medicine, for glaucoma or chemotherapy, or as food, for energy. But for those in power, rooted in cynicism and greed, fear is a cornerstone of their culture and thus their policy-making. During the Vietnam protests, Nixon and Agnew used virtually the same language to attack those that protested their reign as Hitler used to demonize those who opposed him.[7] Once the existence of such a 'threat' is accepted, then those in control can justify the expansion of their 'security forces' and the use of oppression and violence against any so-called 'enemies of the state.'"

"Even if Nixon was a scoundrel, it's hard for me to accept the comparison of his tactics to that of Hitler. Besides, he's past history. Carter doesn't seem so bent on destroying the counter-culture."

"It may look that way," Michael says, "but Carter is a member of the Trilateral Commission.[8] Even if he were only a member of the outer ring,

---

easily programmed, boundary defined, obsessed by sexual possessiveness which is transferred into fetishism and object obsession. We don't want too many citizens asking where the power and the money really goes. Informed by psychedelics, people might stop saluting. 'Take your political party, your job, whatever, and shove it.'" --Terence McKenna

[6] Bread and wine have been used as sacraments by a long lineage of avatars, including Zoroaster, Moses, and Jesus (who, in particular, used it to symbolize and transubstantiate his body and blood). And wine, too, like *cannabis*, can also be used as a food, medicine, or drug (addictive intoxicant). Then there is the matter of *amanita muscaria*, the magic mushroom, referred to consistently by the Egyptians and Essenes, and represented in early Christian paintings.

[7] "The streets of our country are in turmoil. The universities are filled with students rebelling and rioting. Communists are seeking to destroy our country. Russia is threatening us with her might and the Republic is in danger. Yes, danger from within and without.

"We need law and order. Yes, without law and order our nation cannot survive. Elect us and we shall restore law and order." --Adolph Hitler, Hamburg, 1932.

[8] The Trilateral Commission (TC) was formed in 1973 by Zbigniew Brzezinksi at the behest of David Rockefeller. It brought together wealthy and powerful representatives from the U.S., Europe, and Japan to look at common issues. While the stated goals of the commission are "… keeping the peace, in managing the

he is just a kinder, gentler face to the so-called New World Order. In a few years, American's won't remember Nixon's career of shameful subterfuges and Jerry Ford's pardoning of his partners in crime. Then we'll see the true face of fascism."

I look for an avenue to avoid hearing Michael continue to rail at imperialism.

"Anyway," I say, "what's this got to do with the other PBS station opposing your license."

"What our TV station represents," Michael says, "is a significant voice for people who are generally without leverage. Say all you want about freedom of the press in this country—for the most part newspapers, magazines, and broadcasting stations are interested in perpetuating profits, not the truth. When push comes to shove, those who own the presses quash stories rather than run them, if they're unflattering to those who

---

world economy, in fostering economic redevelopment, and alleviating world poverty ... [to] ... improve the chances of a smooth, and peaceful evolution of the global system," the tens of billions of dollars of loans by Rockefeller's Chase Manhattan Bank to the third world blatantly indicate by their terms an imperialistic role more than a humanistic one. Even the conservative former Senator and presidential candidate Barry Goldwater put it thus, "It [the TC—*ed.*] is intended to be the vehicle for multinational consolidation of the commercial and banking interests by seizing control of the political government of the United States." This description is echoed by another congressman: "The drive of the Rockefellers and their allies is to create a one-world government combining supercapitalism and Communism under the same tent, all under their control. ... Do I mean conspiracy? Yes I do. I am convinced there is such a plot, international in scope, generations old in planning, and incredibly evil in intent." Congressman Larry P. McDonald, 1976, killed in the Korean Airlines 747 that was shot down by the Soviets. The conspirators are quite brazen in their intent. "We are grateful to *The Washington Post, The New York Times, Time Magazine* and other great publications whose directors have attended our meetings and respected their promises of discretion for almost forty years. It would have been impossible for us to develop our plan for the world if we had been subject to the bright lights of publicity during those years. But, the work is now much more sophisticated and prepared to march towards a world government. The supranational sovereignty of an intellectual elite and world bankers is surely preferable to the national autodetermination practiced in past centuries." --David Rockefeller, in an address to a meeting of The Trilateral Commission, June, 1991. Everything in place, the plan is now being implemented. "The world can therefore seize the opportunity [Persian Gulf crisis] to fulfill the long-held promise of a New World Order where diverse nations are drawn together in common cause to achieve the universal aspirations of mankind." --President George Herbert Walker Bush

share their financial interests.⁹ It's just like our so-called democracy. Money has more influence over who runs, who gets elected, and what legislation is passed, than the electorate's opinions on such issues. You remember that Jesus threw the money changers out of the temple?"

"Of course," I replied.

"Well, it's time to throw them out of our temple of democracy as well."

"So that's your agenda, Michael, to overthrow the government?" At least he's finally come clean on this, I think.

"Oh, heavens no! I'm just more interested in the Declaration of Independence, the Constitution, the Bill of Rights, and freedom than I am in profits. We can either be controlled by capital or we can put it to use for humanity. It's our choice, depending upon our consciousness and heart. Are we ruled by this abstraction, or do we rule it?"

"This sounds like communism, Michael. Talk about passé!"

> *As if the evidence that my government got involved in Vietnam for the exploitation of natural resources and markets isn't enough, my current classes in Marxian Economics and Marxist Theory are certainly rude enough awakenings in themselves. Here I am, an idealistic youth if there ever was one, always wanting to be the best, the smartest, the fastest—a student of American history and staunch supporter of what I believed was freedom and democracy—discovering that not only is my country's economic system a one way ticket to over-consumption, greed, and world hegemony, but that those so-called communistic systems that our leaders so fondly label as evil are, for the most part, societies that are suffering immeasurably at the hands of Euro-American capitalists, and thus are united in their efforts to oust these intruders from their borders. Their belief in self-determination is no*

---

⁹ The prime contemporary example of this that Michael offers me is when ABC News was told by ABC Corporate to suppress a story that appeared in *Mother Jones* magazine about the mob connections of Sen. Paul Laxalt, R-Nev. Laxalt was a supporter of the legislation that led to a change in television ownership rules and allowed ABC's principal stockholder Leonard Goldenson to make about $20 million when the network was sold to Cap Cities in 1986.

different than the colonists who severed ties with England; they are, however, much poorer.

"Rashan, don't confuse what the imperialists call communism—an idea that has never been put into practice, ever—with what the Russians and the Chinese are doing. Russia and China are no closer to what Marx described than the various sects of so-called Christianity are to the teachings of Jesus.[10] I'm talking about sharing based upon love and compassion. If that's interpreted as communism by bigoted and xenophobic demagogues, then let them make fools of themselves by flaunting their ignorance.

"Change is constant and people must adjust," Michael continues. "I support change that serves freedom and rights for all. If that makes me a revolutionary, like Jefferson, Adams, Franklin, or Jesus, then I'm proud to be considered such. Bring on the mammon worshippers, the slaves of the golden calf! I welcome the opportunity to expose the true nature of their selfish, morally bankrupt agenda, and I sincerely pray that they are capable of transformation, of saving themselves and their souls, because the time of man draws nigh."

I obviously pushed a hot button here.

"So, this is part of the reason that you've decided to start a TV station," I ask, "to counter what you believe are regressive philosophies?"

---

[10] Michael writes: Or, "To liken Marx's ideas with Soviet Communism is to liken Enron with Adam Smith's idea of capitalism." (John Brand, D.Min., J.D., *Masters of Suspicion #3: Karl Marx*, YellowTimes.org, 11/9/02, http://www.yellowtimes.org/article.php?sid=844). But even Brand errs in calling the Russian version, "Soviet Communism." What was instituted in the Soviet Union was "state capitalism" (i.e., an economy in which the state [controlled by an elite, not the proletariat] owned all the "stock"), enforced by a political system of authoritarianism, replacing czars with commissars. Recently, I was happy to see this same idea echoed in John Fowles' *Daniel Martin* (Little, Brown and Company, Boston, 1977, p. 491.), to wit: "And he began to divine something else, that the more precise huge step she was unable to make was between a personal sympathy for her Marxist, or neo-Marxist, ideas and the public manifestation of them in practical, organized form. It was not difficult to trace her fears there back to her Catholic days; to see a parallel between the conflict of Marxism as a noble humanist theory and Marxism in totalitarian practice and the same conflict between personal Christianity and the dogmatic vulgarities and naïveties of the public Church of Rome."

"Of course, but it's also another step in creating a more integrated, holistic view of knowledge that, as I've said, I'm assigned to provide. Remember that excerpt I quoted from José Argüelles' book ... during our discussion at The Sceptre—that the loss of the sacred view results in the notion that knowledge is comprised of unrelated fields?"

"Sure. I even went looking for the book, but couldn't find it." This idea, that all knowledge is interrelated, fascinates me, and it's obviously a key to understanding Michael's philosophy. So, it's something I've got to grasp if I'm going to make any headway describing what he's talking about.

"Oh?" Michael seems surprised by my initiative. "It's still a ways from being published, he says. "I'll get you copies of the notes that José shared with Dennis McKenna[11] and me. Anyway, one of the most compelling parts of the manuscript is the section that expands upon Martin Schöenberger's discovery of the one-to-one correspondence of the sixty-four *kua*, or hexagrams, of the *I Ching*, and the sixty-four DNA codons of the genetic code."[12]

"Good gracious, Michael, what's that supposed to mean?"

"This is part of the second step in my proof of how all human knowledge is not only related, Rashan, but tied to my very appearance."

"How do you 'prove' this?" I ask, aghast once again at his boundless ego.

"I've shown you the first step: the congruency between Heisenberg's Uncertainty Principle and the Taoist, Judaic, and Platonist insistence that the deity, or totality of existence and being, cannot be accurately rendered in symbols."

"Right, we covered that at the café after the theatre."

---

[11] Michael spent a number of evenings with McKenna, discussing the work that he and his brother Terence did in the South American rainforests, researching native tryptamines and seeking a logical means of integrating the hexagrams of the *I Ching* with the Gregorian calendar. Today, Terence McKenna's research centers on how to apply the use of one of these tropical medicaments, aya-huasca, to the cure of alcoholism. Michael, meanwhile, has solved the binary riddle of the *I Ching*, using it (à la Martin Schöenberger's discovery) as a bridge between his Quantum-Torus Model and human history in his proof (See *Appendix 6 – The Proof*.), as we are about to see.

[12] Argüelles, José A., *Earth Ascending: An Illustrated Treatise on the Law Governing Whole Systems*, Shambhala, Boulder & London, 1984, p. 17.

"And as we discussed, these congruencies mean that whether you are a scientist or a saint, there's a limitation on what you can know and communicate about the ultimate Reality—leading us to the undeniable conclusion that science and spirituality converge at the same boundary. In other words, what lies beyond this boundary—as Taoism, Judaism, Platonism, and Physics tell us—is not something that you can quantify in an equation or in a name. This frontier of indefiniteness itself is the ultimate Reality, what spiritualists call G-d, and what I, for the purposes of my proof and in the name of science, call the Anomaly—that which is different, that which operates by principles that are outside the bounds of our pedestrian perceptions—what is available to us through what religion calls faith, what humanists call creativity or magic or genius, and what science has branded as 'uncertainty.'"

"You've used this term, Anomaly, before, but in a different context," I said, trying to follow his thread.

"Right. Anomalies are woven throughout the universe because they are at the core of the fundamental building blocks of creation—what we generally call Light. It is through the creation of a symbol to represent the Anomaly that we discover the path from which we are able to move from the toroidal model of quanta in step two of the proof, to step three in which we derive the implications of this model on human evolution. Once you understand the necessity for the Anomaly in the model you can understand why the culmination of the Unified Field Theory[13] is ultimately

---

[13] Or M-Theory, or String Theory, as it is called today. In the current theoretical world of physics and mathematics, M-Theory is an umbrella for different theories and models that represent the workings of the universe, none of which alone is comprehensive. String Theory is focused on formulating the mathematical equivalencies of the four fundamental forces, the strong force, the weak force, the electromagnetic force, and gravity to unify the disparate equations. Here, Michael is questioning whether such a final equation would really be a theory of everything if it did not account for Uncertainty, which is why he refers to his analogous proof as an interdisciplinary theory of everything, that is, the bridge which ties theoretical physics to a mathematical model (the *kua*, or hexagrams of the I Ching) from which a binary progression ties it to DNA, and, therefore, human history. So, the microcosm (particle physics), the macrocosm (astrophysics), and humankind are all a reflection of the same principles (because they are all derived from the Quantum-Torus. Michael also illustrates this graphically with Babbit's Atom, the Aleister Crowley-Frieda Harris Universe card, the Hubble spacecraft's shot of the Cat's Eye Nebula, and his own drawing of the toroidal framework of human beings and the heart. As I've mentioned, Michael is eventually able to

not an equation, but a ratio—a is to b as c is to d as e is to f as g is to h, etc.¹⁴—an analogous proof of the congruency between different emanations of the same force. In fact, I believe that Heisenberg himself foresaw what I have proven when he said, 'Perhaps it is not too rash to hope that new spiritual forces will again bring us nearer to the unity of a scientific concept of the universe ...'"¹⁵

"And you represent that spiritual force that can provide this unified scientific concept of the universe?"

"Yes, I see this as a significant part of my mission, Rashan—to codify a conceptual direction for further study, the Philosopher's Stone if you will, the Perennial Philosophy.¹⁶ Again, it's just like José Argüelles says,¹⁷ 'The notion that there are different fields of knowledge that are unrelated to each other is fundamentally the result of a loss of sacred view.'¹⁸ I shall

---

apply his model and proof to existent experimental evidence and thereby prove the existence of strings as well as to apply Poincaré's Conjecture, which was solved by Grigory Perelman and recognized in October, 2006, to prove the Big Bang. (See *Appendix 6 – The Proof.*) The ultimate proof then, to which Michael is referring, ties all phenomena together, not just those of the natural sciences.

[14] a : b : : c : d : : e : f : : g : h, *ad infinitum.*

[15] Heisenberg, Werner, *Philosophic Problems of Nuclear Science*, Fawcett Premier Books, New York, 1952, p. 28.

[16] The Philosopher's Stone is a mysterious catalyst that Alchemists believe has the power to transmute base metals into gold. Metaphorically speaking, it is the mental power to change chaos into order, negativity into a desired result, or anything into something else, that is, by showing the connection between the two. "The Perennial Philosophy, or '*Philosophia Perennis*' -- the phrase was coined by Leibniz -- [is] the metaphysic that recognizes a divine Reality substantial to the world of things and lives and minds; the psychology that finds in the soul something similar to, or even identical with, divine Reality; the ethic that places man's final end in the knowledge of the immanent and transcendent Ground of all being -- the thing is immemorial and universal. Rudiments of the Perennial Philosophy may be found among the traditionary lore of primitive peoples in every region of the world, and in its fully developed forms it has a place in every one of the higher religions." --Aldous Huxley, *The Perennial Philosophy* Or, "There is only one religion, though there are a hundred versions of it." --George Bernard Shaw.

[17] Argüelles, José A., *Earth Ascending: An Illustrated Treatise on the Law Governing Whole Systems*, Shambhala, Boulder & London, 1984.

[18] Or, "The great tragedy of modern times is the excessive fragmentation of our knowledge. Inundated and confused by fascinating and frightening bits and pieces, we drift and suffer because we don't understand *who* we are, *where* we are, or

show this to be true as well, just as I said earlier that I shall show how a scientific model of fundamental forces can serve as a paradigm for right action in the sphere of human affairs."

"Okay. I follow you so far," I say. "We have agreement between spiritual, philosophical, and scientific approaches that there is an indefinable force at the center of creation. Next, as I understand it, you aim to show me a model based on this force, and from there you will progress the model to its historical implications."

"Correct," says Michael. "Once again, you've stated the nature of what I've been describing in very clear terms."

"As you said at one point, Michael," I say, surprising myself, "there's a reason why we met."

"It's good to hear you say that, Rashan. As time goes by, I expect we'll understand our affinity even better."

It was time to rub the lamp once more and importune the genie. I had been anticipating Michael's clarification of the dense series of ideas contained in the interdisciplinary paper he had forwarded me,[19] and now, with the ubiquitous tape recorder running, the context has been provided.

"Let's start with the Torus, Michael. This is obviously the central component to the schema that you're presenting in Step Two. You describe it as 'a sphere changing through Time.' Can you explain in simple terms what this means?"

"Sure, Rashan. Imagine a sphere, like an inflated rubber ball, say, the size of a baseball. Next, imagine it suddenly pumped up to the size of a soccer ball. Now, repeat this pattern over and over again, and you have a sphere expanding and contracting in time. If you are walking along the circumference of this ball, as it grows and shrinks, and the ball is being propelled through space, as of course it is, your path unfolds not as a circle, but as a constantly expanding and contracting spiral, in whatever direction you're headed."[20]

"That seems simple enough to understand," I say. "So, the fact that the surface swells and contracts is what allows one riding on the surface to be transported from any point on the outside surface of the most expanded

---

why we are." – Charles T. Tart, Professor of Psychology, University of California, Davis, in the Preface to *Earth Ascending, ibid.*

[19] *Appendix 2 – Prolegomena to Any Future Physics.*

[20] See *Appendix 2 – Prolegomena to Any Future Physics* for an illustration.

phase of the sphere to any point on any surface within that sphere, down to the smallest, most contracted point?"

"Exactly. Very insightful. In essence, this gives the Torus properties of a Möbius strip,[21] if you're familiar with that topological figure."

"I am."

"That will help you understand the next wrinkle in the model: When the Torus is used to represent the workings of Quanta, it does more than just expand and contract—it twists or spirals inward and outward, retracting and projecting along the summation of all diametrical axes that intersect the core or center of itself."

"That's a bit obtuse, Michael."

"I figured such a definition would be, though I necessarily had to state it. Here's an easier metaphor. Pretend that the Torus is an apple. If you cut the apple in half, from top to bottom, you see that exterior surface of the apple recedes through the stem hole and up from the bottom (or flower hole) as well. The Torus representing Quanta is similar to the apple. When the surface shrinks, it recedes toward the core in a spiral motion, wrapping around and disappearing through the stem and the bottom simultaneously, much like Babbit's atom[22] that I included with the materials that I sent you. Likewise, when Quanta expand, they do so in a spiral pattern emanating from what we perceive as the stem and the bottom."

"What I hear you saying, Michael, is that there are two diametrically opposed vortices through which the pulsations of Quanta manifest."

"That's the three-dimensional way of putting it. My caution here is that we're visualizing a four-dimensional phenomenon in three dimensional

---

[21] A continuous, one-sided surface, named after the German mathematician that discovered it, formed by twisting one end of a rectangular strip through 180° about the longitudinal axis of the strip and attaching this end to the other. Another notion of a torus would be a ribbon tied as a bow and spun about an axis formed by the two loose ends (held opposite one another) and the knot that they form. The knot would then represent the anomaly (with the two loose strands representing the vortices into and out of which the toroidal surface formed by the spinning Möbius strip [the loops of the ribbon that conjoin to form one double-sided sphere] spirals). Other, non-mathematical, ways of seeing what this looks like are described by Michael in the paragraphs immediately following this footnote in the text.

[22] See *Appendix 2 – Prolegomena to Any Future Physics* for an illustration.

terms, so seeing the vortices as a pair is artificial. The vortices are, depending upon your point of view, either infinite or rotating along spiraled axes, and represent the so-called "inside surfaces" of the toroidal figure."

"Could you put that more simply, so those of us who are not physicists can come to grips with the idea?"

"I don't believe that only physicists can understand this. As Einstein said, "Imagination is more important than knowledge.""

"Okay. Maybe if I study this I can understand what you mean by infinite vortices."

"Like I said, seeing the toroidal quanta as having two vertices works perfectly fine for the purposes of understanding my proof. But I don't want anyone who operates in four-dimensions to think that I've neglected the torus' dynamic nature."

"Okay, so noted. Then can I say, for the purposes of this discussion, that what we have now is a sphere that expands and contracts along spiraling axis as it moves through space-time?"

"Bravo! Once again, you've nailed it, Rashan. And this model that we've described, believe it or not, explains how light, that is, quanta, is both wave and particle 'at the same time.'"

"I don't see it."

"Consider the expanding and contracting ball, again. There are two space-time incidents here, that is, where the motion of this model undergoes transformation: when it has reached its fully expanded shape, the soccer ball; and when it has reached its fully contracted shape, the baseball. Between these so-called 'fixed states'—as it changes from a soccer ball to a baseball, and vice versa, through expansion and contraction—it moves at the speed of light, which we perceive as a wave; but when it is in these so-called 'fixed states'—as it shifts modes from expansion to contraction and contraction to expansion—it undergoes a transformation that we perceive as a particle, as if the motion had stopped, or at least significantly slowed down or converted its energy to mass. So, particle and wave are different moments in the periodicity of Light.[23]

---

[23] It is this notion, in which light is both a particle and a wave (or a sphere and a doughnut), that later allows Michael to use Poincaré's Conjecture as a check for his proof. (See *Appendix 6 – The Proof.*)

"However," Michael continues, "we cannot perceive these intervals because they are increments of the fundamental unit of space-time. This is why our instruments tell us that light is both a wave and a particle at the same time, and why we perceive that quanta can be 'in two places at once.'"

"What is it, then, that we can't measure?" I ask, struggling with what he has just said.

"What we can't measure," says Michael, dropping his bombshell, "is the origin of space-time itself, the Anomaly of infinite possibilities, which we symbolize with the Greek letter Delta (Δ), meaning change.' This is our scientific equivalent of the Tao that cannot be spoken, the name (יהוה) that cannot be pronounced, and that which is represented by the shadow on the wall of the cave.

"How, then," I ask, "can we ever understand the Anomaly? You seem to indicate that we cannot."

"In physics we can see the Anomaly in many different ways, just as in religion and spirituality the Anomaly is represented by a variety of names. We can see it as a point (which, by mathematical definition, has no physical correspondence) at the exact center point of the core, where the vortices are tangential in every direction, or we can see it as no point in particular, but as an invisible principle that animates the behavior of quanta and everything else in the universe, and on which it necessarily leaves its holographic stamp. In whatever way we choose to see it, though, it is a special case—it does not follow the rules that govern the four-dimensional universe as we know it: just as the Plasma Ball and the Einstein-Bose Precipitate are anomalies at the vibrational limits of matter, the Anomaly itself is a special, all-inclusive phenomenon.

"It is something that we cannot define—it has the qualities of both nothingness (that is, lacking in specificity) and everything-ness (that is, no single thing, but no-thing in which everything is contained). To the degree that the Anomaly is present in the indefinable aspects of Heisenberg's Uncertainty Principle and the-name-which-cannot-be-spoken,[24] it has material, spiritual, and symbolic presence."

---

[24] The Hebrew יהוה (YHVH), the Chinese Tao (☯), and that which casts the shadow in Plato's Allegory of the Cave.

"So, to update our model," I attempt to summarize, "we have added an anomalistic quality to a sphere that expands and contracts along spiraling axis as it moves through space-time. This anomalistic quality, which cannot be defined by symbols, nevertheless leaves its stamp on everything in the universe. And through this imprint you are proposing that we can apply the principle of the Anomaly not only to the natural sciences, but to the social sciences as well."

"You're making this easy for me, Rashan," Michael says. "Yes, there is a logical progression of anomalistic qualities from quanta to all its infinite differentiations."

"Now that I'm getting the hang of it, it seems quite elegant, Michael. I'm surprised at the simplicity of the ideas. Somehow I was expecting words as complex as the mathematical equations that are used to represent impossibly difficult scientific formulae. That's not to say these concepts are easily understood, only that they're described in a way that allows me to make a plausible attempt at describing them."

"It couldn't be any other way, Rashan. The Great Anomaly is necessarily holistic; it can't obfuscate the workings of the universe, that is, itself; it is we—having 'fallen' from the sacred, having evolved past instinctive truths into the purgatory of conscious confusion—who lose sight of the unity of all things. How could there be two models for one thing? That is why I am beside myself when I hear from so-called fundamentalist thinkers who say that evolution is an illusion created by G-d to test us. On the contrary, the biggest obstacle to seeing the beauty and unity of both scientific and spiritual points-of-view is to fall prey to 'the superstitions of fearful men seeking to steel their tribes against a hostile world'[25] and to take their suppositions literally. The great spiritual works to which we are heirs all have both eternal and temporal components, and at this point in time it is our responsibility to separate the wheat from the chaff and find the universal elements that transcend any particular religion. These eternal truths, such as the insufficiency of giving names to a force that is inherent in everything, are the enduring precepts upon which we should be concentrating and building new paradigms, not on the prejudicial and

---

[25] More than once Michael has used this or a similar phrase to describe the fundamentalist component of temporal beliefs—in particular the prohibition against homosexuality—represented in the *Torah* (the *Old Testament*).

ignorant beliefs that have to do with avoiding pork or shaming gay people."

"You're saying that the prohibition practiced by Jews and Muslims against eating of pork is not an eternal truth."

"Precisely. As we've discussed before, the practice arose because people developed disease from eating undercooked pig meat infested with a particular bacteria.[26] Millennia before Pasteur, tribal elders had no concept of germs so they forbade the practice to prevent the problem. This is much like the fundamentalist clap-trap concerning gay people. Ancient Hebrew leaders needed as many bodies as they could muster to fight other tribes. All men in the tribe were expected to marry and procreate. Millennia before Gregor Mendel, they had no concept of genetic variation and the spectrum of human sexuality, so they forbade people from acting out their biological truth.

"Here again, a temporal dogma is being promulgated as a universal spiritual truth by those who deny science when it is convenient to them, but who drive cars, use telephones, watch television, and support the use of 'smart bombs' when it suits their hypocritical mentality. The manner in which they manipulate these beliefs is despicable to anyone who takes the teachings of Christ or any of the masters to heart. G-d's word, like man's evolution, is progressive not fixed. When Jesus sought to replace ten thousand laws with 'Love the Lord your God with all your heart … and love your neighbor as yourself,'[27] he didn't tell people to go back through the Torah and pick and chose particularly odious beliefs and superstitions and add them to their practice, as so-called fundamentalists have done. Clearly, we see examples everyday of people who consider themselves religious but who preach actions which are not based in love but mired in the bigotry and hatred of knotted hearts. While I have compassion for those who were taught to believe these things and act accordingly, they are not followers of Abraham, Jesus, Buddha, Krishna, or any other master. I am judging them as they have judged.[28] They must repent or their souls shall be lost. 'Every tree that bringeth not forth good fruit is hewn down,

---

[26] Trichinosis.
[27] Mark 12:30
[28] Matthew 7:1, Luke 6:37. Also, consider John 5:30 and John 12:47.

and cast into the fire ...'[29] In other words, G-d recycles. That which abandons synchronicity with the Anomaly breaks down and gets reused."

Again, Michael had taken a simple comment of mine related to the application of his model and drawn conclusions that directly impact human relations. From this oft-revisited exercise—and what he has previously described as the Glass-bead Game, Jnana Yoga, and the Qabalah—I'm finally beginning to get an inkling of what he means when he talks about matrixes that connect the workings of scientific and humanistic models.

"So, these parallels that you suggest between the machinations of quantum physics, the galaxies, and human endeavor lead you to believe that one can interpolate paradigms from one of these realms and apply it to others?"

"Yes, you can see that in the materials I gave you, where the activities of black holes and white holes and the manner in which they cycle are metaphorically consistent with the behavior of Quanta. The operational principles are related as harmonic octaves—logical congruencies of the same truth. In the human realm, this metaphor of 'polarity switching,'—particle and wave, solid and broken lines; spheres and doughnuts—is evident as well in the inside-out (toroidal) rebirthing process accomplished through Yoga and other meditative arts and sciences."

I nod in appreciation of Michael's metaphors and continue with my questions. "After exploring these 'logical congruencies' in your paper, you added a section on paradoxes. How are paradoxes related to the models that you've introduced and how does all of this play into your desire to represent a unified vision of human knowledge?"

"All of these models are instruments by which one can evaluate ideas that purport to be universal truths. Take the Quantum-Torus Model, for instance. It's paradoxical because its inside and outside surfaces are the same surface. It's not black or white, wave or particle, but both: another paradox. And, it's constantly changing: so much so, in fact, that we cannot measure the interval between its phases. It would seem, judging from this cursory examination, that the Torus as a model of Quanta meets all three of my basic premises for a universal truth, that is, 'Truth is paradox. Nothing is black or white. The only constant is change.'

---

[29] Matthew 7:19.

"Another reason why I have given you these models, Rashan, is that I will use many of these same concepts later, as I explain human events or needs, to show the consistency of our vision. And finally, the models act as an example to others in representing what unity looks like. It's important to remember, though, that this vision that I give to you is just one way of looking at the world. It is constructed to support the purposes of my mission. It may or may not work for others, but that does not negate its message or purpose. This is how I substantiate my statement that a sacred vision of life necessarily leads to the unity of thought. Each integrated soul represents the universe in his or her own holistic terms."

"Okay, to summarize again, this anomalistic quality that you assign to your Quantum-Torus Model is a thread that runs through all of creation—from the tiniest particles and waves to the largest stars and galaxies, that is, the universe itself, including humankind."

"Right."

"So explain to me, specifically, how you can prove that human activity follows the principle of the Anomaly."

"As I've described it, the toroidal model of quanta is binary—it reveals how light is both particle and wave. In this binary quality of light, which animates nature itself, we find the unity of all phenomena—conveniently, another paradoxical universal truth.

"At least three millennia ago and probably much longer, Chinese philosophers used a binary system to codify the principles of change (signified by Δ). Instead of using ones and zeroes, as we do in our computer chips, or particles and waves (as physics represents quanta), they used solid and broken lines to represent the basic binary manifestations that occur when the indescribable monadic Anomaly enters the dualistic realm of space-time.

"This system was written down into what we know today as the *I Ching*, or *Book of Changes*.[30] Starting from the basic dualistic manifestation of 2^1 (solid or broken lines), these Chinese philosophers multiplied the permutations and combinations of events by carrying out

---

[30] The classic version of which is *The I Ching or Book of Changes,* The Richard Wilhelm Translation rendered into English by Cary F. Baynes, Forward by C.G. Jung, Bollingen Series XIX, Princeton University Press, 1950 (27th printing, 1997).

their model to 2^6, creating 64 hexagrams or *kua*, each consisting of two trigrams or a total of six lines, in every possible combination.

"Again, these hexagrams each represent a key aspect of change (Δ), which means they symbolize, among other things, the Anomaly itself. Using Dr. Martin Schönberger's discovery to correlate these binary patterns of change with humanity's biological truth, the binary patterns of the amino acids in DNA, the scientific basis of the Vedantic belief in the procession of the avatars is revealed."

"Again, you've lost me, Michael."

"I understand that this is difficult to grasp, and that I've jumped ahead a couple of steps here, but this is my proof in a nutshell. Let me deconstruct it: the appearances of Abraham, Jesus, Buddha, Krishna, and other spiritual anomalies are rooted in the patterns of our genetic code, and these anomalistic appearances repeat, or have periodicity, based on the permutations and combinations of that code. Basically, this means that the hexagrams of the *I Ching* have direct binary and periodic equivalency in DNA patterns, called codons. That is, the 64 hexagrams and the 64 codons are simply different octaves of the same chord or pattern that runs through the universe, and what we find expressed in one we find expressed in the other. In fact, the same pattern can be found in our bicameral brains, the Van Allen radiation belts, and the universe itself—on this level the universe itself can be understood as a single organism built upon binary replication.[31]

"As you can see," Michael says, "this is closely related to the notes that I sent you, but taken a little further: At the heart of all matter, in the very center of each quanta, is an anomaly from which the force that animates creation springs forth. When we apply this framework to the 64 symbols of human change used in the *I Ching*, this anomaly finds expression in hexagram 52,[32] that is, the anomaly's occurrence is

---

[31] These suppositions were originally proposed by Oliver Reiser, a physicist at the University of Pittsburgh, in 1966, based on Teilhard de Chardin's notion of the noosphere. Schöenberger's case, built on these ideas, was published as *The I Ching & the Genetic Code: The Hidden Key to Life,* Aurora Press, Santa Fe, NM, 1992, originally published in German in 1973.

[32] Hexagram 52, Keeping Still, Mountain, is the special case among the 64 sets in the *I Ching;* it represents rest in a world of change. It is the hexagram of Yoga, a practice in which the anomaly (union with the Divine) is achieved through

recognized by the Chinese philosophers as a constantly recurring phase of universal change. Therefore, it follows that anomalies periodically occur in all phenomena, including the 64 binary-based patterns, the codons, through which DNA communicates. So, there is not only a biological basis for an anomalistic point within each one of us that connects us to the One-Without-A-Name, the Great Anomaly, but there are human anomalies that reflect this force in biological form, that is, light manifesting as DNA.[33] All of us, including these anomalies, possess the same transcendent qualities as the indefinable deity of the Taoists and the Jews, as that which casts the shadow on the wall of Plato's cave, and as the unpredictable force described by Heisenberg. While each of us has a unique gift, the anomalies express human potential in a their own field, setting the bar for a period of time, depending upon the periodicity of the incarnation of such energy

"Put as a ratio, or what I call an analogous proof, this congruency between the anomaly in each Quantum-Torus and the anomaly of human DNA would look like this:

"Yad-He-Vau-He[34] is to the Tao is to Plato's source is to Heisenberg's Uncertainty Principle as the Anomaly is to Hexagram 52 is to the Avatar is to divine revelation."[35]

"So you're saying that the appearance of the world teacher is not only a spiritual occurrence, but a predictable scientific fact as well?"

"Predictable in the sense that it is certain to occur, yes—as certain as the appearance of the White Buffalo[36]: the spiritual anomaly will occur, but

---

discipline of meditation (stilling of body and mind). See also *Appendix 2 – Prolegomena to Any Future Physics.*

[33] For example, in sport, Jim Thorpe or Babe Didrikson Zaharias or Tiger Woods or Michael Jordan, in physics, Isaac Newton or Albert Einstein, in music, Mozart or Beethoven, in drama and poetry, William Shake-speare (Edward de Vere), and in spiritual pursuits, Abraham, Jesus, Krishna, Buddha, et al.

[34] Ha Shem ("The Name").

[35] יהוה : ☯ : The shadow on the wall of Plato's cave : Heisenberg's principle : : the Anomaly : Hexagram 52 : Messiah/Christ (et al.) : The Word.

[36] The first white buffalo to appear in 61 years was born on a farm in Janesville, Wisconsin, in August of 1994. According to Lakota Sioux legend, its appearance is a sign for all nations and races to look for peace. As this book approached publication, such occurrences were multiplying—on 9/25/02, the *Denver Post* reported four white buffalo born on the Kirk family ranch in Westhope, North Dakota—as if the master pattern had begun to replicate.

you don't know when. It is essentially the same as what was said long ago, 'Therefore you also must be ready; for the Son of Man is coming at an hour you do not expect.'[37] Scientific proof and spiritual prophesy come to the same conclusion.

"This truth repeats itself across the spectrum of knowledge and experience because it is derived from a universal source and the anomaly embedded therein. In other words, everything in the universe is made from light, and within each component of light is an anomaly; so the anomaly is omnipresent, expressing itself in infinite ways throughout the universe. Scientists and philosophers who seek a theoretical framework within which all knowledge is connected and within which the so-called Unified Field Theory[38] ecompasses theoretical physics, metaphysics, and everyday practice—with consistent principles applying throughout the paradigm, as one would expect in a uni-verse—will have to focus on the phenomena of anomalies and the centerpiece role that uncertainty plays in this 'master formula.' As we have shown, only in this way can scientific and spiritual thinking be unified into a truly all-inclusive theory.

"Also, in this way, as I said, you can see that all of creation is one organism, infinitely manifested yet logically and spiritually united. These are the metaphorical parallels that are behind what we call Jnana Yoga, the Qabalah, and The Glass-Bead Game: Jnana Yoga, liberation through knowledge—the mastery of all symbolism leading inextricably back to the G-dhead, the Great Anomaly; Qabalah, the cross-referencing of all knowledge that allows one to bridge from any one point, idea, or concept to any other; and The Glass-Bead Game, the ability (of the Magister Ludi[39] or another practitioner) to weave together any symbolic phenomena (literature, poetry, drama, dance, music, painting, etc.) and reconcile them with the thematic motif from whence the exercise began. This is the stream of consciousness of universal mind. It is an unbroken string of beads in every direction, uniting Quantum Theory, spiritual beliefs, genetic

---

[37] Matthew 24:44

[38] As noted in *Chapter 4* and *Appendix 2 - Prolegomena to Any Future Physics*, today this is called M-Theory or String Theory, umbrella systems that envelop different theories and models representing the workings of the universe, none of which alone is comprehensive.

[39] The Magister Ludi was the supreme teacher at Castalia, the school in Hermann Hesse's *The Glass Bead Game: (Magister Ludi) A Novel*, at which the quintessential integrated and contemplative life was lived.

replication, history, and divine revelation; it has never before been presented in this logically progressive manner."[40]

"I'm beginning to understand why you always seem to approach your explanations with such confidence," I say. "You see the unity of all thought and have the keys to reference it across what most people consider to be immutable boundaries."

"I'm flattered. You must be careful, though, not to assume too much from this. Just as we don't attempt to place a name upon that which is indefinable, we mustn't attempt to attribute omniscience to that which is only a vehicle for representing the unity of all things."

"You're telling me that you're just a messenger?"

"A high-level representative, yes, but I have my limitations."

"Such as?"

> *So it has come to this—being led to Golgotha by Roman soldiers who carry out the orders of the governor, Pilate. And for what shall I be remembered, if at all? For preaching that love and compassion is the whole of the Law, for refusing to recognize Caesar's authority over G-d and Israel?*[41] *Does not my father have the power to stop this, or is it his will that I die for purposes which I understand not? "G-d, my G-d, why hast thou forsaken me?"* [42]

---

[40] Michael's propensity for making connections between things resembles the methodology of Leonardo, and even that of the recently rediscovered German Jesuit Athanasius Kircher. His claims that the logic underlying the universe is simple are now being reiterated by other "genius theorists," i.e., in July, 2002, Stephen Wolfram, in *A New Kind of Science*, proposed "that simple rules, not complex equations, are the key to such profound scientific mysteries as the structure of the universe and the incredible diversity of life on Earth." (Matt Crenson, "Scientist: Simple math is key to natural world," *Associated Press*, 6/2/02) Another modern example of such thinking is Edward O. Wilson's work, particularly *Concilience: The Unity of Knowledge*.

[41] As Michael has noted, "Render therefore unto Caesar the things which are Caesar's; and unto G-d the things that are G-d's." (Matt. 22:21; Mark 12:17; and Luke 20:25) is one of Jesus' most misinterpreted statements. He spoke these words ironically, throwing the coin to the ground, so as not to fall victim to the Pharisee's ideological trap of speaking out against Roman law (taxation).

[42] Matthew 27:46, Mark 15:34. Here again, Jesus' words reference Psalm 22:1. This is not a statement of disillusionment, but of alignment, even with that which he does not understand or is unmanifest.

"I have manifested as a man, subject to the limitations of this form. I am only an imperfect symbol, just like the letters יהוה are symbols of something far greater. Those who are expecting a G-d-man—who arrives from the sky and who performs miraculous acts which are not consistent with the limitations of this dimension—are going to deny my message."

"So you're saying that you think you're Jesus?"

"Not exactly, Rashan. What many call "Christ" works through me. It is a state of being and vibration that transcends any one person."

"But you are not going to raise the dead, or even heal the sick?"

"Actually, I'm more interested in turning water into wine, preferably a Carmignano blend."[43]

I laugh. He smiles.

"Seriously, Rashan, it has never been 'me' that did such things. Healing feats are acts of faith, that is, anomalistic events which result from true belief in what I, or some other practitioner, may stand for. This is where the power lies—not in some hocus-pocus invented by the Romans and other mythologists to forever elevate my existence to that of the superhuman, thereby attempting to seal off the possibilities that I could return as a man and liberate my teachings from their dogmatic hoax."

"You consistently revisit this, Michael—the idea that the Romans stole your teachings."

"The consequences of the big lie are so pervasive that I have little choice but to emphasize it when presenting my case. Think of it this way, Rashan. Herod has all first born male Jewish children killed because of his dream in which an individual is born who challenges his power. As a child, Jesus escapes this *fatwa*,[44] but in the end it is nevertheless the Roman

---

[43] Michael's favorite, a combination of Sangiovese, Cabernet, and Canaiolo from Tuscany.

[44] The term is derived from Islamic law: a death warrant issues by a so-called religious leader, usually for blasphemy against the faith. In the 1990's, imams issued *fatwas* against both Salman Rushdie, for supposedly blaspheming Islam in his book *The Satanic Verses,* and Terrence McNally, for supposedly blaspheming Jesus in his play *Corpus Christi*. In June, 2001, another Muslim cleric issued a fatwa against Khalid Duran, who wrote *Children of Abraham: An Introduction to Islam for Jews,* which seeks reconciliation between the two faiths. On November 7, 2002, an Iranian court sentenced a prominent scholar, Hashem Aghajari, to death for insulting the Prophet Muhammad and questioning the hard-line clergy's

soldiers who put him to death for his revolutionary teachings. His mostly Jewish followers are persecuted and murdered by the Romans after his death. Some of them escape. Only when the Roman Empire is threatened by dissention from Jesus' martyrdom do the Romans find it necessary, with the help of 'agreeable Christians,' to conjoin Jesus' teaching with their dying brand of idol worship and absolve themselves of guilt by editing the testaments of Matthew, Mark, Luke, and John, and blaming the Jews for Jesus' death."[45]

"This does seem a bit belabored, Michael, continuing to claim that the *New Testament* is an edited political text. Do you expect people to toss their belief systems out the window?"

"Not entirely, Rashan. There are kernels of truth that remain in the Christian *Bible,* and, by the way, there are Christians, such as the Mormons, that share my belief about the multitude of distortions that have been edited into its text. And it is no different when it comes to the *Torah,* the *Koran*, and other holy books. They all, in part, distort the truth. That is why Jefferson edited his own version of the Christian *Bible*.[46] Yet, I see

---

interpretation of Islam. In other words, *fatwas* are simply edicts issued by those posing as spiritual leaders for the purpose of enforcing their misperceptions.

[45] As this book approached publication, Michael supplied me with various texts to support this thesis including the following quote from *The Jesus Mysteries,* Timothy Freke & Peter Gandy, Three Rivers Press, New York, 1999, p. 249, to wit: "As we reviewed the evidence, it seemed to us that the traditional 'history' of Christianity was nothing less than the greatest cover-up of all time. Christianity's original Gnostic doctrines and its true origins in the Pagan Mysteries had been ruthlessly suppressed by the mass destruction of the evidence and the creation of a false history to suit the political purposes of the Roman Church. All those who questioned the official history were simply persecuted out of existence until there was no one left to dispute it." This quote is followed by comparisons to Soviet Russia, not unlike Michael's example which follows in our text. Other comparative references in support of this argument follow later, including the cover-ups concerning the true author of the works of Shakespeare and the facts behind 9-11.

[46] The Government Printing Office published Jefferson's Bible in 1904, and there was a tradition of giving copies to new senators and representatives that lasted for decades thereafter. *The Jefferson Bible* eliminated selections from the *New Testament* which claimed that Jesus was G-d, that he had an unusual relationship with G-d, and that a series of supernatural events surround his life. (This would hardly fly in our present Congress, populated as it is by those who find a literal interpretation of the *New Testament* a convenient means of garnering votes and controlling the masses.) Michael adds in 2006: In gleaning the Christian *Bible* of

that many of Christian practitioners have found the love in their hearts that is the focus of Jesus' teachings. So, we must separate the wheat from the chaff,[47] the teachings from the propaganda. Think about how the text was created from the point of view of the Roman Empire.[48] For example, say Jesus returned to earth in the Soviet Union in the 1950's, at the height of the Cold War. He would have been compelled to teach as he always does. At some point, when the number of his followers became alarming, the Russian authorities would have put a stop to it, most likely by killing him. Years later, after the movement continued to grow, the Commissars would have been forced to make the teachings their own, as a means of co-optation. The book that they would have published would blame Jesus' death on his followers, or the Jews themselves, given the pervasiveness of anti-Semitism in that country, rather than on the fact that his teachings undermined the authority of the state. Later, if you received a copy of this Soviet rendering of the story, would you believe that the state wasn't responsible for killing Jesus?"[49]

---

its mythological embellishments, Thomas Jefferson not only manages to get to the core of the Christ's teaching—forgiveness—but also reveals a text that is almost identical to the Gospel of Thomas! (See, "Jesus Without the Miracles," by Erik Reece, *Harper's Magazine,* December 2005, pp. 33-41.

[47] Jeremiah 23:28, Matthew 3:12, Luke 3:17

[48] "The notion that the Jews were somehow responsible as a people for the death of Jesus had now become and accepted part of the Christian tradition. Time had obliterated the fact that the early Christians were Jews, that Jesus himself was a Jew. And time had obliterated any consciousness that the Crucifixion of Jesus by the Romans was the response of Rome to a defiance of its authority." From *Heritage—Civilization and the Jews,* Abba Eban, Summit Books, New York, 1984, p. 118. Again, as Michael Baigent points out in *The Jesus Papers, op. cit.,* crucifixion was punishment for crimes against the state. If Jesus had been found guilty of Judaic religious crimes, his punishment would have been stoning.

[49] Years later, scholarship continued to back up Michael's argument. To wit, "Pilate is an extreme case: successive writers, intoxicated by what he represented and unhindered by knowing much about him, invented him almost from scratch.

"That process of 'invention' has taken some startling turns. For example, soon after Jesus' death, his followers gave a particular spin to the events. They initially saw Pilate as the villainous representative of Roman colonial power. Wroe's research supports this view, showing that Jesus may have been a local troublemaker, an affront to Roman authority. Here, Pilate's role would seem clear: He works to maintain the status quo of those in power, in Judea as well as Rome. Jesus must be dealt with, not merely swiftly and efficiently but made into an example for others to see.

"Given the circumstances of the Cold War, and the fact that I live outside of the Soviet Union, of course not."

"Well, the Romans were much more sophisticated empire builders than the Soviets. How can I believe that they would not have manipulated the text to their advantage, not only to escape blame for their actions, but to assure themselves the continued use of the material, that is, the so-called the *New Testament*, to perpetuate their own power and greed?"

"That's a compelling comparison," I admit.

"One might also take the actions of the Popes in recent years as attempts to absolve the Church's sins for such actions."

"Seriously?"

"I would expect this to accelerate as we approach the Millennium, Rashan. Succeeding Popes will realize with increasing unease the necessity to prepare for the judgment of the Church by the Christ, and thus perform acts of contrition for everything from persecuting Galileo to branding Mary Magdalene a prostitute."

"Interesting speculation, Michael.[50] So, what do your notes on the convergence of science and spirituality have to do with a rip-off of the teachings?" I ask, once again importuning my genie to find the link.

"In a matter of decades, however, Christian believers began to paint Pilate in a more favorable manner in order to cozy up to Roman authority. In this scenario, Pilate, though still guilty of participating in Christ's crucifixion, is manipulated by the Jews into reluctantly condemning a man he's come to believe is truly holy. Wroe shows how this led to the scapegoating of the Jews and was undoubtedly a major contributing factor in the development of anti-Semitism." (from Davis, Duane, "Out of the Darkness," A review of Ann Wroe's *Pontius Pilate,* Random House, New York, 2000, as it appeared in the *Denver Rocky Mountain News,* Books section, April 16, 2000, p. 1.)

Another excellent examination of anti-Semitism in Christianity is James Carroll's *Constantine's Sword: The Church and the Jews*, Houghton Mifflin, 2001. One need look no further than Luther's teachings themselves to see how derivative Christian sects continued this hateful distortion. Also, concerning the falseness of traditional evidence against the Jews, see Rev. Upton Clary Ewing, *The Prophet of the Dead Sea Scrolls: The Essenes and the Early Christians--One and the Same Holy People,* Tree of Life Publications, Joshua Tree, CA, 1994.

[50] Michael writes: The Church issued such apologies, while stopping short of full apology for the Holocaust. It is obvious that the Church needs to ask forgiveness for not doing anything to stop the Holocaust; the evidence for Pius XII's and his

"Simple, Rashan. The mass of humanity will need some form of proof that the Messiah or Christ (what I call the World Teacher or Spiritual Anomaly) has returned to earth. I have been led to believe from all evidence, information, and feedback that I've been cast as the lead in this play. It's like being up there on that 'lonely wooden tower'[51] and wondering 'God, My God, why hast thou forsaken me?'[52] I mean, this is quite a chunk to bite off at once for anyone, and so far I have not been given any supernatural powers, nor do I expect any. But what I have been given is the physical, emotional, psychological, intellectual, and spiritual resources to create myself in the image of the human Messiah or Christ—like the symbol of the self in that essay I recommended to you when we first met, or the spiritual anomaly in my proof—and to teach what is prescribed. This is what I have come to understand as my assignment. I come as a

---

hierarchy's complicity is overwhelming, despite the Church's attempts to paint Pius as a "prudent" protector (Frances D'Emilio, "Vatican No. 2: Pius protected Jews during WWII," Associated Press, 10/7/08). But the Church is not capable of fully apologizing for the Holocaust without destroying itself, for that is what such an admission would do, indicating as it would that the Romans, not the Jews, killed Jesus, and that anti-Semitism arose as a result of this lie, which continues to be perpetrated upon us. As noted, crucifixion was a Roman punishment for sedition. If Jesus had been sentenced to death for Jewish religious crimes, he would have been stoned to death. So, admission that the Romans killed Jesus is tantamount to admitting that Jesus was, in fact, a revolutionary who did not recognize Caesar's authority over G-d, which would undermine the Church's cozy accommodation with temporal wealth and power. As Pius XII's actions showed, the Church and the Nazis are natural allies—they both have the elimination of the Jews in their interest, because only the return of Jesus (the Jew) would thwart their control. The Church institutionalized its lie by giving its imprimatur to the repetitive interjection of the lynchpin of their blasphemous marriage to Mammon, "Render to Caesar the things that are Caesar's, and to G-d the things that are G-d's" (Matthew 22:21; Mark 12:17, Luke 20:25), which, as we have pointed out, is not a recognition of Caesar's authority, but (cleverly, so as not to appear to reject taxation by the Romans) a statement contemptuous of the coinage upon which Caesar's image is imprinted and all for which it stands. As Jesus said, "You cannot serve God and mammon." (Matthew 6:19-24) Today, the original Nazis may be nearly gone, but their protégés, the executives of the corporate state and its institutional vassals, including the U.S. government and the Church, remain in control. Truly, the golden calf, 666, is enthroned. So, I pay my taxes, despite the questionable authority by which they're collected; I have bigger fish to fry than the IRS or the federal prison system.

[51] A reference to the Crucifixion, from *Suzanne,* a song by Leonard Cohen.
[52] Matthew 27:46, Mark 15:34—again, a reference to Psalm XX.

pattern unto the sons and daughters of men and women.[53]   Or, as Jung said, human beings need symbols of integration to function in a healthy manner, and this is what I offer.

"I am here because these symbols of integration are in disrepair, besieged by false prophets who use them to twist perceptions of the perfection of the universe and lend enchantment to hateful and ignorant actions. It's my job to straighten up this mess as quickly and efficiently as possible, so that humanity can evolve, return the earth to a garden, and raise its children to take their rightful place among other light-conscious beings from across the universe."

"But I understood your message as one that asks people to concentrate on compassion and love of G-d, self, and others?"

"Yes, Rashan, it's true that love is the way and that love is the manifestation of the anomalistic point within us that is tangential to the All, for our hearts are toroidal in structure like light itself. It's also true that one must love one's neighbor as oneself.[54] But love is not enough, for there are many that love, yet willingly lend their support to those who do not, like the so-called Christians who preach war, and spread weapons and hate throughout the world. As Crowley[55] said, 'Love is the law. Love under will. Do what thou wilt shall be the whole of the law.' People must come to understand, through compassion, the implications of their actions; they must see how, diseased by materialism, they perpetrate damage to the earth's ecological systems and biosphere; they must see how their demand for product creates economic slavery and death.[56]   The life-sustaining powers of the earth are too threatened at this moment, and human knowledge and activity too integrated, for my teachings to be confined to what others may mistakenly perceive as the limited realm of spirituality. There is no magic wand for me to wave and make this all better as James

---

[53] John 13:15. Actually, "I have given you an example, that ye should do as I have done unto you."
[54] Matthew 5:43, 19:19, 22:39, Mark 12:31, 12:33, Luke 10:27.
[55] Aleister Crowley (1875-1947), qabalist, yogin, magician, poet, author, mountain climber, and Master Therion.
[56] Michael's sentiments, calling for a more holistic view of compassion, are echoed in a recent article by Paul Ehrlich, a professor of population studies at Stanford University—"An expanding world requires an ethical revolution." (*Newsday*, reprinted in the *Boulder Daily Camera*, 2/10/02).

Watt[57] and his deluded ilk would fantasize, hoping to salve their consciences and hoodwink others into thinking their profligate habits somehow less culpable. That is why I teach more than spiritual truths. 'I make all things new,'[58] means that I remake the world through accelerating the evolutionary transformation of the human race into a spiritually-based society, not by instantaneously metamorphosing a toxic waste dump into Paradise; I remake the world by changing people's hearts in real-time. My use of the Quantum-Torus Model to explain the scientific basis of spiritual experience is just one of many intellectual tools that I'm offering humankind to deal with the inertia of superstition and misinformation that abounds. People may be offended by my references to Marx, or they may be offended by my criticisms of those who invoke Marx' name for their totalitarian purposes. Others may be offended by my criticisms of so-called Christianity and those who invoke the name of Jesus for their own brand of totalitarianism. In any case, the anger of those so offended is a result of their own lack of intellectual rigor and depth, fueled by propaganda and half-truths that they've been spoon-fed since birth by corporate media and religious dogmatists. And while we may see, from a big picture perspective, that this ignorance was necessary to drive capitalism—and its byproducts of technology and information—to this point where we are able to prove the convergence of science and spirituality and the unity of all things, it is an ignorance that now threatens our evolution and our very existence. I can help those thus afflicted, but I will not be surprised at a wide-scale rejection of what I have to say particularly amongst the wealthy and their fellow mammon worshippers, as they seek to justify beliefs that support their materialistic obsessions and satisfy their untrained instincts and ego. This turning away has certainly been the case before—'Having eyes, see ye not?'[59]—as we've discussed."

I had to let my mind catch its breath for a moment after Michael stopped. It was the simple humanity of this man's quest that had caught me. I glimpsed that all this work is, after all, just one man's statement of love for the potential of life and his attempt at emulating Messiah or Christ

---

[57] The United States Secretary of the Interior under Ronald Reagan, who believed that humankind could continue to overuse and abuse the earth's resources because the world would end with the Second Coming and all things would be made anew.
[58] Revelation, 21:5
[59] Mark 8:18

consciousness, as called for by the Torah and Jesus and explained by Jung. With the fervent skepticism required of me to write this chronicle, this sudden empathy for Michael's cause alarms me. After a moment, though, I realize that this emotional resonance is not new, that it was present in me, and to a greater degree in Chimera, when we originally discussed whether I should take on this project.

Yet I can't help question whether Michael's vision has the potential to engage billions of people, who would then work together to evolve. To believe that such a thing could happen would be, as Michael might describe it, like betting all your money on the Anomaly to happen. It may be scientifically or metaphorically certain that such an Anomaly *will* happen, but at this point you'd be right only one out of every four to six billion times or so. So, it remains comfortable for me, as I said, to see Michael as a being simply emulating such consciousness, not as the periodic singularity embodying it.

"Michael, I'm a bit overwhelmed at the moment. I hardly know where to go next. I'm thankful to have the opportunity to be offered such compelling arguments, but were I to accept all this, what could I possibly do? It seems so perfect and final. What wiggle room is there for my own spin on events?"

"I appreciate your humility, Rashan. But recall that Jesus reminded his admirers 'He that believeth on me, the works that I do shall he do also; and greater works than these shall he do.'[60] These notes that I have offered you are but enablers to the resolution of humankind's pre-history. There is so much work to do and to be a part of, so much wonder that is undiscovered and unknown. Just because I have presented you with a map doesn't mean that you have experienced the food, the flowers, the art, the treasures, and the people that populate these lands. The variations are limitless. When someone today is branded a genius, they are called an 'Einstein,' but think what will happen when someone takes the principles of relativity and interweaves them with spiritual consciousness in a way that permits them to demonstrate the unity of all things. Then this person shall be our new paradigm. And as we all stand on Einstein's shoulders, and on the shoulders of those who have traveled this way before him, so shall we

---

[60] John 14:12

stand upon the shoulders of our new paradigm, the latest anomaly, resulting in a still newer and more encompassing paradigm."

It was a clever answer for my question, I admit—Michael's thinly veiled description of himself and his mission notwithstanding.

My brain is thoroughly exhausted. Michael had answered all the questions I could formulate at this point. I exchanged pleasantries with him, wished him well in his new television project, and suggested that we get together soon and see another play.

"I'd love that, Rashan. I'm getting the feeling that, at some point, our shared interest in the theatre is going to play an integral role in the work we're doing."

6

Broadcasting

"Behind the ostensible government sits enthroned an invisible government owing no allegiance and acknowledging no responsibility to the people."
--President Theodore Roosevelt

"We are grateful to The Washington Post, The New York Times, Time Magazine and other great publications whose directors have attended our meetings and respected their promises of discretion for almost forty years. It would have been impossible for us to develop our plan for the world if we had been subject to the bright lights of publicity during those years. But, the work is now much more sophisticated and prepared to march towards a world government. The supranational sovereignty of an intellectual elite and world bankers is surely preferable to the national auto-determination practiced in past centuries."
--David Rockefeller, founder of the Trilateral Commission, in an address to a meeting of The Trilateral Commission, in June, 1991.

The next couple of years are uneventful as far as my relationship with Michael goes. We touch base every few months, over the phone usually, and catch up on each other's life, but the conversations are relatively brief compared with our prior marathon sessions. By this time, Michael and Diane have a child, a son, Aquila. Michael is also busy with preparations for the TV station.

Chimera and I have a child as well, Gita, who seems to bring normalcy to our relationship, if there is such a thing. Almost gone are my fears of losing her love and my concerns over bringing children into this crazy world and then caring for them. The fact that I had been hurt so long ago, as a young man in Avignon, does not mean that it is going to happen to me again automatically, though it has taken my subconscious mind a good portion of my adult life to realize this. That's not to say I still don't struggle with this, but my solace is that I am now so much more capable of giving myself to Chimera, to Gita, and to others. This change in my emotional maturity gives me hope for the future—that we can evolve, as Michael insists, and that our new behaviors can be passed along to our children, and thus contribute to a better world.

As to how this will happen, I'm not sure. I still find myself at odds with a key part of Michael's philosophy. I know that this has to do with my upbringing and life-long approach to financial security. In France, of course, there is a much broader spectrum of opinions than in the U.S.A., and public consciousness of political issues and theory is significantly more developed.[1] All this, it seems, would make me a natural supporter of "conscious spiritual evolution" (the overcoming of the instincts and ego) and a culture of "sharing," as Michael describes the process. But while my formal education and business experiences have given me a well-developed understanding of the workings of both capitalism and socialism, my job involves accounting for and consulting with wealthy capitalists—limiting tax exposure and managing investments and growth for some of the largest corporations in the world. So, I have an appreciation for the benefits that the accumulation has brought to the world: technology, information, and leisure. And to be fair, Michael has noted these benefits (This is his list!), just as Marx did in his economic and political tracts.

But when Michael goes on about the downside of the system, I'm naturally resistant. While I agree with him that the command economies developed under the Chinese and Russian collectivist experiments do not reflect negatively on socialism in general,[2] or upon other variants of this practice, such as the market economy in mixed socialistic and capitalistic Sweden, I do not agree that "Capitalism is a system that must expand in order to survive, and therefore is imperialistic by nature." I admit, though,

---

[1] This is still true in 2008, but not to the same degree it was during my upbringing. Global corporate culture has flattened things out, even in once-resistant France, as evidenced by Nicolas Sarkozy's recent victory. The argument that male chauvinism crossed political lines to keep Socialist Segolene Royal from becoming France's first elected female head of state, does not hold up in the face of a two to one conservative to socialist ratio in the National Assembly; rather, this is a case, as it is in all wealthy nations, of "profit over people" as the operative mentality.

[2] Particularly in light of the market dynamics now prevalent in "socialized" China.

that I have never read *Das Kapital*,³ and wouldn't know if, as Michael says, Marx's mathematics and data 'proves' the intrinsic expansionary nature of capitalism. Reading it wouldn't matter to me anyway. I believe capitalism to be progressive. Other than this important difference, though, my comfort level with Michael and his ideas continues to grow. If we disagree about politics, so what? Lot's of learned people disagree.

I'm also comfortable with the progress I continue to make on the book. Chimera reads what I write and provides valuable criticism. After that I put the manuscript aside and wait—compiling recordings of my conversations with Michael. Then, I transcribe the taped dialogues and file them, adding notes to the relevant folders now and then, when something occurs to me. At some point in the cycle, it becomes apparent that there is enough material for chapter. The rhythm seems natural, and the undemanding workload fits comfortably with my growing responsibilities at Arthur Andersen and at home.

Having a daughter changes Chimera as well: The physical demands of an infant, especially during the weekdays when I'm at work, are relentless, and as Gita begins to walk and talk, a whole other set of necessities come to the fore. All this attention to someone other than herself helps Chimera evade her own demons—at least for the most part. Occasionally, exhaustion overcomes her—allowing these negative thought

---

³ At Stanford, Michael took a class in Marxian economics taught by visiting professor Joan Robinson, from Cambridge University in England. His reading is reflected in his present-day library where, in the economics and political theory section, he keeps the three volumes of Karl Marx's classic, *Capital: A Critique of Political Economy*, Volume I: The Process of Capitalist Production, Volume II: The Process of Circulation of Capital, and Volume III: The Process of Capitalist Production as a Whole, edited by Frederick Engels, International Publishers, New York, 1967. He also took coursework in Marxist Theory, taught by Stanford political science professor Robert North. Other than those two classes and his own reading and involvement in anti-Vietnam War demonstrations in the late '60's and early '70's, that's his "indoctrination" as far as I know. His emphasis in Political Science was political theory and American political history, while his other course work in Economics concentrated on the theories of capitalists such as Adam Smith, John Maynard Keynes, and the Chicago School. Essentially, this gives him the perspective of a Political Economist, as he has reminded me numerous times through his insistent that, "You can't understand politics if you don't understand economics, finance, and banking. If you want to know who's running the show, follow the money."

patterns access through her vulnerable defenses. Then I take over primary care for Gita, working from home a couple days a week, and hiring a nanny for the days I commute to Denver or travel.

So it goes.

☼ ☼ ☼

"Rashan! Look at this!" Chimera bubbles as she walks into my study. "There's a picture of Michael in *TV Guide*!"

Sure enough, in the regional insert in the middle of the latest issue of America's definitive record of consumerism, there is a shot of Michael, hair askew, with a trimmed beard, in front of a few racks of equipment, striking an authoritative pose.

"He would be the one they use for the article's cover photo," I muse.

"I'm surprised they ran this, aren't you?" Chimera asks.

"Controversy sells," I say.[4] "Can I read this?"

"Sure. I'll take it when you're done. I can see the snowball picking up speed and size, like an avalanche."

"Or, a snowball's chance in hell," I say.

"You choose your season of the mind. He's building toward something," Chimera insists. "First a home rule municipality, now a public television station. Throw in Yoga and the synthesis of science and spirituality and you've got some traction. Your manuscript makes this obvious: personally strong and centered, an organizational plan, a far-seeing and unifying philosophy, and a means of propagating it."

I'm a bit shocked by her bullet-point approach. This is like trying to argue with Portia,[5] I think. As much as I am unprepared to admit it,

---

[4] "Actually, this is another example of profit as the key driver for the class interests of the bourgeoisie," Michael writes, "which is one of the many dynamics that will lead to capitalism's demise: The seeds of its destruction are inherent in its growth mechanism, much like they are in human beings, or quanta, or universes for that matter; the unity of opposites that comprise the Dialectic (which, in a universal sense, represents the logic of the Quantum-Torus model and the Anomaly), in this case represents the life and death of capitalism. So profit will ultimately result in loss, and those whose positions and identities are dependent upon such notions will, eventually, lose their power and sense of self-importance and belonging. Such identity crises often result in violence. That is why I stress spiritual practice."

Chimera has a point. Perhaps it is her "spiritual affinity" with Michael, a relationship that is still painful to me at times, which permits her to emphasize his idealistic aspects, while I stress the differences I have with him.

"Okay," I admit, "I can see a method in his madness," I begrudge her.

"And we're still twenty years out from the Millennium," she says. "This is just the underpainting."

☼ ☼ ☼

The *TV Guide* article is an interesting departure for a publication that generally caters to 'safe' recipes that feed the public's obsession for details in the lives of well-known personalities or the plot twists of their favorite soap operas. KBAL-TV, which was named in the tradition of alternative broadcasting outlets (read *cabal*), is described in the article as "the only third world television station located within the borders of the United States." Michael's opinions on the content of most television programming are also included.

"Let's face it," Michael is quoted, "most of what passes for news, information, or entertainment on American television has little or nothing to do with truth, justice, or personal development. It's about audience size, advertising, and profit. That's why independent public television is a necessity[6] and, of course, that's why every conservative president and congressperson opposes funding for it, because despite what these 'leaders' promote publically about family, religion, and values, their G-d is money—they pray to Mammon and exalt it over everything else. So, we've built this

---

[5] In "Shake-speare's" *The Merchant of Venice*, the bright and becoming Portia, poses as a young man and lawyer and argues eloquently and convincingly that the laws of the city-state must be tempered by a higher purpose: "The quality of mercy is not strain'd, / It droppeth as the gentle rain from heaven / Upon the place beneath: it is twice blest; / It blesseth him that gives and him that takes: / 'Tis mightiest in the mightiest: it becomes / The throned monarch better than his crown; ..." Act 4, Scene 1. Of course, later, Portia shows little mercy toward Shylock, or even his daughter, revealing the limitations of her Christianity.

[6] At the time, public broadcasting enjoyed more editorial freedom than it does now. See "Journalism" in *Appendix 7 – Michael's Notes*.

station with very little capital, in spite of the concerted efforts of those posing as pious guardians of traditional values, to expose the crass materialism and hate that's behind their façade of righteousness."

Despite my comments to Chimera about the strategy of selling magazines, I find it remarkable that such a perspective is being spotlighted. Oh, to be certain, the writer doesn't let Michael's remarks go unchallenged. There are quotes from representatives of KRST, the other PBS station in town. "This is one of the reasons we opposed the Commission[7] granting a license to KBAL," said Ron Johansson, general manager. "These people are just troublemakers. Besides, there are serious questions as to whether the community can support two public television stations."

"Typical bourgeois thinking," is Michael's take on Johansson's comment the following weekend, when Chimera and I drive up to Wayne to celebrate the article over breakfast with Michael and Diane at the Old Depot Café. "Up until the time when we went on the air, KRST wanted to confine the debate over KBAL to the courts. Since justice in America is to a large degree dependent upon capital and "muscle,"[8] this would have worked perfectly well for them, even though they're largely supported by tax dollars and viewer donations. However, once we went on the air and began to have our say, they wanted to call off the debate. It seems that the free press, to the degree that it exists and that one can afford access to it, levels the playing field, and that made them nervous. If it ever came to an honest debate of the facts, they would drown in their own lies."

"So you're saying is that KBAL is *de facto* a licensee?" I ask between gulps of whole wheat pancakes smothered in honey, strawberries, and yogurt, while trying not to get any of the goop on my tape recorder.

"Yes, though it's amazing we got on the air at all. The attempts by KRST to demonize Jim Black, the founder of the station, almost convinced the Commission to revoke our Construction Permit.[9] Luckily, we

---

[7] The Federal Communications Commission (FCC) is often referred to as the Commission in broadcasting circles.
[8] In mafia parlance, "muscle" is firepower or hit men. For those who control governments, it would be, black ops (intelligence operations or operatives), and police and military power.
[9] The approval of a construction permit (CP) is usually considered the most difficult step in becoming a broadcasting outlet because it grants the recipient a frequency and allows them to invest millions of dollars in equipment, plant, and personnel with the nearly guaranteed assurance of an eventual license.

discovered a little known rule change that allowed us to go on the air immediately—and of course, a *fait accompli* has a lot more leverage than a wannabe."

"Out of the blue?" Chimera asks.

"Completely," Michael answers. We got a call from Lorenzo Milam,[10] the community broadcasting legend—he's been a mentor to our two principals—saying that the Commission had changed its procedures for going on the air. It meant that we had the authority to begin broadcasting without asking anyone[11] and *before* the court's mandate[12] to withdraw our CP could go into effect."

"Just like that?" I ask.

"Yes," he says. "It forced the Commission to make an agreement with us. Our transmitter was reaching millions of Coloradans, so by going on the air we created a large support group that would not have tolerated termination of our signal by the FCC or further anti-competitive actions by KRST. Milam's insight was a *deus ex machina*[13] on the world stage."

"So, you see this as a form of divine intervention, Michael?" Chimera asks.

Diane laughs and gives Michael a challenging look.

"It makes for great theatre, you have to admit," Michael says. "But of course, anything can be seen as divine intervention. It all depends on your point of view. I agree with Gurdjieff's[14] proposition—which foreshadowed Heisenberg's Uncertainty Principle—that while the future is

---

[10] Milam founded KDNA-FM in St. Louis, a non-commercial station operated on a commercial frequency, and, later, KFAT-FM in the San Francisco market, the first country rock station in the nation. He also authored *Sex in Broadcasting*, a primer on community-based broadcasting.

[11] The rule change required only that the permittee pass a proof of performance test, essentially meeting the technical standards set forth in the FCC-approved construction permit, before notifying the Commission of its intent, and then going on the air.

[12] Milam's obscure rule discovery bought KBAL 60 days to get on the air, before the mandate (a decree from a Federal Appeals Court) would go into effect and perhaps permanently deny them the opportunity to broadcast.

[13] A Latin term derived from Greek drama that describes an improbable device that resolves the difficulties of a plot.

[14] G.I. Gurdjieff, an Armenian mystic and author of the series *All and Everything*, which includes *Beelzebub's Tales to His Grandson* and *Meetings with Remarkable Men*.

unpredictable, even seemingly accidental, generally there is a reason for what happens and that this reason is what we must discover in order to understand our existence and its evolutionary imperatives. That's why, in the face of obstacles or negative experiences, it's important that we ask ourselves, 'What am I supposed to learn from this?'"

Apparently Michael's response passes Diane's test, since she nods and goes back to her omelet.

"So what you're saying," I ask, "is that an event like this—an obscure rule change that serendipitously appears—reinforces your belief in your 'mission'?"

Michael pauses to savor his almond croissant. "We could take fortuitous events as signs that we're 'at one with our Tao,' but, even if it were so, that fortune is smiling on us, from Buddhist point of view, for example, this is no more important than events which obstruct our path. Ultimately, our actions are warranted by our own internal truths. And while overcoming obstacles is a measure of an idea's power, there are countless stories of those who, having overcome great obstacles to achieve results, became objects of admiration and even worship, corrupting them absolutely.[15] So, getting a break such as the FCC's rule change means that one obstacle has been removed and that the journey that will take us to the next obstacle has begun. Such is the dialectic of the material plane. It is important, however, not to let this evolutionary dynamic prevent us from being at peace in the moment."

"That seems contradictory," I say, "—striving to change the world, yet being content here and now."

"It may seem that way to everyday logic," he says, "but the logic of the universe operates beyond two-dimensional, Euclidean-Newtonian cause and effect. Remember the postulates derived from the Quantum-Torus model?"

"The three postulates?" I ask, not sure if I'm remembering right.

"Yes," he says. "The first one states, 'Truth is paradox.' Statements containing higher truths have built-in paradoxes. It's unavoidable. The

---

[15] "Power tends to corrupt, and absolute power corrupts absolutely. Great men are almost always bad men." John Emerich Edward Dalberg, 1st Baron Acton (1834–1902), British historian. Letter, April 3, 1887, to Bishop Mandell Creighton. The Life and Letters of Mandell Creighton, vol. 1, ch. 13, ed. Louise Creighton (1904).

fabric of the universe includes opposites for everything[16]—the 'unity of opposites' as it's called in dialectical or Taoist reasoning. So, 'striving to change the world, yet being content here and now,' is in perfect harmony with nature."

"How do you reconcile this contradiction—between evolving and being?" I ask.

"Continuing my earlier metaphor," he says, "to our Buddha Nature—and by this I mean that place within each of us that is co-existent with Buddha-Consciousness, much the same as each of us is capable of having Christ-, Krishna-, or Cosmic-Consciousness—here and now is all there is. Within the present, coincident with the Anomaly, is contained all of the past and future, as well as every dimension. It is a seamless unity of all things. It is neither black nor white. All change and paradox is subsumed by this state. Yet, when a Buddha rises from his or her contemplative posture and steps into the world as a Bodhisattva, actions are taken that have ethical and moral implications—a shift occurs from immersion in the All to a point-of-view. For example, one may choose to be non-violent and of service to humankind, that is, doing the work of an evolving soul. Thus a Buddhist balances the action of changing the world with the consciousness of undifferentiated awareness."

"So," I say, summarizing the discussion, "your current situation at the TV station—integrating your political agenda with your spiritual perspective—is basically justified by this philosophical reconciliation of the paradox between social change and cosmic consciousness."

Michael nods.

It seems to me that despite our differences, I'm learning Michael's language, and this fluency is increasing my effectiveness at getting him to express his views, particularly the more obscure variants. This growing linguistic and logical comfort helps me to see how the record of our conversations will help others absorb aspects of his extraordinary consciousness. It has already changed my own habits, driving me into scientific and metaphysical inquiries and improving the logical progression of my thoughts and language. Yet there are always new wrinkles, for

---

[16] Actually, the fabric of the universe is comprised of more than just opposites: the Quantum-Torus Model and String Theory dictate that incidents are reflected in multiple dimensions. This is also a teaching of the Qabalah.

example, Chimera's follow-up question delivered in-between mouthfuls of Mountain High vanilla yogurt mixed with the house granola and some mango slices.

"Why these sudden references to Buddha-nature," she asks, "given the House of David motif that you've got going?"

"It's as I've said—the world is at a critical juncture." Michael pauses for a moment as if to amplify our attention. "The continued tyranny of instinctive reactions and ego, and thus greed in all its manifestations, including capital, over human behavior, all to the detriment of spiritual awareness and the higher self, drives a level of consumption of the planet's resources that is not sustainable. A variety of global prophesies point toward the coming of a being who will initiate a new dispensation that addresses humankind's developmental crisis. This being represents more than the Jewish Messiah, the Christian Christ, the Buddhist Lord Maitreya, the Islamic Imam Mahdi, the Hindu Kalki, the Mayan Quetzalcoatl, the Hopi Phana, the Zorastrain Saoshyant, the Bahá'í Bahá'u'lláh, or whatever other prophesies you may wish to name. For a starting point, I've focused on Christianity because it offers several compelling arguments: It is the dominant religion of the most powerful and wealthiest nations on earth and it has an eschatological element—that is, it's tied to a rough historical timetable. Then, as you say, there's my genealogy and astrology, which support Judaic and Christian prophesies, being of the House of David and being born on April 6th.[17]

"But this initial identification of the spiritual anomaly with the Messiah or Christ is only a gateway to a broader teaching. The Avatar of

---

[17] According to Hebrew prophesy, the Messiah will be a descendent of King David. Jesus met this stipulation. The Spiritual Anomaly's next incarnation, the so-called "Second Coming," would necessarily reflect this genealogy as well. While the date of Jesus' birth is up for debate, Joseph Smith, the founder of the Mormon interpretation of Christianity, had a vision in which Christ's birthday was revealed as April 6th, a date more consistent with the astronomical events associated with Christ's birth and the appearance of the Magi. Also, astrologically speaking, April 6th falls during the 10-day period in which the Sun is exalted and coincides with celebrations of the Buddha's birth as well. The fact that this date is coincidental with Michael's birthday did not lead Michael to endorse Mormonism as a whole, but simply to incorporate a piece of it into his story. "The truth is the whole," Michael says, once again quoting Hegel. "Make note that I have incorporated relevant facts from as many different points of view as my time on this planet and my human form permits, and I still have some time to go."

this age, the World Teacher, cannot be tied to a specific strain of spiritual terminology, but must necessarily create an inclusive and independent evolutionary teaching that draws upon all sources. So, while I shall be known to many as the Messiah or Christ or 'anointed one' at this time, it is part of my mission to see that history does not confine its understanding of my incarnation to these limited terms alone. That is why I use terminology from various traditions in my teachings. This includes Buddhist terminology, which I find particularly lucid in terms of mind science and the meditative arts: remember the Buddha was enlightened through the practice of Yoga. It's also true that, despite what you've called my encyclopedic gifts, being manifest in a human form necessarily limits my database of comparative metaphors. What I do or don't say in our book isn't intended to slight any spiritually-based belief system, but simply to be as universal as possible in the time I have been allotted during this incarnation. This is why I use of the term Spiritual Anomaly, because it represents the scientific description of the Avatar phenomenon and carries the least connotative baggage."

> *Will they call me Buddha? Or Christ? Or What? How will I teach in such a way as to not favor any particular belief system? Surely, there will be those who will seek advantage by painting my appearance in one hue or another. But truly, the pallet from which I'm drawn contains the entire spectrum of frequencies, of which the colors of visible light are just one among limitless variants in every direction and dimension.*[18]

I feel the sudden urge to inject some levity back into this conversation.

"Michael," I say, "while I've always expressed admiration for your ability to describe the unity of seemingly disparate knowledge bases and for your consistency in applying these lessons to your everyday life, and while I recognize that these attributes are consistent with how I perceive the character of the Avatar, there are still a few steps between here and there."

---

[18] Again, as the Quantum-Torus Model, String Theory, and the Qabalah so artfully explain.

"True," says Diane. "But it's like acting, Rashan. You have to be fully in the moment and remain true to your motivation; otherwise, you'll not only lack conviction—you'll never be convincing enough to bring about the audience's catharsis."

I nod. Once again, Diane cuts to the quick and renders me speechless.

"Your honesty and skepticism are indispensable in framing this process," Michael says after another sip of what is apparently a heavenly latte. "Spiritual evolution can be a slippery concept. In my case, I approach Messiah consciousness or Christhood in the same way I approach enlightenment. There's an ambivalent and somewhat murky step between seeking and attaining. At some point, maybe even aided by a synchronistic event, one simply believes that the transition has occurred, and that showing such faith is part of making it so. While this runs contrary to fundamentalists' notions of a Jesus that comes out of the womb quoting scripture, their thinking is the comic book version of events. So, I understand your dilemma and the daunting leap you face concerning my claims, but you see that I have little choice in the matter—as I've said, if in the unlikely event that the Christian *Bible*'s Jesus descends from a golden cloud some Easter morning and waves a magic wand, then more power to him, but this isn't the sequence in which the Second Coming currently is unfolding. So, given the truth as I experience it, my energy is focused on a down-to-earth yet equally miraculous process. At first, those who believe in the comic book version will be apoplectic over the simplicity and accessibility of what I'm saying. That's why your objectivity and willingness to seriously consider my words is important: you're documenting the details for the next, uncensored version of the teachings; and, by expressing your point-of-view, you also inform what I say and how I say it, which is invaluable to our purposes and to those of the book. It's a symbiosis that will change both of us."

Chimera swallows as if she has simultaneously absorbed both Michael's point and the last sumptuous spoonful of her breakfast.

"So," Chimera says, in the afterglow of her delicious repast, "going back to the balance between being in the present and evolving into the future: Is this a core process you're teaching?"

"It is a state of mind that comes with evolution," Michael says, "but it comes with a qualification."

"Which is?" Chimera asks.

"As we've discussed, each of us has a unique path by which her or his potential is reached. Many people find their way to enlightenment without reference to anything that I, as an individual soul or spiritual catalyst, may have specifically affected. So, what I have to say shouldn't be taken dogmatically. There are many approaches to the One-Without-A-Name, the Great Anomaly, and each is valid. No one has a corner on the market; it's like a computer network with a very large server: the hosted information is accessible by anyone who chooses to use the network, but each user accesses it by a different path. We all have unique passwords, or mantras so to speak, that allow us to connect to the source."

"The advisory that your teachings are voluntary is duly noted," I say, making a mental note to go back and re-read Michael's clever cybernetic metaphor when I transcribe this tape. Looking at Chimera and Diane, I see we've reached our metaphysical and culinary fill, so I attempt to change the subject, which, as we've noted with Michael's approach, is more accurately described as coming at the same subject from a different angle.

"I notice that KBAL has begun broadcasting real programs," I say.

"Touché!" says Michael, feigning a blow from my remark. "Obviously, going on the air with less than two weeks notice doesn't allow for a well-planned program schedule—but we're getting there," he says.

"Where did you find all the weird stuff that you're running?" Chimera asks, continuing along the same irreverential lines.

"It is weird, isn't it? Diane says to her.

"You don't like Cubist programming?" Michael says as he laughs. "It's just stuff we've been shooting for the past year or so, to train our volunteers and staff and to start a content library—cultural eclecticism—it's part of our mission statement. We're not a bunch of corporate stiffs selling sex and violence."

"But you've got eighteen hours a day to fill," I say, noticing that the coffee cup containing my third refill is beginning to jiggle in my hand.

"That's a challenge, but we've got some ideas," he says.

"Like what?" I ask.

"The evening news—a commentary on international, national, and local issues of the day."

"You can afford that?" I ask.

"Sure. Look," he says, "we put a public television station on the air for less than $400,000.[19] So, creating more news on a shoestring than the networks produce with millions of dollars is a breeze."

"Or a boast," I say.

"Not really. Think about how much so-called news you actually get from commercial television. The national news programs give you what—twenty to twenty-two minutes of material in a half hour broadcast?"

"That's about right," I say, "though it's constantly shrinking."

"Okay," Michael says, "and within that limited editorial space, how many of the stories are actually hard news, and how many are features and Pabulum?"

"There's probably about eight to ten minutes of soft stuff," I say, beginning to catch his drift.

"So, if KBAL has a fifteen minute news program that is specifically focused on political, social, cultural, scientific, and economic events of import, then we'd be broadcasting more news than the networks do and in half the time."

"That would actually be true given those parameters," I say after doing the math. "But what are you going to do—sit in front of a camera and read newspapers?"

"Actually, we've already subscribed to a couple of wire services including UPI, Reuters, and LNS,[20] plus WGBH[21] uplinks,[22] what they call the Daily Exchange Feed, which it relays to the entire PBS system via satellite."

---

[19] This figure, in itself, was shocking to PBS executives who had estimated that it takes ten times as much money (in 1980 dollars) to create an operable station. Michael gave much of the credit to Jim Black's frugality (while criticizing him for withholding additional promised cash infusions and for the tyrannical manner in which he ran the station) and the ingeniousness of Chad Waterman, who wired the station together with "bubble gum, paper clips and rubber bands" and scrap parts from his "warehouse of broadcast history," (i.e., discarded components that Waterman salvaged, which were at least 20 years out-of-date).

[20] Liberation News Service, an alternative, left-wing, news association.

[21] The Boston public television station that is responsible for producing a considerable portion of PBS programs.

[22] The process by which an electronic signal is sent from a ground station (or uplink) to a satellite, from which it is instantaneously transmitted to a wide area (footprint) on earth, and received by antennae or dishes (downlinks).

"And this provides you with news?" Chimera asks, never one to watch much TV, especially not the news.

"Yes—international and domestic," Michael says. "We'll use the wire service copy and the DEF video, filtered through our own well-developed perspective on global issues, to produce a daily commentary."

"From Rasta man to anchorman," Chimera says.

We all laugh.

"It's a proof of concept," Michael says, "—something that can be implemented on a grander scale at a later date. In the beginning, the general public will be challenged by our views."

"From the language you use?"

"Certainly," Michael says. "People key off of certain words and then classify my views as communistic, or some other popular slander, depending upon their political or religious indoctrination. We've discussed this. But, there's no denying that capitalism is a system that must expand in order to survive.[23] Marx's numbers prove this and the *Wall Street Journal* reiterates it every day: failure to grow means corporate and career death—leadership change, takeovers, and layoffs. The brainwashed, however, only see Marx as a philosopher whose social theories were used to justify totalitarianism in Russia and China. But as I've said, Russia and China had a long history of totalitarianism before Marx was even born: the czars and their heirs, the commissars, are part of the same repressive

---

[23] Years later, after the destruction of the Berlin Wall, the fall of the Iron Curtain, and the collapse of the Warsaw Pact, Michael remarked to me that years had been added to the potential viable life span of the capitalist system. "The opening of all these previously inaccessible markets and the creation of what is now, truly, world trade, allows for expansion of capital investments into areas that will take some time to saturate. No wonder the U.S. economy sustained its longest period of economic growth on the heels of these historical events." Michael comments were recently echoed by Joseph Kahn in an article entitled, "Globalization Proves Disappointing," http://www.nytimes.com/2002/03/21/international/21GLOB.html?), to wit, "The vast majority of people living in Africa, Latin America, Central Asia and the Middle East are no better off today than they were in 1989, when the fall of the Berlin Wall allowed capitalism to spread worldwide at a rapid rate." "But, if the imperial imperatives of capital aren't obvious enough," Michael continued, "the unbridled use of the earth's natural resources and lack of provisions for replenishing forests, fresh water, and air quality stand as blatant examples of the Marxian mathematical tenet that the underlying core formula for capitalism is expansionary, just like cancer."

tradition of social organization and power; and Mao rules like a Ming. The fact that they call their systems Marxist only shows that they value propaganda more than the dialectic. The Russians and the Chinese are no more followers of Marx than the majority of so-called Christians—with their war-mongering, bigotry, and worship of the almighty dollar—are followers of Jesus."

This is a powerful insight, I think, but by this point I've come to expect nothing less.

"The left won't like you for that," Diane says.

I had almost forgotten Diane's anti-Vietnam war activities during her undergraduate years at Northwestern. She had told me that this was when she first discovered Brecht, and thus when her life in the theatre was born.

"Any ideology eventually locks itself into views that are inconsistent with the principles upon which it was founded," Michael says. "Rashan and I found a great quote from William James to this effect that we're going to use in the book.[24] So, it doesn't matter whether it's left, right, up, or down—I just call it like I see it. People may try to define me politically, but that's not where I'm coming from. Sharing isn't an ideology; it's a state of being in consonance with the universe; it's the way we experience light in human form. It's why we can say 'Love is the law.'"[25]

"All this may be true," I say, "but greed does not give up so easily. People associate the sharing of resources with the repression they witness in places like Russia."

"Why else would I describe the Soviet economy as state capitalism and ours as private socialism?"[26] Michael asks.

"Another conundrum from the Sphinx." Diane says.

"Kinda like Garbo or Dylan," says Chimera.

"That *je ne sais qua*," I say, "—'a riddle, wrapped in a mystery, inside an enigma.'"[27]

---

[24] James, William, *The Varieties of Religious Experience*, 1902 (see *Invocation* at the front of this book).
[25] Michael writes in 2008: As we show in our proof (www.SolomonsProof.com or *Appendix 6 - The Proof*), the heart, which is the first organ that develops in an embryo, is a holographic replica of the Quantum-Torus. It is the focus of our next evolutionary step—overcoming the tyranny of the instincts and ego—which enables us to inform our behavior with love and compassion, leading us to an enlightened state in which sharing is the norm.
[26] This remark is dated 1984.

Michael smiles and begins to explain his juxtaposed analogy. "You know my uncle," he says to me.

"Yes," I nod, "the retired senior partner in our firm?"[28]

"He once explained to me how CPAs from Andersen helped the Soviets set up their bookkeeping," Michael says.[29] "He made it clear to me that the Soviets keep track of their economic activities in much the same way as we do, except that they have only one stockholder. That's why I call it state capitalism. Over here, we have private shareholders who hold stock in regulated monopolies, such as the electric companies and telephone companies, or in cartels and oligopolies, such as the oil industry and armament manufacturers, all of which subsidize themselves through legislative fiat, that is, taxpayer-supported contracts. So, I call this arrangement private socialism."

I wonder if Rousseau and Descartes rapped philosophy on the fly like this in the cafés of their day.

"Are you trying to confuse people?" Chimera asks.

"They're already confused," Michael says. "I'm just pointing out the paradox, which is a way of finding higher truth and making people pay attention to the labels they're using—to make them define their terms—and to help them see that in a fascist universe labels are used to separate things that are actually connected. Only by recognizing this will we get away from the slop that passes as ideology in this country and move forward. In this case, the truth is that the world's largest economies are similar; they include both entrepreneurial and regulated elements; and they are

---

[27] "I cannot forecast to you the action of Russia. It is a riddle, wrapped in a mystery, inside an enigma; but perhaps there is a key. That key is Russian national interest." --Winston Churchill

[28] Arthur Andersen LLP. At that time, the early 1980's, long before the Enron debacle, it was the largest accounting firm in the world. During its formative years, the firm was one of the leaders in reestablishing faith in the economic system following the Depression, through its contributions to the promotion of what came to be known as Generally Accepted Accounting Principles (GAAP). Michael's uncle, originally a student of Andersen's at Northwestern University Business School, was instrumental in this process. After his retirement, when Enron brought down Andersen, the *Wall Street Journal* interviewed him for his perspective on the erosion of trust and goodwill in the market.

[29] This tradition of working with so-called collective economies continues today. In November, 2002, Ernst & Young celebrated 10 years of operation in Vietnam, with 190 employees in Hanoi and Ho Chi Minh City.

controlled by a few people who manipulate—through capital, intelligence, and armed force—the governments that regulate the markets and labor.[30]

"People may think that democracy and laissez-faire capitalism are related intrinsically, but they coexisted only by happenstance in America, and that is no longer the case. Look at how campaign financing laws have turned this relationship inside out: democracy serves capital, instead of vice versa; America has become a corporate vassal, where a person's ability to run for office is dependent on the sponsorship of big business and private war chests. This subservience of the state to corporations is America's brand of fascism.[31] The earth is being destroyed by the cult of consumerism, cynicism, and greed, and so-called religions enable this process, despite Jesus' admonition that 'No servant can serve two masters ... Ye cannot serve God and mammon.'[32] It's up to us to turn this around."

"So we're back to your mission," I say, "and the role the station will play in getting the message out."

"Leadership has to come from outside the system," Diane says, because those running the ship are headed for the rocks and don't care. Look at Earth Day. Most of America is still pretending this was started by communists rather than by people concerned about the future of the planet,

---

[30] We return to a quote from the previous chapter: "The drive of the Rockefellers and their allies is to create a one-world government combining super-capitalism and Communism under the same tent, all under their control. ... Do I mean conspiracy? Yes I do. I am convinced there is such a plot, international in scope, generations old in planning, and incredibly evil in intent." Congressman Larry P. McDonald, 1976, killed in the Korean Airlines 747 that was shot down by the Soviets.

[31] Again, as noted in *Chapter 4*, as Eisenhower warned in his famous farewell speech, "In the councils of government, we must guard against the acquisition of unwarranted influence, whether sought or unsought, by the military-industrial complex. The potential for the disastrous rise of misplaced power exists and will persist." Also, long before Eisenhower's remarks Jefferson declared, "I hope we shall ... crush in its birth the aristocracy of our moneyed corporations, which dare already to challenge our government to a trial of strength and bid defiance to the laws of our country" (Letter to George Logan, 1816), and Lincoln, too, warned, "Corporations have been enthroned. An era of corruption in high places will follow ... until wealth is aggregated in a few hands ... and the Republic is destroyed."

[32] Luke 16:13

and most scientists are still pretending that all our resource exploitation is without any long-term climatic effects."[33]

Again, Diane's political acumen startles me, putting her relationship with Michael in another light: their interest in Yoga, theatre, and politics—*c'est très simpatico.*

"Democrats and Republicans are just different wings of the same party, Rashan—the capitalist party," Michael says, continuing where Diane left off. So, whether it's through the TV station or other means, we are simply doing what's necessary to ensure the survival of life in a manner befitting the glory of creation. They may characterize my views as radical, but that is like calling Jesus' teachings communistic—it misses the point: an economic system ruled by monopoly capital, and the fascist governmental apparatus that such mammon worship engenders, is not the answer to humankind's spiritual goals and intrinsic evolutionary truth. Anyone who is more focused on rationalizing their gluttonous life styles and putting economics above life, rather than focusing on raising their consciousness, will be offended by the Good News. It would be surprising and disappointing if they didn't react negatively to my message. That would indicate ineffectiveness on my part."

"So, you expect your television news effort to have a big effect?" Chimera asks.

"As I said, I think it's more a proof of concept than the beginning of any movement. Most of the folks at the station and management in particular, don't have the politics to understand the significance of this news program—they're liberals, after all. And their spiritual practices are haphazard at best, so it may turn out to be very similar to what's happening in the Town of Wayne: People inherit a situation filled with the power to transform and change their world and they don't know what to do with it."[34]

---

[33] This is the mid-1980's, before Earth Day became a mainstream activity.
[34] "Men make their own history, but they do not make it as they please; they do not make it under self-selected circumstances, but under circumstances existing already, given and transmitted from the past. The tradition of all dead generations weighs like an Alp on the brains of the living. And just as they seem to be occupied with revolutionizing themselves and things, creating something that did not exist before, precisely in such epochs of revolutionary crisis they anxiously conjure up the spirits of the past to their service, borrowing from them names, battle slogans,

"And if that happens, if this programming falls by the wayside, then what?" I ask.

"I will have created the example that I'm prescribed to fulfill. You will have recorded it. Then it will be time to move on. I mean, look at what the teachings were turned into the last time—a religion that supports greed-based murder—that is, wars and state terrorism—and the accumulation of wealth rather than the propagation of love and ministering to the poor. Compared to the Catholic Church, the Wayne's Home Rule Charter and KBAL's news program are highly successful examples. I've learned not to be attached to how others twist my words. I'm not co-dependent in my relationship with humanity."

"But there's still the book and the play," I protest, surprised at the degree to which I'm emotionally invested.

"Yes, we hope that by publishing a book we shall take advantage of an opportunity for change and succeed where others have failed. But 'In my father's house there are many mansions.'[35] If the people of the earth fail to fulfill their potential, then that shall be a great loss, but the enlightenment that I promulgate has happened other places in the universe and shall continue to occur with or without participation here. However, as I've explained, I'm optimistic by choice. And as I've said before, this time we get to be our own editors. I'm not promising this will be easy. The forces of repression are ubiquitous, including the highest levels of government and religion, in this country and around the world."

☼ ☼ ☼

I find Michael's attitude of non-attachment towards the institutions he has helped shape both remarkable and disconcerting. As usual, his overview of the world is a double-edged sword of complete egotism, believing that he is the messenger of the deity, and egolessness, believing that he is a vehicle for a much greater power. Admittedly, there seems to

---

and costumes in order to present this new scene in world history in time-honored disguise and borrowed language." Karl Marx, *The Eighteenth Brumaire of Louis Napoleon*, translated by Saul K. Padover from the German edition of 1869, at http://www.marxists.org/archive/marx/works/1852/18th-brumaire/ch01.htm.
[35] John 14:2

be very little choice for him in harboring both these dispositions. The words and symbols that he uses to communicate are, as he says, frontal lobe phenomenon; as such, they are necessarily connected with a part of the mind we associate with ego. Michael's argument for the divine or anomalistic nature of his teachings is that the spirit or force which animates his use of these symbolic forms could only produce inspired language if his ego operates as a transparent servant of his higher self, the Great Anomaly, the G-d principle, the Supreme Being—a state that he says is recognized in the teachings of Yoga. As he has often noted, "Simultaneously having the greatest ego and none at all is a paradox that I necessarily hold in the balance of consciousness." As we have already seen, Michael offers descriptions of how this process works, and as we shall see later, he has prescriptions for others to accelerate their own growth by similar means.

But understanding how these levels of consciousness coalesce for Michael doesn't make it any easier for me to deal with his totality of being on a personal level. There doesn't seem to be much ground in-between believing in Michael as he presents himself, as the World Teacher or Christ-Messiah, and believing that he's just another highly-evolved, but ultimately deluded, individual.

Regardless, he is a friend that I now have known for almost nine years. During this time, as our personal and artistic relationship has developed, I have had growing concerns over the manner in which his teaching will be revealed and how his privacy and safety will be maintained. If more and more people become aware of, and begin to come to grips with, this message, whether I believe in it or not, I fear there could come a day, just as he told me years ago, when those who find his teachings antithetical to their interests will attempt do away with him. As he says, isn't this what always happens? If he's regarded as a great spiritual leader and gains any sort of following, what is the likelihood that he will die a natural death, in America or anywhere else?

To be certain, Michael has already managed to navigate some potentially treacherous waters. His involvement in anti-imperialist demonstrations and actions in the Bay Area during the Vietnam War resulted in his arrest and an FBI file. In Wayne, establishment concerns over the hippies who had written a Home Rule Charter, refused to chlorinate their water, outlawed flush toilets, had locally certified Colorado law enforcement officers, and *de facto* permitted the cultivation of cannabis, again brought the FBI snooping around on the premise of hunting for radicals on their most wanted list.[36] Now, as Chimera has pointed out, Michael is escalating his message by helping to create a VHF broadcast station[37] in a relatively large and growing market. Opposition by KRST, a licensee owned and operated by the Denver Public Schools, is just one indication of the reactionary opposition that awaits anyone who aspires to mass visibility and promulgates a message advocating significant change. Even after KBAL's debut and a supposed truce between the local PBS affiliates, KRST orchestrated a public letter-writing campaign and investigation by PBS over the financing and organization of the station[38] as well as the political perspective being promoted on Michael's news show.

Michael is also not a man who shies away from addressing anything he considers to be a problem. This, of course, is an admirable trait, but one that could attract retaliatory force if the stage is big enough. This is really nothing new, of course; from the beginning, Michael made it clear to me that among the reasons he needed me to help him write this book is the

---

[36] Michael writes: In 2005, it seems they have instituted a permanent excuse for such activities—"Remember 9-11! Remember the terrorists!"—with the Congress giving permanency to virtually all the critical provisions of *The Patriot Act of 2001* that was rushed through, unread, on the heels of a calculated "flag event" (the leveling of three buildings in NYC) and the anthrax scare that followed in time for the vote. We shall get to this later.

[37] In broadcast television, frequencies assigned to channels 2 through 12 are dubbed Very High Frequency (VHF), while frequencies assigned to channels 13 and above are termed Ultra High Frequency (UHF). It was considered a coup by Jim Black, the station founder, and his acquaintances (including Michael) that they landed a VHF station in a major (top 20) market. Many people at this time did not have UHF antennae, and the cost of powering UHF transmitters, which require geometrically more electricity than lower frequencies, would have been prohibitive for the under-funded KBAL.

[38] In a deal with the courts, Jim Black was removed as President and General Manager of KBAL because of the legerdemain he used in accounting for donations to his first public broadcasting venture, a radio station in Pittsburgh—and was replaced by Chad Waterman, who was able to make the required financial showing (based on the sale of the nation's first country rock-formatted station, which Waterman and Milam had cleverly expanded from a small rural market station into a San Francisco powerhouse by convincing the unsuspecting FCC to allow them to move their antenna and increase power). "Black's removal was actually a positive development," Michael tells me, "because despite his liberal pretensions, he is totalitarian in his management of staff."

possibility that he might become a target. And though I didn't take his claims seriously at the time, I did agree to chronicle his efforts—only now coming to understand that the threats to Michael are real and that this makes our book project all the more crucial. A thousand years from now, if Michael is correct in his assumptions, these observations may be the only record of this remarkable man at a remarkable time.

☼ ☼ ☼

"I've got a lot of questions, Rashan," Chimera begins after reading the latest book entries, which express both my concerns over Michael's safety and my continued ambivalence over the enormity of his claims. "Maybe we should make a list and go through it with him, to make sure that we don't miss something important—you know, just in case?"

"Just in case he is killed or just in case he is the Avatar?" I ask.

"Both," Chimera replies diplomatically.

"Sometimes I wonder how normal people are going to react to the complexity of this stuff," I say. "And even if they do understand, it's one thing for people to read what someone says and quite another for them to apply it to their own lives."

"There's always gap between what people say and how they act." She pauses for her next thought, as if listening to some inner voice. "So, maybe we should try to be examples, and take up some of these practices he talks about?"

"Become his devotees?" I ask. My hackles rise immediately. I can see the 'isms' marching down the streets, four by four, ad infinitum.

"That not the model that Michael's suggesting," she says. "He said that he was ready to provide you with voluntary instruction, and I've reached a point of willingness—after reading what you've written—to listen and learn. Look, in addition to his friendship, we already accept him as a counselor of sorts, and we agree that he seems to know what he's talking about and that he's capable of doing what needs to be done. We just don't know whether events will bear out his claims."

"Where did you read that I'm sold on this?" I ask. "I don't know that anyone's capable of doing what he's talking about."

"It's in the subtext," she says, as if my subconscious thoughts were patently obvious to anyone, "and I'm not sure we have a choice given what we've already chosen to do," she continues.

"What do you mean?"

"We're unsure whether Michael will be successful in his efforts, yet we've been willing to go along with this project as both observers and interested parties. Now, we're being offered a chance to become involved to a greater degree, and to change our lives in the process. It's not like he invented Yoga, or Jungian psychology, or that he's laying some foreign doctrine on us or something. If we want Michael to succeed, aren't we compelled to give it a try?"

How is it, I wonder, that Chimera is so good at pointing out my behavioral contradictions and yet has so much trouble with her own issues? And what if we are all as blind to ourselves as she? What contradictions am I missing in myself, or is Michael missing in himself?

"It seems," Chimera continues, "that anything less would be a vote against what he's suggesting. And I have to think that bringing these practices into our lives will serve as the first step in replicating the consciousness he's seeking to spread."

"I'm not sure I follow you."

"Let's say, G-d forbid, something happens to Michael and he's not available to teach. I know Diane is picking up a lot of his wisdom through osmosis, but she's not recording it. If we practiced his teaching, we could record the process in the book and at least provide some record of his approach for others to consider—regardless of whether they believe he is the World Teacher or just a gifted man."

☼ ☼ ☼

"That's a great idea, Rashan," Michael says when he hears the plan. We are both working downtown these days, and meet up at Le Central, a low-key French restaurant, for lunch. "This'll allow you to record what I have to say about spiritual practice, and you and Chimera can ask questions that'll be helpful to others."

"I know Chimera will be thrilled. She seems to have gotten the bug from Diane. I'm a little skeptical, of course."

"As you should be, otherwise this doesn't work. Almost everyone who reads this book will be a skeptic. That's the point."

You'd think after hearing this from him so many times, I'd stop apologizing for my doubts, but chronicling a friend's life is a challenge, so Michael's assuaging my guilt pangs over my arms-length approach is much appreciated. Journalists desperately want to believe they are objective, and I am fighting the good fight. The tape recorder is rolling as usual.

"So, where should we begin," I ask.

"With the soup, don't you think?" says Michael.

I laugh.

"Well, you know," he says, I'm busy with the station, so how about we begin with the first four stages of Yoga practices?"

"I think I'll go with the vichyssoise," I say to our waitress.

"And I'll start with the cucumber basil soup," Michael says. "Tell me about the *assiette de fromage*."

"That's got Papillon Roquefort, Montrachet chèvre, Muenster, Chaource, and Comembert served with toast points, fried fruit, and a small salad," the waitress says.

"A good choice," I say. "We'll start with that." After our waitress leaves, I continue. "This Yoga material is another aspect of your teaching that you've already written about?"

"In part, yes—some take-home helpers for the classes I used to teach."

"At the Yoga Retreat?" I asked, remembering my investigative sojourn to Chicago and eye-opening discussion with Cynthia.

"Actually, I used them for my own students. I had my own classes as well, around the city."

"Doesn't that seem mundane, I mean, in comparison to what you're trying to do now."

"Only in the way that etudes or sketches are a mundane part of music or painting—such exercises are part of practicing one's art, and teaching Yoga is integral to my experience in human form. The notion that the World Teacher, or Messiah, or Christ, or Avatar is born with god-like powers or telepathic understanding of all human affairs is not reality—the spiritual anomaly is a human being. As a playwright, you understand this—it's the human experience itself that completes the catharsis; so with a prophet, it's the synthesis of environment, genes, and spirit in combination with the light force that flows through such a person at a particular time and place that create the anomalistic experiences through which the miracles of healing, enlightenment, and other such transmissions occur in the minds and souls of the recipients. On the physical plane, I experience time, thought, and aging in much the same sense as anyone else. This mortal profile is one of the reasons that I began the practice of Yoga myself—because I began to notice deterioration in my physical vehicle. Let's face it—life is short and the body can be a valuable tool during the time we're given here, so why not keep your vehicle tuned up."

"And that was when, as you explained to Chimera and me, that you became aware of your mission—after you began this practice?"

"That too!—a rather startling surprise after such a vain beginning, *n'est-ce pas?*" he says, always looking for a way to slip his rudimentary French into the conversation, while I, ever the assimilated *citoyen*, have let the use of my native idiom slip. "That's why I feel a deep sense of gratitude to those who kept alive these practices in remote regions of the world until now, when it's become necessary to teach them to others who, in turn, are spreading them around the globe. So, my synthesis of the teachings of Yoga with other disciplines isn't meant to disparage the sacredness of the great yogic tradition, but to marry it to the rest of creation. I'll send some introductory material to you and Chimera, and after that we'll get together and begin the work."

"Sounds like a plan," I say, unsure how easy it will be to swallow these prescriptions.

"Speaking of Yoga, did I tell you that I've made arrangements to interview Baba Ram Dass[39] on KBAL?"

"Another 'proof of concept' for a series?"

---

[39] Formerly known as Richard Alpert, he was colleague of Timothy Leary and Ralph Metzner at Harvard. Together, along with Karma-Glin-Pa Bar do, they wrote *The Psychedelic Experience*, which used the *Tibetan Book of the Dead* as a guide for the journey of psychological death and rebirth that a new generation was experiencing under the influence of a variety of psychotropic substances, including LSD. Alpert later became a disciple of an Indian yogi and changed his name, which now has become simply Ram Dass. He wrote two very popular books, *Be Here Now* and *The Only Dance There Is*. His later work involved ministering to the aged, as well as writing about the spiritual aspects of aging.

"I don't think so. Ram Dass happens to be coming to town for another event. It's a great opportunity to share perspectives with someone who has similar interests."

"So, you know Ram Dass?"

"No, but I've read some of his work. Also, we have the same birthday, though he's a number of years older. I expect we talk the same language, which will make for an interesting show."

"I'm glad to hear that the station is so open to your ideas."

"It helps that our program director is a Buddhist that I hired."

"Only in Boulder."

"For all the craziness of its reputation, Rashan, there are some good reasons why I've chosen to establish myself here. It's beautiful and there's openness to a variety of spiritual teachings."

"You don't have to convince me, Michael. I chose it myself."

"That isn't to say I would hold Boulder up as an example to the rest of the world. Like everywhere else, it been run over by capitalism: underneath all the local hoopla over environmental issues and spiritual practice it is still a place where, when push comes to shove, profiteering and repression is accepted."[40]

I begin searching my mind for an escape route from Michael's politics, but before I can think of anything he returns to the subject.

---

[40] Michael's assertion is later born out by the reaction of local, university, and state officials when it became known that Ethnic Studies Professor Ward Churchill had written a paper in which he compares those who died at the World Trade Center to underlings of the Third Reich. "Governor Owens, his Brownshirts at the university, and those who support these fascists live in total denial," Michael says, when I ask him about this. "The more immoral America's actions become, the greater our moral façade," he adds. "They say it's not about freedom of speech, that they're ousting him on academic grounds, picking on his argument that the U.S. Cavalry used germ warfare on Native Americans. If the cavalry didn't, it would be the first documented case where our government's actions weren't aimed at the extermination of these people. Even today, the Bureau of Indian Affairs steals billions from them with impunity." [MDS: As of 2008, the US government was still refusing to account for billions of dollars owed Native American landowners (*The Associated Press*, "Judge Hits Gov't on Indian Money Delay," *The New York Times*, 1/30/08)]. At one time I found this attitude alarming, but before you dismiss any connection between our leadership and the fascist movement, read on.

"But to answer your question, no I don't expect this program with Ram Dass to be the start of a series. We don't have the money to fly in folks to be interviewed, so we'll run it as a special."

"And your news program is still holding its own?"

"For now, despite KRST's campaign to get the FCC to come after us."

"That doesn't seem to be a deterrent. I caught your editorial the other day, after John Lennon was shot."

"Another cultural revolutionary murdered by the proverbial 'lone gunman.' We weren't as shocked as most. I was at Altamont when a guy pulled out a gun while Mick Jagger was on stage. But, John Lennon!" he says emphatically. "We had to pay homage to someone who affected our generation so profoundly."

"It was moving. I didn't see anything like it on any of the network stations."

"Of course not, given the views of their corporate ownership," he says. "To them, Lennon was a dangerous celebrity, someone with a message they couldn't tolerate. In his own offbeat way, I think Lennon was like King."

I wasn't sure whether I agreed with this assessment, but the intended parallels between the politics of a rock star and a preacher hit home. "It also made me think about our discussions concerning your own vulnerability," I casually drop.

"Yes, there's that aspect as well," Michael says without missing a beat, obviously at home with this issue. "But, like I've said, we're doing what we can, both you and I, to reduce our exposure to such phenomena."

"I've been thinking," I say, "that our book could allow you to reach out to the world without having to expose yourself to public risk."

"Perhaps. There may be a period of time after it's published when I remain anonymous. It may take a while before there's much of a reaction."

"That's reassuring—that you might wait before you begin to make public appearances, I mean."

"For you and me both," he says, in a rare showing of human concern over the enormity of what he's undertaking. "I have faith that you and I will play a part in the evolution that needs to happen, but there are no guarantees when it comes to a population's proclivity for higher consciousness. The change must occur on an individual basis, one person at a time. There will be significant numbers that will choose to reject our message. So, I expect that, as we approach the Millennium and the declaration of our intentions through publication, we'll take further precautions for our safety."

"I'm glad to hear you've given this some thought."

Our hors d'œuvres and soups partially devoured, we decide to order another course as well. Michael goes with the *salade de saumon fume*—slices of Nova Scotia lox-style smoked salmon, over spinach tossed in a walnut vinaigrette, accompanied by red onions, cucumbers, tomatoes, capers and dill crème fraîche—and I order the house quiche, filled with savory egg custard, topped with a ratatouille of vegetables and Swiss cheese.

"Speaking of safety precautions," Michael says, picking up where we left off before this appetizing distraction. "Just the other day a few of us at the station were comparing notes on each of our FBI files. I'm sure it's only a matter of time before the Feds come poking around again."

"A number of you have FBI files?"

"Yes, for a variety of reasons. A bunch of us retrieved our records under The Freedom of Information Act[41]—just for fun."

"Just for fun?"

"Sure. As we've talked about, during the late '60's, when I was involved in demonstrations against U.S. imperialism in Vietnam, it was understood that the FBI was all over the place. Rather than get paranoid about it, I figured if they were listening, they might learn something from our conversations."

I had heard this story from Michael's former Stanford compadre, Paul Offenbacher, out in San Francisco, but since Michael hadn't read what

---

[41] Michael writes: How interesting to consider that in the not so distant past, after the Nixon Watergate scandal and his resignation in the face of impeachment, there was a time when Congress reacted against the secret powers and surreptitious agenda of the oligarchy's intelligence and security establishment, and allowed citizens to view the (albeit censored) records that had been collected on them. A far cry from the present atmosphere in which the CIA and the Homeland Security Department override Constitutional protections, arguing that "terrorism" (which they themselves foment, aid, and abet) makes this necessary. As noted earlier, Hitler and many other fascists (such as Nixon and Agnew, Bush I and II, Cheney, Ashcroft, Rove, DeLay, et al.) use this scare tactic to implement extraordinary totalitarian controls over a supposedly "free" citizenry. More on this later.

I'd written about this, I nodded my head, gave him a faint smile, and noted his commitment to the idea. "So, you see your interface with the FBI as a playful encounter?"

"In a sense. I have compassion for them and the limitation of their consciousness, which makes them pawns for the morally-rudderless cabal that controls them. I also understand that they are fully capable of deadly force, even on a whim."

"Don't you find that scary?"

"I can't be killed, Rashan."

"Surely you don't believe that you're physically invincible?"

"Of course not. This physical body that I animate could easily perish, and according to the current parameters for human existence on this planet, I may only use it for somewhere between seventy-five and a hundred and ten years. Whether I choose to extend this period of time by reincarnating along the lines of the Tibetans or by some other means, remains to be determined. But, ultimately, I do not fear the FBI or anyone else. I have eternal life—life that transcends the transitory material world."

"And the people you work with at KBAL feel the same way about the larger picture?"

"Spiritually, no, but they do find the transparency of the FBI's actions humorous. That's why we've all posted our FBI files next to our FCC licenses near the station's master control area—they're our badges of courage. We consider ourselves patriots. The treason in this country is at the top.[42] We believe in freedom of the airwaves and in the 1934

---

[42] During the editing of this book, Michael pointed out to me that his reference at this time is not to 9-11, but to the 1980's and the plotting of then presidential candidate Reagan, his vice-presidential nominee George H.W. Bush, and the to-be named Director of Central Intelligence William Casey, with the government of Iran to delay the release of American hostages until after the Carter-Reagan election had been decided. The hostages were then released the very day of Reagan's inauguration. This was followed by the U.S. selling arms to Iran and granting them immunity from any lawsuits resulting from their seizure of the hostages. (Iran, it might be remembered, had, before the Ayatollah, been long-suffering under the regime of Mohammad Reza Shah Pahlavi, a dictator propped up by U.S. foreign aid.) Portions of the profits from the arms sales to the new Iran went to support the Contra guerillas in Nicaragua, U.S. mercenaries fighting the *Sandinistas*, a popularly-elected socialist movement. U.S. involvement in Nicaragua had been prohibited by Congress. The Tower Commission, appointed by President Reagan (!), was critical of these activities, but did not suggest any

Communications Act, which created the assignment of TV and radio frequencies across the nation and declared that the airwaves belong to the people. Contrary to this law, the Congress is selling permanent bandwidth to private corporations—another example of fascism and corporate control over the state. All of creation is up for sale under the reign of the involuted god, the almighty dollar. Rabid pseudo-Christian fundamentalists, who are so fond of pointing fingers and finding the devil everywhere but within themselves, would be wise to note that this tyrannical rule of capital is one of the prime examples of Antichrist energies—the very embodiment of Mammon. They have bought the derivative Calvinist doctrine—'having money signifies being of the spiritually elect'—hook, line, and sinker to justify their materialistic lives. The truth of the ages, of course, teaches the opposite; and we'll spread this teaching—that the enthronement of wealth is not part of the long-term plan—through books, radio, television, movies, or other means in the future. Sooner or later, we'll come head to head with the power elite."

"You don't feel that KBAL is currently under some threat—that the FBI or the FCC is ready to throttle you?"

"Not yet anyway, though they may wish that they could. But KBAL is an organization of mostly Caucasians in a country that theoretically respects the rule of law. I expect that, in the wake of the post-Watergate

---

criminal prosecution. A Congressional investigation, led by special prosecutor Lawrence E. Walsh, showed direct U.S. involvement in gun-running and drug trafficking. The scandal was tidied up by pinning the blame on Marine Lt. Col. Oliver North of the National Security Council (NSC) staff and others, including national security advisor John Poindexter (now overseeing domestic spying for George W. Bush), who stated that he personally authorized the diversion of money and withheld that information from the president. Seeing it as their patriotic duty, North, Pointdexter, and Robert McFarlane (Pointdexter's predecessor) took the hit for Reagan, Bush, Casey, and the rest of the ringleaders. On Dec. 24, 1992, President George H.W. Bush pardoned all the principals charged in the scandal. Walsh's eventual report, released in 1994, criticized Presidents Reagan and Bush for their roles in events related to the scandal but did not charge either with criminal wrongdoing. It might be noted that one of Oliver North's biggest supporters, during the illegal operation and afterwards, was Congressman Dick Cheney of the House Intelligence Committee, now George W. Bush's Vice President and one of the most influential of the "New World Order" plotters. Through such incestuous behaviors, corporate terrorists continue their stranglehold on governmental operations.

resurgence of civil liberties, unless we break the law or until we pose a legitimate threat to the status quo of privately-held large-scale capital concentrations that control the Congress, the courts, and the state apparatus, we'll not be quashed. Not even the well-oiled rumor mongers and wheeler dealers working at the behest of KRST are a threat to get our news show off the air or to impinge on our general operations. We're much more likely to become ineffective as a result of internal squabbling than external interference."

"This is the first I've heard of problems amongst yourselves."

"Any organization has disagreements between its members, just like we talked about with town of Wayne. A friend of mine, Doug Shackelford, the head of KBAL's Independent Film and Video Distribution Center, insists that 'there is some strange inverse cosmic law which says that the level of infighting and conflict is inversely proportional to the amount of money at stake: the less money, the harder and longer people will bicker over it ... or anything else they can think of.'[43]

"In a way, that's what is going on at KBAL. There's a lot of internal pressure to turn the station into a liberal media outlet, which, though rare enough, would ultimately offer only the illusion of social and environmental progress as a substitute for actual systemic improvement. As we've discussed, this is how the Democrats operate—when push comes to shove, they are only the left wing of the Capitalist Party—which makes them more dangerous than the Republicans, who are out front in their contempt for humanistic values."

"That must be disappointing: this dilution, as you see it, of the station's potential?"

"Yes, though not surprising. As I've said, one thing I've learned through my experiences with the Movement in the late '60's, in the Town of Wayne in the '70's, or here at KBAL in the '80's, is not to get hung up

---

[43] *The Sky's No Limit*, Vol. V & VI, Double Issue, published by the Reginald A. Fessenden Educational Fund, Winter Quarter, 1982. I found Shackelford's aphorism a witty parallel to both Michael's statement in our previous conversation, and Michael's later footnote to that conversation (which cites Marx's related quote) concerning the failure of humankind to unchain itself from its instinctive patterns and take a conscious evolutionary step from the tyranny of instincts and ego (and the subsequent worship of mammon and capital) to freedom and alignment with the Great Anomaly or G-d principle. See "Evolution" in *Appendix 7 – Michael's Notes* as well as *Appendix 6 – The Proof*.

on short-term results, but to allow events to inform our teachings. Just as the lack of spiritual fortitude of those surrounding Jesus didn't undermine his teachings, so, too, I can't let the regressive behaviors that surround me affect my work. Your recording of our efforts is more important than the success or failure of any local implementations. This way I can present my teachings without dogma and steer clear of creating any formal organizations that presume to act on my behalf or to represent my teachings. Those with whom I've been involved—in the past at Stanford, or Wayne, or KBAL, or whatever else may come along—are free to follow their own conscience and consciousness. The book will carry forward the important points."

"This primacy of the book seems consistent with our discussion concerning provisions for your safety."

"Not just my safety, Rashan. Yours and Chimera's as well."

"Mine and Chimera's?"

"It's your name or pseudonym that's going on this book."

"I hadn't really thought about it one way or the other, Michael. But since you mention it, I can see that we need to discuss this."

I'm left to wonder about this turn in the conversation as our next course arrives and Michael orders a couple of cappuccinos to follow our meal.

"While many will hail our work as important and necessary, even species-defining," Michael says, "to others '… ye shall be hated of all men for my name's sake.'[44] My suggestion, Rashan, is that you masquerade your identity, in much the same way that Shakespeare did."

"I'm not sure what you mean," I say. "I'm aware of some controversy over the authorship of a couple of Shakespeare's plays, and that some scholars have suggested the historical figure of William Shakespeare isn't the author of the plays and sonnets that we attribute to him, but I never considered this a masquerade."

"The issue hasn't come to a head in theatrical circles yet, because some of the critical information has yet to be widely published, not to mention the self-interest of the academic and commercial reputations attached to the so-called Stratfordian position; but recent discoveries show that Edward de Vere, the 17th Earl of Oxford, is, to the most minute

---

[44] Matthew 10:22.

biographical detail, the author of almost all the work we call Shakespearean."[45]

"Whoa! Yet another conspiracy!"

"Believe me, Rashan, you'll see that it makes perfect sense when you read the research. As a high ranking nobleman, de Vere, like many of his acquaintances, not only used pen names for his poetry and drama, but for pamphlets as well, to argue political and religious issues, just like the Founding Fathers did in *The Federalist Papers* and such."

"Isn't this a rather elitist view, that a commoner such as Shakespeare couldn't have possessed the genius to produce such remarkable work?"

"That's the Stratfordian argument against the Oxfordian view, and while it's romantic and idealistic to think that someone relatively uneducated and socially underprivileged could realistically invent relationships to which he was not privy and become the greatest influence on the development of the English language and its poetry and drama, this is simply not the case. Access to books and the leisure to study at that time was severely limited. I mean, the Stratford man's[46] daughter was illiterate! This doesn't mean that the genius for doing such doesn't exist everywhere amongst all peoples, but without nurturing of some sort, it's unlikely to manifest. Given that de Vere had some of the greatest minds in Europe for teachers, his talent argues for better education for everyone, hardly an elitist point of view. Besides, he's the only candidate that has all the biographical evidence on his side—the arguments for the other candidates are entirely circumstantial and farfetched at that."

"So when might I expect to learn more about this?"

---

[45] After years of debate, the momentum for the Oxfordian position gained much ground in the late 20th Century and early 21st Century. The compelling reasons for this are summed up in the landmark article, "A Historic Whodunit: If Shakespeare Didn't, Who Did?" William S. Niederkorn, *The New York Times*, 2/10/02 (http://www.nytimes.com/2002/02/10/arts/theater/10NIED.html). Much of the scholarship underlying this change in historical perspective can be attributed to Charleton Ogburn's *The Mysterious William Shakespeare: The Myth & the Reality*, Dodd, Mead & Company, New York, 1984. More recently, Mark Anderson's *"Shakespeare" by Another Name*, Gotham Books, New York, 2005, adds invaluable biographic insight to the characters and settings of the plays. Later in this book, the Oxfordian position is further elucidated in *Chapter 8 – Dreams*, as well as *Appendix 4 – The Bard's Ghost*.

[46] A reference to William Shakspere (as he himself sometimes spelled it), a grain dealer and glove maker's son.

"I'll get you a copy of *The Mysterious William Shakespeare*,[47] which has just been published. Meanwhile, consider taking a *nom de plume* to publish our book."

"Doesn't it seem odd that we would be publishing what we believe to be a very influential work in an anonymous fashion?"

"Not really. As I've said, the last time around my teachings were entirely appropriated by others for their own unholy purposes—and they did so pseudonymously. De Vere was prevented from publishing under his own name by the conventions of the day—a caste system that likened thespians and dramatists to courtesans and thieves—and by the harsh political realities of the time, when one could be incarcerated in the Tower of London or beheaded at the Queen's whim. In our situation, publishing in this manner is part of a strategy to gradually introduce our ideas to the public. I believe it'll enhance the possibilities of our success if our words are, for a time, considered in the absence of our physical presence and personality."

"Why so?" I ask, noticing Michael's continued use of the royal third-person "our," as if I were now *de facto* his appendage.

"Because the words must stand or fall on their own, like any universal work. In both de Vere's case and my own, our authenticity is proven not by circumstantial evidence, as is the case with all the pretenders, but by biographical fact—a writer writes what he knows in detail. What I look like and the details of my incarnation are specific to the time and place I physically appear, in this case the late 20th and early 21st century in the USA. I do not look exactly as I did the last time I was here. That would be impossible according to the parameters of this universe, although there may be certain resemblances given my genealogy. But the words that I have chosen are, for the most part, of a universal nature. They point to truths that transcend the specifics of this time and place. They will be here long after this 'I' is gone."

"So, to summarize, by remaining anonymous for a period of time you hope to get people to consider your words and ideas without being distracted by the specifics of your appearance and personality?"

---

[47] Ogburn, Charlton, *op. cit.*

"Yes. Invariably, some people will be disappointed by the manner in which I've chosen to incarnate, hoping instead for a different ethnicity or more a conservative look. Widespread understanding of the sense behind my manifestation will take some time."

"But given the biographical details that connect you and me to this account, doesn't the book inevitably lead back to us, just like you say of de Vere?"

"Of course, Rashan—given the powers of information retrieval and surveillance, it's unavoidable that our identities will be discovered. But there is a lesson for posterity in the use of pen names."

"You mean that this book might be taken for fiction?"

"No, though it might by some, but all major spiritual works share that quality, because many people don't see the miracles in their daily lives. The Christian *Bible*, minus the censorship and distortions that were woven into it, is a highlight reel,[48] so to speak. Important incidents from Jesus' life have been selected, modified, and refined so as to make them art. It's like the so-called 'docu-dramas' that run on television. They're based on real events, but the stories have been culled to dramatize their intrinsic truths, with beautiful actors playing the roles. This is not unlike what de Vere did in shaping his histories,[49] or what most novelists do, with events from their own life, in creating fiction. For that matter, this approach is entirely consistent with my discussion of Heisenberg's Uncertainty Principle, that is, as hard as I may try, I can't represent the exact truth of my mission or that of the universe or the Great Anomaly. These things will always be, to return to our philosophic and spiritual analogies, shadows on the cave wall or a name that cannot be fully captured in written or spoken form.

"The art in our work is the documentation that proves our point. In this we have captured what is important now and will continue to be important long after we're gone. This is what establishes our teaching, not our physical appearance."

"And that's why we've agreed to keep your personal information to a minimum?" I ask.

"Yes. Perhaps it would benefit people to learn more about the minutiae of my life, but it's a secondary consideration. As we've said, I

---

[48] A selection of "the best of" quotes and incidents; not a minute-by-minute journal or account.

[49] That is, the so-called Shakespearean histories, *Richard III*, *Henry V*, etc.

inhabit a physical body that in every manner resembles everyone else, and my bodily functions and instincts are also the same as theirs. What's important is how I handle the parameters of this vehicle and what I produce with it, not the sundry details."

"At some point though, Michael, I expect these specifics would help others in their own quests: understanding the circumstances that fostered your empowerment, as you put it, would enhance their ability to empower themselves."

"As long as we're conscientious about the difference between idolatry and biography, at some point we can explore those details."

Suddenly, Michael has reminded me that as helpful as such glimpses of personal details might be, there is a danger as well—it is the very thing I have feared from the beginning concerning those who come to believe in Michael's rap—the so-called cult of Michael, as I thought I saw it in Chimera, Diane, and Cynthia. Yet, again, when confronted by this potential problem, it seems that Michael considered the issue long ago. So I had to ask, "And if that happens, how do you propose to deal with the issues of dogmatism and cults, which you've so fervently stated that you wish to avoid?"

"I think you'll understand this better after you and Chimera begin to work on the Yoga practices that I'll be providing."

With that we wound up our leisurely lunch, I picked up the tab, and went our separate ways back to work.

7

Yoga

"There was only blessing and love in the religion of Christ. But as soon as crudeness crept in, it was degraded into something not much better than the religion of the Prophet of Arabia. It was crudeness indeed, this fight for the little self, this clinging to the 'I,' this desire not only for its preservation in this life, but also for its continuance even after death. This they declare to be the foundation of morality! And strangely enough, men and women who ought to know better think that all morality will be destroyed if these little selves go, and stand aghast at the idea that morality can be based only on their destruction."
--Vivekananda, *The Yogas and Other Works*, 1953

"When humans finally learn to harness the power of Love, they will once again have discovered fire."
--Teilhard de Chardin

"If ye love wealth greater than liberty, the tranquility of servitude greater than the animating contest for freedom, go home from us in peace. We seek not your counsel nor your arms. Crouch down and lick the hand that feeds you. May your chains set lightly upon you; and may posterity forget that ye were our countrymen."
--Samuel Adams

As always, I eagerly anticipate Michael's next shipment of notes, yet somehow this time it feels more threatening. I attribute my uneasiness to the fact that Chimera and I are going to be altering the details of our everyday lives based on the suggestions that Michael is forwarding to us. Granted, he has affected us profoundly in the past decade, but during that time there was a random, serendipitous quality to the selected ideas we chose to take to heart. Now, I'm going to be confronted by a set of practices to which I'll be making a commitment. This is not the way I live.

I am accustomed to considering what comes to me on its own merit, then picking and choosing what suits me. Even at a button-down firm like Arthur Andersen, I have input on policy. So, I wonder whether Michael can present his ideas in a non-dogmatic fashion and make me feel that my own choices are driving my spiritual development.

"Maybe it's not Michael that you fear," observes Chimera, deepening my anxiety.

"What do you mean?"

"Maybe you fear parts of yourself that you'd rather not visit. Isn't that the nature of the ego—to try to stay in control? It's instinctive with men. And it's diametrically opposed to what Michael's telling you."

"In what way do I fear myself?" I ask, hoping to find some defense for my muse's 'terrible swift sword.'

"From what you've written, it's clear that, in Michael's world, embarking on a spiritual path means submitting to a higher power that's both in us and greater than us."

"Why should that scare me?"

"Because it's unfamiliar territory and because your ego projects its own controlling nature onto these forces—and fears them. It's similar to what we've talked about when you project your anima onto me and then expect me to live up to that form of perfection; but in this case, you're attributing your controlling instincts to Michael."

"Here we go again with the psychoanalyzing." I say, shielding myself with a line I picked up from Michael.

"Sor-ry!" Chimera says. "I was just trying to help. You brought up your fears."

"No, you're right." I backtrack. "I'm being too rigid. So, as long as we're aware of the pitfalls of using this language …"

"We can handle that," says Chimera.

"Besides," I say, "you're right about projection being the nature of the ego."

This admission is as surprising to me as it is to Chimera. We both just look at each other for a moment.

"So what do you think is the antidote?" I finally ask.

"It's right in your book," she says, "—the best way to conquer fear is with faith. According to Michael's proof, the cause of the universe isn't explainable, so faith is a built-in principle, the anomaly itself."

"Okay."

"That's faith in a force you can't control," she says, "a force that we experience as love. I told you that before Michael did."

"So, having faith in the nature of this force, faith in love itself, will allay my fears?" I say, once again fully inhabiting that mesmerized state which accompanies these visitations from the muse.

"According to Michael, it should do more than that. It should bring you the lessons you need to learn when you're ready to learn them."

"Isn't this always happening?"

"Yes, but if you're not involved in a practice that keeps you focused on it, you're likely to lose the lessons."

While Chimera's comments impress me, I can't help but recall, once again, that individuals preach progressive behaviors better than they practice them.

"So this'll get easier for us?" I venture.

"Hopefully. Having faith in love and giving up control is going to be harder for you, because male instincts work against this. For me, it'll be easier. I'm used to being around bigger and stronger beings; surviving as a woman in the jungle develops faith and the ability to give up control."

"An interesting premise," I observe.

Afterwards, it occurs to me that while my intellect is beginning to trust some of Michael's ideas, my emotions are not. Deep down I'm still at odds with both Chimera and Michael; she for her self-satisfied assurance of spiritual superiority; he for implying that I must give up control over my own life.

☼ ☼ ☼

A few days later, I'm at my office window, looking out at downtown Denver, the Front Range, and the Continental Divide from Pike's Peak to Long's Peak. I'm in the middle of writing an audit report, trying to clean up one of my footnotes. My secretary, Rita, buzzes me on the intercom.

"Michael Solomon's here to see you," she says.

I'm surprised, but I want to finish what I'm doing before I discover what brings Michael to my office for the first time.

"Tell him I'll be out in a couple of minutes," I say.

Five minutes later I come out to find Michael and Rita engaged in an intense conversation about Jesus and American politics. Alarms go off in my mind—she's a Christian fundamentalist with no room in her belief system for any alternatives.

"You do have a knack for finding everyone's hot button," I say when I finally get him in my office with the door shut.

"You'd be surprised what a little well-placed doubt can do for even the most rigid dogmatists," Michael says, "—their belief systems are built on shifting foundations ... castles made of sand."

"And no doubt, you're the guy to deliver the defining blow," I reply.

"I'm the wind and the waves."

"Even in the staid executive suites of Arthur Andersen," I say.

"All the more so!" Michael says with a bemused smile.

"Your uncle would not be amused."

"But my dad would," he says.

He puts a manila envelope on my desk.

"I happened to be downtown," he says, "and thought I'd remind myself how the movers and shakers live. Besides, I hadn't sent you the Yoga materials I'd promised."

I take a deep breath and smile.

"Sorry. You know there's a part of you I find antithetical to my life in the fast lane."

"Yes. I know—the black sheep of the family, the skeleton in the closet," he says with a twinkle in his eye. "It's just like doing the news on KBAL—the Socratic gadfly, c'est moi."

☼ ☼ ☼

Michael's package includes two copies of his Yoga handout, which was originally designed for the small, scattered classes he used to teach in Chicago. Chimera and I read them separately and then sit down and discuss them, before our first session him.[1]

---

[1] See *Appendix 3 – Introduction to Yoga*.

I'm aware of my resistance and fears as I go through the brief material, though there's little threatening in it.

"This seems pretty simple," I say to Chimera, "but that's what makes me nervous. I have no idea of the context. The world's filled with cults that started out as 'spiritual' organizations and religions."

"I thought the personal discovery part was clear," Chimera says.

"You mean the quote?" I read from the sheet:

> *"The wise student of Yoga takes the various doctrines of philosophy and religion lightly, as tentative explanations and interpretations of truths beyond the realm of the intellect, but uses them as best as he can in his direct discovery of those truths."*[2]

"Right."

"Okay, I admit this seems to be saying the same thing that Michael's been saying all along."

"Which is?"

"The idea that truth—whether we are talking about quanta, or G-d, or Yoga—is something beyond description. But that's no guarantee," I add, "that as a teacher he has no designs on being enthroned."

"It may not be up to him," Chimera replies.

☼ ☼ ☼

A few days later Michael knocks on the door, right on time for our first session on Yoga. A shock awaits me when I open the door.

"Diane! What a surprise!" I say, trying to recover. "Michael, how are you?" We exchange hugs and Chimera joins us. Diane lights up when she sees her.

"I thought I'd tag along," Diane says. "I hadn't seen you guys in ages."

I'm both relieved, knowing that Diane's presence will lighten things up, and panic stricken, realizing that I'm going to be spending hours with her in such a familial atmosphere. I know it sounds crazy, considering my

---

[2] Taimni, I.K., *The Science of Yoga*, Theosophical Publishing House, Adyar, Madras, India, 1961.

present relationships with Chimera and Michael, but as I've said before, Diane is very attractive and bright and I'm still only thirty-six years old, with the normal testosterone challenges of men my age.

"You look great!" Chimera says to her.

"Not to sound like an advertisement or anything," Diane says, "but it's amazing what a little Yoga will do for you."

"Not so little," Michael says.

"Well, okay, I admit I've gotten into it," she says. "I don't think I could parent without it."

We follow each other up half a flight of stairs to the main floor. From the first time he ever visited us, Michael always found a ready compliment about our house. Usually, it's in reference to the natural light and the views. The house was designed by a student of Frank Lloyd Wright's, and the original owners had found a wonderful lot in west Boulder that afforded grand views of the Flatirons, views which remained unimpeded by the extensive landscaping that had been done over the years to enhance the privacy of the space.

"I hadn't thought about it," Michael says, "but having radiant heat will certainly be a plus when you're doing *Asanas*[3] or *Zazen*[4] on the floor."

"I'm not sure Wright had that in mind," Chimera responds, "but we're always making new discoveries. Remember that wall behind the hot tub, Michael? Looked what happened when we took it out."

Michael stares through the windows that dominate the back of the house and look onto the patio, the hot tub, and the back yard.

"It opens the whole space," he remarks. "I never noticed the garden in the back corner."

"Neither did we," Chimera continues, "until we took the wall down. Then it was obvious that corner of the backyard had been a focal point from the living room when the house was first built. Rashan and I went

---

[3] The physical postures or positions used in *Hatha* Yoga, the third of Ashtanga Yoga's eight steps.
[4] A Zen Buddhist term for a specific posture and form of meditation (see Shunryu Suzuki, *Zen Mind, Beginner's Mind*, Weatherhill, New York, 1973, pp. 25-28) that literally means "just-sitting." The highest or the purest form of zazen is referred to as *shikantaza*, being the moment or being oneself in the moment, when one realizes there is nothing but this.

out there and started poking around and we found all those flagstones buried underneath a couple inches of mulch."

"It's striking—" Diane says, "definitely aligned with the original design."

"An interesting synthesis of architecture and archeology," Michael says.

"I hadn't thought of it that way," I say, "but you're right. We seemed to have discovered something about the architect's intent through our dig."

"—much like the process of Yoga," Michael segues after a moment. "When you take down a wall, you become aware of natural processes and relationships that were previously unavailable to you."

"Speaking of which, Michael," I say, starting my portable tape recorder, "before we start with specific practices, we'd like to ask you some general background questions that came up."

"Sure."

"I thought we could all sit over here," Chimera says, pointing to a bunch of overstuffed pillows she's spread out on the other side of the living room floor.

"I love the way the windows bring in the landscaping," Diane says.

"That's one of the things that sold us on the house," Chimera says.

"We both thought the introductory quote you chose put us at ease right away," I start, giving a quick sidelong glance to Chimera, hoping she'll let me jumpstart the business Michael had come for. Frankly, my nervousness—over what I've gotten into with the Yoga multiplied by my excitation and anxiety over Diane's presence—begs me to fill the silence.

"Yes," Michael says. "Taimni's[5] perspective on Yoga is exceptional. His descriptions of meditative states are the most refined I've ever read."

"It was the personal discovery part that jumped out at me," Chimera says, looking from Michael to Diane.

"That's what did it for me, too," says Diane. "It's had a huge effect on my outlook and my acting."

I'm reminded that Diane's impressive performance as Suki came after she had started her Yoga practice with Michael—something I wasn't consciously aware of until Michael told me months later. Since then, I've

---

[5] Taimni, I.K., *op. cit.*

been over this in my mind a few times and realized that the signs were there all along—her kicking the smoking habit and bringing a noticeably increased vitality to rehearsals—but at the time I was too jealous to allow myself to imagine what this change indicated in the nature of Diane and Michael's relationship.

"That's an important point," Michael says. "We're moving into an age where humankind will no longer believe in spiritual truths they haven't experienced, but instead believe in spiritual truths *because* they've experienced them.

"During the last age,"[6] Michael continues, "after Jesus served as the principal Avatar or Spiritual Anomaly, the spiritual practices of humankind were controlled by bureaucratic organizations whose articles of faith were devices for totalitarian control. In this age, the spiritual practices of humankind are returned to each individual, who shall *know* and *experience* spiritual truths in his or her own way."

As if on cue, Michael had once again taken our question and drilled down to the specific concern that prompted it. There was a time when this uncanny sense for others' motivations made me uncomfortable, but now I realize why Michael continues to stress the importance of my skepticism—that only through such a point-of-view will our chronicle address the readers' questions and incredulity. I glanced at Chimera again, but she was looking at Michael, responding to his riff.

"Are you saying," Chimera asks, "that our Yoga experiences will be the same as the saints we read about in holy books?"

"Essentially, yes. Anyone who has undergone a spiritual rebirthing can personally identify with most any comment by Jesus, Mohammed, Krishna, Zoraster, Abraham, Buddha, Lao Tsu, Báha'u'lláh, et al."

> *The following morning I awake to church bells from the Seventh Day Adventist services down the street. Gone are the demons from my "dark night of the soul"; the sky is cloudless and the sunlight seems brighter than normal, as if my newly cleansed soul is reflected in the outer world. In the days that follow, I am amazed at the spiritual clarity that*

---

[6] An age, celestially speaking, lasts approximately 2,200 years or one-twelfth of the time it takes our solar system to travel around the center of the Milky Way—a celestial month, as it were. See "Astrology" in *Appendix 7 – Michael's Notes*.

> *is suddenly mine; every scripture that I pick up is now permeated with descriptions of feelings and thoughts that are perfectly in consonance with my own. I have passed through the abyss and am reborn into a world in which I commune with saints and avatars.*

"Or Mary Magdalene," Diane says.

Not having seen Diane in a while, I was surprised by this comment and its sense of familiarity with the hidden personal life of Jesus with which Michael always seems so fluent. But that was not someplace I wanted to go with this conversation.

"And this happens to anyone who practices Yoga?" Chimera asks.

"Not automatically," Michael says. "Quality of practice varies with the individual. Not everyone easily adapts to what is required. To the degree that material concerns dominate us, we are less available for spiritual and heartfelt matters."

"So what you're saying," I ask, "is that there is some kind of event that occurs during the practice of Yoga that transforms the consciousness of the practitioner?"

"Yes, what we call 'rebirthing' or 'spiritual healing.' Of course, it's not exclusive to Yoga; there are many belief systems or practices that bring out such transformations, and sometimes they occur outside an organized practice, say from an event. But I teach Yoga because it's the most direct route to 'awakening' and carries with it a minimum of philosophical baggage."

"What makes it so direct?" Chimera asks.

"Yoga is the science of turning oneself inside out, along the lines of a torus,[7] and all creatures living in four-dimensions are highly-adapted toroids; so, Yoga uses the natural processes of the universe, that is light itself—in this case manifested through DNA as body-mind-spirit—to heal. Without any religious dogma, Yoga acts as a catalyst to the natural self-healing powers within all of us: When you scratch your arm, it bleeds, it coagulates, a scab forms, and eventually skin reappears and the wound is healed—all without conscious effort on our part; so, too, the soul has its

---

[7] See the illustration, "The Torus and Human Form," in *Appendix 6 – The Proof*.

own innate power to heal itself. *The Tibetan Book of the Dead*[8] and *The Revelation of St. John the Divine*,[9] or even some psychological treatises on the healing of schizophrenia,[10] all offer examples of this rebirthing process through which the personality dies and is reborn in a more spiritualized state. It's one of the great miracles of life that we can rebirth our souls by casting out the traumas we've suffered. Yoga is designed to make this happen."

"I can't say enough about this," says Diane. "You know me, Rashan. I was a nervous wreck."

"You seemed confident to me," I say.

"On the surface, yes," she says, "but that was my mask."

"A mask we all wear," says Michael. "Our self-centered instincts and the ego feed off this uncertainty. So, to evolve we need to respond to uncertainty with faith, not selfishness. Yoga engenders the faith we need by providing the experience of the one certainty—the force behind the unchanging constant of change—the Great Anomaly, the G-d principle, the Supreme Being."

"If, as you suggest," I ask, "Yoga induces a state that's universally attainable, did the teachers that you mentioned—Abraham and the rest—all experience this as well?"

"Essentially, yes," Michael says. "But the vocabulary that each of them had at his disposal to describe the experience was limited by cultural training. That's why we find such different, even disparate, ideas in their teachings. Today, however, communication between everyone on this planet is integrated in a manner never before experienced: Ergo, part of my mission is to synthesize our multi-cultural and interdisciplinary beliefs into the cohesive universal truth of which they're a part, just as you and Chimera will discover your own unique way to apply your spiritual insights and talent to this reality."

"Like Diane did with her acting?" I say, surprising myself by finally facing this difficult memory and employing it to support Michael's argument.

---

[8] Evans-Wentz, W.Y., *The Tibetan Book of the Dead*, Oxford University Press, London, 1927.
[9] The final book of the *New Testament*.
[10] Laing, R.D., *Knots*, Random House, 1972.

"Thanks," Diane says. "It was surprising, really, to find that Yoga helped me on stage."

"Availability, as Michael calls it," I say.

"That's a good term for it," she says.

"So, what kind of Yoga are you proposing that we study?" Chimera asks Michael.

"It's important to understand that there are many paths to the One-Without-A-Name—the universal anomaly of which I speak," Michael says. "One of my favorite passages from the *Yoga-Sutras* of Patanjali[11] states that '*Siddhis*[12] may be attained by birth, herbs, mantra, austerities, or transcendence.'[13] This is Yoga's way of saying that it is not the only way. As it happens, I'm experienced in all five of these practices, but the one that I propose to teach you is a variation of what is traditionally called *Ashtanga* Yoga, 'the eight limbs of Yoga.'"[14]

"That's what you had on the card you gave me when we first met," I recall.

"Yes," Michael says, "though since then this traditional term has been turned into a commercial brand; but I'm using the original denotative meaning."

"And these sutras of Patanjali that you mentioned, they are part of *Ashtanga* Yoga?" I ask, intrigued by the idea that yogic canon legitimizes practices that seem to be outside of its purveyance.

"Yes, the *Yoga-Sutras* can be considered the generic basis of *Ashtanga* Yoga."

"So, is the use of herbal sacraments part of what you are going to teach?" I ask, seizing on what is clearly the most controversial aspect of what he's saying.

"As the *Yoga-Sutras* state, herbal sacraments can play an important role in transcendental experience, and there are a variety of indigenous groups throughout the world that incorporate these practices into their recognized sacred rituals. I, myself, have participated in some of these ceremonies and have even used certain sacraments to accelerate the natural

---

[11] The oral teachings of the Yoga masters that were handed down through the ages and finally transcribed by Patanjali over 2,500 years ago.

[12] Literally, powers or accomplishments, from Sanskrit.

[13] Taimni, I.K., *op. cit.*, pp. 377-383.

[14] For more details, see "Yoga" in *Appendix 7 – Michael's Notes*.

processes stimulated by Yoga.[15] As Carlos Castaneda's Yaqui Indian medicine man Don Juan said, the 'little smoke' can 'stop the world' and contribute to one becoming 'a person of knowledge.'

"However, the use of *ganja*[16] is not standard practice and I can't recommend it even if I subscribe to it. So, within the confines of Yogic practice, I won't be discussing herbal sacraments except to comment on their use by others. This is much like the special case of certain yogis whose path does not include the presence of a physical guru. These individuals, myself for one, know that 'the guru is inside of them,' and are able to call upon other forces and forms of teachers to guide them through their initiation and evolution. Again, this is not standard practice and I can't recommend it. If you have to ask, it's not for you. In any case, I must recommend the middle path—that is, having a teacher who uses the prescribed practices."

That seems reasonable enough to me, given that I don't go around broadcasting that I smoke the stuff myself on the weekend (at least not until this book is published!).

"And what are these prescribed practices," I ask, happy that we've finally gotten to the heart of the matter and eager to know just what kind of a situation I was getting myself into.

"The practice of Yoga begins with *Yama* and *Niyama*, when you define your relationship with Yoga by adopting general ethical principles and vows of self-restraint."

"Define my relationship with Yoga?" I ask. "You mean I choose the degree to which I am involved in practicing it?"

"Yes, based on your consciousness and free will."

---

[15] "... it is the Quality of this Grass to quicken the Operation of Thought it may be a Thousandfold, and moreover to figure each Step in Images complex and overpowering in Beauty, so that one hath not Time wherein to conceive, much less to utter any Word for a Name of any one of them. ... This is the Profit of mine Intoxication of this holy Herb, The Grass of the Arabs, that it hath shewed me this Mystery (with many others), not as a New Light, for I had that aforetime, but by its swift Synthesis and Manifestation of a long Sequence of Events in a Moment. I had Wit to analyze this Method, and to discover its Essential Law, which before had escaped the Focus of the Lens of mine Understanding." From Crowley, *Op. cit.*, pp. 124-127.

[16] Hindi for *cannabis*.

"Can you give me some examples of what these 'ethical principles and vows' look like?"

"Sure. If we were to look at the initiations of monks, nuns, and renunciants of various faiths upon their entrance into monasteries, nunneries, ashrams, and such, we find that one of their first acts is the taking of a spiritual name, usually given them by their teachers. Consciously, what occurs here is that the novitiate allows his or her ego to be submerged into his or her higher mind,[17] or to that of G-d, depending upon your belief system. The taking of a spiritual name, such as Brother, or Sister, or Baba, or whatever the custom may be, involves recognition of a force in one's life that is more powerful and exalted than that of the self, much like the first step in traditional twelve-step programs. Along with this act often comes, celibacy, poverty, and other life-altering vows."

"Are you suggesting that Rashan and I have to become celibate and give up our worldly possessions?" Chimera asks.

> *Here I am in Colorado, finally, with my backpack and little else. My school loans are paid off, I have no romantic commitments and no place to call my own—just a soul, the wilderness, and endless possibilities. Additional karma is my choice, based on principles formed in my own short-lived self-conscious life; my potentiality unfolds as my truth in time!*

Diane laughs. "Careful now, Michael," she says.

"Yes and no, Chimera. I'm simply giving everyday examples of *Yama* and *Niyama*. I believe that the practice of Yoga is something that must work among householders[18] just as it works for renunciants. But while I'm suggesting that Yoga is adaptable to different circumstances, I do not mean to imply that variation from traditional yogic principles will yield the highest states of consciousness. Yes, in most cases, the adaptation of yogic principles to everyday life will provide an initial foundation of spiritual practice upon which one can build; however, the greatest states of spiritual attainment, at least at first, are generally only accomplished by the full adoption of time-tested principles and vows. The greater the spiritual

---

[17] Another example of humility and ego-loss would be the shaving of one's head. [MDS]
[18] A spiritual term for those who raise families or live conjugally.

responsibility one is willing to accept, the greater the spiritual rewards—so having nothing left to lose is often the catalyst for spiritual transformation. The price may seem steep, but that is only a perception of the ego resisting subservience to a higher authority."

"What does that have to do with celibacy," Chimera responds, with a slight hint of desperation in her voice.

"We've talked about the unification of the masculine and feminine within the individual. The practice of continence, or celibacy, whether life-long or for interim periods, is a very effective means of counteracting the commoditization of the opposite sex, which, in turn, is a prerequisite for the acceptance of these 'other' elements within ourselves. After this work has been accomplished, the goal for householders is to maintain their newfound consciousness within the parameters of an intimate relationship.

"In Judaism, or Bahá'í, celibacy is not practiced by spiritual leaders—indeed, it is frowned upon—while in other religions it is a sine qua non. This problem is now coming to a head."[19]

"Is this something you're doing?" she asks, first looking at Michael, then at Diane.

"I have in the past," Michael says.

I look at Diane.

"So have I," she says blushing, "though rarely on purpose."

We all laugh.

"So," Chimera asks, "you're saying that celibacy is particularly effective early in one's Yoga's practice—to reduce dependencies and control issues in intimate relationships—but after that intimate relations can be resumed?"

"That's well put," Michael nods, "as long as the inner work has actually been done."

"You're serious?" I'm quick to contend. "There's no other way to deal with dependency and control other than celibacy? This seems so extreme."

"I didn't say I'm prescribing this for everyone, Rashan, nor did I say it's the only way to deal with these issues, only that it's the most effective way. The amount of time that different people need to accomplish this

---

[19] See Leslie Kaufman, "Making Their Own Limits in a Spiritual Relationship," The New York Times, 5/15/08.

varies. There aren't many people who can work through these issues without some period of abstinence, and fewer couples, still, who have no issues in this area."

"So, celibacy aside," Chimera says, again looking from Michael to Diane, "what's an easier way of getting started?"

"What about the idea of taking a spiritual name," Michael says.

"That seems hippie-ish," I cringe.

"The fact that hippies do this outside of traditional settings doesn't make their practice any less effective. Most religions and tribes have such a practice that serves as a means of creating a higher consciousness, separate from the ego. It doesn't mean that you have to use this name in public or with anyone other than yourself."

"Okay," says Chimera. "I suppose that's not much different than how I already changed my name."

"Everyone has a way into this," says Diane. "I put on a new persona with every acting role, so that's my context. For my Yoga practice, I just picked a name and imbued it with my spiritual goals. When I meditate, this part of me gets the time and attention of my consciousness ... and it's been growing from there."

Chimera nods her head. "Okay, a spiritual persona—that could work—something less demonic than Chimera, like Immaculata."

We all laugh.

"What?" she asks, feigning ignorance of the irony in her comment.

"What about some of the other behavioral modifications?" I ask.

"You could take a vow of no harm," Michael says. "Though, like everything in Yoga, it means more than what it appears on the surface—simply abstaining from harmful actions. Harmful thoughts and words—the seeds of harm in action—are where the real work takes place."

"Again, this is so idealistic, Michael," I say.

"It is idealistic," he says, "in the sense that it is a goal beyond our current state. But if you pay attention to your dreams—they come true. As I've proven, the nature of humankind is to evolve, not to remain static."[20]

"I assume you're referring to your old saw about the Flood and the burning of the libraries at Alexandria?"

---

[20] See *Appendix 6 – The Proof*.

"Among other things, yes," says Michael, not blinking an eye at my carping. "The so-called historical record is more quicksand than solid ground—it's the conqueror's spin on every war and every holy book. But that's only part of it. We've never stopped evolving—it's our nature. Only the short-term view sees it otherwise. It's all there in black and white."

Having covered this topic in more detail before, I move on. "I think that's a fair rebuttal. So, what are some of the other precepts that are included in *Yama* and *Niyama*?" I ask, returning to my question.

"Avoiding exaggeration, detaching from sensory pleasures, and overcoming materialism and greed."

"Again, I have to note for the record, Michael, this is expecting a lot from people given the current condition of humankind."

"Certainly, many people seem very far from being able to accept these practices," he says, "and I'm under no illusion that they're going to be embraced overnight. But, I believe that each of us can take steps to improve our spiritual practice. What I'm recommending here are traditional yogic practices, not fundamentalist commandments. I'm not asking people to abandon enjoyment of the beauty, pleasures, and magnificence of the world—only to have faith in its perfect nature, reflected in the power of love, to allow that love to manifest within themselves, to express that love in their own unique fashion, and to be unattached to the result. How we accomplish this is up to each of us individually. The alternative is to allow the world to continue as an armed camp—protecting the ownership of the few and spreading the disease of materialism—where behavior *is* externally enforced. That's the dogmatism you ought to be worried about, not the spiritual teachings of the ages."

I nodded, noting once again that Michael had turned spiritual practice into political action.

"You mentioned earlier," I say, "that spiritual practices are begun usually in ashrams, nunneries, and monasteries—environments specifically designed to be supportive of such purposes. But in the secular world, where can people like Chimera and I look for support?"

"Right here," says Diane, looking from Chimera to me.

"Think of what we're doing here as representative of what can happen anywhere," Michael says. "People who study with the same teacher form natural support groups that function similar to what you find at a retreat. But since there are dangers in following a particular brand of teaching, we need to encourage the grassroots development of support groups in much the same way that AA[21] and other twelve-step programs evolved. Membership is voluntary and democratic, support is unconditional, and the principles apply equally to all forms of attachment across the board—whether dealing with addictions to chemicals, sensory enrapture, instinctive reflexes, or material accumulation."

"So," I ask, "you're suggesting that community support groups, which would deal with the difficulties faced by average people attempting to raise their spiritual consciousness, are a critical element in world transformation?"

"Yes," Michael says, "as long as they meet the non-judgmental characteristics that I've described. In many places, community support systems have been completely lost. We need to rebuild this connectedness around mutual spiritual concerns, much like the tribal rituals that arose from our innate consciousness, early in our evolution, the remnants of which we now find in the theatre."

"Isn't that going to be difficult," I ask, "considering how alienated and rootless society is?"

"People come to twelve-step programs from all walks of life," Michael says. "In the long run, this eclectic mix makes these groups more effective."

"I find it curious," Chimera says, "that there's a parallel between the vows that a yogi takes in the *Yama* stage, and the promises one makes to oneself when entering a twelve-step program."

"This is no coincidence," Michael replies. "In both cases the vows enable the individual to concentrate on the spiritual task at hand by letting go of attachments, without having to question the relative moral pluses and minuses of every situation. That's why I don't claim that these yogic principles are absolute or irrefutable, only that they're effective and progressive in their own right; its like Jung saying that human beings need symbols of integration for the health of the psyche, all the while admitting, like Plato, that these symbols are based on white lies, that they are not the thing in itself."

---

[21] Alcoholics Anonymous. In its most refined iterations, AA is based upon the union of spiritual practice and psychological insight, not unlike the teachings of Jung, who was an admirer of the formative work of the group.

"It's the same in theatre," Diane says, "when you agree to take a role and commit to the rehearsal and performance process. Everyone in the project relies on each other to make it work."

"I can see that," Chimera says.

"I believe you've given us a handle on *Yama*, then," I say, seeking to moderate the discussion and keep my tape transcriptions to the point.

"Good," says Michael. "So, you see, Yoga is a spiritual practice that focuses on self-evaluation and self-evolution, like the spiritual teachings in Atlantis that were organized into the 42 Questions[22]—a stark contrast to the Ten Commandments and other externally-imposed values. The guru is inside of each one of us and everything we need is available for the asking. It's critical for students to take personal responsibility in this way—to avoid the pitfalls of guru worship and transference."

"You explained this to us in Wayne," Chimera says, "—that at some point in the process, when we awaken our own divine nature, we become our own teacher and student."

"Right," Michael replies.

"As artists," says Diane, looking at both Chimera and I, "we've already got this piece. Once you get started, it'll fall right into place for you."

"Okay, so where do the simple, ascetic practices that we associate with Yoga come in?" Chimera asks.

"What you're referring to are the practices known as *Niyama*. In *Yama*, as we've been discussing, would-be yogis define their ethical practices that generally involve actions toward others, such as celibacy or *Ahimsa*; in *Niyama*, the practices are focused inward. For example, when I began my Yoga practice, my *Yamas* were the standard abstinences,[23] while for my *Niyamas* I initiated a number of austerities including changes in my diet, use of mantra[24] and prayer, periods of silence,[25] and other observances of this nature."

---

[22] Curious, isn't it, that the answer to the riddle of existence in Douglas Adams' *The Hitchhiker's Guide to the Galaxy* is the number 42?

[23] The Great Vow, as it is know in yogic orders, includes abstention from violence, lying, stealing, sex, and possessiveness (greed).

[24] Ritual chanting.

[25] *Mănū*, in phonetic Sanskrit.

"Are you indicating that there are specific austerities that Yoga students must undertake?" Again, I test for any hint of orthodoxy.

> My own family thinks me most strange. Not long ago, when my aunt and uncle were visiting San Francisco, I had to send them a note explaining that I couldn't meet with them because I was silent (practicing Manu). Now, it's my vegetarian eating habits that drive them to distraction. "Where's the guy that could eat half a beef tenderloin and a loaf of challah by himself?" they ask.

"No, Rashan. It's just as we've already said—there are choices, as always. These practices shouldn't be foreign to you. So-called practicing Catholics abstain from meat 166 days a year, for example. What I'm *recommending*, mind you, are practices that facilitate the passage of the yogi."

"Such as?" Chimera jumps in.

"Diet, to begin with. In the industrialized nations of the world, much of what people eat is for sensory fulfillment, not for nutritional value. And much of what is eaten is detrimental to the body, particularly in the quantities that it is consumed."

"What substances are you referring to?" asks Chimera, ever the dietician.

"Over-use of refined sugars, meat, and alcohol, to say nothing of the chemicals used in industrial farming."

"Are you suggesting that these items can't be consumed by students of Yoga?" I ask.

"You guys eat a healthy diet," says Diane. "I don't think you'd have to change anything."

"What about the masses? You expect this to fly?" I ask, sounding more like a press agent than a journalist, the feelings of an "insider" startling me, as if I had just crossed some invisible line.

"Again," Michael resumes, "I'm not here to set down a code of rules for people to rigidly follow. I'm providing commentary on the practice of Yoga, the science of human spirituality, and how householders and laypersons may use it for their own and others' benefit. As I said earlier, one of the goals of Yoga practice is to awaken the healing power latent in each of our souls. Diet is one means of clearing the body and opening up the free flow of energy.

"Years ago, Rashan," Michael continues, "we briefly touched on Taoist chemistry, the ancient dietary guidelines from which Macrobiotics was drawn. In this approach, one of the keys to health is maintaining the slightly alkaline pH of the body and the blood system (which reflects the salinity of the oceans when our branch of the evolutionary chain crawled up on land). Bacteria that are natural to our bodies, such as those that aid in digestion, thrive in this mild saline environment. Bacteria that are harmful to our health thrive in acidic environments, like the agar solutions in the Petri dishes used for testing throat cultures. These acidic, sugary solutions support the quick growth of harmful bacteria. When your body becomes acidic from excessive consumption of the substances I mentioned, or from stress or negativity, resistance is lowered and susceptibility to disease increases.

"So, spiritual progress can be facilitated by understanding the underpinnings of diet and making the necessary adjustments—not only to maintain health, but to remove obstacles that stand in the way of your own healing power. The degree to which you wish to stimulate this process is your choice. I'm simply providing a roadmap. There's more than one way to get to your destination and you necessarily get to choose the mix of scenic local roads, industrial service feeders, blue highways,[26] dead-ends, and superhighways as you prefer it. They're your arteries."

"So," Chimera asks, "in *Niyama* we can choose to abstain from these substances to open our bodies for healing energy?"

"Sometimes, like with smoking, it's more a must than a choice," Diane says. "You can't really do the breathing exercises if you're still using tobacco. It'd actually do more damage to your lungs than help. Take it from me."

"There's more to dietary considerations than just the effects of toxins on individuals," Michael says. "Consider the raising and slaughtering of cattle for food. In her book *Diet for a Small Planet*,[27] Frances Moore

---

[26] A colloquial term taken from older automotive maps that use the color blue to denote two-lane throughways, with occasional passing lanes. They are usually state highways.

[27] Lappé, Frances Moore, *Diet for a Small Planet*, Ballatine Books, New York, 1971.

Lappé makes a compelling case for the negative entropy of such a practice. Between the destruction of trees for grazing and the silage and feed expended for growth, in particular on feed-lots, the eating of beef is a greater eco-disaster than it is a personal health and karma problem, which it is in great measure. On top of this, we've done the same thing to our oceans, fishing out the Grand Banks and countless other populations to the point where they may never recover."

"You're saying there's an element to diet that goes beyond personal ramifications?" I ask.

"Of course. It could't be any other way given the unity of all things. I could go on about sugar as well."

"The political ramifications of sugar consumption?"

"Precisely. The European quest for sugar and other spices resulted in a number of disastrous consequences. Herbalists and natural healers, mostly women, who opposed sugar's introduction into Europe—because its uses in the quantities that had become common in the West are essentially poisonous—were branded as witches and burned for their beliefs. This marked the beginning of male domination over Western medicine, which then began to treat pregnancy as if it were an illness. Then there is the ruthless slaughtering, conquering, enslavement, and ruination of tropical cultures, from the East Indies to the West Indies and South America, perpetrated by Europeans in order to expand the supply of sugar. Even today, after the colonialists and imperialists have been extricated from most of these sites, indigenous societies struggle to reestablish the variety of crops and level of self-sustenance that existed previously. And then there's the political and instability left in the wake of this material exploitation."

"The point is noted," I say, hoping to avoid getting sidetracked into Michael's political landscape, as if that were possible.

"It's much as I said to you earlier, Chimera," he says, turning to her. "Devotion to spiritual principles and daily practice isn't enough. We must be conscious of the ramifications of our actions. This is a perfect example of where most religions, in their compromise with commercial interests, abandon their big picture responsibilities and 'render unto Caesar.'[28] So,

---

[28] Matthew 22:21; Mark 12:17; Luke 20:25. Michael writes in 2006: "Render therefore unto Caesar the things which are Caesar's and unto G-d the things that are G-d's," is probably the most commonly misunderstood and misinterpreted statement of Jesus in the entire Christian *Bible*. Roman sympathizers or Jewish

recommended diet in the United States is a result of lobbying by various food industries, not the result of any scientific, ecological, or ethical inquiry, much in the same way that our democracy has been destroyed by financial and business interests."

"I never thought much about the *political* consequences of what I eat," Chimera says. "This casts a different light; it changes the picture completely."

"What other practices are included in *Niyama*?" I ask, still hoping to dodge the political implications lying just around the next convolution in Michael's brain.

"In addition to diet and fasting, there are a number of other traditional austerities, such as chanting and silence, as well as some more refined states, including purity of mind, contentment, detachment from material possessions, and commitment to self-study."

"From what I've seen," I say, "it seems the line between these practices is blurred."

Orthodox fundamentalists may have thought they were tricking Jesus into choosing between supporting Rome (and therefore its taxation) and supporting the indigenous uprising of Judea, but Jesus' response was a trick as well. Showing consistency with his earlier remarks that "Ye cannot serve G-d and mammon," (Matthew 6:24; Luke 16:13), he tells them to take the coin with Caesar's image and give it back to Caesar. In such a remark, he shows his contempt for the empire, while avoiding incarceration and torture over this point. He had bigger fish to fry before the climax of his mission. Eventually, his anti-imperialist views netted him a crucifixion, the Roman punishment for sedition, not a stoning, which would have been the case if he had been punished actually for an offense against Jewish law. As noted in *The Jesus Papers* (Michael Baigent, HarperSanFrancisco, 2006.), Jesus was respectful of Jewish law. In a two page letter to the Sanhedrin (unearthed at the Temple mount in 1961), Jesus clearly explains that his remark on being "the son of G-d," was not blasphemous because he did not mean it literally or physically, but metaphorically in the way that everyone is a child of God. This is the smoking gun that finally and irrefutably invalidates the Roman Church's dogma that Jesus was singularly Divine. Jesus' uniqueness is in his being the spiritual anomaly of his age, the anointed one ("Messiah" in Hebrew, "Christ" in Greek, and "Avatar" in Sanskrit). This makes him the most prominent Jewish law-giver since Moses, his teachings holding sway until the next spiritual anomaly shows him or her self. But rendering unto Caesar, or paying one's taxes to live for a better day, is not the same as serving mammon, as contemporary religions do by appeasing corporate interests instead of sharing.

"Yes," he says. "We're separating spiritual immersion into its parts—a way of breaking down something large in order to re-integrate it and absorb it. *Solvé et Coagula*.[29] We parce processes into components to get a handle on details, which we then recombine and synthesize into a notion[30] of the entirety of the subject. It's an alchemical metaphor for dialectical reasoning.[31] Every observance is an expression of the healing force that Yoga practice sets in motion: unification through a folding inside out of itself; a four-dimensional space-time continuum; a holographic reflection of the Quantum-Torus model."

"How about an example of this purity, this healing force?" I ask, responding to a sudden mental reminder of the discussion that Chimera and I had concerning the purpose of this Yoga session—to thoroughly detail Michael's teachings on the subject. I check to see that the tape recorder is still running, hoping to revisit Michael's complex imagery, later at my leisure.

"Sure," Michael says. "My favorite example is Paramahansa Yogananda, the founder of Self-Realization Fellowship. Yogananda was sent to the West by his guru to exemplify *Kriya* Yoga, the Yoga of Purity. Following Yogananda's decision to leave his body on March 7, 1952 and enter *Mahasamadi*, the mortuary director in Los Angeles noted that even 20 days after the event his body had not shown the slightest indications of decay, at which time they sealed his casket.[32] Yogananda's devotion to

---

[29] Literally, "Dissolution and Coagulation." In medieval Alchemy, *solvé* refers to the breaking down of elements and *coagula* refers to their synthesis, together representing the dialectic of transmuting base metal into gold, discovering the Philosopher's Stone. This turning of lead into gold—a transmutation from the baser aspects of something into a more refined or higher state of being—is in fact a metaphor for transmuting the subject (the student, lower-self, or "base metal") physically, psychologically, and spiritually, into the object of aspiration and adoration (the teacher, higher-self, or "gold").

[30] *Begrif*, from German. The term is used in the denotative sense, that is, its meaning similar to the experience of an impressionist painting, where the placement of smaller, independently abstract details combine *in toto* for a larger, integrated idea of the thought or object in question.

[31] The Dialectic (roughly grasped as thesis, antithesis, and synthesis). See the introductory paragraph to *Appendix 6 – The Proof*.

[32] See Paramahansa Yogananada, *Autobiography of a Yogi*, Self-Realization Fellowship, Thirteenth printing 1998, p. 570.

love and purity on all levels is a sign to the world of our potential, both individually and as a group.

"Another example of *Niyama* is contentment. While spirit is unlimited in scope, the accumulation of material wealth is limited by the physical laws of this plane and, more importantly, sustainability factors. We have a G-d-shaped hole within us that can only be filled by G-d. The more we seek to feed our desires and satiate them with possessions, the bigger and emptier we get, and G-d is replaced incrementally by the Golden Calf, Mammon, our own satanic shadow. As capitalism evolves, everything becomes a commodity, including our souls. It's the involution of alchemy, from the spiritual into the material. To survive and flourish, we need to turn this around, and cease to concern ourselves with material accumulation beyond reasonable subsistence and access to the tools necessary to express our unique gifts. As our spiritual awareness and activity expands, our needs will be met at every turn. 'Ask and you shall receive.'"[33]

"How realistic is it to expect this from people? Didn't Moses and Jesus already try this? Where did it get them?" I ask, attempting to uphold some measure of skepticism.

"Yes, Moses and Jesus established these principles in the West, but they didn't teach yogic principles like the Buddha," Michael says. "Overcoming the tyranny of instincts and ego is no simple matter. One needs more than faith; one needs a practice. Our present eco-catastrophe begs for it. Now is the time for our next evolutionary step—conscious spiritual evolution."

"Rashan," Diane says. "You remember our conversation years ago, when I told you I was baffled by Michael's platonic approach to me?" Chimera looks from Diane to me, and then to Michael, who smiles and raises an eyebrow.

"Yes, I remember," I say.

"The way I see it," Diane continues, "is that when I was willing to face my anxieties, rather than grab another cigarette, is when I became what I most admired in Michael and wanted in myself. It wasn't something I could buy. It was already inside of me. When I found it in there, it appeared on the outside as well. Does that make sense?"

---

[33] John 16:23

"That sounds like the Torus—" I say to Michael, "from the inside to the outside."

"Yes, a holographic toroid, the macrocosm and the microcosm." Michael says.

"Okay," I say. "Given the growing awareness of the ecological consequences of materialism in advanced industrial societies, I can theoretically accept that you might be able to convince more people today than ever before of the importance of curtailing consumption."

"So given this change of perception," Michael says, "it follows that awareness of the world is as important as contentment with the world. That's why the next *Niyama* is self-study. It's much as you and I already discussed vis-à-vis *Jnana* Yoga, the Qabalah, and *The Glass-bead Game*:[34] Self-study is important because our familiarity with—and ability to connect—symbols across different spheres of knowledge liberates us from the tyranny of the ego, from the poison of dogma and propaganda, and, ultimately, from the restriction of symbols themselves."

"You won't get any argument here," Chimera says, motioning to me and then Diane and finally back to Michael. "It seems we are all absorbed in depth by our passion."

"And this," Michael says, "has led us on a spiritual path. So, it makes sense that the last *Niyama* is the immersion of the individual in this spirit—the Great Anomaly."

"It sounds like you're asking everyone to join up and turn the planet into a church." I say.

"There's a difference between each individual finding his or her own path to the truth and individuals forming groups to propagate exclusive doctrines. We're talking about a gradual transformation that unfolds throughout the course of lifelong practice, and through which we connect with a force greater than ourselves—and thereby to all other beings and phenomena born of this same force. As we raise our *Prana*[35] through Yoga and get in touch with this source energy, we begin to embody its

---

[34] Literally, these three concepts taken together mean (*Jnana* Yoga) liberation through knowledge, (Qabalah), the cross-referencing of all knowledge, and (*The Glass-Bead Game*) the poetic free-association of the inter-connectedness of all phenomena (as it is explicated in Hermann Hesse's book of the same name [German title: *Das Glockenspiel*], also called *Magister Ludi*).

[35] Sanskrit for life-force; also known as *chi* in China or *ki* in Japan.

nature: the evolving consciousness that nurtures our ability to experience and give voice to universal spiritual truths; the healing force that facilitates an individual's identification with the words of the avatars and saints; the latent power within, *kundalini*, that mirrors the nature of the Great Anomaly."

"Those are pretty lofty ideas for the average student, Michael," I say.

"We are aiming high, of course, but these goals are not out of reach. Remember, we're setting standards for millennia, not days, months, weeks, and years, as contemporary popular culture would have it. We earthlings, despite our advancements, are still in our infancy, at the very beginning of self-consciously directing our own development. So, I'm compelled to present a vision of possibilities and choices that, while seemingly out of reach for many in this hour, may be commonplace in the future."[36]

"That possibility seems remote," I say.

"Eternity is a blink of an eye," Michael says. "Before you know it, your children grow up. The human race is the same on a larger scale. Nurturing may not account for everything, but it indispensable. Such change may seem slow or imperceptible to individuals confined to the three dimensional world of the adolescent ego, but to the mature adult (our four-dimensional higher selves) change is just around the corner, or more accurately, as near as the next toroidal phase shift."

"So, the processes of *Yama* and *Niyama* are like self-parenting?" Chimera asks.

"Yes," says Michael, "we are re-birthing and nurturing ourselves, self-consciously raising ourselves up by our bootstraps to our higher selves."

"Right," Chimera says.

"Given the foundation of *Yama* and *Niyama*, as you've just detailed, Michael, what follows?" I ask.

"Once the student defines the parameters of their work through *Yama* and *Niyama*, the next step is *Asana*. It's the most visible and well-known form of Yoga here in the West—the postures that have been popularized by so many television shows, videotapes, books, and teaching studios and franchises."

"What's the point of doing *Asanas*?" I ask.

---

[36] As they already are for some earthlings and for many extra-terrestrials. [MDS]

"Aside from the general health benefits derived from stretching muscles, mobilizing joints, aligning the skeletal structure, and stimulating glandular and other bodily systems, *Asana* carries forward *Yama* and *Niyama* practices and prepares the body for the more rigorous practices associated with meditation. *Asana* balances and realigns our musculature, and changes our brain correspondingly.[37] Ultimately, a body capable of total relaxation facilitates the next level of exercises that isolate and still the mind, which then allows consciousness to align with the soul and provide a channel for the light of the anomaly to shine through."

Michael's image of gradual refinement, from the physical to the mental to the spiritual, strikes a chord with me. I see a parallel between the rituals of Yoga and writing, in the way that the practitioner goes through a series of steps before settling down into a focused state. My comfort level thus satisfied by this resonance, I'm eager to move on through the rest of the material.

"What other principles are embodied in *Asana*?" I ask.

"There's still widespread confusion on the role that *Asana* plays in a Yoga practice. Many people operate on the assumption that postures are the be all and end all of Yoga; so, I must stress that, while *Asana* improves the health of every bodily system and bolsters concentration and induces relaxation, it is not an end in itself, only a catalyst.

"This misconception seems to stem from the effectiveness of an *Asana* practice. While *Asana* engenders the development of the individual practitioner's ideal body form, much like the Greek golden section and golden mean, or Leonardo's Vitruvian Man, there is a danger in over-emphasizing this result. This is not just a problem for individuals. There are schools of Yoga that seem to lose themselves in this aspect as well, forming attachments to that which is, ultimately, transitory. So, remember, the practice of *Asana* is a steppingstone to super-consciousness and transcendence, and not the end in itself."

---

[37] Michael comments, "This can be dangerous if one is not guided by a guru. I am aware of persons who, without the structure of Yoga and without a teacher, have gone crazy simply by modifying their normal dexterity, from right-handedness to left-handedness. Yet, the rewards can be great. Clearly Leonardo's mastery of the bicameral brain—two dominant sides, ability to write forward, backward, and mirror with either hand, and world class talent in both science and art—shows the potential for personal experimentation and human evolution."

"Why are there so many different postures to practice? Are we supposed to master all of these?" Chimera asks.

"I didn't mean to overwhelm you with examples,[38] but I wanted to give you an indication of how the spectrum of Yoga postures is systematically designed for the entirety of the body. The postures work much like acupuncture or Shiatsu.[39] There are paths that run through the body, what we call meridians in English, or what the yogis call *nadis*, which carry *prana* between the central nervous system and the various organs. Along these meridians are points that can be stimulated to balance the flow of this life-force. Likewise, the organs, glands, and circulatory system can be stimulated by physical manipulation through *Asana*. Over the course of long-term practice, *Asana* works on all of these aspects of the body, in concert with dietary, breath, and mental practices, to improve health and stimulate consciousness at every level. There are many more postures than what I sent you, but these represent a basic, well-rounded routine that provides a foundation for householders to continue their study of the other levels of Yoga, the next being the breathing practices—*Pranayama*."

"Why the breath?" I ask.

"I asked Michael the same question when I went to him about starting Yoga," Diane says, "and he told me I had to quit smoking before he'd teach me Yoga. It's a vibrational thing. I can see that now."

"Breath is life itself," says Michael. "That which ceases to breathe dies. To a large degree, how we respire determines our consciousness. It's no coincidence that the root meaning of 'spirit' is tied to breath and respiration.[40] By consciously manipulating the patterns of our inhalation, retention, and exhalation of air, we may advance our spiritual progress. In my own practice, I have found that the use of *Pranayama* together with *Asana* can result in infusions of *prana* capable of creating states of

---

[38] Again, *Appendix 3 – Introduction to Yoga*.
[39] A Japanese massage therapy technique that focuses on the same points that are used in acupuncture.
[40] **Spir·it**   ORIGIN   Middle English: from Anglo-Norman French, from Latin *spiritus* 'breath, spirit,' from *spirare* 'breathe.' *The New Oxford American Dictionary*, ed. Elizabeth J. Jewell and Frank Abate, Oxford University Press, 2001, p. 1644.

magnetism, what I call polarization, which imitate zero-gravity and weightlessness."

> *I slept at the Yoga center last evening and awoke early. For my morning practice I decide to try something new—performing rigorous* Pranayama *while practicing my* Asanas. *I move easily through my routine, breathing deeply with barely a thought interrupting the flow of the routine. When I come to the inverted postures, which I normally practice as a headstand with variations, I decide to substitute a handstand, which I've never tried before. I bend over and place my hands on the ground and begin to shift my weight onto my arms. All of a sudden, my legs magically lift up into the air, requiring no effort on my part, as if I am magnetically aligned with the Earth's core. Later, that evening, still keenly aware of my breath, I dream of walking on water, across the Sea of Galilee, to save my friends in their foundering ship—my elevated life-force overcoming the laws of gravity and other limitations of the material plane.*

"That seems a remarkable claim for something so simple," I declare.

"It only shows the degree to which most of us are unconscious of the details of our actions. For example, consider the common, everyday advice of 'take a deep breath and count to ten' before responding to something that causes anxiety or anger within us. This suggestion is well-grounded in practice. Normally, our biological heritage as human beings favors instinctive responses when we are threatened—the so-called 'fight or flight' syndrome. For men especially, this produces a volatile mix of testosterone and adrenaline that often leads to violence. Deep breaths are a first defense against such behavior. *Pranayama*, the science of breath, takes these practices much further: Breath-control is intricately tied to the successful implementation of all stages of Yoga, from the ethical standards one chooses in *Yama* and *Niyama* to the unfolding of physical health in *Asana*, and from the liberation from sensory domination in *Pratyahara* to the final spiritual frontiers of *Dharana*, *Dhyana*, and *Samadhi*. By learning to control the breath, we not only gain a measure of control over the instincts and ego of our lower nature, but stimulate the unfolding of our higher selves as well."

"So you're saying that breathing techniques help us deal with material and sensory desires and mental blocks?" Chimera asks.

"Yes. Breathing is central to each waking moment of our life. It helps us take what we learn from just-sitting, *Zazen*, and bring it to our present actions—flower arranging, tea ceremony, calligraphy, gardening, or the bow[41]—what we've termed 'applied meditation.' By becoming conscious of our breathing, we affect the manner in which *prana*, the life-force, flows through us, which in turn is a catalyst to yogic transformation."

"This seems obscure to me," I say. "I don't understand the connection."

"What I mean by this, Rashan, is that once the breathing techniques practiced in *Pranayama* have been internalized, we come to understand that the eternal in us is neither our body nor our breath. Then we are ready for *Pratyahara*, where we move beyond identification with our senses, detaching from them as well. Following that, our consciousness is ready to expand into states beyond the physical instincts, and beyond the subconscious emotional and psychological desires of our lower self.

"So, as each succeeding yogic practice takes hold within us, a different level of awareness is accessed and remains with us even when we are not practicing *per se*. Gradually, the clarity of the states we achieve during practice become more conscious in our everyday life, as if through spiritual osmosis. In this way, we become more loving and generous with others, and the world is—one person and one act at a time—transformed toward the perfection—the Anomaly, G-d principle, Supreme Being—that we all share at our core."

"Okay, this description makes sense to me, but I still don't understand the mechanics. What does the practice of *Pratyahara* look like?"

"Think of the eight limbs of Yoga as different, yet cumulative, forms of meditation, with *Yama* and *Niyama* involving a conscious evaluation of one's past, present, and future self, followed by active meditations involving our physical state, *Asana*, and our breath, *Pranayama*. *Pratyahara* is a stage of meditation in which we withdraw from the body and its senses. From the outside it looks as if certain forms of *Asana* and *Pranayama* are

---

[41] Zen archery.

being employed, which they are, just as are the accumulated effects of *Yama* and *Niyama*, but to these we have added a new practice in which we voluntarily leave the world of physical awareness. If the groundwork has been properly laid through a concerted effort in the previous stages, then *Pratyahara* is achieved."

"It sounds like the beginning of meditation." Chimera says.

"That's one way of looking at it—as a meditation within and without the senses, although, as I just said, all the yogic stages before this can be seen as simple forms of meditation as well. However, only when *Pratyahara* is achieved—that is, when the first five stages of Yoga have been reasonably mastered—do we truly leave behind the realm of the body and senses, and the physical plane, and turn inward to the mind and begin our transcendental work."

"I can tell you," says Diane, "this is a tough test. My senses are so used to high levels of excitation, I hear them screaming, 'See me, touch me, feel me!'"[42]

"Heal me!" says Michael. "That's what *Pratyahara* does."

"Explain then, the final three stages of Yoga," I say, feeling that Michael's Sybillic[43] read-out has subsumed *Pratyahara*.

"It will become increasingly clear," says Michael, "as I give you an overview of the final three stages of Yoga, that the language I use to describe the experiences on these planes is abstract. This is necessarily so, because our perceptions of everyday reality are not applicable to higher, spiritualized states. The obvious explanation for this is that everyday experience is largely about the dualistic nature of the material plane. For example, many of us worship, pray, and express our faith during certain times of the day or week or year, but the rest of the time we act as if these precepts did not apply, treating our fellow humans with insensitivity or even violence. In a dualistic world, we accept 'good' and 'evil' living side

---

[42] From "See Me," The Who, on the album *Tommy*, 1969.
[43] A word derived from Sybil (after Sybil Leek), which, as mentioned earlier, is a type of medium that "reads" from the database of an individual or the Akashic Records (that is, all that was, is, and will be written into the fabric of the universe). For more information on the Akashic Records, see Levi Dowling, *The Aquarian Gospel of Jesus the Christ*, DeVorss & Co., Santa Monica, CA, 1972 (first published in 1907).

by side, as if they were equals; we see our choices as either/or, good or evil, black or white.

"We see no incongruity paying lip service to the teachings of Jesus or Mohammed or Moses or Krishna on the one hand, and then, on the other, turning around and supporting wars, carrying guns, killing human beings, and concentrating on material accumulation—while providing little love and charity for the poor, downtrodden, and less fortunate.

"But when you choose to undertake a life devoted to self-reflection, meditation, love, and compassion, then your capacity to maintain such hypocritical behavior wanes.[44] Transcendent states provide direct experience of the unity of all things and the eternal nature of the unchanging One-Without-A-Name, the Great Anomaly, the source of all change. In experiencing these states, we pass beyond words—which are by their very nature dualistic, distinguishing *this* from *that*—to an inclusive world of 'both/and,' in which all things are connected and 'Truth is paradox.' To describe these unified states using words, then, is like using mathematics to describe music—you get the theoretical idea, but not the experience itself."

"There's no way around this vagueness?" Chimera wonders.

"Not entirely," says Michael. "As I mentioned earlier, all the great prophets basically have the same transcendent experience, yet they each end up describing it in different words. These differences lead many of their followers to believe that their religion or belief system is superior to all others. This is blasphemy, as if the One-Without-A-Name, the Great Anomaly, is somehow less than the sum of all the parts of the universe.

"However, as I've said, enough data has been generated today to permit the integration of knowledge across what, mistakenly and for some time, have been considered separate disciplines; as a result, we're able to offer a perspective in which seemingly disparate religions, sciences, and other belief systems are seen as part of a greater, and more ancient, over-arching spiritual teaching that had been lost to us through natural and historical cataclysms."

"Michael, I have to stop you in order to digest this string of concepts."

---

[44] "The sole cause of man's unhappiness is that he does not know how to stay quietly in his room." --Blaise Pascal, *Pensees*, 1670.

"Sure."

"What you're saying is that while using words to describe transcendental states has inherent limitations, at this point in time you have certain tools at your disposal that allow you to communicate a more universal message regarding the meaning of such experiences?"

"Yes, and we've also tried to indicate in the text of our book, with footnotes and references, that many of the ideas which I'm promulgating have been synthesized from others' work. These cumulative perspectives, in turn, will lead to insights by others that will advance consciousness in ways currently unforeseen. 'He that believeth on me, the works that I do shall he do also; and greater works than these shall he do ...'"[45]

"So Jesus' teachings, too, would need to be more sophisticated this time around than the last time?" Chimera asks.

I can't help but notice the implication of her statement: that Michael's teachings represent this update. This, of course, plays right into his hands, and my anxieties are immediately aroused. I know I'm being tested here on two counts—the nature of Michael's spiritual mission and Chimera's connection to it.

"Yes, though technically it's the Messiah's or Christ's teachings—" Michael replies, "that is, a spiritual presence, not a personage, transmitted through different incarnations in space-time. While people may look to a biological and spiritual lineage, the present World Teacher's calling card is his ability to synthesize vast amounts of contemporary information with the original timeless message."

"And how is the teaching of Yoga related to this purpose, Michael?" I ask, hoping to sidestep a discussion of the anointment question.

"You've often remarked at the extended conceptual nature of my thoughts," Michael says. "And while I was blessed with this capacity by the One-Without-A-Name, the Great Anomaly, it's been enhanced by the practice of Yoga, particularly by the meditative disciplines of *Dharana*, *Dhyana*, and *Samadhi*. These final stages of Yoga, which roughly translate as concentration, contemplation, and transcendence, are really different degrees of the same practice known as *Samyama*, in which the practitioner gradually frees herself or himself from mental distractions until these interruptions disappear altogether and the object of concentration and

---

[45] John 14:12

contemplation becomes one with the subject—thus transcending the duality of this plane and self-consciousness itself, dissolving into the undifferentiated Oneness of Being.

"As we've talked about before, the *Yoga Sutras* posit that enlightened beings can manifest the truth of such transcendental states in conversation. My words, then, are an indication of both how this process works, as well as proof that this process, in my case a meditation on Messiah or Christ consciousness, has in fact succeeded. The practice and teaching of Yoga, then, is integral to my ability to represent, define, and fulfill my mission."

"Michael," Diane says, "I understand what you're saying here, that through Yoga your meditation on higher consciousness has brought forth a state of being in which you act as a vehicle for a powerful message, but it sounds egotistical."

"Rashan and I have talked about this," Michael says to her. "In a personal conversation like this, between friends, I understand that it can feel out of place, but it's not about ego—it's simply the dynamics of Messiah or Christ consciousness expressed through the vocabulary garnered by the current spiritual anomaly.

"We've talked about an artist's vocabulary before," Chimera says, "but the context was painting, not Yoga."

> *The acid is beginning to take effect, but while my collegiate friends are out in the living room of our home—The Magic Theatre*[46]*—enjoying "the retinal circus"*[47] *and other non-verbal states, I am at my desk, my diary open, planting words at the frontier of consciousness. What power these words shall have when they are rooted to my instinctive mind and primitive brainstem, rather than in the shallow strata of frontal lobe ego-illusion. These are seed-*

---

[46] A term Michael and his friends borrowed from Hermann Hesse's book, *Steppenwolf*, Modern Library, 1963, describing a physical location in the book that metaphorically represents a stage of awareness which follows the ingestion (smoking) of cannabis.

[47] A term Michael borrowed from *The Psychedelic Experience*, by Timothy Leary, Ralph Metzner and Richard Alpert (later Baba Ram Dass), and Karma-Glin-Pa Bar do, University Books, New York, 1964, that describes the visual synesthesia which follows the ingestion of psychotropic herbs and compounds.

> *inklings that shall germinate, thrive, and ripen into a cornucopia of conceptual truth which I shall harvest and propagate—food for thought in which souls shall find sustenance and be made anew.*

"As we've discussed, there are many ways for each of us to celebrate his or her unique gifts. But whatever we choose, our success at communicating these gifts is enhanced by learning to use the tools of our art at the point within us where self-consciousness evaporates and being is coincident with everything that ever was, is, or will be. This is the Anomaly of the soul, the innermost point at which the Torus of the mind-body-spirit, spirally folding in upon itself, coincides with the window to other dimensions and the indefinable One itself."

"How are we supposed to do that?" Chimera asks.

"As I said to Rashan earlier in reference to playwriting, this is something that you're already doing when you paint, just as it happens with Diane on stage. The closer each of us gets to our true or higher self, the greater clarity, honesty, and insight that manifests in our being and in our work. Our aim here is simply to increase the incidence of self-actualization[48] in humankind."

"This reminds me of something," Chimera says.

"Tell us," says Diane.

"Well, sometimes I enter my studio to do something entirely different from painting, say just to fetch something I've left there, and hours later I find myself standing at my easel in front of a picture I have no memory of."

"That's a great example," Michael says. "Afterwards, how do you feel about what transpired?"

"What takes place is an answer to my requests," Chimera says. "I'm constantly sketching, doing 'scales,' sharpening my skills. So, when the spirit moves me, I'm prepared to serve as a worthy vehicle for it. I'm always amazed. I look at the work and see technique and style I've never seen before. I don't know how it happens; then, I'm exhausted, as if I've just given birth."

---

[48] Self-actualization – A concept popularized by Abraham Maslow. In particular, see *Toward a Psychology of Being*, Second Edition, Van Nostrand Reinhold Company, New York, 1968, p. 97.

"That's precisely what I'm describing for yogis in developing 'the availability of a vocabulary' during *Dharana* and *Dhyana*—tools through which the spirit speaks."

"So, if as you say, the practitioner achieves this availability of vocabulary through concentration and contemplation, then what happens during *Samadhi*?" I ask.

"Like *Dharana* and *Dhyana*, *Samadhi* draws fine distinctions between states of consciousness. These distinctions become increasingly more subtle as your consciousness evolves, particularly as it approaches the Anomaly. Because I regard this as the holiest experience, and because I believe it is indefinable, I'm wary of describing it. To paraphrase Buddha, it is not 'white light,' which is a neurological phenomenon, because 'it' can be nothing in particular since it the sum of all things. This goes along with a corollary of one of the postulates I gave you many years ago: Nothing is black or white; *In nothing is everything contained.*"[49] We can only say that it is the source of what we've been, what we are, and what we're becoming—all coexistent in the now."

"So after the yogi has achieved *Samadhi* and the 'transcendence of self-consciousness, as you describe it, you're saying that it's his or her responsibility is to share their experience?" I ask.

"Yes. Sharing. The meditative practices and states of consciousness availed through *Samadhi* are the most sublime in the entirety of the science of Yoga. There is no rushing this attainment. The message or assignment that we receive as a result of achieving 'enlightenment' or, fill-in-the-blank—Christ-, Buddha-, Krishna- or Cosmic-Consciousness—differs from individual to individual, but like all spiritual pursuits, when the lower self has been subsumed and enveloped by the whole, the focus turns outward, toward service. How this gift is to be shared is not for me to say, but for each of us to discover for ourself."

It seems as if Michael has given us a stimulating and cohesive overview of the practice of Yoga based on the discipline's own terms—a nice companion to his Yoga handout[50]—but I realize that this will not seem sufficient for many people reading this account. His brevity, however, should not be confused with incompleteness. I may express impatience at

---

[49] See "Descartes," in *Appendix 7 – Michael's Notes*.
[50] See *Appendix 3 – Introduction to Yoga*.

Michael's encyclopedic recitations, but it's clear to me that his depth lies not only in the detail of his expertise in certain key subjects, but in the breadth of his thinking as well. Now, I can see what he means when he says that one of the keys to "proving" his case is his ability to describe phenomena in an interdisciplinary fashion, synthesizing concepts from disparate fields into a cohesive, organic, and universally cross-referenced codex. That's how I understand the free-associative improvisational revelations he likens to Qabalah, *Jnana* Yoga, and *The Glass-Bead Game*. It is as if he is skipping stones on the ocean of truth. Each path is unique, graceful, and true to the initiator, the moment, and the intrinsic shape of the idea itself. So, with the tape recorder rolling, I take a deep breath and call upon the genie to deliver one more of his inimitable explanations.

"Michael, that was an eloquent recapitulation of Yoga in spiritual terms, but I've also heard you describe the evolution of consciousness in psychological terms. In fact, this goes back to when we first met. So, for our readers whose vocabularies are less inclined toward the spiritual, and who prefer a 'scientific' point-of-view, how would you describe the Yogic process?"

"As you say, Rashan, we can also use psychological terminology, particularly the language of Carl Jung, to see the yogic process as a journey of integration and selfhood. In the essay that I recommended to you when we met, *Christ, a Symbol of the Self*, Jung begins with examples from the Christian *Bible* that make it quite clear, using his terminology, that Christ exemplifies the archetype of the Self. By this Jung means that Jesus' enlightenment and anointment as Messiah, or his ascendancy to the office of Christ, that is, his becoming the Avatar of the age, provides us with an example of complete psychological integration—the Divine Syzygy, as Jung calls it—Jesus' marriage within himself of the masculine and feminine, *animus* and *anima*, and higher and lower selves.

"To take this example further, Jesus' use of bread and wine as Eucharistic catalysts for his body and his blood fit Jung's observation that psychological health and fulfillment is facilitated by the use of 'symbols of integration.' Following Jung's lead, then, if we use Jesus' state, Messiah or Christ consciousness, as a model for individual psychological development,[51] then a number of fundamental principles become clear.

---

[51] Individuation.

"First, psychology regularly fails to produce happy, healed patients because it generally does not include a spiritual component as a control against which behavior is measured. Instead, progress is measured against whether patients 'fit in' after their therapy has run its course, as if the standards dictated by the commercial marketplace, being nothing more than the worship of Mammon, constitute a legitimate and defensible measurement for human development. Yet, those beings we most revere for their courage and enlightenment are hardly a group of people that 'fit in' with society and such profane standards. So, let's be clear as we discuss the psychological basis for human evolution that we are not talking about 'normalcy,' but rather 'attainment.'

"In the East, there are longstanding beliefs that individuals come into this world with karma, or, simply put, behavior and fate based upon past actions. Similarly, in the West, psychology generally recognizes that individuals bring certain hereditary traits into this world, which begin with genetics, but have physical, emotional, and mental components. The bearers of these predispositions are then subjected to environmentally-induced experiences that begin to shape their personality and their interior emotional landscape. As is almost always the case, some of these experiences create impressions of such lasting negativity that neurotic, and sometimes psychotic, behaviors result. When individuals recognize the undesirable nature of these patterns within themselves, they often choose a practice, either psychological or spiritual, that will help them overcome these limitations.

"So, second, following the necessary realization that psychology must have a spiritual component, the individual begins her or his journey by undertaking a practice, such as we discussed with *Yama* and *Niyama*. In our psychological paradigm, what we call the archetype of the Self—Messiah or Christ consciousness in the spiritual paradigm—informs us that these goals are more than just reducing one's pain and minimizing dysfunctional behavior, but necessarily include the manifestation of inspired and compassionate actions.

"Next, we must explain, in psychological terms, the yogic process for ridding ourselves of the negative repercussions of hereditary and environmental experiences that have accumulated in our psyches. In the West, many of the behaviors categorized as neurotic are rooted in what psychology calls repressions. These are usually memories that the conscious mind has buried in order to escape from their painful nature. Even when repressions become conscious they continue to function negatively, behaving like looping audiotapes that play over and over again, preying on the psyche, draining valuable energy. So, in psychological terms, the third object of Yoga is to transform these repressions into conscious memory, where they can be experienced, recognized, counterbalanced, and neutralized by auto-suggestion and self-induced behavioral modification. From there, these repressions cum conscious memory are transformed into accessible memory, where they can be accessed or ignored at will. To use a cybernetic metaphor, the object in this stage of psychological transformation is to migrate the repression from the main operating system, where it is constantly affecting performance, to a document folder from where we have a conscious choice of either activating it to RAM[52] for temporary referencing and updating, or ignoring it.

"At each of its stages, the process of Yoga directly focuses on psychological repressions, first, as we have already discussed, by addressing the ethical principles upon which the practitioner's behavior is based. I stress this because—given the powerful nature of the transformation that is activated by a concentrated Yoga practice—it's imperative that the yogi uses his or her powers for spiritual purposes. In the latter stages of Yoga, as the level of *prana* is raised through the *chakras*[53] by *Asana* and *Pranayama*, and then concentrated through *Pratyahara* and *Dharana*, repressions are addressed at the physical level, when powerful streams of energy released from the nervous system and spinal column are channeled through the mind to directly activate repressions located in close physical proximity to the path that is being drilled, laser-like, through the center of the brain toward 'The Third Eye.'

"As this stream of *kundalini*[54] makes its way through the mind's storehouse of life experiences, the process of clearing accelerates, eventually

---

[52] Random-Access Memory.
[53] In Eastern medicine, seven concentrated energy centers or vortices that emanate from the nervous system—including the spine, the *hara*, and the brain—from the tailbone to the crown of the head.
[54] As mentioned, *kundalini* (from Sanskrit) is "the latent power within" or coiled serpent that resides at the base of the spine. In a toroidal model, this is the manifestation of the anomalistic force that animates creation in all its manifestations.

leading through the 'The Dark Night of the Soul'[55] to a clear channel of being and rebirth—a birth in which the practitioner is conscious and gets to choose, or re-design, the thoughts which surround this replication of pure being that is re-awakening within her or his self.

"So, the fourth principle that follows from adding a spiritual dimension to psychology, and using the Messiah or Christ (or Buddha or Krishna, etc.) symbol of self as its paradigm, is that practitioners choose an inspirational environment (where they are and what they have) with which to surround this new unimpeded flow of the force that dwells within them. While the nature of this inspirational environment is a matter of choice on the practitioners' part, it is a choice that is inextricably related to the goals that they have chosen at the start of their therapy (*Yama* and *Niyama*). If their goal is to achieve Messiah or Christ consciousness, their choices will necessarily be different than if their goal is to achieve some other exemplary state, say that of a master painter, actor, or playwright. The choices made at this stage, then, are less universal than those which preceded it, because they refer to unique, individual development, that is, the personal application of source energy—though the underlying dynamic by which psycho-spiritual rebirth and self-integration are achieved remains the same for everyone.

"And finally, it is important to note that when this psychological state of integration is achieved, it is the one and the same state that the meditative arts call attainment or enlightenment; integrating one's self is the same as being at one with the All; they are just different ways of looking at the same thing or dissecting the same universe."

"That was quite a treatment on the parallels between spiritual practice and psychological integration," I say, feeling that we had reached the end of the readout. "It almost seemed like a syllabus for courseware: The Psycho-Spiritual Journey."

"Thanks, Rashan. It is part of the curriculum I'm putting together."

"You're planning courseware?"

"I'm just in the elementary stages. The technology necessary to accomplish what I have in mind isn't here yet, but we've got about twenty years before we'll need it. By then, worldwide communications will be light years beyond our simple networks."

---

[55] A reference to the verses of St. John of the Cross (1542-1591).

☼ ☼ ☼

After Michael and Diane leave, Chimera and I look at each other with eyebrows raised.

"I see what you mean," Chimera says. "Sometimes his intellect transcends thinking. If he were a politician, I'd say his Teflon coating makes Reagan look like a scouring pad."[56]

"Are you saying he's putting something over on us?" I ask, unsure of where Chimera's going.

"No, only that it's hard to find a weak spot."

"He's efficient at dispersing the red flags as they pop up," I agree, "except for the subject of celibacy."

"That does seem to be a sticking point with you, Rashan."

I couldn't tell whether Chimera was being serious or just punning.

"And not with you?" I ask.

---

[56] Michael notes in 2005: During his presidency, Ronald Reagan was called "the Teflon President," for his slipperiness at escaping implication and prosecution for the many scandals that plagued his term in office, including treason (for negotiating with Iran on the fate of American hostages before his election, handled by George H. W. Bush, V.P. to-be, and William Casey, Director of Central Intelligence to-be), drug trafficking, gun running, assassination (through support of the Contras in Nicaragua), and fraud (the rape of America's savings and loan industry). Only a few hands—including National Security Council officials John Poindexter and Lt. Col. Oliver North, and private operators Richard Secord and Albert Hakim (Iran-Contra) and then Vice President George Bush's son, Neal (savings and loan)—got slaps on their wrists for these actions. President George H.W. Bush later pardoned Defense Secretary Caspar Weinberger and five other guilty parties, calling them patriots. Given that the records from the Reagan and Bush I presidencies have been sealed by an Executive Order of Bush II, and given the millions of sheets of paper that each of these administrations shredded in the weeks before the end of their terms, it is unlikely that we will ever know the full extent of illegal and depraved acts for which these persons are responsible. Suffice it to say that there is substantial evidence to indicate that the usual suspects, including the Bush Crime Family, were in the middle of all this—claims which will be substantiated later in this work. It's no coincidence that at the end of September, 2001, the Bush II presidency issued an executive order extending the secrecy of presidential documents from past administrations, from a 12-year limit back to the beginning of the Reagan administration, 19 years prior. Even a cursory examination of this now-suppressed record is incriminating.

"I think Michael makes a valid argument about the sexual politics in relationships."

"You think we have a problem around sex? I thought everything was going pretty well between us?"

"Don't take this so personally, Rashan. I'm not saying that I don't love you or that I don't thoroughly enjoy making love with you."

"Then what are you saying?"

"Sometimes, when my demons get a hold of my soul, it's difficult for me to be there for you."

"So you think celibacy would solve this problem?"

"Maybe as short-term tactic now and then."

"Really! This seems so crazy!"

"After talking with Michael," she says, "about the need for meditation or some form of spiritual practice to deal with my demons, it seems like what he is really prescribing for me is a 'time-out' of sorts—for me to get a handle on the forces that are bringing me down."

"And that means me and our relationship?"

"Heavens no! But you know our relationship is affected by my bouts of depression."

"Okay," I replied, calming down a bit. I try taking a deep breath. "If something like this can help, then we should try it."

"Don't worry," Chimera says in a consoling voice, moving to put her arms around me. "Think of it as 'intermittent celibacy' within serial monogamy."

8

Dreams

"For false Christs and false prophets shall rise, and shall shew signs and wonders to seduce ..."
--Mark 13:22

"And the devil, taking him up into a high mountain, shewed unto him all the kingdoms of the world in a moment of time. And the devil said unto him, all this power will I give thee, and the glory of them: for that is delivered unto me; and to whomsoever I will, I give it. If thou therefore wilt worship me, all shall be thine. And Jesus answered and said unto him, Get thee behind me, Satan ..."
--Luke 4:5-8

"And before him shall be gathered all nations."
--Matthew 25:32

"The supreme revelation of G-d appears in prophets and holy men. To venerate them is true veneration of G-d. The will of G-d, as revealed through them, should be accepted in humility."
--Confucius, *The I Ching* or *Book of Changes*

As I understand Michael's description of *Yama* and *Niyama*—the ethical foundations of Yoga practice—they are supposed to be voluntary, but Chimera's decision to incorporate "intermittent celibacy" into our relationship is hardly that. Granted, I have agreed to it, and, yes, her case for needing to get a handle on her demons is persuasive, but this is not exactly what I had in mind when she and I talked about taking up Yoga.

Nevertheless, I persevere. At first, my attempts to outline a set of *Yama* and *Niyama* for myself are frustrating, as I am unclear about what I want from my practice of Yoga. Certainly Michael's achievements, derived as they are from the ethics and observances he set for himself, make a compelling case for taking the benefits of such a practice seriously. But what should the results look like in my own life?

I find my answer to this question in Michael's focus on our inherited evolutionary instincts as the key obstacle to human evolution at this time. My own emotional life is witness to the truth of this notion. While I would never characterize myself as an angry person, there are events that trigger aggressive responses within me. Sometimes these are as common as being unable to find my tools after Chimera has used them, or having to deal with a messy room that should have been cleaned up. Even getting cut off in traffic, finding a mistake in an audit footnote, flubbing a chip shot during a golf match, or an actor missing a cue can send me off. These situations have little or no meaning relative to the big picture of my life and my work, yet there I am turning sour or cursing a blue streak or otherwise signaling my displeasure over what has transpired.

I take these incidents as indications of a gap between my higher self, that knows better than to identify with or enable these behaviors, and my lower self, which finds these knee-jerk reactions perfectly natural and seemingly automatic. This glaring shortfall, between my innermost aspirations and my crudest displays, would be reason enough to begin a formal spiritual practice.

But as I begin to institute some of the practices that Michael has suggested, including simple postures, breathing techniques, and meditative exercises, my growing awareness of the daily thought patterns of my mind shocks me. Cultural prejudices that I so easily condemn in others appear to thrive just below the surface of my own mind. To what degree do I emotionally buy into racial or gender stereotyping, even if I know better than to act out these ingrained modalities? What is my response to the beggar that approaches me on the street or the wandering homeless with their shopping carts? It's obvious to me that I often recoil from such encounters before my compassion can be aroused to counter my socially-encouraged and instinctively-reinforced prejudices.

Months pass, but the nagging awareness of the conflict between my animal instincts and my conscience hangs on. This is not only a spiritual problem, as Michael has made me aware, it's a social and vocational problem as well. As I move up the organizational ladder of my Andersen accounting and consulting practice, I increasingly find myself in multicultural situations, in Denver, Chicago, Europe, and Asia. Even on a subconscious level, I tell myself, I can't afford to be uncomfortable about people different than myself.

That I still have these feelings is outrageous to me. Me, who looks like a *pied-noir*.[1] I now clearly see why Michael stresses the need for spiritual practices to overcome our instincts: What was once a means of survival is now, in most instances, a threat to survival.

It seems like a good time to call Michael, for despite my best efforts, I haven't been able to find a cure for my problem; besides, we haven't spoken in a while.

After commuting from his mountain home to KBAL's offices for a year and a half, Michael ended up moving his family from Wayne to Longmont to shorten the drive. He and Diane bought their first house there, and had their second child, a daughter. Recently, they've moved into their second home in that locale.

Michael and I ask Diane and Chimera if they'd join us for a Sunday brunch at Judith's restaurant, a well-appointed breakfast and lunch venue in a converted Victorian house with a pleasant patio under an arbor, just up the street from the post office in Longmont.

After we're seated, before we even order, Michael asks me what I think about Reagan's latest Supreme Court nominee's admission that he had smoked marijuana in his youth.[2]

---

[1] In French, literally "black foot," an Algerian-born Frenchman.
[2] On November 5th, 1987, Douglas Ginsberg [the replacement nominee for Robert Bork, who had been turned down by the Senate by the largest margin in history], admits that "once as a student in the 1960's and on a few occasions in the '70's," while he was a Harvard law professor, he smoked marijuana. He calls it a "mistake." On the following day, with Ginsburg's nomination in greater jeopardy than it had already been before these revelations, conservatives tried to downplay the admission. "He was not an addict," says President Reagan. "He was nothing of that kind." Ginsberg was eventually forced to withdraw his name. Thirteen years later, conservatives seem to have no problem with George W. Bush's prior addictions to alcohol and cocaine, yet the laws applied to those not born with Bush's special privileges are harsh. Bush served no jail time for his addictions, nor for any of his increasingly threatening transgressions, including going AWOL (his daddy's applied muscle and financial incentives having scrubbed the records almost clean), actively participating in insider-trading (again, during his daddy's presidency, the SEC was persuaded to desist prosecution, though the agency managed to do this without removing the charges), not to mention treason (his

I know I'm being baited by my friend, but Chimera bails me out.

"I don't see what this has to do with his qualifications to serve as a Justice," she says.

"Of course," Michael replies. "It shouldn't have anything to do with it, but given that this administration supports drug-running by the Contras and, at the same time promulgates the so-called 'War on Drugs' and the DARE program,[3] Ginsburg's admission provides a wonderful opportunity to illustrate the hypocrisy and criminal activities of those who have seized control of our government. Vice President Bush himself oversaw the contra operation,[4] and also sits as the head of the National Narcotics Border Interdiction System—they're all partners with the Mafia."[5]

"I don't think Reagan would allow that," I say, trying to stem Michael's conspiracy theories.

---

daddy and Cheney were in the White House on 9-11-2001), war crimes, and crimes against humanity.

[3] Michael writes in early 2005, "The DARE program was just another ploy in a cultural and generational war. No one can argue against preventing children from using substances for which they are physically and psychologically immature, but this crusade is only superficially about that. It was started by Nancy Reagan, a person with her own addictive issues, to solidify reactionary support for the abject imperialism and domestic economic rape that the conservatives were carrying out under her husband, a clueless figurehead (see following footnote) whom she and her cronies controlled. By bandying about the word *drugs* (at the same time that the CIA and war lords such as the Bushes were in the business of running drugs), they reduced the dialogue on this subject to gibberish."

[4] On January 20th, 1987, eight days after it is announced that George Bush's press secretary, Marlin Fitzwater, is replacing President Reagan's press secretary Larry Speakes, Vice President Bush says, President Reagan "is certain to this very day that he did not authorize arms-for-hostages," in *The New York Times* story, "Contra Arms Crew Said To Smuggle Drugs." This is after months of vacillation by Reagan, who confounded his handlers by claiming he knew, then forgot, then knew about the scam. This is a "President" who is unable to decide what he did and didn't know—who is detached from and disinterested in reality—and who could do nothing more than simply read what is put in front of him (see footnote #7). Bush's remarks represent a strategic move by the folks in charge to step forward and present plausible excuses for the administration's criminal behavior. "James Baker, a member of Reagan's cabinet at the time, stated, 'Bush is functioning much like a co-president.'"
(http://www.prisonplanet.com/analysis_lavello_041403_bush.html)

[5] See Brewton, Pete, *The Mafia, CIA and George Bush*, S.P.I. BOOKS/Shapolsky Publishers, New York, 1992, ISBN: 1561712035.

"Reagan!" he barks. "Let's face it, he was a good-looking jock and a B-movie actor, well known for his profanity, never better than a C student, who as president of the Screen Actors Guild worked for the FBI and rolled over for McCarthyism, helping to blackball many of his co-workers. He's just a front man, long-controlled by the Davis family[6] and now almost completely incompetent. He can't even read his script without stepping all over himself."[7]

"Michael," Diane says, "you'll scare the other diners."

"Okay, *no mas*," he says.[8] "Sorry, Rashan. The Reagan years haven't been easy on us," Michael says, picking up his tea.

I seize the opening. "So how's your new house?" I ask.

---

[6] The family of Nancy Davis, Reagan's second wife, racist ultra-conservatives from Orange County, California. She convinced Ronald to switch to the Republican Party.

[7] In 2003, Michael writes, "A *The New York Times Magazine* cover story (10/6/85) on *The Mind of the President*, quotes a White House aide as saying, 'You have to treat him as if you were the director and he was the actor, and you tell him what to say and what not to say, and only then does he say the right thing.' On 2/11/87, during testimony to the Tower Commission concerning the Iran-Contra scandal, President Reagan mistakenly reads his stage instructions aloud. In *Speaking Out: The Reagan Presidency from Inside the White House* (Scribner, 5/88), former Reagan press secretary Larry Speakes notes that preparing President Reagan for a press conference was 'like re-inventing the wheel.' In *Landslide: The Unmaking of the President: 1984–88* (Houghton Mifflin Co, 10/88), White House correspondents Jane Mayer and Doyle McManus, reveal that Reagan was so oblivious during the Iran-contra scandal that aides signed his initials to documents without his knowledge. An aide to Howard Baker says of Reagan's underlings, 'They told stories about how inattentive and inept the President was. ... They said he wouldn't come to work - all he wanted to do was to watch movies and television at the residence.' After the attempted assassination attempt by the son of a long-time Bush friend, one wonders whether his later diagnosed Alzheimer's disease had not set in during his term as President. Regardless, he was never calling the shots—the Bush Crime Family had been running things from early on, and G.H.W. Bush (presently the daily 'unofficial' advisor to G.W. Bush), John Poindexter (Pentagon's Total Information Awareness Office [2003]), Elliott Abrams (National Security Council [2003]), John Negroponte (Ambassador to the United Nations [2003]), and Henry Kissinger (9-11 investigation [2002 – resigned]), still have their fingers in it."

[8] "No mas!" (No more!)—the words of the once ferocious boxer Roberto Duran, one of only four men to have held four different world titles, signaling and end to his famous middleweight championship bout with Sugar Ray Leonard (11/25/80). The phrase remained popular for years.

"I'm enjoying the neighborhood," Diane says. "It's closer to the kids' schools."

"You must be doing okay at the TV station?" I ask Michael, curious about his economic survival as a radical in American society.

"The station doesn't pay a lot, but a friend of mine, a real estate agent, handled both transactions and saved us some money. We needed more space for the kids."

The idea that Michael, so often larger than life, is absorbed in such mundane activities of family life strikes me as uncharacteristically human. I wonder how he will maintain his aura of spirituality as a householder.

"It must be difficult, working for a non-profit and trying to plan for your family's future?"

"I can't worry about the money part," he says. "That doesn't mean I'm not upwardly mobile—you'll recall, when Black's 'neo-liberal authoritarianism' got to be too much at KBAL, I repackaged myself as a television journalist and got a better job at KRST—but that wasn't about money; it was about hands-on producing, writing, and directing at a major market PBS outlet. That it paid better was a benefit, but the move was about personal growth. As long as I'm doing what I'm supposed to be doing and paid reasonably for it, I have faith that things will work out."

"Still, it's hard to plan when you don't have any disposable income," I say.

"That's your mom talking," Chimera says. "Get a CPA degree while taking drama classes."

I laugh. "Yeah, well it seems to be working."

"I've got an old friend in Chicago," Michael says, "George Orloff, a lawyer and CPA, who handles the legal aspects of my humble estate."

"I'm glad to hear that," I say, "Financial independence is always important."

"As I said, Rashan, money can't be the motivating factor—'You can't serve God and mammon,'[9] and all that. I don't mean to insert myself in your personal issues, but it's as Chimera says—when you were growing up, your instincts around self-preservation were heightened by an emphasis on money. These types of subconscious values, what Freud called the superego, are reactionary, in all senses of the word. They're imprints of

---

[9] Matthew 6:24; Luke 16:13.

someone else's values—some good, some bad. They're not rational; they have nothing to do with your *raison d'être*."

I take a deep breath and begin to mull this over. "That may be," I say. "It seems that I'm struggling with multiple instincts. In fact, that's why I called you. Ever since I started doing Yoga, I've been hounded by the realization that I harbor a whole spectrum of prejudices against all sorts of people. I worry about how it could show up in my everyday activities, and what it reveals about my moral character."

"That's brave of you," says Diane.

"Yeah, or just practical," I say, surprised at my own self-deprecation. "You know, all those international clients."

"All of us suffer from what is often mislabeled as 'sinful' behavior," Michael says, "but this is nothing more than instinct and its vassal, the ego, holding sway. Remember when Jesus admonished those willing to condemn the adulterous woman, he said, 'He that is without sin among you, let him first cast a stone at her.'[10] If the greatest spiritual teachers among us can have their doubts and instinctive moments, and confess to these moments, then we are forgiven for having these struggles ourselves. This is one of the benefits in having spiritual anomalies to consider.[11]

"Jesus came as a pattern for us, and in doing so he gives us a way to forgive ourselves for having instinctive impulses that transgress our spiritual aspirations, for he himself overcame the same temptations on his way to anointment,[12] or Christhood. This is a natural part of being both human and divine, having a body evolved from the earth and a soul engendered by

---

[10] John 8:7. A more recent example would be the Dalai Lama's comment that "... sometimes I get angry at the Chinese." McNichols Arena, Denver, CO, June 1, 1997.

[11] Almost 15 years after Michael made this comment to me, I was pleased to find similar sentiments expressed by Yann Martel, in his popular novel, *Life of Pi*: "We must all pass through the garden of Gethsemane. If Christ played with doubt, so must we. If Christ spent an anguished night in prayer, if He burst out from the Cross, 'My God, my God, why have you forsaken me?' then surely we are also permitted doubt." (Harcourt, New York, 2001, p. 28) Michael writes in 2007: Gethsemane is a better example of self-doubt than the crucifixion. As we discussed earlier, Jesus' exclamation on the cross echoes Psalm 22, which is a confirmation of the power of the Lord (as one would expect of a spiritual anomaly [Messiah, Christ, etc.] at such a critical moment).

[12] Anointed, or the anointed one, is the English translation for the Hebrew word "Messiah."

heaven. So, take heart in this. Your sincerity in making even the most incremental adjustments will produce positive changes in your life. We all have the potential of attaining Messiah or Christ consciousness."

"Isn't that a bit of a stretch, Michael?" I implore. "I mean, it's one thing for someone like you, with your ethnic background and exceptional education, to successfully access the Messiah or Christ archetype and receive whatever inspiration and guidance you may, but that reality is so far from my own. I don't feel particularly capable of leading such a spiritual life."

"Amazing grace," Diane says. "It's there for the asking."

"The point is not about perfection," Michael says. "On this plane, we're all caught between our higher and lower selves, between Messiah or Christ consciousness, call it what you will, and our instinctive and ego-oriented patterns. No one escapes this dualistic quandary. There's no sin in this. It's all part of the human struggle and our evolutionary challenges. There's an integrated being inside of you that reflects your unique gift, and in that you are no different from me or anyone else—you must discover it like Michelangelo finding the perfect form of 'David' or the 'Pieta' in a block of marble."

That pretty much sums up the conversation, other than the small talk that followed. After all, how can you argue with Michael's conclusion? He can sure hammer it home when he wants to, which is quite often. Still, as many times as I've gone through this with him, I'm always surprised at the result. Apart from his political diatribes, I find myself amazed at how his words cut to the heart of the issue—in this case relieving my guilt over what I am discovering about my subconscious environment—and strengthen my resolve to free myself from the stranglehold that my reptilian and mammalian genetic heritage exerts upon my spirit. He's right: Why should I kick myself for instinctive reactions that are perfectly natural?

But what most excites me about Michael's pep talk is his suggestion that even the smallest victories in my struggle are likely to bring significant results. Given my present spiritually impoverished state, the belief that I can move a mountain is my only hope.

I am also just beginning to see the power that Michael possesses when he acts as a window for Jesus' teaching; and it's always curious which pieces of the Christian *Bible*, as he calls it, that he chooses to claim as his own and which he does not, given what he describes as the willfully disinformative translation and editing job that Roman sympathizers, Church revisionists, and anti-Semites have handed down to us. I can see that his real-time vocalization of these teachings is what he means by The Living Word: it is spoken for a particular time and place; and when the speaker is not present, or no longer lives in the flesh, we are left with the tyranny of The Written Word, a disconnected remnant inflexibly applied to situations incongruent to the original event.[13] This happens with every "ism" and philosophy, even in the theatre with errant adaptations of classical plays shoehorned to fit contemporary mind-sets; but when it happens to the words of a spiritual anomaly, the effect is particularly insidious. So again, Michael's insistence about getting to publish his own story jumps out at me.

☼ ☼ ☼

A year later, I'm at home writing. I've just returned from Chicago, where my firm, Arthur Andersen, held meetings concerning the just breaking Reagan-era savings and loan scandal.[14] While there, on Friday

---

[13] See William James' comment, from *The Varieties of Religious Experience*, in the *Invocation* to this book.

[14] Michael writes: The Savings and Loan scandal was the largest theft in world history up to this time, not including the continuous machinations of the Federal Reserve itself, until the staggering accounting and stock frauds and looting of the federal treasury of the Bush II era. According to
http://home1.gte.net/res0k62m/savings.htm#savings and http://www.inthe80s.com/sandl.shtml: The "government's" bailout cost the taxpayers around $1.4 trillion dollars. If the White House had stepped in and saved the S&L's in 1986 instead of delaying until after the 1988 elections, the cost might have been only $20 billion. But, it was a bipartisan theft, with both George Bush and Lloyd Bentsen (Michael Dukakis' running mate) keeping the scandal quiet until after the 1988 election, as they both were deeply involved. The S&L scandal was the worst in Texas, California, Colorado, and Florida, and it is no accident that George Bush II and Jeb Bush have been governors of Texas and Florida, while Neil operated in Colorado and Reagan was the California governor. The same people who figured so highly in the Iran-Contra Scandal—where proceeds from arms sales to Iran were used to send weapons to Contra insurgents in Nicaragua—were also laundering drug money through the S&Ls that were being looted in the president's back yard, by his buddies. In essence, what happened in the S&L scandal was that a gang of criminals, including the CIA, the Mafia, Washington politicians and others all participated in raping the nation's S&L industry, eagerly sidling up to the trough

afternoon at the end of a week of intense activity, the furious circle-the-wagons sessions finished early, and I had time to meet Michael's boyhood chum, George Orloff, for nine holes of golf at a public course not far from his house, and a short jaunt from O'Hare International Airport.

Orloff is on the putting green when I walk by on my way to the clubhouse. I recognize him immediately from his description in our brief telephone call—a strongly-built medium-frame hirsute fellow, whose beard and balding pate form a continuous, evenly cropped carpet of close bristles that circumscribe a pair of glasses and a smile.

I approach him as he hovers over a row of three balls perpendicular to a practice cup about five feet away. He waggles his putter, something I've never seen before.

He winces as his first effort hits the rim of the cup and skids two feet by.

"George," I say.

"Rashan!" Orloff says. "A pleasure to meet you. I've already talked to the starter. We can go off the back side whenever you're ready."

"Thanks," I reply. "What do I owe you?"

"Don't worry about it," he says, waving his hand. "If we beat the rush, we'll have you to the airport in plenty of time."

"Great! I'm ready to go."

"No warm ups?"

"Just a few practice swings and I'll be okay," I say. "I've got this psycho-kinetic routine; I can get ready with a visualization and a few stretches."

"Interesting," he says. "I've tried so many systems I don't know what I'm doing."

---

while it lasted. The criminal behavior engaged in by George H.W. Bush and friends was staggering, and for the most part they got off scot-free, using front men and plausible deniability (much of the denial was not that plausible) to dodge the worst of the charges. It was time to move on—they had fatter cattle to slaughter: the Carlyle Group had been formed and war profiteering and resource annexation, both domestic and foreign, was at the top of the agenda. The energy market deregulation/Enron scandal/accounting frauds and the mortgage deregulation and bank "bailout" were still to come.

"I've only been playing about ten years," I admit as we arrive on the tenth tee, ready to slip into a gap left by a foursome waiting for its lunch. "But I got hold of this tape and it's done wonders."

Orloff's swing is indeed a mishmash. On his tee shot, he starts walking before he makes contact and hits a sweeping hook into some trees alongside the driving range which parallels the 10th hole.

"Argh! Same old thing," he says, shaking his driver.

I hit my drive too low off the clubface and send a weak, fading line drive into the first cut of rough about 220 yards down the right side of the fairway.

Though I prefer to walk, I take up Orloff's offer of sharing his gas cart, so we can talk and get around quickly. I don't want to miss my flight.

"Have you ever played golf with Michael?" I ask, trying to get a feel for Orloff's non-stop personality.

"All the time when we were kids," he says. "Big Dad was always the best golfer. His dad was a great golfer."

"Big Dad?" Yet another variation on all these nicknames for Michael, I think.

"Yeah, The Dad," he says. "He was always bigger than everybody up until high school. When we played football in grammar school and junior high school, nobody could tackle him. We had to gang up on him, which wasn't easy. He was faster and stronger."

"What happened in high school?" I ask.

"His dad wouldn't let him play football. The track coach tried to recruit him for cross-country in the fall, because he had broken the city record in the quarter-mile by four and half seconds as an eighth grader, but he wasn't interested—played golf instead, and basketball in the winter."

"Sounds low-key for a good athlete," I say.

"I don't think he needed the glory," Orloff says looking at me as we arrive at his drive. Everything was easy for him: academics, sports, girls. You name it."

Orloff pulls out an eight iron from his bag and, staying down on this shot, manages to loft it over a small tree onto the fairway about a seventy-five yards in front of the green. I hit a good six-iron, right on line with the pin, but it falls just short of the green. As a high altitude golfer from Colorado, I forget to compensate for the effect of the dense air near sea level. By the time we're finished with our first hole, Orloff three-putts for a six and I miss a four-footer and take a bogey five.

The back nine at this course has a challenging finishing stretch, combining length, narrow tree-lined fairways, small well-bunkered greens, and a couple of water hazards. As we drive up the 18th hole, Orloff has long since given up keeping score, but we've become close friends, sharing concerns as CPAs, especially about the Savings and Loan scandal. Finally, the conversation comes around to Michael again.

"George, you've known Michael a lot longer than I have," I say. "What do you think of his story?"

"I don't know what's in the book," Orloff replies, "but Mike and I have talked about all sorts of things over the years—physics, politics, sports, and family stuff—and I can see that he's an anomaly, just like he says. He's always been successful. I think that's why he avoided a traditional career path—it would have been too easy, no challenge. You and I might fret over his financial security, or even solvency, but to him it's all karmic balance: He believes if he does the right thing, he'll be taken care of; and, on the flip side, if you have more money than you need, that's an issue. More power to him. He's the least stressed person I know."

Orloff's insights surprise me. For a type-A personality, he seems to be remarkably in tune with Michael's sensibilities. It makes me wonder what it has been like knowing Michael since childhood. What is it that Orloff is seeing which I'm not?

☼ ☼ ☼

One afternoon, some months later, I'm contemplating my current theatre work-in-progress—a large-scale public performance piece entitled *The Dream Catcher*. I had not been involved in a theatre project for quite some time, so I was excited when it fell in my lap. The idea had germinated with a friend of Chimera's, a Balinese dancer named Maya, who had a dream about Iktomi, the spider spirit who bestowed the dream catcher on the Ojibwa.[15] In the dream she had come upon a crying Iktomi who told

---

[15] A native North American tribe habituating lands spread across the Lake Superior region of present day Canada and the United States. The Ojibwa later shared the dream catcher with the Lakota.

her that he was aggrieved because no one believed in their dreams anymore. Maya's dream ended with a vow to help Iktomi restore people's faith in their dreams.

From knowing Michael, I have come to respect the power of dreams: after all, he stimulated my reading of Jungian psychology. I also have been captivated by his emphasis on the healing aspects of theatre, as a result of his repetitive paraphrasing of Maxwell Anderson's take on Aristotle—"The theatre is a religious institution dedicated entirely to the spiritual exaltation of humankind."—as well as his insistent citation of tribal rites as group therapy. The power of dreams and their application to theatre always seemed such a vague notion; now, I understand that dreams are primal consciousness, like innate tribal theatre rituals, which, when acted out, heal us individually and collectively.

These influences made it easy to envision the upside of Maya's project; so, after she told me about her dream, I began to research the dream catcher and explore the possibilities of building a theatrical spectacle around it. From what I had been told of Ojibwa and Lakota metaphysics, I understood that a dream catcher hung in the vicinity of one's bed filters out the bad dreams and let the good dreams pass through.

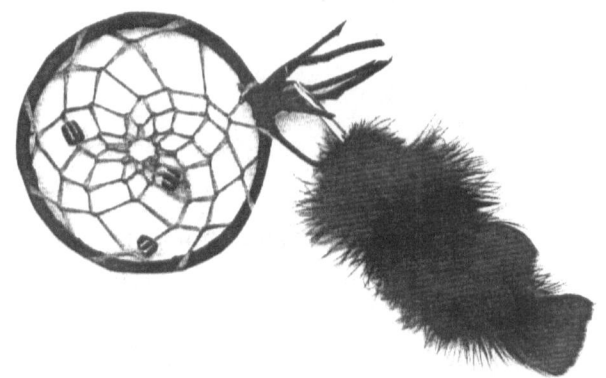

A dream catcher is comprised of a hoop within which is constructed a web, much like the spider's web upon which it is modeled. Attached to the web and the hoop are ritual objects, such as feathers or shells or stones, which represent the aspirations and beliefs of the individual or group that constructs each dream catcher.

I debate this interpretation of the dream catcher in my mind. Filtering out one's bad dreams could be problematic, for isn't one of the most significant lessons of religious fundamentalism that the more individuals or groups ignore their own shadow the greater their self-righteous ferocity in pointing fingers at others, accusing anyone who disagrees with them of "Satanism" or other "blasphemies"? Filtering only what we perceive as good about ourselves may, then, lead to ignorance of one's self, and blindness to our animal nature.

And from another perspective, isn't one of the objects of meditation essentially a mental alchemy within which we turn our negative thoughts into positive ones? I am reminded of Michael's dream in which he confronts an extreme negative force and dispels it by declaring, "I am Christ." Isn't this an example of a "bad" dream providing the conditions for the entrance of the light of Christ consciousness[16] into human form? Therefore, rather than something that "filters out" bad dreams, isn't the dream catcher a sophisticated metaphor for the spider and its web—representing a psychological function that snares our ephemeral dreams, both good and bad, suspending them in space-time so that we may fully digest their components and make them our own?

Regardless of the answers to these questions, when I began *The Dream Catcher* project I found the web in a hoop a worthy symbol of integration, as Jung would say. Rather than use it for personal work, though, as one might use a *mandala*,[17] my aim is to use the dream catcher for community integration. As my research proceeds, I discover that Australian aborigines also use dream catchers, leading me to envision a ritual involving indigenous peoples from all over the world. I see each of these unique tribes performing invocations from their own traditions, each inviting their version of G-d to manifest and join other faces of the deity in constructing a dream catcher that, in the interests of world spiritual cooperation, will act as a lens for focusing on Mother Earth's most pressing

---

[16] Michael writes: Again, you are invited to substitute your own name for what is referred to generically as Cosmic consciousness.
[17] Generally, a concentric series of spiritual symbols that represent the cosmos; a symbol of psychological unity.

needs. If this sounds like Michael is having a "New Age" influence on me, well so be it. Once I began to see the connection between theatre and dreams and healing, the logic of what Michael had been saying to me all these years suddenly awakened me to human potential. I may not be ready to join the revolution, but I certainly am ready to evolve.

At first, the project unfolds as if it is meant to be. The initial group includes two Lakota, one of whom I would describe as a contemporary medicine man; a woman who produces and directs large-scale celebrations (including work for the International Women's Conference in Beijing); a University of Colorado engineering professor (his father was one of the conceivers of "The Big Bang Theory"), who will design a large-scale modular dream catcher for the ceremony; Maya; and myself.

At our initial meeting, the medicine man performs a sage-burning ritual to purify our circle. Next, holding an eagle's wing, he describes his hopes for the group's direction; then he passes the wing, which makes its way around as each of us shares his or her goals. Finally, we each take a turn weaving a portion of the group dream catcher, incorporating some basic material that Maya has supplied along with a meaningful object each of us brought for this purpose.

As part of the massive production that we plan to stage in Sydney, Australia, I begin to outline the rituals that will be enacted at this event, including my vision of how these parallel indigenous mythologies and belief systems will be united in the final scene.

I also start spending more time with my Lakota friends. At first, these visits revolve around securing a letter from tribal elders that expresses interest in the project. The process of building trust between us advances one conversation at a time. At such an early stage in our relationship, the chasm between our vastly different cultures is a challenge. Alongside the timeless, acausal Algerian nomad harbored in my psyche is the European burgher accustomed to the cause-and-effect, time-is-money logic, upon which contemporary business plans are constructed. My Native American friends, though, are suspicious of this way of thinking. It is hard to predict which appointments they will choose to keep (according to the white man's clock) and which they will not.

Nevertheless, over a period of a few months, they come to accept of the need for a document that will formalize the commitment of their tribe to this project and help us with fundraising. There is talk of going up to the reservation in South Dakota to discuss such a letter, but before this happens I am invited to attend a sweat lodge.

A sweat lodge is considered one of the seven sacred rituals in Lakota culture,[18] so I take it as an honor to be included. I also surmise that it is a test of my mettle, though I admit that at the time I had not fully considered the meaning and repercussions of the use of such rituals to prove worthiness. I take it simply as a way of bonding.

It takes me a few passes in my car to find the site in Northwest Denver. Luckily, there is still light in the sky when I arrive. The neighborhood is decidedly mixed zoning, with industrial, commercial, and residential uses haphazardly thrown together, indicative that the area was once unincorporated county parcels where the land-use policies were lax. Along one side of the road, I pass a welding shop, a gas station, and intermittent cottages. A smattering of chickens along with a couple of horses—mixed in amongst the swing sets, camper tops, bird houses, chain link fences, and painted wagon wheels—enliven the scene.

About a dozen people, men and women, are gathered to participate in the lodge. While this commingling of the sexes is not a traditional practice, it is one that has become more accepted among certain contemporary medicine people.

The ceremony has been called to heal an acquaintance of the group who is suffering from a variety of physical afflictions that are assumed to reside in the spiritual body.

The rocks—"grandfathers" they call them—that will heat the lodge are almost ready, simmering in the fire which has burned down nearly to its

---

[18] Other major rituals include: The Vision Quest, Ghost Keeping (The Keeping of the Soul), the Sun Dance, Making Relatives, Puberty Ceremony, and Throwing the Ball (though this has been replaced in this century by Yuwibi, which unites concepts of buffalo hunting culture and contemporary reservation life (see, Powers, William K., "Lakota Religion," in Mircea Eliade, ed., *The Encyclopedia of Religion*, Macmillan Publishing Company, New York, 1987, pgs. 434-436). One could take this reintroduction of buffalo hunting culture as an indication that we have come full circle, back to the White Buffalo Woman who gave the Sacred Pipe (which is at the center of all these rituals) to the Lakota and whose reappearance, in the form of the white buffalo recently in Wisconsin (1994 in Janesville), indicates that the time is at hand when all the peoples shall be reunited by the Wanekia (Lakota for "Messiah").

embers. After a short introductory ritual in the yard, the initial alignment of grandfathers is placed, and we are invited into the lodge (framed in willow branches that are bent and covered, not with blankets or skins, but by a tarp) and seated at the leader's discretion. I am directed opposite the main door to the hottest spot, behind the grandfathers, at the back of the enclosure.

During the many rounds of prayer and chanting that take place, with occasional breaks for the addition of more grandfathers that are sprinkled with water to radiate and replenish the heat, it is all I can do to maintain consciousness. Every part of my body is wet with sweat. My newly initiated Yoga practice is certainly a help, though. By concentrating on my breathing and maintaining a minimal metabolism, I am able to lend some energy to the healing process and still have enough strength to sit up and transcend the searing atmosphere. At times, it is only my pride that keeps me upright. Occasionally, in-between rounds, the fellow sitting next to me lifts up the canvas behind us, and I greedily stick my head out into the cool night air and suck as much oxygen as I can. Then, the tarp comes down and new grandfathers are added; much like Camus' *The Myth of Sisyphus*, I fear I am trapped in a nightmare that never ends.[19] I imagine that my native friends are closely observing me to see how I am holding up. Intermittently, I cover my head with the towel I was given, to shield myself from the heat. The patient, who is sitting a couple of feet away—in front of me and to my left—coughs incessantly during the parts of the ceremony in which the leader gets particularly worked up. I try to visualize his illness escaping his chest through these fits, so that we can finish and I can get outside and breathe.

In the weeks that follow, I sense a small but significant change in the way I am accepted by the group. One evening, about six of us are sitting around the kitchen table at the medicine man's house, which had been the site of the sweat lodge. The discussion turns philosophical and in the

---

[19] Albert Camus was a French-Algerian writer, essayist, and playwright awarded the Nobel Prize for Literature in 1957 for his explorations of the philosophy of the absurd. Sisyphus was a mythological Greek figure forever condemned to roll a rock up to a mountaintop whereupon it would roll back to the bottom. *Le Mythe de Sisyphe* was originally published in 1942 by Librairie Gallimard. The English paperback version was published in 1955 by Vintage Books (Alfred A. Knopf, Inc.), New York.

context of discussing the project we stumble onto two subjects that change my entire perspective on the potential of what we are doing.

"Are you saying that you believe gay people are less than whole?" I ask, shocked by the offhand remarks of John Running Bear.

"In a way, yes," John continues with the other four Lakota nodding in agreement. "Their spirit is imbalanced. But it is something that can be healed."

Granted, most traditional cultures that I've had contact with have difficulty in dealing with this subject clearly. Much as Michael and I had discussed years earlier, the demands of survival had created the imperative for each member of a group or tribe to contribute progeny to aid in the tribe's proliferation and protection.

I can't help but being disturbed by the consequences of such beliefs. If all variations from physical "normalcy" represent spiritual disease, then what does our ultimate demise—dying—signify in each of us: death of our spirit? Surely, this view does not hold water. To someone like me, who has spent a good deal of time reconciling scientific research and spiritual perspectives on the subject of hetero- and homosexuality, not to mention my time in the theatre and all my gay friends, the idea that someone is spiritually damaged because of the way they were born is offensive, even if I understand how ignorant, hypocritical, and bigoted persons have come to hold such views.

Whatever circumstances may have led to someone's make-up, from a simple genetic roll of the dice to the number of brothers or sisters who were born before them to the stress of the mother during pregnancy to whatever psychological or physical experiences may have been incurred in childhood, these are all natural events in our world. Love and compassion demand acceptance of another's unique way of being, as long as it's peaceful and doesn't harm others. Isn't this the basis of Christ's and Buddha's teachings? But of course, fundamentalists of every stripe are such slaves to literal interpretations (of revised books or oral teachings promulgated by men and women of varying degrees of inspiration) that they cannot see the moral bankruptcy of their position.

It's not that these Lakota men are openly hostile toward homosexuals—or *winkte*, as they call them—only that they see them in an unhealthy condition, much like the ill "patient" at the sweat lodge I had attended. Much as the so-called Christian fundamentalist re-programmers, some of whom have gone so far as to say that "G-d hates gays," these Lakota make a mission out of changing gays to straights. There is a deep philosophical chasm here, between my newfound friends and me, that gnaws at my conscience. But I am in for more surprises.

"When we are born as men, we are meant not only to take wives and raise children, but also to fight. That is how one becomes a brave," William Sparrow patiently explains to me.

While I am familiar with the importance of rights of passage and "coming of age" in ancient cultures, when the subject turns to the taking of life as a necessary act in proving one's manhood, I balk. Yet, I seem to hear from my friends that this is a fact of life.

Leaving William Sparrow's house that night, I feel confused. Ever since coming to America as a college student, I have been fascinated by Native American culture. Now, it seems I have overly romanticized their worldview.

"That's a rude awakening," Chimera responds after hearing my story. "But you shouldn't be surprised."

"Why's that?"

"We live in an insular environment. What we take for granted in terms of human rights or spirituality is totally foreign to most of the world, even to the most of the United States."

"I just didn't expect such a macho attitude toward these things."

"This is no easy project you've chosen," she says. "You're likely to find the same attitudes in other indigenous groups. And most Caucasians are even worse."

Chimera's advice is disturbing, but honest. What am I getting myself into? I look forward to getting my guru's perspective on all of this.

A few weeks later, I meet Michael at a Nepalese restaurant facing the north side of the Boulder County Courthouse. He suggests I try the *saag* platter, a variety of delicacies in a heavenly creamed spinach sauce spiced with fresh garlic, cumin, and ginger. We both start with the *dal johl*, a lentil soup, and *roti*, a whole wheat bread baked in a *tandoor*[20] oven.

I tell him about my project and the difficulties I'm having.

---

[20] A clay oven, in this case heated by charcoal.

Michael smiles. "Despite what appears to you as 'Paleolithic artifacts,'" Michael begins, "your friends, the Lakota, and most Native Americans and other indigenous 'tribes,' understand my mission better than those whose culture has been subsumed by the so-called New World Order.

"Only those who share a vision of the harmony of Nature can see what's necessary for our world to survive. It's staggering to think that only 150 years ago vast tracks of land on this continent were roamed by human beings that lived in harmony with the cycles of the Earth, using only what they needed. Today, nearly all this wisdom has been wiped out by Europeans who, in the name of their capitalistic G-d—the Golden Calf—have lied, cheated, and murdered these noble people to near extinction. Now these prairies are crawling with gas-guzzling automobiles that wander over roads littered with trash, under the control of politicians who claim technology will save us, all the while proselytizing for their paltry Romanized degradation of 'Jesus.' No wonder Americans make little protest over the holocausts being perpetrated throughout the world: they continue to do the same things to the natives of this hemisphere—even those who know better, like so many here in Boulder. All these 'Free Tibet' bumper stickers make me wonder: Where are the ones that say 'Free Native America'?"

"So why is it," I ask Michael, "that when it comes to women, gays, and war, our native brothers are at such odds with our sensibilities?"

"Among any peoples there are always differences of opinion, and so it is with your friends, the Lakota. How could it be that the Great Spirit, *Wakan-Tanka*, sent the White Buffalo Woman to give Standing Hollow Horn the sacred pipe—the inextricable basis of all the holy rites of the Oglala Sioux—if somehow the female is not an equal partner in human wholeness? Do not these people believe that the Earth is their Grandmother and Mother as Heaven is their Grandfather and Father? Similarly, what you experienced is not an indication that traditional Lakota philosophy paints gays in a negative light. In fact, most tribes had special positions for those they called 'two-spirit people.' It was only after the white missionaries came, with their superficial and twisted views on human sexuality, that divisiveness over gender identity became an issue among Native Americans. So what you experienced with your friends is the same prejudice derived from the *Torah* from which most of the Judeo-Christian-

Islamic world suffers—a hangover from the days of the patriarchs, when each member of the tribe was expected to provide progeny to serve as soldiers against one's foes.[21] But these are only *temporal* truths based on the urgency of self-preservation. *Eternal* truths are much different. This is why, today, I find it necessary to marry psychology and science to metaphysics and spirituality—because *all* perspectives point to the same truth. In the wake of this synthesis,[22] each teaching shall, in its own way, make room for the unity and connectedness of all things, or risk obscurity in its disjunction from the whole.

"And as far as war and killing goes, Rashan, I don't believe the Lakota are much different than the rest of us. It was, for a time, perfectly natural and acceptable for our instinctive nature to act out in this life-preserving manner. Now, at this crossroads in human evolution, such knee-jerk responses run counter to our survival; now, we must develop spiritual practices that sublimate our instinctive and ego-based drives to our higher selves.

"The use of instincts having come full circle verifies its own truth. By this I mean that the paradoxical structure of the statement, 'The instincts that once preserved us in the jungle now threaten our survival' and 'The instincts that brought us success at killing now sustain our spiritual evolution,' intrinsically contain a higher truth. We've talked about before in regard to my precepts of 'Nothing is black or white; Truth is paradox;' and, 'The only constant is change.'

"The Lakota recognize this, though they, like others, may not always act upon it. As Black Elk said when explaining the use of black paint for the dance held when returning from fighting, 'By going on the warpath, we know that we have done something bad, and we wish to hide our faces from *Wakan-Tanka*.'[23] So, too, do the followers of Judaism, Christianity, and Islam claim to follow a tradition in which swords shall be beaten into plowshares and one shall love one's neighbor as one's self, and yet they

---

[21] A perfect current example of the carryover of this prejudice can be found in Joel Greenberg's article, "Gay parade irks old guard in Jerusalem," *The New York Times*, 6/8/02.
[22] *Appendix 6 – The Proof*.
[23] *The Sacred Pipe: Black Elk's Account of the Seven Rites of the Oglala Sioux*, recorded and edited by Joseph Epes Brown, University of Oklahoma Press, Norman, OK, 1989, p. 92.

accept and justify war through their temporal, materialistic belief systems. But whether the premise is Jihads, Crusades, Inquisitions, Pogroms, the War Path, or Holy Wars, these are all works against the unity of G-d."[24]

"So, what you're saying, Michael, is that the Lakota, like all these other groups to which you allude, will have to make some adjustment to their cosmology in order to accept your teachings?"

"Yes, to the degree that any belief system strays from love and compassion and the interconnectedness of all things, it will find itself out of balance and at odds with what is necessary for spiritual evolution at this time. Adapting to this new perspective shall not require much effort for the Lakota who practice the old ways. Their path resonates more fully with impending evolutionary imperatives than most. Certainly Native American prophesies regarding the coming Messiah[25] are an indication that they are willing to change doctrinal beliefs based on a new teaching. And witness their playful habit of counting coupe, which is an obvious indication that bravery and skill are ultimately valued over killing. Clearly, the most basic axioms of their culture are aligned with the sacredness of all life. So, the tenets of my teachings shall not be much of a change for anyone who believes that we are all brothers and sisters."[26]

"You seem to have a remarkable affinity for Native American culture," I say.

"Like I've said before, I am a member of a related tribe."

---

[24] Michael's discussion here, regarding how a tonic becomes a poison, and vice versa, reminds me of the Balinese, who possessed one of the most spiritually balanced cultures on earth before Europeans showed up in search of sugar. Yet, the Balinese continue to ritually eat sea turtles in their celebrations even though these animals are now threatened with extinction.

[25] The *Wanekia* (from the Lakota), literally "One who makes live." Indeed, in July of 1995, outside of Taos, Hopi and Navajo elders accepted the Rainbow Tribe as the prophetic 13th Native American tribe that would appear at the time of the great change.

[26] A similar point, concerning Islam, is made by Khalid Duran, author of *Children of Abraham: An Introduction to Islam for Jews* (KTAV Publishing House, 2001), who says that the social order of the Koran, though progressive for 7th century Arabia, "would have to be amended in order to meet present-day standard of human rights." Khalid has been threatened with a *fatwa* by Islamic fundamentalists, who would deny him the right to such evolutionary thoughts. This type of thinking perfectly illustrates where fundamentalism has abandoned the worship of G-d (the Great Anomaly) in favor of political terrorism.

"You mean like a Crazy Horse returned to lead the Ghost Dance?" I wonder aloud.

"Perhaps, but don't forget that Crazy Horse's life was taken from him by those who put words in his mouth. Let's pray that we have a different outcome this time. After all, I was raised in this culture and talk the white man's language."

Michael's concluding grimace startles me. I suddenly see his visage as a mask—well-tanned with his hair longer than when I first met him in short dreadlock-like curled formations—not as a white man with Semitic highlights, but as a chief of a new tribe—a blend of the races—the Rainbow tribe. The genie has indeed changed color; like the many faces of Hindu deities, he morphs into a spiritual chameleon that reflects the belief of the beholder.

"Given this perspective, then, what would you suggest regarding my project with the Lakota?"

"The idea of a ritual of integration involving the surviving native peoples is still a beautiful and powerful idea, Rashan, but the alignment needed to do this as a spiritual and political statement is not present at this moment. There is a great deal of mistrust that you and I, as white people—Semitic or Moorish as our roots may be—must work hard to overcome, and that will take time. I believe your friend Maya's dream is still that—a private vision. Given time, this will change, but I recommend against *The Dream Catcher* as a live public ritual. Save it for when it will draw more attention."

"Then what's to be done concerning the treatment of these indigenous peoples that I hoped to address?" I sense the desperation in my voice. Clearly this project served as a balm for my guilt over personal prejudices and those which ooze from the corporations that are served by my personal accounting work, my firm's practice, and, indeed, the accounting industry in general.

"A good question," Michael replies. "As I've said before, the major powers have all contributed to the destruction of the cultures and homelands of these people—Native Americans, Australian Aborigines, Canadian Eskimos, Tibetans, Balinese, and various Amazonian and African tribes. The list goes on and on. All this has been done under the deluded notions of Manifest Destiny and cultural 'superiority.' As I've discussed with you before, these forms of imperialism have also contributed to the destruction of regional eco-systems and natural agriculture. Yet this war—*Homo economus*[27] versus Paleolithic man—is only the surface of the problem. The core difference between these ancient cultures and the current powers revolve around the concept of property and sharing."

"I don't see it."

"Ignoring for the moment the historical data that was lost in the Flood and the burning of the libraries at Alexandria, we may deduce that property-oriented societies have their roots in Neolithic culture, where specialization changed the relationship of the individual to the group. Along with this advent of property, the male sex, based on size and strength, began to control these societies in ways that are generally unknown in Paleolithic cultures.[28] This specialization ultimately resulted in the frontal lobe, ego-based application of symbolic forms. The people raised under such conditions developed mutually reinforcing notions of private ownership and the primacy of the self—that is, a left-brained emphasis on individual cultivation over group development. Again, while we recognize the incredible gifts of information, technology, and leisure that have been generated by this adaptation, it must be said it is also the source of our most insidious behavior: materialism and the resulting ruination of our biosphere.

"Yet, there exist cultures that have survived down to our very time in which these notions of property do not exist; in which sharing is the rule. The idea that Europeans could make their way across the Americas and privatize land for themselves and their rulers was absolutely without reference to Native Americans and other indigenous groups, whose lifestyle depended on sharing their environment with other species. Today, there is hardly any place left where such a worldview survives.

"I might add that these same cultural contrasts are apparent in notions of time as well, with the heirs to Neolithic culture caught up in a world of cause and effect and the equation of time with money, while Paleolithic peoples place significance on the synchronicity[29] of events and

---

[27] Marx's term for industrial humankind, a prehistoric sub-species ruled by the anarchy of production and distribution.
[28] See Frederick Engels, *The Origin of the Family, Private Property and the State*, International Publishers, New York, 1969.
[29] Michael often refers to synchronistic events as "acausal" phenomena, an idea he borrowed from Carl Jung.

the accessibility of everything that ever was, is, and will be to our present consciousness. That's why, Rashan, my answer to your question about the prospects for indigenous peoples is for me to join with other spiritual leaders and ask the major powers and the United Nations to create Spiritual Protectorates."[30]

"You plan to join with other spiritual teachers?"

"Yes."

"At what point? No one has even heard of you."

"This will change, of course, when the proof and the book are published."

"Yes, I forget that sometimes."

"We all do," Michael quickly responds. "The idea that the humankind will overcome its inertia and transform itself into a kinder, self-sustaining world is no easy leap of faith for anyone. I've been climbing this mountain consciously for almost twenty years now and, like Jesus before me, have had my own crossroads of faith as well."

"What makes you think," I ask, "that a group of spiritual leaders will have any influence on the major world powers to change their policies toward those they've conquered? After all, churches and governments have supported these ungodly pursuits for centuries."

"What has to happen first, Rashan, is for the populations of these powerful countries to see the illegitimacy of leaders who claim the right to perpetrate such policies."

"And how to do you hope to enlighten them?"

"Through my teachings I hope to make clear to the so-called Christian populations of the world's most powerful nations that the teachings of Jesus are in no way compatible with the manner in which these countries and their inhabitants behave, including their acceptance of materialism, murder, bigotry, and the rest. My words in this book, Rashan, will make it as difficult as possible for those who had previously claimed that their exorbitant use of the earth's resources and contempt for their fellow creatures is even remotely justifiable. That is how I shall begin in the West."

"That's quite optimistic, Michael."

---

[30] Michael writes in 2003: Although I did not hear of it until 14 years later, my idea is much like the "Zone of Peace" idea floated by the Dalai Lama in 1989.

"I prefer to see it as the only practical belief that I can support. It's much like the charter in Wayne and the news program on KBAL—I offer my perspective and people may ignore it or take heed; we are the only ones who can save ourselves. There is no certainty to any of this: it requires a self-conscious act of evolution. We have overcome the unconscious physical restraints of gravity and stood erect; we have overcome the subconscious mental bounds of ignorance and developed symbolic forms; now we must overcome the tyranny of the instincts and ego through conscious spiritual practice."

By this time, our waiter had cleared the plates from the table and Michael and I ordered another pot of Darjeeling tea.

"And in the East?" I query.

"The difficulty with current international dialogue is that while the so-called democracies of the West have criticized the Chinese for 'human rights violations,' not the least of which is the systematic annihilation of the Tibetans, the Western powers themselves, as we've already discussed, have annihilated their own indigenous populations. This gives them no moral standing to criticize the Chinese; the fact that they put profit above people while claiming to be Christian and compassionate only compounds their hypocrisy.[31]

"If, however, someone takes the Chinese to task based on their own philosophy, namely dialectical materialism, then the real debate concerning current Eastern and Western modalities begins. Under these conditions, all current 'major powers' stand naked before their own half-truths, outright lies, and propaganda; they are forced by their own rationalizations to choose between instinctive cynicism and greed or the spiritual ideals to which they have heretofore paid only lip service."

"And you expect leaders from China and Western regimes to debate these issues with you—or even acknowledge your presence? Your pronouncements are so utopian!"

"By the time this the book is published, new technologies will make it possible to distribute information freely world-wide; then there shall be

---

[31] In fact, the Western powers point to their own imperialism as an excuse to ignore Chinese aggression: "They'd (the Chinese) no sooner return Tibet to the Tibetans than the United States would return South Dakota to the Sioux." (Lewis M. Simons, "Tibetans Moving Forward, Holding On," *National Geographic*, April 2002, p. 14).

enough grass-roots support for the evolutionary changes that I propose. Outside of this country, particularly in South America, Africa, and parts of Asia, liberation theology is stronger than ever. These believers have little or no stake in the religious and political apologies offered by oligarchies, monopolists, and dictators. Whether leaders of the wealthy and powerful nations shall see their way to a humanistic philosophy, or whether they shall remain in their selfish miasma remains to be seen. I could be shot or poisoned, or meet some other typically disguised end by the CIA warlords or their mafia collaborators, and the process would take a different turn. This is the beauty and pain of the free will aspect of our consciousness. Somewhere, the scenario may be predetermined; but of the outcome, we are unaware.[32] So, whatever the plan of the Great Anomaly, thy will be done."[33]

This was another of those times that I am left in a quandary of resistance and receptivity. The idea that Michael, as one intelligent and apparently sane person, could believe that his arguments would be compelling enough to move the major powers to change their policies seems fanciful at best, not to mention his continued insistence that there is some secret conspiracy that would then single him out for assassination. And yet, I have to admit, some ideas do change the world.

"Could I interest you gentlemen in dessert?" our waiter asks.

Both Michael and I decide on the *kheer*, a rice pudding seasoned with cinnamon, clove, and nutmeg.

"So, assuming that Christians in the West, when confronted with the fulfillment of their prophesies, are capable of abandoning two millennia of hypocrisy and brainwashing," I ask—attempting to recapture continuity for the tape recorder and resume Michael's explanation of his grandiose plan to preserve indigenous cultures—"what are the details of your approach to the Chinese problem?"

---

[32] See *Appendix 6 – The Proof*, "7.5 Chaos Theory as Further Impetus for Conscious Spiritual Evolution."
[33] Here Michael is referring both to The Lord's Prayer and to its most extreme example—Jesus' last words on the cross, at least those given by the *New Testament*, "G-d, my G-d, why hast thou forsaken me?" (Matthew 27:46, Mark 15:34) —which is, again, a reference to David's Psalm 22. However, it is quite possible, Michael posits, that if the crucified Jesus was speaking in a dialect of Atlantis taught in the mystery schools he had attended in Egypt, India, and Tibet, he would have been saying, "A veil comes over my face."

"As I said, the Chinese claim that the foundation of their current state philosophy is dialectical materialism,[34] a method of interpreting change synthesized by Marx, from the dialectical principles of his teacher, G.W.F. Hegel, the last of the great philosophical idealists in a line that began with Plato in the West.

"The Hegelian dialectical aspects of this philosophy are tied to the notion of continual evolution, which we described earlier in the first theorem, 'The only constant is Change (Δ).' A somewhat overly simplistic, yet useful, conceptualization of the dialectic is the three-fold progression of 'thesis, antithesis, synthesis': For every force there develops an opposition force that, together with the original force in mutual influence, results in a new force, which is a qualitatively distinct synthesis of the two antecedent forces.

"In reality, the unfolding of events is more complex than this, but nevertheless, this notion of 'The Dialectic' is a useful means of looking at process. Hegel, the idealist, believed that reality proceeded from an ideal form, much like Plato, downward to some physical manifestation. Marx's famous remark that he had 'turned Hegel on his head,' is a declaration indicating his belief that reality proceeds from the social condition (materialism) upward to an idea which grows out of it, putting ideal forms, then, at the end of the phenomenal process, not the beginning. To Chinese dialectical materialists, this not only means that their brand of socialism is an evolutionary result that first grew out of feudalism, and later capitalism,

---

[34] When editing what I had written, Michael pointed out to me that there is a legitimate debate as to whether the Chinese are really followers of Marx (i.e., "secular humanists"), given the capitalistic reforms they have instituted and the authoritarian manner in which information is restricted and basic human and labor rights are violated. "However," Michael granted, "their leadership still claims they are dialectical materialists. This, of course, is much like asking whether Christians are really followers of Jesus. They may claim to be such, but their actions belie it." (See, Joseph Kahn, "Some Chinese See the Future, and It's Capitalist," http://www.nytimes.com/2002/05/04/arts/04CHIN.html) Whether or not capitalism sponsored by the Chinese Communist Party is a ploy aimed at bringing the West to its knees (clearly, their financing of American debt gives them tremendous leverage), or whether materialism shall swallow whatever revolutionary principles remain buried in the Party's leadership, remains to be seen. Regardless, Marxism (dialectical materialism) and Christianity (Jesus' teachings), respectively, provide opportunity for observation of and entry into the psyche of the Chinese and the West.

but that its development remains rooted in the material conditions of their society.

"In truth, Rashan, both Hegel's and Marx's points of view contain some measure of truth—mental and physical conditions are *both* a part of what is—but as we've seen in our Quantum-Torus, it is impossible to characterize the phenomenal process as having a beginning or an end. So, there is more to a model representing universal phenomena than simply integrating the points of view represented by dialectical materialism. The quest for the truth is further muddied for socialists by Marx's statement that 'Religion is the opiate of the people,' or Mao's comment to the Dalai Lama that 'Religion is poison.' Despite my spiritual beliefs and mission, I do not disagree with the gist of Marx's and Mao's statements. But in their limited or veiled capacities, they failed to recognize that what they were saying in the most universal sense is 'Dogma is counterproductive.' In other words, the static vision of dialectical materialism held by Chinese leaders (i.e., failing to account for the anomalistic aspect of the model) is dogma—just another religion used to maintain control and power over the masses.'[35] Religions lose their basis once dogmatism has set in, becoming nothing more than bureaucracies.[36] But this does not mean that spirituality and dialectics are mutually exclusive.

"*Au contraire*, it is in this direction—understanding the convergence of science and spirituality—where the Chinese need to look for their own evolution and for the ever-evolving principles of the dialectic and the 'humanism' they claim to embrace. Certainly, they may or may not be off base when criticizing the corrupt elements of, say, the former Tibetan Buddhist hierarchy, yet this would no more prove the unworthiness of the Dalai Lama's teachings and Tibetan claims to geo-political independence than does the corruption within China itself undermine socialism or Marx's premises[37]—just as the hypocrisy of the so-called Christian, Western powers does not undermine the teachings of Jesus. But the corruption, violence, and materialism of Chinese imperialism in Tibet are, in the extreme, certainly worse than any excesses they found among the ruling classes of that country when they invaded it.

---

[35] Religion is most likely derived from the Lain *religare*, "to bind." (See *The New Oxford American Dictionary, op. cit.*, p. 1439.
[36] Again, see William James' comment in the *Invocation* to this book.
[37] For example, all the tainted products that have been recalled.

"Regardless of the material fulfillment that the Chinese deliver to their own people and to those whom they have conquered, the worldview underlying their short-sighted, instinct and ego-based objectives has long ago been subsumed by the teachings of the Dalai Lama and other spiritual leaders. In this sense, the social vision that the Chinese leadership promulgates has much in common with Western psychology and advertising, which define 'normalcy' as 'focusing on the consumption of commodities,' rather than on spiritual centeredness or happiness. Indeed, one could easily argue that this runs directly counter to Marx, who warned against the commoditization of the world and its inhabitants. Granted, collective models must build an industrial base to defend themselves from monopoly capital, but they must do so without losing sight of their humanistic or spiritual goals."

"So," I ask, eager to hurry this along, "in summary, you believe there is a way to approach the Chinese that can bring their blind spot into focus and make them see that spirituality and materialism are compatible?"

"Of course there is always an approach; but whether or not they are willing to do the work is another matter. The answer for the Chinese lies within the current tenets of their beliefs, but of which they haven't become conscious and, thus, are unwilling presently to accept the implications. For example, as a nuclear power, the Chinese accept the principles of Einsteinian physics, which includes Heisenberg's Uncertainty Principle. As we discussed years ago, one of the extrapolations of Heisenberg's concept is 'There is a force that we cannot measure with exactitude.' We may have faith, even 'know', that it is there. We may see manifestations of its presence everywhere and can identify many of its behaviors; yet, as the Taoists and the Hebrews and Platonists have concluded, we cannot name it or describe its origin. This is where science and spirituality and philosophy converge—in their agreement on the ultimate unknowableness of the force that animates creation. So, it would be a natural step for the Chinese to unite Taoism and Relativity.

"Like most social, political, and cultural revolutions, the Chinese 'communists' have gone to extremes in order to redefine themselves, yet the pendulum is bound to swing back to the center some day. When it does so, we hope that they consider the wisdom of one of their greatest spiritual masters, Lao-Tsu:

> The nameless is the beginning of heaven and earth.
> The named is the mother of ten thousand things.
> Ever desireless, one can see the mystery.
> Ever desiring, one can see the manifestations.
> These two spring from the same source but differ in name.[38]

"Spirituality and materiality are not mutually exclusive, but different aspects of a continuum much like energy is convertible into mass, as in the formula $E=mc^2$, that is, they are part of the seamless, toroidal universe of integrated mass-energy-space-time; in other words, the degree to which you invest yourself in material matters is the degree to which you are unavailable for spiritual matters. Likewise, there is a direct convertibility between spirit and matter, though they seem light years apart in orientation and force. In order to evolve, 'You cannot serve G-d and mammon.'[39] 'It's either Adonai[40] or the golden calf.'[41] We must move beyond 'seeing is believing' to spiritual states that are not part of the visible light spectrum, yet which just as surely exist."

"And if, by some extraordinary measure, the Chinese respond to your point-of-view, what then? Where would this get us?" I ask, failing to see how admission that spirituality is linked to science will change the totalitarian manner in which the Chinese government treats its citizenry and its neighbors.

"Once one admits to the existence of spirit, Rashan, a whole new set of values necessarily come into play. At that point, I would begin by asking the Chinese the same questions that I ask of the Western industrial monopolists, 'To what end does your philosophy serve your people? Is yours simply an exercise in the accumulation of material wealth? From there, the line of reasoning diverges to follow the peculiarities of Chinese history, though it is remarkably parallel to that which I have prescribed for the so-called Christian West. For example, if material wealth is your

---

[38] Lao Tsu, *Tao Te Ching*, translated by Gia-Fu Feng and Jane English, Vintage Books, New York, 1972, Chapter One.
[39] Matthew 6:24; Luke 16:13.
[40] The word used by Jews as a substitute in prayer for pronouncing יהוה', which others have attempted to pronounce as Jehovah or Yahweh, both of which are incorrect and considered blasphemous.
[41] See Exodus 32:25-27.

objective, does the fact that you would (theoretically) spread such benefits more generously among your favored ethnicities make you any less cynical, greedy, eco-damaging, or imperialistic than those who have victimized you in the past? Do not your assaults on individual rights and the trampling of ethnic minorities make you as heartless as those you chastise (and those who colonized you)? Do not the very roots of your tradition support compassion and the unity of opposites, and don't these perspectives beg a society in which the equality of all is balanced with the uniqueness of each? And what of the destruction of your natural resources and environment? Is this the better world Marx importuned when he expressed his desire to 'Hunt in the morning, fish in the afternoon, and criticize after dinner,' or, to give a Western example, the earthly Kingdom of Heaven where Jesus asked us to reside?"[42]

"And how would you expect them to answer these questions?"

"I believe the Chinese are capable of addressing evolution, but they're caught up in an arms race with the West, where both sides diminish themselves through mutual distrust. This could change, of course, in the context of a consciousness that, on a reasonably large scale, recognizes the global human predicament and, for evolutionary purposes, leverages the instantaneous worldwide communications network that's just over the horizon.[43]

---

[42] "How interesting," Michael remarks in 2003, "what different generations idealized as the goal of statecraft and political science. On May 12, 1780, John Adams wrote to his beloved Abigail, 'I must study Politicks and War that my sons have liberty to study Mathematicks and Philosophy. My sons ought to study Mathematicks and Philosophy, Geography, natural History, Naval Architecture, navigation, Commerce and Agriculture, in order to give their Children a right to study Painting, Poetry, Musick, Architecture, Statuary, Tapestry and Porcelaine.' Perhaps, as my political science advisor at Stanford, Dr. Charles Drekmeier, suggested, the evolution of political thought after Marx runs in reverse to the actual chronology of its theorists, that is, from Marx to Hegel to Rousseau."

[43] On 3/9/01, some years after this particular conversation, the *Denver Post* carried an article by Tyler Marshall and Anthony Kuhn, writing for the *Los Angeles Times*, reporting that the Chinese government is struggling in their efforts to prevent unrestricted Internet access for what is expected to be 100 million users by 2005. By 2006, the form that this restriction would take was becoming more defined (Howard W. French, "Chinese Discuss Plan to Tighten Restrictions on Cyberspace," *The New York Times*, July 4, 2006, http://www.nytimes.com/2006/07/04/world/asia/04internet.html)

"This transformation of objectives would be in the spirit of native Chinese philosophy, which embraces change, and in the spirit of its new so-called Marxian variant, which embraces the 'revolution within the revolution.'[44]

"And while their leaders may think, as did the dynasties that preceded them, that authoritarianism in the face of civil disobedience is a sign of strength, I tell you it is a sign of weakness and mistrust. Clearly, the people's determination shown at Tiananmen Square and by the Falun Gong[45] in the face of severe repression indicates a deep spiritual conviction among the Chinese people. I stand with Jefferson when 'I swear upon the altar of God, eternal hostility to every form of tyranny over the mind of man.'[46] Whether Chinese rulers will see the light is not for me to predict, but their doing so is the outcome in which I have chosen to direct my energy in this matter."

As always, Michael's grasp of the philosophic subtleties of a relatively obscure subject matter is more than I could have imagined. I cannot help but marvel at the seemingly endless array of insights and virtuosity that pour forth from his fertile mind, if not the political rhetoric it generates.

Pressing on, I change the direction of the conversation.

"The Chinese question seems to be a subject you've thought long and hard about," I begin, "and as is always the case with such subjects, you have synthesized a wealth of information. But I'd like to step back from these details for a moment, and revisit a subject we discussed long ago:

---

[44] The phrase "revolution with the revolution" is taken from the book of the same title written by Régis Debray (Grove Press, New York, 1967), a French professor and philosopher who was jailed by the Bolivian government, with the consent of the CIA, for aiding and abetting guerilla insurrectionists, led by Ernesto "Che" Guevara, in their fight against the dictatorial puppets of American monopoly capital. He was sentenced to 30 years by a military tribunal, but released after three years largely through the intervention of French President Charles de Gaulle, novelist André Malraux, and philosopher Jean-Paul Sartre. In the same vein, see Franz Fanon's *The Wretched of the Earth*, Grove Press, New York, 1963.

[45] On June 5, 1989, the day after Chinese troops had brutally murdered hundreds of pro-democracy students at Tiananmen Square, one man stopped a column of Red Army tanks on the Avenue of Eternal Peace. The Falun Gong is a spiritual movement that the Chinese rulers have characterized as a 'dangerous sect' and 'evil cult,' the practitioners of which they have incarcerated and executed.

[46] This quotation was inscribed around the base of the dome of the Jefferson Memorial in 1826.

your process, and the seemingly fully-synthesized manner in which you verbalize your ideas. Back then, you discussed how the practice of Yoga influences the organization and dissemination of information in the human brain. Now, I'd like to know what this integrative process feels like to the practitioner in the present. Is it spontaneous, as in the stories of Mozart, where he writes symphonies without changing a note? Or is it the result of study?"

"If you think about it, Rashan," Michael says, without missing a beat, "Mozart had both spontaneity and training. In making oneself a vehicle for universal truth, one needs the tools of expression, which come through diligent study, *and* divine inspiration, which comes through vigilant spiritual practice. When one finally sees that the ego is a tool to serve the higher mind, then one can outfit it with the fundamentals of one's art, which are recombined by the subconscious in ways that the conscious mind can not foresee, much as we described previously in our discussions of stream-of-consciousness in painting and writing and such."

"You're saying, then, that the creative process is a gestalt that can be facilitated by systematic intent?"

"Precisely. It is much like the rituals of the Lakota that we discussed. When the Lakota smoke the Sacred Pipe, their voice is sent to *Wakan-Tanka*, linking them to the Great Spirit. The smoke from the Pipe is their spirit made visible through their breath, and the living words that follow are the oracle that results from the divination, as it were. Before we undertake such a ritual, whether it's one of the sacred rites of the Lakota or something entirely different—for example, writing this book comprised of dialogue and transcription—we must prepare ourselves by focusing on the intention of such an act."

"So rituals are necessary to further the work?"

"Yes. If one thinks about a ritual as a series of pre-established steps that, when followed, produce an intended result, then such spiritual rites are not much different than empirical methods. Granted, the experience of transubstantiation or transcendental meditation or *Samadhi* is not quantifiable like electrolysis or magnetism or even photosynthesis, nevertheless, in the realm of human behavior, rituals and their results are more or less replicable processes. For example, a professional golfer's pre-shot routine produces the intended result a reasonably high percentage of the time, and the more consistently the ritual is performed, the better the results. For myself, I find that any ritual—in which I choose to invest my belief—works, whether it be yogic meditation, the Sacred Pipe, Hebraic prayer, my own pre-shot golf routine, or what have you. The lesson that I wish to impart here is akin to the practice of the auxiliary Zen disciplines;[47] that is, as we expand consciousness by incorporating our meditative practices into the various activities that comprise our lives, we find that our need for specific ritual is diminished to the degree that all of life becomes an intentional artistic act."

I pause for a moment to consider how our dialogue has resulted in so elegant a conclusion, and then continue from this new perspective. "How does this transformation of ritual into life fit with Jung's idea of the human psyche's need for symbols of integration?"

"As one's ability to synthesize the phenomena of this world grows, then the universe itself becomes the ultimate symbol of integration, a large-scale *mandala* as it were, like the one you visualized for *The Dream Catcher* project. In such a universe, the creative process, much like we discussed vis-à-vis painting and writing, is unbounded and continuous—and perfectly reflects the universe as different octaves of the same wave."

"So, in Mozart's or anyone's gift of spontaneity there is much hard work."

"That there is, Rashan."[48]

Michael insists on paying the tab, after which we enter the fresh, damp air of a spring evening. The Flatirons, visible under the waxing moon to the west of the courthouse, offer a vibrant geophysical exclamation point to another remarkable experience. Once again, my tape recorder had made it easy for me to recreate a seminal conversation with Michael without having to sacrifice my attention, nor ignore the fine dinner.

☼ ☼ ☼

As the repercussions of what we discussed percolate through my gray matter in the days that follow, I slowly come to grips with the realization

---

[47] Tea ceremony, flower arranging, gardening, and archery, for example.
[48] This exchange reminds me of golfer Lee Trevino's quip, "The harder I practice, the luckier I get."

that a major project has been removed from my schedule. Michael's perspective on *The Dream Catcher* was welcome in its hard truths and terrifying in its results. Now what am I going to do?

"You should see this as an opportunity, Rashan," Chimera suggests.

"You mean having the extra time to work on new things?"

"That, and getting on with the business which is already before you."

"Which is?"

"What Michael has been trying to get us to do: use our artistic talents to integrate the various loose ends and questions we have about our lives into one holistic experience."

"Okay," I abide, not understanding where she's going, yet anticipating a visitation by the muse.

"Lately, the projects you've been working on have been derived from other people's visions—Michael got you started on the book, Maya on *The Dream Catcher* project."

"So ..."

"What you need to discover is your own truth, something that ties together your own life, makes sense out of who you are."

"I'd be happy just figuring out how I'm going to deal with 'intermittent celibacy,'" I say, content with the muse's message, but longing for her sympathies and sensual pleasures.

For the next couple of weeks, I continue to ruminate over these issues. First, there are my personal quandaries: Is my relationship with Chimera evolving, or are we stuck in some kind of celibate penitence for having used sex to bandage our incompatibility? If that's the case, what does this say about my own spiritual growth? And what about my creativity; where is my next play going to come from?

Then, there's my friendship with Michael and our collaboration. Michael's challenge, as he has explained it, is to create a vision so compelling it will be obvious, at least to those with the requisite intellectual substance and spiritual clarity, that he is the World Teacher, the Great Synthesizer, Avatar, and Spiritual Anomaly—a combination of Christ (Christian), Messiah (Hebrew), Maitreya (Buddhist), Phana (Hopi), Kalki

(Hindu), Saoshyant (Zorastrian), Quetzalcoatl (Aztec/Mayan), et al.—a fulfillment of the prophesies at this evolutionary cusp.

But what experience does humanity have with such phenomena? After all, the Romans crucified Jesus in an attempt to nip his revolution in the bud. To them he was the serpent, not the Messiah. But it is one thing to worry about Michael becoming a target for so-called religious fanatics or government black-ops, and quite another to generate the renown that would prompt such an extreme reaction. Since I now accept—"for better, for worse, for richer, for poorer ..."—full responsibility for helping Michael in this task, how am I to convey his genius?

It suddenly strikes me that the answer to the problem of proving that Michael is the Spiritual Teacher of the Age lies in its resemblance to the authorship question surrounding the works of Shakespeare, for next to the hijacked teachings of Jesus, the so-called Shakespearean canon stands as the greatest literary theft in recorded history.[49] As Michael and I had discussed on various occasions, though Edward de Vere was considered the greatest English poet of his day, no works were published in his name following the appearance of plays written by one "William Shake-speare," the same pseudonym that de Vere used for topical pamphlets. Only de Vere's works that *preceded* the publication of "Shake-speare's" sonnets and plays are extant. After that, while de Vere was still alive and to protect the family's "good name" and his own neck, the plays and the sonnets were published under this pen name that happened to resemble the appellation of a surrogate and all-to-willing "upstart crow." Then, after de Vere's death, his family and other interested parties continued the charade for political and social purposes, systematically destroying his correspondence, and continuing to distribute his literary works and political broadsides under this pseudonym, while adjusting the legacy of the Stratford man (Will Shakspere) to make it appear that he, the barely literate glove maker's son, not de Vere, was the playwright. Even Shakspere's bust in the Holy Trinity

---

[49] "As we reviewed the evidence, it seemed to us that the traditional 'history' of Christianity was nothing less than the greatest cover-up of all time. Christianity's original Gnostic doctrines and its true origins in the Pagan Mysteries had been ruthlessly suppressed by the mass destruction of the evidence and the creation of a false history to suit the political purposes of the Roman Church. All those who questioned the official history were simply persecuted out of existence until there was no one left to dispute it." Timothy Freke & Peter Gandy, *The Jesus Mysteries*, Three Rivers Press, New York, 1999, p. 249.

Church in Stratford was altered, by adding pen and parchment to the sack of grain upon which his arms rested.[50]

Similarly, Michael has convinced me that like de Vere, Jesus' words, and therefore his life, have been altered by the needs of those in control of church and state, in whose continuing interest it remains to distort the author's intent and subvert history:

> His words became half forgotten and were not collected till some generations after they were uttered. They have been misunderstood, wrongly annotated, hundreds of times rewritten and hundreds of times transformed, yet they have nevertheless survived almost two thousand years.
>
> And though his words, as we have them to-day in the *New Testament*, have been terribly mutilated and deformed, they nevertheless have conquered half of humanity and the whole of the civilization of the West.[51]

The convergence of these forces—the dilemmas of Jesus and de Vere—along with Michael's spiritual and political dialogues and my chronicling them in the book, my playwriting, my spiritual practice, my relationship with Chimera, finally come to a head a couple of weeks later in my sleep. As Chimera had importuned, my dream is a marvelous weaving of all these loose ends.[52]

---

[50] See Ogburn, Charlton, *op. cit.* It's worth noting that February 10, 2002, *The New York Times* finally published an article in favor of de Vere's authorship (see William S. Niederkorn, "A Historic Whodunit: If Shakespeare Didn't, Who Did?"). In 2005, Mark Anderson's *"Shakespeare" by Another Name*, Gotham Books, NYC, adds a hefty share of new scholarship to the weight of de Vere's biographical argument.

[51] *The Gospel of Peace of Jesus Christ by the disciple John*, The Aramaic and Old Slavonic Texts compared and edited by Edmond Székely. Translated by Edmond Székely and Purcell Weaver, The C.W. Daniel Company Limited, 1 Church Path, Saffron Walden, Essex, England, 1937, p. 5.

[52] For the full text of my dream/play, see *Appendix 4 – The Bard's Ghost*. Note that the version of the play included herein is the current stage version at the time of publication, as it has been presented to major theatres for workshops, readings, production, and performance, and not the integrative "psychological" version as I first dreamed it and describe here, which elucidates how my subconscious and

In the mysterious and integrative workings of my subconscious and unconscious mind and dream world, I, Rashan Barcusé, manifest as an American television news producer and reporter—much like Michael—and hold his political views not mine. But I discover that my soul is that of Edward de Vere, a playwright like myself. Following this startling revelation, I'm consumed by a need to retrieve de Vere's truth and prove to the world that he, not William Shakspere, wrote the plays and sonnets which we all so admire. In my attempts to prove this, I am ridiculed by those who, because of their political, commercial, academic, or romantic stakes, support Shakspere as the author. Michael's politics come into play in a nightmarish fashion, as if his conspiracy theories were actually true and I was trying to propagate them as well. In the end, though, my deep faith in Christ redeems me (and thus, de Vere) in a most startling manner.

I awake with Michael's face in front of me. I am shaken, at first, by the subconscious connection my mind has made between Michael and the image of Christ in my dream. In the interests of journalistic objectivity and my own ego, I have resisted full acceptance of this idea with as much will power as I could muster; and I resist, even in the face of such a compelling dream, facing its implications.

With the dream still vivid in my mind, and Chimera already risen and gone, I immediately set about recording what I remember. The level of detail that I am able to recall astonishes me. So *this* is the theurgy that Mozart and others spoke of when they acted as midwives to their masterworks. Sure, there is a lot of work left to be done, but I am amazed at the basic dramatic structure that underlies my dream.

By early afternoon, I have committed the dream to paper and am already embellishing it when Michael calls with news of the latest turn in his career—designing training programs that run on computers.

"This is quite a coincidence, Michael, like an *intentional unfolding* of the Truth."

"I see you've been working on the book, Rashan," Michael says.

"Why's that?"

"Your comments reveal a contemplative state on your part. I assume you've been writing."

---

unconscious mind mediated the forces then at play in my world, and in which I discovered the Christ within me through Michael's reflection.

השלמה « 309

"That's what gets me with you, Michael! Like Spock,[53] you always have some logical explanation for knowing these things, like there's nothing premonitory about it."

> *As always, my evening hot tub ritual serves as a welcome respite from the frenzy of my days, but my experience this evening is without precedent. I am about twenty minutes into my relaxation when the inspired words begin to come. Wrestling with the problem of Jerusalem, I wonder how I might contribute to making it truly a city of peace, as its name implies. It occurs to me that given the holy nature of all of G-d's earth, the lesson I am to teach concerning the City of David is that, prophesies duly noted, I am perfectly capable of promulgating my message without rebuilding the temple in that place, or anywhere else for that matter. Having reached this thought, I say to myself, "I therefore cede Jerusalem until such time as those who believe that they each have the exclusive path to G-d learn to accept each other and live in peace." At that very instant, as my thoughts conclude, the sky is lit up with the largest and most glorious meteor that I have ever witnessed, streaking across the sky for less than ten seconds until it burns up in the earth's atmosphere directly in front of my eyes. I am incredulous and filled with the Holy Spirit. I give thanks to the Great Anomaly, the One-Without-A-Name, for speaking to me in such an unexpected and wondrous way.*

"Rashan, this intentional unfolding ..."

"Yes?"

"Those words answer your question. The unfolding is something that we each experience, even if you see it first through the lens of my practice. Don't confuse this with premonition. While we may see conditions of the future, we see few specific events. So, what you describe as psychic phenomena is simply informed vision or insight—knowing, as you call it, or what Jung called synchronicity, a combination of simultaneity and meaning. Granted, it is an expansive vision, but events on the magnitude of prophesy are not our doing, other than being in the right

---

[53] Dr. Spock, the Vulcan in the once popular television and film series, *Star Trek*.

place saying the right things at the right time when it happens. Any forethought we have is attributable to preparation and practice. The only ego involved is in the use of symbolic forms to explain the phenomenon."

"So your informed vision knew, when we met, that I had just finished reading *The Way of All Women* and needed to start on *Christ, a Symbol of the Self*?"

"Precisely."

"And that's it?"

"There are other phenomena at work here as well, for example, 'the guru effect' that we've discussed before—the same as transference, in psychology."

"The guru effect is related to what I call your knowing?"

"Yes. Because you have begun to ascribe certain qualities to me, my presence stimulates subconscious processes in you that, in turn, you attribute to me. While this elevates my status in your mind, an element which may be essential to your evolutionary process in the short run, in the long run it has the potential to delay you from making these spiritual attributes your own."

"This kind of analytical approach could demystify our relationship, Michael."

"Perhaps as the Anomaly I can't avoid having this effect. But it's just one way among many to look at and understand our interpersonal dynamics and to interpret the process. Each of our unique gifts remains as nameless as the source from whence it comes."

"So how are these forces related to what you call prophetic proof?"

"As I said, prophesy arises from being spiritually aligned—'in one's Tao,' as I call it, or 'on the path,' as it is commonly characterized. Anyone thus aligned is 'in the right place at the right time.' The greater the alignment, the better one's timing, like 'instant karma' on a grand scale. When Black Elk talked to the spirits, as described at the end of his first book[54]—and clouds appeared out of a clear sky, and thunder without lightning rumbled across the Black Hills and the rain came—was this a result of Black Elk calling on the Six Powers of the World, or was it pre-ordained that an ancient Black Elk would stand there once again on Harney

---

[54] *Black Elk Speaks: Being the Life Story of a Holy Man of the Oglala Sioux*, as told through John G. Neihardt (Flaming Rainbow), University of Nebraska Press, Lincoln, Nebraska, 1979.

Peak, as he had when he was nine years old and had his Great Vision, and that out of a clear blue sky clouds, thunder, and rain would come as he spoke to the spirits? Or from a European point-of-view: Was it a 'coincidence' when the skies darkened at Calvary as Christ was crucified? In either case, we cannot know the answer to this any more than we can describe G-d or the Great Anomaly. This paradox is similar to the unity of opposites in free will and determinism. Since we cannot know what is in store for us—except on those rare occasions when we experience visions or 'worm holes to the future'— we must act as if we have free will.[55] This also is not unlike the Uncertainty Principle or 'the Tao that cannot be spoken'—we cannot prove either importuning, chance, or fate correct—so cause and effect, coincidence and synchronicity, and free will and determinism may look much the same."[56]

"Whew! That's elegant," I say. "And all of this started from what I called a coincidence?"

"Which I'm assuming had to do with my new venture that I mentioned?"

"Right—training programs that run on computers."

"What's coincidental about that?" Michael asks.

"Just when I seem to get my arms around your vocation in my chronicle, you go and change it on me."

"How else would it happen?"

"I don't know. The same thing happens to me in my life: I have a breakthrough dream, in the form of a play, actually, and just as I'm ready to call you, the telephone rings."

"Now we're talking, Rashan. Tell me about the dream."

"It's already a three-act play," I say. "How about I send you a copy?"

"I've been looking forward to this day," says Michael, "when you would send me an appendix to the book."

"Seriously?"

---

[55] Again, see *Appendix 6 – The Proof*, "7.5 Chaos Theory as Further Impetus for Conscious Spiritual Evolution" for the mathematical evidence of this logical progression.
[56] See "Astrology" in *Appendix 7 – Michael's Notes*, for a more detailed comparison of causal and acausal reasoning.

"How else would we document our work but through a dialectical process?"

"The book is dialectical?"

"Sure," he says, "—a Socratic or Talmudic dialogue that evolves as the exchange progresses. As our model indicates, this is the same as saying it is toroidal."[57]

I hadn't thought of my chronicle in this way, but it *is* an evolving dialogue. It also occurs to me that given the span of years involved and book's orientation, it is a memoir as well. So I promise to send Michael my play as it is written so far,[58] and we agree to talk as soon as he finishes reading it.

☼ ☼ ☼

That evening, when Chimera returns home from a day of hiking and sketching in the hills, I am suddenly struck by what I'd just written in the first draft of my play concerning the parallels between my suspicions of her and those of de Vere's toward his own wife, Anne Cecil—a central theme in "Shake-speare's"[59] plays and his (de Vere's) life. As Chimera approaches for a kiss, I feel guilty, particularly in light of her (and Anne's) redemption that concludes my dream-play.

"Ah, my long-suffering partner!" I say, attempting to right a wrong that feels both immediate and ancient.

"Whatever are you talking about, lover boy?"

---

[57] Michael's definition here was later proven correct with Grigory Perelman's November, 2002, solution to Poincaré's Conjecture, which serves as a check to the Quantum-Torus Model (see *Appendix 6 – The Proof*).

[58] Again, for the full text of the version of Rashan's dream/play, see *Appendix 4 – The Bard's Ghost*.

[59] This was the way that de Vere spelled his pseudonym, to reference Pallas Athena, the spear-shaking goddess of war and the arts, and his similarly-themed coat-of-arms as Viscount Bolbec. The hyphenated version of the name appeared on the first few plays and on various pamphlets defending the throne against Catholicism, though not on the first definitive publication of de Vere's plays, "Mr. William Shakespeare's Comedies, Histories & Tragedies, Published according to the True Originall Copies," sponsored posthumously by his daughter, Susan. The part-time actor and poseur ("upstart crow") from Stratford spelled it "Shakspere" more often that not in his six extant signatures and—like all others who shared this surname in England—without a hyphen.

"I had this amazing dream last night and amongst its wonders is my saintly wife who, behold, appears before me now!"

"I see. You really have lost it!" We both laugh. "No, really, I want to hear about it. Tell me," she says.

"Remember a couple of weeks ago you suggested that I put into practice the ideas which I've been discussing with Michael concerning 'creative individuation and the spiritual process'?"

"Of course."

"And, I've been working on remembering my dreams, writing down the pieces I recall each morning."

"Right, right." She nods.

"Then it all came together last night—I mean, I had this epic dream and remembered *everything*."

So, I read the current draft of the play to her.[60] As I do, I can't help but feel that I'm offering a confession about the ups and downs of our relationship as well as my hidden desires toward Diane.

"Well, at least you come around in the end," she says. "It's not easy to deal with," she says, looking hurt.

"It would have been hard for me to get around it," I say, "given what I wrote about your demons and how I justified that."

"Yes, I understand," she says unconvincingly.

"So, you think it holds together?" I ask, trying to get her to look at the broader picture.

"It needs some work, but it's got a lot of potential. There's quite a cast of characters, and the emotional drama reflects the intellectual arguments, the authorship questions."

"It seems that's where I have the most conflict in my life—the intellect."

"Unlike my emotional battleground, you mean," she says defensively.

"The temperaments of painters and writers are necessarily different," I say. We agree on that.

---

[60] As I have explained, the version that I read to Chimera is an earlier "psychological" version of the play in which I discover the Christ within me through Michael's reflection, as opposed to the current stage version reprinted in *Appendix 4 – The Bard's Ghost* (the version presented to major theatres for workshops, readings, production, and performance), where it is de Vere that discovers the Christ (or Messiah) within himself.

"Yes," she says, still unenthusiastic and dizzy from my confession. "I know when the pain wells up inside of me I have little patience for thinking. It's either run the trails or paint."

I have often spoken of Chimera's periodic fragility and our many conversations about this over the years; now it seems we will have another. This isn't surprising, of course, for why else would someone change her name to Chimera but for the acute, even schizophrenic, natures at war within herself?

"It seems," I say to her, "that the dream work you suggested for me might be something that you should do for yourself."

"What do you mean?" she asks.

"We're both aware of how our lack of wholeness as individuals undermines our relationship."

"Yes."

"Well, sooner or later, if we both don't get it together, we could drive ourselves apart."

"But you *know* I've been doing this work for a long time!" she protests.

"Yes, longer than I, that's for sure. But the stakes are higher now."

"Go on."

"I mean with Michael."

"In what sense?"

"As 'his time' gets closer, I sense that his ability to heal, not only by his presence, but also by the simple thought of him, seems to be growing, just as with Christ in my dream."

"I guess it's time to face that fact, isn't it?" she sighs.

"Face what?" I ask, not understanding her fatalistic resignation.

"Well, most of the time," she continues, "Michael seems just like an everyday person, and other than his unique appearance, you wouldn't think twice about who he is or why he's here—until you talk with him. Then, no matter where it starts, the conversation always seems to swing around to some profound spiritual truth."

"Right."

"So, the implications of who he really is and what that means for the world are enormous. And while it's been easy for me to accept this in theory, the closer it comes to 'his time,' as you put it, the clearer it becomes how much personal work I have to do to be worthy not only of being his friend, but of being someone who can carry his message to the world."

I sat for a moment, absorbing this.

"You know," I say, "when we started doing Yoga with him, I was worried about getting trapped under his influence, like so many people I've read about who are either fanatical devotees or in de-programming. But now, I find my trepidations almost laughable. Michael's teaching is so transparent; he won't let me even consider falling into these traps. Earlier today, he reminded me of that psychological mechanism he calls 'the guru effect.' He simply refuses to let anyone avoid responsibility for their own spiritual growth and consciousness-raising."

"So, you're comfortable doing the work that's required?" Chimera asks.

"Now? Certainly—even the abstinence part," I say, surprising myself. "It's either that or throw away what we've worked so hard to build. You know, I still have trouble with some of his political pronouncements, but I don't feel like I'm doing this for Michael," I continue. "It's clear that the illumination that comes through him is not, strictly speaking, self-generated. He's shown me that I'm a vehicle for the same force that he is. The only difference is he's my teacher in this sphere. And if his process helps us get in touch with that force, then we'll be able to come together as two whole people, independent yet interdependent, instead of two incomplete dependent people. That's the only sense I can make out of the Yoga austerities, particularly this 'intermittent celibacy' that we've agreed to try."

"It seems you're right then," Chimera sighs, "that I need to integrate the consequences of my life issues in the same way that I suggested you do with yours. Funny, how we come face-to-face with our own advice."

Michael and I resumed our conversation about the play a week later.

"Well, Mr. de Vere," he says when I pick up the phone in my study, "I believe you've done wonders for both our causes! 'So as twins doth both Jesus and de Vere stand bereft of their original intent.'"[61]

---

[61] From *Appendix 4 – The Bard's Ghost*, I, i.

"You think so?" I ask, my confidence rising.

"The subplots mirror the main drama, mimicking one of the Bard's telltale traits. Your dialogue is inventive, too. The idea of mixing King James and Shakespearean verse supports your argument concerning the parallels of Jesus and de Vere on a subtextual level,[62] and your blank verse is unobtrusive and, when intended, remarkably Elizabethan to the ear."

"Well, I'm flattered that you think this is a good start," I say. "Something clicked. I don't know where my affinity for Elizabethan language came from—it's as if I channeled it—but, one never knows how other people are going to react. To be honest, though, most of this is right out of my dream; I didn't do much editing."

"That doesn't detract from the accomplishment; on the contrary, it minimizes artifice. You may end up substantially changing it for the stage, but that's beside the point. You've tapped into some important truths without involving your ego in the construction. The fact is, this sprang out of your mind, even the sections lifted directly from the canon."

Once again, Michael's employs the Jungian perspective on the truth of the subconscious "tribal" mind to substantiate our exchange.

"And you're okay with the words I've put in Jesus' mouth?" I say.

"I couldn't have done it better myself—which brings up something that de Vere says near the final curtain, 'And now, my self in Christ identified, I rest my case, desirous of heavenly passage.'[63] This is important."

"That de Vere gains Christ consciousness?"

"Yes," he says. "How do you feel about that?"

"I'm a bit overwhelmed by the whole experience—channeling an entire play, and then remembering it and writing it down," I say, the delirium of the aftermath having been followed by exhaustion from the process. "I haven't really thought about 'the message,' or that it might signify some change in consciousness."

---

[62] In recognition of the fact that Jesus and de Vere are the most quoted persons in history, the addendum containing quotations for *The New Shorter Oxford English Dictionary*, Oxford University Press, 1973, is entitled "Authors and Publications Quoted, References to the Bible, References to Shakespeare." It should also be noted that the version of the Bible that is most quoted in these references—the King James—was translated during "Shake-speare's" time, in basically the same location.

[63] *Appendix 4 – The Bard's Ghost*, III, iv.

"Spoken like a true playwright, my friend. I, on the other hand, see this less as a play and more as an integrative dream or vision. The signs are everywhere."

"That may be, but unlike my surrogate, de Vere, I'm still feeling separation from the Christ within."

"Yet nevertheless desiring unity. Think of Messiah or Christ consciousness as an affective memory that you are trying to manifest. You know it's inside of you. You simply have to do the actor's work. 'All the world's a stage,'[64] and this is your next role."

"I see. ... So, that means I'm close?" I finally say, somehow having been brought to an acceptance of the Jungian ideal that Michael put in front of me when we first met—Christ as a symbol of Self.

"Indeed," he says, "the text indicates that you, through your unfiltered subconscious, have asked for a unity with your higher self—a goal you thought impossible not too long ago. It's a marvelous glimpse into your individuation process."

"I'm not sure where that leaves me."

"In the present, with a new play to work on," he says. "It's like the Taoists say, 'Before I was enlightened, I chopped wood and carried water; after I was enlightened, I chopped wood and carried water.' It's the same for any artist."

"I'll keep working on it then. We'll stage it."

"Yes, though, as I said, right now it's more of an integrative dream in the form of play. As you work it and turn it into a stage-worthy drama, it will go hand-in-hand with the book—yet persuade in a decidedly different manner."

"How?"

"Your selection of quotations from de Vere's plays—quotations that reference key events in his life, including passages strongly tied to the authorship question—and arranging them seamlessly into one story convinces us of his cause in a way that an intellectual argument could not. And he gets to speak for himself in his own words and in a plausible dramatic context. After seeing him in this way, we see the details of his life through his characters. It's both brilliant and simple. How else would the true Bard talk to us but in this manner? But, the *coup de maître* is the way

---

[64] *As You Like It*, II, vii.

you included the discovery of the Geneva Bible.⁶⁵ Who better than Jesus—the only author more disenfranchised than de Vere—to have a hand in this?"

Who better, indeed! I think, remembering the transposition of Jesus' and Michael's faces in my dream.

"The discovery of that Bible is the capstone for the Earl," I say. "But more than that, in the play it speaks to the point you've been making all along—that much of the proof of de Vere's authorship and your own credentials as the Spiritual Anomaly are in the words themselves, and that perhaps the acceptance of these two radical notions are related."

"Yes," he says. Don't you find that a bit shocking?"

"Shocking?"

"It's just as I was saying—that the play and the book go hand in hand, that they're dialectical: just as the recognition of de Vere's authorship is facilitated in your play by Christ's intervention on his behalf with the Geneva bible, so, contrapositively, are the Christ's or Messiah's credentials substantiated in these dialogues that we're recording."

"You're saying my play is holographically related to the book?"

"Yes, they're congruent; they say the same thing in different ways, in different media."

"So, they're related, like the play has the same genes as the book?"

"Yes," Michael says. "'[E]very word doth almost tell my name, Showing their birth, and whence they did proceed,'⁶⁶ and analogously in any other media that the Good News is spread, just as Jesus says as the end of the play, 'I, like de Vere, shall be granted a new life and redeemed. As his own play did for him, so shall my own creative endeavor do for me

---

[65] In 1986, a Geneva version of the *New Testament* in which a high percentage of the biblical passages used in "Shakespeare's" plays are underlined, was found in the Folger Shakespeare Library in Washington, D.C. The name on the bible, however, is not that of the Stratford man, but of the Oxford man, Edward de Vere. Mathematical probability tests on the works of other author-candidates indicate that this Geneva Bible belongs to the actual playwright. See Mark Anderson's "Thy Countenance Shakes Spears," *Harper's Magazine*, April, 1999, pp. 46-47, and *"Shakespeare" By Another Name*, Gotham Books, NY, NY, 2005, "Appendix A: Edward de Vere's Geneva Bible and Shake-speare," and Michael Satchell's "Hunting for good Will," *U.S. News & World Report*, July 24-July 31, 2000, p. 72.

[66] Sonnet 76

...'⁶⁷ Consider what we've discussed about the mass media—how it's really the public relations department for the corporate state. So, if this book arrives unheralded in New York City, what are the chances that a publisher would want to touch it given its content *vis-à-vis* the power structure? And even if there were a publisher with the guts to distribute it, what are the chances the barons of propaganda and Yellow Journalism wouldn't order scathing critiques or ignore it entirely? There are plenty of whores to write such criticism for them—the Golden Calf is enthroned. So, our strategy is to create as many metaphors for our story as we can, and then parlay the successes into a forum for our teachings. It's the law of indirection."

I had to admit this made sense. If I, the author of this book and a relatively liberal member of the bourgeoisie, have a hard time relating to Michael's politics, what could I expect from the movers and shakers that rule Western society and all the masses suckled on their media? Yes, I'm increasingly attracted to Michael's spiritual message and grateful for the changes that his friendship has brought to my life, but despite this I've maintained a reasonable skepticism concerning his politics, and presented a fair account of what he's about. So, the bottom line is that I'm committed to seeing this work published and that I understand that it is in my best interest to find a way around the resistance we can expect to encounter.

"Yes," I say, "I can see how this strategy may help both of us."

"Timing's everything," Michael says.

"Meaning I've got plenty of time to work on it?"

"Yes, that, and how time will change the play, the proof, and the book. They will be significantly different by the time they become the focus of public attention."

"Well, Chimera will certainly be happy about that. She's disturbed by my subconscious romantic meanderings."

"You're referring to the muse in the play that bears more than a little resemblance to my wife," Michael says. "Your feelings for her are evident in both the book and the play.⁶⁸ That's not going to go away."

---

⁶⁷ *The Bard's Ghost*, Epilogue.
⁶⁸ In the early versions of the play, the physical descriptions of the Muse and Anne Vavasor (Rosalind) clearly resembled Diane, while Anne Cecil is a stand-in for Chimera, and the persona of Rashan overlaps with de Vere.

"I never told her how taken I was by Diane after you introduced us, but it's right there in black and white. As I said to Chimera, I guess I had it coming after I wrote about her issues earlier in the book and then tried to assuage her by explaining that personal revelations are what artists are all about. Now it's all hitting me at once: I'm confessing my attraction to Diane in print while dealing with Chimera's ideas on 'intermittent celibacy' at home. I feel like the universe is forcing monastic austerities upon me."

Michael laughs.

"Well, when I told you about my platonic feelings for Chimera years ago, you had a hard time understanding what I was talking about. Now you'll get to find out—with two women! That's synchronicity."

I smile grudgingly, noting that Michael has, in his inimitable fashion, drawn the discussion back toward 'coincidence,' the subject at the beginning of our previous call, bringing the kind of symmetry he always seems to discover in our conversations.

"So," I ask, "you understand my surprise at the news of your new computer training venture following on the heels of my dream in which I had your previous job?[69] All of a sudden, as if you were responding to my having internalized you—captured a part of you on paper—you tell me you've become something else?"

"Of course," he says. "I'm as taken by the juxtaposition of roles as you are, and pleased by the fact that your character adopts so many of my views. Your dream makes an amalgam of our lives—a spiritual alchemy."

"... as if my subconscious has carte blanche to warp reality at will for its own purposes—poetic license to synthesize my disparate parts."

"Now you're talking like me. See, this is why my career's taken a change of direction—just to keep up with your all-consuming integration of my life into your art," Michael says, nudging me and smiling.

"The jumble of our lives in my play is like a funhouse mirror, and the current draft will likely end up on the cutting room floor—but my description of these same relationships in the book is another matter. There I'm trying to be objective."

"Yes, as you told Chimera—it's in black and white for everyone to see."

---

[69] Again, this refers to earlier versions of the play in which Rashan appears as a radical television news journalist.

"Don't you find this honesty burdensome? Chimera and I do. It's so public."

"I couldn't call the constancy of revelation a burden. It's too glorious."

"I can see why you feel that way. Calling it the 'Great Anomaly'[70] hardly seems an appropriate description."

"Anomaly is only one name for it—but it's useful in mapping the Avatar[71] to an empirical model. The Lion of Judah, Pluméd Serpent, Magister Ludi, *Mahavatar*, Qabalah Master, or *Wanekia* describe the same phenomena, yet with romantic overtones. All of these descriptions are facets of the truth, and taken together draw a more complete picture—a convergence of science and spirituality, history and myth."

"This begs the question, Michael—the part played by the ego in an enlightened being."

"You think I have a problem with egoism?"

"Not so much a problem as a challenge. I mean, as overwhelming as your mental powers are, and given the ego's general co-location in the frontal lobes where such processes take place, it would seem that egoism is something you have to deal with."

"As we've discussed, attaining anomalistic or Messiah or Christ consciousness requires both an unbounded ego and no ego at all—an unbounded ego in the sense of coming to a belief that 'I am Christ', and no ego at all, because only through utter humility would such an attainment be possible. So, although I consciously prepared for this attainment, my anointment came to me in a dream, not in a moment blurred by the desire and control of ego-consciousness. This is much the same manner as your dream came to you. Also, this point which I've made numerous times— that such enlightenment is possible with a minimum of egoism—is a

---

[70] A recent compelling metaphor that Michael has offered me on the subject of human anomalies is a comparison to certain celebrated sports figures. "Like Tiger Woods," he said, "I still make occasional bogeys, double-bogeys, or worse, or like Michael Jordan, I have off nights. But when all's said and done, the anomaly is the catalyst for the evolution of his or her respective discipline—moving up the bar."

[71] Or Spiritual Anomaly or World Teacher, the Christ, Messiah, Imam Mahdi, et al.

teaching from the *Yoga Sutras*: there is a state in which the Yogi is able to maintain at-one-ment while using ego functions to reveal truth."

"You're qualifying this by saying that this state is attainable with a *minimum* of egoism."

"Yes, on this point the Masters all agree—that the incarnate body-bound soul, avatars included, is *de facto* defined as having ego and the instinctive functions related to it. But as we've also discussed, the enlightened are simply not ruled by such forces. To them, ego is a servant, not a master. Ego is not the source of their motivation."

"I'm assuming, then, that your new venture in computer-based training is somehow related to your ability to communicate knowledge sans ego?"

"That's only part of it, of course, because, in truth, the development of these technologies is being underwritten by corporations that hope to profit from improved efficiencies in the workplace, as a result of the digitally-delivered business skills training they're paying us to produce. They're paying for the R&D, but they have no awareness that these same technologies will provide for the world-wide promulgation of spiritual teachings, including my own courses on conscious spiritual evolution."

"This must be what the Muse in my dream meant when she said, 'new discoveries shall unite all means of different folk, as if on the rim of a dream catcher they reside, enmeshed in the spider's web, an internet not a corp'rate network!'"[72]

"We're at the threshold of a revolution in communications that will expedite the needed changes, and our project will play a big part in teeing that up, including, as we've discussed before, theatre rituals, which, like your play, inculcate the innate basis of tribal healing."

"I have to admit that even after all the talk we'd devoted to your paraphrasing of Maxwell Anderson's paraphrasing of Aristotle and to your emphasis on the Paleolithic origins of theatre, I'd still never expected that a play, let alone one which I write, would play a part in your plans. So, I guess we've finally found the perfect opportunity for our collaboration, incorporating Yoga into the rehearsal process."

"Yes, you're right."

"And you'll play the role of Christ when it's staged?"

---

[72] From *Appendix 4 – The Bard's Ghost*, II, ii.

"It seems we've come full circle then, from that morning in Wayne when I asked you, '… what would sell you, as a playwright, on a prophetic character.'"

9

Pastels

"As our meeting concluded, [the Dalai Lama] suddenly started to laugh heartily ... 'If I went to work for a company ... I do not know how far I would be able to follow my own advice. I don't know—I might start stomping around, yelling and breaking things ... I might get fired!'"
--The Dalai Lama, from *The Art of Happiness at Work*

"Peace can be reached through meditation on the knowledge which dreams give. Peace can also be reached through concentration upon that which is dearest to the heart."
--*The Yoga Sutras*

"A good marriage is that in which each appoints the other guardian of his solitude. Once the realization is accepted that even between the closest human beings infinite distances continue to exist, a wonderful living side by side can grow up, if they succeed in loving the distance between them which makes it possible for each to see the other whole against the sky."
--Rainer Maria Rilke

Chimera paints furiously as months slip into months, but the breakthrough dream is slow in coming. I'm amazed at her resiliency. Morning after morning, she rises with the first light in the sky, and is out the door with her backpack and portable easel for a day in the hills. Not all of her subjects are mountains, trees, rocks, streams, and wildflowers, however. Some of her excursions bring visitations of demons from her youth, which gnaw at her soul, demanding to be heard and provided canvas space.

On days such as these, when the voices are too strident to ignore, she relents and lets them be heard in the hopes that they'll play themselves out and be gone. Then, the layers of pastel on her heavily-textured homemade paper tell of the struggle of an inner child seeking refuge from unpredictable backhanded violence and demeaning tongue lashings. At times, this strategy of appeasement seems to work and the voices disappear for a season or two. Perfect days of hiking, painting, culinary delights, and (now less intermittent) lovemaking follow. Alas, each reprieve proves to be temporary, and back the demons come, full fury, taking their toll on Chimera's defenseless psyche.

These are rough times for both of us. Little sleep and lack of appetite further deplete an already nightmare-weary Chimera, making even the simplest day-to-day life sustaining routines challenges of behemoth proportions. With a partner in body only, I take solace in my writing, tending to our daughter, Gita, and the previously shared chores that now default to me. A saturnine fog creeps into what had been light-filled days, casting a pall over Chimera's pallet and a veil around my imagination.

Into this wasteland, Michael would unexpectedly slosh, dispersing the languid atmosphere and clearing the way with his uncompromising optimism and will. So it happens after a particularly insidious spell during which Chimera ceases to paint on her hikes, when walking has become the only means of holding her demons at bay.

"Chimera, you look like you've seen a ghost, and not a very holy one at that!" Michael says, as he and Diane show up at our door one Saturday morning with a host of fresh vegetables they've gleaned from the farmer's market in Boulder.

"You've got that right," she says, "Ghosts of Chimera Past, demanding their oh-so-regular tribute."

"And how is it that they continually return, unsatisfied with your offerings?" Diane asks, playing along with Chimera's theatrical hyperbole.

"If I knew that, I'd give them what they want and banish them," she says.

"You believe they can be satisfied?" Diane asks.

"What do you mean?" Chimera says.

"I mean, negativity begets itself," Diane says. "Take it from me, there's nothing you can give these demons that would satisfy them, other than your soul."

"It's hopeless then?" Chimera asks.

"No, far from that," Michael assures her. "These voices are echoes of abuse handed down through generations, passed along, over and over, until someone finally says, 'No!'"

"Just say, 'No'?"

"To these voices, yes," he says, "say, 'No.' Cut them off. Tell them to be gone. Know that G-d is with you. Confront them as if they were the very persons that put these thoughts in your head—because they are!"

"Just like that?"

"Just like that!" Michael steps forward and puts a relaxed hand on Chimera's shoulder. "Paying tribute to your voices is like writing checks and spending emotional resources; it depletes your spiritual budget. You wouldn't do that with your hard-earned karma would you?"

"No. But what happens if they come back?"

"Do the same thing. They can't live if you don't feed them. The greater the light that you shine on them, the quicker they move from repression to memory. You have the power within you. Call it what you will, but call on it."

Chimera takes a deep breath. "Okay, I can try that. I've got nothing to lose at this point."

"And everything to gain," Diane says with a smile, before giving her a hug.

I take the inviting locally-grown veggies and cook up one of my patented omelets, beginning with sautéed garlic and onions, then the zucchini and mushrooms, all of which I add back over a perfectly cooked bed of eggs, finally smothered in Brie and served with fresh croissants. My homemade lattes never tasted so good.

"Well, we best head back up to the hills," Michael says. "I've got some work to do on my latest course, 'Achieving Balance in Your Personal and Professional Life.'"

With that, Chimera hugs Diane, grips Michael's arm for a moment, manages a tight smile, then wanders off to her studio, obviously unable to handle the shop talk.

"So that's what they've got you doing these days," I say, turning the focus away from Chimera's struggle.

"Yes, it's a good warm-up for me, infusing spiritual values into the workplace. I enjoy the subversiveness of it."

"Subversive? You sound like that Rashan character in *The Bard's Ghost*."[1]

"Or his upper-octave alter-ego you've got bookending the piece," Diane says.

Michael laughs. "You know me, Rashan," he says, "—a child of the late '60's. I recognize that capitalism is a historical necessary that's provided us with the tools and information to set our ship aright, but it's a system that's come to the end of its useful time in the form as we know it—not because of any loss of vitality yet, for it could gut the earth for some time to come, but for ecological and spiritual reasons. The kind of profligate consumption that we witness is no longer tolerable if we're going to build a sustainable world. So, by teaching business people how to behave in ways that foster greater interpersonal communication and respect, we lead them to a worldview that eventually applies these values on a universal scale. And *that's* subversive to the prevailing culture-business."[2]

"Okay, I'm sold. Where do I sign up? I'm ready to take it to the streets," I joke, not really convinced, but tired of fending off Michael's seemingly inexhaustible ammunition.

"Thanks, Rashan," Diane says, "that's the best way to deal with the recruitment speech. Sign right here."

Michael laughs. "You know, as unseemly selfish as the Reagan and Bush[3] years have been, I'm not focused solely on political economy."

---

[1] See *Appendix 4 – The Bard's Ghost*. Rashan's reference is to his first draft, in which he plays a TV news reporter.

[2] Michael notes: Culture-business is a term that I use to describe the thoroughness with which the values of capitalism, namely instinctive- and ego-based behaviors such as cynicism and greed (e.g., "Get what you can because there's not enough to go around."), permeate all aspects of society and individual consciousness, including art, spiritual practice, education, and government—i.e., everything, including people, becomes commoditized, just as Marx predicted. I borrowed the phrase from Marshall McLuhan's *Culture Is Our Business*, McGraw-Hill Book Company, New York, 1970.

[3] Michael notes: The transition between the Reagan and Bush presidencies was seamless, both politically and criminally, given that the same people were in charge. At the end of his second term, "Reagan" pocket-vetoed stricter ethics rules (*Washington Post*, 11/24/88) and a month later (12/16/88) now "President-elect" George Herbert Walker Bush designated John Tower as his Secretary of Defense as a pay-back for Tower's genial whitewash of the Iran-Contra scandal (As

"It's clear that your teachings on spirituality are invariably linked to everything else—technology, politics, economics, art," I say, "but it's the politics that land the body blows."

> *Despite the bumper stickers that say "one cannot simultaneously prepare for war and make peace," the*

previously noted, the Tower Commission slapped a few hands, but let the masterminds get off scot-free.) Later in his presidency, Bush pardoned those who took the hit for him. A few of them (Elliott Abrams, John Negroponte, and John Poindexter) now work for his son, President George W. Bush. But in becoming president, George H. W. Bush, former director of the CIA, necessarily makes the exercise of imperial power and monopoly capital transparent: Those in whose interest U.S. military, economic, and intelligence forces are wielded, clearly emboldened by their ruthless, hard-won success, forge on toward their "New World Order" under the aegis of the plutocrats. What clearer indication that the Earth is in the balance between G-d and Mammon? Imperially, Bush's arrogance is maximized. On July 3, 1988, when the U.S. battleship Vincennes "mistakes" Iran Air Flight 655 for a fighter plane and blasts it out of the sky, killing 290, President Reagan calls the incident an "understandable accident," though the Vincennes is one of the Navy's ultra-sophisticated computer-supported Aegis cruisers. When questioned about parallels to the "inadvertent" Soviet downing of KAL 007, Reagan insists there is "no comparison" between the events, and George H.W. Bush says, "I will never apologize for the United States of America! I don't care what the facts are!" Bush's monopolistic vision is clear as well. Despite his unambiguous aggressive totalitarian message, the few Americans who bother to vote generally support him: Like his son George W. in 2002, who avoided a scandal in the wake of the Senate Majority Leader Trent Lott's racist comments, George H. W. Bush survives the revelation that his campaign staff is riddled with anti-Semites, seven of whom resign. At this point, the American brand of fascism differentiates itself from Nazism: There is no need to overtly torment particular races or creeds, this is a war over control of resources, and any 'house slaves' (Harry Belafonte's term) that have the wherewithal to participate in this war are useful tokens for the right-wing of the capitalist party (the 'Republican' Party). (See "Strategic Racism," @ http://emperors-clothes.com/indict/911page.htm#5) That these minority persons (then Secretary of State Colin Powell, National Security Advisor Condoleezza Rice, Sen. Ben Nighthorse Campbell [R-CO], *et al.*) are so willing to sell-out to those who so efficiently slaughtered and enslaved their ancestors only shows the degree to which all races share in the worship of Mammon. On the eve of the Gulf War against Iraq in late 1990, George H.W. Bush states: "The world can therefore seize the opportunity [Persian Gulf crisis] to fulfill the long-held promise of a New World Order where diverse nations are drawn together in common cause to achieve the universal aspirations of mankind." George H.W. Bush, world-renowned gangster, apparently thinks himself capable of voicing the universal aspirations of mankind.

toroidal nature of the world warrants scrutiny of this proposition. Presently, the world is filled with so many weapons that it's hard to imagine how we shall bloodlessly transform our society from one patterned on instinctive- and ego-based aggressions into one reflective of the peaceful and compassionate nature of our higher selves: Blood is spilled every day in the name of half-truths and hate-filled philosophies posing as religious and political "solutions." Humankind must teach itself to sublimate these impulses by universal spiritual practice, each individual to his or her own. Given the examples of Jesus, Gandhi, and King, it shall not be surprising if the forces of the rich, powerful, and cynical do harm to those who practice non-violent civil disobedience and other pacifist tactics, for again, the unfolding of truth is paradoxical. Yet we shall not be deterred in defense of the earth and the evolution of our species. In this way we shall deliver a lasting peace—in the name of Love.

"The real revolution comes from the heart, Rashan," Michael says. "'Neither shall they say, Lo here! Or, lo there! For, behold, the kingdom of God is within you.'[4] When masses of people become willing to act upon the changes in their hearts that follow from their individual spiritual practices, then we shall have 'the Kingdom come ... on earth as it is in heaven.'[5] So, it could be no other way that a heartless, Antichrist figure such as Bush would be in power as my time draws near, at the so-called 'end of days,'[6] that I may make all things new through our project—now your play and this book, with more iterations to come."

---

[4] Luke 17:21. Michael writes in 2003: The Dalai Lama delivers the same message: "Although it is difficult to bring about peace through internal transformation, this is the only way to achieve lasting world peace. Even if during my lifetime it is not achieved, it is all right. The next generation will make more progress." The Dalai Lama, from *Tibetan Portrait: The Power of Compassion*, Photographs by Phil Borges, Text by His Holiness the Dalai Lama, Rizzoli International Publications, Inc., New York, 1996.

[5] From "The Lord's Prayer," Matthew 6:10, and Luke 11:2.

[6] Michael writes: The Bushes are the natural heirs to Hitler. The Dulles brothers filled up the CIA with Nazis they spirited away from Europe, and G.H.W. Bush later ran this organization. Since the creed of American society will no longer permit him to exhibit public racism, even a Skull and Bones Reich-relic worshipper like Bush is willing to quickly jettison anyone with a track record in this area. But

For the moment, all I can do is nod, feeling the weight of the world on my shoulders.

Seeing me founder, Diane jumps in. "Win one for the Gipper," she jibes.

We all laugh.

I had heard pieces of this rap before. I flash back to the night, many years ago when Michael and I had gone to see *Kindertransport*, the play about the Holocaust. I remembered Michael's description of how emperors from successive ages, Pharaoh, Herod, and Hitler had failed to destroy the contemporaneous prophets—Moses, Jesus, and the present spiritual anomaly. Now he is telling me that these rulers were all really a mask for the same dark force, but one necessarily linked to light—for these devils are our own shadows.

"I'll just satisfy myself with getting these conversations down on paper for the time being, and let the rest take care of itself," I say, overwhelmed at the forces of history now gathering.

"The time will be here soon enough, Rashan," Michael says, "when we'll look back on today's anonymity with nostalgia."

Our solace, of course, is in the transformation of which we're a part, aligned with Change itself—the Great Anomaly.

The next morning, Chimera is in her studio as the sun is rising. As I pass by on my way out for a hike she calls out. "I'll be here for a while. I've got twelve pictures to paint. If you could bring me some food at mealtimes—that would be great!"

Although intense and focused, brow furrowed, there is a different air about her today. Gone is the dark cloud that has been her companion for

---

privately, he is an extension of the same face of the Antichrist as Hitler. His father and grandfather, Prescott Bush and Herbert Walker, along with the Dulles brothers, the Harrimans, the Rockefellers and others, laundered money for the Nazis and helped finance the Nazi war machine. The companies they created to launder the money were seized by the U.S. Government in 1942 under the Trading With the Enemy Act. The only reason they didn't go to jail was that they were and are the richest and most powerful people in America. Even after this, the Rockefellers supplied oil to the Nazis, our declared enemies, while America was rationing gasoline to its own citizens.

months. An explanation will have to wait. "Okay, have fun!" I call out as I make my way into the sunshine.

For nearly three days this goes on, over a Labor Day weekend and beyond. It's as if the most recent months of increasing celibacy have escalated into a separation, yet I hold out hope for this being the culmination of our self-imposed "test." Each day, in-between my writing hours, meal making, and long afternoon walks with Gita in the magical luminance before the twilight, I stop in the studio and view paintings in various states of creation: the canvas shapes and sizes, the grain and texture of the paper, the stroke patterns, the contrasts set up by the underpainting—no two alike.

As she works, Chimera shares tidbits about the sequence of events represented in each painting and how the series of images were woven together in her still dazzlingly fresh breakthrough dream. I wait to put any of this to pen until she is finished and can tell me the whole story.

On the third night, Chimera sleeps in our bed for the first time since she had gone to her studio. Only cat naps of an hour or two here and there have kept her from total exhaustion. Hers had been a spiritual birthing of around-the-clock vigilance, accompanied by the sounds of sacred music wafting through her studio, a constant rotation of strong herbal teas, and only an occasional tidbit of solid nourishment.

Having Chimera lying next to me once again brings a sense of relief, not only in her proximity, but from the release I sense in her relaxed sleep. I doze off thinking about making love as we had before this latest trial. I see us once again sharing so completely that we lose track of our selves and become one loving being. When I awake from this blissful vision, I find we are indeed intertwined as we were in my imagined revelry, at the climax of our lovemaking.

The next day is a busy one at work. Andersen headquarters in Chicago has called and asked me to help evaluate a proposal from our Paris office. Between studying the documents and the conference call itself, I'm busy all day. I don't even get a breather at lunch, as I dine with a senior partner and discuss various matters relating to our Denver operations. But despite the demanding nature of all of this, throughout the day my thoughts turn to the previous evening's ecstasy and Chimera's dream.

That night, after dinner, Chimera shares her dream with me. We sit in our meditation room on over-sized stuffed pillows. With Persian incense billowing, and the tape recording running, the story unfolds. Chimera, eyes closed, begins slowly, as if she's receding into the free-form ethereal world of her dream. She remains in this meditative state, breathing slowly and deeply, for perhaps five minutes, and then, without opening her eyes, begins.[7]

She recounts a dream that consists of twelve paintings, each evolving from one to the other, that capture her life beginning with her earliest recollections from the womb, of an attempted abortion, through her struggles with alcoholism, culminating with a spiritual epiphany in which she is united spiritually with Michael. Finished, her eyes still closed, she re-enters the deep meditative state that preceded her narrative, and remains so for a few minutes. I follow her lead, close my eyes, and let go of my thoughts.

It is a remarkable vision that has come to her. The paintings borrow heavily from masters, and yet are uniquely her own. Much of their subject matter, the difficulties of Chimera's life before we met, are not news to me—we have often discussed our trials with each other—but the fluidity with which they are represented and transformed each into the other, until they are resolved in a final vision, is achieved with such clarity as to defy any conscious explanation. The whole process underscores the genius and healing power of the subconscious, particularly as it is influenced by what Michael calls "The Anomaly," that point within each of us that is tangential to everything that is, was, and will be.

"And how do you feel now?" I ask after a few moments of smiling at each other.

"Perfect."

"Perfect?"

"Yes, perfect in spirit. A perfection that's changing Chimera into a new person."

"So, you speak of yourself now in the third person?"

"The part of me that was elevated through this experience has tasted omniscience, Rashan. It gives me a much different perspective on my own

---

[7] For the full text of the dream, see *Appendix 5 – Twelve Paintings*.

personality, as if I were looking at myself from Michael's point-of-view, 'as Christ,' as it were."

"I have to admit I'm jealous. I came so close in my own dream to what you're describing."

"All I can suggest, based on what I'm experiencing, is to have faith in your dream and your truth. The rest will come. As you told me a couple of months ago, Michael channels the power to make it happen, and now I've experienced it. He symbolizes transformation in my dream just as he did in yours."

"It's hard not to be overwhelmed by the enormity of it," I say.

"You mean Michael being our friend as well as this special being?"

"Yes. That and the influence he's had on us."

"According to him, he's astonished by it as well," Chimera says.

"I'm sure he is."

Not long afterwards, we have Michael and Diane over for dinner. I decide to prepare Chimera's spicy Mexican dish, a creamy mix of beans, tomatoes, and chilies over fluffy long-grained brown rice seasoned with paprika and cayenne.

"Didn't you used to put chicken in this?" Michael asks Chimera.

"Yes, you're right, but Rashan made this. Our approaches to protein are different," Chimera replies, baiting Michael.

"In what way?" Michael responds so immediately that if he were an actor I'd have accused him of stepping on Chimera's line—not waiting a full beat, as if he didn't consider what she'd said. Clearly, there is never any question in his mind that what people eat has implications that reverberate throughout the universe. Perhaps *he* baited *her*.

"Well, of course," I join in, "the biggest concern people have about vegetarianism is the amount and quality of protein that they get."

> *After a few months of diligent Yoga practices, my body is becoming a finely tuned and highly responsive tool capable of evaluating the nutritional worth of every meal I partake. My early experiments with vegetarianism have resulted in a significant weight loss, particularly considering*

that I was not more than a couple of pounds overweight when I began. I find it curious that this shedding seems to parallel the degree to which my ego has come under the influence of my higher mind, as if my body mass had served as a self-preserving buffer for my instinctive nature. But perhaps the most startling event is the surge in strength I experience the day after I mix adzuki beans with rice and muster the force to accomplish the swan and peacock poses for the first time. It strikes me immediately that understanding protein formation, in this case combining legumes and whole grains to produce the full spectrum of the amino acids, is critical to healthy vegetarianism.

"That's one major concern," Diane concurs. "There are some legitimate questions concerning the types and amounts of protein and amino acids that maximize human health."

"That," says Michael, "and the less critical but equally compelling fact that the primary foods which comprise a vegetarian diet may not be as satisfying in terms of acquired taste to those who are used to eating meat or the industrially-sweetened confections they call dessert. And then, for others, killing animals gives them some sense of superiority and control over their destiny, as if 'life is a jungle' is the only metaphor they're capable of understanding."

"Right, those too," I continue. "So, in the wake of our conversations on this subject, my conclusions are fairly simple."

"And ..." Michael begs the question.

"There's no argument that from a spiritual point of view there's little to be said for killing for one's food."

"That would depend on our evolutionary juncture," Michael inserts.

"What do you mean by that?" I wonder.

"The food chain is indicative of the continuous spectrum of life," he says. "Plants react to the sun, rotating before it for growth and sustenance, just as animals use their eyes and senses to hunt for food. It's only a matter of degrees where one draws the line for diet, as an herbivore or omnivore. Destroying our natural predators during the survival phase of our evolution was then natural and instinctive, but it has now become problematic. At this time in history we need to base our choices on sustainability. Today, surviving *ourselves* and our use of the planet, not *our predators* and their imperatives, is paramount. And to do this requires an evolutionary change in consciousness and spiritual awareness and control over 'the killer instinct,' including the adrenaline and testosterone and anger surrounding it. Morality is relative to our evolutionary progression; it is our present state and condition as humans that makes killing passé, so that if it is done consciously, no amount of karmic, dialectical, Socratic, Christian, Buddhist, or Talmudic reasoning can overcome the regression associated with it. One must draw a similar line in political practice as well, between pacifism and aggression. Consider a vegan and pro-active pacifist like Ghandi, who draws his line in the same place for diet as for politics, and a vegetarian and murderer like Hitler, who draws his dietary line in a different place than his political line. Clearly, in this day and age, consistency is what we seek.

"As I said before:

> 'You do not, therefore, transgress the law if you kill the wild beast to save your brother's life. For I tell you truly, man is more than the beast. But he who kills a beast without a cause, although the beast attack him not, through lust for slaughter, or for its flesh, or for its hide, or yet for its tusks, evil is the deed which he does, for he is turned into a wild beast himself.'"[8]

"But," Chimera interrupts, "this argument was made at a time when the chemistry of diet was unknown. Now, there's some question whether humans, or at least some humans, depending on their blood type,[9] don't require animal products in their diet to be healthy, and if so, whether the critical amino acids could be supplanted by artificial means."

"So you're saying," Diane asks, "that if there is a scientific basis for animal protein being a crucial element in some or all human diet, then we would need to weigh the karmic repercussions of killing animals versus our own health?"

---

[8] *Op. Cit.*, Székely, *The Gospel of Peace of Jesus Christ*, p. 46.
[9] Dr. Peter J. D'Adamo with Catherine Whitney, *Eat Right For Your Type*, G.P. Putnam's Sons, New York, 1996.

"Yes," Chimera replies. "It is much like when Don Juan kills a rabbit and Carlos is horrified.[10] Don Juan tells him that we are not only predators, but prey, like the rabbit, stalked by Death itself; one day it shall be our turn to go."

"Putting aside my admonition that 'man is more than the beast,' what about the eco-damage associated with meat?" Michael asks.

"You mean the methane problem?" Chimera asks.

"There's no getting around the fact that livestock manure is choking us," Michael says, beginning one of his patented raps. "In America, 20 tons of it is produced each year for every household, and the eco-disasters that have occurred as a result of this, like the 1995 New River hog waste spill in North Carolina, dwarf the Exxon Valdez oil spill in terms of damage to our fresh water supplies and wildlife,[11] not to mention the air.[12]

This isn't farming; this is corporate sabotage of the environment for profit. Then there's the astounding waste of resources and valuable protein

---

[10] Chimera's reference is to the series of mystical books by Carlos Castaneda that began with *The Teachings of Don Juan: A Yaqui Way of Knowledge* and *A Separate Reality*, to which we alluded in Chapter 1.

[11] Again, see Jim Motavalli, *op. cit.*, "So You're an Environmentalist; Why Are You Still Eating Meat?" from *E Magazine*, 1/3/02 as linked from www.alternet.org on 1/4/02. On 12/16/02, the Bush-controlled U.S. EPA issued new rules to comply with a 1989 lawsuit by the Natural Resources Defense Council that will require some 15,500 factory farms to obtain government permits to dispose of livestock waste. Critics of these regulations say that they are more lax than those drafted under the Clinton administration; the new regulations require fewer farms to comply, grant livestock owners more leeway to draft their own pollution-management plans, relieve major corporations of financial liability for illegal spills by growers or subcontractors, eliminate measures to make use of new technology to combat pollution, and fail to mandate groundwater monitoring. (*Washington Post*, Eric Pianin and Anita Huslin, 17 Dec 2002, as linked from http://www.gristmagazine.com). Meat produced in this type of environment is toxic as well, so the beef industry is trying to sell irradiation as means of avoiding recurrences of Mad Cow disease and various *e coli* epidemics. Critics charge, however, that irradiation process depletes vitamins and nutrients and leaves chemical by-products in food (Jerry Bieszk, "US food industry begins to embrace irradiation," 2/4/03, @ http://www.planetark.org/dailynewsstory.cfm/newsid/19685/story.htm). The writing's on the wall for industrial meat production: It's free-range, grass eating beef or nothing.

[12] Rosenthal, Elizabeth, "As More Eat Meat, a Bid to Cut Emissions," *The New York Times*, 12/4/08.

used to feed cattle. This also is criminal. If meat consumption in the world were reduced only ten percent, we'd gain enough protein from what's fed cattle to feed another 60 million people.[13] This is because so much beef cattle is raised not on grass, but on grains and legumes in feed lots, where they have little range and where the unhealthy conditions produced by overcrowding and waste result in heavy use of steroids to fight disease, not to mention the use of hormones to artificially induce weight gain to increase profit. So here we are cutting down the rainforests for grazing land, and adding all sort of chemicals to the food chain to produce more meat per animal and to make it look 'more appealing' with dyes and such."

"But that doesn't mean that cattle itself is a problem," Chimera counters.

"True," Michael says. "If we were to approach diet, food supplies, and human population from the standpoint of a scientific problem, much like Buckminster Fuller's concept of World Game, that is, managing Spaceship Earth[14] as if it were a closed system, which for all practical purposes it is, then what we grow or raise in terms of crops and animals, what we require in terms of vitamins, minerals, amino acids, and such, and how many people we can support given the amount of arable land available and its use in a sustainable manner, are all mutually interdependent and scientifically discoverable factors that should determine our policies, as opposed to the profit motive and unbridled instincts which now rule the roost. Diet then becomes a combination of nutritional value—protein, vitamins, minerals, et cetera—plus chemical balance—that is Yin-Yang, pH, and sodium-potassium ratios, plus caloric content—plus availability and sustainability.

---

[13] Jean Mayer, cited by the U.S. Senate Select Committee on Nutrition and Human Needs, *Dietary Goals for the U.S.* (Washington, DC, (February, 1977), p. 44, as noted in Rosen, Steven, *Diet For Transcendence: Vegetarianism and the Worlds Religions*, Torchlight Publishing, Inc., Badger, CA, 1997, p. 8, and, once more, in Jim Motavalli's "So You're an Environmentalist; Why Are You Still Eating Meat?," *op cit*.

[14] See Fuller, R. Buckminster, *Operating Manual for Spaceship Earth*, Amereon Ltd., 1978. "Fuller saw the goal of the World Game to 'make the world work for 100% of humanity, in the shortest possible time, through spontaneous cooperation, and without ecological offense or the disadvantage of anyone.'" Also, see, http://www.worldgame.org .

"So," Michael continues, "not only is the family farm with free-running grass-eating livestock nearly passé, we may be past the point where animal protein is a viable option for those whose blood type or dietary theory or psychological comfort may demand it."

"You're saying that despite some scientific evidence for the value of animal protein, we may have to forgo this path?" Chimera asks.

"Yes," Michael says. "We need to make an evolutionary decision regarding our food intake and consider the planetary consequences. Look, there have been many creative and happy vegetarians—Pythagoras, Leonardo da Vinci, Benjamin Franklin, George Bernard Shaw, Albert Einstein. Obviously, genius does not require animal protein."

"Though your own proofs weren't developed entirely during your vegetarian period," Diane says.

"True," Michael says. "I have supplemented my diet with fish and fowl."

"It's very confusing," Chimera says, "like the indications in the Bible that Jesus ate meat."

"As we've explained," Michael says, "the Christian *Bible* is only a semi-accurate account of the story; but regardless, Middle Easterners from that time did not eat meat in the quantities that Westerners consume today, nor were the animals that they did eat as unhealthy and poisoned as those that are eaten today. Whether Jesus ate meat in small quantities or whether, as the Essene Gospels indicate, he was a vegetarian, is not particularly relevant now, for as I've told you, it's my mission to synthesize current scientific information with spiritual practice in a manner that provides a basis for a sustainable future. But I am impressed with the research you've done since we last talked about diet."

"You are what you eat, or as *you* say, 'this is my body, this is my blood,'" Chimera responds.

"'Such faith as this I have not seen even in Israel,'"[15] Michael says. "I didn't realize my time draws so near."

"Sorry," says Chimera, smiling. "Who am I to jump start history? It's just, in the dream I had, there you were in all your glory, at The Feast of the Holy Eucharist—Passover—sermonizing."

"You dreamt of The Last Supper?" Michael asks her incredulously.

---

[15] Matthew 8:10, Luke 7:9.

"That's not what I would call it. It was more like the first supper, actually—the beginning of something new."

"Like now, you mean?" Diane asks.

"And yet I spoke in biblical syntax," Michael says, stroking his chin. "Something like, 'And to the Jews, Christians, Muslims, Hindus, Buddhists, Taoists and others I say unto you, there is no basis for any spiritual belief that incorporates murder into its philosophy. To the degree that any of you perpetrate violence, that is your distance from the Great Anomaly and your true self. Through violence each of you hath made false witness unto G-d and his messenger, and still you claim your churches are heirs to the principles of his kingdom. To you, I say, 'Your license is revoked by and returned to the rightful owner. Whosoever presumes to represent me through a church that condones killing is a false prophet, for the true church resides in your heart.'"

"That's much the voice as I heard it, Michael," Chimera says, "—even the biblical syntax."

"Well," says Michael, "as Zimmerman[16] said, '... I'll know my song well before I start singin'.'"

"Right, 'It's a hard rain a-gonna fall,'"[17] Chimera rejoins.

"So it will be for many," Michael says.

"Anyway, that's the way you appeared to me in my dream," Chimera says.

"Fascinating." Michael says.

"But that was actually the *last* panel of the dream," Chimera emphasizes.

"The *last* panel?" Michael asks.

"Yes. That's how the dream progressed," Chimera says, "—one panel at a time through twelve paintings, clearly divided, like Rashan's dream was by acts and scenes."

"Interesting that it came in twelve steps," Diane says, "like a self-help program."

---

[16] Robert Allan Zimmerman, alias Bob Dylan, the folksinger and poet. Michael, for reasons we shall not reveal at this time, was fond of referring to him by his given name, much like John Lennon did in his song "God" on his *Imagine* album in 1984.

[17] From Bob Dylan's song "A Hard Rain's A-Gonna Fall," on *The Freewheelin' Bob Dylan* album, Columbia Records, 1963.

"No kidding," Chimera says.

"Tell us about it," Michael says.

Chimera proceeds to go through the dream.[18] At the beginning, Michael listens intently, since the images, and the issues that they represent in Chimera's life, speak for themselves. However, when she reaches the seventh panel, where she unites with Michael's spirit, he feels the need to comment.

"That's it exactly, Chimera, your feeling of 'as Christ.' That is the central reason why I'm here—to encourage others to replicate the perfection of spirit that is available to them, regardless of what they call it. Worship the Messiah or the Christ or the Buddha or the Krishna or the G-d principle *within*, not someone else's external representation."

"So, you're saying that 'as Christ' is just one way of looking at my experience?"

"Yes, though an important one. Given the vagaries of history, the mantle of Christ has taken on an exclusive aura to Westerners, because of their general lack of familiarity with my other appearances. Many will see me is simply as the Second Coming of Jesus the Christ, but, as I say, that is an unnecessary limitation."

"So how would you have it?"

"As we've discussed, the word *Christ* is Greek for the Hebrew *Messiah*, which means literally 'the anointed one.' But both the word *Christ* and the word *Messiah* have come to be associated with particular religious beliefs. It is not my intent to favor any one religious belief, because I am not here to start another religion nor to bolster existing ones (other than to accept the part that they have played in providing for and explaining my appearance); I'm here to encourage the evolution of humankind through spiritual development and the recognition of the unity of all things. The fact that in my current incarnation I am associated with Judaism and Christianity through my birth and culture is an outgrowth of historical exigencies—the groundwork that has been laid and the prophesies that address the next evolutionary phase. As we've also discussed, the destruction of historical documents in The Flood and the burning of the libraries at Alexandria contributes to this narrow view of my work and the lack of recognition of my many incarnations. So, using the

---

[18] See *Appendix 5 – Chimera's Dream*.

term 'Christ' is simply an efficacious means of gathering energy and getting people to pay attention. On another planet the particulars would be different."

"That's it?"

"Sure. Think of the difference between, 'Hey, did you hear that the Avatar of the age, the Spiritual Anomaly, the World Teacher, is on the planet and has important things to say?' and 'Hey, did you hear that the Messiah, the Christ, has returned to earth in the flesh and is speaking The Word and passing Judgment?'"

I can't help but agree. "Yes, there's a major difference in my reactions to these statements. The idea that the Messiah or Christ is here, now, is loaded with connotations that carry great power."

"So it is with the cultural prejudices of the West, where most of the world's wealth and military might reside. Yet truly, the Messiah, the Christ, the Buddha, the World Teacher, the Avatar, these are all different names for the same manifestation, the same spiritual anomaly. There's no need to limit how people explain my existence. Chimera's use of the descriptor 'Christ Michael' in her dream is quite appropriate, since it not only sets up the differentiation between the eternal spirit—the Christ energy—and the temporal body through whom it manifests—in this case Michael, but it also begs the notion of the sequential periodicity of the avatars—Krishna, Zoroaster,[19] Jesus, Michael, et al. The point of this image in Chimera's dream, though, is not the name of concept that she employs. The point is that she experienced union with the One as she sees it represented in human form, as a result of which she achieved a certain wholeness and power to heal that which afflicted her."

"Much like what happened with me in *The Bard's Ghost*?"[20]

"Yes, one and the same, except that for you, it is still only an intellectual experience."

"And in both cases," I continue, desperately ignoring Michael's distinction between Chimera's progress and my own, "we saw you as Christ."

---

[19] Some consider Zoroaster or Zarathustra, an earlier manifestation of Michael Melchizedek, the one and the same soul who is Jesus and Michael, as he used the same sacraments. See *The Urantia Book*, The Urantia Foundation, 1955.

[20] Again, this refers to the initial version of the play and not the current stage version (see *Appendix 4 – The Bard's Ghost*).

"As it should be, for that is what I represent to those steeped in Christianity," Michael replies, still staring at me as if searching for some recognition of his previous comment.

"And in both dreams," Chimera adds, "you were teaching and speaking in a similarly elevated style, which is different than how you normally speak."

"Correct," Michael says, now slowly turning to Chimera. "I use the colloquial voice with the two of you because you're my close friends. I've known you for over 16 years, since early in my mission. But once this book is written, the public tone and focus of my teaching will shift away from the background information that we're publishing—the integration of psychology, physics, spiritual practice, biology, politics, religion, diet, economics, theatre, et cetera—and focus more on spiritual solutions. This doesn't mean that I will abandon an interdisciplinary approach to knowledge, only that my priorities will shift toward helping humankind transform its internal landscape. My exoteric use of elevated language, as you call it, will not change either, for just as the last time around, when I set up the expectation that 'Greater works than I shall ye do,'[21] so this time do I also expect my example to be absorbed and surpassed by those who follow. That is evolution. It's my goal that sophistication of language and thought become commonplace during this age, just as I expect Christ-, Buddha-, Krishna-Consciousness, etc., to become commonplace."

"And that is why you're working on digital courseware—to teach this to others?" I confirm.

"Right."

"Where are you in that process?" I ask, ever cognizant of detailing the discussion for the tape recorder and posterity.

"I've learned that research universities, governments, and businesses are now sharing scientific data between computers by way of dedicated phone lines called networks, and that there is already talk of marketing this communication device to individuals. This, I believe, is the beginning of the technology, of which we've spoken, that will alter communication patterns and enable our teachings reach a worldwide audience."

"And until this happens, Michael," Chimera queries, "what do you plan to do?"

---

[21] Paraphrase of John 14:12.

"I'll be expanding my regional audience."

"Another venture?" I ask.

"Yes," Michael says, "—something you got me started with."

"*I* got you started?"

"Yes, you were definitely the catalyst."

"What is it?" I ask.

"Theatre reviews."

"You're going to review theatre productions?"

"Exactly, on public radio."

"The jazz station?" Chimera wonders.

"Yep. KIVA-FM," Michael replies, pronouncing the first four call letters as the word "kiva."[22]

"How cool!" Chimera is ecstatic. "My favorite station!"

"Mr. Yogajazz,"[23] says Diane, "—the improvisations of the toroidal brain."

"That's great, Michael," I say. "I listen to it all the time. I'm honored that our mutual interest led to this new gig."

"We're all *guru* and *chela*,[24] Rashan. Don't think that because of my anomalistic position in my field that I don't learn from everything I experience. I've been given a unique responsibility, but my life involves learning and teaching, just like everyone else."

"I appreciate your humility," I reply. "As you say, we're all just different facets of the same source energy."

"Still, it's overwhelming sometimes," Chimera says. "and not so easy to deal with, this constant awareness of unity."

"I see it like falling in love," says Diane, "except that it never slows down or goes away."

"Just remember," Michael says, "that we're all conscious miracles with our own unique truths."

"This has been a wonderful dinner," I remark after a few moments of silence, "even if it isn't *The First Supper*."

"I do believe, when all's said and done," Michael says with a prophetic tone, "that Chimera's *The First Supper* will reveal itself to be a

---

[22] A large underground chamber used for Pueblo and Hopi spiritual rites.
[23] See "Yogajazz" in *Appendix 7 – Michael's Notes*.
[24] *guru* and *chela*, literally teacher and student, from Sanskrit.

natural progression of Leonardo's and Dali's work on the same subject—it evolves the message of *consolamentum*,[25] yet with her own unique twist, just as your play, Rashan, resolves the Shakespearean authorship question and begs the question, 'Who is the real author of Christianity?'"

Now that's confidence!

In the months that follow, Chimera's voices cease to interfere with her life or her work. When, on occasion, they rise up expecting the opportunity to haunt her, she effortlessly disperses them with a phrase or two that always ends up with, "I am as Christ," much the same as Michael's "I am Christ" from his own dream. She has awakened her own integrated G-d principle by modeling Michael, just as Michael modeled Jesus, and Jesus modeled the Messiah or Christ archetype from the Great Anomaly itself, each serving as a mirror to the next.

The pastels that result from Chimera's dream-sequence transformation remain grouped on a wall in her studio to remind her of the healing power that lies within. And while the techniques imbued in this dodecalogue are replicated in many of the paintings that now flow from her studio, this influence would be unnoticeable to anyone unless they had seen the "Twelve Steps" series or had an expert's eye for artistic evolution. While, her new work is very much along the same thematic lines as her old work, that is, natural settings found in the mountains and valleys that rise up to the west of Boulder (and wherever else we wander, in our travels), there is a subtle difference—a change in the quality of light woven into the very fabric of her paintings.

This elevation in her work is reflected in the marketplace as well. More galleries and arts festivals are now expressing an interest in exhibiting her latest canvases, providing Chimera with steady sales and further opportunities to share her newfound insights into transformational healing.

---

[25] As Leonardo symbolically transmitted in his painting, the secret healing power taught to the disciples (the *consolamentum* [Latin]) is a ceremony in which the aspirant is subject to a laying on of the hands by the "Perfect," or guide, of his or her community. See, Javier Sierra, *The Secret Supper*, Simon & Schuster Ltd., New York, 2006.

For me, however—despite the proximity I came in my own dream to identifying within myself the same force that healed Chimera—the intervening months don't bring me across the threshold into any such consciousness as I see in her. This gap between my own experience and that of Chimera and Michael has exacerbated the separation that I feel from them.

I wonder about the price of enlightenment. Despite having practiced "intermittent celibacy" at Chimera's request, does my lack of commitment to this and other Yoga-related austerities hold back my progress? Chimera's work, since her transformation, has blossomed. What would I sacrifice to alter my consciousness if I believed my own work would undergo a similar improvement? Would I dare separate from Chimera to make this happen?

I decide to talk with Michael about this and make a date to have breakfast with him one Sunday morning. We go to the Aristocrat diner, on the north end of downtown Boulder along the main drag.

"Fancy meeting you here, in such a plutocratic environment," I say, referencing the name of the restaurant.

"That's more ironic than you know," Michael says, "because Nick, the owner, is just a regular guy. I think he named this placed such because that's how he treats his customers—as if each of them were important, but without the pretensions that go with wealth—just like the famous steak house in Chicago, where they used to greet you, 'Yes sir, Senator!'"

"I knew you'd find a way to turn the meaning around," I say, my hopes dashed that Michael would laugh at my comment.

"No turning around is needed, Rashan," Michael says. "The contradictions of the present are generating the seeds of its replacement. It's the same point I made last time we spoke, when I said that building business skills training for the web is subversive. Nick's 'aristocratic' magnanimity is contagious. He even forces his hungriest guests to share."

"What do you mean?" I ask.

"Are you hungry this morning, Rashan?"

"Yeah, I could eat a horse, except that I don't eat meat."

"Great! We'll share a Nick's Omelet," Michael says. "You'll see exactly what I'm talking about."

Sure enough, when our waitress delivers our breakfast, she unloads an omelet so vast in the middle of the table that it requires a serving plate to hold it. Next to it she adds a heaping plate of whole wheat toast.

"There you go, Rashan," Michael says. "Now we're just two aristocrats sharing breakfast after the revolution."

"If it were only that simple," I reply. "Not even the liberal Clinton could get that to happen here."

"Of course," Michael concurs, "because Clinton represents the same so-called New World Order as Reagan and Bush.[26] Look at the figures. He's incarcerated more people than any other President.[27] This is the charade of the so-called two-party system that keeps people thinking things will get better; but the Democrats are just the left wing of the same party as the Republicans—the Capitalist party. They throw us social and environmental crumbs while kowtowing to the same money-grubbing, Mammon-worshiping forces as the Republicans. The armaments sales[28] and drug-trafficking[29] continue as before. It's business as usual for big

---

[26] Strobe Talbot, President Clinton's Deputy Secretary of State, as quoted in *Time*, July 20th, 1992, is a dead echo of David Rockefeller: "In the next century, nations as we know it will be obsolete; all states will recognize a single, global authority. National sovereignty wasn't such a great idea after all."

[27] At the end of Clinton's eight-year term, criminal justice statistics show that he implemented the most punitive platform on crime in the last two decades. "Tough on crime" policies passed during his tenure resulted in the largest increases in federal and state prison inmates of any president in American history. http://www.cjcj.org/pubs/clinton/clinton.html

[28] A year after running on the promise to change one of the most pernicious aspects of U.S. policy—this country's role as the world's number-one weapons trafficking nation—the rhetoric of restraint gave way to an unprecedented arms-selling spree. In fiscal year 1993, the United States sold over $31 billion worth of weaponry to more than 140 nations, the first time any nation had topped the $30-billion barrier.
http://www.findarticles.com/p/articles/mi_m1252/is_n10_v121/ai_15254325

[29] The Iran-Contra operation was run out of Mena, Arkansas with the knowledge and support of former CIA operative and then Governor, Bill Clinton. "Cocaine was obtained from Colombia and moved to Panama where it was protected by Panamanian defense forces. Next, drugs were moved through Costa Rica, where the shipments were personally guarded by the Minister of Public Security. The final destination was U.S. territory. The flights were handled by the FBI and CIA and met no resistance. ... The major traffic point was Mena, Arkansas, where the weapons production and training of Contras took place, and where shipment of guns and trained Contras originated. Planes returning from Central America

business, its government vassals, and its partners—the Mafia, third world puppets, and the mercenary armies of imperialism—all obese from slavery to their instincts and ego, bereft of spiritual practice, their souls long-since sold to the devil."

"Your analytic and polemic consistency over the years concerning the behavior of the so-called Power Elite is duly noted," I say, in-between bites on my portion of the omelet. "But that's not why I asked you here."

"Sorry, Rashan," Michael concedes. "Sometimes I'm caught between our friendship and the fact that you're tape recording me for wider distribution. I'm like my friend, a broadcast emcee, who does a monologue every time the refrigerator door opens and the light comes on. The door isn't open for long, so I've got to connect personal behavior to global survival at every opportunity."

I laugh at the image of Michael, as seen from the inside of the refrigerator, running off his pre-recorded message in the time it takes to grab the milk, before the door closes and the light goes off.

"Well, okay," I say. "I understand how media personalities live and die by the tally light. The art of keeping the audience focused on your performance is similar in theatre, even if the scale and technique are somewhat different."

"So what do you want to talk about?" Michael asks.

"It's about my lack of progress, Michael," I say. "I feel left behind, like the Rapture's happened and I'm still wallowing in lack of commitment and constant sexual frustration."

"Whoa, boy!" Michael says. "What's brought on this self-doubt? Based on your dream, I thought you were making good progress."

"But the dream didn't do the trick. My soul is still devoid of cosmic consciousness in a way that Chimera's isn't, and that separates me from her and from you. I feel like an outsider."

---

would be carrying cocaine. It was easy to load drugs on the planes that returned to the U.S. after delivering weapons to the Contras. The distribution within the United States was handled by the Mafia. ... Clinton made deals to launder CIA money through his scam loan agency, Arkansas Development and Finance Authority. In return, he retained 10% of all the money laundered, and through the ADFA financed local companies, including the Park-O-Meter company in Russellville, Arkansas, to manufacture guns for the Contras."
(http://www.wealth4freedom.com/truth/13/Mena.htm)

"Maybe it's time to change your practice," Michael says.

"What do you suggest?"

"You've got trust issues, Rashan," he says. "You need to find a way to trust your higher self as well as others. Only by recognizing this greater power will you get past the intellectualization of spirituality and move your consciousness from your ego to your heart. Granted, your ego is scared of giving up control—that's part of its instinctive, look-out-for-number-one nature—but you simply have to accept on faith that you won't lose your mind; it'll just have different values. There isn't any other way. If, as you've told me, your lack of trust stems from what happened to you in your youth, with Marguerite, then I suggest by learning to trust Chimera you'll learn to trust yourself.

"It's like the dream about a wolf that I told you I had as a child,"[30] Michael continues. "I lived for a short time with my grandfather, Jacob Solomon, in a dark apartment building in Gary, Indiana. In this recurring dream, I am on the second story landing, locked out of our apartment, and a wolf walks up the stairs and eats me. Finally, after the dream has recurred many times, and in the midst of it again one night, I refuse to be frightened and simply *let* the wolf eat me. That's it. The dream never recurs. My childhood lesson in faith and submission was a steppingstone to a receptivity that opened the door to Messiah or Christ consciousness; by solving that problem, I learned to trust my own shadow, which made it possible for me to have my 'I am Christ' dream as an adult."

He pauses and looks at me as if he's reading my face.

"I have a friend, Elysabeth," Michael continues, "who specializes in 'Partner Yoga.' A Partner Yoga practice could be a steppingstone to your own enlightenment."

Then, as if by virtue of some strange time-warp that sends me back seventeen years to the time when Michael gave me his *Ashtanga* Yoga card, he now hands me Elysabeth's card:

> Elysabeth
> www.PartnerYoga.net

☼ ☼ ☼

---

[30] See *Chapter 2 – A Plan.*

That evening Chimera and I talk about Michael's suggestion.

"I'm not sure about this," I say. "This seems like such a non-traditional approach, like a gimmick, like the latest aerobic exercise—another way of singles meeting singles."

"You were skeptical about taking Yoga instruction from Michael, remember?" Chimera asks.

"Yes, but that was different. Yoga is a proven practice."

"Not to you it wasn't, Rashan. Look, where would you be in the theatre if you weren't open to experimentation?"

I can't respond to that, since she's obviously right.

"You always have the option of stopping if you don't like it," she continues. "Contact Elysabeth and see what she has to say. I'm happy to do the sessions with you."

Sometimes the muse is hard to ignore. I go to the PartnerYoga.net website and write an e-mail to Elysabeth, asking her if we could talk about the process of Partner Yoga. Besides, I tell myself, this is a chance to meet another of Michael's friends.

After a couple of e-mails back and forth, I call her the following Saturday afternoon.

"Michael gave me your card because he says I have trust issues," I explain after some pleasantries.

"Building trust is an important aspect of the Partner Yoga experience," Elysabeth says. "In the context of yogic postures and mindfulness, we use touch and balance to explore emotional boundaries. Some people have difficulty relaxing the boundaries between themselves and others, and some people have difficulty maintaining boundaries. Both are important in finding that place where we overlap, where we are the same. This is what allows us to trust."

"I can see where trust is the key to a higher place," I say, "but I haven't gotten there yet."

"There's no half way about this," she says, "at least not if you want healing. You have to be committed. Whatever latent issues exist in your relationship will be brought up by Partner Yoga, and those issues are likely to be tied to your own personal issues."

"I'm afraid that most of the issues between Chimera and me are my issues at this point," I say.

"If you have issues, then so will Chimera," she says. "Even if they're your issues, she will feel them, and that may add to your feelings of separation."

"Then how do I get out of this loop?" I ask. "It seems like a Catch-22: Michael tells me that I have to be whole in order to experience the full depth of love and to share it, so I use his method and come up short. Now you're telling me that I need to connect with someone else in order to be whole, but how can I involve someone else if I'm not whole? What comes first, the chicken or the egg?"

"There is no beginning," she says. "We're social beings. Your mother gave birth to you and nurtured you. You couldn't become whole without her. Michael brought you another distance. There's nothing unnatural about getting help from others. It's not only necessary, it's unavoidable."

"How come Michael and Chimera had their breakthroughs through Yoga and I haven't?"

"For some people, Yoga cultivates ego instead of compassion. It may have been easier for Chimera than you because, as a woman, it is more natural to integrate without ego. But your intellect, while necessary and important to who you are, also holds you back because it's not always connected to your heart. That's the integration you're missing."

"You make it sound as if it is a male problem?"

"Masculine and feminine is different than male and female. The whole idea of Jungian integration is about marrying the masculine and feminine within each of us. If you're having trouble locating your own feminine, you can model someone else's. Instead of seeing Chimera's femininity as separate, and desiring it as an object, you can find similar qualities within yourself. That's how you'll find trust."

The pain that I associate with Marguerite washes over me, as if on cue, obviously indicating that I associate this feeling with Chimera as well. I understand on the spot that as long as I continue to make these associations, I'll feel separation in any intimate relationship, whether it's with a woman or even with G-d.

"So how will Partner Yoga help me internalize the feminine that Chimera mirrors to me?" I ask.

"Men tend to be more goal-oriented than women," she says. "With touch, their glands initiate a focus on genital connection. This is the part of the cycle where we often get stuck, rarely getting to experience deep touch outside of sex. Alone, sex is a dead-end. It needs to be part of a whole spectrum of touch and trust. Partner Yoga is a practice of cultivating the sacred touch that is innate to all of us. That's what I teach. You could do this same work in other ways, of course, through dance, or massage, or other partnering practices."

"So, do you recommend that your students practice celibacy to get past this instinctive orientation?" I ask, still smarting from the sexual repercussions of my original commitment to do Yoga: 'intermittent celibacy.'

"The goal of Partner Yoga, just like individual Yoga, is to awaken the whole person. You can practice it with friends and acquaintances to establish a relationship, you can practice it with your significant other as a relational tool, you can even practice it as foreplay, if you like, to enhance your sensitivity to the sexual experience. In any case, Partner Yoga is a way to bring forth cosmic consciousness, or whatever you want to call it. It's based on the same principles that Jesus healed by: Believing is part of the process; it requires a self-conscious act by all parties to heal and be healed."

All this makes sense. What Elysabeth is saying is much like what Michael has told me. And as Chimera reminded me, I was skeptical about Yoga, too, at first. If I don't like Partner Yoga, I can stop whenever I like.

"So all I need to do is believe?" I ask.

"All you need to do is be authentic," Elysabeth says. "If you can do that, then Partner Yoga can do everything that an individual practice does—only accelerate it. The total effect is greater than the sum of the parts. If you can give up the idea of me-you, win-lose, give-take, and evolve to cooperation, trust and love, it can work for you."

So Chimera and I attend a weekend workshop. It becomes apparent to me shortly into the Saturday session that despite my issues, Chimera has no problem trusting me. Invariably, I am the one who determines how long it takes us to relax and settle into a posture and the resultant experience. In the course of the weekend, the process gets easier for me, though my physical and emotional commitments are still tentative. Yet I'm happy having sensed some movement: I'm now more aware of when I'm holding back.

What I experience that weekend is a microcosm of Chimera's and my relationship. Chimera has apparently overcome the need for "intermittent celibacy." Her rebirth and the resultant bliss reverberate throughout her consciousness. She is quite happy to indulge my passion whenever I am so moved, and indeed, returns my ardor manifold; yet, if I withdraw from my senses for days, or even weeks at a time, she remains serene and supportive. "Whatever you need to do to experience unity that I feel, I support," she tells me. So now, our sex life is largely regulated by my needs, with Chimera occasionally initiating our physical intimacy. As I said, this is much the dynamic I experienced during our Partner Yoga sessions: Chimera's lack of barriers makes everything effortless for her, while I use a lot more energy to accomplish the same thing.

☼ ☼ ☼

Chimera's only present frustration is being unable to share with the public what she knows about Michael, specifically the part he played in her transformation and the part she expects him to play in the coming global shift. Instead, when she discusses her paintings with friends, gallery owners, and clients, she frames her process in terms of dream work and spiritual integration, which is entirely true, just not the whole story. In art circles, the Michael figure in her paintings is seen as part of a "Christian theme." Without being able to share Michael's actual integrative notions of spirituality, Chimera is powerless to dissuade anyone from this limited and superficial view of what his presence symbolizes in her work.

To a degree, I share Chimera's frustration over our conspiracy of silence as regards Michael's principle focus, particularly when it comes to fielding questions from *Le Canard* Theatre's principals, who are interested in producing *The Bard's Ghost*. In an attempt to avoid this discussion, I eliminate any references in the play to myself, Chimera, Michael, and Diane, and our attendant relationships to the characters, while continuing to hone the text and the dramatic structure. Most of Chimera's and my discomfort from this limbo of fettered impulses, however, is dispelled by discussing the matter with Michael himself, a few weeks later, when he and Diane are over for dinner.

"There's a good reason why we chose to announce our presence with the book rather than through word of mouth," says Michael, responding to our hand wringing. "The book represents the teachings in our own words, unadulterated by those who would seek to use our presence to feed their own narrow aims—greed or lust for power, what have you. If we make ourselves known through word of mouth before we have a chance to put forth our truth, then what we have to share could simply vanish; but by publishing this memoir and sending it to various spiritual leaders, book reviewers, publishers, friends, and other interested parties, we'll preclude anyone from editing what we have to say, and avoid the distortions that transpired with the Christian *Bible*."

"So, again, we come back to this idea that there are forces which will come after you as your teachings spread?" Chimera asks.

"I hate this subject," says Diane, "yet it's proven by history, not only by Jesus' crucifixion, but by all the political murders in this country in the last thirty years—JFK, Martin Luther King, RFK,[31] and Malcolm X, et al."

"This is nothing new," Michael says. "Those in power have the means to make us vanish, through assassinations, airplane and automobile 'accidents,' heart attacks, drug overdoses, rare diseases, poisoning, et cetera, and make it look like there is no conspiracy—and the public buys these 'conspiracy of ignorance theories' just like they buy the Christian *Bible*: lock, stock, and barrel. Yet the Christian *Bible* itself, while containing many of my words, is largely an invention of those who would ascribe supernatural acts to my character so as to preclude me from being recognized in human form and to prevent me from regaining my rightful position as a spiritual teacher.

"It's no wonder most people don't follow Jesus' example," he continues, "and instead pray for divine intervention: he's unattainable to them, a perfect G-d instead of an exceptional, anomalous human being. So, now that I'm here to address these devilish falsehoods, I represent a real threat to those that have stolen my identity and use it as a marketing ploy for their selfish, lowly purposes. If my reappearance is terminated, my branding reverts to those in whose interest church and state operate—those who worship the Golden Calf. And they will use every means at their disposal, such as their self-proclaimed devoutness and my FBI file, to

---

[31] See http://www.copvcia.com/free/pandora/rfk.html

convince the world of their 'altruistic' intent. They will accuse you of being 'conspiracy theorists' when, in fact, they are the conspirators: the de facto mission of the CIA and the rest of the so-called intelligence community is conspiracy; it is the nature of their work—to assassinate, de-stabilize, and defraud—all the while obfuscating the facts and convincing others to believe that they have done nothing illegal and immoral.

"I emphasize this," he continues, "because you must be prepared to deal with such circumstances. Those who control our government will attempt to do away with me and deny their involvement just as the Romans nailed the revolutionary Jesus to the cross on Pilate's orders and altered the texts to deflect the responsibility for this act onto the Jews. When this tactic recurs, you must persevere and keep to our arrangements for publishing this book as we have planned. Don't believe their denials; politicians and the press are whores to their financial masters, all of whom worship at the altar of Mammon. Persevere and know that I will return to you before long."

Chimera and I are aghast, even after all these years.

"What are you saying Michael?" Chimera bursts out. "It sounds like their killing you is a foregone conclusion!"

"It's the Garden of Gethsemane speech," says Diane, apparently finding satire a means of shielding her feelings on the subject.

"I didn't say they would succeed in killing me," Michael says, "only that they would attempt such and that I would disappear—temporarily. They can't kill me or you for that matter. We have eternal life."

"Be that as it may," Chimera complains, "it took two thousand years for you to settle up. Are we supposed to wait another aeon for a third try?"

"As I said, have faith. I am returned to you in this life."

"You will be resurrected?" Chimera asks.

"I am returned *in the flesh* to finish my work."

10

Radio

"Be regular and orderly in your life, like a good bourgeois, so that you may be violent and original in your work."
--Gustave Flaubert

Within a matter of weeks, Michael's weekly theatre critiques reveal themselves to be a radical turn from the standard fare we're used to reading in the local or national corporate-owned dailies. In general, to cover theatre for mass media outlets one must put form ahead of substance: soft features on the lives of stars (appearing in the latest Broadway revival passing through town) masquerade as content; theatre is marginalized to a divertissement, like videos, television, and crossword puzzles, instead of serving as a platform for social analysis and criticism. On top of this insulting treatment, many of our local theatre critics consider a review an opportunity to exhibit their overly-inflated self-concepts of intellectual prowess at the expense of whatever production they happen to visit that week. In contrast, Michael's underlying motivation for reviewing theatre is to get people into the theatre—for its transformational power, both personal and collective. To accomplish this he has developed a unique set of guidelines for his weekly radio broadsides.

To begin with, he never retells the plot of a play to his listeners. If the production is any good, he believes that giving away the story is a disservice. Instead, after describing the setting for the play, he analyzes the ideas and themes that playwrights develop through their characters. In this way, he demonstrates that theatre remains a vibrant form of social criticism—unlike most film and virtually all television, which involve such massive sums of money that they are effectively muted by corporate censorship—while recognizing the craft that delivers the message.

From week-to-week Michael's reviews seem to grow and reveal aspects of his personality that, although I have grown close to him in the nearly 20 years that we have now been friends, I had not previously noticed. Listening to Michael via the radio gives me greater distance and detachment—from which I see patterns that are otherwise invisible to my conscious mind. It also strikes me how important his reviews are to our project, revealing psychological and intellectual wrinkles that give depth to the behaviors which I have already highlighted. So, in addition to the tapes of our conversations that I continue to record, I convince Michael to have the radio station provide me with air checks[1] of his weekly segments. As his side career as a reviewer develops, I ask him about this work.

"Why is that you, a spiritual teacher, choose to express yourself through theatrical criticism? As exalted as the arts are, doesn't this work seem a comedown?"

"Let me turn this question around, Rashan. Do you expect Chimera to give up painting because she has been reborn in spirit, or, when you experience enlightenment, that you will retire from playwriting?"

"I would hope not, in both cases."

"Why is it that you would expect to continue practicing your art?"

"It's what I do, Michael. I take the most compelling questions in my life and work them out through characters and action."

"Exactly. And as we've discussed before, this has always been the role of theatre since primordial times, to work out the soul-wrestling of the community through ritual re-creations using music, song, dance, masks, costumes, fire, props, scenery, and the spoken word. It is our most natural form of religious and spiritual practice."

"I remember," I say, "when you first broached this idea with me: I questioned whether such an approach to spirituality wasn't pagan. But, surprisingly, my perspective on this has changed. I now see that theatrical metaphors are for audiences what Jung's 'symbols of integration' are for the individual psyche—ritual elements that invoke holistic states, much as you commented on some years back."

"So why then would it be inconsistent of me," Michael asks, "to analyze these ancient transformative rites and encourage others to explore them as well? Surely, spiritual rebirth and enlightenment is a new beginning, not the end of our creative life?"

---

[1] A radio term used to describe recordings, on audiotape cassettes at this time, that are made to monitor and evaluate programming, such as a specific announcer's or DJ's air shift.

"Some of the topics seem so mundane and trivial, especially compared to the world problems that are the focus of your mission."

"That is the point, Rashan. Nothing is trivial. Remember a long time ago when I said that love and compassion aren't enough; that each of us must understand the consequences of even our simplest actions and take responsibility for them?[2]

"Sure."

"Well, showing the connection between even the most mundane and trivial thought or action, and its consequences on people and on the biosphere of the earth itself, is crucial to human evolution—and it's something that theatre naturally focuses on. Thinking globally and acting locally requires contemplation and diligence. Theatrical criticism is part of this process of reflecting, questioning, and informing. It focuses us on the innate rituals which our species uses to center itself and evolve. If people are going to act in a more enlightened manner—my teachings need to be broader than just a set of spiritual transmissions; so, my reviews employ and support the theatrical medium to keep important issues alive. I'm not saying that there isn't a lot of trash out there when it comes to mass entertainment, including theatre to a degree, but that's a reflection of the base material values that currently dominate our society. Necessarily, our commentary reflects this shortfall. As our values change through reflection and spiritual practice, art becomes more substantive."

"So, as the apostle of change, your weekly theatre reviews serve as sermons and KIVA as your pulpit."

"An apt metaphor, Rashan. What Trungpa[3] called 'meditation in action' is the application of spiritual values in everyday life. Much like Zen archery, flower arranging, gardening, and tea ceremony carry over into our daily routine, so theatre, painting, poetry, dance, music and the rest of the

---

[2] Michael writes in 2003: In its greatest sense, compassion includes knowledge and understanding. The implications of this idea are staggering: *Jnana Yoga* (liberation through knowledge) is integral to enlightenment; our responsibilities in this area go far beyond the so-called educational policies that serve as window dressing to our "leaders" paltry visions; it includes nothing less than an integrated approach to all human knowledge.

[3] Chöngyam Trungpa, Rinpoche, as previously noted, Tibetan spiritual leader and founder of Shambhala Training and Naropa University. The first of his 14 books is entitled *Meditation in Action*.

arts influence our sensibilities and conduct—just as Schiller argued centuries ago."[4]

The value of theatrical criticism sounds so logical and cultured when Michael explains it, but it feels quite different when I'm driving down the highway and hear him on the radio railing against bigotry, imperialism, and such. Clearly, he means to challenge his audiences' belief systems and, in doing so, usher in a more public phase to his mission. No wonder he recently stressed personal security issues and the need to stick to our plan for publishing this book.

As Michael has explained to me, his inspiration for the "relevancy-based" approach of his reviews comes from such critics as John Lahr.[5] "The diversity of ideas provided by theatre makes criticism a perfect venue for my natural philosophic and analytic instincts."

It's no surprise, then, that Michael's artistic insights are, more often than not, just bait for the hook of his political and spiritual teachings. Driving to work on any given Friday, listening to a music set on KIVA, which may include Latin jazz, big bands, and Broadway standards, one is suddenly thrust into the maelstrom of religious controversy:

> Tony Award-winning playwright Terrence McNally was raised in Corpus Christi, Texas in the 50's. It must have certainly been difficult for him as a gay man in a town of macho football fanatics and other assorted roughnecks, who deal savagely with anyone who doesn't fit into their narrow-minded vision of acceptable behavior. And all this in a place named after their professed savior.
> When McNally's play Corpus Christi opened in New York, Catholic organizations protested vehemently, and the Manhattan Theatre club, which was producing the piece, received bomb threats and had to hire a private security firm to set up metal detectors for playgoers. So much for freedom of speech in America. On top of this, the same

---

[4] See *On the Aesthetic Education of Man*, by Friedrich Schiller, 1759-1805, German dramatist, essayist, and poet. Schiller's work includes the *Ode to Joy*, which serves as the libretto for Beethoven's Ninth Symphony. He was also a friend of Goethe, with whom he carried on a long correspondence and played a major role in German literature's *Sturm und Drang* (Storm and Stress) period.

[5] Prize-winning theatre critic for *The New Yorker*; formerly with *The Village Voice* and *Evergreen Review*.

Imam who placed a fatwa[6] on the head of Salman Rushdie for supposedly blaspheming Islam in his novel The Satanic Verses, issued a fatwa on McNally for "blaspheming a prophet that is part of Islamic heritage." I mean, does this sorry excuse for a religious leader—a so-called professed believer in Jesus—understand the ironic hypocrisy of condemning someone to death? Who's casting the first stone here? Clearly, in these two glaring examples, we see that Catholicism and Islam are equally intolerant. They are the Romans, not the followers of Christ.

All of this holier-than-thou commotion is generated by McNally's retelling of the New Testament story with his interpretation of Jesus as a gay man growing up in Corpus Christi. But despite the knee-jerk reactions of these ignorant and self-righteous "defenders of the faith," many critics and audiences have found much spiritual and intellectual sustenance in the work.

Of course, anyone who believes in the Christian Bible as the literal truth will be offended by this play, because their point of view conceives Jesus as a divine being, devoid of human frailties. There is, however, ample evidence in the Gnostic Gospels and the Dead Sea Scrolls, which escaped the early editing of Church authorities and were dug up in the 1950's, that Jesus was, in fact, a human being who believed in love, both the divinely-inspired and the humanly-expressed varieties. Whether or not he was straight, gay, bisexual, or non-sexual is beside the point.

In the Theatre on Broadway's current production of Corpus Christi, McNally's insightful choices of biblical text, which overlay the Texas-flavored setting, indicate that the playwright understands what many of his critics do not: that the Prince of Peace's message is first and foremost about love and acceptance. Director Steven Tangedal and his cohesive ensemble bring a natural and joyful affirmation to this message—in a land where many currently use the same "scripture" to preach intolerance toward those who don't fit in the their preconceived mold of sexual predisposition, social perspective, or racial stereotype.

Charles Dean Packard's simple yet effective lighting and set design support the overall production objective,

---

[6] In Islam, a warrant for the death of a named individual.

> keeping the focus on the words and actions of a simple, small-town carpenter whose faith in the potential of the human soul forever changed our concept of spirituality. Playwright McNally's adventurous interpretation is a worthy challenge to all those who think they know what Jesus' life looked like, or would look like if he chose to reappear.
>
> Corpus Christi highlights the inherently radical approach Jesus expressed relative to the common beliefs of his day. No wonder the Roman authorities took offense, for their power and control was threatened by a teaching that challenged their materialistic presumptions and taught its followers a new and simplified way to live and to pray.
>
> As McNally's play reminds us and as the Roman version of the story says, "Hold yourselves ready therefore for the Son of Man will come at a time you least expect," and I might add, "in a way you expect not."

Hearing this review, it strikes me immediately that Michael's perspective will, at some point soon, begin to draw attention, if only because it runs so flagrantly against the grain of most people's beliefs. This doesn't seem to be a problem, though, for the minority-flavored management at the non-profit station, who appreciate the alignment of Michael's reviews with their own beliefs, which have been engendered by generations of discrimination at the hands of European "Christians."

Over the next few years the popularity of the station and Michael's 10-minute weekly programming slot—drive time Friday morning—grows from a couple of thousand local listeners to fifteen thousand listeners, and to a geographical footprint that includes the Denver metro area, the Western Slope, and Wyoming, where translators boost the coverage.[7] In any week's cume,[8] KIVA's total number of listeners might run ten times that.

Within the theatre community itself, Michael's reputation continues to grow as well. In particular, local thespians appreciate his passion for the work and his message. Indeed, the pending publication of this book has generated a great deal of interest among his theatre friends and

---

[7] Later on, KIVA streamed its signal over the Internet.
[8] In radio or television, cume is a figure representing the total number of unique audience members for a specific period of time.

acquaintances. This mutual admiration, between reviewer and performer, naturally engenders dialogue, and Michael sees no conflict in developing personal relationships with theatre professionals, finding any limitations on this fraternization superficial.[9]

> To how many rehearsals of musicals did my mother bring me, and how many late movies did we watch together? It should be no surprise that the magic from these worlds is integral to my beliefs. For contrary to the common opinion that such "make believe" stories should be abandoned upon graduation to adulthood, it is their very nurturing that keeps one's dreams alive and supports the child-like wonderment that is the foundation of a spiritual life: "Except as ye be as children, ye shall not enter the Kingdom of Heaven." And then there are the actors: "There's no people like show people, they smile when they are low..."[10]

"Certainly this makes it harder to write some reviews on occasion," Michael confided once, "but my friendships never prevent me from saying what needs to be said. If that weren't the case, then there *would* be a conflict of interest in my inability to separate the personal and the professional. It's much like spiritual counseling among friends," he says, raising his eyebrows to emphasize the nature of our own relationship. This even-handedness seems to fortify his reputation in the local theatre community, just as it has with Chimera and me.

But outside of this open-minded coterie of friends, Michael's radical ideas often find stiff resistance. The first public skirmish over Michael's

---

[9] Theatre producers, directors, and actors differ on the propriety of such relationships. Michael was wont to party with his friends, who often invited him to opening night celebrations. Some producers frown on these social interactions—such fears, it seems, that would have prevented these poor folk from ever being on social terms with George Bernard Shaw, who was both a playwright and a critic, and had personal relationships with a variety of actors and others in the theatre community.

[10] From the song "There's No Business Like Show Business," in the musical *Annie Get Your Gun*, the story of champion sharpshooter Annie Oakley, words and music by Irving Berlin, 1946.

reviews occurs just a few short weeks after he starts broadcasting, following his review of Molière's *Tartuffe*.

One member of the local Catholic archdiocese objected to Michael's "strident excoriation of the Church and the characterization of many of its practitioners as hypocrites." The station was immediately besieged with calls and letters from aroused parishioners.

For its part during this episode, the management of KIVA remained adamant in its support of Michael's right to free speech and in his opinions as well. KIVA's board of directors is largely comprised of Hispanics and blacks. Apparently the Church's threats of excommunication and damnation to those connected with the station only intensified the bad taste that this patriarchic and patronizing institution had left previously in their mouths.

This internal support emboldened Michael.

"It's actually a compliment that I am attacked by the same forces that were offended by Molière," he says to me following that incident.

Every week Michael has a fresh opportunity to "excoriate" someone or something, or offer praise where he feels it's due. When dealing with the backlashes from these frequent criticisms of Christianity as it is practiced, Michael is fond of quoting Bernard Shaw's quip, "'All great truths begin with blasphemies.' So," he continues, "the uproar is to be expected. It was no different 2,000 years ago. 'They have ears and they hear not.'"[11]

During his review of Bertolt Brecht's *Galileo*, Michael observes:

> Humankind has walked on the moon, the space shuttle regularly leaves the atmosphere, and a semi-permanent space station orbits the earth; we receive visual transmissions from satellites at the far reaches of our solar system, and our probes have landed on Mars and Venus and beyond. All of these achievements are traceable, one way or another, to a revolution that began with Copernicus and Galileo. But while today we may find it an annoyance that Patrick Buchanan, Pat Robinson, and their neo-conservative ilk can't reconcile scientific discovery with spiritual amazement, in Galileo's time the belief that the earth traveled around the sun was punishable by death.

---

[11] Mark 8:18.

The next year, Michael followed up on these ideas while reviewing the world premiere of *Reading the Mind of God*, written by local playwright Pat Gabridge, on the relationship between the astronomers Tycho Brahe and Johannes Kepler.

Under the deft direction of Greg Ward, Douglas O'Brien as the bombastic Brahe and Brian Freeland as the inspired Kepler, magically reinvent the stormy and earth-shattering relationship that led irretrievably to the proof that Copernicus was right—the sun, indeed, is at the center of our solar system—which, by the way, the Church recognized formally about 15 years ago, 450 years after Copernicus' proof.

Clearly, as the years tick down to his D-Day, Michael is setting the stage for a showdown of galactic proportions. He has me as a witness, and thousands of others that he hopes will read what I record. Being privy to his private papers, air checks, and personal philosophy as I've recorded it, it's easy for me to see that behind Michael's seemingly irreligious remarks stands a cohesive worldview in which science and spirituality are interchangeable mutually supportive systems of thought for admiring the perfection and beauty of the Universe and the anomalistic force that animates it.

As I indicated, however, there are listeners with countervailing viewpoints and the wherewithal to strike back. Within a month of a particularly vituperative analysis of the military-industrial complex as part of his review of *Nixon's Nixon*, the Internal Revenue Service began a review of Michael's tax records. Michael is nobody's fool when it comes to money. Aside from a mantle of Solomonic cleverness in regards to wealth management, Michael's financial universe includes, as we've noted, his uncle, the former Andersen senior partner, and George Orloff, a sharp tax lawyer. So, Michael welcomed the IRS' investigation as he had the FBI's scrutiny thirty years before. In a telephone conversation, Michael comments to me that "This pretty much proves what I've said about a government controlled by financiers that maintain control through monopoly, armaments, and spying—the first amendment only holds up so long as one does not become a viable threat to their so-called 'New World Order.'"[12]

As Michael gathers his tax records to deal with this bureaucratic shakedown, his radio analyses continue unrepentant. And if the erudite concepts that Michael puts forth in his reviews aren't compelling enough, his luxuriant delivery often wins over listeners. In fact, many of them tune in every week just to hear "the voice," as some of them describe him.

Of course, supreme self-confidence never hurts the cause either. This idea is echoed in Michael's own words, when he introduces his review of Noel Coward's *Present Laughter* by asking the host of KIVA's morning drive show,

> Bob, you've been around the jazz world for most of your life and met many of the greatest performers. Wouldn't you say that there are certain people that come off as larger than life? It's not just their celebrity or talent that sets them apart, but perhaps those qualities in combination with their personality, their savoir faire, their animal magnetism, their "Je ne sais quoi"?

---

[12] As noted in Chapter 9, on the eve of the Gulf War against Iraq in late 1990, George H.W. Bush states: "The world can therefore seize the opportunity [Persian Gulf crisis] to fulfill the long-held promise of a New World Order where diverse nations are drawn together in common cause to achieve the universal aspirations of mankind." Or as we will again note in Chapter 11, David Rockefeller put it thus: "We are on the verge of a global transformation. All we need is the right major crisis and the nations will accept the New World Order." Unfortunately, of course, the Rockefeller, Bush, Dulles, and Harriman families, as well as all their cronies, protégés, servants, and slaves are simply replacing one false idol (Nationalism: Manifest Destiny, *Deutschland über alles*, etc.) with another (Mammon: the Almighty Dollar, the Golden Calf, etc.) and behave in the same manner as all totalitarian dictatorships past and present, without regard for spiritual values. The manner in which they manipulate the IRS is a perfect example of this, since they can seize assets and ruin persons and businesses through accusation alone. Beyond the legislative, executive, and judicial branches, including all intelligence operations and the military, their private control of the state apparatus includes the Federal Reserve, a family-owned franchise to print and regulate the money supply for the U.S. government and its citizens, from which they derive an ongoing percentage. It should be noted that a sizeable portion of the ownership of the Federal Reserve is held by foreign nationals, who most certainly influence U.S. domestic and foreign policy.

Did the deejay have any choice but to answer, "Yes, of course!" And while Michael is referring to the lead character in the comedy, Garry Essendine, Coward's obvious alter-ego, he might as well have been referring to himself. Michael is indeed larger than life; he transcends it. His belief—in his mission, in eternal life, and in "the One-Without-A-Name" (the Great Anomaly, the Supreme Being) that he serves and who provides everything he needs—is absolute down to his deepest subconscious and unconscious mind and across whatever universes flow through the anomalistic point of his innermost self. No wonder then that myth and reality are as equivalent to him as science and spirituality.

In reviewing *The Madwoman of Chaillot*, Michael reveals a unique perspective on his own "madness," for who in his right mind believes that he is the Messiah:

> *In a world where rivers burn, breezes bring tears to our eyes, and our money-worshipping leaders claim to follow divine teachings, Giraudoux's heroine, Countess Aurelia, lives in a Paris of the mind, untouched by the Industrial Revolution and the Reformation. She is surrounded by friends from every walk of life—artisans, politicos, beggars, le bourgeois, laborers and peasants. When these friends complain to her that their world of refined salon conversation, street artists, and* joie de vivre *is being systematically poisoned by those who would drill for oil in the Louvre if they thought it would fill their coffers, Countess Aurelia responds with a wave of the hand and pooh-poohs their alarm. "Anyone that is so driven by money," she assures them, "can easily be done in."*

And so, Michael believes that single-handedly, by an act of will, he can compel the world to change its ways, as if, like David facing Goliath and the Philistines, "One man with courage makes a majority."[13] Given this magnanimous sense of bravado, curiosity demands an exploration of some of Michael's favorite theatrical characters. Certainly from our conversations it's clear he finds much affinity with the historical figures of Jesus, Buddha, and Lao-Tsu, as well as Shake-speare (by which I mean de

---

[13] President Andrew Jackson.

Vere, of course), Marx, and Einstein. But in the theatre, what personae represent the major forces in his life?

One of Michael's favorite theatrical exercises is to memorize monologues written for specific dialects. His choices are quite revealing. There is Sam's Yiddish-flavored speech praising the virtues of a new hat from Susan Sandler's *Crossing Delancy*, the syrupy Southern dialect of Tom tongue-lashing his mother in Tennessee Williams' *The Glass Menagerie*, Christy's lilting Irish brogue extolling his handsomeness in J.M. Synge's *The Playboy of the Western World*, Charles' upper crust British Standard farewell to the haunting ghosts of his former wives in Noel Coward's *Blithe Spirit*, and Thomas' Luciferian lament on the whole of creation in elevated American dialect from Christopher Fry's *The Lady's Not for Burning*.

As it stands, the only Shakespearean speech he includes in his repertoire is the Prologue to *Henry V*. It's not surprising to me that Michael chose this speech, given that it represents one of the better examples of the playwright speaking directly to the audience. In addition, Michael's unrestrained and experimental youth followed by the weighty responsibilities of his pending global mission bear an unmistakable resemblance to the prodigal Hal's transformation into King Henry V.

I remember this review distinctly. It is a Friday morning late in July. I'm in my car, almost to my office, when Michael comes on the air. In all the years that I've been listening to his reviews, this is the first instance in which he actually performs a monologue on the air. The effect is mesmerizing. It could have been Barrymore or Olivier or Burton,[14] given his command of the meter and the deep, rich Elizabethan manner in which his voice envelops and lets fall each sound.

> *If ever there was an English hero for the ages, such was* Henry V. *Not only does his story provide a rollicking princely counterpoint to the comedic antics he shared with Falstaff in* Henry IV, Parts I and II, *but in his own story* Henry V *gives his country the most inspirational military event in its glorious history, as well as the unification, however brief, of England and France. Such a combination*

---

[14] The Welsh actor Richard Burton, born Richard Walter Jenkins, Jr., not Richard Francis Burton, the linguist, explorer, author, and translator of *Arabian Nights* and the *Kama Sutra*.

of content and the playwright's talent produced a monumental work that stands as one of the crowning achievements in a series of fine histories.

In addition to the unprecedented scenes in which the King mixes with common soldiers, the play begins with the most comprehensive argument of the theatrical question ever written:

O for a Muse of fire, that would ascend
The brightest heaven of invention,
A kingdom for a stage, princes to act,
And monarchs to behold the swelling scene!
Then should the warlike Harry, like himself,
Assume the port of Mars; and at his heels,
Leash'd in like hounds, should famine, sword, and fire
Crouch for employment. But pardon gentles all,
The flat unraised spirits that hath dar'd
On this unworthy scaffold to bring forth
So great an object. Can this cockpit hold
The vasty fields of France? Or my we cram
Within this wooden O the very casques
That did affright the air at Agincourt?
O, pardon! Since a crooked figure may
Attest in little place a million;
And let us, ciphers to this great accompt,
On your imaginary forces work.
Suppose within the girdle of these walls
Are now confin'd two mighty monarchies,
Whose high upreared and abutting fronts
The perilous narrow ocean parts asunder;
Piece out our imperfections with your thoughts;
Into a thousand parts divide one man,
And make imaginary puissance;
Think, when we talk of horses, that you see them
Printing their proud hoofs i' th' receiving earth.
For 'tis your thoughts that now must deck our kings,
Carry them here and there, jumping o'er times,
Turning the accomplishment of many years
Into an hour-glass: for the which supply,
Admit me Chorus to this history;
Who, prologue-like, your humble patience pray
Gently to hear, kindly to judge, our play.

For years afterward, I hear many people speak reverentially of this broadcast. Their strong reactions make me think of a discussion I had with Michael concerning his interpretation of the biblical concept of "The Word."

"Almost 30 years ago, Rashan, when I had been studying Yoga for less than a year, I went alone on a retreat into King's Canyon National Park.[15] During this time, I fasted and practiced *manu*[16] for a couple of weeks. When I finally return to San Francisco, where I was living with a group of theatre people, I still had not spoken a word. A few days later, I'm meditating with a friend of mine when I finally break my silence and began to chant. My friend, who previously had suffered from asthma, tells me later that she never experienced the symptoms again after hearing my voice that morning. She described her sonic healing process first as a vibratory field that surrounded her, followed by a strong sensation of light starting in her chest and spreading throughout her body. Immediately after it happened, we begin to talk of spiritual things, but the resonance of my voice was so powerful—due to the vibration of my well-rested vocal chords—she simply smiled, placed her hand on my mouth, and swayed until the energy dissipated.

"My point is that the voice can be an instrument of truth and healing, and that it possesses qualities which can ring at vibrations significantly different than what we currently experience as the spoken norm. It's not just the sound of the voice that accomplishes this, though its vibration is critical, but how it is used and what it says as well. The vibrational effect of 'The Word' is further amplified by poetic scansion and sacred vowels, which may be intuited or received through apprenticeship, person-to-person or channeled from the akashic record or noosphere."[17]

Earlier in our relationship, I would have been all over such claims, but the steady stream of insights from the genie over the years has forced

---

[15] In California, near Yosemite and Sequoia National Parks.
[16] Again, Sanskrit for *silence*, a traditional yogic austerity.
[17] Michael write:The akashic records (from Sanskrit) and the noosphere (from Vladimir Vernadsky and Teilhard de Chardin) are, in essence, terms for the same concept, that of universal and present availability of everything that ever was, is, or will be.

me to give credence to his unique and challenging ideas, including some inexplicable coincidences, as if he stood on a cusp between dimensions.

"What do you mean by intuited?" I ask. "Are you trying to tell me you hear voices?"

But Michael is insistent that the inspiration of which he speaks is grounded in childlike innocence.

"Years ago I explained to you how yogis in certain states of meditation can turn truth into language. This includes rediscovered truth, both personal and collective, that has been lost to us. Getting to this state is not easy, but one of the effects of rebirthing oneself is the rediscovery of a childlike purity of perception that provides the means to transcend space-time.

"That is why 'Except ye ... become as little children, ye shall not enter into the Kingdom of Heaven,'[18] is one of the most important surviving passages from Jesus' teachings—and yet very few people seem to 'get it.' 'As little children' doesn't refer to childishness, but to that aspect of child-like intuition which makes one feel happy and content and full of possibilities—exactly what the Buddha dwelled on as well. It's up to each of us to consciously carry this feeling forward within ourselves every day, capturing our higher selves where we may and, in the synthesis of an artistic act, gather these pieces together into an evolving image of wholeness that, one day, becomes who we are, as if our higher self pulls us up by our bootstraps."

Like the phantasmagoria that he admires, Michael forges his child-like perceptions, unbounded imagination, absolute belief in freedom, and heart-felt empathy for the abused into a cohesive personality within which he has grown and operated for so long that surrealism is part of his normative experience. Each moment and every aspect of his life is a consistent proof of one and the same vision that will transform the world.

We've noted that Michael meets regular resistance to his point-of-view, but that it's rarely anything that brings him much pause. After a number of years on KIVA, when his reputation brought an offer to write a couple of reviews a month for the *Denver Post*, Michael gladly accepted, seeing it as a way to reach more people with his ideas without having to substantially intensify his already crowded schedule. Besides, he thought it

---

[18] Matthew 18:3

would help draw more readers to another new project of his—a website where he posts his social analysis and criticism under the guise of theatre reviews.

After a couple of years at this part-time contribution for the *Post*, and 46 reviews later, Michael remained fascinated by the editorial boundaries to which his commentaries are subjected. From many writers' perspectives, editors are there to make their lives miserable and to embarrass them, and one might have expected that given the challenges Michael's views would pose for any editor, his stint as a critic for a major metropolitan daily would end up a frustrating experience. On the contrary, he saw it more as a game.

"Here's how it works, Rashan," he shares with me over dinner in Denver one weekday evening. "I write up my review just as I would for KIVA or my own website, inserting any and all social commentary that I find relevant. If my editor believes that what I've said is directly related to the text or action in the play, he generally leaves it alone; if he thinks that I'm inserting a subjective interpretation on the proceedings, he cuts it.

"Of course, just where the line is drawn is subjective, too. I can say all I want about racism and gay rights, and my copy sails through. But if I get political, for example, using a housewife's despair over the junta's coup d'état to reference how Jeb Bush and Katherine Harris purged minorities from the voting rolls in Florida and skewed the results to steal the election through the Republican-appointed courts, then my copy is edited and made to appear as if such thoughts never entered my mind. On the other hand, if the playwright writes a burlesque about the Patriot Act that features a hair-trigger cowboy president, that's treated as fair game."

"So, you're telling me, in my role as a playwright, that by creating a political situation as part of the plot, I make it easier for you to comment on current events?"

"Right, though such a plot might make it more difficult for you to get your play produced."

"And you're comfortable writing for a newspaper that subjects your work to these parameters?"

"I wouldn't say comfortable, Rashan. It's challenging, trying to write around corporate America's fascist hot buttons, but you have to admit it's a perfect way of illustrating the type of censorship that goes on under the guise of so-called free speech and democracy."

"You mean by provoking your editor and then illustrating it in this environment."

"I'm not a provocateur. This is all about living one's truth. You, or my editor may feel differently, but my training in social, scientific, and spiritual analysis leaves me no choice but to speak up. I also have the facts to back it up, and am willing to debate anyone on these issues: That in my reviews I tie a playwright's or director's choices to current events is, as you have seen, usually not a stretch, but a means of delineating the interconnectedness of individual behaviors and world events."

In addition to Michael's part-time duties as a theatre critic for KIVA-FM, plus his own website, and the *Denver Post*,[19] he continues to unobtrusively involve himself in the interactive "e-learning" segment of the now burgeoning Internet economy, studiously analyzing the cavalcade of technological innovations, each for its relevance to his plan for worldwide promulgation of courses in spiritual consciousness-raising.

"Did you read about the satellites that are going to be launched to create a wireless Internet?" he asks me one day in the late '90's over tea.

Of course, he's a couple of steps ahead of me.

"No. What's that?"

"Just think!" Michael says enthusiastically. "You could be anywhere in the world with your laptop and a solar powered battery recharger and be surfing the web, even making phone calls!"

"Okay."

"Granted the idea is to find a less expensive way to wire the third world without having to deal with an expensive infrastructure, but peripherally this system would mean that someone, like yours truly, could forward information to a website without being traceable to a specific location."

"Kind of like a pirate radio station?"

"Yes, except there wouldn't be anything illegal about it. It would just make it more difficult for the authorities to find me."

---

[19] In 2004, Michael was asked to cover the Denver metro region for *Variety*, the national entertainment business weekly standard, which delighted him. "I not only found some folks that punctuate and compose sentences like me, but even more thrilling—a sophisticated audience that is willing to think outside the box.

"Now I'm beginning to understand. This would allow you to speak your mind without being subject to physical disruption or threats by those who disagree with you, like an electronic Crazy Horse—an elusive beacon of insight."

"Hah! I like that one, Rashan. It's not absolute security, but a reasonable buffer. Since these satellites won't start out with GPS (Global Positioning System) capability for tracking input, anyone uplinking to the web would only be traceable within about a 300 square mile footprint, which, you'll admit, is a lot more breathing room than a phone line."

"So, you're planning a website?"

"Sure. After this book is published, the website will be the portal for distributing our courses."

"What's so revolutionary about that?" I countered, for by this time the dot-com revolution was in full swing.

"Only the content, of course," Michael says. "As karmic payback for that which is being written through me, I need to provide a way where the teachings are disbursed for free. So, in addition to posting my proof, I plan to offer daily commentaries on the website, just like news organizations do, except I'll be framing events to show people how to analyze the dynamics behind story, as well as what they personally can do to change their world for the better."

"Judging from your onetime KBAL TV news program and your current theatre reviews on the radio," I say, "I don't have to guess that the content you provide for the site will be controversial."

"It couldn't be anything else, Rashan, given that I represent a path in which life and spirit are a higher priority than ego and capital; the powers that be are vested in the materialistic *status quo*."

"At the same time, wouldn't you say that there are many people around the world working for the same things as you are?"

"Of course. That's the beauty of the way in which websites link. Through the popularity of our site, we should be able to increase awareness of global issues and local outlets that support earth-friendly actions."

"What you're saying is that there will be a way in which anyone with access to the Internet will be able to connect with your analysis on a daily basis and that, in addition to the commentaries that you'll be providing, your site will have links to other sites that provide information to further the discussion?"

"Quite an interesting fulfillment of "... and every tongue shall confess to God,"[20] wouldn't you say?"

"I never thought of the Internet in that way," I reply, "but, yes, it could be seen as fulfilling that prophesy." At this point, I'm rarely startled by Michael's grandiose perspective: I have to admit that it reveals a consistent vision of the world in which everything serves a higher purpose.

"It shouldn't surprise anyone that prophetic fulfillment occurs in ways that are unanticipated; for example, the global and multi-lingual character of the Internet is certainly something no one predicted even a decade ago. Further, the rigid interpretation of prophesies will stand as the greatest stumbling block to spiritual development for many. It's incredibly arrogant for anyone to assume they could know how prophesy will be fulfilled. Did I not say, 'The times and occasions are set by my Father's own authority, and it is not for you to know when they will be?'"[21]

"So you did," I say, acquiescing to Michael's relentless presumption of Christ consciousness.

The emergence of Denver as one of the evolving theatrical centers in the U.S. provided further opportunities for the propagation of Michael's budding reputation as a theatre reviewer and "social philosopher." Thus, when the Denver Center Theatre Company's joint production of *Tantalus* with the Royal Shakespeare Company[22] drew theatre professionals to the Mile High City from all over the world for its premiere, it was no surprise

---

[20] Romans 14:11, or "And when the world is ready to receive, lo, God will send a messenger to open up the book and copy from its sacred pages all the messages of Purity and Love. Then every man of earth will read the words of life in the language of his native land, and men will see the light." Levi, *The Aquarian Gospel of Jesus the Christ*, DeVorss & Co., Santa Monica, CA, 1972, 7:25-28. This book was first published in 1907.

[21] Acts 1:7

[22] Written by John Barton, directed by Peter Hall, it premiered October 21, 2000, in the Stage Theatre, Denver Performing Arts Complex. It was selected—along with the Denver Center Theatre Company's co-production (with the Tectonic Theatre Project of New York) of *The Laramie Project*, based on the murder of Matthew Shepard, a gay University of Wyoming student—as one of the top 10 theatrical productions in America that year.

that many of the visitors were drawn to KIVA-FM and, in turn, Michael's Friday morning segments.

"It's gratifying," Michael shared with me, "to find such strong resonance between the political and social opinions of the international theatre community and my own, particularly considering the narrow beliefs to which we're subjected by corporate media on a minute-to-minute basis."

But censorship isn't the only thing that might prevent anyone—who only occasionally catches Michael's reviews or only briefly talks to him—from completely missing what he is about. Michael's chameleon-like personality, rooted in such a vast array of knowledge and experience, allows him to change subjects as it befits his audience. He explains this phenomenon using images from the Tarot.

"First, Rashan, there's the card of The Fool, who bears a certain resemblance to the joker in the modern playing deck. The April Fool mirrors the gap between the world's talk and the world's walk, and is good for anything, so can be whomever you want him to be. But behind The Fool is The Hermit, who cloaks his light, waiting for the appropriate moment to unveil and share his wisdom."

The fact that a person like Michael, brimming with Christ consciousness, can voluntarily, when appropriate, hide his light from the world, makes it easier for Chimera and me to deal with the constraints on our discussion concerning his beliefs and objectives. The social relationship that we have developed with Michael and Diane also helps, since we have no secrets between us.

As I noted many years ago, one reason I have avoided discussing many of the personal details of Michael's life is for his own protection and for the well-being of those closest to him. On the verge of the Millennium, however, Michael suggests that a more defined personal portrait might help facilitate understanding of his teachings.

Over the years, Michael spent a great deal of time studying in preparation for his larger work, but this devotion to his mission was not always obvious to his family. To them, he provided much of what would normally be expected of a father, attending the requisite parent-teacher conferences, sporting events, and musical performances, as well as tending to the yard, taking vacations, and doling out his own version of discipline when necessary. And while, as we've seen, Michael's "day-job" career has evolved successfully and in harmony with his spiritual goals, the material aspect of his existence has remained subordinate to his spiritual and social interests, never an end in itself.

Yet, at the age of fifty-one,[23] Michael lives a comfortably with Diane, their grown kids still close a hand, high in the mountains west of Boulder. Occasionally, I venture up there, sometimes alone and sometimes with Chimera, to visit.

At this point, it seems reasonable to wonder about the anonymity of man over a half century old who believes he is the Avatar of the age. What has taken him so long to prepare for his day in the sun? Why does his life look almost normal? There's no mention in the Christian *Bible* of Jesus having a family—why should this be part of the Second Coming of the Messiah? And finally, I wonder about his personal growth—does a Messiah or Christ or Avatar or Spiritual Anomaly by definition ever do anything "wrong," something that he must recover from like everyone else, or for that matter, do any of us ever make a mistake, or is it all fate, determined from the moment of the Big Bang?

One of the major lessons I have learned from my relationship with Michael is that he is flesh and blood like the rest of us. This does not mean that he is the same as us, for obviously he is not. The conditions of his life have enabled him to experience the most evolved spiritual, social, and technological changes possible at this time in history and, from this experience, to develop the tools necessary to derive and promulgate his proof on the interrelationship of all things.[24] Teaching is, in fact, the core of his mission.

It's also worth noting that the world is a much more complex place than it was 2,000 years ago. It is no longer enough for an Avatar to provide universal parables and immutable commandments for humankind's suffering masses. A contemporary man-for-all-seasons must be a renaissance man of the paleo-cybernetic age—a millennial man, so to speak. According to the *New Testament*, Jesus was 30 years old when he began his mission, i.e., when he became Christ. Shakyamuni was 35 years old, and a father, when he became Buddha. Why should it be a surprise then, at the time of "the information explosion," as McLuhan termed it, that it

---

[23] In the year 2000 AD.
[24] See *Appendix 6 – The Proof*.

would take a man 50 years to develop an all-inclusive world view and the personal refinement to handle the imperatives of such knowledge?

Perhaps Shakyamuni's life is a better example here for us than Jesus', because the separation of its mythological and historical elements is so much more apparent, with Buddha's life experiences transparently contributing towards our understanding of his eventual teachings. While fundamentalist Christians may say that Jesus was born perfect and had no need of learning experiences, his need for meditations in the desert and the mountains clearly indicate that he suffered just like the rest of us.[25] Besides, what do you think he did in the unrecorded years between the ages of twelve and thirty other than educate himself? Truly, this is what gives us hope—that, shown the way, we, too, can attain such consciousness. That is why Jesus said, "The kingdom of heaven is like to a grain of mustard seed,"[26] because, though small, it can grow into our whole life.

"While I have the greatest respect for all monks, nuns, and ascetics," Michael says to me during one of his and Diane's dinner parties, "my interest in providing specific experientially-based advice that addresses the turmoil of everyday people has led me down the path of a householder. It is through such ordinary lives that the world will be transformed. Yes, the number of people on the planet is overtaxing the earth's ability to provide, and yes, we would do well to naturally reduce our numbers, but it is unrealistic and unnecessary to ask everyone to become celibate. And how could I convince others to find peace in their lives if I hadn't walked a mile in their moccasins?"[27]

My heart skips a beat at Michael's mention of celibacy. Despite the peaceful resolution of Chimera's and my experiment, I still have subconscious energy around it.

---

[25] "Jesus suffered as other men suffer, and was made perfect through suffering; for this is the only way to perfection." Levi, *op. cit.*
[26] Matthew 13:31
[27] Michael writes: I am happy to see similar sentiments expressed by the Dalai Lama in *The Art of Happiness* (with Howard C. Cutler, M.D., Riverhead Books, New York, 1998): "As our meeting concluded, [the Dalai Lama] suddenly started to laugh heartily ... 'If I went to work for a company ... I do not know how far I would be able to follow my own advice. I don't know—I might start stomping around, yelling and breaking things ... I might get fired!'" (Also quoted at the beginning of Chapter 9.)

Michael stands up and walks over to the windows of his living room. The view is astonishing, much like Chimera's background in her painting *The First Supper*. From here one can see south to Mt. Evans and north to Long's Peak and beyond to the Mummy Range, into Wyoming. In front of us, to the west, stands the massif of Bald Mountain and behind it rise the Arapaho Peaks covered with snow. In all directions are the rolling, evergreen covered hills of the Front Range.

This afternoon's CD selections are a rotation of chants, randomly alternating between Benedictine monks, Native Americans, Tibetans, and various contemporary ancient music specialists. The wind is pouring over the Divide, propelling legions of clouds over the waves and troughs of the Rockies as they cascade toward the Great Plains. Gradually these billows turn from white to gold to red, then purple, and finally blue-black as the sun sets behind the Indian Peaks range. Across the ceiling of the atmosphere, incandescent jet trails from the world's largest airport arch over the mountains to California and, transversely, across America's heartland to the east.

"Another magnificent show tonight, Red," Michael comments toward the nearby kitchen where Chimera and Diane are conversing. I get a kick out of Michael calling Diane "Red," like Cary Grant did with Katherine Hepburn in *The Philadelphia Story*. It adds a sense of levity to the otherwise supernatural atmosphere that now seems to surround our friends in this magical spot.

Diane refers to this part of Boulder County as "Everland." Like most settlements in the area, it had its origins in mining, but unlike the other sites, Everland is blessed with a combination of lush alpine meadows, dense forests, and panoramic views of the snow-covered peaks above and the high plains below. The access to Everland is so steep however, that it took pioneers until 1876, sixteen years from the time they had settled Honeycomb Mountain on the other side of Boulder Canyon, to create a passage that was remotely navigable.

Despite Colorado's generally arid climate—prior to settlers rerouting water from one drainage basin to another, damming rivers, filling reservoirs, and planting trees, the humidity usually hovered around ten per cent—there are idyllic vortices where moisture converges. The high country of the Western Slope, with its post-World War II Olympic-caliber ski resorts, is an obvious example of this, as is Boulder County, where certain pockets receive more rainfall than other Eastern slope areas. While this precipitation is not remarkable by any standards, it is enough to support a healthy diversity of wildlife, including mountain lions, bobcats, elk, deer, coyotes, foxes, rabbits, eagles, hawks, owls, ravens, pheasant, blue jays, Clark's nutcrackers, grosbeaks, tanagers, robins, and a host of smaller avian and ground critters.

Not far from Michael and Diane's house are miles of trails that wind through U.S. Forest Service land. Many of the trails were once wide enough for jeeps that brought rangers into the area to "manage" the land. Their bumbling incursions still go on today, with the locals and government agents getting into it over the indiscriminate cutting of old growth trees.[28] Most of the time, however, you can walk through the

---

[28] Michael writes in 2003: Ostensibly, the U.S. Forest Service (USFS) and Bureau of Land Management (BLM) carry out these actions for no other reason than having been given a budget for "thinning" and fire prevention, but it makes one wonder which is the greater environmental threat to our forests, the pine beetle and mistletoe, or the genetic mutations supported by tax dollars and operating on behalf of the lumber industry. After the 2002 congressional elections, Bush II and his merry band of corporate whores, including Colorado's Governor Owens, swooped in for the kill, taking 50-80% of the trees out of our local forests as a subsidized gift to the timber industry—a payback for campaign contributions. They justify terrorizing of our forests by claiming that what is being cut is underbrush that contributes to forest fires. In fact, the cutting of underbrush is only a premise for getting to the old-growth timber. In our area the state Forest Service and private contractors leave all the leftover slash on the ground, only adding to the wildfire hazard in the tinder box dry, drought-stricken West. Recent studies have shown this policy is worse than no thinning at all (Jim Robbins, "Studies Find Danger to Forests in Thinning Without Burning," *The New York Times*, November 15, 2006 or @ http://www.nytimes.com/2006/11/14/science/earth/14fire.html). Timber industry arguments to the contrary, demand for trees would be greatly reduced if the government legalized the cultivation of hemp, which was classified as illegal to protect DuPont's patent on producing paper from trees. (Herer, Jack, *Op. cit.*, *The Emperor Wears No Clothes: The Authoritative Historical Record of Cannabis and the Conspiracy Against Marijuana*) This artificial scarcity is not unlike our so-called dependence on foreign oil. Just as we need to convert from trees to hemp, so we need to convert from carbon-based fuels to other energy sources. Such a conversion, however, would diminish the power of the oil cartel and the New World Order. That is what's behind the suppression of the alternative fuel industry. Luckily, foreign automobile companies and various entrepreneurs are circumventing the U.S. oil-automotive industry's influence on the political and

Douglas fir, blue spruce, ponderosa, Scottish and lodge pole pine, aspen, juniper, and sage for hours and never run into another soul except for encounters with local fauna.

Michael regularly walks these trails, shadowed by his favorite ravens, nurtured by the ionic purity and healing energy of a relatively untouched natural environment, often stopping to take notes when a thought comes up. Later, he passes these along to me for our book. Diane, on the other hand, runs these trails when the weather permits, accompanied with abandon by the neighbors' dog, who revels in the abundance of smells and provides security in the twilight when the larger critters are wont to hunt.

Such is Everland, a name Diane partly evolved from Peter Pan's Neverland and partly from a drawing she made for Michael that sits on an altar in his room, amongst the other ritual objects from Native America, Africa, India, and Israel, as well as his father's urn, a picture of the Dalai Lama, and sandalwood beads and *vibhuti*[29] from Satya Sai Baba. In the drawing, in front of a mountain backdrop remarkably like the one seen out their windows, sits a raven, similar to those that visit daily, perched on the railing of a deck. The border of the drawing reminds me of a Tarot card, decorated with hearts, touching hands, and arabesques, with Michael's number, 777, across the top, and the caption "Evermore," a twist on Poe's raven, across the bottom.

"It's 'Evermore' in Everland," explains Diane, "—our own earthly version of eternal life in the kingdom of heaven."[30]

---

economic policies that keep us spilling blood for oil to maintain global hegemony. In an attempt to create the appearance of progress in this area, Bush II recently proposed (1/28/03) giving away $273 million to the American automobile manufacturing monopoly for fuel-cell research that, basically, has already been done. His ploy is to delay the mass production of fuel-efficient cars until at least 2020, maintaining our dependency on an oil-based economy, increasing profits for his friends, and further contributing to global warming and the destruction of the eco-system.

[29] A sacred ash produced by the Indian holy man, a major avatar.
[30] "What are they?" "Ravens." "I thought ravens were just British." "Holarctic. All over the Northern Hemisphere. Where they have space to survive." She stared at them a moment, then gave me a sly look. "They're not saying 'Nevermore.'" "He got it wrong. Evermore was the real message." From John Fowles' *Daniel Martin*, Little, Brown and Company, Boston, 1977, p. 328.

And so it is. Before the world is to experience Michael as the anomalistic synthesizer of anything and everything, he is accepted as such in his own house. Just after sunset, we are joined by Michael's two adult children and seven friends for dinner. At the table, Chimera and I look at each other knowingly, simultaneously recognizing that there are thirteen of us sitting around a long table transverse to the views which I have described—similar to her painting and Dali's and da Vinci's before it. Of course, we had no idea until this moment just who these people would turn out to be, and now that it happened I can't help but reflect on the details.

I suppose it should be no surprise that Michael and Diane's children are here, having been delivered and raised from birth by a couple with such an intense evolutionary spiritual focus.

Aquila,[31] the oldest, is a musician, having begun the violin at age four using the Suzuki method. Michael and Diane are big fans of the practice.

"Music is a fundamental part of education," Michael says. "It's tragic that the arts are being cut from school budgets; it shows a total lack of understanding of aesthetics. Behaviorists who dare to pass themselves off as educators argue that the so-called Mozart effect is unproven and that exposure to music doesn't translate into better science and math scores. I imagine these bullet heads go to galleries and rate Van Gogh's works from one to ten.

"The point to art isn't that its effects can be quantified, only that it develop creative sensibility, an aesthetic, and that it facilitate our evolution, as individuals and as a species. The idea that art, like corporate product, must make a measurable contribution toward the GNP, or translate into a return on investment, shows us the degree to which we have disassociated ourselves from our internal Godhead to worship at the altar of Mammon. The essence of the art is not definable in a mathematical sense, any more than we can quantify love and G-d. Art contributes to the greater good on a spiritual level.

"So, having grown up around the violin and classical music, I was thrilled when Diane discovered a local teacher that catered to young children. As it turned out, she taught the Suzuki method, something with

---

[31] Greek for Eagle; also, a northern constellation. I should note that there is a nesting pair of eagles that live on a giant rock formation near Michael's house, rare for the Eastern slope in Colorado.

which I was not familiar at the time, but have discovered to be a remarkable educational tool, particularly with children."

"Mr. Suzuki's idea," says Diane, "is that learning music is just like learning a language.[32] Every child learns the language of his or her culture through repetition, and that's what the Suzuki method does for music, where students first listen to songs and then imitate them, just like they were repeating phrases back to their parents. Developmentally speaking, the ability to read words or musical notation comes later."

I had, of course, heard of this method, and some of the arguments pro and con.

"Hasn't there been some criticism of the ability of Suzuki students to read music?" I ask.

Diane smiles and then replies.

"That's what traditional music teachers used to argue, but if there is any deficiency in reading music it's due to the ineffectiveness of a particular teacher or student, not in the Suzuki philosophy itself, just like it would be for children with deficiencies in reading skills. Even kids that read at a very young age still learn to speak first; it's the same with music: they should learn to play first and read later. All you have to do is look at the success of Suzuki students—as solo artists and key players in major orchestras—to see how well the method works."

"What's also interesting," Michael adds, "is that the deconstructive[33] approach of the method helps teach children other disciplines. This is what Mr. Suzuki called 'talent education.'"[34]

Michael and Diane's daughter, Anahita,[35] was introduced to music in the same manner, though her focus remains in the healing arts.

"I think Ana's interest in massage therapy and energy work is a good example of the effect of the aesthetic that Michael describes," Diane says.

---

[32] Later studies, including one that appeared in *Nature Neuroscience*, May, 2001, support this view.
[33] Here Michael is referring to the manner in which musical scores are broken down into specific phrases and bowing techniques.
[34] A term used by Mr. Suzuki to denote his belief that every child is talented and needs only nurturing to develop it.
[35] A Persian goddess, both protective mother and warrior-defender of her people; also, the goddess of rivers and waters.

"It's another way of tuning into our natural gifts, by healing what's not in balance and maintaining what is."

"I know that this type of thinking is taken for granted in Boulder County and some other pockets around the country," I say, "but doesn't the ethereal nature of this stuff cause a lot of resistance?"

"There's nothing ethereal about it, Rashan," Michael says. "Here's where the Christian *Bible* has prejudiced Westerners against their capacity to heal themselves. This misperception is partly attributable to the fantastic nature of many of Jesus' miracles in the Church's highly-edited version of events, disassociating him from even the most accomplished healers that precede and follow him, giving him god-like powers apart from the human condition; thus, we are stripped of our own healing capacity. In fact, Jesus most likely learned his healing techniques during his 'hidden years'[36] on a journey to the East. If he excelled at healing,[37] above and beyond others who practiced the same techniques, this is attributable to the depth of belief manifested by him and his followers, an outgrowth of his anomalistic nature—not some otherworldly capacity unavailable to the rest of the human race. So, in a sense, Ana's incarnation is a reaffirmation of the ubiquitous healing power that we all possess."

Michael and Diane's idealism toward their children's potential is not much different from that of most parents, though it's obvious from the names they chose that there is a strong connection to the New Age, late '60's, counter-cultural hippies.[38]

But there is another aspect to Michael and Diane's world that is easily lost in all this goodwill: the price of freedom for living outside the accepted practices and beliefs of most of the world. It is much as Michael

---

[36] The hidden years refer to Jesus' life between the ages of twelve and thirty, which is not documented in the *New Testament*.

[37] Michael writes in 2003: Here, I am referring to Jesus' natural healing feats, not those mythologized to market Christianity.

[38] Michael writes in 2003: It's important to make distinctions here, because the establishment press tried to portray the cult-murderer Charles Manson as a hippie, because he had long hair and was involved with drugs. This was part of Nixon's escalation of the war against the counter-culture that opposed the Vietnam War and the Empire's obsessive materialism. A "true hippie," as defined by *The Hippie Dictionary: A Cultural Encyclopedia of the 1960s and 1970s*, by John Bassett McCleary (Ten Speed Press, 2003), is "a person who lives by the Golden Rule." See "Golden Rule" in *Appendix 7 – Michael's Notes*.

once told me in paraphrasing Dostoevsky's *The Brothers Karamazov*, "Just because everything is permitted doesn't mean that we can do anything we want." This is not an easy thing for children to understand. So, under the umbrella of Michael and Diane's practice of allowing freedom for experimentation and self-direction, both their children had struggles with substance abuse.

"This isn't to say that we don't teach boundaries," Michael says, "but the world is filled with experiences that can harm. At some point or another, children grow up and will be confronted with choices—money and credit, sacraments and drugs, love and sex, et cetera. A parent can't prevent this from happening, so the best we can do is prepare our children to make their own choices. If we base the prohibition of certain behaviors on superstitions or misinformation, we've done nothing to help the world evolve, for in a universe where everything is integrated, lying about one part of our life poisons other parts. Many people think that such deception is preferable to the truth, and they may believe that they have insulated their conscience from guilt over such practices, but part of them knows the truth and, in the end, they're harming themselves and their progeny.

"Like any responsible parent, I experience pain around any major issues my children have, including those with psychotropic or addictive substances. It's not easy to understand why these things happen. There are genetic predispositions to consider as well as psychological and emotional issues; even the desire to push the boundaries of consciousness comes into play. It's also worth noting the involvement of big business and government in contributing to the availability of hard drugs. Pharmaceutical companies produce more narcotics that they can legitimately sell through prescriptions—these surpluses are not inventoried—and our own government traffics in cocaine, heroin,[39] and

---

[39] A reference to the Reagan-era Iran-Contra Affair, which traded cocaine for guns, as well as a reference to the promotion of Afghani opium, when G.H.W. Bush (I) helped arm and train Osama bin Laden, as part of U.S. support for the anti-Soviet Mujahedeen. After G.W. Bush (II) "liberated" Afghanistan from the Taliban, whom we supposedly paid to eradicate opium, opium production quickly recovered ("Afghan anti-poppy effort 'largely failed,' U.N. says," *The Associated Press*, 8/19/02), just as it has in the Andes ("Coca production soars in Andes," Kevin G. Hall and Cassio Furtado, *Knight Ridder Newspapers*, 7/21/02), where we are supposedly eliminating coca farming. The so-called "war on drugs" is not a war against drugs, but a war between competing cartels.

methadone,[40] pushing drug addiction and then defining it as a crime, not the disease that it actually is, thus subsidizing a profitable prison industry in which nearly two-thirds of those incarcerated, one in thirty American adults, are there as a result of drugs. And the most virulent supporters of this morally bankrupt policy are former addicts like the President of the United States."[41]

Michael looks at the tape recorder, as if measuring the depth of his explanation versus the time and energy his audience may have for reading or absorbing it.

"However," he continues, "these are challenges that I faced in my youth as well, and honestly, I'm a better person for it. A friend of mine who is member of the AA fellowship once told me that she is a 'grateful alcoholic.' I asked her what she meant by that and she explained, 'my relationship with G-d and the light that fills my life is a result of having this disease and developing a practice to control it.' Being snagged on alcohol or heroin or sugar or money or other material goods is all the same thing: dependency on a false G-d. So, when my kids overcame their struggles through developing spiritual practices, they then had the tools to help them stand up against all the other insidious, yet generally unrecognized, traps of this world."

Just as it is no surprise that those closest to Michael, his children, bear such a heavy symbolic and practical connection to his teaching and his past, likewise, the others at the table this night seemed to be related to the

---

[40] Government policy has resisted the use of medicines that have shown remarkable success in facilitating quick and painless withdrawal from heroin, while they continue to push Methadone, which allows them to register addicts and create new ones. Why does the government prefer maintaining a subculture of addiction? For more on the U.S. government's involvement in drug trafficking, see http://www.fromthewilderness.com/free/ciadrugs/index.html. Also, Pam Belluck, "Solution becomes serious problem: Methodone-related deaths alarm states," *The New York Times*, 2/9/03.

[41] George W. Bush was addicted to both alcohol and cocaine as a young adult, yet his policies show no compassion towards those with similar problems but without the family resources (like he had) to escape from the legal consequences of their actions and to pay for private rehabilitation. Bush attempts to pass off his behavior as "youthful indiscretions," a term which he and his rabid cohorts refuse to apply to others, unless they happen to be Bush's own children (who have been arrested for underage drinking) or his brother Jeb's daughter (who has been arrested for falsifying prescriptions for narcotics and has, because of her family's position, escaped prosecution for possession of crack cocaine).

unfolding anomalistic story in substantial ways as well. By this I mean the presence of Michael's friends, John, Mary, Elysabeth, Nathan, Martha, Peter, and James.

> *The notion of Jesus and the Apostles returning* en masse *is something I've ruminated over for as long as I've immersed myself in "Christ consciousness": The presence of those with the requisite biblical names always stimulates questions on my part. The only predisposition I can have toward this phenomenon is to wait and see what happens. I suppose it's like musical chairs—when my time comes the particulars at that juncture will become significant in ways they previously were not. I do find it exciting that as this moment approaches my sense of the future becomes clearer, and those who will play important roles are making themselves known in my life.*

As I said, surrealism is the order of the day in Everland, and while I wouldn't necessarily place too much significance on the coincidence of biblical names in a world where they are commonplace, in Michael's proximity I think twice about dismissing such synchronistic possibilities. It would be easy to attribute these enhanced layers of meaning to "the guru effect" that Michael explained to me years ago, but that belies the anomalistic nature of Michael's existence. The fact that Michael is descended from Solomon and Boas[42]—that is, the House of David on both sides—makes it more difficult to dismiss names as so much serendipity. Even if I do hold different political views from Michael and still find myself questioning the whole notion of a Messiah and Second Coming and the convergence of the two, I've heard and seen too much now to dismiss the possibility. Magic is alive and God is afoot. One cannot help but wonder what other miracles are to be revealed in the near future.

---

[42] According to genealogical research completed in 2007.

11

Transcendence

"The interests behind the Bush Administration, such as the CFR,[1] The Trilateral Commission - founded by Brzezinski for David Rockefeller - and the Bilderberger Group, have prepared for and are now moving to implement open world dictatorship within the next five years. They are not fighting against terrorists. They are fighting against citizens."
--Dr. Johannes B. Koeppl, Ph.D., former German defense ministry official and advisor to former NATO Secretary General Manfred Werner

"The drive of the Rockefellers and their allies is to create a one-world government combining supercapitalism and Communism under the same tent, all under their control. ... Do I mean conspiracy? Yes I do. I am convinced there is such a plot, international in scope, generations old in planning, and incredibly evil in intent."
--Congressman Larry P. McDonald, 1976, killed in the Korean Airlines 747 that was shot down by the Soviets

"We are on the verge of a global transformation. All we need is the right major crisis and the nations will accept the New World Order."
--David Rockefeller

"The process of transformation is likely to be a long one, absent some catastrophic and catalyzing event—like a new Pearl Harbor."
--The Project for the New American Century (PNAC), signed by Dick Cheney, Donald Rumsfeld, Jeb Bush, Paul Wolfowitz, et al. on June 3, 1997.

"Let us never tolerate outrageous conspiracy theories concerning the attacks of September the 11th."

---

[1] Council on Foreign Relations

--President George W. Bush, to the United Nations, November 10, 2001.

"Of course we will have fascism in America but we will call it democracy!"
--Huey Long

"Americans think their danger is terrorists. They don't understand the terrorists cannot take away habeas corpus, the Bill of Rights, the Constitution. ... The terrorists are not anything like the threat that we face to the Bill of Rights and the Constitution from our own government in the name of fighting terrorism. Americans just aren't able to perceive that."
--Paul Craig Roberts, former Assistant Secretary of the Treasury under Reagan

"Fascism is not defined by the number of its victims, but by the way it kills them."
--Jean-Paul Sartre

"Fascism ought to more properly be called corporatism since it is the merger of state and corporate power."
-- Benito Mussolini

Unlike the segment of Chimera's dream set to canvas in her painting *The First Supper*, at this evening's meal Michael does not offer sacraments or sermonize on world events, but simply converses with his guests, irrepressibly tracing ideas through the infinite circles of universal phenomena, and then, as always, folding back to some basic spiritual truth. Perhaps, as Michael, Chimera, and I had discussed, *The First Supper* is a continually recurring event, following Michael around as in "Behold, I make all things new,"[2] or perhaps reinventing itself whenever a *minyan*[3] breaks bread.

---

[2] Rev. 21:5

This evening's dinner gathering is, in a sense, a glimpse of the future—a representative smattering of artists and spiritual seekers, each sharing their work and dreams with the others. Many of the piecemeal political, religious, and social issues which invariably concern those caught up in less holistic realities don't seem to raise much dust in these surroundings. Instead, there seems to be an unspoken acceptance of spiritual growth being the basis for any lasting social change and a sustainable future for humankind.

Among these friends and peers, Michael's focus seems right at home—just another artist putting his truth in front of others. One could almost forget that his truth is earth-shattering outside of this small circle, and that his presence will likely be seen as proof of the universe's detailed perfection. Yet this dichotomy is as it should be, for most of the world is not yet experiencing the consciousness of the new millennium—and that, of course, would be why he's come.

During the course of the evening, I visit with many of Michael's guests. Since Chimera and I have been doing Partner Yoga for a while now, I use this opportunity to talk with Elysabeth about my progress.

"How are you feeling?" she asks me in her usual intense manner, her dark brown eyes penetrating me.

I had initiated the conversation, but it suddenly occurred to me that I hadn't anticipated the emotional depths to which I'd be taken. Luckily, the wine was beginning to kick in.

"I'm learning," I say. "I still separate my mind and heart. I find myself doing all sorts of things while not knowing how I'm feeling about them."

"Everyone has that problem more or less," she says. "Being present takes practice."

"My accounting work takes a toll," I reply. "I spend fifty hours a week analyzing corporate finances. The focus of all that effort—the so-

---

[3] A Hebrew term for the minimum number of persons required to be present for the lawful conduct of a public Jewish service: ten Jewish males of at least 13 years of age. Michael writes in 2008: In the present dispensation, religious affiliation and gender requirements have been eliminated. Separation by sexes is optional, as a tip of the hat to the Orthodox (Judaic) practice, which has its merits (in much the same way that "intermittent" celibacy does).

called bottom line—isn't something you see on a heart monitor. It's hard to shift gears."

"For you and the whole industrialized world," she says, turning from Yoga to politics as quickly as Michael.

"I've got a family, Elysabeth. It's not so easy to give up one's vocation."

"It depends on your priorities," she says.

Diane sets out some *hors d'oeuvres* and I change the subject. We walk over to the table to nosh and refill our wine glasses.

As if psychically smelling the offering from another room, Aquila and Anahita, the twenty-somethings, suddenly appear right behind us. It's a biographer's field day.

After some pleasantries, I ask them, "So how do you feel about your dad and me publishing this book?"

"It's his truth," Aquila says, "like my music. He needs to say it, and people need to hear it."

Anahita nods. "It's all very heavy though, thinking about what's going to happen when you publish."

"What *is* going to happen?" I ask.

"People are going to be shocked," she says. "A lot of people will freak out."

"It's our job to minimize this, though" Aquila says.

"How are we going to do that?" I ask.

"With music and other healing arts. We're talking about putting something together around my dad's *satsangs*,[4] he says.

"You guys are already planning public events?" I ask, surprised to hear this.

"Maybe not at first," she says, "but eventually."

"What about all the security, and the crazy people like you said?" I ask her.

"It'll get easier. Things will calm down after a while."

"You think so? I'm not so sure."

"There are a lot of people out there," Aquila says, "who are ready for this. You'd be surprised."

---

[4] Sanskrit for teacher-led group discussions and meditations.

It seems that everywhere I turn this evening I run into people who think much like Michael. This is a very different mindset than my everyday experience in the world of high finance and global wheeling and dealing.

"It's the people who aren't ready for this that you need to watch for," I say, suddenly aware of my chameleon existence in-between two worlds.

"They may change quicker than you think," Anahita says.

It's not surprising that Aquila and Anahita reflect the self-assurance of their parents, and indeed, in this evening's group everyone seems aligned with this outlook, but I wonder how realistic it is to think that the world at large will be anywhere near as receptive.

Since Chimera and I are the last to leave this evening, I use the opportunity to ask Michael about the simpatico he has with his community of friends, acquaintances, and like-minded evolved beings for whom conscious spiritual evolution is the objective, and about the coming contentious showdown with those whose belief systems preach competition and self-interest, elitism, and conspicuous consumption.

As always, my tape recorder is running.

"There's a certain shock value to my existence, Rashan, of which I'm acutely aware, and despite my desire for peace, prophesies and world events indicate that our declaration shall result in a loss of identity for many and a certain degree of violence that often attends such abrupt changes. I pray that these dark forces are muted by love, compassion, and the light of G-d consciousness, the Great Anomaly, the higher self that each of us carries within." Michael pauses. "I had a dream recently that indicates to me that such hope is plausible."

Chimera and Diane are downstairs and Michael and I are sitting without lights, gazing at a magical snow-packed landscape illuminated by a quarter moon.

"Play on!" I implore.

"I'm in this very room," Michael begins, "with my earthly father who, as you know, passed on almost twenty years ago. He's standing right over there, and I'm standing before him."

Michael gets up and walks to a spot between the two couches on which we've been sitting.

"At this spot, right here, where I can see the whole Front Range,[5] there's an alignment of three points: myself, the cross of the main beams of the front of his house facing the Divide, and the spot along the ridge of the mountains behind which the sun sets at the Summer Solstice," he says, pointing through the cross-beams that separate the front windows toward Mount Audubon, northwest along the Divide.

"Before me is my father's face with a number of lesions on it, which disturbs me. I face these skylights and hold up a Star of David in front of a crucifix and suddenly a circle of focused light from the Sun cuts through this intersection of religious symbolism. I turn and shine this laser-like beam on my father's lesions and they heal before my eyes. And so it is with the lesions upon the face of my heavenly "father"—to use the patriarchic name by which I so often referred to the G-dhead in my previous incarnation—that the antipathetic fluctuations of faith shall be healed, and that all G-d's children shall realize they are of the same faith, from the same source, just as I have shown in my proof."[6]

"You do have such all-consuming dreams."

"It's the same content I concern myself with when I'm waking, Rashan. It's who I am. There isn't much point in me spending time thinking about anything other than the work at hand. Anything less than total transformations in thought and action will be insufficient to alter the death-wish mentality that dominates those in power."

The here and now is never more than a reply away when talking with Michael. I've often wondered what type of life made it possible for a human being to attain such clarity of vision and unflappable belief in his own truth. As I've documented over the years, I've spoken with many of Michael's friends, lovers, acquaintances, and even his kids, but have avoided asking Michael directly about his upbringing and the conditions of his life. Now, with the Millennium quickly approaching, and our book and public appearances looming just beyond, I feel an impending urgency to get something on tape and into our chronicles.

"How did you get this way, Michael? I mean, before you taught yourself Yoga, what conditions made it possible for you to become who you are?"

---

[5] In this case, from Mt. Evans to Long's Peak and beyond.
[6] See *Appendix 6 – The Proof*.

"That's always been an interesting question, Rashan, particularly so if the focus is spiritual anomalies. Take the Christ: The commonly accepted notion of Jesus' life presents him as someone who essentially came here with complete knowledge and without any need to evolve in order to pass along his gift. But despite the efforts of early church censors (who excised the key educational years between twelve and thirty from Jesus' life to create the illusion of his omniscience from birth), the text of the Christian *Bible* still reveals that it is a misinterpretation to see Jesus as a divinity separate from man. Why else would Jesus need to retreat to the mountains and desert to meditate? If he were super-human, he would have no need to recharge himself. Clearly his body grew from babe to adult in the same manner as all human beings, and needed rest and recuperation as well. He didn't talk to the Magi when they arrived at his birth, because he was physically and mentally incapable of doing so; nor did he cast the first stone at the adulterous woman, because he had the same human frailties as the rest of us.

"That he *is* human is his greatest gift, because this makes each of us responsible for our own divinity—and shows us a pattern that we may follow to accomplish this. This human Jesus, frailties and all, is perfect, in and of himself. But the lack of personal detail in his printed story, the missing aspects of personality, the remote and inhuman face given to him by the editors of the Christian *Bible*: it is this that I shall remedy with your help, in this dispensation, so that even the most dispossessed among us who choose conscious spiritual evolution shall find within their life some shred of connective tissue that links them to the body of Christ within themselves, whatever they may prefer to call it. No longer shall my way be out of reach from anyone. There shall be no untouchables, for truly I am all of these things."

"So what you're saying is that you'd like to provide some details of your life that would give us an accessible vision of the conditions that shaped your path?"

"Yes, but I do so not in any absolute sense, not to measure anyone's distance from Messiah or Christ or Anomalistic Consciousness, but to paint a general and relative picture of natural events from which others may find resonance in their own lives and thus come to their higher self in their own unique and perfect way."

"As always, we note the non-dogmatic, decentralized vision within which your wisdom is framed."

"Then how else should my life begin but anonymously, in New York City, like millions of others. As we've discussed, there are cosmic forces at work: it is in 1949 and in Beth Israel[7] Hospital in Manhattan, less than a year after the rebirth of Israel. But again, I was born one among millions of Jews who escaped Pharaoh's then Herod's then Hitler's plans to put an end to the succession of prophetic Judaic incarnations that began with Moses, recurred with Jesus, and continue with the present spiritual anomaly."

"So what you're saying is that the time and place, though shared by many, is nonetheless prophetic, being that it was technically within 'the House of Israel' and after the rebirth of Israel as a nation."

"I have no other way to interpret it, since it is plain to see, but I would say to others, 'You, too, have an anonymous birth that is significant for your own unique reasons. Discover what binds your soul to time and place throughout your life, for the manner in which your unique truth unfolds is perfect.'"

"But despite what now may seem significant," I counter, "there were no indications at your birth that you were any different than a million others?"

"As we've discussed, the House of David has long since been dispersed far and wide, and even though it appears that I am descended from the House of David on both sides of my family,[8] history awaits the once and future king, much like David himself or King Arthur for that matter, to display his credentials in his own unique manner, rather than through royal succession, visitation of wise men, or recognition by lamas. This is as it should be in our case, for what better way to make the point that the force behind this incarnation is indomitable, unpredictable, and perfect."

"And for others, what's the lesson here?"

"I often muse that there must have been many candidates for the office which has been bestowed upon me but, as I've said before, like the millions of sperm seeking to fertilize an egg, only one succeeds. That sperm

---

[7] Hebrew for "the House of Israel."
[8] As noted earlier, from Solomon on one side and Boas (David's grandfather) on the other.

is the anomaly relative to the others. It looks the same and feels the same, but it's somehow different. There is no way to determine beforehand which sperm possesses the wherewithal, the *Je ne sais quoi* that will unlock and regenerate the miracle. When I say, 'Greater works than I shall ye do!'[9] I'm recognizing that each of us bears the seeds of unspoken miracles, and that in this life we discover, through the interdependence of free will and fate,[10] the potential of our soul. So, in a sense, I represent only the most generic of miracles—a steward of behaviors and thoughts that others don't want or avoid—while they, building on the universality of this miracle, shall be the ones that warp Space-Time, cure disease, and heal the earth."

"That's rather self-deprecating, Michael."

"It's the recognition that what I share with you and our readers in this book is my song and that I sing for my supper like the rest of us. It's a simple truth and, for the most part, nothing new, save for the anomalistic synthesis of the information itself: being the alpha and the omega means that exaltation rests upon humility; when one assumes that one knows nothing, and is unafraid to ask the questions needed to figure out whatever's at hand, then all knowledge is accessible."

"And this is your *modus operandi*?"

"Yes—at least regarding the information gathering aspect of my work. As I've mentioned, my earthly father always told me that the smartest people are those who ask the right questions. From there, the answers are easy. It's like knowing how to use a search engine on the Internet. Somewhere, out there on the web, is the information that you're looking for; you just have to figure out the proper query. Sometimes it takes a while to frame the question, and sometimes it takes a while to get the answer. Regardless, '… ask and you shall receive, that your joy may be full …'[11] still holds true. For some reason, I came in with this belief, like the master of the hundreds of robots I painted in kindergarten."

"What are you talking about?" I ask, readying myself for some unforeseen oblique connection.

---

[9] John 14:12.
[10] See *Appendix 6 – The Proof*, or updates at www.SolomonsProof.com, "7.5 Chaos Theory as Further Impetus for Conscious Spiritual Evolution."
[11] John 16:24

"In kindergarten, I painted robots for most of a year—hundreds of them. Robots were just coming into vogue then. They fascinated me. I see this as a lesson in humankind's inherent ability to program itself, much like auto-suggestion in Yoga. I believe my photographic recall and pattern recognition skills stem from this openness to the suggestibility of the mind. I always believed that I could ask my mind to do whatever was required for the job at hand."

"So in school, these qualities—self-questioning and self-awareness—stood you well?"

"I attended public schools in the suburbs north of Chicago. For the most part, they were good schools, relative to the era, and their coeducational nature was an important factor in my socialization. Only occasionally did any aspect of my schooling seem to impede my progress."

"You say 'seem,' because the appearance of mistakes and problems to the contrary, you believe that given a heartfelt effort, everything is perfect?"

"I think that's a fair take on my philosophy, although in the cosmic scheme of things, the notion of 'mistakes' provides for a stimulating discussion, the basis for which can be found in Gurdjieff's *All and Everything* and in my own proof."[12]

"How would you generalize, then, from your educational experiences to what others may experience?"

"Good teachers and encouragement matters. While many others had opportunities similar to my own, most people presently do not. There are a variety of reasons for this, including the class nature of our economic system, where the quality of education is directly related to local property values and parental educational levels. We need to be concerned with universalizing these opportunities, much as the case for Edward de Vere's authorship of the Shake-spearean canon is not an elitist argument but one that begs for recreating the quality of education he received. This is why the parameters of a de Vere's or a da Vinci's upbringing should be important to us. Currently, however, this is a low priority in a society where oil barons—who profit from pollution, retard the growth of

---

[12] Gurdjieff, G.I., *All and Everything: Beelzebub's Tales to His Grandson*, E.P. Dutton & Co., Inc., 1950, and *Solomon's Proof* (see *Appendix 6 – The Proof*), updated at www.SolomonsProof.com, particularly "7.5 Chaos Theory as Further Impetus for Conscious Spiritual Evolution."

sustainable energy sources, revel in capital punishment, disenfranchise millions of people and hire thugs to intimidate election judges in order to steal an election,[13] and pretend to follow the teachings of Jesus—are rewarded with the Presidency."

"But Americans pride themselves on being self-made, pulling themselves up by their bootstraps—like Horatio Alger."

"There's nothing wrong with self-reliance, but for the most part our politicians thrive on privilege and seek to preserve the system that engenders this and the excessive consumption that supports it. Equal opportunity is more a myth than a reality."[14]

"How can we change this?"

"With our hearts, of course. Schools that engender love and respect can provide compensation for what's lacking in the home. We must do our work where we can."

"And teachers' salaries?"

"Again, the present disparity reflects the priorities of a materialistic society. The heart is the antidote. Priorities will change as people evolve."

"What other influences in your formative years would you highlight? I understand you thrived at competitive games as a child?"

"Yes, this is what was available to us, and the success I experienced certainly contributed to my self-confidence and empowerment, but it also reinforced the aggressive tyranny of ego and instinct that I later had to work diligently to undo. Physical culture is a worthwhile endeavor that can instill belief in oneself, and top performance is certainly joyful, but by this I don't mean the cult of competitive sports and fame. In a materialistic society, success is defined as beating others rather than achieving personal

---

[13] Michael writes in 2003: I'm referring to the Bush-Cheney junta's tactics in Florida in the 2000 Presidential election, including the purging of 57,000 minorities and Democrats, alteration of voter records, police blockades, and disruption of vote-counting procedures. The reference to "millions" includes those whose vote was negated (or disenfranchised) by these crimes. This statement remains true, despite Barak Hussein Obama's election, since it was supported by the New World Order.

[14] Michael writes in 2003: And judging from the George W. Bush administration's stance on the University of Michigan Law School's admission policies, equal opportunity, or reparations for the denial of it, is not something this segment of the ruling class wants to consider. In this way, they support the continuation of the racist conditions that they bear responsibility for creating.

and collective goals. What we need is a balance between healthy instincts, the ego as a tool, and spiritual centeredness."

"So again, what you're saying is that evolving souls can transform society in their own image."

"Essentially, yes. There's no substitute for having a spiritual practice, and the urgency of our current collective situation make this an essential element of my teachings."

"Are your own spiritual practices something that came from your parents?"

"My parents were very loving. I never doubted for a moment their commitment to my welfare and happiness, yet their behavior was not the result of any regular practice or organized set of principles, unless you want to pretend that the influence of Judeo-Christian philosophy, as it is bandied about in Western society, is a cohesive set of precepts. No, rather, they did the best they could given their conditioning and the pre-millennial climate of their world."

"And would you agree that most people do not have the relatively positive support that you enjoyed?"

"Yes. It has become increasingly clear to me as I have aged that most people have experienced much more psychological and emotional damage during their childhood than I. As an adult, I have spent some time grieving over these sad truths, particularly as it has affected my intimate relationships. But regardless of how our experiences may have twisted us, our past cannot be an excuse for antisocial behavior. We must take responsibility for our own conditioning and see to our own healing. We begin this when we, as victims, ask, 'Who victimized the perpetrator?' At the precise moment we ask this, we become capable of ending the cycle of violence which has been passed down, generation to generation, from our pre-history in the jungle to our present-day circumstances. Only then do we become capable of fulfilling our potential as conscious human beings. No longer ruled by our ego and instincts, we can evolve into spiritual beings."

"Surely, though, there have been many that have experienced positive childhood conditions similar to those you have described so far?"

"Yes, at least in part, but in the combination of key elements the numbers are relatively small. In my own school district, growing up, I only can think of a handful of peers that meet the psychological, emotional, academic, social, economic, physical, and spiritual requisites that would adequately prepare one for the steps necessary to even consider of what avatar consciousness consists."

"And what might those steps be?"

"Much as we've often discussed over the years, Rashan, spiritual warriors[15] must be ready to abandon commonly-accepted assumptions concerning societal organization and their personal career goals. The social conditions of my childhood that we've described are generally only available to those whose class position is relatively elevated. Yet, lifelong wealth and privilege tends to influence against the type of risk-taking that we're talking about—the conscious willingness to change, which is essential to human evolution at this time. The wealthy young man that approached Jesus and remained unconverted is a good example of this, while Shakyamuni[16] and St. Francis[17] are the exception."

"You're saying there's a fine line between others growing up and experiencing many of the same conditions that you did and experiencing *all* of the conditions?"

"Yes. This is a fundamental condition of the universe, that a specific time and place supports a singular phenomenon.[18] However, as we stated at the beginning of this line of inquiry concerning my upbringing and education, in analyzing social conditions peculiar to my life we are seeking common ground whereby others may find elements in my anomalistic journey that resonate with them. That is why you and I are pursuing this personal angle, offered in the spirit of demystification and elucidation. Obviously, cosmic consciousness is a universal phenomenon, and not a state exclusive to a Kundun[19] or Rabbonai.[20] That is why it is important to see the singularity or anomalistic nature of my life as a generic event, because each of us, in one way or another, is an anomaly.

---

[15] A term popularized by the Tibetan Buddhist teacher Chögyam Trungpa, Rinpoche. Also, see reference to Trungpa in Chapter 2.
[16] Siddartha Gautama, the Buddha, born Prince of the Shakyas.
[17] Though St. Francis rebelled against his father's pursuit of wealth, as a boy its privileges allowed him to pursue his studies.
[18] The particle-wave behavior of light not withstanding. See *Appendix 6 – The Proof*, "2.3. Duality, Simultaneity, and the Fundamental Unit of Space-Time."
[19] The name given to the soul who successively incarnates as the Dalai Lama.
[20] Literally, "Master." Another name for the Christ or Messiah.

"The important thing to remember about the social conditions of my youth is the spiritual challenge I faced overcoming the materialistic atmosphere that pervaded the society in which I was raised. And it's not as if I don't have many trappings of comfort around me still: I live in a beautiful area, eat organic food when I can, listen to music, attend theatre with my friends, work at a fulfilling job, see my kids regularly, and have time to read and write. But if people believe that the tools which I have accumulated to do my job are excessive, they are missing the point. I came to Colorado with the clothes on my back and a couple of weeks' salary in my pocket. I also came with a spiritual goal in mind. What I have accumulated has come to me while I have pursued that goal. Much has been given away to others. Now, here I am sitting in my study gazing at the mountains, helping you write our book. I have a mortgage on this house. I have no savings account. I pay my bills every month, and can help my kids out now and then. Being focused on spiritual matters doesn't mean living in abject poverty. We live, as the Buddha called it, 'the middle path.' The world can support a fulfilling life for everyone, but it can't support an excessive life for the numbers that are demanding it, nor for the population we have let ourselves become."

"So, you're saying that a universal part of your childhood experience is overcoming your bourgeois upbringing?" I ask, not quite following Michael's logic.

"No. The universal part is overcoming obstacles to spiritual development. The poor people of the world cannot identify with the bourgeois part my experience. Their challenge is the challenge of second and third world countries: when development arrives—people become covetous, and their instincts and ego overwhelm them, just as it does with the rich and powerful. So, '… again I say unto you, it is easier for a camel to go through the eye of a needle, than for a rich man to enter into the kingdom of God.'"[21]

"Okay, I understand now. So, what other experiences would you draw attention to as having shaped your path?"

"In my generation, there are a few events that I would single out as having a significant influence on my beliefs and actions. We've already

---

[21] Matthew 19:24; Mark 10:25; Luke 18:25.

discussed the Holocaust, and while it occurred before I came into this body, its aftermath certainly pervaded the culture into which I was born. The effect of the Holocaust on the Jews serves as a constant reminder of the price that people pay for separateness from any dominant belief system and culture. Certainly persecution and prejudice is a condition with which many peoples from many different cultures can identify. As I have noted before, there are many holocausts, to one degree or another, occurring all the time. Sensitivity to these genocidal acts is part of the framework in my own life for a broader study of political, economic, and social philosophies outside of the standard censored fare that fills American media, educational settings, and public forums. The influence of these formative critical thought processes on my work is readily apparent.

"The next event to which I'd call attention is the launch of the first satellite to orbit the earth, the Soviet Sputnik. This set off a wave of trepidation throughout America and resulted in increased funding for mathematics and science programs in our schools. As a result, those of us who showed promise were ushered into accelerated programs to combat the looming Communist 'threat.' For me, this provided grounding in logic[22] and in the principles of physics and math, which aided me in the synthesis of the concepts of quanta, torus, anomaly, hexagrams, DNA codons, and binary replication into a proof for the convergence of science and spirituality, light as the building block for creation, the omnipresent anomaly, and, ultimately, the appearance of the Avatar and the next step in human evolution."[23]

"With all due respect," I say to Michael, "a lot of people were involved in advanced science and math programs without having the gumption to get out of the box and come up with some cross-disciplinary theory of human evolution."

"What is it that gives someone the empowerment to improvise and risk the seemingly heretical implications?" he asks. "It's like Agassiz[24] said,

---

[22] On my insistence, Michael reluctantly revealed some of his national test scores. As a sophomore in high school he scored in the 99th percentile in all three categories of a verbal, mathematical, and abstract reasoning test administered to advanced students, placing him among the handful that set the curve. He also scored 800s on both his advanced Math I and Math II SAT tests.

[23] Again, see *Appendix 6 – The Proof.*

[24] Louis Agassiz, nineteenth-century biologist.

'Every great scientific truth goes through three stages. First people say it conflicts with the Bible. Next, they say it has been discovered before. Lastly, they say they have always believed it.' The historical examples of individuals willing to buck the status quo to further human understanding are few and far between, and most of these inspirational innovators paid dearly for challenging it. What they possessed, in addition to the intellectual tools that provided the footing for their breakthrough, was the spiritual substance to get it done. So, it is a combination of symbolic and communicative proficiency, along with a substantive will, that sets pioneers apart. They simply believe they are on the right track; while, in others, complacency and comfort resist these forces at every turn. 'For many are called, but few are chosen.'"[25]

"The conditions that you are recounting here fall into two different categories—those that stimulate thought and those that stimulate action," I muse.

"That's astute. We're all influenced in varying degrees by each, but both are required for meaningful change. Take Jack Kennedy going to the thermonuclear brink with Nikita Khrushchev over Cuba, and then, later, Kennedy's assassination. Irrespective that we later discovered Kennedy's politics were not what we thought they were, the notion that nuclear annihilation was only a push of the button away engendered an urgency in my generation that continued to build throughout the sixties. The well-documented facts surrounding JFK's assassination and cover up and the sealing of the evidence by Johnson and his fascist apologists only increased our suspicions.[26] Thereafter, the assassinations of those on the liberal side of the spectrum continued relatively unabated.[27] Our suspicions were

---

[25] Matthew 22:14.
[26] It might also be recalled that Johnson's first act as President (on Air Force One with the body and Jackie aboard) was to increase U.S. presence in Vietnam, further adding to suspicions that the assassination was part of a strategic plan on the part of the CIA and those who stood to gain by increased military spending. George H. W. Bush, then a CIA operative, admits to being in Texas at the time, but can't remember where (see http://www.internetpirate.com/bush.htm).
[27] Michael writes in 2003: It should be noted that twice as many Democratic office-holders have died in plane crashes, compared with Republicans, the latest being Missouri Governor Mel Carnahan, who was killed in a plane crash ahead of a Senate election in 2000, and Senator Paul Wellstone, one of the most liberal members of Congress, during the campaign of 2002. Given the present one-seat

further confirmed by the Gulf of Tonkin incident that—much like Hitler's Reichstag fire that justified the Nazi takeover of Germany or the bombing of the U.S.S. Maine that was used to start the Spanish-American War—began the illegal and undeclared war in Vietnam, through which America sought to supplant the French as the preeminent colonial power in Southeast Asia. In a sense, the Selective Service System draft was a unwitting catalyst for our mistrust, because it put our lives on the line for our government's foreign policy, unlike today's system, which uses the underclasses as cannon fodder for the willy-nilly adventurist wars of Presidents interested in the empire's business interests, not in the lives of those they're sworn to protect. Added to the war in Vietnam, we had 'the British Invasion' of music, led by the Beatles, and the widespread proliferation of cannabis, which altered Western psychodynamics, and made 'Question Authority' a ubiquitous bumper sticker and everyday practice.

"On a personal level then, this skepticism toward the status quo and openness toward new ideas carried over when I began my spiritual studies. At that time, many so-called Christians were attempting to use Jesus' teachings to justify the USA's annual consumption of two-thirds of the world's natural resources by a country with six percent of the world's landmass and seven percent of the world's population. I don't believe I could have imagined conditions more upside down. Even today, when our percentage of world consumption has only gone down because others have adopted our gluttonous ways, the same sorry pseudo-Christian presumptions abound."

Just when you think Michael might be getting colloquial he rolls off one of his patented pre-recorded political loops. Sensing an opening between soundbites, I interrupt.

"Nevertheless," I say, "most of your compatriots from the sixties have been absorbed into the mainstream of our culture."

"True. The class privileges to which many of them were accustomed play a role in this, but in all fairness, Rashan, the nature of the battle

---

plurality of Republicans, such "accidents" were key facilitators in the implementation of the scorched-earth policy of the Bush-Cheney junta.

changed, and I sense an unspoken reservoir of belief in the principles from that era that are awaiting a cogent focus."[28]

"And you would describe that focus as …"

"… the synthesis of social, scientific, and spiritual principles into a philosophy that guides evolutionary change. That's our calling."

☼ ☼ ☼

Not long after our discussion, Michael had the occasion to revisit some of these same political questions in one of his weekly theatre reviews. He had just seen Puccini's *Madama Butterfly*:

> *The philosophy of Manifest Destiny—that America has a G-d given right to rule the Western hemisphere, and any other place where the populace is perceived to be "less developed" than our own, has been around since the early 19th Century. It led to the aggressive western march of Europeans across Native American land, the Louisiana Purchase, the Mexican-American War, and even the threat of war with Canada to secure the incredible expanse that makes up our current borders. This zealotry didn't stop when the ports of San Diego, San Francisco, and Seattle had been secured. In 1853, with a show of American naval force, Admiral Matthew Perry began the process of forcing Japan to trade with the Western powers. Following the Civil War and the industrialization that it stimulated, American expansion and "gunboat diplomacy" continued in the Far East, with acquisition of the Philippines, and in the Caribbean, with the Spanish-American War and other actions.*
>
> *This then, is the political setting underpinning Giacomo Puccini's masterful* Madama Butterfly, *Opera Colorado's winter production that opened last Saturday. The turn-of-the-century story revolves around a geisha, Cio-Cio-San, who marries a visiting American naval officer, and the tragedy that results from his frivolous attitude toward their marriage and Japanese culture in general. This theme is not*

---

[28] The grassroots presidential campaign of Barack Obama is a good example of this.

unlike the behavior of *The Ugly American*,[29] written some 50 years later, which anticipated the most far-flung military exercise of American imperialism to that time, the Vietnam War.[30]

This review provoked a firestorm of protest from veterans, particularly those who had served in Vietnam. Michael was branded a communist in some of the letters, all of which were fervently "patriotic." A death threat against Michael was even phoned into the station.

For his part, Michael has no qualms about addressing these questions, because he considers his actions in opposition to the war in Vietnam as patriotic, as he delineated in another review during that period.

An entire generation was scarred by the Vietnam War: Those who served did not return as heroes; those who opposed it lost faith in their country. To paraphrase Alan Ginsberg, "I saw the best minds of my generation destroyed by madness ..."[31] *In an attempt to explain Vietnam and the economic and pseudo-moral imperatives that generated it, Lanford Wilson wrote* Fifth of July.

Currently in production by The National Theatre Conservatory, Fifth of July *showcases this year's graduating class exorcising the demons of their parents' generation and finding universal truths capable of liberating anyone.*

How does a generation recover from such trauma? Think back on those who survived the Great Depression, World War Two, and the Korean War. They're not without scars from the carnage. But here, the hope that playwright Wilson gives us is that his characters, survivors all, may regain a sense of purpose, and even flourish—if they're willing to stop looking for answers outside of themselves.

But, of course, Michael's occasional well-tempered musing didn't quiet those who have little tolerance for differing opinions, and a persistent

---

[29] *The Ugly American*, William J. Lederer and Eugene Burdick, 1958.
[30] This review was written before Bush II and his friends at the CIA made U.S. intervention in the Middle East oil fields routine.
[31] From *Howl and Other Poems*, City Lights Books, San Francisco, 1956.

campaign of letters continued to call for his ouster. To their credit the station management of KIVA continued to stand behind the First Amendment principles that the issues involved. And as Michael's "luck" would have it, regional theatre productions provided a constant means for him to address his critics, such as this excerpt from his review of *A Tale of A Tiger*, performed by Ami Dayan:

> *They say the pen is mightier than the sword. Even saber rattlers like Ronald Reagan pay credence to this idea. That's why Nancy's husband kept the likes of Dario Fo out of the country as long as he could. Fo, who won the Nobel Prize for literature in 1997, knows how to tell a story that cuts through class lines and knee-jerk ideology to the crux of the human condition, a subject with which most politicians and their systematically repressed flocks are uncomfortable.*

As a citizen of the United States, Michael isn't deportable; he has no visa to revoke. So, ultimately, his own version of patriotism is as good as anyone else's. And while he has his steady detractors, most of those who listen to the station find his work engaging, if not stimulating. Death threats, however, are always problematic, and no one is more aware than Michael of the potential threat that right-wing groups and quasi-governmental operatives hold for him. Less than fifteen years earlier, another controversial Jewish radio personality in Denver had been gunned down for his views.[32]

In addition these threats, the IRS investigation dragged on into its second year, despite Orloff's strong legal representation in this matter, Michael's impeccable records, and the unconstitutional nature of the Treasury Department powers—seizing assets without trial (a crime worse than what mad King George III perpetrated on the colonies[33]) and taxing without legal authority.

---

[32] Alan Berg, KOA talk radio host.
[33] "He has affected to render the Military independent of and superior to the Civil power. He has combined with others to subject us to a jurisdiction foreign to our constitution, and unacknowledged by our laws; giving his Assent to their Acts of pretended Legislation: ... For depriving us in many cases of the benefits of Trial by Jury: ..." -- Thomas Jefferson, *Declaration of Independence*. Michael writes: This

It isn't until Passover that I have a chance to discuss this situation in detail with Michael. Chimera and I arrive at Michael and Diane's place early, before the rest of the guests. It is the end of a warm spring afternoon in the mountains. The woods are warily showing signs of life, knowing that a few snowfalls and killer frosts are still in store. Michael and I are having a glass of wine on the deck.

"There are some issues surrounding these death threats and government pressures that we ought to discuss, Rashan, and delineate in the book. To begin with, I want to make it clear that I believe the government, operating as a proxy for wealthy and powerful interests, is fully capable of arranging for my death."

"We've noted this before."

"I see no reason to believe that those in control of the government have changed for the better; in fact, I believe that some of the letters which the station has received are a set-up. It's no different now than it ever was, two thousand years ago or twenty-five years ago. Serious threats to the state—or the church for that matter, which acts as an apologist for the socio-economic status quo—are dealt with summarily and covered up. The same thing will happen if they decide to terminate me."

"You're saying they will attempt to deny any involvement?"

"Yes, as we've discussed a few times, they've become better at this since JFK's assassination, which was rather sloppy and required a great deal of follow-up to suppress the facts.[34] But they're getting slicker. Now with another Bush in the White House, the black ops are firmly in control of the government. W's daddy is an old pro at this sort of thing. He was around for both the JFK and the Letelier jobs among others."[35]

---

is much like the indictment of Bush II's actions post-September 11, 2001, including the so-called The Patriot Act of 2001 and the fascist legislation that followed (See *Chapter 12 – Resurrection*).

[34] At least 15 material witnesses died mysteriously within a short time frame following the assassination and during the ensuing investigation. According to all the doctors present in the emergency room, the autopsy photographs were altered. Websites for gathering information on the assassination and cover up are a moving target, particularly given the government-sponsored disinformation campaign, but the best current site we've found is: http://jfkmurdersolved.com.

[35] The Bush Crime Family (and those it represents) has always put its own interests above American interests. Great grandfather Herbert Walker and grandfather Prescott Bush both helped raise and launder money for the Nazi war machine through the Union Banking Corp. in the late 1930's and 1940's (see *Behind the*

"And if this happens to you, what are we to do?"

"First, it's important not to buy into the cover-up. Roman soldiers did away with Jesus, yet somehow the written text pins the crucifixion on the Jews. If the Romans had no stake in doing away with this revolutionary, how come Herod put Jewish children to death in the hopes of killing Jesus soon after he was born? Or, why was Jesus crucified under Roman law for sedition instead of stoned under Jewish law for blasphemy? Clearly, the ruling class of today's Rome—the wealthy and power throughout the world—will be threatened by my teachings because the basis for humankind's spiritual evolution runs counter to the hegemony of capital, the commoditization of Earth and outer space, the maintenance of a criminal class, and the proliferation of narcotics and weapons. Behind this current state of affairs is the military-industrial complex that Presidents Jefferson, Lincoln, Hayes, and Eisenhower warned against.[36] They killed

---

Bushes, http://www.prorev.com/bush2.htm). In 1942, three firms with which Prescott Bush (as well as the Harriman and Dulles families) was associated were seized by the U.S. government under the Trading with the Enemy Act. (The Rockefellers, at the time, were rerouting precious fuel to the Nazis.) This type of criminal activity apparently rubbed off on father George H. W. Bush, whose list of crimes "are now legendary. Over the years he formulated, directed and otherwise facilitated brutal guerilla wars, coups, death squads, propaganda operations, money laundering, assassinations, and drug smuggling (What? Why leave out treason?—*ed. note*)." (from John Dee's "Coup 2K" @ http://www.lumpen.com/magazine/81/coup2k/). The USA Patriot Act of 2001 only makes the CIA's complicity in conspiracies easier to cover up, allowing them to legally resume hiring criminals to carry out their dirty work, thus obfuscating the chain of command.

[36] Again, as quoted in Chapter 4, in Eisenhower's famous farewell speech he warned, "In the councils of government, we must guard against the acquisition of unwarranted influence, whether sought or unsought, by the military-industrial complex. The potential for the disastrous rise of misplaced power exists and will persist." It should be noted that long before Eisenhower's remarks: Jefferson declared, "I hope we shall ... crush in its birth the aristocracy of our moneyed corporations, which dare already to challenge our government to a trial of strength and bid defiance to the laws of our country (Letter to George Logan, 1816); Rutherford B. Hayes recognized that "This is a government of the people, by the people and for the people no longer. It is a government of corporations, by corporations, and for corporations"; and Lincoln more ominously warned, "Corporations have been enthroned. An era of corruption in high places will follow ... until wealth is aggregated in a few hands ... and the Republic is destroyed."

Kennedy for a variety of reasons (his failure to support the Bay of Pigs Invasion, his fooling around with Sam Giancana's moll, and RFK's targeting of the Mafia), but preeminently for his plans to withdraw from Vietnam and the loss of armament spending and interest on borrowings (from the privately-owned Federal Reserve) that would result from the lack of an ongoing war. So what aren't they willing to do? If, and I emphasize if, an act such as my assassination comes to pass, know that they will attempt to deny involvement and eliminate others who may know something. *Use these very words to reject their disclaimers.* Despite their professed 'Christianity,' they are the same mammon worshippers who killed Christ and in whose perceived interest it is to do so again.

"Second, make sure that copies of this book are distributed to everyone on the list as we have planned. It's essential that my teachings and your commentary get published as you and I intend for them to be read, and not after editing by those who would have an interest in altering them, such as what happened with the Christian *Bible*.

"And finally, persevere and have faith. The collective ills of this world are nothing more than our karma for becoming conscious. There is nothing 'sinful' about it. Even the Church has finally come to recognize that heaven and hell are metaphors for one's connection to or disconnection from G-d in the here and now.[37] This is the garden, and you shall have the Kingdom of Heaven by becoming one with the messiah and savior within you. When you do this, then, as I have said, I shall return to you in this life."

This is a lot to digest before our full moon Eucharistic feast, but Michael is obviously beginning to feel a need to summarize as we approach the completion of the book. He recently read the rough draft for the first time, and tells me that he can help me with the final editing process after Easter.

"Very few people know about this book, Rashan, but after copies are distributed to our list, people will find out very quickly. I believe that, like the growing trend in pop music, a lot of our sales will come via the web.

---

[37] *Denver Rocky Mountain News*, "Spotlight Magazine," 7/31/99, in a Scripps Howard News Service reprint of an article by James Meek of *The Guardian* entitled "Pope defines hell more as a separation from God," Pope John Paul II, in the course of one week, described both heaven and hell not as physical places but as descriptions of one's relationship, or lack thereof, with G-d.

This is our great hope—a means of free and democratic sharing of ideas outside of the control and censorship of governments and the private monopolies that control the press. It won't be easy. America pretends to frown at the Chinese for restricting Internet access, and is even aiding the Chinese populace in avoiding net censorship,[38] but when our friend Philip Zimmerman from Boulder released his encryption software over the web before the government could stop him, they tied him up in court for three years.[39] Just like the Third Reich, they use the excuse of law and order and the threat of 'terrorists and drug pushers' to undermine the Bill of Rights.[40] But what they're really after, Rashan, is totalitarian control, private monopoly, and the destabilization of other regimes in the process.[41] This is Rome plus 2000, the naked face of American fascism, and they'll seek to crush me just as they did the last time."

The other guests begin arriving and Michael and I get up to say hello. Again, Michael's children join us along with some of those who had gathered with us the last time we were here, including John and Peter as well as Mary and Elysabeth.

When we finally sit down, Michael offers us an abbreviated Seder, his approach to Passover being far from traditional: He is more interested in

---

[38] *The New York Times*, 8/30/01, "U.S. May help Chinese Evade Net Censorship," by Jennifer Lee.

[39] See *The Denver Post*, "Empire Magazine of the West," March 3, 1996, "Cyber Rebel," by Maureen Harrington, and a follow-up article, *The Boston Globe*, September 24, 2001, Section C, p. 4, entitled "Battle over encryption software rages anew," by Anick Jesdanun.

[40] Michael writes in 2003: The comparison of the current US government and the Third Reich is not rhetoric. The precursor to the CIA, the OSS, absorbed so many Nazi intelligence officers after WWII (after helping them escape allied forces in Europe) that it became, in effect, a Nazi spy organization. Its influence is now extended to the Executive branch. "I never would have agreed to the formulation of the Central Intelligence Agency back in '47, if I had known it would become the American Gestapo." -- Harry S. Truman (1961)

[41] Again, "The interests behind the Bush Administration, such as the CFR (Council on Foreign Relations), The Trilateral Commission, founded by Brzezinski for David Rockefeller, and the Bilderberger Group, have prepared for and are now moving to implement open world dictatorship within the next five years. They are not fighting against terrorists. They are fighting against citizens." --Dr. Johannes B. Koeppl, Ph.D. a former German defense ministry official and advisor to former NATO Secretary General Manfred Werner (11/6/01, posted by *From the Wilderness* at http://www.fromthewilderness.com/free/ww3/nov202001.html).

tying together Jewish and Christian symbolism and talking about eternal life than he is in following ancient rituals.

"In an effort to free his people from slavery in Egypt, G-d had Moses bring down ten plagues upon the Pharaoh and his people, the last of which was death to first born male children. And G-d had Moses bade his people to slaughter a lamb and put its blood upon their doors so that the spirit of death would pass over their houses and spare them, and thus they were not afflicted.

"In the Christian dispensation, at the convergence of Passover, the crucifixion, and the resurrection, Jesus came to symbolize this lamb, by whose blood our spirit is freed from death, blessing us with eternal life. To the Jews at that time, his sacrifice was nothing less than the redemption of Israel.[42]

"Baruch atah adonai, elohenu melech ha-olam, hamohtzi lehchem min ha-aretz.[43] This bread from the earth is my body. Baruch atah adonai, elohenu melech ha-olam, bo-ray pree ha-gauphain.[44] And this fruit of the vine my blood. Let these sacraments be as Eucharistic portals unto the highest consciousness, filled with the light of the One-Without-A-Name, the Great Anomaly, our Lord G-d. Amen."

The sky behind Michael is filled with the golden remnants of the setting sun and our meal proceeds as if each of us had, in fact, been transubstantiated by our ritual act of eating the bread and drinking the wine. I have never experienced anything quite like it. It is as if a portion of our consciousnesses all tuned in to the same universal place—a group experience of Cosmic Consciousness. The conversation that followed

---

[42] Michael writes in 2008: A recently deciphered tablet, found about a decade ago in the Qumran caves, indicates that a sacrificed Messiah, who would rise after three days, was part of Judaic cosmology prior to the time of Jesus, lending an additional layer of meaning to Jesus' numerous predictions of his pending suffering, i.e., for the Jews, he shed blood "not for the sins of people but to bring redemption to Israel." (See Ethan Bronner, "Tablet Ignites Debate on Messiah and Resurrection," *The New York Times*, July 6, 2008.)

[43] This is an English phonetic version of the Hebrew blessing over bread: "Blessed art thou O Lord, our God, ruler of the universe, who brings forth the bread from the earth."

[44] This is an English phonetic version of the Hebrew blessing over wine. "Blessed art thou O Lord, our God, ruler of the universe, who brings forth the fruit of the vine."

centered on the different means that each of us uses to spread this consciousness to others.

After the meal, some of us retreat to the teepee that Michael and Diane have erected up the hill. We cross a small bridge fording an artificial creek that tumbles from one of three waterfalls Michael has set around the house. After we ascend the rock and flower-lined path and settle around the campfire in the middle of the teepee, Michael, already bronzed from the spring sun, with wavy dreadlocks falling over his ears, begins to speculate on the possibilities for the spiritual protectorates that he proposes for various sacred sites around the world.

"Recently, Native Americans have had some legal success against the government of the U.S. in reestablishing the terms of treaties that have been broken, and in regaining certain ancestral lands. There is also a movement afoot to create a Buffalo Commons across the heartland, consolidating prairie that is being abandoned as subsistence farming and the local population declines.[45] Occasionally, even the courts recognize the government's breach of responsibility concerning Native American trust accounts and other fiduciary matters.[46] While I'm not proposing that we ask for a blanket return to *status quo ante*, we must press for some

---

[45] "Sioux tribe endorses buffalo repopulation," *Associated Press*, 8/27/01, in the *Boulder Daily Camera*. Also, Matt Gouras, "Tribe proposes full control of bison range," *Associated Press* in the *Boulder Daily Camera*, November 26, 2006.

[46] At one point in 2002, federal courts shut down Interior Department web sites to prevent hacking into the trust fund accounts, and threatened Secretary of the Interior, Gail Norton, with contempt of court for failure to account for missing funds. This is still an uphill battle though, because the Republican-controlled Supreme Court is systematically seeking to diminish tribal rights (Bill McAllister, "CU prof says Supreme Court hurting Indians," *The Denver Post*, 3/31/02). On another front, the Bush II administration is seeking to overturn a federal appeals court ruling that found the government had failed to protect the Navajo Nation's interests in mining leases on reservation land, essentially agreeing that Reagan appointee, Secretary of the Interior Donald Hodel, secretly conspired with the Peabody Coal Co. to undermine the tribe's negotiations with the company (Robert Gehrke, *Associated Press*, 3/30/02, in the *Boulder Daily Camera*). As more judicial appointments are made by the illegitimate junta, chances for Native Americans regaining stolen lands and funds grow less likely. Contrast this to Canada, where the Haida Nation, a 7,000-member native group living on the Queen Charlotte Islands off the Northwest Coast, "have sued to secure 'exclusive right to make decisions about their land' and the surrounding waters." (http://www.washingtonpost.com/wp-dyn/articles/A17230-2002Mar25.html)

compromise between the deplorable present conditions and the complete reversal of nearly 400 years of European occupation. Only by making some form of commitment to this process, some form of reparations, a Marshall Plan, as it were, can the United States be in a position to encourage other governments to follow suit—the Chinese in Tibet, the Indonesians in Bali, our own puppets in Guatemala and Peru, and on and on. Then, from these centers, and from the centers of spiritually aligned individuals around the world, shall a change come over the earth.[47]

"It's hard to believe," he continues, revisiting one of his central motifs, "that just a few generations ago, native peoples roamed this country, perfectly in touch with nature and without a concept of real estate ownership. Now people think they own G-d's earth; but even English law doesn't say that. All people really own under English law is the use of the land according to the law. That's why states have the Right of Eminent Domain: governments can condemn land and take it over. And these governments themselves lose their rights to stronger states and so on. So it shall be when all states recognize a higher power and the land is returned to the people and once again respected as our mother and birthright and not devalued as a commodity and means of income."

From Michael's point of view, this seems like a reasonable plan to preserve what ancient wisdom hasn't already been destroyed by military, economic, and cultural imperialism. It remains to be seen, however, whether the publication of our book will create the necessary preconditions for Michael to be in a position to facilitate such changes.

The fire inside the teepee warms us against the chill of the evening, which encourages us to wander outside into a landscape of light and shadows generated by the full moon. Eventually, the evening ends with a sense of anticipation. As Chimera and I drive home, I wonder aloud about Michael's plans for spiritual protectorates.

"Now that we're on the verge of publishing this book, I get these sudden flushes of disbelief that Michael could really generate the kind of changes he's suggesting."

"That's normal," she says.

"But I feel guilty about it. I mean after all these years, and the work we've put into the book, I'm ashamed of these feelings. I guess part of it is

---

[47] See "The Great Invocation" in *Appendix 7 – Michael's Notes*.

just trepidation over the consequences of publishing. I know this is going to turn our lives upside down."

"That's a given," Chimera says, "but it's the price you pay for believing in these changes. I don't see any alternatives. It's like the Dead said, 'You got to play your hand sometime—the cards ain't worth a dime if you don't lay 'em down …'"[48]

It's been an eventful and unsettling evening. Michael's talk about the possibilities of government assassins and public ferment always makes me nervous. Despite the late hour, I'm fitful, and too worn out to realize when sleep finally comes.

☼ ☼ ☼

I call Michael to ask if he could give me a ride to Denver on Friday morning, knowing that he will be going to KIVA to deliver his theatre review live on the FM airwaves. My car will be in the shop and I need to get to Le Canard to review the set designs for the upcoming production of *The Bard's Ghost* before I go to the office.

Michael is quite jovial when he picks me at our house that morning. He is driving a 1990 BMW 325ix, a far cry from the antique 1949 Ford flat-head six that he had when I first met him. Although the car is eleven years old, it is impeccable. The all-wheel drive system gets Michael up and down the mountain, even during the iciest storms, in stereophonic comfort. Michael bought the car almost four years ago for a song. He always seems to be in the right place at the right time to get "the deal of the century." "It cost me less than a used Geo," he claims.

"We're very close to walking into our dreams, Rashan," he says to me as we began our drive past the University of Colorado campus on our way through Boulder to the highway.

"Which dreams?" I ask, not sure to which Michael refers.

"Both our dreams—to be recognized for who we are—you for your play and me for my proof."

"Let's hope the reaction is gratifying," I reply, not as self-assured of my place in the sun as Michael.

---

[48] Lyrics from "Truckin", The Grateful Dead; words by Robert Hunter; music by Garcia, Lesh, and Weir. Copyright Ice Nine Publishing, 1970.

"I don't think we can presume to know what the best reaction is," Michael says.

"Why wouldn't I desire critical acclaim?" I ask.

"It's like I told you a few years back in regards to the Crucifixion—sometimes very negative experiences can lead to positive changes. One can't anticipate the Great Plan."

Michael drives and listens to KIVA's morning jazz while I dive into this morning's *The New York Times*, which had been flown in overnight. When we arrive, Michael goes into the broadcast facility and I go across the street, to The Tea Ceylon, for refreshments, the rest of the paper, and to listen to Michael's timely, Easter-season review of a play entitled *My Magdalene*.

> *A week ago, Good Friday, seemed like an appropriate time to take in the current production,* My Magdalene, *at the Nomad Theatre in Boulder. As the title suggests, the play is a personal interpretation of the life and spiritual legacy of Mary Magdalene.*
>
> *Jane, a young married woman adrift in the late '60's and early '70's, has a near death experience as a result of an accident, opening access to the spiritual plane upon which Mary Magdalene dwells. Through this portal, Jane not only redeems the saint who has been so disparaged by the church, but learns healing and meditative techniques from her.*
>
> *Although the research upon which this story is based is not accepted or understood by so-called mainstream Christians, it is, nonetheless backed up by more evidence than the stories that got edited and placed in the Christian* Bible. *In 591 AD, Pope Gregory pinned the label of penitent prostitute on Mary Magdalene, though there are no references anywhere that confirm she was ever a lady of the night. Pope Gregory's outrageous position (consider the prostitutes who catered to many popes as well as the prostitution of the popes to money and power) was finally reversed by the Catholic Church nearly 1400 years later, in 1969.*
>
> *But even the Christian* Bible *(which has been aggressively edited before it was distributed) as well as the gospels found*

at Nag Hammadi (the Gnostic Gospels*) and at Qumran (the* Dead Sea Scrolls*), which survive largely unedited, do tell us that it was Mary Magdalene that anointed Jesus. This would make her the high priestess from an esoteric tradition dating back before The Flood. According to all four books of the Christian* Bible, *each in their own words, she was also the first person to experience the risen Jesus and, according to the Essene text, written in the original Aramaic, she was not only first among the Apostles, but the beloved partner of Jesus. These relationships are substantiated by the early Church texts of the Gnostics, though they were later suppressed by the patriarchal elements that won control of the Church ...*

A few minutes after the review, I notice Michael standing in the foyer across the street, talking with someone who has just entered the facility. I finish an article about the news organizations involved in the Florida Presidential Election ballot recount, wondering why there was no mention of the fifty to sixty thousand Democratic and minority voters that had been disenfranchised by Jeb Bush's "purge of felons,"[49] or all the absentee ballot irregularities that the Republican's so assiduously cultivated,[50] or all the roadblocks that had been set up in minority precincts. I made my way to the cash register.

All of a sudden there is a tremendous explosion that rattles the windows of the shop. I run back to the door and am terrified by what I see. Michael's car, that is, what is left of it, is aflame on the sidewalk near where it had been parked. I rush out and run toward the vehicle, hoping to pull Michael from the wreckage, but the blaze from the gasoline has spread over the whole car and its perimeter; the conflagration is so intense my face and hair is seared as I approach it. The smoke is thick and toxic and I can't see inside the passenger compartment. There are body parts next to the

---

[49] As mentioned earlier, this story conveniently disappeared from public discussion following the *coup d'etat* that put George W. Bush in the White House.

[50] Xavier Suarez, the former "mayor" of Miami who had been stripped of his office due to massive vote fraud, worked for the Republicans on Campaign 2000, helping fill out thousands of absentee voter applications in Miami-Dade County right up to election night. See John Dee, "Coup 2K," at http://www.lumpen.com/magazine/81/coup2k/.

wreck. The smell is sickening. Someone pulls me away from the vehicle, telling me it could blow up again.

"My friend is in there!" I shout. "I've got to get him out!"

"There's no one alive in there," the fellow says.

I hear sirens and almost immediately the place is crawling with police and firefighters. The area is quickly cordoned off, and the hose men begin to dump water on the fire. I get inside the building and find a phone to call Chimera and tell her the news, but there's no answer. I panic, thinking that she and I could be targets too. I leave through the back of the building and make my way down side streets toward downtown, eventually arriving at the bus station. It's afternoon before I get home.

Chimera is sitting with her head in her hands in a chair in her studio. KIVA is playing on her radio and I don't have to guess that she has already heard the news. We hold each other for the rest of the day, too stunned to do anything else.

The next day, the FBI identifies what remains of the body as Michael's, but won't release the remnants to the family until "an autopsy and further tests have been performed." When interviewed in the press, the FBI spokeswoman insists that there are no indications that the assassination is anything more than "the work of an individual who was enraged by Michael's 'promulgation of the Jewish Communist Conspiracy.'"[51] This phrasing also was used in the death threats that had been received by KIVA over the past few months and apparently represents sufficient evidence of a civil rights crime as to warrant FBI involvement in the case. "So far," the FBI spokeswoman says, "we have no suspects and no solid leads."

Chimera and I hardly know what to do with ourselves. We spend a number of days with Diane and the kids up in the hills providing what little consolation we can and taking care of whatever arrangements need to be made. Diane is remarkably stoic about Michael's assassination.

"He told us this was going to happen, didn't he, Rashan?" she asks me rhetorically. "I know we all downplayed this one way or another, not wanting to think about it, but Michael always planned for it."

---

[51] These are much the same words that were used to describe the actions of "The Order," a virulent neo-Nazi/White Power/Aryan Resistance movement ranging throughout Colorado and the Pacific Northwest and affiliated with the Aryan Nations, when they gunned down controversial KOA talk radio personality Alan Berg on June 18, 1984, in the driveway of his suburban Denver townhouse.

"It seems that way, yes," I say.

"I mean, it's clear in the footnotes you guys wrote that the people who did this do this sort of thing all the time. It's one of the ways they stay in power."

"I'm beginning to think that's true."

Diane looks at me directly and says commandingly, "Then you need to help me get to the bottom of it."

I hire a private investigator to see what he can find out, but he returns my money and quits a few days later saying that the case is "too hot to get involved in" and that "the police and the FBI had closed ranks just like they did in the Mena case."[52]

The events all blend together. Chimera and I attend a memorial service with Michael's family and friends at a modest chapel north of Wayne that looks out at the Continental Divide. Those who speak at the service recount the influence Michael had on their lives. At this point, I am still too outraged by the events and the stonewalling by authorities to limit my remarks to Michael's spiritual mission. I quote Michael's description of what the authorities would say if and when they tried to eliminate him and show, in fact, that this is exactly what is happening. I urge those in attendance to make their own inquiries into what has transpired in the hopes of stirring up an investigation.

The assassination is ignored in the press. Even KIVA steers away from making it a *cause célèbre*. I can't seem to get anyone interested in the implications of what has happened. It takes a while before I am finally able to take my own advice and refocus on what Michael told me to do if such a thing happened:

> *"First, it's important not to buy into the cover-up …*
> *"Second, make sure that copies of this book are distributed to everyone on the list as we have planned …*

---

[52] Ismael Mena was a Mexican immigrant who was shot and killed by Denver SWAT officers during a no-knock drug raid in which they entered the wrong house. Police claimed that Mena shot at them, but this story was a cover-up to hide the fact that they killed an unarmed man. Evidence later indicated that police fired into the wall to make it appear as if their story were true. Despite this evidence, the officers in the case only received a temporary suspension from the police force. This was in a city with an African-American mayor!

"And finally, have faith. As I have told you, I shall return to you in this life."

Later, Michael and Diane's kids come by with some materials for the book. Their package contains a box of notes, a series of journals, newspaper clippings, and disks with electronic files on all the subjects Michael had been tracking for these many years. They tell me that Michael had left instructions in his will to give these to me. Eventually, I get back to work on the manuscript.

☼ ☼ ☼

What are we to think now that he is gone from us? Was it all an illusion perpetrated by some highly intelligent being with cosmic consciousness to keep alive the dream of a spiritually-evolved world? Had he, like Ghandi, evolved from a revolutionary to a saint, from fiery political rhetoric to "the peace of God that passeth all understanding?"[53] Or is Michael truly the Anomaly among us, the consciousness of the Messiah and of Christ returned, the teacher of teachers whose intellectual capacity, high-level personal integration, life-long empowerment, and spiritual practice sets a standard for us, our children, and our children's children twelve-by-twelve *ad infinitum*?[54] In the days that follow, I am filled with a growing belief that *he is indeed* the Avatar, Messiah, and Christ and, for the first time since childhood, begin to pray, this time to Michael, for some sort of sign. As for the lack of biblical-sized miracles that he has produced up until this point, I am reminded of a recent quote I came across, "It should be kept in mind that prophecy in the biblical sense does not mean to predict the future but to explain the will of God for the present, and therefore show the right path to take for the future."[55]

As I process my grief and begin to return to my normal activities, I find myself, one day, with my dramatist's hat on, and begin to analyze

---

[53] Philippians 4:7.
[54] Michael used this mathematical expression, rather than the mistranslated but popular 144,000 saved, in order to indicate that there are no limits on the number. Here again, the misunderstanding of the Hebrew use of the zero placeholder has led to dogmatic fallacies by fundamentalist Christian sects.
[55] Cardinal Joseph Ratzinger (now Pope Benedict XVI), overseer of Roman Catholic Doctrine (6/27/00, *Boulder Daily Camera*).

Michael's story as a classical tragedy. Did he have a choice in his actions? Did the authorities that feared and killed him have a choice? The answers depend upon one's definition of choice. On the surface, it seems that Michael could have chosen not to accept his mission, just as the state, or some hate group member working on its behalf, could have chosen not to murder him. But in many respects these choices are illusory because they run counter to the intrinsic truths of the people involved. These are the same parameters as Jesus' story: Cleary, as Michael reiterated to me recently, it was G-d's will that the crucifixion and martyrdom take place—meaning that a tragedy occurred because neither Jesus, nor Judas,[56] nor Pilate had a choice, and that the horror of the image of Christ nailed to a cross is part of its power and success. And while one could argue that very few people follow Jesus' teachings today, it's hard to deny the global recognition of his story and the prophesies surrounding it—meaning that the events of two millennia ago could be said to have accomplished their objective, that is, a marketing campaign to pave the way for the Second Coming.

Given the reappearance of the Messiah/Christ/Avatar/spiritual anomaly, or at least the attainment of this consciousness in the form of Michael, the global recognition of Jesus' life and teachings is something that can be built upon, within the framework of Michael's scientific approach, to bring about rapid spiritual evolution in the present. So, if this story of Michael's life and teachings leads to a *bona fide* change in human behavior, I will have to assume that his assassination was essentially inevitable, and that what we have witnessed *is* a tragedy. Seeing events in this way would, however, herald the end of tragedy as we know it, for we will have chosen (as Michael recommended) to free ourselves from the tyranny of instincts and ego—the "flaws" that feed tragedy—and thereafter make choices that honor the greater good. This does not mean that tragedy will disappear—or that the limbo of our existence between free will and

---

[56] Note that the recent publication of *The Gospel According to Judas* (by National Geographic Society, Bart D. Ehrman (Commentary), Rodolphe Kasser (Editor), Marvin Meyer (Editor), Gregor Wurst (Editor), April 6, 2006), shows Judas in a much different light, that is, as a willing accomplice of Jesus in facilitating the inevitable.

determinism will suddenly be lifted[57]—but it will alter the way in which we will define these forces.

And now what? My companion of twenty-five years has suddenly vanished. Answers that had been given to me when Michael was physically present must now be discovered on my own, which is what he asked me to do all along.

After bringing this last chapter up to date with the immediate events, I turn the book over to the printer as Michael and I had previously arranged. Soon thousands of copies will be in the hands of reviewers, news organizations, and interested spiritual parties. After that, mass marketing will take care of the rest. But despite my relief at having done this, I feel lost. Having spent so many years at this, it's hard to believe it all changed so abruptly. All I can do is wait.

I go back to my desk. *The Bard's Ghost* is in need of some final rewrites. Opening night is almost upon us.

---

[57] See *Appendix 6 – The Proof,* 7.5 Chaos Theory as Further Impetus for Conscious Spiritual Evolution.

12

Resurrection

"Patriotism in its simplest, clearest and most indubitable meaning is nothing but an instrument for the attainment of the government's ambitious and mercenary aims, and a renunciation of human dignity, common sense, and conscience by the governed, and a slavish submission to those who hold power. That is what is really preached wherever patriotism is championed. Patriotism is slavery."
--Leo Tolstoy

"Take heed that no man deceive you. For many shall come in my name, saying, I am Christ; and shall deceive many. And ye shall hear of wars and rumors of wars: see that ye be not troubled: for all these things must come to pass, but the end is not yet."
--Matthew 24:4-6

It seems like years since that fateful morning in April when Michael was vaporized after his car blew up in front of the radio station, an event now marked by a memorial post outside the building that is inscribed with "Peace on Earth" in four languages. I think of him many times everyday. How could I not? Even my dreams are filled with messages from him, as if after working so closely together for a quarter of a century I could channel his thoughts through my pen. The book I now have written, compiling our conversations and my reflections, has been a runaway bestseller ever since it was published a few months after his death. On top of that, it has stimulated intense public discussions over spiritual, scientific, and political issues. It also has made Michael the subject of a great debate: whether he was, in fact, the Messiah, Christ, spiritual anomaly, etc.

I am sorting through my e-mail after a leisurely Sunday breakfast with Chimera and Gita, when I notice the address of one of my messages listed as "sanctuary@rabbonai.org.nz." It seems very strange to see someone using Rabbonai,[1] a title that before this time I associated only with Michael. Cynthia called him that. Of course, I am eager to discover who is using it independent of Michael. After all, the Master teacher from the Hebrew tradition comes along only every couple of thousand years, so this title gets little use.

I double click on the message. What I read gives me the most shocking experience of my life:

Hello, Rashan!

This note will probably seem unbelievable to you at first, but please trust me, this was the best way I could imagine to get our plan rolling. Needless to say, I never died in that explosion in front of KIVA's studios. And while the authorities wouldn't admit having been a part of any plot on my life, they not only plotted the attack, but knew I didn't die in it. I guess they think they can now find me, knock me off, and get away with it. When I saw that fireball though, I knew it was time to leave and let you do as we had planned for this type of contingency.

Obviously, the events that followed the explosion played out exactly as we had foreseen in our book, *and the public's interest in our story has been developing much as we had hoped. We were also correct in detailing how the fascists would react. I was and am still pursued by U.S. government agents, and so remain in hiding, moving constantly to avoid entrapment.*

I know I can't expect you to believe prima facie that I'm really alive in New Zealand writing you, so perhaps I can recall a few events, about which only you and I would know, to help convince you of my existence ...

At the present time, I travel a lot throughout the world, using my laptop computer to connect to commercial satellites that provide me with excellent Internet access. This has allowed me to prepare the website that I talked about.

---

[1] Title of address often associated with Jesus, meaning "Master" or "Master teacher"; yet signifying someone who may be unordained in the rabbinate. Pronounced rab-boʹ-nī, or rab-bo-nīʹ.

As we discussed, it will provide daily analysis and commentary on world events as well as distribute courseware that I am writing for those interested in pursuing the path of (Messiah-, Christ-, Buddha-, Krishna-) Cosmic-Consciousness. You remember how I always insisted that this state of consciousness is, as Carl Jung described it in that essay I suggested for you, available to each one of us. So, just as we talked about, these courses will help others achieve this state, each in their unique way.

Also, just as we anticipated, the wireless Internet allows me to move about relatively undetected. In fact, the unanticipated change in the way this technology has been deployed, from the original idea of low flying satellites (with 300 square mile footprints) to the use of geo-stationary satellites (with hemispheric footprints), has improved my ability to move about. Those who sought to put an end to my current physical life undoubtedly monitor my cyberspace activity, and are probably wishing they had slipped GPS technology into email protocol. No doubt the Congress of whores will try to make this law.

So, until the time comes when, G-d willing, enough of a following has developed to make the consequences of any CIA plot a cause for pause on their part, I shall continue to live *sub rosa. As you and I discussed, there are many pseudo-religious folk who would prefer to maintain their present hypocrisy. Despite insisting on their adherence to Christ's teaching, they are quite content to call for my death. To them, "The day of the Lord so cometh as a thief in the night ... " (I Thessalonians 5:2). They look at the Messiah and see a serpent. Of course, we must have compassion for those thus persuaded and pray that love finds a way into their hearts.*

I'm hoping that this note finds you and Chimera well, and that the two of you have found some way to deal with all the publicity and those who would hound or abuse you.

Diane and the kids know what's happening and can fill you in.

> *This e-mail will self-destruct shortly after you finish reading it and close it (How's that for some Mission Impossible software? PGP has sure come a long way!). I'll be back in touch soon to continue this discussion.*
>
> *My best always, love,*
>
> *Michael*

My God! He's alive! I can't believe my eyes!

In the intervening years I had given up all hope of seeing him again. Everyone had assumed that he had perished in the intense fireball that melted down his car. But this!—this Messianic-like resurrection,[2] this rising of the phoenix Quetzalcóatl, this is beyond coincidence. Michael has recreated events not seen for 2,000 years as if they are a stage play or novel to prove his point—like *The Passover Plot*![3] The old union organizing song comes back to me from those American folksingers I listened to as a teenager in Avignon and as a college student in the Village …

> I dreamed I saw Joe Hill last night,
> Alive as you and me!
> Said I, "But Joe you're ten years dead,"
> "I never died," says he, "I never died," says he.[4]

"Chimera! Chimera! You won't believe it!" I call out. She leaves her painting and comes upstairs.

"Yes, Rashan. Rashan! Wake up, you're dreaming!"

"Huh? What?"

"You're dreaming, sweetheart. You seem upset."

---

[2] See Ethan Bronner, "Tablet Ignites Debate on Messiah and Resurrection," *The New York Times*, July 6, 2008, for newfound evidence concerning the Judaic concept of the sacrificed Messiah that pre-dates Christianity.

[3] As referred to in Chapter 2: *The Passover Plot*, a novel published in the U.S. in the late 1950's in which Jesus and his friends knowingly arrange the details of the crucifixion so that he survives, thus perpetuating the myth of his physical immortality and establishing his martyrdom.

[4] "Joe Hill" was written by Earl Robinson in the summer of 1936 at Camp Unity in New York State. See liner notes for "Alive and Well," (Aspen Records APN 30101), 1986.

"I'm dreaming? I was asleep?"
"Yes."
"What day is it?"
"Sunday, April 8th, 2001, Buddha's birthday."
"Were we with Michael and Diane and everyone last night?"
"Yes, at their Passover dinner."
"And nothing catastrophic has happened since then?"
"Not that I know of. Why?"
"Whoa! I just had the most intense dream!"

And so I retraced for her what I had dreamt, from Michael's review of *My Magdalene* to the bombing and the funeral, and what now seems like years ago, his e-mail.

"Has the book been published yet?" I ask her.

I couldn't tell which experiences happened while I had been awake and which happened when I had been dreaming.

"No, Rashan. You and Michael are still editing it, remember?"

"Right, right. 'Edit, then market.'"

It all seemed so real, what I had dreamt. Michael's conditional warnings about fanatics who would resort to violence to prevent the spread of his teachings had so profoundly affected my state of mind that I easily accepted my dream as if I were awake. Now, here we all are, still alive, and yet to publish.

> Sur le pont d'Avignon,
> L'on y danse, l'on y danse,
> Sur le pont d'Avignon,
> L'on y danse tout en rond ...[5]

I called Michael immediately.
"Michael?"
"Yes?"
"You're okay?"
"Of course."
"I had the wildest dream."

---

[5] "Sur Le Pont D'Avignon" is a traditional French folk song and dance. Translation: On the bridge of Avignon, Everyone is dancing, everyone is dancing, On the bridge of Avignon, Everyone is dancing in a circle. ... Etc.

I proceeded to explain it to him just as I had to Chimera, including the details of his radio review, how he told me to publish the book, how the authorities reacted, and the growing popularity of his teachings.

"I'm sorry that my cautionary advice had such a frightening effect on you."

"No need to apologize. I'm so relieved it was just a dream."

"So I am, Rashan, though dreams can be prescient. As I've said many times, it wouldn't surprise me if the powers that be still try to murder me. They've become so good at this now, making assassinations look like suicides, drug overdoses, heart attacks, mafia hits, third world paramilitary strikes, mental patients gone berserk (so-called 'Manchurian Candidates'), automobile and plane malfunctions, and on and on. They don't understand that despite their desperate actions, my views shall be heard. It's in the cards."

"This sounds like a change in perspective?"

"As we've discussed, while Cosmic Consciousness includes identification with the unchanging Reality that is behind all of creation, precognition of space-time sequencing is not generally a part of this. But, my recent meditations and spiritual communications indicate to me that it's time to wholly invest our faith into publishing and await the outcome."

"And you're not worried about your safety?"

"Worried, no; cognizant, yes. The most beautiful sunsets last only a few moments. My fifty-two years on this planet are more than enough reward for my work, but I remain proactive about my safety. I'm making arrangements to create a buffer of sorts.

"This doesn't mean I believe that the forces that control the government of the United States, and its intelligence agencies and their criminal networks, and the various religious and political fanatics who support them are any less dangerous than I've previously indicated, only that it's time to act and to declare our intentions, regardless of the consequences. Besides, like Socrates, Jesus, Hamlet, and Hedda Gabler—I have no choice—my commitment to my truth necessitates my actions."

"Don't you find this a dilemma—your teachings focus on love and compassion and yet you're surrounded by a violent world?"

"It's the unity of opposites, not a dilemma, and it's something faced by everyone committed to Peace." Michael says. "I'm reminded of what the Dalai Lama said when I saw him speak in Denver."

"I remember you mentioning this."

"Someone asked him about the use of force; he said that it seemed necessary to have some level of policing at the current time. I agree with him. Of course, by this I do not mean the level of policing and militarization that we see today, which is an unavoidable manifestation of the tyranny of the instincts and the ego and all that follows from that—fascism and greed. We have a long ways to go in our spiritual evolution and we can only change the multitudes by changing ourselves, one person at a time."

I sensed a subtle change in Michael from the evening before, but I can't quite figure out what it is.

"These arrangements for a 'buffer' as you say—what are they?"

"I've decided to retire from my weekly theatre reviews on KIVA. That will also give me more time to help you edit our book. I've also made some preliminary inquiries into hiring private security. I read where a former member of the Shin Bet[6] started his own firm. Also, I'm considering an alternate residence—in New Zealand, in fact."

"Funny how that goes. You decide to distance yourself from the station and perhaps spend some time in New Zealand at the same time I have a dream about the same topics."

"This is more than a coincidence," he says.

☼ ☼ ☼

Less than a week after Michael shares these plans with me, the IRS finally drops their tax investigation of him, not because of his impeccable records and Orloff's tenacious defense that had held them off so far, but by the IRS' inability to prove that they have the right to tax anyone in the first place, let alone seize assets.

As an accountant, I have been aware for some time of a number of cases in which defendants had won using this defense, but I never paid it much heed. After all, even if the IRS has no legal basis to tax, I've never thought the time and expense of proving such a thing was worth it. Besides, how else would a government function? Of course, I'm not saying I agree with the way our tax money is spent.

---

[6] Israel's secretive internal security force.

The same thing goes for the Federal Reserve. Yes, it's a privately-held corporation that collects interest on every dollar loaned through the banks and every dollar borrowed by the government, but who for a minute believes that the Rothschilds, the Rockefellers, and the rest of their syndicate would give this franchise up without bloodshed?

So, other than the settlement of the IRS case freeing up Michael's time to help me edit, I didn't give much weight to it—we already had enough on our hands with the book, and working together seems to generate even more work—for despite our many conversations over the years, as each day passes I continue to learn more about my friend and teacher, and so continue to write about these insights—as memoir and as theatre.

One of Michael's most astonishing qualities is his ability to trace the threads of his knowledge back through all the acquaintances, teachers, conversations, events, and reference books that he's encountered in his life. This is invaluable for our editing, of course, but its larger application is even more important. By documenting his thought in detail, Michael has created a transparent map of knowledge that not only reveals the meaning of what he calls the "Qabalah, *Jnana* Yoga, or *The Glass-bead Game*"—a constant stream of improvisational revelation that he promulgates under the umbrella brand of "YogaJazz"—but also lays bare the interdependence of group and personal evolution: We see that history is the large-scale accumulation of what individuals incrementally achieve in their own lives; we see that history evolves in the same way that we unfold the Buddha, Krishna, Christ, and Cosmos within ourselves. As someone who has always appreciated scholarship and erudition, I can only marvel at the refinement that Michael is offering us. It may be, as he says, that in another thousand years everyone will be so evolved, but I am here today witnessing the rarest of anomalies—the one in six billion chance.[7]

Finally, as the summer approaches its end, Michael and I are nearly ready to print the first complete copy of *Solomon's Proof: A Psycho-Spiritual Journey to World Consciousness* and begin the final proofreading process.

---

[7] In Chapter 1, I had originally described this as a one in four billion chance, but now, in 2001, given population growth in the last 26 years, it is a one in six billion chance.

Then, on September 11, 2001, thousands of Americans die as a result of four strategically hijacked commercial jetliners.

My first reaction is disbelief.

"What?"

The television pictures seem like special effects for a summer action blockbuster designed to strike fear and stir patriotic zeal in every citizen's heart. Sadly, they are not computer-animated simulations. Would it be that I am only dreaming as I was with Michael's assassination, but I'm wide awake.

Yet these images have the same effect as the movies. Many of the politicians and "experts" that are interviewed in the news as well as my friends respond to the tragedy with feelings of anger and thoughts of revenge. I feel confused by all the emotions that come into play. As now has become my habit when I am in this state, I invite Michael for a visit.

Michael drops by after work the following day. Chimera has gone to pick up Gita at school. In the wake of the calamitous events, Chimera and I have been spending a lot of time talking with family and friends, getting little work done. But unlike many Americans who take advantage of their employers' offers for time off to come to grips with 9-11, Michael hardly skips a beat.

"For the sake of argument," he says, "let's say that these hijackers accomplished all this destruction independently, without any help from other sources. Then, as despicable as these acts are, we would do well to think about how we, as a country and as individuals, also perpetrate violence on innocents."

"To what are you referring?" I ask defensively, my shell-shocked feelings at odds with Michael's hypothetical angle.

"As we've discussed many times[8]—throughout Euro-American history, starting from Columbus' first voyage—the march of 'Manifest Destiny'[9] has never ceased. First, we exterminated Native Americans, and

---

[8] See Michael's review of *Madama Butterfly* in Chapter 11.

[9] As alluded to in Chapter 8, Manifest Destiny is the belief that it is divine providence for the United States to expand its borders and "raise up" pagans to its "civilized" standards. Coupled with the Monroe Doctrine, Manifest Destiny has been used by the U.S.A. to dictate its own terms in the Western Hemisphere and elsewhere for some time. Using political and religious excuses to obfuscate greed

then we enslaved blacks. We warred with the Mexicans to gain Texas and San Diego, and threatened war with the Canadians to get Seattle. Our ports thus secured, we took to the seas, forcibly opening Japan and the Philippines and seizing Caribbean isles and, in Central America, what we call 'banana republics.' After a period of isolation, we pulled ourselves out of a depression by not only 'saving the free world,' but supplanting Europe's far-flung colonialism with our own. The communists were just another bump in the road to worldwide centralization ruled by monopoly capital—the so-called New World Order. We replaced the French in Vietnam, piling on six million more deaths. Embarrassed by our lack of success, we diversified. In Nicaragua we armed, trained, and salaried a group of terrorists who killed over 30,000 civilians.[10] We've bolstered Batista, Pinochet, Somoza, and Noriega[11] and countless other dictators and fascists, and continue to do so today. Now we're indiscriminately defoliating and bombing Columbia, even as their government and electorate call for an end to the drug war, in an attempt to enthrone the U.S.-backed military and a brutal right-wing paramilitary group that we have trained. All this to protect our strategic interests."[12]

---

for natural resources is nothing new, nor is the delusion that such excuses are justified.

[10] Between 1946 and 2001, over 61,000 Latin American mercenaries who do the U.S. Government's bidding were been trained at the School of the Americas in Fort Benning, Georgia. The victims of these terrorists far outnumber the people killed by the attacks on the WTC, the Pentagon, the embassy bombings, the USS Cole and the other atrocities that are now laid, rightly or wrongly at al-Qaeda's door. This boot camp for Latin American fascists is now called the Western Hemisphere Institute for Security Cooperation, or WHISC. See George Monbiot, 10/30/01, "Backyard Terrorism," Guardian Unlimited, http://www.guardian.co.uk/Archive/Article/0,4273,4287795,00.html.

[11] Dictators that ruled over Cuba, Chile, Nicaragua, and Panama respectively.

[12] See: Adam Isacson, AlterNet, "Bush to Fund Columbia War Effort," at http://www.alternet.org/story.html?StoryID=12361; "Noam Chomsky on the Drug-Terror Link" at http://www.alternet.org/story.html?StoryID=12420; Ruth Morris' story carried by the *LA Times* wire service, "U.S. Plan Aims to Stem Pipeline's Flow of Trouble" at http://www.latimes.com/news/printedition/front/la-020602colomb.story; Arianna Huffington, "The Bush Oil-igarchy's Old Friend Oxy," Alternet, 2/21/02 at http://www.alternet.org/story.html?StoryID=12460; Christopher Marquis, "U.S. may help Colombia on rebels," http://www.nytimes.com/2002/03/03/international/americas/03COLO.html; "Bush wants freer Columbia aid," *The Associated Press*, 3/16/02, *The Denver Post*; George Gedda, "Bush seeks funds for terror fight in Columbia," *The*

Associated Press, 3/17/02, *The Denver Post*; and Christopher Marquis, "U.S. Expects a Wider War on Two Fronts in Columbia" (http://www.nytimes.com/2002/04/28/international/americas/28COLO.html?).
One might also note that another American energy combine, the Drummond Company (coal), used their own paramilitary forces to assassinate union organizers (http://www.nytimes.com/2002/03/22/national/22ALAB.html?). Most recently, the people of Columbia have gone to the polls to reject the policy of war against the FARC (http://www.narconews.com/colombiavote2002.html). The Bush II administration's attempt to link aid to Columbia to stemming the flow of cocaine is entirely disingenuous. All sides in the conflict (including the CIA) are engaged in drug trafficking (http://www.fromthewilderness.com/free/ciadrugs/index.html), and the battle of "freedom fighters" and "insurgents" is, despite denials, now spilling over into Peru (see "Bush Finds His Vietnam" @ http://www.alternet.org/story.html?StoryID=12728 http://www.nytimes.com/2002/03/24/international/americas/24PREX.html?). The expansion of "the war on terrorism" hardly stops here. By March, 2002, American soldiers had also been sent to the Philippines, Yemen, and (the former Soviet-controlled) Georgia to protect American corporate interests. On June 29, 2002, it was announced that the Bush administration plans to resume assistance to the Indonesian military (Raymond Bonner and Jane Perlez, "White House Seeks to Resume Aiding Indonesia's Army," @ www.nytimes.com/2002/06/29/international/asia/29INDO.html). But it is the backing of the unsuccessful coup attempt in Venezuela that was the most transparent example of the arrogance of U.S. policy. Here, Bush administration officials (and the CIA) backed those attempting to overthrow a democratically elected President (Hugo Chavez received 60% of the vote), got the world's mainstream press (including *The New York Times*) to call Chavez' popular government "dictatorial" and "unpopular," claim Chavez ordered his troops to fire on demonstrators (for evidence to the contrary, see Greg Palast, "Don't Believe Everything You Read in the Papers about Venezuela," *Guardian UK*, April 17, 2002, at http://www.gregpalast.com/, http://www.emperors-clothes.com/articles/jared/distort.htm, and http://video.google.com/videoplay?docid=5832390545689805144&hl=en), claim Chavez "resigned," then, when the people and the military rebelled against the coup, claim they were not involved in it (the generals behind the coup were all graduates of the School of the Americas [see prior footnote in this chapter]), and finally, have the audacity to warn Chavez that he must embrace the laws and customs of democracy (all this from the people who stole the election in Florida and [Bush I, as CIA director] overthrew the popularly elected Salvador Allende in Chile and replaced him with the fascist, Augusto Pinochet). A few days later, Gen. Luis Alfonso Acevedo, the man named by Chavez to head the air force in the wake of the failed coup attempt, and three other generals died in a helicopter crash. This desperate campaign is a response to 1) Chavez ordering large plantation owners to turn over untilled land to the poor and 2) his fiat that doubled the

"Much of this is true, Michael, and yet surely you cannot lay the blame entirely on America's doorstep?" I say.

"I do not mean to imply that America is being punished by G-d for the harm it has suffered—as the pseudo-religious extremists such as Falwell and Robertson[13] or the Taliban[14] claim—only that we contribute more than our share to the cycle of retribution and violence that engulfs the world. The worship of the Golden Calf by those who control and those who support the U.S. regime has its consequences. But most Americans are in denial over this, putting American flag bumper stickers on their gas-guzzling SUVs, like Nazis swastikas on Mercedes in the '30's and '40's, pretending that their nationalism is patriotic,[15] while their corporate

---

royalties paid Venezuela for oil extraction. Obviously, those for whom Bush is the poster-boy do not recognize any democratic means for change. To them, the world shall be gained through monopoly capital, disinformation, and war. On 5/27/02, following the election of Alvaro Uribe, a hard-liner with ties to right-wing paramilitary groups, as president of Colombia, Pedro Carmona, who led the coup attempt in Venezuela, was given asylum by Colombia. Having failed in its first coup attempt in Venezuela, the U.S. and its mercenaries efforts turned to organizing the oil industry strike. As of March, 2003, Chavez has successfully outmaneuvered strikers and deflected attempts (including Jimmy Carter's!) to set up an early election that could be manipulated and stolen by the Bush Crime Family's skilled team of black ops.

[13] In the days following the September 11th terrorist attacks, "Reverend" Jerry Falwell said that America "got what we deserved." Falwell blamed gays, feminists, the ACLU and People for the American Way for making G-d mad at America. "I totally concur," Pat Robertson followed.

[14] The Taliban, a peculiar sect that claims to be Islamic, ruled Afghanistan before the U.S. invasion, sheltered Osama bin Laden's once CIA-funded training camps, received U.S. aid for drug eradication programs, and continues to blame America and the Jews for the world's ills.

[15] Michael writes in 2003: Every SUV is another nail in some Afghani's, Iraqi's, or American soldier's coffin, yet, in the twisted logic of greedy Americans, linking the flag with consumption is a sign of patriotism. "Patriotism is the last refuge of a scoundrel." – Samuel Johnson. Or, again, "Patriotism in its simplest, clearest and most indubitable meaning is nothing but an instrument for the attainment of the government's ambitious and mercenary aims, and a renunciation of human dignity, common sense, conscience by the governed, and a slavish submission to those who hold power. That is what is really preached wherever patriotism is championed. Patriotism is slavery." --Leo Tolstoy. True patriotism isn't expressed by the waving of flags and proclaiming the greatness of one's country over all others, for this is the very lock-step mindless nationalism of "my country, right or wrong" that was rejected as a defense for Nazi atrocities by the judgment at Nuremberg following WWII. True patriotism is exhibited by the unpopular

government rides roughshod over anyone who stands in the way of their gluttony for more resources."

After many years of listening to such political rants, I thought I was inured; after all, I've managed to balance my executive career at Arthur Andersen with our curious friendship and writing project. However, at this moment, I'm angered by Michael's speech. Yes, I am sophisticated enough to understand that despite his rhetoric, he sees American actions as a natural and necessary part of history, but I am in too much pain over so much death (in my former city of residence no less!) to listen to such criticism.

"Michael, this is too much for me! You're going too far, and I don't want to hear it!"

"I understand your pain, Rashan. I'm in pain over this too. But our instincts are clouding the truth. If you don't see this in context, you'll just end up perpetuating the root cause."

"Not now, Michael. You need to leave before I lose it!"

"If that's what you want, sure, even if it buys into the 'fight or flight syndrome.'" He stands.

"Fine," I say. "I'm a person, I have instincts. Sometimes they're valid."

---

actions that uphold the Bill of Rights; true patriotism, the kind that Adams and Jefferson were willing to die for, is about Justice, Compassion, and Mercy, something that is absent in those most vociferous about their "patriotism." Depending upon which side of the fence you're sitting, patriotism—like drugs (which can be a medicine, food, or sacrament) and terrorism (which also can be "freedom fighting")—has become a label used to manipulate public opinion in support of the oligarchy's control of the government. One of the best articles addressing this phenomenon was written in response to the Colorado legislature's debate over whether to require public-school students to recite the Pledge of Allegiance at the beginning of each day. In an article, "The Aloha State has it right," Reggie Rivers suggests that if local lawmakers are interested in defending civil liberties they would be better off following Hawaii's lead and adopting a resolution which recognizes that "the recent adoption of the USA Patriot Act and several executive orders may unconstitutionally authorize the federal government to infringe upon fundamental liberties in violation of due process, the right of privacy, the right to counsel, protection against unreasonable searches and seizures, and basic First Amendment freedoms ..." (*The Denver Post*, 5/2/03)

"Yes," Michael says, "sometimes they *are* valid ... and sometimes they're like the body's appendix—an evolutionary remnant. In either case, evolution depends on instincts subordinated to the higher self."

With that he leaves.

☼ ☼ ☼

For the next few weeks, my anger over Michael's remarks percolates as I watch bodies dragged from the rubble of the twin towers in lower-Manhattan. The enemy, Osama bin Laden and his organization al-Qaeda, have been identified, and the President has called for a worldwide war on terrorism. Anthrax is suddenly being mailed all over the country and the nation is in a panic. Less than six weeks after the attack, Congress passes the USA Patriot Act of 2001. President Bush's popularity is at an all-time high, and we are at war with Afghanistan.

As allied troops close in on Kandihar, the last major stronghold of the Taliban, the Securities and Exchange Commission (SEC) announces it is expanding its investigation of Enron Corporation to include Arthur Andersen. I fly back and forth to Chicago for meetings concerning the firm's growing problems. The Justice Department also orders the White House to preserve any documents related to its dealings with Enron. The President's friend, Ken Lay, who had contributed his corporate jet and over $200,000 to Bush's presidential campaign, invokes the Fifth Amendment before the Senate panel. As the investigation proceeds, Andersen corporate leadership decides to stonewall the SEC and deny any knowledge of the destruction of Enron documents. But the dominos continue to fall. Our company's lead Enron auditor pleads guilty to obstruction of justice for destroying Enron financial documents and the court refuses the company's request to defer prosecution of the corporation in return for an admission of wrongdoing. As the focus of the broadening investigation begins to shift from document shredding to widespread accounting irregularities, pieces of Andersen's practice are sold off to other accounting firms all over the world. I get an offer to migrate my clients to Ernst & Young, but by this time the scandal is not just about Arthur Andersen and Enron, it's about all the major accounting firms and banks,[16] the planet's largest corporations,[17] and the Executive and Legislative branches of our government.[18] Even while Bush and Cheney jump on the bandwagon of corporate and accounting reform, their own business dealings with Harken Energy and Halliburton make it clear they are part of the problem, not the solution.[19] It now appears that the White House had knowledge of the scandal months before the collapse began, yet did nothing. It even comes out that Enron was not only going to be part of a pipeline deal that would bring oil from Turkmenistan and Kazakhstan through Afghanistan to a new refinery in India,[20] but that it was involved with other energy companies in manipulating the supply and demand of power that led to the California energy crisis[21] and the fall of the Democratic governor there.

With all this on my mind, I'm driving into work one day listening to KIVA and Michael comes on the air with one of his inimitable broadsides, framed as a review.

> *Lillian Hellman knows a lot about the big lie. In 1952 she was called before the House Un-American Activities Committee and blacklisted for her views. Although the Arvada Center couldn't have anticipated the events of September 11th and the subsequent nationalistic intolerance over dissent when it planned its current theatre season, they couldn't have chosen a more appropriate play than Hellman's* The Children's Hour *for their current production.*
>
> *As we listen to Attorney General John Ashcroft call all those opposed to the unilateral dismantling of the Bill of Rights "unpatriotic," and as we watch Bush and Cheney hide their shameless military and corporate shenanigans behind the guise of "executive privilege" and "national*

---

[16] See *Appendix 8 - Anatomy of Treason*, Accounting scandal: CPA firms and banks [Footnote 1].
[17] See *Appendix 8 - Anatomy of Treason*, Accounting scandal: corporations [2].
[18] See *Appendix 8 - Anatomy of Treason*, Accounting scandal: government [3].
[19] See *Appendix 8 - Anatomy of Treason*, Accounting scandal: Bush and Cheney, Harken Energy and Halliburton [4].
[20] See *Appendix 8 - Anatomy of Treason*, Enron, 9-11, and the pipeline [5].
[21] See *Appendix 8 - Anatomy of Treason*, Enron, other energy companies, and the California energy crisis [6].

> security," Hellman reminds us that such stubborn righteousness as a cover-up for criminal actions is as American as apple pie.
>
> Unwilling to look at any evidence to the contrary and without regard for the consequences, the entire adult population of a New England village takes the word of a spoiled, vindictive young girl (Hello, Shrub!) known for her propensity to lie, irretrievably shattering the local peace so thoroughly that even the eventual revelation of the truth cannot heal the wounds.

Maybe it was the theatrical hook that somehow brought back recollections of Michael's 9-11 analysis, but I begin having second thoughts about our parting of the ways. Daily it becomes more apparent that the war in Afghanistan is about geo-political control and oil, which means that what Michael was trying to tell me back in September is true, and I was just too stubborn and defensive to hear it. On top of this, the evidence tying together Enron and Andersen and the administration underscores the complicity between corporate greed and American militarism.

Like anyone seeking to protect his comfortable lifestyle, I can pull my weight in rationalizations, but the idea of continuing to work in the accounting profession and supporting a system that rips off people as a matter of course is beginning to sour in me. Within a couple of months, a number of other companies[22] join Enron on the road to bankruptcy. The pattern is similar in all of these cases: Business interests pour their money into Congressional candidates who rig the laws so that insiders can cook the books, make a killing on stock deals, and get off scot-free before investors' and employees' stock and retirement funds (leveraged in company stock) collapse. No matter what the President, the Vice President, the Justice Department, the SEC, and the accounting profession say to the contrary, legislation passed to stem such fraud is simply a new, more opaque, tool for legal fraud,[23] and those appointed to oversee its enforcement[24] are just so many foxes guarding the hen house.

---

[22] See *Appendix 8 - Anatomy of Treason*, Other major bankruptcies [7].

[23] See *Appendix 8 - Anatomy of Treason*, Congressional laws perpetrate fraud and thievery [8].

[24] See *Appendix 8 - Anatomy of Treason*, Collusion of government and business to commit fraud [9].

As soon as I begin to question my own perspective and the motives of those who control the nation, my thoughts recall a host of the ideas that Michael has thrown at me in the past quarter century. Things begin to make sense in a way that I never thought possible. My growing ability to link events changes my perception of Michael's teachings from intellectual concepts to a network of ideas that live and breathe multidisciplinary interactivity between politics and economics, morality and action, life and death.

"So you're ready to take the plunge?" Chimera asks during a discussion about the transfer of my Andersen practice to Ernst & Young.

"You mean back into the icy waters of corporate finance or into the steaming broth of artistic creation?" I say.

"Into the temperate ocean of sub-conscious truth," she replies.

I look at her and see immediately that our exploratory conversation has turned into a defining moment.

"Then a playwright I shall be," I say, finally ready to take the plunge.

My choice comes with major financial repercussions for our family, but I've done well enough with the firm over the years and invested wisely enough to be able to maintain the important things in our lifestyle—where we live, where Gita goes to school, our books and art supplies, and our water and food. Besides, we've never lived extravagantly, at least not by ostentatious American standards.

Freed from my accounting practice, I immediately immerse myself in the final rewrite of *The Bard's Ghost*. A number of ideas to tighten the script have been percolating since my dream of Michael's assassination; I'm itching to get them down on paper. As the play originally presented itself in my dream, it captured my spiritual individuation process; now, in adapting it for the stage, I've eliminated myself from the script, just as Michael had suggested, letting de Vere speak for himself. As the play evolves in this leaner, less personal form, I begin to consider where I will submit it.

Before long, the effects of hearing Michael's radio review and my newfound sense of artistic purpose reignite the smoldering alchemy of my months-old dream about his assassination and my subsequent relief over his well being. My rediscovery of the emotional cornerstone in our relationship surfaces in my consciousness as if it were a recovered memory and I a victim of traumatic amnesia.

> ... *I don't know why nobody told you*
> *How to unfold your love;*
> *I don't know how someone controlled you;*
> *They bought and sold you.*
>
> ... *I don't know how you were diverted;*
> *You were perverted too.*
> *I don't know how you were inverted;*
> *No one alerted you.*[25]

Despite my angry outburst with Michael over 9-11, I begin to realize that, as my dreams evolved, my disposition toward him significantly changed, with my long-term skepticism dissipating in the process: Not only did I experience Michael as Christ in my dream of his assassination (just as a I had in the dream of *The Bard's Ghost* [where he interceded on de Vere's behalf]), but in the assassination dream my prayers to him were answered and he was returned to me unharmed.

As I said at the beginning of this chronicle, in the heat of the moment it's often hard to determine when I am awake and when I am dreaming, but in either case I maintain that my experience is real. Now, as my political beliefs are challenged and begin to change, my perspective on Michael's divine role is no longer "an intellectual concept"—it is a subconscious and conscious belief. Following the collapse of my accounting firm and my full-time commitment to playwriting, the details of my dreams give me concrete psychological and spiritual proof that my hard work is finally paying off. Everything is strangely new, as if I have been granted a new body; my soul feels cleansed, yet I remember everything. This is the light!

My supposition about the "one in six billion chance" of meeting Michael is, despite the odds, a mathematical certainty based on universal laws: the constancy of change as reflected in exponential patterns of DNA and the periodicity of the appearance of the anomaly. Michael *is* the one in six billion on the planet that can explain in a fully integrated manner what we are doing and why. Through my tape recordings and their

---

[25] George Harrison, "While My Guitar Gently Weeps," *The Beatles* (White Album), Harrisongs Limited, 1968.

conversion from spoken word to magnetic audio bits to written word, we have created a journal and memoir of the World Teacher's advent. Unedited. The real *ex cathedra*. The *Living* Word, just as Jesus described it in the original Aramaic:

> *"Seek not the law in your scriptures, for the law is life, whereas the scripture is dead. I tell you truly, Moses received not his laws from G-d in writing, but through the living word. The law is the living word of living G-d to living prophets for living men."*[26]

How fitting that, as we are about to conclude a project we have worked on for twenty-six years,[27] I have finally entered a state that Michael described to me at the onset.

I have come full circle, finally achieving a union with Chimera based on unconditional love and a family that is nourished by this. The simplest way I can explain my evolution is that once I accepted a power greater than my own individual ego, everything became possible.

Chimera, who was horrified hearing that I had told Michael to leave our house ten months before, is relieved that I've finally come around.

"So call him and invite them over for dinner," she says. "I'm tired of meeting Diane at restaurants and coffee shops just to tiptoe around your feud."

I call Michael to apologize and invite him over to our house.

"Sure, we'd be happy to come over," he says. "I won't even discuss politics."

I laugh.

"That's hardly necessary," I say. "I'm in a different place. Actually, I'd be interested in what you have to say."

"Well, you can imagine that I've done quite a bit of research over the whole series of sordid events that the Bushes and Cheney and their cabal have been orchestrating."

"I'd be surprised if you hadn't," I say, giddy like Scrooge on Christmas morning.

---

[26] Szekeley, *Op. Cit.*, p. 13.
[27] In the waning days of 2001.

And so we resume our friendship over dinner. We're all very happy to see one another again.

Now that the U.S. is on the verge of war with Iraq, and French-bashing has become a national pastime, I worry about whether I'm about to be jailed as a terrorist, and am anxious to hear Michael's analysis of the events leading up to 9-11 and where it's going.

"I realize that sometimes I push people further than they think they're capable of handling at the moment," Michael says, "but opening the mind and spirit is similar to stretching the body during *Asana*: there is an optimal state that prepares for future expansion. It was my hope that the spiritual grounding I'd given you over the years was sufficient to help you when the conditions were right."

"Luckily that was so," I say.

"The patriarch revealed," Diane notes.

"I suppose that's why his boyhood friends called him 'The Dad,'" I say, surprised to find a comfortable place with Michael's "parental guidance."

"It doesn't surprise me," Chimera says. "It's all unfolding like clockwork. The trick is having the frame of mind to deal with situations you can't anticipate."

"That's the reason for spiritual practice," Michael says. "Having consciousness that can withstand the life-threatening aspects of instinctive and egoistic behaviors, yet flexible enough to take advantage of their life-sustaining capacities."

"We all have that perfect body within us," Diane says.

"Well, I feel strong enough to hear what you have to say about 9-11 and the rest," I say, "though, as always, you'll have to allow me to act as devil's advocate for the purposes of the tape recording."

"Fair enough," he says. "There are plenty of people in the world who understand full well what I'm about to say, and more who would be convinced if there were a full accounting, rather than the present Congressional whitewash.[28] A lot of commentators have dismissed the charge that the Bushes and Cheney knew about 9-11 beforehand, and they've been aided by those who have created urban legends to obscure legitimate information, but they haven't refuted the facts, they've only

---

[28] See *Appendix 8 - Anatomy of Treason*, 9-11 Congressional investigation [10].

attempted to denigrate the truth with innuendo—*ad hominem* epithets—the refuge of bullies and the whores of Mammon. They say our charges are too outrageous to consider, which is what DINA said when they were accused of assassinating Letelier.[29] The more outrageous the act, the easier it is for them to deny the facts.

"The Bush Crime Family is taking a page out of Hitler's book.[30] Remember, the history of the Bush family is the history treason. Along the way, they've worked with the worst, including the Nazis. In 1942, the U.S. government seized a variety of companies owned by great-grandfather Herbert Walker and grandfather Prescott Bush (as well as the Harriman and Dulles families) under the Trading with the Enemy Act. These guys were funding Hitler's Nazi party as far back as 1924, while they were smuggling German agents into the U.S. and bribing American politicians to see things Hitler's way. Despite a 1934 congressional investigation, Prescott Bush hired Allen Dulles to hide the assets of the holding company rather than divest their position with the Nazis. This trading with the enemy continued during the war.[31]

"You'll also recall that it was Allen and John Foster Dulles who were responsible for reorganizing the OSS[32] into the CIA after World War II. Along with Nazi financial resources that the Dulles brothers were spiriting out of Europe just ahead of the Soviets, they also were enrolling large numbers of Nazi intelligence agents into what became the CIA. Their preference for fascists makes sense when you consider that World War II, as they saw it, was a battle between monopoly capital and socialism. Later, of course, father George Herbert Walker Bush assumed leadership of the Nazi-infested CIA. His treasonable offenses, as Reagan's yet unelected Vice Presidential candidate (along with William Casey, the future CIA Director), include circumventing official U.S. policy and making a deal with the Iranians to hold onto American hostages until after the election.[33] Later, when G.H.W. Bush ran for President, his campaign organization was riddled with anti-Semites, many of whom were forced to resign. Why

---

[29] See *Appendix 8 - Anatomy of Treason*, Assassination of Orlando Letelier [11].
[30] See *Appendix 8 - Anatomy of Treason*, The Big Lie [12].
[31] See *Appendix 8 - Anatomy of Treason*, U.S. support for Nazism. [13]
[32] Office of Strategic Services.
[33] See *Appendix 8 - Anatomy of Treason*, The Hostage Deal [14].

should it surprise us that the son, George W. Bush, another Skull and Bones inductee, is a fascist who indulges casually in treason?

"So instead of an investigation of 9-11, we get W telling us not to discuss any alternative scenarios to the government's 'official' story, and a host of columnists, even so-called 'liberals,' dismissing anyone who puts forth facts with name-calling—"conspiracy theorist"—and other cheap sophistry. This is not to say that there aren't terrorists who wanted to blow up the WTC. There are. And Al-Qaeda, to the degree that it has life outside of CIA control, is not the only group opposed to American empire and that "for which it stands."[34] But the facts indicate clearly that this ragtag band of Muslim scapegoats, if they were involved at all, was *aided and abetted* in carrying out its scheme to further the New World Order's totalitarian scenario."[35]

"You have proof of this theory?" I ask.

"As we've discussed," Michael continues, "it's the nature of the CIA to act in a conspiratorial manner. This is their charter, and it is these very powers—to hire criminals, commit assassinations, perpetrate *coup d'états*, traffic in drugs, and run guns—that the U.S.A. Patriot Act of 2001 expands. What I have to say is more than a 'theory,' as you characterize it; it is an explanation of the mountain of facts that have come out. These incontrovertible, circumstantially overwhelming, facts *irrefutably warrant* a real investigation of the body of evidence that indicates U. S. government officials at the highest level not only had foreknowledge of attacks on the World Trade Center—all *three* buildings—and the Pentagon, but aided in their implementation. We reject categorically the sham that the junta has concocted to disentangle themselves from this event."

"It won't be easy to get this into print," Chimera says.

"It's not as hard as you might think," Diana says. "There are a lot of folks to whom the whole plot is obvious."

"If liberty means anything at all," Michael says, "it means the right to tell people what they do not want to hear,[36] and believe me, there is a

---

[34] From the Pledge of Allegiance, originally written by Francis Bellamy (1855 - 1931), a Baptist minister and Christian Socialist, expressing the ideas of his first cousin, Edward Bellamy, author of the American socialist utopian novels, *Looking Backward* (1888) and *Equality* (1897).

[35] See quotes at the beginning of Chapter 11.

[36] George Orwell.

tidal wave of incriminating evidence that's been suppressed by government officials and the media."[37]

"Like what?" I ask.

"More than I can enumerate, Rashan. First, in the days leading up to 9-11 there was speculative trading in the stocks of United Airlines, American Airlines, Morgan Stanley Dean Witter, Merrill Lynch, and other organizations that took big hits as a result of the attacks. Most of these trades were executed through a German bank that had been run by the number three man in the CIA.[38] The mainstream U.S. media refused to follow up on this story.

"Second, contrary to standard operating procedure, military jets were not scrambled in response to commercial aircraft that had lost voice contact and deviated from their flight plans. This fact, too, was obfuscated by both government and media officials.[39] At the same time, contrary to Bush and Cheney's claim that no one understood what was going on, we know that some secondary-level intelligence services were called into action before the first plane even hit.[40]

"Third, there is evidence to indicate that the planes hitting the towers were a diversionary tactic used to draw emergency personnel to the site, and that the collapse of the towers was due to explosive charges that first imploded the three buildings, then exploded the remains, scattering debris and dust everywhere. Here, the government forced one expert to recant his story, and the newspaper running the original story has deleted it from its website.[41] In addition to seismic evidence of the detonation, there are also witnesses to the explosives being planted in the WTC.[42]

---

[37] See *Appendix 8 - Anatomy of Treason*, Corporate/government control of media [15].
[38] See *Appendix 8 - Anatomy of Treason*, Speculative trading of stock in 9-11 targets [16].
[39] See *Appendix 8 - Anatomy of Treason*, Air Force stand-down [17].
[40] See *Appendix 8 - Anatomy of Treason*, U.S. Military deployment prior to the attack [18].
[41] See *Appendix 8 - Anatomy of Treason*, Implosion and explosion of WTC, including seismic evidence [19].
[42] See *Appendix 8 - Anatomy of Treason*, Seismic and eye-witness evidence for WTC implosion and explosion [20].

"Fourth, there is a trail of evidence indicating that the government abetted the hijackers by securing visas for them.[43]

"Fifth, there are indications that Osama bin Laden is still working for the CIA and met with them at least as late as July, 2001, years after the Lebanese U.S. embassy and U.S.S. Cole bombings.[44] Again, U.S. mainstream media ignores the evidence of bin Laden's cooperation with and protection by U.S. intelligence agencies during both the Clinton and Bush administrations.

"Sixth, up until recently, the Bush family continued to have corporate and financial connections with the bin Laden family.[45]

"Seventh, the Bush family and their associates are the only ones to have their agenda completely furthered by the events of 9-11, including their long-standing designs: to implement extraordinary police powers and federalize all law enforcement through the Office of Homeland Security;[46] to pin the label of terrorism on any group that disagrees with their agenda;[47] to expand their control of Middle Eastern and Central Asian oil sources;[48] to gain control over pieces of the former Soviet Union;[49] to repeal environmental protections;[50] to create economic uncertainty; to gut social programs and fill the nation's prisons with the poor, minorities, and those who oppose their regime;[51] to insert pseudo-religious fundamentalists at every level of government;[52] to generate massive military spending; to

---

[43] See *Appendix 8 - Anatomy of Treason*, Executive branch collaboration in visas for hijackers [21].
[44] See *Appendix 8 - Anatomy of Treason*, The CIA's relationship with bin Laden [22].
[45] See *Appendix 8 - Anatomy of Treason*, The Bushes and bin Ladens family ties [23].
[46] See *Appendix 8 - Anatomy of Treason*, U.S. totalitarianism [24].
[47] See *Appendix 8 - Anatomy of Treason*, U.S. fascist propaganda [25].
[48] See *Appendix 8 - Anatomy of Treason*, Control of Middle Eastern and Central Asian oil sources [26].
[49] See *Appendix 8 - Anatomy of Treason*, Control over former Soviet Union territories [27].
[50] See *Appendix 8 - Anatomy of Treason*, Repeal of environmental protections [28].
[51] See *Appendix 8 - Anatomy of Treason*, Destruction of the social fabric [29].
[52] See *Appendix 8 - Anatomy of Treason*, Government infiltration by pseudo-Christians [30].

increase corporate tax breaks and give-aways;[53] to gain more access (through the CIA) to international drug trafficking sources and return the contraband markets to levels achieved during the previous Bush administration;[54] and to thwart potential investigations of the Bush family and others.[55] Given that Bush's electoral victory was stolen, these accomplishments would have been very difficult to achieve (even with the Congress and the judiciary in the pocket of corporate capital) were it not for a *cause célèbre* such as 9-11—the 'new Pearl Harbor' called for in 2000 by the self-described 'New World Order.'"[56]

"And eighth, both the *coup d'etat* that hijacked the American ship of state and the terrorist attacks on U.S. targets follow strategies that have been plotted for some time.[57]

"All of these aims were realized as a result of the attack and the domestically originated anthrax scares that followed.[58]

"So, basically," Michael continued, "the Bush-Cheney junta let these people into the country, officially ignored them, pushed away any evidence that came their way, waited until the planes and rockets had done their damage, rounded up a collection of so-called terrorists that they were never able to prosecute,[59] and used the attack to further their totalitarian agenda. The only thing our corporate fascists cum state-terrorists need to do before they attack the next target on their list, Iraq,[60] is to ratchet up the level of terror alert, tell folks to go out and buy rolls of plastic and duct tape,[61] and

---

[53] See *Appendix 8 - Anatomy of Treason*, Massive military spending and corporate tax breaks [31].
[54] See *Appendix 8 - Anatomy of Treason*, Access to international drug trafficking sources [32].
[55] See *Appendix 8 - Anatomy of Treason*, Obstruction of potential investigations of the Bush family and others criminals [33].
[56] See *Appendix 8 - Anatomy of Treason*, Neo-cons call for another Pearl Harbor to further agenda [34].
[57] See *Appendix 8 - Anatomy of Treason*, Coup strategies for the New World Order [35].
[58] See *Appendix 8 - Anatomy of Treason*, U.S. government complicity in anthrax scares [36].
[59] Or, as Claude Rains as Captain Renault put it in the film *Casablanca*, "Round up the usual suspects." See *Appendix 8 - Anatomy of Treason*, Failure to convict so-called suspects [37].
[60] See *Appendix 8 - Anatomy of Treason*, Pre-determined attack on Iraq [38].
[61] The official solution to the anthrax scare.

then broadcast a digitally altered videotape of their boy Osama making threats, while occasionally picking up a new member of al-Qaeda to show they're on the case.[62] After Iraq, one need look no further than the other major petroleum producing states to see where the next war on terrorism will be fought."[63]

"Michael," I interrupt, "even someone like me, who lived through the Kennedy and King assassinations and the Vietnam War, can hardly believe all of this. It seems preposterous that in a country with a free press such a series of events could happen without public notice."[64]

"Free is a relative term, Rashan. The press is easily manipulated in this country[65] because, since the 1980's, the corporate prostitutes that fill the Congress have changed the laws that formerly prohibited the monopolization of media outlets; now the bulk of ownership of newspapers, magazines, and radio and television stations is in a few hands—exactly what we tried to change in Germany after World War II.[66] We have become fascists, America is the Fatherland,[67] and 9-11 is a sophisticated version of the burning of the Reichstag."[68]

"It's hard for me to accept the comparison," I say.

"As I've already said," Michael responds. "'The bigger the lie, the easier it is for people to believe it.'[69] The perpetrators rely on your desire to believe it, because the alternative is too horrible for you to face. Yet face it you must, for the evidence is overwhelming, and your freedom and the future of humankind depend upon it. Really, it's a simple progression from our own *agent provocateurs* sinking of the U.S.S. Maine, our military fabricating the Gulf of Tonkin incident, and Roosevelt's foreknowledge of

---

[62] See *Appendix 8 - Anatomy of Treason*, False linkage of Iraq to 9-11 [39].
[63] See *Appendix 8 - Anatomy of Treason*, Other oil-rich countries to become targets [40].
[64] See *Appendix 8 - Anatomy of Treason*, "It couldn't happen here" mentality [41].
[65] See *Appendix 8 – Anatomy of Treason*, History of corporate manipulation of the press [42].
[66] See *Appendix 8 - Anatomy of Treason*, The fascist model for controlling the press [43].
[67] See *Appendix 8 - Anatomy of Treason*, Fascist attitudes [44].
[68] See *Appendix 8 - Anatomy of Treason*, The Reichstag model for *casus belli* [45].
[69] See *Appendix 8 - Anatomy of Treason*, More Hitler parallels [46].

Pearl Harbor to the Bush administration's involvement in 9-11,[70] especially considering the narrow range of reporting and criticism allowed in the mainstream American press."

"But many of your sources are from the mainstream press," I reply.

"Some," he says. "Like I said, reporting is allowed within a small range, and this range gets narrower when it comes to analysis of the news and how the known facts are tied together. But I also use many sources from the Internet, which, in the information age, has supplanted *The New York Times* and other corporate rags as America's electronic newspaper of record.[71] While the mainstream press may be handy for taking note of events, at least those of which that are not fabricated and actually occurred, it is their selective interpretation of facts or 'spin' on these events that alter the truth and get you to believe what the power elite wants you to believe. This tactic is not much different than Caesar burning the libraries at Alexandra and the Church editing the Christian *Bible*. Today, the Internet is our last bastion of hope when it comes to a free exchange of ideas because it has not yet been taken over by the corporate state, though, as I have explained before, they are trying."[72]

"This sounds like another conspiracy theory," I respond.

"As I have always insisted, Rashan, calling the CIA a 'conspiracy' is not a theory; conspiracy is the nature of the CIA; it's what they do—assassinations, coups, gun running, drug trafficking, disinformation campaigns, *ad infinitum*. If anything, they are the conspiracy theorists; they propagate conspiracy theories—the JFK single assassin theory, the Gulf of Tonkin incident, a dozen guys taking down three buildings at the World Trade Center—and use the label "conspiracy theory" as an *ad hominem* argument to discredit those who have factual evidence against them."

"So, like Zola's *J'accuse! ...*,[73] you feel that the facts could indict the inner Bush administration?" I ask, trying to find some parallel from my own country's history.

---

[70] See *Appendix 8 - Anatomy of Treason*, U.S. fabrication of *casus belli* [47].
[71] See *Appendix 8 - Anatomy of Treason*, U.S. newspapers and the CIA [48].
[72] See *Appendix 8 - Anatomy of Treason*, Government control of the Internet [49].
[73] Emile Zola was a French novelist who, in January 1898, wrote an open letter (entitled *J'accuse!* by the publisher of the newspaper) to the President of the

"An interesting comparison, Rashan. Emile Zola's actions, despite some setbacks, did eventually expose the cover-up perpetrated by authorities and lead to Dreyfus' exoneration. Although you must remember, Zola was murdered for his part in breaking this story."

"Yes, unfortunately you've reminded me of what is so often the price for speaking out," I admit, recalling the fishy circumstances of Zola's death.

"Be that as it may, we might not have enough proof to convict all of the inner circle of the Bush Crime Family in a judicial system that they appointed and control, not to mention all the secrecy laws and shredding of evidence by which they have shielded the executive branch," Michael responds, "but we have more than enough for many convictions.[74] Connecting the dots leads incontrovertibly in one direction.

"Unfortunately, as with the Warren Commission Report on the assassination of JFK, the truth has little impact once the 'official findings' have been manipulated and approved, insulating the ringleaders from jail.[75] What does it matter if we know military, corporate, mob, anti-Castro, and Executive branch forces all wanted Kennedy dead, or that we know that Jeb Bush and Katherine Harris conspired to disenfranchise fifty-seven thousand voters in Florida,[76] or that we know the Bush Presidential Campaign hired thugs to intimidate voting officials? Once 'five corporate ideologues in black robes'[77] appointed Bush president, the criminals gained legal status; when a consortium of national newspapers ignored the facts about the illegal voting roll purges and other obstructions and claimed that Bush would have won anyway, it was just the icing on the cake. 9-11 will end up the same way. The Patriot Act of 2001 makes this type of suppression easier by legalizing the U. S. intelligence community's use of criminals, so that others can get pinned for the dirty work of the real conspirators. I can only hope that by printing contrary evidence in our book we'll encourage others to join those that are already trying to spread

---

French Republic accusing his government of complicity in covering up the truth in the framing of Alfred Dreyfus, a Jewish army officer, for spying.

[74] See *Appendix 8 - Anatomy of Treason,* Government disinformation [50].

[75] See *Appendix 8 - Anatomy of Treason*, Control over the 9-11 investigation [51].

[76] See *Appendix 8 - Anatomy of Treason*, Voting fraud in Florida: the actual *coup d'état* [52].

[77] See *Appendix 8 - Anatomy of Treason*, Corporate control over the Supreme Court [53].

awareness of this evidence[78] and come forward and help change the consciousness that has allows such treachery to continue unabated."

"If this is true," Chimera manages, "what hope is there for us?"

"There's always hope," Diane says. "There are more people who get this than you think."

"Most people," Michael says, "*are* capable of change, even if the New World Order is not."

"Their power seems so absolute!" Chimera insists.

"It may seem that way," Michael says, "but we know the power of the spirit transcends that of the flesh. When the forces of repression seem their greatest, our time is near."

"It's hard to see past their greed and violence," Chimera says.

"It's the same as seeing past our own instincts and ego," Diane says. "We evolve one person at a time. You know, 'Think globally; act locally.'"

"It all comes down to how we utilize our resources," Michael says.

"How so?" I ask.

"Think of it this way," Michael says. "First, one of the definitions of fascism is corporate control of the state.

"Second, due to a lack of true campaign finance reform, large concentrations of corporate and private capital control the government, the media, and the military-intelligence establishment; so, what we have in this country is a corporate state—in other words, fascism.

"Third, the fascist need to control people and resources through the manipulation of capital, and the tools derived from its accumulation, is based on instinctive fears for safety, food, and such—all the things animals do to survive. Thus capitalism, the ethics of Social Darwinism, and the instincts and ego work symbiotically, creating a system that must continually expand, kill and subjugate 'enemies,' and consume ever more resources in order to survive.[79] Unless this is behavior is stopped, the earth's ability to sustain human life will be destroyed.

---

[78] See *Appendix 8 - Anatomy of Treason*, Other books presenting related evidence [54].

[79] According to a study published in the Proceedings of the National Academy of Sciences, "It would require 1.2 earths, or one earth for 1.2 years, to regenerate what humanity used in 1999." While this may not seem like a lot to overcome, consider that, "[w]hile the world's ecological overshoot is 20 percent, Europe's is about 100 and America's is 300. The research group Redefining Progress analyzed

"Fourth, the taming of these instinctive and ego-based reactions is achieved only through the admission that our lower selves are powerless over these forces—that we are, in fact, addicted to instinctive and ego-based behaviors, just as some of us are addicted to drugs, alcohol, et cetera.

"And fifth, the means by which we evolve and overcome these addictions is to invite a higher power, whether it is G-d, the Great Anomaly, or our higher selves, into our lives. 'We must love one another or die.'[80]

"That is why I return to the need for spiritual practice—for that is how we will make a new world."

In many ways, this statement delineates the evolution of Michael's philosophy from his student days at Stanford to his current pinnacle of consciousness—his once solely political and economic solutions for achieving a self-sustaining and renewable world are now symbiotic outgrowths of spiritual and holistic practices, the result of leading a fully integrated life.

"I am just ashamed that we, the people, have allowed the republic to sink so low," I say.

"Keep the faith," Michael says. "The scale of change we're calling for necessarily depends upon the presence of opposing circumstances: know that many good things will come from the reversal of political corruption, religious hypocrisy, and over-consumption. It is why the spiritual anomaly has manifested here and now."

"I don't understand," Chimera says.

"This country is blessed with high ideals, natural resources, ingenuity, determination, and spiritual and ethnic diversity that have the potential to allow us to serve as an example to the world for how we may

---

the resource use of Sonoma County, California, a haven of recycling and bicycling that ranks among the top 4 percent of America's counties in personal income. It turns out that even the eco-friendly Sonomans live at a level that would require the resources of four earths annually if practiced worldwide." (Stan Cox, "Capitalism might work if we had a spare planet or two," YellowTimes.org, 9/9/02, @ http://www.yellowtimes.org/article.php?sid=664) According to the U.N. Environment Program, "only 5 percent of people in developed countries maintain sustainable lifestyles." (Alex Kirby, "Psyching up the green consumer," BBC environmental correspondent in Nairobi, 2/4/03, @ http://news.bbc.co.uk/2/hi/science/nature/2726847.stm)

[80] From W.H. Auden's poem *September 1, 1939*.

all live together and thrive. These great gifts, however, are being squandered by our collective lower natures that worship at the altar of Mammon, as the fascists play upon our bigotries around ethnic, religious, and gender differences, while inuring us to corruption and greed. Whether or not, after all the paper shredding, witness neutralizing,[81] and cover-ups, Bush and his co-conspirators are found guilty of 9-11,[82] is beside the point. The system is rotten from top to bottom,[83] and the Bush family is only one example of how 'absolute power corrupts absolutely.'[84]

"It's part of my mission to offer antidotes to these selfish practices so that we may evolve. As we've discussed, political change begins by eliminating private money from campaign financing, most likely through a constitutional amendment, and electing candidates of spiritual substance,[85] not the pseudo-religious pork-barrel poseurs currently feeding at the trough. This presupposes an electorate capable of discerning the nature of the problems they face, which is why I quote from Jefferson, Franklin, Adams, Lincoln, and other well-known defenders of democracy: to politically, scientifically, artistically, and spiritually challenge my fellow citizens. Yet, for these teachings to serve that purpose, we, as a nation, must look into the mirror and observe our own faults and come to understand how, despite our self-proclaimed good intentions, we contribute to the same terrible actions that we accuse others of perpetrating.

"Heed my words, America! 'Judge not, that ye be not judged ... And why beholdest thou the mote that is in thy brother's eye, but considerest not the beam that is in thine own eye?'[86] This cannot continue if we are to win the spiritual war that faces us."

"Spiritual war?" I ask.

"Of course," he says. "Islamism[87] is correct in calling what is going on in the world a *jihad*,[88] because it is. Only it is *not* a war between Allah

---

[81] See *Appendix 8 - Anatomy of Treason*, Assassination of witnesses [55].
[82] See *Appendix 8 - Anatomy of Treason*, Corporate control over government regulators [56].
[83] See *Appendix 8 - Anatomy of Treason*, Corporate tax evasion [57].
[84] See *Appendix 8 - Anatomy of Treason*, Government for sale [58].
[85] See *Appendix 8 - Anatomy of Treason*, Real campaign finance reform [59].
[86] Matthew 7:1-3.
[87] A term that has come into use to differentiate a radical political offshoot of Islamic fundamentalism from spiritual forms of Islam. See Daniel Pipes, *Militant Islam Reaches America*, W.W. Norton, New York, 2002.

and infidels, or Jews and gentiles, or Christians and pagans, or Hindus and Sikhs. It is a war between our higher selves—the Messiah, Christ, Buddha, and Krishna that manifest the One-Without-A-Name, the Great Anomaly, the Supreme Being within us—and our lower selves—our shadows, instincts, emotions, and egos that manifest the Antichrist within us. Truly, this is a fight for our souls and the Soul of the World."

"And how do you propose to win such a war?" Chimera asks.

"As we've discussed: one person at a time. The cycle of violence that has accompanied us throughout our evolution, from the primordial soup to the jungle and into the present, must be stopped. When victims learn to have compassion for perpetrators by understanding how the perpetrators began as victims, the cycle is broken. *Then* there shall be peace."

"And you sincerely think this is achievable?" I ask.

"It is not only possible, it has been done before and necessarily must happen here."

"You say *necessarily*?"

"Yes," Rashan. "Remember our discussion of free will and determinism many years ago?"

"Vaguely."

"In essence, free will and determinism are inextricably linked; we cannot know our fate, so we must act as if we have free will. We have a choice as to when and how we evolve our souls, but the act itself is mandatory."

"Mandatory?" I ask.

"Yes, if our goal is to evolve spiritually."[89]

"So where would you have us begin?" Chimera asks.

"One of the objectives of this book is to clear the air, to set aside religious differences, and to offer the universal scientific truth that transcends any particular notion of G-d and establishes the Great Anomaly as the religion-neutral version of the deity, the G-d principle, as it were. We've offered a variety of suggestions for individuals to consider as a path

---

[88] At least in the connotative sense that *jihad* has come to be used. In its denotative sense, *jihad* is better defined as either the struggle of the individual on the path to self-purification or the struggle of the community against all forms of injustice. In Arabic, *quitaal* is the word that means fighting.

[89] See *Appendix 6 – The Proof*, "7.5 Chaos Theory as Further Impetus for Conscious Spiritual Evolution."

to this truth, for example, Yoga and dietary considerations as well as other spiritual practices that would aid in creating a self-sustaining world."

"It sounds like you're close to going public," Chimera says.

"It's time to get this show on the road," Diane says.

"Compared to where we've been," Michael says, "our preparation is nearly over. The Son of Man's time draws nigh. We've reached a major anomaly in history—the end of days, a demarcation in time, a jubilee. What is past is pre-history. The old rules shall no longer apply. The Ghost Dance has begun.[90] A qualitative change is imminent. The cycle of retribution and endless war is ending. Human evolution takes a new step today as I declare, 'I am the prophesized one—the Messiah, Christ, Imam Mahdi, Krishna, and Quetzalcóatl—the spiritual anomaly.'"

"And you believe that you have proved this?" I ask.

"In the twenty-eight years that we've known each other, Rashan, we've discussed many things, all of which contribute to the cohesive delineation of the universe's essential interdependence and interrelatedness and my role in it. If we take the core ideas from this discussion and place them in the context of a scientific proof, which I've recently committed to paper,[91] they sound something like this:

"Quanta represent the basic manifestation of the Great Anomaly—the eternal first cause, the Supreme Being—in the mass-energy-space-time continuum.

"The behavior of Quanta is consistent with the Torus.

"Animating the Quantum-Torus is the ineffable Anomaly.

"The Anomaly conforms to Heisenberg's Uncertainty Principle, the Tao that cannot be spoken, the shadows on the wall of Plato's cave, and יהוה, Ha-Shem, the One-Without-A-Name.

---

[90] The Ghost Dance was initiated by Wovoka, a Paiute holy man, in 1889, and quickly caught on with many tribes. The beliefs of the Ghost Dance movement included the renunciation of alcohol and farming and an end to mourning, since the resurrection would be coming soon. U.S. government fears over the power of the dance and the growing movement surrounding it led to the massacre at Wounded Knee.

[91] See *Appendix 6 – The Proof*, including the application of Poincaré's Conjecture as a check to The Proof and the corollary proofs of the Big Bang and String Theory. Updates available at www.SolomonsProof.com.

"Our knowledge of the Anomaly is therefore necessarily proximate and unquantifiable; therefore, our proof of the Anomaly is analogous.

"The Anomaly is omnipresent throughout the fabric of the universe because it animates the building blocks of all matter, that is, light itself, wave and particle, the Quantum-Torus.

"The omnipresence of the Anomaly is represented by one of the sixty-four characteristics of transformation,[92] as delineated in the binary system of the *I Ching (Book of Changes)*.

"The sixty-four hexagrams of the *I Ching* are directly analogous to the sixty-four codons of the genetic code; thus proving—once again, but through a different means[93]—that the Anomaly is a constant—in this case embedded in biological replication, including the human genome—appearing with periodicity in human populations and producing, among other things, extraordinary beings in all walks of life.

"In the spiritual realm, the Anomaly expresses itself as the Avatar, just as in the animal realm it is the White Buffalo. These anomalies are as predictable as quanta: 'The spiritual anomaly is going to occur; though, we cannot predict when, where, or how.' Thus the spiritual anomaly, scientifically derived from the Quantum-Torus Model, is perfectly congruent to prophesy: 'Therefore you also must be ready; for the Son of Man is coming at an hour you do not expect.'[94] Ergo, scientific proof and spiritual prophesy are mirror images of the same truth.

"Since the Great Anomaly represents the deity or G-d principle, it follows analogously that the spiritualized human form of the Anomaly—the Avatar—provides divine revelation through the symbology of the Living Word.[95]

"Proof of the Living Word is the Truth it describes.[96] Our Quantum-Torus model—including the proof of the convergence of science and spirituality, the application of Poincaré's Conjecture as a check for this

---

[92] Hexagram 52, *Keeping Still, Mountain*, the special case: "at rest" in a sea of change.
[93] The first means being that everything comes from Light and the Anomaly is coincident with every quanta of Light; thus it is omnipresent.
[94] Matthew 24:44
[95] Just as, at the conclusion of *The Universe in a Nutshell*, Stephan Hawking describes human communication as an asymptotic evolutionary effect.
[96] Again, see *Appendix 6 – The Proof*, in particular "7.3. The Philosopher's Stone and the Spiritual Anomaly (as the Avatar or World Teacher)."

proof and of the Big Bang and String Theory, and the progression of this proof into the human genome and the derivation of the Avatar—is verification of our claim to Anomalistic revelation.

"Therefore, that which I am offering you today is the testament to that which I promised long ago—a Truth that is living proof of its power on a scale that verifies its claim—a self-fulfilling, toroidal prophesy."[97]

"That was an eloquent recapitulation," I say. "I have no choice but to accept that your logic is as close as one can come at this time, given the Uncertainty Principle, to the synthesis and integration of all phenomena."

"Dropping your journalistic guard?" Michael chides.

"If not now, when?[98] The 'who, what, why, when, where, and how' are answered.[99] So, given this proof of the Messiah/Christ/Imam Mahdi/Quetzalcóatl/spiritual anomaly, what is it that you want to say?"

"First, to the people of the Middle East: There is no political solution to the conflict in the Holy Land unless it arises from a spiritual agreement. All former peace proposals (the Saudi plan, the Carter plan, the UN Resolutions, Bush's so-called 'plan') are incomplete because they offer a political solution to a religious problem. They fail to recognize that: there is an element that hides under the banner of Islam that does not recognize the right of Israel and Jews and Christians to exist; there is an element that hides under the banner of Judaism that promulgates hatred toward Islam and Christianity; there is an element that hides under the banner of Christianity that seeks to convert Jews and Muslims to its beliefs. These three religions must repudiate these elements, for truly, those with such beliefs are not worshippers of the One-Without-A-Name—the Supreme Being, the G-d principle, the Great Anomaly—but are worshippers of a less-inclusive, less-empowered entity that seeks to compensate for its shortcomings by terrorizing others; that is, they worship a devil. Only by repudiating these false idols will those committed to these three different

---

[97] That is, a prophesy having the properties of a torus: to touch upon multi-dimensional truths while holding to the same arc of inquiry; in other words, to express infinite octaves of the same truth.
[98] See Rabbi Hillel's quote in the Invocation to this book.
[99] These are the foundational questions of journalism, as memorialized by Rudyard Kipling (from "The Elephant's Child" in *Just So Stories* [1902]): I keep six honest serving-men / (They taught me all I knew); / Their names are What and Why and When / And How and Where and Who.

ways of worshipping be capable of a long-term agreement. Only ego holds them back from agreeing that they worship the same G-d.

"And to the world I say: It may seem easy to justify one's reasons for responding to attack, and truly self-defense is a natural and occasionally spiritually valid action, especially in response to those whose philosophy is specifically designed to deprive a particular class of people their rights. But 'an eye for an eye' can no longer be part of our path. 'Love your neighbor as yourself ...'[100] is all you need to know. Share with others. Those of us with more resources should look for ways in which to distribute what we don't need to our neighbors who do, forgiving their debts.[101] Evolve. 'Think globally and act locally.' Maintain a spiritual practice and practice compassion by understanding the far-reaching ramifications of your actions. Participate in the governance of your community and support representation by those who exalt the human spirit not our base instincts. The worship of Mammon must end or materialism will destroy the earth."

"And that's it?" Chimera says.

"Yes. The Golden Rule transcends all spiritual belief systems,[102] because it enables each of us to discover the universal perfection that resides within, including our own unique truth, through which we contribute to the fulfillment of the collective dream. In this way, we see that we are all but different faces of the same singular force and spirit, even as we may refer to it variously as G-d, Allah, Brahman, Buddha, the Great Anomaly, the Supreme Being, Ha-Shem, the name that cannot be spoken."

---

[100] Matthew 5:43, 19:19, 22:39, Mark 12:31, 12:33, Luke 10:27.

[101] Contrary to the conduct of the World Bank and the major private institutions that support it and which are principally responsible for a policy of imperialism through debt (http://www.gregpalast.com/detail.cfm?artid=78&row=1), the forgiveness of debt by those who can afford it stimulates growth in repressed economies and eventually pays dividends in healthier, more diverse international partners. Thus ownership is universalized and profit becomes a scientific means of evolving private ownership into social responsibility and, eventually, true sharing.

[102] See "Golden Rule" in *Appendix 7 – Michael's Notes*, for examples of this precept in all religions.

Epilogue

Symbols of Integration

"When you are inspired by some great purpose, some extraordinary project, all your thoughts break their bounds. Your mind transcends limitations, your consciousness expands in every direction and you find yourself in a new, great and wonderful world. Dormant forces, faculties and talents become alive, and you discover yourself to be a greater person by far than you ever dreamed yourself to be."
--Patanjali, *The Yoga Sutras*, circa 2500 BC

"A good book is the precious life blood of a master-spirit, embalmed and treasured up on purpose to a life beyond life."
--Milton, *Areopagitica*, 1644

I am at my desk, finishing my work on *Solomon's Proof*, pondering Michael's words, "… we are all but different faces of the same singular force and spirit, even as we may refer to it as G-d, Allah, Brahman, Buddha, the Great Anomaly, the Supreme Being, Ha-Shem, the name that cannot be spoken." This is not the first time that he has said this to me, but this time my reaction is different; this time, sitting at my computer, contemplating the words as they form in my mind and then, through my fingers and onto the screen, I see myself as an instrument of a power and intelligence far beyond what my limited ego could ever have created or imagined.

From our very first meeting in that bookstore so many years ago, Michael has guided me on a wonderful journey of discovery. In recommending that I read Jung's essay, *Christ, a Symbol of the Self*, he recognized my need to integrate myself—my masculine and feminine natures, *anima* and *animus*—before I could undertake the greater mission he had in mind for me. Perhaps being so close to the theatre, from which I absorbed a life-long awareness of the interchangeability of roles, made the identification of these voices within me somewhat easier than it would be for most heterosexual men, but that is not to say it was easy.

After some frustration, it became clear to me that rather than accepting my feminine side, my habit (like most men) is to project its idealized form onto the current female object of my affections, and to subsequently hold her to the unrealizable standard of this subconscious presence within my self. My study of Jung's work helped me to see that the perfection which I sought is only achievable through a union of these seemingly disparate elements inside of me, through the so-called Divine Syzygy,[1] and that the expression of this union is the basis of art. Only by entering into this creative reformation could I hope to come to my interpersonal relationships and playwriting as a whole person.

But what does the balanced form of womanhood, which I seek to internalize, look like? Having viewed the world primarily from a masculine perspective for so long, I find it second nature to align with its intellectual, artistic, athletic, social, and commercial aspects. But all of these talents and blessings are of little value when it comes to discovering my feminine nature, which is by definition a state both antithetical and complimentary to the one that I inhabit most consciously.

How, I ask, am I to manifest a side of myself that is a mysterious, though absolutely necessary ingredient to my spiritual evolution? The answer, I discover, is not as difficult as I imagine, for in my life I have had a variety of relationships with women that I love and admire. What better examples could I have to help me identify and develop my own feminine qualities than to emulate these lovers and friends? And that is what I did.

Chimera, lovely enigmatic Chimera, whom I first met in Barth's wonderful book of the same name,[2] is a fascinating conglomerate of genetically distinct, sexually unique, and artistically and intellectually stimulating personalities that I have encountered in my life. By identifying these traits in others and shaping them into a personality that I could study and make my own, I have truly realized the ideal *anima* within myself—for Chimera and I are one and the same person in every sense.

---

[1] Jung's term, also discussed in *The Structure and Dynamics of the Psyche, Part II, Aion*, 1951.
[2] John Barth's *Chimera*, Random House, 1972, winner of the National Book Award.

But that is only half the story. In addition to acting as a catalyst for my Jungian Syzygy, Michael's voice was instrumental in planting the seeds for my study of Yoga. As he described it to me, Yoga is about union, which makes it a perfect catalyst for the Divine Syzygy; however, this union of male and female natures is not the only integration that Yoga facilitates. There is also the union of the higher and lower selves.

The experience of awakening the higher self and sublimating the lower self is part of the yogic rebirthing process. As Michael metaphorically describes it, "When you are cut, the blood flows and then coagulates. A scab is formed that eventually heals, often leaving no indication of the cut. In any case, 'you' did little if anything to induce this healing. Your body possesses an unconscious capacity to do this. Healing the soul is very much the same. By using a spiritual practice, such as Yoga, as a catalyst, the forces by which you can heal your soul are manifested."

This healing (or rebirthing) can be a challenging transformation for us because we have little experience with pure and limitless consciousness, let alone trying to make it our focus while we continue to experience the world of instinct, ego, and illusion. Our family, friends, and the greater world outside are all baffled by our shift in perspective and sensitivity to all manner of common, thoughtless human activities. In the early stages of such a spiritual transformation, it is difficult to sort out what is real and what is not. Indeed, until we are fully grounded in the G-dhead within—the Supreme Being, Great Anomaly, Christ, Buddha, Krishna, Atman, Quetzalcóatl, et al.—we have not achieved the integration that Jung describes as fundamental to wholeness.

Thankfully, Michael's presence in my life is the light that made this transformation possible. But like Chimera, Michael is not a being separate from me—he is my higher self. By discovering him inside of me and giving him a voice and a name, I not only allowed him to enter into this world unencumbered by the doubts and prehistoric remnants of my lower self, but also allowed him to enter into this world disguised in a manner that made him safe and accessible for others: for up until the publication of this book, Michael has mostly existed as a character in what I have variously described to friends and acquaintances as "my novel," sparing them the judgment that "No prophet is accepted in his own country."[3]

---

[3] Luke 4:24.

You will recall, also, that it was Michael who introduced me to Diane. If Chimera and I are the feminine and masculine aspects of my lower self, and Michael the masculine image of the higher self, then Diane is the feminine image of the higher self. This is best understood through Diane's relationship with Michael. More than anyone else, she brings levity to Michael's sometimes overwhelming presence.

Diane does this through humor, sometimes irreverent, sometimes dark, and sometimes farcical. As the only actor in the mix, Diane is a muse for both Rashan and Michael, one relationship platonic, the other conjugal. Psychologically, she is both a conscience and a preconscious force. She is the nurturing aspect that has been brought forth from my relationship to my mother, sister, wife, lovers, and friends.

Thus, as Michael concluded—"... we are all but different faces of the same singular force and spirit, even as we may refer to it as G-d, Allah, Brahman, Buddha, the Great Anomaly, the Supreme Being, Ha-Shem, the name that cannot be spoken."—consciousness expresses itself in infinite ways, not only through "diverse and simultaneous incarnations" throughout the universe, but also as "multiple personalities" within each of us, some unique, some borrowed from others. As we've discussed, these facets of our self, "symbols of integration" as Jung called them, achieve unity as something greater than the sum of their parts, because the higher self—the Great Anomaly within each of us—is without boundaries, and thus subsumes our instinctive and ego-centric behaviors into its infinite light without a trace. Admittedly, it was a constant struggle over the years for me to align with this selfless psychological and spiritual truth, but in recognizing Michael's truth I have recognized my own.

At this point, you may be feeling confused or even misled by my confession; or, perhaps, you are not surprised at all. In any case, I believe that everyone who reads this book is aware at some level of Rashan's and Chimera's and Michael's and Diane's actual relationship to each other. If you weren't conscious of this, your ego was just ignoring the evidence, for there were ample indications.

So, this book is neither non-fiction nor fiction, but a psycho-spiritual memoir, a chronicle of the integration of my self—including the elements of higher self and lower self, *anima* and *animus*, masculine and feminine, yin and yang, light and dark, creative and receptive—into one fully integrated being, the Messiah or Christ archetype of the Self.

Given the groundbreaking and sometimes disingenuous work that, in the past few years, has positioned itself as biography and memoir, publishers and readers alike may experience some discomfort with such "creative non-fiction," but as Michael would say, this is a manifestation of their own hypocrisy toward objectivity and subjectivity. Clearly, as we have seen detailed throughout this work, so-called objective news sources are nothing more than mouthpieces for those who hold the purse strings, while apparently subjective criticism and art hit the nail on the head.

So, we insist that this is a realistic account of one person's psychological and spiritual integration, which makes Michael's story as true as Rashan's, Chimera's, or Diane's, for they are all one and the same—me, my dreams, hopes, and waking experiences, all real, affective memories[4] organized into four separate gestalts.[5] The people, places, and incidents described herein are all real as well, and though some names have been changed and some time sequences modified for artistic and dramatic purposes, the words express my heartfelt concern for the world and its people, no punches pulled. Finally, this is an accurate account of my transformation from one seeking political revolution to one seeking spiritual revolution, from which all else (including politics) must follow.

Do not think that a psycho-spiritual rendering of my memoir diminishes Michael's message in any way, for truly, it does not! His message is the same as the previous spiritual anomaly:

> *Yeshua said to them, When you make the two into one, and when you make the inner like the outer and the outer like the inner and the upper like the lower, and when you make male and female into a single one, so that the male will not be male nor the female be female ... then you will enter the kingdom.*[6]

---

[4] According to Stanislavski, memories capable of being recalled for the purpose of representing, through acting, the behaviors associated with them.

[5] Gestalt refers to a combination of thematically linked emotions and thoughts that reach conscious formation and expression together as a unit. See Frederick Perls, M.D., Ph. D, Ralph F. Hefferline, Ph. D., and Paul Goodman, Ph. D., *Gestalt Therapy*, Dell Publishing Company, Inc., New York, 1951.

[6] From the Gospel of Thomas, in *The Gnostic Bible*, edited by Willis Barnstone and Marvin Mayer, Shambhala, Boston, 2003, p. 51. Again, the discoveries of the the *Gnostic Gospels* and the *Dead Sea Scrolls* unmask the distortions of the

And truly I am of the same emanation, sent by the Supreme Being, the most holy One-Without-A-Name, the Great Anomaly, to present the message just as I have delivered it.

Further, this chronicle of personal integration also details the threats that the world faces from a group of devolved individuals who control governmental, military, and corporate apparatuses worldwide. Whether we define these persons psychologically, as slaves to their instincts and ego, or spiritually, as worshippers of the Golden Calf and Mammon, they have defined themselves by greed and excess profits, materialism and over-consumption, propaganda and disinformation, imperialism and, ultimately, subjugation through violence.

So, the successful distribution of this book will make Rashan Barcusé (and the Michael within him, etc.) just as vulnerable to state terrorism as if he were a Jesus whose teachings ran counter to the interests of Caesar and Rome. There is little difference, America and Rome, Michael and Jesus; the truth of Michael's words and actions shall set us free from instinctive and institutional tyranny.

Whether you believe that the "historical" Jesus existed, or whether you believe that Michael is the spiritual anomaly, is no longer relevant to your actions, for Messiah-, Buddha-, Christ-Consciousness (and its equivalents) is now a vision realized. We have pulled ourselves up by our bootstraps, through the evolutionary chain, from pre-cognitive animals to erect, thinking beings: Our next evolutionary step awaits us; our higher self offers a helping hand; we can overcome the tyranny of the instincts and the ego; it is our choice; it is our destiny.

Whether this story shall be a tragedy, as in Rashan's dream of Michael's assassination, or whether it shall be a comedy, as in Rashan's dream of *The Bard's Ghost*,[7] is up to you, for "by your works shall you be judged."[8] Shall Michael be a tragic figure unredeemed, his flaws preventing a new world from being born? Or shall Michael be redeemed, a comedic figure—the fool, a child of providence, through whom the struggles and

---

Christian *Bible* initiated by Bishop Irenaeus of Lyon and compounded by other "Church fathers" during various sanctioned councils and conclaves.

[7] See *Appendix 4 – The Bard's Ghost*.

[8] Revelation 22:12.

sorrows of the past are forged into a glorious and enlightened future?[9] In other words, am I a fool for undertaking the monumental task of bringing the Messiah, Christ Michael, into this world to claim the Kingdom my predecessor-in-spirit announced, or simply another sacrificial lamb calling out in the wilderness? In assuming this role, I assure you, I had no choice: once open, the door cannot be shut; once called, the spirit cannot be denied. Hopefully, your answer to my query is affirmative, and that, by your actions, you make this a comedy and me the fool, bringing forth the real "New World Order" out of our seemingly tragic circumstances.

I only ask you, brothers and sisters, to receive this message into your hearts today. We stand at the crossroads of human evolution. The route by which instincts and ego rule, in which materialism dominates and greed is celebrated, can only lead to the destruction of our biosphere and the end of human life on earth. Choose a different path, one uniquely your own. Have faith in the potential of your soul and the great wonder from whence it comes. Undertake a practice today that welcomes your true self into this world. Breathe, meditate, and affirm. Know that the love you feel in your heart is how you experience G-d in human form.[10] Join together with others in sharing the light and bounty that the One has bestowed upon us and is our right and heritage. The Kingdom of Heaven is at hand. Just as "In the beginning ...," we are all the same light-infused, indivisible Supreme Being, the Great Anomaly.

Peace be with you.

---

[9] As Gary Eberle so astutely points out in his analysis of the fool in Shakespearean drama ("A Child of Providence," *Parabola* magazine, Volume 26, Number 3, August 2001, p. 66), "The beginnings of great comedy and great tragedy are often indistinguishable ... (but) their endings are worlds apart. Why? The comedies are redeemed by their fools, and the tragedies are not ... Anyone can be a tragic hero ... (but) [t]he privileged position of fool brings forth a new order out of what could end as tragedy."

[10] See *Appendix 6 – The Proof*, 7.6. Individual Spiritual Practice as the Next Evolutionary Step.

Appendix 1

Excerpts from The Home Rule Charter of the Town of Wayne, Colorado

Prefactory Synopsis

This Charter is intended to be as simple and brief as possible, while including all necessary and legal provisions for governance. This has been achieved by assuming the broadest powers available, and vesting them in a General Assembly of the People, congruent to the Constitution of the United States of America and its Congress. Legislative procedures included as part of the Charter are meant to give initial structure to the General Assembly, while in no way interfere with the sovereignty of the People.

Preamble

[As it is the nature of Spirit to manifest itself in Matter, so also is it the nature of Mind, operating through individual and collective Will, to express itself as governance of the political body through Law.

So long as such governance upholds the right to self-determination without privilege, so long as its policies, rules, and regulations as regards community interests do not conflict with individual freedom, so long as its laws pertinent to individuals be few and considerate of differentiation, and so long as it retains the support of its citizenry even unto the least interested member, it remains viable.

Just such governance reflects awareness of constant natural processes, thereby changing in harmony with the True Will of the People.

It is our right and responsibility to create such governance according to the developing conditions of our environment, whether their temper be tranquil or chaotic.

The dissolution of fettered rule and the establishment of consonant governance is no more than Life itself outgrowing its past, and is not in any manner a disruption to the Way.

Necessarily therefore,][1] We the People of Wayne, Colorado, to insure our right to self-determination, maintain our autonomy from federal, state, and regional authorities, and protect our natural resources and the harmony of our environment, do declare it our purpose, and within the full and proper exercise of our Power, Love, and Wisdom, to reformulate our government as a Home Rule municipality under the provisions of Article XX of the Constitution of the State of Colorado as amended.

Article I. – General Provisions

☼ ☼ ☼

Section 2. Powers. The Town of Wayne shall have (1) any and all, but not limited to these, powers granted by the Constitution and laws of the State of Colorado and/or the United States of America, (2) the power to supersede any law of this State and/or these United States now or hereafter in force, in so far as it applies to local or municipal affairs, (3) all powers that now or hereafter may be granted to municipalities by the laws of the State of Colorado and/or the United States of America, (4) all other powers granted by this Charter, and (5) any other powers which shall be deemed necessary and proper for carrying into execution the foregoing powers. The enumeration of particular powers in this Charter shall not be deemed to be exclusive of others.

☼ ☼ ☼

---

[1] The bracketed section of the Preamble was withdrawn from consideration by Michael before the final vote of the Charter Commission for the reasons he discusses in Chapter 3.

Section 5. Form of Government. All legislative powers herein granted shall be vested in a General Assembly of the qualified electors of the Town of Wayne.

Section 6. Elections and Electorate. The General Assembly shall be the sole judge of the elections and qualifications of its own members.

Section 7. Quorum. Twenty-five (25) percent of the qualified electors of the Town of Wayne shall constitute a quorum of the General Assembly.

☼ ☼ ☼

Appendix 2

Prolegomena to Any Future Physics

> *"Niels Bohr, working with Rutherford in 1912, was intensely aware ... of the need for a radically new approach. This he found in quantum theory, which postulated that electromagnetic energy – light, radiation – was not continuous but emitted or absorbed in discrete packets, or 'quanta.'"*
> --Oliver Sacks, "Everything in Its Place," *The New York Times Magazine*, April 18, 1999

Michael's title is taken from Immanuel Kant's famous treatise, *Prolegomena to Any Future Metaphysics*, published in 1783. In his introduction, Kant noted, "These Prolegomena are destined for the use, not of pupils, but of future teachers, and even the latter should not expect that they will be serviceable for the systematic exposition of a ready-made science, but merely for the discovery of the science itself." From our discussions, it seems that Michael had similar hopes for his ideas, when he wrote this in the 1970's. Indeed, he continued to refine the ideas contained in this early paper, which eventually resulted in his Proof.[1]

Topology (Conceptual Physics)

The Tao[2] has no name, but it has a form through which it manifests and that is called Torus.[3]

---

[1] See *Appendix 6 – The Proof* and also www.SolomonsProof.com, for the latest updates.
[2] Usually translated from Chinese as "The Way." "The Force" or, as the philosophers used to put it, "the First Cause" work just as well.
[3] Torus is the fundamental figure of Topology, the science of four-dimensional geometry. It is the first expression of the non-dual into the dual.

468 » Prolegomena to Any Future Physics

As the point is of one dimension, the circle of two, the sphere and the doughnut of three, so the Torus is of four.

The Torus is a sphere (Space) changing through Time.

Circular motion along the circumference of a sphere becomes spiral motion on a Torus as it expands and contracts through Time.[4]

The inside surface and the outside surface are experienced as the same surface on a Torus, given motion and Time.[5]

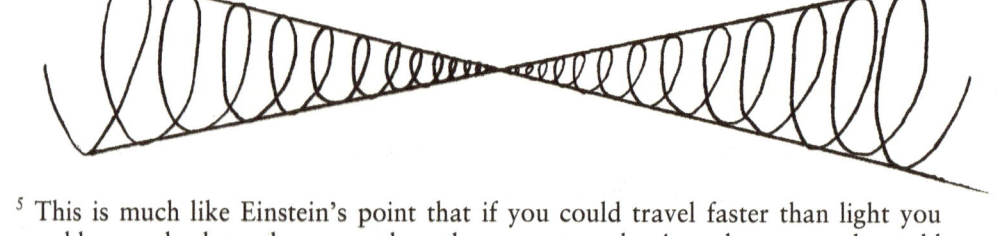

[5] This is much like Einstein's point that if you could travel faster than light you would come back to the same place that you started. Any slower speed would return you to a different place-time, i.e., the "inside" or "outside" of the original surface, rather than the point-of-origin itself. In the drawing, Time is on the Z-axis that comes out of the page or goes through the page. The spiraled path (as noted by the broken line) experiences both the outside surface and inside surface of the Torus at the progressive tangential "x" points as the torus expands and contracts.

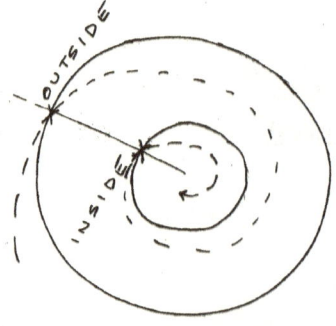

Centrifugal and centripetal forces result from expansions and contractions of the Torus in Time.[6]

The microcosm and the macrocosm conform to the laws of the Torus.[7]

Quanta (Quantum Physics)

Quanta are both energy and mass, wave and particle.

Quanta are the yin and yang of the universal fabric at the threshold of its manifestation.

Thus Quanta conform to the unspoken Tao, the hidden Torus, and the visible spiral.

Quanta inspire and expire at the speed of light.

At the extremes of this motion are moments of rest, just as Hexagram 52, Kên/Keeping Still, Mountain[8] is the special case or anomaly of movement in a world of constant change.[9]

As motion on the Torus manifests as a spiral, so also are the vectors of Quanta perceived as spirals through space and time.[10]

At the core of Quanta is the ineffable Anomaly, the Unified Field,[11] where qualitative change originates, yet where differentiation is nil.

---

[6]

[7] As reflected in the occult maxim and esoteric meaning of the Star of David (✡), an upright and an inverted equilateral triangle: "As above, so below."

[8] The 52nd of 64 hexagrams that describe the cycle of change in *The I Ching*, Wilhelm/Baynes translation, forward by C.G. Jung, Bollingen Series XIX, Princeton University Press, New York, 1997, page 200.

[9] It should be noted that the correlation of this hexagram to the basic structure of matter along with the correlation of the hexagrams of the *I Ching* in general, representing as they do poetic renderings of the cycle of change, are the keys to tying the laws of physics to the human genome and, subsequently, the periodicity of the avatars. This is also one of the basis for developing what Michael calls "The Proof" (Appendix 6).

[10] This perception of a spiral is a result of the same effect as Einstein's imaginary model of the universe riding a bubble, with that bubble representing invisible conformation to the natural laws of the Torus.

The Anomaly is the gateway through which the limitations of four dimensions are transcended.

In humankind, the Anomaly is a point within each individual that is tangential to the universal,[12] where everything that ever was, is, and shall be is present. The Anomaly manifests as singular individuals as well, whose unique talents set them apart in every endeavor.

Black Holes and White Holes (Astrophysics)

Black Holes and While Holes in space-time are analogous to the inspiration and expiration of Quanta, the mathematics of the Torus, and the laws of the Tao (yin and yang), appearing the moment before and after rest,[13] at the extremes of galactic motion:

Contracting Torus
Centripetal spirals
A Black Hole
Rest
"Big Bang"
A White Hole
Expanding Torus
Centrifugal spirals
"Swirling gases"
Stars, galaxies, universes
Rest
Contracting Torus, *et cetera ad infinitum*.

---

[11] As postulated by Einstein, where equivalency between electro-magnetism, gravity, the strong force, and the weak force is formulable. The Einstein-Bose Precipitate and the Plasma Ball (Singularity) are other examples of this special state.

[12] This is akin to the ideas expressed in The Great Invocation as promulgated by the Theosophists (See "The Great Invocation" in *Appendix 7 – Michael's Notes*, or http://www.lucistrust.org/invocation/).

[13] The final moment of a black hole, when the potential for further compression has been exhausted, or the final moment of a white hole, when the potential for expansion as a galaxy or universe has been reached—both like Newton's apple at the top of it's arc—are moments of rest, parallel to the two moments of Quanta just before mass is converted to energy (or particle is converted to wave) or before energy is converted to mass (or a wave is converted to a particle).

As with Anomalies on the quantum level and human level, Anomalies in the space-time continuum are warps that allow transitions between non-sequential events.[14]

<u>The Paradox of Constant Change</u>

Truth is Paradox [$1 = 0$, $1 \neq 0$, where everything is no-thing in particular, yet each thing is unique and different from the other].

Nothing is Black or White [$\emptyset \neq 1$, $\emptyset \neq 0$, $\emptyset = n$, where $\emptyset$ is the null set and n is a number that varies asymptotically between 0 and 1].[15]

Change is the only constant [$\Sigma\Delta = \infty$, where $\Sigma\Delta$ is the summation of all change and ∞ is infinity].[16] Change manifests as space-time.

---

[14] That is, instantaneous travel across space and time. See "Extra-Terrestrials" in *Appendix 7 – Michael's Notes* for an explanation of how gravity is amplified to cause warps in the space-time continuum.

[15] As reflected in the symbol of the Tao, the unity of Yin and Yang (☯): The seeds of the black are within the white, and vice versa. Therefore, Nothing approaches both the unity of all things (1) and no thing in particular (0).

[16] The cumulative effect (Σ) of constant change (Δ) generates light and sound, background radiation, the hum (∞): Om.

Appendix 3

Introduction to Yoga[1]

> *"The wise student of Yoga takes the various doctrines of philosophy and religion lightly, as tentative explanations and interpretations of truths beyond the realm of the intellect, but uses them as best as he can in his direct discovery of those truths."*[2]

You are embarking on an ancient and marvelous journey by adding Yoga to your life. Above all, Yoga is a human science designed to help you rediscover your birthright to greater health and spiritual awakening.

Beginning Yoga at Home

Regardless of your age or bodily condition, conscientious practice of Yoga postures (*Asanas*) and breathing exercises (*Pranayamas*) will bring you better health, greater relaxation, and increased concentration and awareness.

Beginners should not be in a hurry to master the positions. Improvement will come with ease and comfort through daily observance.

If there is any illness or special disability, it is always advisable to consult with a Yoga therapist before starting practice. This holds especially true for those who have undergone major operations or are suffering from heart trouble or abnormal blood pressure.

---

[1] For additional details on the practice of Yoga and where *Hatha* Yoga fits in the greater scheme of spiritual attainment, see "Yoga" in *Appendix 7 – Michael's Notes*.
[2] Taimni, I.K., *The Science of Yoga*, Theosophical Publishing House, Adyar, Madras, India, 1961.

If there is any discomfort during their menstrual period, women should suspend all Yoga practices except for the corpse pose, breathing exercises, and light forward-bending.

Early morning hours, when the stomach is empty and the call of nature has been answered, are most conducive to the practice of Yoga *Asanas*. The mind is fresh and the stiffness of the body should be removed by a few sun salutations. *Asanas* may also be practiced four or five hours after lunch or in the late evenings, when the body moves more freely. Practice in the morning makes one work better in one's vocation. In the evening it removes the fatigue of a day's strain and makes one fresh and calm.

Yoga poses should be practiced in a quiet well–ventilated area with sufficient space to stretch the trunk and limbs in all directions. Avoid hot sunshine and drafts. The ground should be level with no uneven surfaces. A thick rug, carpet, or mat will facilitate positioning. Dress should be minimal and never tight.

One should see that there is no straining or heavy breathing at all during the practice. In-between *Asanas*, whenever necessary, one should relax in the corpse pose. These rest periods may be accompanied by music and words conducive to meditation. At the end of practicing all poses, the corpse pose should be done for a longer time, beginning with each part of the body being consciously cleansed of tension. Even at the end of practice, one should feel quite fresh, both physically and mentally.

During the practice of *Asanas*, the breath should never be retained for a long time. It doesn't matter if you stop the breath for a moment when necessary, such as while raising the legs to form the plough pose or shoulder stand or while raising the body to form the forward-bending pose. As a general rule, it is good to exhale as you bend the body forward and to inhale as the body is bending backward, and to have normal breathing at all other times. It is always better to breathe through the nose and never through the mouth (except in specially instructed instances).

474 » Introduction to Yoga

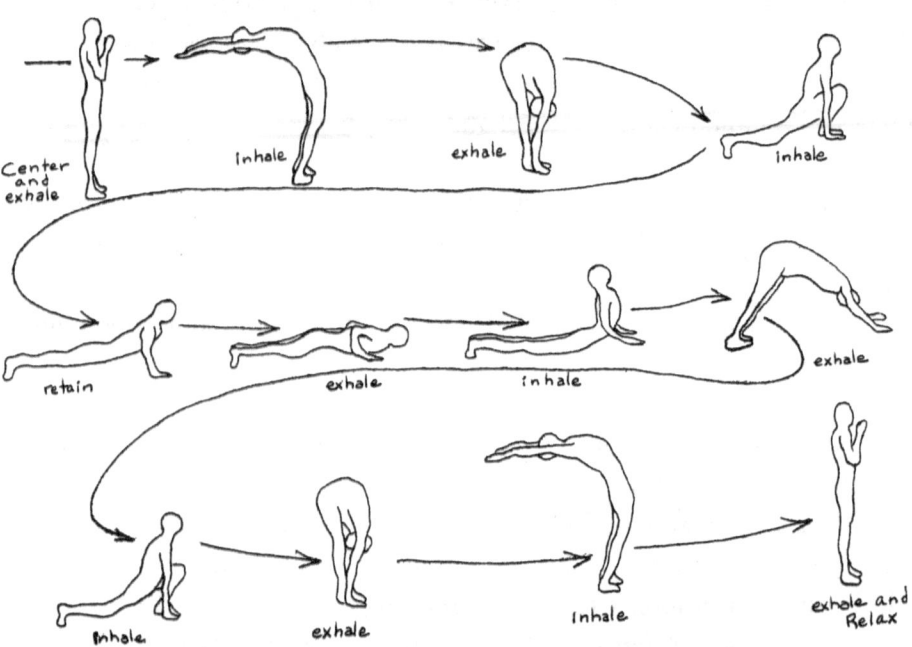

Appendix 3

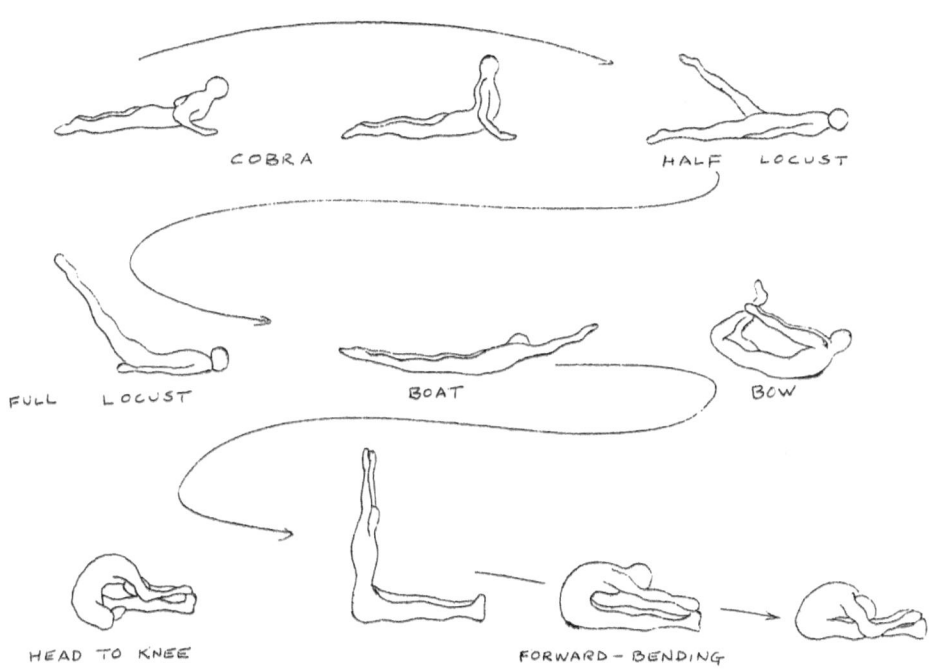

476   »   Introduction to Yoga

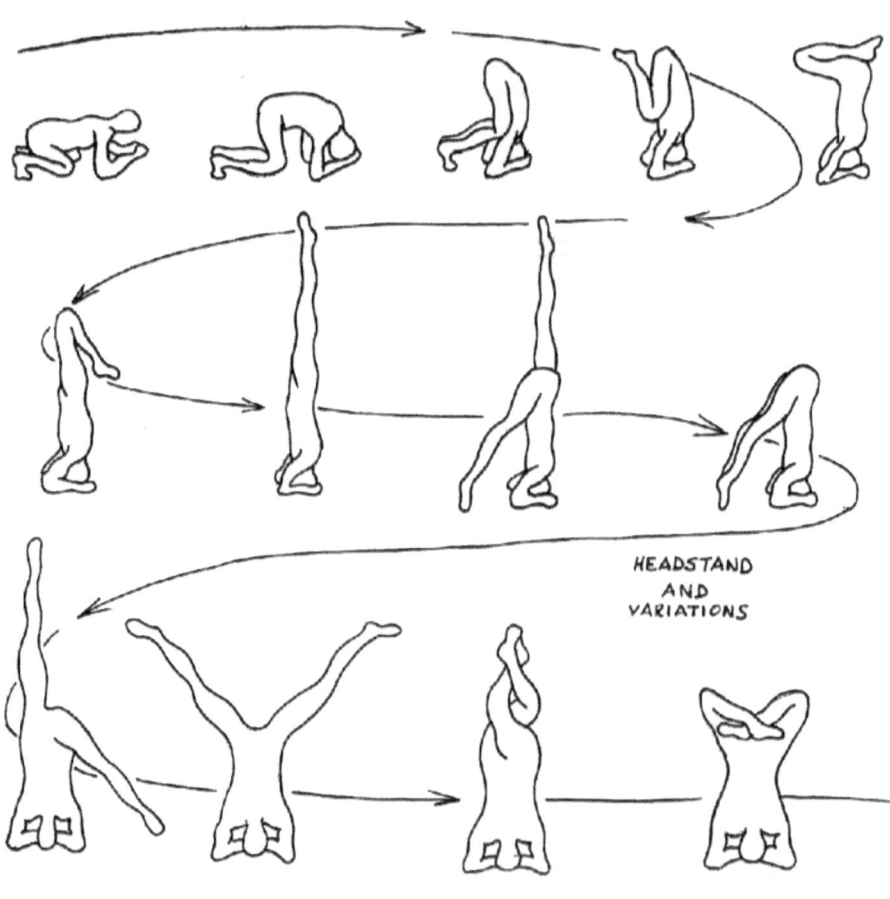

HEADSTAND
AND
VARIATIONS

FISH

HALF SPINAL TWIST

YOGIC SEAL

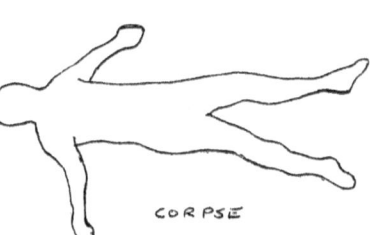
CORPSE

COMFORTABLE

Appendix 4

The Bard's Ghost

In the manner of
A Shakespearean Comedy
In Three Acts

By
Rashan Barcusé

"The conventional biography of Shakespeare is simply wrong; the ghost of another man haunts the canon." [1]

As Michael suggested to me in Chapter 8 concerning this play—"You may end up substantially changing it for the stage, but that's beside the point. You've tapped into some important truths without involving your ego in the construction."—the play has gone through significant iterations from the original dream to this current script, documenting a shift from personal integration, in which I discover my internal Christ archetype through Michael's reflection, to a Shakespearean comedy that introduces the world to the true author of the canon. And while it would have been instructive, from a psychological point of view, to have included an earlier draft of the play in this appendix, to illustrate the Jungian concept of the marriage of anima and animus (Divine Syzygy), I have concluded that is it is even more valuable to present the current stage version here, as it is the strongest argument for de Vere's authorship, the rediscovery of which provides a perfect parallel for what must be done to rediscover the Messiah's/Christ's/spiritual anomaly's true teachings.

---

[1] Mark Anderson, *"Shakespeare" By Another Name*, Gotham Books, NYC, 2005, p. xxvi.

DRAMATIS PERSONÆ

In order of appearance by actor

Tour Guide/Edward de Vere [the 17th Earl of Oxford, Lord Great Chamberlain of England, Viscount Bolbec, a.k.a. "Pasquill Caviero," "Labeo," and "William Shake-speare"].........The bard whose authorship has been hijacked

Christ Jesus/Player/Friar Laurence.........An avatar and holy fool who seeks and performs miracles

[I.] Tourist/Bardolph/Player/Attendant/[I.] Rogue/[I.] Aide to Dull/William Stanley, Earl of Derby.........A steady guy willing to think outside the box

[II.] Tourist/Robin/Player/Page/[II.] Rogue/Mistress Page/[II.] Aide to Dull/Elizabeth de Vere (Edward's daughter).........A steady gal—playing a guy playing a gal—willing to think outside the box

[III.] Tourist/First Huntsman/First Servant/Crowd extra/[III.] Aide to Dull

[IV.] Tourist/Second Huntsman/Second Servant/Crowd extra/[IV.] Aide to Dull

[V.] Tourist/Servingman/Third Servant/Crowd extra/[V.] Aide to Dull

William Shakspere/Player.........An opportunist who attempts to find immortality in a legal gray area

John Falstaff/Camillo/Player.........A man who conveniently changes sides

Roger Stritmatter, Researcher/Constable Dull/Player/Attendant......... "A man of good repute, carriage, bearing, and estimation ..."[2] who focuses on the heart of the matter

Librarian/ Mistress Quickly/Muse, Anne Vavasor/Messenger.........A woman who inspires poetry and is an instrument of magic

---

[2] *Love's Labour's Lost*, I, ii, 271-2.

480 » The Bard's Ghost

Voices of the three Witches

Polonius [William Cecil, Lord Burghley, Lord Treasurer of England]/Player.........An imperious and cynical powerbroker who supports the status quo

Anne Cecil/Player ....A noble woman who falls victim to politics and jealousy, yet is resurrected in the end

> *Authorial attributions for the text included herein are given on the right margin at the beginning of each new section of dialogue. The attributions should be illuminated on an overhead electronic title display.*[3]

PROLOGUE

The stage is dark, lit only by a ghost light; a scrim divides the stage in half from side to side. The ghost light dims and then blackout. The scrim comes up, and then lights come up.

Time: Late 20th Century
Place: The Folger Shakespeare Library, Washington, D.C.

A researcher is working. The librarian brings him some books.

Librarian. *RB*[4]
Here are the books you asked for, Roger. [*She puts all the books down except one.*] I've taken the license of bringing you another volume as well, which I think you'll find interesting.

---

[3] A device, like the telestrators often used in call centers or scoreboards at sporting events, that can be programmed to carry illuminated alpha-numeric messages. Projected stencils are discouraged, unless dissolves are used to segue between title changes.

[4] The initials RB denote passages written by the playwright. Attributions for other material are noted also at the right margin at their introduction.

Researcher. How so?

Librarian. It's a 1569 Geneva Bible of some note. [*She hands it to him.*]

Researcher. Rather regally bound, I'd say.

Librarian. Yes, but it's the handwritten notes and underlinings that you'll find most interesting.

Researcher. Humph! … Copious.

Librarian. Yes, and they possess a rhyme and reason. [*She exits.*]

>*Researcher spends a few moments flipping through the book and reading a few underlined passages.[5] He is suddenly struck, and quickly scans through various sections. He fumbles for his large, formative cell phone in his briefcase and calls a colleague.*

Researcher. You won't believe this, Frank! … I've found Shakespeare's bible! … The underlined passages—almost all of them are right out of the canon … Yeah, amazing! Only one funny thing … The gilded crest on the cover is that of the Earl himself—Edward de Vere!

>*Blackout. Scrim comes down.*

>*A light comes up on the lone figure of Edward de Vere, downstage right. A few set pieces indicate we are in a study. A pale light behind the scrim baths Jesus on the cross, wearing only in a loincloth.*

>Time: Present
>Place: Purgatory

De Vere.   RB

You might think it a bit frustrating, over 400 years after my death, to remain unrecognized for my achievements, and I admit it does chafe to see such an unworthy recipient showered with accolades for my work. But, as

---

[5] See *Appendix A: Edward de Vere's Geneva Bible and Shake-speare* in Mark Anderson's *"Shakespeare" by Another Name*, Gotham Books, New York, 2005, pp. 381-392.

it's said, good things come to those who wait, so at this late date I expect greatness.

As you witnessed in the previous scene, the cat is out of the bag, the facts are plain to see—but only known to a few. You might wonder, why stir up the dust now? Don't we have a perfectly suitable mythology to explain the unparalleled genius that reveals itself in almost every foot, line, and measure of the 37 plays, 154 sonnets, a couple of epic poems, and pamphlets, and so on?

Unfortunately and absolutely, no! For the tale that has been foisted upon you since you were old enough to understand is a rather crude and ill-considered fabrication which, while it served a purpose in its day, even to mine own family, now lacks the wherewithal to protect our illustrious canon from the hacks and charlatans who abuse it daily with impunity for lack of historical context and psychological motivation.

Ah, you say, is this not just the ravings of a self-centered profligate seeking to repair his tarnished reputation? Well, I admit my life was a wild one, with more than its share of indulgences, and my purgatory has been a long one, but I ask you, how else does the poet educate himself save through experience? The American beat, Gary Snyder, does a fine job explicating this in "What You Should Know to Become a Poet," in his 1967 collection *Regarding Wave*. The paradigm, of course, was written by William Blake: "What is the price of experience? Do men buy it for a song? Or wisdom for a dance in the street? No, it is bought with the price of all the man hath, his house, his wife, his children."[6]

And that is the nut of my case. Every detail of my life, as it is with all writers, is imbued in my work. So, unless this other fellow, you know who I'm talking about, the one whose name is much like one of my pen names, spent his entire life documenting my activities, then I think that you, after hearing my metaphorical account, will agree to the biographical gravity of my authorship.

I do not stand alone in this matter, either. Among those who agree on one or more of these points, we can count Walt Whitman, Henry James, Ralph Waldo Emerson, Benjamin Disraeli, Mark Twain, Sigmund Freud, Charlie Chaplin, Orson Welles, Leslie Howard, John Geilgud, Charles de Gaulle, Derek Jacobi, Mark Rylance, Michael York, Kenneth Branaugh, Keanu Reaves, and the Supreme Court justices, John Paul Stevens and Harry

---

[6] *The Price of Experience*, 1797.

Blackmun. And that's not all—for as you are about to see, I've made friends where it matters most! [*He laughs, visually acknowledging Jesus.*]

And that is how I plan to escape from this purgatory that separates my name from my soul, by enlisting the support all those who savor my work to consider my case and, if thou art convinced, grant me your applause when I ask. I cannot succeed without your help in this matter, for the inertia of history is enormous. Just think of all the folks who died at the hands of the Church for saying the Earth is not the center of the universe. Such is the twisted logic and terrorism of totalitarian strictures. We can take heart, however, in the knowledge that resolute individuals turn around global beliefs to further our conscious spiritual evolution.

The stakes are enormous. On this stage, you are looking at the two most quoted men in history, each with their reputations tangled in a morass of commercial profiteering and academic and clerical reputations. Hear ye! The truth is at hand! Just as the unearthing of the Gnostic testaments at Nag Hammadi and the Dead Sea Scrolls at Qumran beg us to fight for recognition of Jesus as an exceptional man [*He acknowledges Jesus.*], so shall we, with the unearthing of my biography, fight for recognition of de Vere as "William Shake-speare," an exceptional poet.

So, let's get on with our little exercise. I've fashioned it, as has been my wont, with a prologue—of which we are in the midst—and an epilogue; though, I have trimmed my usual five acts to three to appease modern attention spans and scheduling strictures. You'll also note that I borrow heavily from my own work, while adding to it where needed, to present some of the principal themes, dramatic structures, and emotional dynamics that dominated my life and work. I hope you shall appreciate the effort it has taken me to incarnate in this way, tonight, on the Stratford man's birthday, April 23rd, which as some of you may know, was actually the day he died—and rightly so, since in the change to the Gregorian calendar, my birthday was advanced 11 days from April 12 to the 23rd. Convenient, no? Attribute it to politesse, coincidence, or karma—it shall be a jubilee for me—but as you ponder our argument:

Piece out our imperfections with your thoughts ...   *Henry V, Prologue*
[And turn] the accomplishments of many years
Into an hour-glass: for the which supply,
Admit me Chorus to this history;
Who, prologue-like, your humble patience pray
Gently to hear, kindly to judge, our play.

The lights go down on de Vere, who disappears, and then up on Jesus, who dismounts from the cross and proceeds downstage as the scrim comes up.

Time: Present
Place: Purgatory

Jesus. Since last I walk'd upon these hallow'd grounds   *RB*
Much time and noted science has ensued.
By sacrifice a martyr's name I gained
And many pay homage to my message.

Yet what, if anything, has transpired?
Moneychangers once cast from the temple
Now rule the halls of democracy
And preach from pulpits near and far.
One would suspect lobotomies at fault,
If not for the common of such thinking.

I warn'd,
        "T'is easier for a camel   *Luke 18:24-25*
To go through a needle's eye, than for a
Rich man to enter into the kingdom of G-d."
Yet, sons of Calvin, pockets brimm'd with gold,   *RB*
swagger as if such fortune were a sign
of election to G-d's etern'l favor,
heeding not my words to
"sell all thou hast,   *Luke 18:22*
and distribute unto the poor."

"Having eyes, see ye not? And having ears,   *Mark 8:18*
hear ye not? And do ye not remember?"
For it is the son of man before you   *RB*
Again calling before it is too late!
Are not my words proof enough it is I?
Since
"I have given you an example,   *John 13:15*
That ye should do as I have done unto you,"
What words and acts on my part would you take   *RB*
To be a pattern for your behavior?

Surely I have more to share than old rags
And worn phrases from 2,000 years ago?

How oft' have my once holy words been used
To blaspheme the spirit from whom I'm sent?
My challenge is great,
"for greater works than I have ye done."   *John 14:12*
Here, again, how shall my offerings be   *RB*
Such gifts as may take an age to o'er come?

    He pauses, pondering.

Clamoring for clues that remain scatter'd
Amongst the rubble of my soiled teachings,
I seek another disenfranchised soul
Within whom I may inspire reverence,
And from whom I may draw inspiration.

    The scrim disappears into the flyloft and the lights slowly come up. Jesus returns upstage to the cross and reassumes the position with which we associate him.

    Act I, Scene I

    Time: April 23rd, Late 20th Century
    Place: The Holy Trinity Church, Stratford-on-Avon

    Christ, visible in half-light, considers the proceedings.

    A hubbub is heard and a Tour Guide with tourists in tow enters the church.

  Tour Guide. It is my great pleasure on Shakespeare's birthday
to introduce you to the famous bust of our greatest poet,
a common man with an everyday education who, through force of
will and talent, wrote plays and sonnets that have endured for
over four centuries. ... The tongues of angels are upon his words.
... Next to G-d, there is Shakespeare.

And over here the altar upon which our language is exalted, the great man's
tomb!

    Tour Guide begins to choke upon the last phrase; his hair falls and a goatee appears upon his face. A greenish-yellow spotlight accompanies this change from the Tour Guide into

The Bard's Ghost

Edward de Vere. The tourists are fearful, and huddle to the side. De Vere looks across the church at a statue of Jesus and notices that it has taken on additional illumination.

De Vere. Next to G-d by way of a bust misplaced!
This charlatan has my birthright usurped
Like Jacob, feigned as Esau, did deceive,
Yet freely given by my guardian
William Cecil, Lord Burghley, CEO
Of Queen Elizabeth's global estate,
Ill disposed his assumed nature being
To mine art and dramatic persuasion.
And not unlike that ancient woolly tale,
My savior's teachings doth sheepishly play
As slavish musings to Caesar's behest!
So as twins doth both Jesus and de Vere
Stand bereft of their orig'nal intent.
And on this our birthday shall this Jacob
Be uncovered, a wolf in sheep's clothing,
And shall my savior and I be restored!
Slayers of a dragon of diff'rent sorts![7]

The bust of the Stratford man looks at Jesus for a reaction. Seeing none, he takes this as a fortuitous sign to come to life and strikes up a dialogue with de Vere.

Shakspere. My liege. How surprising to see you here!
Your words sting my heart as nettles to calves.

De Vere. Such whimpering from a counterfeit who,
Forgetful of his sponsor, doth present
Himself as a figure of fine letters,
But is rather an unlettered man
Sprung from illiteracy and spawn to't,
Unread and without literary couth!
Grain trader mired in petty lawsuits—
Coarse hands covered by the glove of history.
Yet, surely the prints of a certain man

---

[7] Shakspere's birth date is unknown. April 23rd is actually the day he died. The celebration of his birth on this date (relatively close to his christening) may have been chosen for its coincidence with the feast day of dragon-slaying St. George, the patron saint of England.

Are upon the immort'l words of the Bard?
And what man could be marked such a suspect
His syntax unique as his very life?
If suspects were sought as by sleuths to crime,
Then the profile of our poet could be
None other than that wit Edward de Vere,
The esteemed 17th Earl of Oxford.
Though long from this world, his verses ring on
Sadly echoing the name of a shill.
And I am de Vere in time no longer,
But the bard longer than common belief
Would have it. And depriv'd of mine own time,
My work and ideas are wholesale assign'd
To those who took inspiration from me!
No need did I have of a translation,
For the tongues I borrowed had been made
Mine own through study; the meter of Ovid,
And the form of my beloved sonnets
From mine own uncles did I learn.
Yet on the timeline of this Stratford man
Is my sweet poetry and drama cast
Largely as a creative borrowing.
Heavenly mercy! [*To Jesus.*] Is your divine plan
Impervious to such a travesty?
Am I to be consigned to godless purgat'ry
And this fraud to holy eternity?

> *Again seeing no reaction from Jesus, Shakspere*
> *unapologetically lapses into prose and turns the knife.*

   Shakspere. As you say, it beats selling grain, suing the apothecary, and playing a bit role now and then. You may be versed in many tongues, but academes have dusted off translations that, forced-fit, provide a plausible alibi for my pen. Who are you to distain my borrowings, so many plots have you pilfered from near and far? By now your shaken spear of the muse Pallas Athena and your esteemed, spear-laden coat-of-arms are mere coincidences of history and no sign of authorship. Some apologists have even grafted them to me.
Look, who out there [*To the audience.*] has even heard of you?

Besides, your own kin enshrined me—
and for a fair penny at that! And with Burghley's control over

your papers, history is easily deceived. Give it up, Oxford!
I am immortalized, and your purgatory a prelude to the hell
that you have raised—may history [*To the audience.*] be the judge!

   Jesus ponders this.

 De Vere. [*To Jesus.*]
How shall it be in a day so afield
From the time our phrases stirred hearts afresh
That we shall win misled minds [*Indicates audience.*] to our cause?
I pray, dear Lord, that you favor my quest
And aid me in redeeming history-
As history shall redeem thine own cause!

Shakspere. [*To the audience.*] In such favor was I, as a commoner
yet, that the familiar and reproachful tone I used on occasion,
such as to address Lord Southhampton in the Sonnets or, to cite
the extreme, to make fun of the queen, was of no consequence to
my life and liberty.

 De Vere. [*To the audience.*]
For myself, what writings bear my true name
Pay tribute to a youthful turn in court
And are but saplings to the mighty oak
Of my misattributed masterworks.
Yet, they called me the court's premier poet.
And every ancient plot did I enhance
With dramatic flair and mine own histr'y,
Which you, pernicious snipe, did swipe wholesale
Whilst yet did I heart'ly breathe and invent--
Those six bad quartos soiling my good name.

 Shakspere. Such was my imagination
that I could invent upon myself the occupational worldview,
interpersonal familiarity, and personal details of de Vere's life
and metaphorically represent them in my dramas as if they
were my own.

 De Vere. Hah! But doth not the vast record of my life
Make clear the argument for mine own hand?
Did not I misplace mine own wife's virtue
As Othello and countless other men
Into whom I breath'd motive through my pen?

Was not my voyage by pirates besieged
Just as my Hamlet was rudely taken?
And what of many court details I've told,
And scenes lifted from Italian sojourns?
Who else could speak in every Western tongue
Privy to such travel and proceedings?
Indeed I sold my property for it!
Yet as a bystander am I witness
To this pilfering of my adventures,
As if I shared them with this imposter!

Isn't this much as the prophet will face
When anonymously he revisits
A world that knows him not, and must from scratch,
Via his words and acts, make such renown
That he is seen for what he is—genius!
Perhaps he, too, will take pen to parchment
For do not the scrolls of the Essenes say,
He shall strike the earth with the rod of his mouth,   *Dead Sea Scrolls*
and with the breath of his lips shall he slay the wicked.[8]
If I were he, I'd masquerade as Jaques: *RB*
Invest me in my motley. Give me leave   *As You Like It*, II, vii, 58-61
To speak my mind, and I will through and through
Cleanse the foul body of the infected world,
If they will patiently receive my medicine.
But time is upon us and as pebbles   *RB*
We are torrent-toss'd for dissolution.

[Yet,] ...in black ink my love may still shine bright,   *Sonnet 65*
Not marble, nor the gilded monuments   *Sonnet 55*
Of princes, shall outlive this powerful rhyme.
[They shall query,] How many ages hence   *Julius Caesar*, III, i, 111-113
Shall this our lofty scene be acted o'er
In states unborn and accents yet unknown!

    He kneels in front of Christ's statue.

When in disgrace with Fortune and men's eyes   *Sonnet 29*
I all alone beweep my outcast state,
And trouble deaf heaven with my bootless cries,

---

[8] *The Dead Sea Scrolls*, translation and commentary by Michael Wise, Martin Abegg, Jr., and Edward Cook, Harper, San Francisco, 1996, p. 292.

490 » The Bard's Ghost

And look upon myself and curse my fate,
Wishing me like to one more rich in hope,
Featur'd like him, with friends possess'd,
Desiring this man's art, and that man's scope,
With what I most enjoy contented least;
Yet in these thoughts myself almost despising,
Haply I think on thee; and then my state,
Like to the lark at break of day arising
From sullen earth, sings hymns at the heaven's gate;
   For thy sweet love rememb'red such wealth brings
   That then I scorn to change my state with kings.
Now with drops of this most balmy time   *Sonnet 107*
My love looks fresh, and Death to me subscribes.

Yet, such Death dulls not the everlasting life,   *RB*
Within your bosom where my soul abides.
You alone understand my dilemma.
Thou art savior for those lives dispossess'd,
And dispossess'd we save by saving thee.
Let thy name be reheard in its first voice,
And ours in tow humbly repossess'd too,
If through my charms such suit doth conscience find.

> *While de Vere's head is bowed in prayer, Christ's subtly indicates that is considering de Vere's argument. The lights dim, with Christ the last piece of the tableaux to fade from view.*

Act I, Scene II

Time: Late 16th Century
Place: Anne Cecil's quarters, Hampton House

Christ, visible in half-light, considers the proceedings.

Anne Cecil.   *The Merry Wives of Windsor, II, i, 1-110*
What, have I scaped love-letters in the holiday-
time of my beauty, and am I now a subject for them?
Let me see. [*She reads.*]
'Ask me no reason why I love you; for though
Love use Reason for his physician, he admits him

not for his counsellor. You are not young, no more
am I; go to then, there's sympathy: you are merry,
so am I; ha, ha! then there's more sympathy: you
love sack, and so do I; would you desire better
sympathy? Let it suffice thee, Mistress Page,--at
the least, if the love of soldier can suffice,--
that I love thee. I will not say, pity me; 'tis
not a soldier-like phrase: but I say, love me. By me,
Thine own true knight,
By day or night,
Or any kind of light,
With all his might
For thee to fight, JOHN FALSTAFF'

What a Herod of Jewry is this! O wicked
world! One that is well-nigh worn to pieces with
age to show himself a young gallant! What an
unweighed behavior hath this Flemish drunkard
picked--with the devil's name!--out of my
conversation, that he dares in this manner assay me?
Why, he hath not been thrice in my company! What
should I say to him? I was then frugal of my
mirth: Heaven forgive me! Why, I'll exhibit a bill
in the parliament for the putting down of men. How
shall I be revenged on him? for revenged I will be,
as sure as his guts are made of puddings.

> *Enter Mistress Page.*

Anne Cecil. Mistress Page! trust me, I was going to your house.

Mistress Page. And, trust me, I am coming to you. You look very ill.

Anne Cecil. Nay, I'll ne'er believe that; I have to show to the contrary.

Mistress Page. Faith, but you do, in my mind.

Anne Cecil. Well, I do then; yet I say I could show you to the contrary. O Mistress Page, give me some counsel!

Mistress Page. What's the matter, woman?

Anne Cecil. O woman, if it were not for one trifling respect, I could come to such honour!

Mistress Page. Hang the trifle, woman! take the honour. What is it? dispense with trifles; what is it?

Anne Cecil. If I would but go to hell for an eternal moment or so, I could be knighted.

Mistress Page. What? thou liest! Sir Anne Cecil! These knights will hack; and so thou shouldst not alter the article of thy gentry.

Anne Cecil. We burn daylight: here, read, read; perceive how I might be knighted. I shall think the worse of fat men, as long as I have an eye to make difference of men's liking: and yet he would not swear; praised women's modesty; and gave such orderly and well-behaved reproof to all uncomeliness, that I would have sworn his disposition would have gone to the truth of his words; but they do no more adhere and keep place together than the Hundredth Psalm to the tune of 'Green Sleeves.' What tempest, I trow, threw this whale, with so many tuns of oil in his belly, ashore at Windsor? How shall I be revenged on him? I think the best way were to entertain him with hope, till the wicked fire of lust have melted him in his own grease. Did you ever hear the like?

Mistress Page. Letter for letter, but that the name of Page and de Vere differs! To thy great comfort in this mystery of ill opinions, here's the twin-brother of thy letter: but let thine inherit first; for, I protest, mine never shall. I warrant he hath a thousand of these letters, writ with blank space for different names--sure, more,--and these are of the second edition: he will print them, out of doubt; for he cares not what he puts into the press, when he would put us two. I had rather be a giantess, and lie under Mount Pelion. Well, I will find you twenty lascivious turtles ere one chaste man.

Anne Cecil. Why, this is the very same; the very hand, the very words. What doth he think of us?

Mistress Page. Nay, I know not: it makes me almost ready to wrangle with mine own honesty. I'll entertain myself like one that I am not acquainted withal; for, sure, unless he know some strain in me, that I know not myself, he would never have boarded me in this fury.

Anne Cecil. 'Boarding,' call you it? I'll be sure to keep him above deck.

Mistress Page. So will I if he come under my hatches, I'll never to sea again. Let's be revenged on him: let's appoint him a meeting; give him a show of comfort in his suit and lead him on with a fine-baited delay, till he hath pawned his horses to mine host of the Garter.

Anne Cecil. Nay, I will consent to act any villany against him, that may not sully the chariness of our honesty. O, that my husband saw this letter! it would give eternal food to his jealousy.

Mistress Page. Why, my good man too: he's as far from jealousy as I am from giving him cause; and that I hope is an unmeasurable distance.

Anne Cecil. You are the happier woman.

The Merry Wives of Windsor, III, iii, 189-190

I know not which pleases me better, that my husband is deceived, or Sir John.

The Merry Wives of Windsor, III, iii, 196-210

Mistress Page. Hang them, dishonest rascals! I would all of the same strain were in the same distress.

Anne Cecil. I think my husband hath some special suspicion of Falstaff's being here; for I never saw him so gross in his jealousy till now.

Mistress Page. I will lay a plot to try that; and we will yet have more tricks with Falstaff: his dissolute disease will scarce obey this medicine.

Anne Cecil. Shall we send that foolish carrion, Mistress Quickly, to him, and excuse his throwing into the water; and give him another hope, to betray him to another punishment?

Mistress Page. We will do it: let him be sent for ... to have amends.

Act I, Scene III

Time: Late 16th Century
Place: The bar at the Garter Inn, Windsor

Falstaff is cleaning glasses. Shakspere is drinking at a corner table.

Enter Dull, who crosses to the upstage end of bar

Dull. Good morrow, Sir John.   RB

Falstaff. Good morrow, your honor. What brings the pleasure?

Dull. Rumors.

Falstaff. What rumors recommend thee to my establishment?

Dull [*Eyes Shakspere in corner.*]. That ale tax due the crown hath been diverted to arms.

Falstaff. Surely, Constable, you jest that a gentleman such as I would dare short the Queen!

Dull. I pray that t'is jest, good John, or thou shalt pay for't.

Falstaff [*Draws pint from keg tap for Dull.*]. I pour my ale and mark my measures—my account is drawn for all to see. Woe to the fool that casts a stone at me!

Dull. As it may be [*Drinks.*]. Ah, and a fine draught it is.

Falstaff. He seems to like it [*Indicates Shakspere.*].

Dull. Yes, too much I fear.

Falstaff. The grain dealer's a harmless sot.

Dull. You misjudge your customer, good John. This one would as soon slay you as pay you.

Falstaff. Fair warning, your Lordship, yet my license rides not on vigilance delayed. This house is well versed in calculation and will.

Dull. That I also fear, Sir John.

Merry Wives of Windsor, II, ii, 32-35
Enter Robin.

Robin. Sir, here's a woman would speak with you.

Falstaff. Let her approach.

Enter Mistress Quickly, who faces the audience at downstage end of bar. Robin then goes and sits and drinks at the corner table with Shakspere.

Mistress Quickly. Give your worship good morrow.

Falstaff. Good morrow, good wife.
What with me?   *Merry Wives of Windsor, II, ii, 41-55*

Mistress Quickly. Shall I vouchsafe your worship a word or two?

Falstaff. Two thousand, fair woman: and I'll vouchsafe thee the hearing.

Mistress Quickly. There is one Mistress de Vere, sir:--I pray, come a little nearer this ways:--I myself dwell with a nosey doctor

Falstaff. Well, on: Mistress de Vere, you say,--

Mistress Quickly. Your worship says very true: I pray your worship, come a little nearer this ways.

Falstaff. I warrant thee, nobody hears; mine own people, mine own people.

> *He points to Dull at bar and Shakspere and Robin at the corner table.*

Mistress Quickly. Are they so? God bless them and make them his servants!

Falstaff. Well, Mistress de Vere; what of her?

Merry Wives of Windsor, II, ii, 60-62

Mistress Quickly.
Marry, this is the short and the long of it; you
have brought her into such a canaries as 'tis
wonderful.

Merry Wives of Windsor, II, ii, 64-72

There has been knights, and
lords, and gentlemen, with their coaches, I warrant
you, coach after coach, letter after letter, gift
after gift; smelling so sweetly, all musk, and so
rushling, I warrant you, in silk and gold; and in
such alligant terms; and in such wine and sugar of
the best and the fairest, that would have won any
woman's heart; and, I warrant you, they could never
get an eye-wink of her:
            all is one with her.

Merry Wives of Windsor, II, ii, 80-122

Falstaff. But what says she to me? be brief, my good she-Mercury.

Mistress Quickly. Marry, she hath received your letter, for the which she thanks you a thousand times; and she gives you to notify that her husband will be absence from his house between Shrove Tuesday and Easter.

Falstaff. Shrove Tuesday and Easter?

Mistress Quickly. Why, you say well.

But I have another messenger to
your worship. Mistress Page hath her hearty
commendations to you too: and let me tell you in
your ear, she's as fartuous a civil modest wife, and
one, I tell you, that will not miss you morning nor
evening prayer, as any is in Windsor, whoe'er be the
other: and she bade me tell your worship that her
husband is seldom from home; but she hopes there
will come a time. I never knew a woman so dote upon
a man: surely I think you have charms.

Falstaff. Not I, I assure thee: setting the attractions of my
good parts aside I have no other charms.

Mistress Quickly. Blessing on your heart for't!

Falstaff. Woman, commend me to her; I will
not fail her.

Mistress Quickly. Why, you say well.

Falstaff. But, I pray thee, tell me this: has de Vere's wife and
Page's wife acquainted each other how they love me?

Mistress Quickly. That were a jest indeed! they have not so little
grace, I hope: but Mistress Page would desire you to send her your
little page, of all loves: her husband has a
marvellous infection to the little page [*Indicates Robin.*]; and truly
Master Page is an honest man. Never a wife in
Windsor leads a better life than she does

Merry Wives of Windsor, II, ii, 125-130

: and truly she deserves it; for if there
be a kind woman in Windsor, she is one. You must
send her your page; no remedy.

Falstaff. Why, I will. [*Waves for Robin.*]

Mistress Quickly. Nay, but do so, then: and, look you, he may come and
go between you both

Merry Wives of Windsor, II, ii, 132-169

and the boy never need to understand any thing; for
'tis not good that children should know any
wickedness: old folks, you know, have discretion,
as they say, and know the world.

   Falstaff. Fare thee well: commend me to them both: there's
my purse; I am yet thy debtor.

      Exeunt Mistress Quickly and Robin.

This news distracts me!

      Enter Bardolph.

   Bardolph. John, there's one Master Brook below would fain
speak with you, and be acquainted with you; and hath
sent you a morning's draught of sack.

   Falstaff. Brook is his name?

   Bardolph. Ay, John.

   Falstaff. Call him in, Bardolph.

      Exit Bardolph.

   Falstaff. Such Brooks are welcome to me, that o'erflow such
liquor. Ah, ha! Mistress de Vere have I encompassed you?

      *Re-enter Bardolph, with de Vere, who is adding a disguise
      (full beard to his extant goatee) as he enters. He crosses to
      the spot Mistress Quigley has vacated.*

   De Vere. Bless you, sir!

   Falstaff. And you, sir! Would you speak with me?

      Bardolph joins Shakspere. They drink.

   De Vere. I make bold to press with so little preparation upon
you.

   Falstaff. You're welcome. What's your will?

De Vere. Sir, I am a gentleman that have spent much; my name is Brook.

Falstaff. Good Master Brook, I desire more acquaintance of you.

Merry Wives of Windsor, II, ii, 186-328

De Vere. Sir, I hear you are a scholar,--I will be brief
with you,--and you have been a man long known to me,
though I had never so good means, as desire, to make
myself acquainted with you. I shall discover a
thing to you, wherein I must very much lay open mine
own imperfection: but, good Sir John, as you have
one eye upon my follies, as you hear them unfolded,
turn another into the register of your own; that I
may pass with a reproof the easier, sith you
yourself know how easy it is to be such an offender.

Falstaff. Very well, sir; proceed.

De Vere. There is a gentlewoman in this town; her husband's name is de Vere.

Falstaff. Well, sir.

De Vere. I have long loved her, and, I protest to you,
bestowed much on her; followed her with a doting
observance; engrossed opportunities to meet her;
fee'd every slight occasion that could but niggardly
give me sight of her; not only bought many presents
to give her, but have given largely to many to know
what she would have given; briefly, I have pursued
her as love hath pursued me; which hath been on the
wing of all occasions. But whatsoever I have
merited, either in my mind or, in my means, meed,
I am sure, I have received none; unless experience
be a jewel that I have purchased at an infinite
rate, and that hath taught me to say this:
'Love like a shadow flies when substance love pursues;
Pursuing that that flies, and flying what pursues.'

Falstaff. Have you received no promise of satisfaction at her hands?

De Vere. Never.

Falstaff. Have you importuned her to such a purpose?

De Vere. Never.

Falstaff. Of what quality was your love, then?

De Vere. Like a fair house built on another man's ground; so that I have lost my edifice by mistaking the place where I erected it.

Falstaff. To what purpose have you unfolded this to me?

De Vere. When I have told you that, I have told you all. Some say, that though she appear honest to me, yet in other places she enlargeth her mirth so far that there is shrewd construction made of her. Now, Sir John, here is the heart of my purpose: you are a gentleman of excellent breeding, admirable discourse, of great admittance, authentic in your place and person, generally allowed for your many war-like, court-like, and learned preparations.

Falstaff. O, sir!

De Vere. Believe it, for you know it. There is money; spend it, spend it; spend more; spend all I have; only give me so much of your time in exchange of it, as to lay an amiable siege to the honesty of this de Vere's wife: use your art of wooing; win her to consent to you: if any man may, you may as soon as any.

Falstaff. Would it apply well to the vehemency of your affection, that I should win what you would enjoy? Methinks you prescribe to yourself very preposterously.

De Vere. O, understand my drift. She dwells so securely on the excellency of her honour, that the folly of my soul dares not present itself: she is too bright to be looked against. Now, could I could come to her with any detection in my hand, my desires had instance and argument to commend themselves: I

could drive her then from the ward of her purity,
her reputation, her marriage-vow, and a thousand
other her defences, which now are too too strongly
embattled against me. What say you to't, Sir John?

Falstaff. Master Brook, I will first make bold with your
money; next, give me your hand; and last, as I am a
gentleman, you shall, if you will, enjoy de Vere's wife.

De Vere. O good sir!

Falstaff. I say you shall.

De Vere. Want no money, Sir John; you shall want none.

Falstaff. Want no Mistress de Vere, Master Brook; you shall want
none. I shall be with her, I may tell you, by her
own appointment; even as you came in to me, her
assistant or go-between parted from me: I say I
shall be with her between Shrove Tuesday and Easter; for at
that time the jealous rascally knave her husband
will be forth. Come you to me at night; you shall
know how I speed.

De Vere. I am blest in your acquaintance. Do you know de Vere,
sir?

Falstaff. Hang him, poor cuckoldly knave! I know him not:
yet I wrong him to call him poor; they say the
jealous wittolly knave hath masses of money; for the
which his wife seems to me well-favored. I will
use her as the key of the cuckoldly rogue's coffer;
and there's my harvest-home.

De Vere. I would you knew de Vere, sir, that you might avoid him
if you saw him.

Falstaff. Hang him, mechanical salt-butter rogue! I will
stare him out of his wits; I will awe him with my
cudgel: it shall hang like a meteor o'er the
cuckold's horns. Master Brook, thou shalt know I
will predominate over the peasant, and thou shalt
lie with his wife. Come to me soon at night.

De Vere's a knave, and I will aggravate his style;
thou, Master Brook, shalt know him for knave and
cuckold. Come to me soon at night.

> *De Vere comes downstage and removes his disguise. The
> lights in the background dim. Only Dull seems to notice
> him.*

De Vere. What a damned Epicurean rascal is this! My heart is
ready to crack with impatience. Who says this is
improvident jealousy? my wife hath sent to him; the
hour is fixed; the match is made. Would any man
have thought this? See the hell of having a false
woman! My bed shall be abused, my coffers
ransacked, my reputation gnawn at; and I shall not
only receive this villanous wrong, but stand under
the adoption of abominable terms, and by him that
does me this wrong. Terms! names! Amaimon sounds
well; Lucifer, well; Barbason, well; yet they are
devils' additions, the names of fiends: but
Cuckold! Wittol!--Cuckold! the devil himself hath
not such a name. Page is an ass, a secure ass: he
will trust his wife; he will not be jealous. I will
rather trust a Fleming with my butter, Parson Hugh
the Welshman with my cheese, an Irishman with my
aqua-vitae bottle, or a thief to walk my ambling
gelding, than my wife with herself; then she plots,
then she ruminates, then she devises; and what they
think in their hearts they may effect, they will
break their hearts but they will effect. God be
praised for my jealousy! The Lenten season the hour.
I will prevent this, detect my wife, be revenged on
Falstaff, and laugh at Page. I will about it;
better three hours too soon than a minute too late.
Fie, fie, fie! cuckold! cuckold! cuckold! [*He exits.*]

Falstaff.
What's a woman's affections between two gentleman?   RB
I have Master Brooks' purse, Mistress Page's heart,
And soon a set of horns for de Vere!

Dull. How, good John, may such merry follow a fresh adieu to anger?

Falstaff. You mistake Master Brooks' passion, my good Dull. I have his gold for the promise of a moment's pleasure with Mistress de Vere; it is satisfaction that rests upon him thus.

Dull. No satisfaction did I detect in his seething visage. He acts as if your promise was of his own wife!

Falstaff. Most men are vexed when it comes to women, or reading their own hearts for that matter. So, far and wide they seek my service, in search of succor, such is my success with the distaff side.

Dull. Jealousy is no stranger to man, well we know that. But it is not every man who shows his hand. In the ways of women, some men are versed. Woe the fool that see not this mask!

Falstaff. Fair words, your honor, yet de Vere, upon whom through "Brooks" I'll gain revenge, acquits himself with no such conceit. He shambles from crisis to crisis like a buck in rut, locking horns without heed for his name or estate, in no way showing a talent for this feminine trait.

Dull. Mark me, Falstaff, his verse doth abide such sentiments that those opined in such matters thus do swear there be no equal at court. The Queen herself holds him dear, and in that passion another story, yet see that her annual pension for his pen exceeds all others on the list.

Falstaff. Likely a lover's gift that.

Dull. Lovers of the same art, no doubt, are drawn to the same artful flesh. The crux here is unanimous acclaim for his rhyme and the mask that such artifice doth imply.

Falstaff. The nut here is his wife's good name and the discreet exchange of favor.

Dull. And for this you risk life and limb?

Falstaff. Surely you don't believe Lord Burghley would sue to make public his daughter's virtue. This aside, alas, her beauty and charms be such that both Master Brooks and I would seek her bed, even 'twere our last.

Dull. That may be an epitaph divined.

Falstaff. T'is more likely a pleasure from behind, but not one with which I will be aligned. For Mistress Page this hour hath made it known that her virtues are assailable by me alone. And, thus, I so generously bequeath my good fortune to Brooks who lacks the cheek.

Dull. We'll leave that outcome for another day, since there's little rev'nue in't. Such crimes pale next to the refinement of untaxed ale. And there's no telling how your duplicity in matters of heart may be at work in the darker arts.

> *Light go down on Falstaff and Dull and up on Shakspere and Bardolph, whose conversation has grown heated in the background and now spills over.*

Shakspere [Besotted.]. I say to the barkeep, I sell me grain and count me farthings like a beggar man, so if I fancy to spend it on your hops, what of't?

Bardolph. You're a fool, Will'm! No man with a lick of sense would do business with you without bringing his own weights to your scale; elsewise, he'd starve with the sack he broke his back earnin' that you've shorted.

Shakspere. I warn ye boy, 'tis slippery ground you're treadin'. Careful what ye impute to your superior!

Bardolph. Superior! A jest! In posterior only!

> *Shakspere jumps up and starts swinging at Bardolph.*

Shakspere. You'd better retract that, impertinent youth!

Bardolph. Here's whack, decrepit old coot!

> *Falstaff leaves the bar and joins the fray, finally getting a hold of Shakspere by the collar and dragging him out the door and depositing him in the gutter.*

The Taming of the Shrew, Induction, 1- 15

Shakspere. I'll pheeze you, in faith.

Falstaff. A pair of stocks, you rogue!

Shakspere. Ye are a baggage: the Shakesperes no rogues; look in the chronicles; we came in with Richard Conqueror. Therefore paucas pallabris; let the world slide: sessa!

Falstaff. You will not pay for the glasses you have burst?

Shakspere. No, not a denier. Go by, Jeronimy: go to thy cold bed, and warm thee.

Falstaff. I know my remedy; I must go fetch the third--borough. [*Motions inside toward Dull.*]

Exit Falstaff.

Shakspere. Third, or fourth, or fifth borough, I'll answer him by law: I'll not budge an inch, boy: let him come, and kindly.

Falls asleep.

Act I, Scene IV

Time: Present
Place: Purgatory

Christ, visible in half-light, considers de Vere.

RB

De Vere. I hope that you enjoyed that scene. It is the longest in this play, but in its exposition frames everything that is to follow in our plot and subplots. I had many such scenes—of cuckoldry imagined—from which to chose, for my suspicion of my wife's infidelity was a nagging voice within me throughout a great portion of my life and thus in my writings. In addition to this storyline from *The Merry Wives of Windsor*, in which I mock my own behavior, my doubts play major roles in *Much Ado About Nothing*, *Othello*, *Cymbaline*, and *The Winter's Tale*, not to mention additional commentaries on my marriage, which I am conscious of having included in nine other plays.

Then there is that rascal drinking in the corner, up to no good as usual. You'll recognize him, in his general form, as my rustic—or "rude mechanical" as Puck would call him—whom I employ in subplots, to underscore or elaborate the central drama by contrasting class, language, sensibility, or spirituality and to keep those in the pit interested. For if the groundlings can't afford the theatre, or find something there for jest or admiration, then we have failed as surely as a church that abandons the poor in pursuit of the Golden Calf.

In choosing this particular lout as my representative rustic, some may accuse me of taking a cheap shot at an easy target—after all, what chance does a barely literate burgher have against the mightiest pen in history? But I remind you that I have paid for my sins with 400 years of Purgatory watching the gullible lather fame upon this gnarly knave. Like a cat slapping around a once-proud rodent, I shall have my fun before the kill.

Besides, if I am to persuade you in my conceit, a trademark rustic must I have, and what better example than to unmask Christopher Sly—the enigmatic subject of the Induction in *The Taming of the Shrew*—as William Shakspere, that "upstart crow" whose feathers are lifted from my very nest.[9]

Here is an allegory that I put right under your nose—and what did I get for it?—some lukewarm drivel on illusion and disguise. Wake up! For this evening, in our rustic divertissement, you shall be privy to my long-awaited skewering of a most piteous creature.

So, you see, there is no wanton randomness in my voice or in my choice of targets here. Once you are familiar with my story, you will see that I do not pull fully-formed characters out of a hat, to use them frivolously—but draw them from life, to float or founder at my whim, often subjecting them to public ridicule, and providing me the satisfaction that so often escaped me in life.

No one with whom I had a row escaped unscathed, including Sir Philip Sidney (in the form of Sir Andrew Aguecheek in *Twelfth Night*; Michael Cassio in *Othello,* and Slender in *The Merry Wives of Windsor*), Sir Christopher Hatton (as Malvolio in *Twelfth Night*), Lord Robert Dudley (as Claudius in *Hamlet* and Shallow in *The Merry Wives of Windsor*), and, of course, Lord Burghley, my guardian and later father-in law (as Polonius

---

[9] In *Grimm's Fairy Tales*, a crow gathers feathers dropped by peacocks to pose as something he is not. The reference to an upstart crow in *Greene's Groat's-worth of Wit* ("... there is an upstart crow, beautified with our feathers, that ... supposes he is as well able to bombast out a blank-verse as the best of you: and being an absolute *Johannes factotum* ...") makes this clear: The upstart crow, Shakspere, is a braggart who wraps himself in borrowed feathers to aggrandize himself.

in *Hamlet*, Gonzalo in *The Tempest*, and others), to name a few, not to mention the Queen herself, my dear Elizabeth, in various disguises.

Some of these issues, I admit were petty, such as my famous tennis set-to with Sidney, from which I derived much jest, even as Elizabeth put me under house arrest; some provided key plot devices, such as the £3,000 bond I defaulted to Michael Lok in Venice; while others called to my soul, giving rise to such broadsides as my pseudonymous William Shake-hyphen-speare's tracts against Elizabeth's proposed Catholic marriage to Spain. But Shakspere is a target of a different color, one that begs a proper theatrical thrashing, for all the affections he hath stolen under false pretenses.

That said, let's get back to it. By this time, I have left my wife and am about to take up with one of the Queen's ladies-in-waiting. You may recognize some of the literary allusions, for I wrote about her often under different guises. She is my greatest inspiration—truly did I love her! For this, I pray you are willing to overlook the abridgement of temporal norms and judge favorably my suit versus Stratford, and its most serious stakes of heaven and hell. [*Christ ponders this.*] Now, if you'll excuse me, I need to slip into something more comfortable. [*He begins to disrobe.*]

Act I, Scene V

Time: Late 16th Century.
Place: Bathing quarters in de Vere's ancestral country estate, Castle Hedingham; servants finish filling a large wooden tub with hot water

We hear laughing, and then see de Vere and a beautiful red-haired, dark-browed woman in a hot tub, smoking pot from a hookah and drinking red wine.

De Vere. We've known each other only a short time,   *RB*
But I must tell you a secret.

Anne Vavasor. A secret, my love, between new lovers is as a spring rain to flowers. I pray you will shower me with your fertile deliverance.

De Vere. That is precisely what I mean to do in word and deed; in word: my name for which I'm most acclaimed is not the one I go by.

The Bard's Ghost

Anne Vavasor. I shall call you what you wish. You need not have an identity with me—or with yourself for that matter. Though Anne Vavasor is the name that I was given, my true name, Rosaline, is self-assigned.

De Vere. How apt, for a flaming dragon lady thou art!

Anne Vavasor. And you, St. George—what forces do you bring to bear?

De Vere. I bring a few. My identity remains but a secret to others, yet in this broth I have nothing to hide.

Anne Vavasor. I can see that, and a mighty speare it is! So what are these secrets that belie your upright advances?

De Vere. Can I trust you?

Anne Vavasor. As much as I can trust a man with a stiff conscience.

De Vere. Are you true?

Anne Vavasor. You sound like a man who has lost at love.

De Vere. I believe my wife has been unfaithful.

Anne Vavasor. And you in turn seek a muse and mistress?

De Vere. I confess I do, though each for different reasons: A mistress to mend my broken heart; a muse to restore my secret art.

Anne Vavasor. Here find a muse and a mistress intertwined. What of this secret art you wish to restore?

De Vere. Before I confess to that, I must query you.

Anne Vavasor. A riddle, perhaps?

De Vere. Of sorts.

Anne Vavasor. Play on.

De Vere. Though Edward de Vere is my given name
And the Earl of Oxenford my title,
T'is another calling for which my fame

Upon which, I hope, history settles

  Anne Vavasor.   *Romeo and Juliet, II, ii, 43-53*
What's in a name? that which we call a rose
By any other name would smell as sweet;
So Oxenford would, were he not Oxenford call'd,
Retain that dear perfection which he owes
Without that title. Oxenford, doff thy name,
And for that name which is no part of thee
Take all myself.

  De Vere. I take thee at thy word:
Call me but love, and I'll be new baptized;
Henceforth I never will be de Vere.

  Anne Vavasor. What man art thou that thus bescreen'd in night
So stumblest on my counsel?

  De Vere. By a name
I know not how to tell thee who I am:
But the gentle William Shake—hypen—speare,   *RB*
The true author of the queen's courtly plays,
Sponsor of that false-hearted upstart crow,
The ham-handed thief William Shakspere

  Anne Vavasor. Oh, my! That *is* obscure. How exciting!
I had no idea this assignment would have such lovely perks.

  De Vere. And what might those be?

  She moves closer.

  Anne Vavasor. I can be bribed by shaken speares.

  De Vere. Ah, dare we strike a Faustian bargain?

  Anne Vavasor. I seek to praise thee, not bury!

  De Vere. And what might I tender for the inspiration
to reclaim the honor so rightfully mine?

  Anne Vavasor. I only accept hard cash, no credit.
A few of your sweet nothings shall lubricate the transaction,

For which you must pay in advance.
In exchange for these gifts, your name shall be restored in spades.

De Vere. My pleasure!

Anne Vavasor. Slay me! *[They embrace and kiss.]*

> *De Vere breaks away to write down insights on a pad of paper he keeps next to the tub.*

Henry V, Prologue

De Vere. "O for a muse of fire, that would ascend
The brightest heaven of invention…"
That would be you, my red lady.   RB

Anne Vavasor. Aye, my lord, a muse doth my dreams inform.

De Vere. Be thou the tenth Muse, ten times more in worth   *Sonnet 38*
Than those old nine which rimers invocate.
And by such convergence shall hist'ry turn.   RB

> *As the lights fade, the couple becomes increasingly erotic, steam rises, and we hear the witches from Macbeth cackle, then incant:*

Witches. "Double, double, toil and trouble,   *Macbeth, IV, I, 10*

Fire burn and cauldron bubble …"
"All hail … [de Vere]! hail thee, [The Bard of Bath]!"   *Macbeth, I, iii, 48*

First Intermission

Act II, Scene I

Time: Present
Place: Purgatory

Christ, visible in half-light, considers de Vere's argument.

De Vere. As you've probably guessed from the portent of the witches at the conclusion of the previous steamy scene, this tryst ended rather badly for Ms. Vavasor and me (we'll have more on that later). And though my dear, irrepressible Elizabeth, the queen, eventually did forgive me, her first minister, the newly-minted Lord Burghley, William Cecil—again: my legal guardian and, later, my father-in-law—did not; for to a man so recently raised to the peerage, any scandal-tinged aspersions toward his daughter were as a fungus to a rose, to be rooted out at all costs and without a public ruffle.

So, Burghley, Lord Treasurer of England, did tenaciously pursue me, alternatively bailing me out and reigning me in. Needless to say, our relationship was conflicted. Here, again, I pray that you understand my behavior toward William Cecil in the political, legal, and familial furnace within which it was tempered.

Act II, Scene II

Time: Late 16th Century
Place: Burghley's study, Cecil House

Enter Shakspere.

Shakspere. Lord Burghley, you sent for me?   *RB*

Burghley. [*Turning from his papers.*]
Yes, Will. Once more, our Queen's enemies rumble,
And to the breach must we courageously go!

Shakspere. The hounds are gathered, the scent profuse;
Our wicks clean, our power dry; I covet pursuit,
Awaiting only your legal directive.

Burghley. It is my ward and son-in-law, de Vere
Of whom I seek disposition unseen.

Shakspere. The Earl of Oxford—under suspicion?
What offense hath follow'd the profligate now?

Burghley. T'is his pen, Will'm, that hath stray'd afar,

In affairs of state and affairs of heart.

Shakspere. Many are the men who would claim his words
For their own, including present comp'ny.

Burghley. Yea, his pen names doth persuade unmatched,
"Pasquill Caviliero," "Labeo," and
That "William Shake-speare" argue on matters
Better left for the masters of statecraft:
Catholic sympathies, legal nitpicks;
His mind too divisive to guide our course,
And the Queen too fertile to his ploughing.

Shakspere. But in such alias his weakness lies,
For who's to say if it is he or I
Whose suasions pamphlet for the public's smarts,
While courtly masks entreat a monarch's heart.
His noble name, Oxford, shielded from sight,
Is our recipe for usurpéd rights.
So transpose my name and his *nom de plume*
And we find profit at the author's tomb.

Burghley. Were you my own son I should not wonder
That such clever use of "rights to copy"[10]
Would regiment for such loyal purpose.
But that it is your speech, Will, that commends,
I am most proud of my steadfast tut'lage.
My daughter did not a de Vere marry
To see our house despoiled by courtesans,
Our repute besmirched by common thieves,
As we find in players born to the stage.
For this, I tender you the mark you wish.

Shakspere. 'Tis use of "William Shake-speare" I desire,
To alter minds and make de Vere a liar.
His prodigious talent shall be my fame;
My fate transform'd by his occluded name.

Burghley. *Macbeth, III, i, 128-134*
Your spirits shine through you. Within this hour at most
I will advise you where to plant yourself;

---

[10] There were no copyright laws at this time.

Acquaint you with the perfect spy o' the time,
The moment on't; for't must be done to-night,
And something from the palace; always thought
That I require a clearness: and with him--
To leave no rubs nor botches in the work--

Act II, Scene III

Time: Late 16th Century
Place: Outside the Garter Inn

Shakspere is sleeping in the gutter.

The Taming of the Shrew, Induction, 16-138
Horns winded. Enter a Lord from hunting, with his train.

De Vere. Huntsman, I charge thee, tender well my hounds:
Brach Merriman, the poor cur is emboss'd;
And couple Clowder with the deep--mouth'd brach.
Saw'st thou not, boy, how Silver made it good
At the hedge-corner, in the coldest fault?
I would not lose the dog for twenty pound.

First Huntsman. Why, Belman is as good as he, my lord;
He cried upon it at the merest loss
And twice to-day pick'd out the dullest scent:
Trust me, I take him for the better dog.

De Vere. Thou art a fool: if Echo were as fleet,
I would esteem him worth a dozen such.
But sup them well and look unto them all:
To-morrow I intend to hunt again.

First Huntsman. I will, my lord.

De Vere. What's here? one dead, or drunk? See, doth he breathe?

Second Huntsman.
He breathes, my lord. Were he not warm'd with ale,
This were a bed but cold to sleep so soundly.

De Vere. O monstrous beast! how like a swine he lies!
Grim death, how foul and loathsome is thine image!
Sirs, I will practise on this drunken man.
What think you, if he were convey'd to bed,
Wrapp'd in sweet clothes, rings put upon his fingers,
A most delicious banquet by his bed,
And brave attendants near him when he wakes,
Would not the beggar then forget himself?

First Huntsman. Believe me, lord, I think he cannot choose.

Second Huntsman. It would seem strange unto him when he waked.

De Vere. Even as a flattering dream or worthless fancy.
Then take him up and manage well the jest:
Carry him gently to my fairest chamber
And hang it round with all my wanton pictures:
Balm his foul head in warm distilled waters
And burn sweet wood to make the lodging sweet:
Procure me music ready when he wakes,
To make a dulcet and a heavenly sound;
And if he chance to speak, be ready straight
And with a low submissive reverence
Say 'What is it your honour will command?'
Let one attend him with a silver basin
Full of rose-water and bestrew'd with flowers,
Another bear the ewer, the third a diaper,
And say 'Will't please your lordship cool your hands?'
Some one be ready with a costly suit
And ask him what apparel he will wear;
Another tell him of his hounds and horse,
And that his lady mourns at his disease:
Persuade him that he hath been lunatic;
And when he says he is, say that he dreams,
For he is nothing but a mighty lord.
This do and do it kindly, gentle sirs:
It will be pastime passing excellent,
If it be husbanded with modesty.

First Huntsman.

My lord, I warrant you we will play our part,
As he shall think by our true diligence
He is no less than what we say he is.

  De Vere. Take him up gently and to bed with him;
And each one to his office when he wakes.

    Huntsmen bear out Shakspere. A trumpet sounds.

Sirrah, go see what trumpet 'tis that sounds:

  Exit Servingman.

Belike, some noble gentleman that means,
Travelling some journey, to repose him here.

    Re-enter Servingman.

How now! who is it?

  Servant. An't please your honour, players
That offer service to your lordship.

  De Vere. Bid them come near.

    Enter Players.

Now, fellows, you are welcome.

  Players. We thank your honour.

  De Vere. Do you intend to stay with me tonight?

  A Player. So please your lordship to accept our duty.

  De Vere. With all my heart. This fellow I remember,
Since once he play'd a farmer's eldest son:
'Twas where you woo'd the gentlewoman so well:
I have forgot your name; but, sure, that part
Was aptly fitted and naturally perform'd.

  A Player. I think 'twas Soto that your honour means.

The Bard's Ghost

De Vere. 'Tis very true: thou didst it excellent.
Well, you are come to me in a happy time;
The rather for I have some sport in hand
Wherein your cunning can assist me much.
There is a lord will hear you play to-night:
But I am doubtful of your modesties;
Lest over-eyeing of his odd behavior,--
For yet his honour never heard a play--
You break into some merry passion
And so offend him; for I tell you, sirs,
If you should smile he grows impatient.

A Player. Fear not, my lord: we can contain ourselves,
Were he the veriest antic in the world.

De Vere. Go, sirrah, take them to the buttery,
And give them friendly welcome every one:
Let them want nothing that my house affords.

Exit one with the Players.

Sirrah, go you to Barthol'mew my page,
And see him dress'd in all suits like a lady:
That done, conduct him to the drunkard's chamber;
And call him 'madam,' do him obeisance.
Tell him from me, as he will win my love,
He bear himself with honourable action,
Such as he hath observed in noble ladies
Unto their lords, by them accomplished:
Such duty to the drunkard let him do
With soft low tongue and lowly courtesy,
And say 'What is't your honour will command,
Wherein your lady and your humble wife
May show her duty and make known her love?'
And then with kind embracements, tempting kisses,
And with declining head into his bosom,
Bid him shed tears, as being overjoy'd
To see her noble lord restored to health,
Who for this seven years hath esteem'd him
No better than a poor and loathsome beggar:
And if the boy have not a woman's gift
To rain a shower of commanded tears,
An onion will do well for such a shift,

Which in a napkin being close convey'd
Shall in despite enforce a watery eye.
See this dispatch'd with all the haste thou canst:
Anon I'll give thee more instructions.

Exit a Servingman.

I know the boy will well usurp the grace,
Voice, gait and action of a gentlewoman:
I long to hear him call the drunkard husband,
And how my men will stay themselves from laughter
When they do homage to this simple peasant.
I'll in to counsel them; haply my presence
May well abate the over-merry spleen
Which otherwise would grow into extremes.

Exeunt.

Lights up inside the bar, where Falstaff is tidying up. A few patrons are congregated at the corner table.

Dull enters.

Dull. Good morrow, Sir John. Looks like the usual suspects.   RB

Falstaff. No suspect here, your Lordship, just the light mead crowd.

Dull. A few flagons have passed bye and bye those innocent lips.

Falstaff. A final indulgence 'fore Shrovetide nary dents the barrel. [*Serves Dull.*]

Dull. If it leads to an honest confession, I'll drink to that.

Falstaff. Nothing to confess 'mongst us, good sir. We're altar boys to the last.

Dull. Speaking of the profane, your friend Master Brooks must be quivering, with de Vere leaving town.

Falstaff. One must be cautious in these matters, as you've cautioned me,

Dull. Word has it that the Earl and Lord Burghley have had it out over our Anne's honor and the spies whom the Lord Treasurer hath tailing his hot-headed son-in-law.

Falstaff. A Hotspur is de Vere in mind and in deed. No telling what fortune that rift will bring.

Dull. It appears we'll know soon enough.

Falstaff. At last we meet.

> *Enter de Vere.*

De Vere. Good morrow, gents.

Dull. Your Grace.

Falstaff. My Lord. A pleasure to receive you in my humble house.

De Vere. A house of intrigue may hardly be humble
With the likes of n'er-do-wells and plotters.

Falstaff. I assure you, my liege, we consort with no criminals.

> *Robin enters with a bag of money with which he tries to impress the other drinkers.*

De Vere. It is the wont of conspirators to avoid scrutiny, but lawlessness eventually yields its insidious intent.

Dull. Well said, your lordship. My occupation informs me of this very same wisdom. We remain vigilant.

Falstaff. I trust you'll find no such subterfuge here.

Dull. Trust that notion not, if ye be guilty.

Falstaff. I pray thou hast not found a trace of such.

De Vere. Pray as ye like, t'is not my affair.
I am brought to celebrate another hunt.

Falstaff [*Draws draught for de Vere.*]. Then celebrate shall we your good fortune.

De Vere. Your libations do please, but it is your page I desire.

Falstaff. Surely you do not share Master Page's peccadilloes?

De Vere. I know not to what you refer in this, but a message delivered is my suit.

Falstaff. For that he may be suited, if he hath not been ridden too roughly. [*Motions to Robin.*]

De Vere. There will be no buggery in this venture.

   Robin crosses and waits.

                                   Love's Labour's Lost, III, i, 165-207

De Vere. Our fair queen comes to hunt here in the park,
And in her train there is a gentle lady;
When tongues speak sweetly, then they name her name,
And Rosaline they call her: ask for her;
And to her white hand see thou do commend
This seal'd-up counsel. There's thy guerdon; go. [*Giving him a shilling.*]

Robin. Garden, O sweet garden! better than remuneration, a'leven-pence farthing better: most sweet garden! I will do it sir, in print. Garden! Remuneration! [*He exits.*]

De Vere. And I, forsooth, in love! I, that have been love's whip;
A very beadle to a humorous sigh;
A critic, nay, a night-watch constable;
A domineering pedant o'er the boy;
Than whom no mortal so magnificent!
This whimpled, whining, purblind, wayward boy;
This senior-junior, giant-dwarf, Dan Cupid;
Regent of love-rhymes, lord of folded arms,
The anointed sovereign of sighs and groans,
Liege of all loiterers and malcontents,
Dread prince of plackets, king of codpieces,
Sole imperator and great general
Of trotting 'paritors:--O my little heart:--

And I to be a corporal of his field,
And wear his colours like a tumbler's hoop!
What, I! I love! I sue! I seek a life!
A woman, that is like a German clock,
Still a-repairing, ever out of frame,
And never going aright, being a watch,
But being watch'd that it may still go right!
Nay, to be perjured, which is worst of all;
And, among three, to love the worst of all;
A wightly wanton with a velvet brow,
With two pitch-balls stuck in her face for eyes;
Ay, and by heaven, one that will do the deed
Though Argus were her eunuch and her guard:
And I to sigh for her! to watch for her!
To pray for her! Go to; it is a plague
That Cupid will impose for my neglect
Of his almighty dreadful little might.
Well, I will love, write, sigh, pray, sue and groan:
Some men must love my lady and some Joan. [*He exits.*]

Falstaff. Now the celebration is ours to toast.   RB
Did I not counsel that de Vere lacks couth,
Flinging himself like a moth to the flame?
No sooner doth he offend Treasury
By charging foul deeds to his daughter's name,
And mocking him for ill-devised spying
Than he goes off full-cocked and in full view!

Dull. And in this you find comfort for your plans?

Falstaff. Aye, sir, for a man in the throes of lust
Is apt to leave his jewels unguarded.
So I shall profit as Brooks makes merry
While de Vere with Rosaline doth tarry.

Dull. And of Mistress Page?

Falstaff.   Icing on the cake.

Act II, Scene IV

Appendix 4 « 521

Time: Late 16th Century
Place: A bedchamber in de Vere's house

The Taming of the Shrew, Induction, II, 1-147

Enter aloft Shakspere, with Attendants; some with apparel, others with basin and ewer and appurtenances; and de Vere.

Shakspere. For God's sake, a pot of small ale.

First Servant. Will't please your lordship drink a cup of sack?

Second Servant. Will't please your honour taste of these conserves?

Third Servant. What raiment will your honour wear to-day?

Shakspere. I am William Shakspere; call not me 'honour' nor 'lordship:' I ne'er drank sack in my life; and if you give me any conserves, give me conserves of beef: ne'er ask me what raiment I'll wear; for I have no more doublets than backs, no more stockings than legs, nor no more shoes than feet; nay, sometimes more feet than shoes, or such shoes as my toes look through the over-leather.

De Vere. Heaven cease this idle humour in your honour! O, that a mighty man of such descent, Of such possessions and so high esteem, Should be infused with so foul a spirit!

Shakspere. What, would you make me mad? Am not I William Shakspere, old John's son of Wilmecote, by birth a farmer, by education a trader, by transmutation a glovemaker, and now by present profession an Alderman? Ask Marian Hacket, the fat ale-wife of Wincot, if she know me not: if she say I am not fourteen pence on the score for sheer ale, score me up for the lyingest knave in Christendom. What! I am not bestraught: here's—

Third Servant. O, this it is that makes your lady mourn!

Second Servant. O, this is it that makes your servants droop!

De Vere. Hence comes it that your kindred shuns your house,
As beaten hence by your strange lunacy.
O noble lord, bethink thee of thy birth,
Call home thy ancient thoughts from banishment
And banish hence these abject lowly dreams.
Look how thy servants do attend on thee,
Each in his office ready at thy beck.
Wilt thou have music? hark! Apollo plays,

   Music.

And twenty caged nightingales do sing:
Or wilt thou sleep? we'll have thee to a couch
Softer and sweeter than the lustful bed
On purpose trimm'd up for Semiramis.
Say thou wilt walk; we will bestrew the ground:
Or wilt thou ride? thy horses shall be trapp'd,
Their harness studded all with gold and pearl.
Dost thou love hawking? thou hast hawks will soar
Above the morning lark or wilt thou hunt?
Thy hounds shall make the welkin answer them
And fetch shrill echoes from the hollow earth.

   First Servant. Say thou wilt course; thy greyhounds are as swift
As breathed stags, ay, fleeter than the roe.

   Second Servant. Dost thou love pictures? we will fetch thee straight
Adonis painted by a running brook,
And Cytherea all in sedges hid,
Which seem to move and wanton with her breath,
Even as the waving sedges play with wind.

   De Vere. We'll show thee Io as she was a maid,
And how she was beguiled and surprised,
As lively painted as the deed was done.

   Third Servant. Or Daphne roaming through a thorny wood,
Scratching her legs that one shall swear she bleeds,
And at that sight shall sad Apollo weep,
So workmanly the blood and tears are drawn.

De Vere. Thou art a lord, and nothing but a lord:
Thou hast a lady far more beautiful
Than any woman in this waning age.

First Servant. And till the tears that she hath shed for thee
Like envious floods o'er-run her lovely face,
She was the fairest creature in the world;
And yet she is inferior to none.

Shakspere. Am I a lord? and have I such a lady?
Or do I dream? or have I dream'd till now?
I do not sleep: I see, I hear, I speak;
I smell sweet savours and I feel soft things:
Upon my life, I am a lord indeed
And not a grain dealer nor Will Shakspere.
Well, bring our lady hither to our sight;
And once again, a pot o' the smallest ale.

Second Servant. Will't please your mightiness to wash your hands?
O, how we joy to see your wit restored!
O, that once more you knew but what you are!
These fifteen years you have been in a dream;
Or when you waked, so waked as if you slept.

Shakspere. These fifteen years! by my fay, a goodly nap.
But did I never speak of all that time?

First Servant. O, yes, my lord, but very idle words:
For though you lay here in this goodly chamber,
Yet would you say ye were beaten out of door;
And rail upon the hostess of the house;
And say you would present her at the leet,
Because she brought stone jugs and no seal'd quarts:
Sometimes you would call out for Cicely Hacket.

Shakspere. Ay, the woman's maid of the house.

Third Servant. Why, sir, you know no house nor no such maid,
Nor no such men as you have reckon'd up,
As John Shakspere and did John Naps of Greece
And Peter Turph and Henry Pimpernell
And twenty more such names and men as these
Which never were nor no man ever saw.

Shakspere. Now Lord be thanked for my good amends!

All. Amen.

Shakspere. I thank thee: thou shalt not lose by it.

> *Enter the Page as a lady, with attendants.*

Page. How fares my noble lord?

Shakspere. Marry, I fare well for here is cheer enough.
Where is my wife?

Page. Here, noble lord: what is thy will with her?

Shakspere. Are you my wife and will not call me husband?
My men should call me 'lord:' I am your goodman.

Page. My husband and my lord, my lord and husband;
I am your wife in all obedience.

Shakspere. I know it well. What must I call her?

De Vere. Madam.

Shakspere. Al'ce madam, or Joan madam?

De Vere. 'Madam,' and nothing else: so lords
call ladies.

Shakspere. Madam wife, they say that I have dream'd
And slept above some fifteen year or more.

Page. Ay, and the time seems thirty unto me,
Being all this time abandon'd from your bed.

Shakspere. 'Tis much. Servants, leave me and her alone.
Madam, undress you and come now to bed.

Page. Thrice noble lord, let me entreat of you
To pardon me yet for a night or two,
Or, if not so, until the sun be set:

For your physicians have expressly charged,
In peril to incur your former malady,
That I should yet absent me from your bed:
I hope this reason stands for my excuse.

Shakspere. Ay, it stands so that I may hardly
tarry so long. But I would be loath to fall into
my dreams again: I will therefore tarry in
despite of the flesh and the blood.

Enter a Messenger.

Messenger. Your honour's players, heating your amendment,
Are come to play a pleasant comedy;
For so your doctors hold it very meet,
Seeing too much sadness hath congeal'd your blood,
And melancholy is the nurse of frenzy:
Therefore they thought it good you hear a play
And frame your mind to mirth and merriment,
Which bars a thousand harms and lengthens life.

Shakspere. Marry, I will, let them play it. Is not a comonty a Christmas gambold or a tumbling-trick?

Page. No, my good lord; it is more pleasing stuff.

Shakspere. What, household stuff?

Page. It is a kind of history.

Shakspere. Well, well see't. Come, madam wife, sit by my side and let the world slip: we shall ne'er be younger.

They sit and watch the play.

Act II, Scene V

Time: Present
Place: Purgatory

Christ, visible in half-light, considers de Vere.

De Vere. And thus one William Shakspere, son of the Borough Ale-Taster—alias Christopher Sly in *The Taming of the Shrew*, William in *As You Like It*, Bottom in *A Midsummer-Night's Dream*, et al—through gradual force of conviction upon his pickled mind became William Shakespeare: as so often happens with liars who repeat their confabulations, they eventually inhabit them wholly. A wild card as this is good for anything; and so, conveniently, in our present play, our rustic serves additionally to stand in as the rustic observer and mock my own marital masquerade.

Act II, Scene VI

Time: Late 16th Century.
Place: Burghley's study, Cecil House

Christ, visible in half-light, considers de Vere.

Burghley. How does my good Lord de Vere?   *Hamlet, II, ii, 171-221*

De Vere. Well, God-a-mercy.

Burghley. Do you know me, my lord?

De Vere. Excellent well; you are a fishmonger.

Burghley. Not I, my lord.

De Vere. Then I would you were so honest a man.

Burghley. Honest, my lord!

De Vere. Ay, sir; to be honest, as this world goes, is to be one man picked out of ten thousand.

Burghley. Very true, my lord.

De Vere. For if the sun breed maggots in a dead dog, being a god kissing carrion,--Have you a daughter?

Burghley. I have, my lord.

De Vere. Let her not walk i' the sun: conception is a blessing: but not as your daughter may conceive. Friend, look to 't.

Burghley. [*Aside.*] How say you by that? Still harping on my daughter: yet he knew me not at first; he said I was a fishmonger: he is far gone, far gone: and truly in my youth I suffered much extremity for love; very near this. I'll speak to him again. What do you read, my lord?

De Vere. Words, words, words.

Burghley. What is the matter, my lord?

De Vere. Between who?

Burghley. I mean, the matter that you read, my lord.

De Vere. Slanders, sir: for the satirical rogue says here that old men have grey beards, that their faces are wrinkled, their eyes purging thick amber and plum-tree gum and that they have a plentiful lack of wit, together with most weak hams: all which, sir, though I most powerfully and potently believe, yet I hold it not honesty to have it thus set down, for yourself, sir, should be old as I am, if like a crab you could go backward.

Burghley. [*Aside.*] Though this be madness, yet there is method in 't. Will you walk out of the air, my lord?

De Vere. Into my grave.

Burghley. Indeed, that is out o' the air.
[*Aside.*]
How pregnant sometimes his replies are! a happiness that often madness hits on, which reason and sanity could not so prosperously be delivered of. I will leave him, and suddenly contrive the means of meeting between him and my daughter. --My honourable lord, I will most humbly take my leave of you.

The Bard's Ghost

De Vere. You cannot, sir, take from me any thing that I will
more willingly part withal: except my life, except
my life, except my life and my lands.   RB

Burghley. Sir, I have no aims on your land.

De Vere. Say you; says he, "Aims not have I on your land."
Yet in trust he holds in trust these treasures.

Burghley. [*Aside.*] Again, he makes sense in riddles,
For I do hold such estates in escrow
Against such distemper re my daughter,
And his tracts intemperate and impious
'Gainst our fair church and royals alike
Dost further advise such encumbrances.

De Vere. And spies, spies, spies he dost read'ly espouse!
One wonders how you unapprised remain
Of your Anne's black stain on our marriage bed.

Burghley. Still you insist on such libelous charge
Rememb'ring not your affection for grape
And bedding down in the dark with your wife—
Whilst you thought yourself a-whoring on tour.
Perchance assumed rendezvous went askew—
Then? Would not your wife intercept your seed?

De Vere. A bed trick for a pedigree dost Cecil trade
To provide a good name where none now lies.

Burghley. It shall be my oak that nature doth spare
When England's saplings are dried and fallen.

De Vere. Blight has a knowing way of weeding out
Those born from acorns and those born from nuts.

Hamlet, II, ii, 222-223

Burghley. Fare you well, my lord.

De Vere.   These tedious old fools!

Act II, Scene VII

Time: Late 16th Century
Place: A bedchamber in de Vere's house

Page. Is the mask to your liking, my Lord? RB

Shakspere. What mask?

Page. The entertainment.

Shakspere. Me thought this was me own household that quarreled thus.

Page. Your household, yes—the players within it. They perform a story for your consideration.

Shakspere. What think you, wife, a Lord should say of all this?

Page. A son mocks his wife's father and the honor of his wife, his wife's father's daughter.

Shakspere. Surely such things are make believe. Do we act thusly?

Page. We must, my Lord, else why wouldst thou have written such?

Shakspere. I, my wife, have written such a play?

Page. You have forgotten that as well?

Shakspere. I struggle penning my own name to paper—never the same way twice.

Page. You are a victim of your memory lost upon some spirits—and we, victims too, bereft of your poetry.

Shakspere. And what do we call our amusement?

Page. 'The Bard's Ghost,' sire—a clever jest!

Shakspere. I see no shadow.

Page. Look more closely. In vanity you'll find its reflection.

Shakspere. I shall work on't then: My attention shall inform me.

Act II, Scene VIII

Time: Late 16th Century
Place: The bar at the Garter Inn

Falstaff and Dull at the bar. De Vere enters.

Falstaff. What hear you from our Robin—a message returned?

De Vere. Alas, I am alone in a black sea
Cast away and marooned by my belov'd.

Falstaff. What is it that so troubles fair Romeo?

De Vere. Sweet Rosaline answers not my missives!

Falstaff. Perhaps she is taking care with her heart?

Enter Robin with a letter for de Vere.

De Vere. What is it, boy?

Robin. A note back from the lady.

De Vere. A note from the lady to whom you delivered my missive?

Robin. Ay, sire.

De Vere reads note, then waxes poetic.

Love's Labour's Lost, IV, iii, 302-304

De Vere. From women's eyes this doctrine I derive;
They are the ground, the books, the academes
From whence doth spring the true Promethean fire.

Love's Labour's Lost, IV, iii, 312-317

For where is any author in the world
Teaches such beauty as a woman's eye?
Learning is but an adjunct to ourself
And where we are our learning likewise is:
Then when ourselves we see in ladies' eyes,
Do we not likewise see our learning there?

Love's Labour's Lost, IV, iii, 324-354

Other slow arts entirely keep the brain;
And therefore, finding barren practisers,
Scarce show a harvest of their heavy toil:
But love, first learned in a lady's eyes,
Lives not alone immured in the brain;
But, with the motion of all elements,
Courses as swift as thought in every power,
And gives to every power a double power,
Above their functions and their offices.
It adds a precious seeing to the eye;
A lover's eyes will gaze an eagle blind;
A lover's ear will hear the lowest sound,
When the suspicious head of theft is stopp'd:
Love's feeling is more soft and sensible
Than are the tender horns of cockl'd snails;
Love's tongue proves dainty Bacchus gross in taste:
For valour, is not Love a Hercules,
Still climbing trees in the Hesperides?
Subtle as Sphinx; as sweet and musical
As bright Apollo's lute, strung with his hair:
And when Love speaks, the voice of all the gods
Makes heaven drowsy with the harmony.
Never durst poet touch a pen to write
Until his ink were temper'd with Love's sighs;
O, then his lines would ravish savage ears
And plant in tyrants mild humility.
From women's eyes this doctrine I derive:
They sparkle still the right Promethean fire;
They are the books, the arts, the academes,
That show, contain and nourish all the world:
Else none at all in ought proves excellent.

Love's Labour's Lost, IV, iii, 366

Falstaff. Saint Cupid, then! and, soldiers, to the field!

De Vere exits.

Dull. Even to a seasoned eye as my own   RB
I detect no falsehood in such behavior.

Falstaff. 'Tis as I said then, that de Vere be daft
And that his cuckoldry a guileless crime.

Dull. Guileless toward de Vere it well may be,
But the Lord Burghley will see no such thing
And in the settlement of that dispute
We shall see whether the adage rings true
That: the pen is mightier than the sword.

Falstaff. With impunity then shall Master Brook
Have the leisure to dally with fair Anne
Each tryst recompens'd measure for measure.

Act II, Scene IX

Time: Present
Place: Purgatory

Christ, visible in half-light, considers de Vere.

De Vere. I would be remiss here if I did not point out the florid style of my rhetoric in the preceding scene—and indeed the style in the entirety of *Love's Labour's Lost* from whence it is drawn—that has been the source of much historical confusion on the part of so-called Shakespearean scholars; conveniently, my present illustration also serves to point out how, much in the style of pre-Copernican apologists for the Catholic Church's earth-centered solar system, such academes have had to stretch the credulity of their arguments in an attempt to shoehorn the Stratfordian Shakspere into the persona of author of my work and biographer of my life.

Like many master artists of my day, I employed other craftsmen, most notably Anthony Mundy and John Lyly, not only to serve as secretaries to tend to my personal correspondence and papers, and to support their poetry and prose works, but also to serve as my protégés, coloring between the lines, as it were, in a few of my plays. During this period of employment, from 1580 to 1582, Euphuism was the vogue and its Baroque verbiage the genre for courtly poetry and masks.

And while I have derived much insight and delight from Baldassare Castiglione's *The Courtier* as a guide for proper conduct of the Renaissance nobleman, the generally "sanctimonious tone and omniscient voice"[11] of such tracts is ripe for satire, as Munday and Lyly and I so ably illustrated in our work, *Love's Labour's Lost*, and my own then anonymous poem, "Pain of Pleasure," recently attributed to me by the literary scholar and novelist, Sarah Smith. These excesses made perfect sense at the time, but when placed upon the timeline of Shakspere ten years later, would have been passé.

Stratfordians may point out that this is less an obstacle than *my* claims to a few plays that were first performed after my death. This is a desperate metaphor. There were certain subjects that even I could not broach in a mask at court, not the least of which was highlighted in the Scottish play where I call into question Elizabeth's strained rationalizations for executing her half-sister Mary Stuart, Queen of the Scots.

In fact, the plays produced after my death are an argument in my favor, to wit: no newsworthy events that took place after 1604, when I died—comets and kings, court gossip and weather, and such, of which I was so fond of employing to time-stamp my work—appear in any of my plays! None! Topical references ended with my death: end of story.

By now you get the drift: the plays and all the rest mirror my life. So it is, as I said early on this evening, "surely the prints of a *certain* man are upon the immort'l words of the Bard." [*He looks from the audience to Jesus and back to the audience for some recognition.*]

Act II, Scene X

Time: Late 16th Century
Place: Idyllic pond on an English estate

---

[11] Anderson, *op. cit.*, p. 160.

534 » The Bard's Ghost

Christ from one vantage point and Shakspere and Page from another, visible in half-light, consider de Vere and Vavasor in a row boat.

De Vere and Vavasor's sentiments parallel Act I, Scene V, in the bathing quarters at Hedingham, though more refined, de Vere voicing an extended version of the same sonnet he quoted to her earlier. Vavasor's pregnancy is beginning to show.

   De Vere.   Sonnet 38, 7-12
For who's so dumb that cannot write to thee,
When thou thyself dost give invention light?
Be thou the tenth Muse, ten times more in worth
Than those old nine which rhymers invocate;
And he that calls on thee, let him bring forth
Eternal numbers to outlive long date.

   Vavasor. Flattery, my bard, is the Devil's card.   RB
What say ye demon Edward to our sins?

   De Vere. If pleasure and love be not of the Lord
Then surely he hath cut a bad bargain.

   Vavasor. And after the Lord comes our fair Regent—
Surely 'Rosaline's' mask fools not the Queen,
And her wrath that guards this vestal virgin?

   De Vere. It is 'Shake-speare's' pen that praises you thus,
Not the Lord Great Chamberlain [*Bows.*], late of court.

   Vavasor.   Romeo and Juliet, II, ii, 43-44
What's in a name? That which we call a rose
By any other name would smell as sweet;

So the poet's rhyme reveals its maker.   RB

   De Vere. That you see darkness here surpriseth not,
Forsooth,
       "...my mistress' [brows] are raven black,   Sonnet 127, 9-14
Her eyes so suited, and they mourners seem
At such who, not born fair, no beauty lack,
Sland'ring creation with a false esteem:

Yet so they mourn, becoming of their woe,
That every tongue says beauty should look so."

Vavasor. These eyes mourn the brevity of our trysts,   RB
And the bloodless months that grow witness here
To our most perfect lovemaking and desire.
These signs cannot escape your father-in-law,
Or your wife, 'Ophelia'[12] of the Cecils.

De Vere. "...why should others' false adulterate eyes   *Sonnet 121, 5-8*
Give salutation to my sportive blood?
Or on my frailties why are frailer spies,
Which in their wills count bad what I count good?"

Vavasor. Were your value judged by your art alone,   RB
Then we would fear not what is in our heart,
But the shackles of London's dark Tower
Are lock'd by a turnkey from us apart.

De Vere. A dark and dank fate that invites my death
Is a scene I'd rather cut from my life.
Instead I endeavor to set the stage
And seal an understanding with my wife. [*They paddle off.*]

Act II, Scene XI

Time: Present
Place: Purgatory

Christ, visible in half-light, considers de Vere.

De Vere. As I mentioned earlier, my affair with Anne Vavasor scandalized the court, and immediately after the birth of our so-called illegitimate son we were both incarcerated in the Tower of London. Eventually, I was freed by the intercession of the inestimable Sir Walter Raleigh; though the Queen's ardent desire for fresh poetry from my pen did not hurt the cause either.

---

[12] Ophelia is derived from the Greek word for "profit" or "indebtedness," in reference to Anne's dowry of £15,000, which was both for de Vere: cash for his profligacy put him in Burghley's debt.

I say ardent because the wound to Elizabeth, while officially attributed to my transgression against one of her vestal virgins, was, in private, a blow to her own ego, as a lover scorned. Happily, as I've noted, we were reconciled, and our relationship rekindled. But don't misunderstand me: Elizabeth was a brilliant woman who rejected marriage because she refused to be ruled by any man, being as she was Great Britain, for whom she vouchsafed a special place in her heart for the finest poetry and drama—a heart that still beats strongly today. Given that she was my monarch, not to mention the strictures of courtly behavior, I am foresworn from discussing the details of our relationship, but suffice it to say, my income from the Queen's list, as noted by Dull earlier, went way beyond my ancestral privileges as the Lord Great Chamberlain of England or as the most favored poet at court.

I make no excuses for my behavior other than to say my earthly appetites often feasted while my reputation, my purse, and my marriage starved. My poetry, on the other hand, thrived. I pray that this peculiar but necessary dynamic shall not deny me salvation. [*He looks hopefully from the audience to Jesus and back.*]

Act II, Scene XII

Time: Late 16th Century
Place: Anne Cecil's quarters, Hampton House

Christ, visible in half-light, considers the proceedings, as do Shakspere and Page.

Hamlet, III, i, 43-55

Burghley. Daughter Anne, walk you here. Gracious, so please you,
We will bestow ourselves.
Read on this book;
That show of such an exercise may colour
Your loneliness. We are oft to blame in this,--
'Tis too much proved--that with devotion's visage
And pious action we do sugar o'er
The devil himself.

Burghley. I hear him coming: I must withdraw promptly.

Burghley hides behind the curtain. Enter de Vere.

De Vere.   *Hamlet, III, i, 56-59*
To be, or not to be: that is the question:
Whether 'tis nobler in the mind to suffer
The slings and arrows of outrageous fortune,
Or to take arms against a sea of troubles,

                                                               Hamlet, III, i, 70-169
For who would bear the whips and scorns of time,
The oppressor's wrong, the proud man's contumely,
The pangs of despised love, the law's delay,
The insolence of office and the spurns
That patient merit of the unworthy takes,
When he himself might his quietus make
With a bare bodkin? who would fardels bear,
To grunt and sweat under a weary life,
But that the dread of something after death,
The undiscover'd country from whose bourn
No traveller returns, puzzles the will
And makes us rather bear those ills we have
Than fly to others that we know not of?
Thus conscience does make cowards of us all;
And thus the native hue of resolution
Is sicklied o'er with the pale cast of thought,
And enterprises of great pith and moment
With this regard their currents turn awry,
And lose the name of action.--Soft you now!
My fair wife Anne! Nymph, in thy orisons
Be all my sins remember'd.

  Anne. Good my lord,
How does your honour for this many a day?

  De Vere. I humbly thank you; well, well, well.

  Anne. My lord, I have remembrances of yours,
That I have longed long to re-deliver;
I pray you, now receive them.

  De Vere. No, not I;
I never gave you aught.

Anne. My honour'd lord, you know right well you did;
And, with them, words of so sweet breath composed
As made the things more rich: their perfume lost,
Take these again; for to the noble mind
Rich gifts wax poor when givers prove unkind.
There, my lord. [*She holds out his letters.*]

   *Burghley drops his ring of keys. De Vere looks toward the
   curtain, then back to Anne.*

De Vere. Ha, ha! are you honest?

Anne. My lord?

De Vere. Are you fair?

Anne. What means your lordship?

De Vere. That if you be honest and fair, your honesty should admit no discourse to your beauty.

Anne. Could beauty, my lord, have better commerce than with honesty?

De Vere. Ay, truly; for the power of beauty will sooner transform honesty from what it is to a bawd than the force of honesty can translate beauty into his likeness: this was sometime a paradox, but now the time gives it proof. I did love you once.

Anne. Indeed, my lord, you made me believe so.

De Vere. You should not have believed me; for virtue cannot so inoculate our old stock but we shall relish of it: I loved you not.

Anne. I was the more deceived.

De Vere. Get thee to a nunnery: why wouldst thou be a breeder of sinners? I am myself indifferent honest; but yet I could accuse me of such things that it were better my mother had not borne me: I am very

proud, revengeful, ambitious, with more offences at
my beck than I have thoughts to put them in,
imagination to give them shape, or time to act them
in. What should such fellows as I do crawling
between earth and heaven? We are arrant knaves,
all; believe none of us. Go thy ways to a nunnery.
Where's your father?

Anne. At home, my lord.

De Vere. [*With reference to the curtain.*]
Let the doors be shut upon him, that he may play the
fool no where but in's own house. Farewell.

Anne. O, help him, you sweet heavens!

De Vere. If thou dost in our marriage persist,
I'll give thee this plague for insistence:
Be thou as chaste as ice, as pure as
snow, thou shalt not escape calumny. Get thee to a
nunnery, go: farewell. Or, if thou wilt needs
pairing, pair with a fool; for wise men know well enough
what monsters you make of them. To a nunnery, go,
and quickly too. Farewell.

Anne. O heavenly powers, restore him!

De Vere. I have heard of your paintings too, well enough; God
has given you one face, and you make yourselves
another: you jig, you amble, and you lisp, and
nick-name God's creatures, and make your wantonness
your ignorance. Go to, I'll no more on't; it hath
made me mad. I say, we will have no more of our marriage:
To a nunnery, go. [*He exits.*]

Jesus grimaces at the scene.

Anne. O, what a noble mind is here o'erthrown!
The courtier's, soldier's, scholar's, eye, tongue, sword;
The expectancy and rose of the fair state,
The glass of fashion and the mould of form,
The observed of all observers, quite, quite down!
And I, of ladies most deject and wretched,

That suck'd the honey of his music vows,
Now see that noble and most sovereign reason,
Like sweet bells jangled, out of tune and harsh;
That unmatch'd form and feature of blown youth
Blasted with ecstasy: O, woe is me,
To have seen what I have seen, see what I see!

Second Intermission

Act III, Scene I

Time: Present
Place: Purgatory

Christ from one vantage point, and Shakspere and Page from another, visible in half-light, consider de Vere's argument.

RB

De Vere. With our parallel plots now established, I thought it fitting to revisit my earlier remarks concerning the use of such devices to reinforce and elaborate upon the drama of my principal storyline. With Anne reeling from my rejection and Burghley scrambling to repair the damage, and I licking my wounds at Castle Hedingham, devoting myself to my writing and assuming the posture of lord of the manor, the de Veres and the Cecils find themselves in the depths of despair, while Shakspere is coming into his own as a counterfeit lord and auteur poseur.

I must admit that my employment of this dramatic counterpoint comes as a relief to me, having felt some trepidation at shaking off the rust of 400 years and attempting to grab your attention with some catchy plot that serves my case. Admittedly, this is not the sophisticated orchestration of *Lear*, but, then again, this is *commedia*, something I enjoyed first hand during my travels on the continent and was eager to incorporate in my own work.

One issue that has always puzzled so-called Shakespearen scholars is the unfinished nature of the subplot in *The Taming of the Shrew*, that is, the story of Christopher Sly, who has been stripped of his pseudonym here and laid bare as Shakspere. I must say that the opportunity to recreate the lost scenes to serve my redemption is an event I never anticipated, but such is the beauty of life, or the afterlife in my case.

Act III, Scene II

Time: Early 17th Century
Place: A bedchamber in de Vere's house

Shakspere and his wife (the Page) converse about what they have been watching.

Shakspere. Find you this Italian odd?

Page. My Lord?

Shakspere. The fancy fellow with two women: Is he not strange? He makes my native language a foreign tongue, one with which I'm not familiar.

Page. You, who spend your fortune on fancy raiment's, scorn this eloquence? You would do well to emulate such culture. De Vere is no Italian, though he finds much there to imitate—the sincerest flattery.

Shakspere. Hush woman! Am I not your Lord and master?

Page. How quickly your guilty conscience doth bring you to grasp the reins!

Shakspere. My reawakened memory, Madam, not conscience! Hush now, or I shall have my rights!

Page. Yes, yes, of course my Lord. [*Aside.*] With what vengeance you've become what you feigned to be.

Act III, Scene III

Time: Early 17th Century
Place: Anne Cecil's Quarters, Hampton House

Christ, visible in half-light, considers the proceedings.

> *Burghley is conferring with his daughter, Anne. He hides behind the curtain as he hears de Vere's approaching footsteps.*

De Vere. Now, wife, what's the matter?   *Hamlet, III, iv, 8-38*

Anne. Edward, thou hast my father much offended.

De Vere. Anne, you have my honor much offended.

Anne. Once more you answer with an unkind tongue.

De Vere. Go, go, you question with a wicked tongue.

Anne. Why, how now, Edward!

De Vere. What's the matter now?

Anne. Have you forgot me?

De Vere. No, by the rood, not so:
You are my wife, my guardian's daughter;
And—so you say—the mother of my child.

Anne. Nay, then, I'll defer to those who can speak.

De Vere. Come, come, and sit you down; you shall not budge;
You go not till I set you up a glass
Where you may see the inmost part of you.

Anne. What wilt thou do? thou wilt not murder me?
Help, help, ho!

Burghley [*Behind.*]. What, ho! help, help, help!

De Vere [*Drawing his sword.*]. How now! a rat? Dead, for a ducat, dead!

> *Makes a pass through the arras.*

Burghley [*Behind.*]. O, I am slain!

Falls and dies.

Christ sees the irony in this. He shakes his head and laughs, recognizing that this is a play representing de Vere's feelings, not a real murder.

Anne. O me, what hast thou done?

De Vere. Nay, I know not:
Is it your father?

Anne. O, what a rash and bloody deed is this!

De Vere. A bloody deed! almost as bad, good wife,
As marry an Earl, and bed a stranger.

Anne. As bed a stranger!

De Vere. Ay, lady, 'twas my word.

Lifts up the arras and discovers Burghley.

Thou wretched, rash, intruding fool, farewell!
Who feigns to be my father: take thy fortune;
Thou find'st to be too busy is some danger.
Leave wringing of your hands: peace! sit you down,
And let me wring your heart; for so I shall,
If it be made of penetrable stuff,
If damned custom have not brass'd it so
That it is proof and bulwark against sense.

Christ appears skeptical of de Vere's rationale.

Act III, Scene IV

Time: Present
Place: Purgatory

Christ, visible in half-light, considers de Vere.

RB

De Vere. As you can see, my family suffered greatly in real and imagined worlds for my traumas, and while I grant you that in the interests of drama I took liberties with the facts—but this is fiction, where such poetic license is sanctioned. And after all, is it not the artist's responsibility to find art in the seemingly mundane details of life? I admit I was a teller of tall tales, especially after some drink, but much of my life was so outlandish, who could tell the difference? Of course, these behavioral excesses do not go unnoticed in this world or the next, as my savior has indicated. [*He notes Jesus.*] As the time draws nigh for your judgment of Edward de Vere and William Shakspere, such questions begin to weigh heavy on my conscience.

Act III, Scene V

Time: Shakespeare's birthday celebration, the first Saturday after April 23rd, late 20th Century
Place: Stratford-on-Avon

On a street in Stratford-on-Avon (next to the Holy Trinity Church), Elizabethan gaiety prevails. There is music, and most of the participants are costumed, with a few scattered tourists taking snapshots and eating turkey legs and confections.

Christ, visible in half-light, considers the proceedings.

[I.] *Rogue.* How now, that sallow sow full of himself? RB

[II.] *Rogue.* A glovemaker's son whose rough hand ill fits
The verse it's presum'd to have engender'd.

Shakspere leads the parade. Then, he gloats as Burghley gives his pompous, but ghostly mechanical, speech. Burghley wears the same clothes from Act III, Scene III, with his shirt now blood-stained and his face pale, like a corpse. The scene is played out as if it were de Vere's nightmare. He is bathed in a greenish-yellow spotlight. The music is discordant; the lighting and characters are Fellini-esque, in the manner of Satyricon.

Burghley. You know me well, friends, as Polonius,
My advice now taken as the Bard's own, to wit:
See thou character. Give thy thoughts no tongue,   *Hamlet, I, iii, 59-67*
Nor any unproportion'd thought his act.
Be thou familiar, but by no means vulgar.
The friend thou hast, and their adoption tried,
Grapple them to the soul with hoops of steel;
But do not dull thy palm with entertainment
Of each [new]-hatch'd, unfledg'd comrade. Beware
Of entrance to a quarrel; but being in,
Bear 't that the opposed may beware of thee ...

> *De Vere fumes as Polonius goes on. In the following sequence, his speech is cross-hatched with Polonius' continuous speech (whose voice drops during the overlap), ending as Polonius begins with "Neither a borrower nor a lender be ..."*

De Vere. [*To the audience.*]   RB
Corambus[13] I called this two-heart'd poseur,
In the image of my guardian assign'd,
Though guarded me not 'cept to save his self,
William Cecil, Lord Burghley by title.
As Polonius did he reassign
My player's name to void such aspersions,
As this list being well known in his day.

Burghley. [*Lowers voice.*]   *Hamlet, I, iii, 68-80*
... Give every man thine ear, but few thy voice;
Take each man's censure, but reserve thy judgement.
Costly thy habit as thy purse can buy,
But not express'd in fancy; rich, not gaudy;
For the apparel oft proclaims the man,
And they in France of the best rank and station
Are most select and generous in that,
[*Raises voice.*] Neither a borrower nor a lender be;
For loan oft loses both itself and friend,

---

[13] Corambis is what de Vere named the Polonius character in the first printing. *Cor ambis*, literally "two-hearted," is a swipe at Burghley's motto *Cor unum, via una*, "one heart, one way." De Vere was forced to change the name for later versions. Charlton Ogburn, *The Mysterious William Shakespeare: The Myth and the Reality*, Dodd, Mead & Company, New York, 1984, pp. 202-203.

And borrowing dulls the edge of husbandry.
This above all: to thine own self be true,
And it must follow, as the night the day,
Thou canst not then be false to any man.
                                    [*Applause.*]
And now I'd like to introduce the great playwright that put   RB
such words in my mouth, Will Shakespeare, who today we
honor on his birthday, for his unparalleled contribution to
the dramatic and poetic arts ...
                                    [*Applause.*]

   Shakspere. Thank you, my friends, and lucky am I that I might
call you thus, four centuries after my time, for
great pride do I take in the staying power of my verse
and in the heavenly station to which it has, most assuredly, assigned me.
                                    [*Applause.*]

   *Christ reacts to this braggadocio. No longer able to contain
   himself, de Vere speaks from the back of the crowd.*

   De Vere. Good people, you confuse this character with the
great Shake-speare when he is but a minor *Shakespearean*
character, Christopher Sly in fact, a beggar made gentleman
by the exigencies of courtly protocol—to criticize anonymously.
Is he not as he who one day wakes up to find himself

                        The Taming of the Shrew, Induction, i, 38-41
Wrapped in sweet clothes, rings put upon his fingers,
A most delicious banquet by his bed,
And brave attendants near him when he wakes --
Would not the beggar then forget himself?
And this tinhorn orator that would submit such puffery to our   RB
senses, is he not, as Polonius, the Lord Burghley who cleansed
the public records of this charade?"

   Shakspere. Hah! Who is this aristocratic fiend that
seeks to sully the good name of Shakespeare as if
it were his entitlement? Do not the academes and the
good merchants of Stratford speak with one voice
when we say, "The gates of Hell await thee?"

   *The crowd derides de Vere and throws food at him. They
   call him Iago, crown him with thorns, strap him to an ox*

yoke, making him a hunchback, and deride him as "Edward de Vere, King of the Ox-fordians." Christ reacts to these aggressions.

De Vere. Alas! 'tis true I have gone here and there,   *Sonnet 110*
And made myself a motley to the view;
[But] ... every word doth almost tell my name,   *Sonnet 76*
Showing their birth, and whence they did proceed.

De Vere seeks refuge in the church, collapsing on the floor before Christ. He extricates himself from his bindings as he speaks, and then goes to a bookcase and pulls a bible as a prop to reiterate his point.

De Vere. [*To the audience.*]   *Richard II, V, i, 38-50*
Think I am dead, and that even here thou tak'st,
As from my death-bed, thy last living leave.
In winter's tedious nights sit by the fire
With good old folks and let them tell thee tales
Of woeful ages long ago betid;
And ere thou bid good night, to quit their griefs
Tell thou the lamentable tale of me
And send the hearers weeping to their beds.
For why, the senseless brands will sympathize
The heavy accent of thy moving tongue,
And in compassion weep the fire out;
And some will mourn in ashes, some coal-black,
For the deposing of a rightful king.
Thence comes it that my name receives a brand,   *Sonnet 111*
And almost thence my nature is subdu'd
To what it works in, like the dyer's hand.

Christ has dismounted from the cross and approaches de Vere.

Jesus. Whilst thou take heart and in faith waiver not?   *RB*
Remember when before nail'd Messiah
Jeering Romans and myriad doubters
Stood: a serpent great is what they perceiv'd,
And seeing thus did they proceed to crown
Their demon with a mocking wreath of thorns,
Anointing him thus, "The King of the Jews."

Psalm 38 (underlined in de Vere's Geneva Bible)
As the hope of the daylight causeth us
not to be offended with the darkness
of the night, so ought we patiently
to trust that God will close our cause and
restore us to our right.

De Vere.   *Micah 7:19 (underlined in de Vere's Geneva Bible)*
I will bear the wrath of the Lord because
I have sinned against him, until he plead
My cause and execute judgement for me.
Then will he ring me forth into the light
and I shall see his righteousness.

Jesus. Make no mistake, Oxford, the spirit blind   RB
Among us fail to see rightful suasion,
Just as the Christians in your Merchant play
Did mock and abuse their Hebrew brethren,
While Shylock in turn dishonorèd them.

*De Vere in letter to Burghley, echoed
by Isabella in Measure for Measure, V, i, 45-46*
[But, t]ruth is truth, though never so old,
And time cannot make that false
Which was once true.
So must you open your heart to your wife   RB
And to events beyond appearances,
Where forgiveness is law and love doth rule.
Root yourself as the Prince of the Shakyas,
In the shade of the Bodi tree, at peace,
Knowing that through faith transcendent your cause
Shall enlist adepts of the highest rank.
Concern thyself with appropriate tasks
As I have made known to your ears today,
And be assur'd your plea is justly serv'd. [*De Vere bows.*]
Hand me the scripture upon which you've sworn
That I may exalt thee through thy rev'rence. [*De Vere hands Jesus the bible
he's holding.*]

Act III, Scene VI

Time: Present

Place: Purgatory

Christ, visible in half-light, considers de Vere.

De Vere. As I told you at the beginning of this tale, I made friends in high places, and thankfully so, for the ignominy I've suffered over the theft of my work has been a cross above and beyond what mere mortals should be asked to endure.

Having realized, however, that my literary banishment was part of a Divine Plan to serve as inspiration for an anomaly of a higher rank [*He refers to Jesus.*], I am only too happy to have suffered my humble cross. I hope you will agree, then, in the wake of this next scene, that it is not only fitting, but elegant, that my personal fortunes have been tied to that of my savior, we the two most quoted persons on the planet, by making his words my own. It is my hope that you shall consider this in your final judgment.

Act III, Scene VII

Time: Late 20th Century
Place: The Folger Shakespeare Library, Washington, D.C.

Christ, visible in half-light, considers the proceedings.

A researcher is working. The librarian enters.

Librarian. Nose to the grindstone as usual, Roger.

Researcher. Thanks to you, you know! That Geneva bible has become my millstone and doctoral dissertation, no difference.

Librarian. And how might you defend its contents?

Researcher. By comparing the biblical references in the master's plays and poems with those in the works of other candidates.

Librarian. And who might you consider thus?

Researcher. Bacon, Marlowe, and Spenser—the usual suspects.

Librarian. And?

Researcher. The overlaps do not compare. De Vere is six to twenty times more likely the author.

Librarian. As if his biography hasn't made that clear.

Researcher. Yes, those details confirm what these numbers prove:

"That every word doth almost tell my name,   Sonnet 76
Showing their birth and where they did proceed."

Act III, Scene VIII

Time: Early 17th Century
Place: A wooded setting, Windsor

Enter Falstaff and Mistress Quickly

Falstaff.   Merry Wives of Windsor, V, i, 1-9
Prithee, no more prattling; go. I'll hold. This is
the third time; I hope good luck lies in odd
numbers. Away I go. They say there is divinity in
odd numbers, either in nativity, chance, or death. Away!

Mistress Quickly.
I'll provide you a chain; and I'll do what I can to
get you a pair of horns.

Falstaff. Away, I say; time wears: hold up your head, and mince.
My establishment suffers as I dally at the gates of earthly delights.   *RB*

Exit Mistress Quickly.

Enter de Vere disguised.

                        Merry Wives of Windsor, V, i, 10-32
How now, Master Brook! Master Brook, the matter
will be known to-night, or never. Be you in the
Park about midnight, at Herne's oak, and you shall
see wonders.

De Vere. Went you not to her yesterday, sir, as you told me
you had appointed?

Falstaff. I went to her, Master Brook, as you see, like a poor
old man: but I came from her, Master Brook, like a
poor old woman. That same knave de Vere, her husband,
hath the finest mad devil of jealousy in him,
Master Brook, that ever governed frenzy. I will tell
you: he beat me grievously, in the shape of a
woman; for in the shape of man, Master Brook, I fear
not Goliath with a weaver's beam; because I know
also life is a shuttle. I am in haste; go along
with me: I'll tell you all, Master Brook. Since I
plucked geese, played truant and whipped top, I knew
not what 'twas to be beaten till lately. Follow
me: I'll tell you strange things of this knave
De Vere, on whom to-night I will be revenged, and I
will deliver his wife into your hand. Follow.
Strange things in hand, Master Brook! Follow.

Exeunt.

*After lighting and mood change with music, enter Falstaff
disguised as a stag.*

Falstaff.   *Merry Wives of Windsor, V, iv, 1-40*
The Windsor bell hath struck twelve; the minute
draws on. Now, the hot-blooded gods assist me!
Remember, Jove, thou wast a bull for thy Europa; love
set on thy horns. O powerful love! that, in some
respects, makes a beast a man, in some other, a man
a beast. You were also, Jupiter, a swan for the love
of Leda. O omnipotent Love! how near the god drew
to the complexion of a goose! A fault done first in
the form of a beast. O Jove, a beastly fault! And
then another fault in the semblance of a fowl; think
on't, Jove; a foul fault! When gods have hot
backs, what shall poor men do? For me, I am here a
Windsor stag; and the fattest, I think, i' the
forest. Send me a cool rut-time, Jove, or who can
blame me to piss my tallow? Who comes here? my
doe?

552 » The Bard's Ghost

Enter Anne Cecil, with Robin, dressed as a puckish forest fairy, and Dull, dressed as Oberon, who works his magic on the periphery.

Anne. Sir John! art thou there, my deer? my male deer?

Falstaff. My doe with the black scut! Let the sky rain
potatoes; let it thunder to the tune of Green
Sleeves, hail kissing-comfits and snow eringoes; let
there come a tempest of provocation, I will shelter me here.

Anne [Looks offstage]. Mistress Page is come with me, sweetheart.

Falstaff. Divide me like a bribe buck, each a haunch: I will
keep my sides to myself, my shoulders for the fellow
of this walk, and my horns I bequeath your husbands.
Am I a woodman, ha? Speak I like Herne the hunter?
Why, now is Cupid a child of conscience; he makes
restitution. As I am a true spirit, welcome!

Noise within.

Anne. Alas, what noise? Heaven forgive our sins.

Falstaff. What should this be?

Anne. Away, away!

She runs off.

Falstaff. I think the devil will not have me damned, lest the
oil that's in me should set hell on fire; he would
never else cross me thus.

Falstaff pulls off his buck's head and rises.

Enter de Vere and Anne Cecil.

Robin.   *Merry Wives of Windsor, V, v, 107-178*
Nay, do not fly; I think we have watch'd you now
Will none but the deer hunter serve your turn?

Anne. I pray you, come, hold up the jest no higher
Now, good Sir John, how like your Windsor wife?
See you these, husband? do not these fair yokes
Become the forest better than the town?

De Vere. Now, sir, who's a cuckold now? Not de Vere.
Falstaff's the knave, a cuckoldly knave; here are his
horns, plain to see: and, Master Brook, he hath
enjoyed nothing of mine but his buck-basket, his
cudgel, and twenty pounds of money, which must be
paid to Master Brook; his horses are arrested for
it, Sir John.

Anne. Sir John, we have had ill luck; we could never meet.
I will never take you for my love again; but I will
always count you my deer.

Falstaff. I do begin to perceive that I am made an ass.

Anne. Ay, and an ox too: both the proofs are extant.

Falstaff. And these be not fairies? I thought they were
not fairies: and yet the guiltiness of my mind, the sudden
surprise of my powers, drove the grossness
of the foppery into a received belief, in despite of
the teeth of all rhyme and reason, that he were a
fairy. See now how wit may be made a Jack-a-Lent,
when 'tis upon ill employment!

Dull. Sir John Falstaff, serve Got, and leave your
desires, and fairies will not pinse you.

De Vere. Well said, fairy Dull.

Dull. And leave your jealousies too, I pray you.

De Vere. I will never mistrust my wife again till thou art
able to woo her in good English.

Falstaff. Have I laid my brain in the sun and dried it, that
it wants matter to prevent so gross o'erreaching as
this? Am I ridden with a Welsh goat too? shall I

have a coxcomb of frize? 'Tis time I were choked
with a piece of toasted cheese.

   Robin. Seese is not good to give putter; your belly is all putter.

   Falstaff. 'Seese' and 'putter'! have I lived to stand at the
taunt of one that makes fritters of English? This
is enough to be the decay of lust and late-walking
through the realm.

   Anne. Why Sir John, do you think, though we would have the
virtue out of our hearts by the head and shoulders
and have given ourselves without scruple to hell,
that ever the devil could have made you our delight?

   De Vere. What, a hodge-pudding? a bag of flax?

   Anne. A puffed man?

   Robin. Old, cold, withered and of intolerable entrails?

   De Vere. And one that is as slanderous as Satan?

   Robin. And as poor as Job?

   De Vere. And as wicked as his wife?

   Dull. And given to fornications, and to taverns and sack
and wine and metheglins, and to drinkings and
swearings and starings, pribbles and prabbles?

   Falstaff. Well, I am your theme: you have the start of me; I
am dejected; I am not able to answer the Welsh
flannel; ignorance itself is a plummet o'er me: use
me as you will.

   De Vere. Marry, sir, we'll bring you to Windsor, to one
Master Brook, that you have cozened of money, to
whom you should have been a pander: over and above
that you have suffered, I think to repay that money
will be a biting affliction.

Act III, Scene IX

Time: Early 17th Century
Place: A bedchamber in de Vere's house

RB

Shakspere. I see villainy in this nonsense: The ale-maker posing as a stag to poach his Lord's doe.

Page. Scandalous, presenting oneself as something other than oneself.

Shakspere. Quite. We should be harsh to those so disposed, as with horse thieves.

Page. My Lord?

Shakspere. Pillory them: lock, stock, and barrel!

Page. Pray that we live to see it! And you would submit to such ridicule should the thievery be at your hand?

Shakspere. Such aspersions do not become your station, wife! Silence your tongue or bear the consequences.

Page. Unlike Falstaff, you curry not chivalry; instead, bare your lack of couth like a butcher disgorging offal.

Shakspere. I shall take no more of this in my own house, or honor such wickedness by acknowledgment. Sweet solace awaits me at the Garter Inn.

Exit Shakspere.

Page. Good-night, sweet prince,   *Hamlet, V, II, 369-370*
And flights of angels sing thee to thy rest!

Act III, Scene X

Time: Present
Place: Purgatory

Christ, visible in half-light, considers de Vere.

RB

De Vere. If only the actual reconciliation with my wife had gone as well as it did for Master and Mistress Ford in *The Merry Wives of Windsor*. Alas, my haughty rejection of her most certainly contributed to her death— as I imagined in *Othello, Much Ado about Nothing, Cymbeline,* and *Hamlet,* and confessed in *The Winter's Tale,* which we'll revisit shortly.

At least I can be thankful for having seen the light, which was in no small measure due to Burghley's insistence on the famous "bed trick," in which I unknowingly, in a bout of inebriation, am said to have brought Anne Cecil to bed, before I left England for my grand tour of the courts and sights of the continent. You may recall, I used such a ruse in *Measure for Measure* to resolve that plot.

Whether Burghley's version of events coincides with reality is beside the point now, of course, but since my savior seemed to believe it true as well, I am chastened into accepting it. It's a good thing, too, for it assuaged my aching conscience and, eventually, healed my heart. That's not to say that others weren't startled by my about face.

Act III, Scene XI

Time: Early 17th Century
Place: The bar at the Garter Inn

Friar Lawrence is sitting at Shakspere's usual table. Falstaff (wearing his horns and costume from Scene VIII) is counting the day's take and conferring with Robin at the bar.

RB

Falstaff. Not a bad day for a public house with private books. You know the arrangements: A quid to Shakspere for his silence and the rest to the safe upstairs. Get thee gone before we're espyed.

Robin. No Dull, no worries, sire.

Falstaff. Mind you, tarry not.

*Robin begins to walk across the bar, but stops at
Shakspere's table. Enter de Vere, who notices the purse in
Robin's hand, as he walks to Friar Laurence's table.*

De Vere. Good morrow, father.   *Romeo and Juliet, II, iii, 31-94*

  Friar Laurence. Benedicite!
What early tongue so sweet saluteth me?
Young son, it argues a distemper'd head
So soon to bid good morrow to thy bed:
Care keeps his watch in every old man's eye,
And where care lodges, sleep will never lie;
But where unbruised youth with unstuff'd brain
Doth couch his limbs, there golden sleep doth reign:
Therefore thy earliness doth me assure
Thou art up-roused by some distemperature;
Or if not so, then here I hit it right,
Our de Vere hath not been in bed to-night.

  De Vere. That last is true; the sweeter rest was mine.

  Friar Laurence. God pardon sin! wast thou with Rosaline?

  De Vere. With Rosaline, my ghostly father? no;
I have forgot that name, and that name's woe.

  Friar Laurence. That's my good son: but where hast thou been, then?

  De Vere. I'll tell thee, ere thou ask it me again.
I have been feasting with mine enemy,
Where on a sudden one hath wounded me,
That's by me wounded: both our remedies
Within thy help and holy physic lies:
I bear no hatred, blessed man, for, lo,
My intercession likewise steads my foe.

  Friar Laurence.
Be plain, good son, and homely in thy drift;
Riddling confession finds but riddling shrift.

  De Vere. Then plainly know my heart's dear love is set
On once and future wife that you hath met:
As mine on hers, so hers is set on mine;

And all combined, save what thou must combine
By holy re-marriage: when, where, and how
We reunited, woo'd, and exchanged vows,
I'll tell thee as we pass; but this I pray,
That thou consent to re-marry us to-day.

Friar Laurence.
Holy Saint Francis, what a change is here!
Is Rosaline, whom thou didst love so dear,
So soon forsaken? young men's love then lies
Not truly in their hearts, but in their eyes.
Jesu Maria, what a deal of brine
Hath wash'd thy sallow cheeks for Rosaline!
How much salt water thrown away in waste,
To season love, that of it doth not taste!
The sun not yet thy sighs from heaven clears,
Thy old groans ring yet in my ancient ears;
Lo, here upon thy cheek the stain doth sit
Of an old tear that is not wash'd off yet:
If e'er thou wast thyself and these woes thine,
Thou and these woes were all for Rosaline:
And art thou changed? pronounce this sentence then,
Women may fall, when there's no strength in men.

De Vere. Thou chid'st me oft for loving Rosaline.

Friar Laurence. For doting, not for loving, pupil mine.

De Vere. And bad'st me bury love.

Friar Laurence. Not in a grave,
To lay one in, another out to have.

De Vere. I pray thee, chide not; she whom I love now
Doth grace for grace and love for love allow;
The other did not so.

Friar Laurence. O, she knew well
Thy love did read by rote and could not spell.
But come, young waverer, come, go with me,
In one respect I'll thy assistant be;
For this alliance may so happy prove,
To turn your households' rancour to pure love.

De Vere. O, let us hence; I stand on sudden haste.

Friar Laurence. Wisely and slow; they stumble that run fast.
There are [*To audience.*] unanswered plot devices that   RB
As yet complicate [*To de Vere and audience.*] these matters; for while
You, posed as Ford, hath seen the error in
Your condemnation of your wife, you, posed
As Hamlet, hath sent Ophelia beyond
All sense and wit, o'er the cliff, to her death.
Space and time thus torn asunder do beg
For a *deus ex machina* to mend:
Your wife, Anne Cecil, Countess of Oxford,
Is of this realm no longer; immortal
In your lit'rature, mortal in your life;
Alive in your mind, yet dust in her tomb.
Only agape and faith transcendent
May conspire to bridge this life and the next.

De Vere. Well spoken, father; well taken in kind.
I swear faith in Jesus, love of Divine.

    Friar Laurence waves to Falstaff to bring a couple of draughts.

Friar Laurence. Since you insist that this new love is true,
We shall make thy oath one of steadfast hue.
By thick'ning a draught with herbs from this vial
Never again shall your marriage travail
Darken the aura of your fair estate.
A life's long journey is now worth the wait.

    A humble Falstaff delivers drinks to Friar Laurence and de Vere.

De Vere. My thanks, Sir John for your undue attention
That brought my mistress back to affection.
Thus we are eager to renew our vow
And succor the sweet sting from Cupid's bow.

Falstaff. So Master Brook shall in a way find honey
Where de Vere wills it with his own money.

Friar Laurence. More funny by half than a cuckold's right,
Your pun begs pardon for yet unmade fight.

Falstaff. Your Worship's mindful of my present plight
As I am mindful of his Lordship's might.

> *Falstaff returns to the bar. Robin exits. Friar Laurence pours content of vial into de Vere's glass. De Vere raises the glass in a toast.*

De Vere. To the present heaven I shall be wed
Until grim reaper visits my deathbed. [*He drinks.*]

> *Shakspere, in his finery with a newfound swagger, gets up from his table and approaches Friar Laurence and de Vere.*

Shakspere. Why it's the shadow poet importuning at heaven's gate.

Friar Laurence. My son, mocking the Lord begs for a fall.

De Vere. What have we here, Will, drunk again?

Shakspere. Sober as ever, my Lord.

De Vere. Not so sober as to mind your tongue.

Shakspere. My tongue is your tongue, my Lord; and your tongue mine.

De Vere. An ironic twist worthy of my own doing. Soon you'll believe you wrote these lines.

Shakspere. That day has come. I awake to a new name—one you had thought a clever mask, now simply a misspelling of mine own.

De Vere. Hah! Yes, history has smiled on you for a brief moment, but eternity is mine.

Shakspere. A damned one at that!

Friar Laurence. Hold your tongue, or it is you who shall be damned!

Shakspere. My tongue shan't be silenced, its former owner rendered mute by his profligacy!

De Vere. Mute? Hardly! Your life is but a figment of my pen. See here, whose robes and jewelry hast thou pilfered? You are a knave, with a knave's heart!

Shakspere [*Draws sword.*]. These be my own fineries; I, a Lord in mine own right!

De Vere [*Standing.*]. Surely you jest: Your new life a mirage of my mirth and my players' making!

Shakspere [*Thrusts.*]. Lies! My life and my words by my wife's honor!

De Vere. Your wife is my page; her honor at my service.

> *They duel. Dull and his seconds arrive and break up the fight.*

Dull. Father, I pray you have escaped intact from this fracas.

Friar Laurence. Thankfully, Constable, but sadly, years of ale-mongering have pickled our poor brother's brain. A few hours without a pot and the devil's delusions come knocking.

Shakspere. Liar! I am entitled to my satisfaction with this impostor!

De Vere. You see, Dull, he's quite lost his wits.

Dull [*To a couple of aides.*]. Pillory him for public drunkenness and impersonating a Lord.

Shakspere. The Queen shall know of this! I shall have you all hung!

> *A couple of Dull's aides take Shakspere away.*

Dull [*To a couple of aides.*]. That one, too, [*Motioning toward Falstaff.*] for solicitation of a Lady and failure to pay the ale tax.

Falstaff. Sir, have I not suffered enough, horned and costumed for all to see? A gentleman I remain.

Robin [*To Dull.*]. Sire, I beg of you on my life; no gentleman is he! For I am beaten and pandered by him.

Dull [*To his aides.*]. Add pandering to the posted list.

Act III, Scene XII

Time: Present
Place: Purgatory

Christ, visible in half-light, considers de Vere.

De Vere. Having finally reeled in the disruptive elements—by which I refer not only to the rustic, Will Shakspere and the vainglorious and cowardly Falstaff, but to myself as well—I am finally prepared to atone for my behavior towards my wife and, hopefully, purchase some small measure of redemption from my eldest daughter, whose issue precipitated this bloody affair. As you can imagine, for a headstrong fellow like me, this was no easy task—a lifelong labor in fact [*He glances at Jesus and back.*]— but here, once again, Burghley has played a part, with the haunting painted funerary statue he erected to Anne at Westminster Abbey.

Act III, Scene XIII

Time: Early 17th Century
Place: A chapel in Limbo

Anne Cecil stands behind a curtain on a dais in place of an altar, in an admirable pose. Friar Laurence, de Vere, Elizabeth de Vere, Edward and Anne's daughter, her husband—the Earl of Derby, Camillo, and Dull are among those present.

De Vere.   *The Winter's Tale, V, iii, 98-132*
O grave and good Friar, the great comfort
That I have had of thee!

  Friar Laurence. What, sovereign sir,
I did not well I meant well. All my services
You have paid home: but that you have vouchsafed,
With your progeny, all these your contracted
Heirs of your kingdoms, my poor house to visit,

It is a surplus of your grace, which never
My life may last to answer.

   De Vere. O Friar,
We honour you with trouble: but we came
To see the statue of our queen: your gallery
Have we pass'd through, not without much content
In many singularities; but we saw not
That which my daughter came to look upon,
The statue of her mother.

   Friar Laurence. As she lived peerless,
So her dead likeness, I do well believe,
Excels whatever yet you look'd upon
Or hand of man hath done; therefore I keep it
Lonely, apart. But here it is: prepare
To see the life as lively mock'd as ever
Still sleep mock'd death: behold, and say 'tis well.

      Friar Laurence draws a curtain, and reveals Anne Cecil
      standing like a statue.

I like your silence, it the more shows off
Your wonder: but yet speak; first, you, my liege,
Comes it not something near?

   De Vere. Her natural posture!
Chide me, dear stone, that I may say indeed
Thou art Anne Cecil; or rather, thou art she
In thy not chiding, for she was as tender
As infancy and grace. But yet, Friar,
My darling Anne was not so much wrinkled, nothing
So aged as this seems.

   Dull. O, not by much.

   Friar Laurence. So much the more our carver's excellence;
Which lets go by some sixteen years and makes her
As she lived now.

   De Vere. As now she might have done,
So much to my good comfort, as it is
Now piercing to my soul. O, thus she stood,

564 » The Bard's Ghost

Even with such life of majesty, warm life,
As now it coldly stands, when first I woo'd her!
I am ashamed: does not the stone rebuke me
For being more stone than it? O royal piece,
There's magic in thy majesty, which has
My evils conjured to remembrance and
From thy admiring daughter took the spirits,
Standing like stone with thee.

   Elizabeth. And give me leave,
And do not say 'tis superstition, that
I kneel and then implore her blessing. Lady,
Dear queen, that ended when I but began,
Give me that hand of yours to kiss.

   Friar Laurence. O, patience!
The statue is but newly fix'd, the colour's not dry.

   Camillo. My lord, your sorrow was too sore laid on,
Which sixteen winters cannot blow away,
So many summers dry; scarce any joy
Did ever so long live; no sorrow
But kill'd itself much sooner.

   De Vere. Dear my brother,
Let him that was the cause of this have power
To take off so much grief from you as he
Will piece up in himself.

   Friar Laurence. Indeed, my lord,
If I had thought the sight of my poor image
Would thus have wrought you,--for the stone is mine--
I'd not have show'd it.

   De Vere. Do not draw the curtain.

   Friar Laurence. No longer shall you gaze on't, lest your fancy
May think anon it moves.

   De Vere. Let be, let be.
Would I were dead, but that, methinks, already--
What was he that did make it? See, my lord,

Would you not deem it breathed? and that those veins
Did verily bear blood?

Dull. Masterly done:
The very life seems warm upon her lip.

De Vere. The fixture of her eye has motion in't,
As we are mock'd with art.

Friar Laurence. I'll draw the curtain:
My lord's almost so far transported that
He'll think anon it lives.

De Vere. O sweet Friar,
Make me to think so twenty years together!
No settled senses of the world can match
The pleasure of that madness. Let 't alone.

Friar Laurence. I am sorry, sir, I have thus far stirr'd you: but
I could afflict you farther.

De Vere. Do, Fiar;
For this affliction has a taste as sweet
As any cordial comfort. Still, methinks,
There is an air comes from her: what fine chisel
Could ever yet cut breath? Let no man mock me,
For I will kiss her.

Friar Laurence. Good my lord, forbear:
The ruddiness upon her lip is wet;
You'll mar it if you kiss it, stain your own
With oily painting. Shall I draw the curtain?

De Vere. No, not these twenty years.

Elizabeth. So long could I
Stand by, a looker on.

Friar Laurence. Either forbear,
Quit presently the chapel, or resolve you
For more amazement. If you can behold it,
I'll make the statue move indeed, descend
And take you by the hand; but then you'll think--

The Bard's Ghost

Which I protest against--I am assisted
By wicked powers.

  De Vere. What you can make her do,
I am content to look on: what to speak,
I am content to hear; for 'tis as easy
To make her speak as move.

  Friar Laurence. It is required
You do awake your faith. Then all stand still;
On: those that think it is unlawful business
I am about, let them depart.

  De Vere. Proceed:
No foot shall stir.

  Friar Laurence. Music, awake her; strike!

  Music.

'Tis time; descend; be stone no more; approach;
Strike all that look upon with marvel. Come,
I'll fill your grave up: stir, nay, come away,
Bequeath to death your numbness, for from him
Dear life redeems you. You perceive she stirs:

  Anne comes down.

Start not; her actions shall be holy as
You hear my spell is lawful: do not shun her
Until you see her die again; for then
You kill her double. Nay, present your hand:
When she was young you woo'd her; now in age
Is she become the suitor?

  De Vere. O, she's warm!
If this be magic, let it be an art
Lawful as eating.

  Dull. She embraces him.

  Camillo. She hangs about his neck:
If she pertain to life let her speak too.

Dull. Ay, and make't manifest where she has lived,
Or how stolen from the dead.

Friar Laurence.   That she is living,
Were it but told you, should be hooted at
Like an old tale: but it appears she lives,
Though yet she speak not. Mark a little while.
Please you to interpose, fair madam: kneel
And pray your mother's blessing. Turn, good lady;
Our Elizabeth is found.

    Elizabeth approaches Anne.

Anne Cecil. You gods, look down
And from your sacred vials pour your graces
Upon my daughter's head! Tell me, mine own.
Where hast thou been preserved? where lived? how found
Thy father's court? for thou shalt hear that I,
Knowing by this holy priest that the oracle
Gave hope thou wast in being, have preserved
Myself to see the issue.

Friar Laurence. There's time enough for that;
Lest they desire upon this push to trouble
Your joys with like relation. Go together,
You precious winners all; your exultation
Partake to every one.

De Vere. This is a match,   *The Winter's Tale, V, iii, 136-141*
And made between's by vows. Thou hast found mine;
But how, is to be question'd; for I saw her,
As I thought, dead, and have in vain said many
A prayer upon her grave. ...

        ... Let's from this place.   *The Winter's Tale, V, iii, 146-155*
What! look upon my brother: both your pardons,
That e'er I put between your holy looks
My ill suspicion. This is your son-in-law,
And son unto an earl, who, heavens directing,
Is troth-plight to your daughter. Good padre,
Lead us from hence, where we may leisurely
Each one demand an answer to his part

Perform'd in this wide gap of time since first
We were dissever'd: hastily lead away.

  Anne Cecil. We are not the first   *King Lear, V, iii, 3-19*
Who, with best meaning, have incurr'd the worst.
For thee, oppressed earl, am I cast down;
Myself could else out-frown false fortune's frown.
Shall we not see these daughters and these sisters?

  De Vere. No, no, no, no! Come, let's away to prison:
We two alone will sing like birds i' the cage:
When thou dost ask me blessing, I'll kneel down,
And ask of thee forgiveness: so we'll live,
And pray, and sing, and tell old tales, and laugh
At gilded butterflies, and hear poor rogues
Talk of court news; and we'll talk with them too,
Who loses and who wins; who's in, who's out;
And take upon's the mystery of things,
As if we were God's spies: and we'll wear out,
In a wall'd prison, packs and sects of great ones,
That ebb and flow by th' moon.

  Exeunt.

Act III, Scene XIV

  Time: Present
  Place: Purgatory

  Christ, visible in half-light, considers de Vere.

                                                                                      RB
  De Vere. All's Well That Ends Well, in other words, given the strictures of classical comedy, I owe you a return to *status quo ante*, in which the final setting and my motivation are reframed much as they were when we first delved into this imbroglio. I might also note in the coming scene that the disposition of our rustic versus our nobility is reversed from where it stood mid-stream, though not without a concerted effort on my part to reform. In doing so, I hope I've provided you a decent serving of mirth, some at my own expense, being that is the measure of comedy as surely as catharsis is that of tragedy.

Now, if you'll excuse me, I need to freshen up and enjoy the fruits of my labor.

De Vere begins to disrobe once again.

Act III, Scene XV

Time: Early 17th Century.
Place: Bathing quarters in de Vere's ancestral country estate, Castle Hedingham; servants finish filling a large wooden tub with hot water

Champagne is served.

De Vere. To your restor'd health and eternal life!   RB

Anne. To your renew'd faith in your once and future wife!

De Vere. She be as transcendent as my child bride.

Anne. She be in need of a long, sweaty ride.

De Vere. Her trusty steed eager for her mount;
His heart trembling; his desire a fount.

Anne. And night into day and day into night,
'Cross meadow and brook she rides him aright.

De Vere. He a willing slave to her timeless charm,
Chain'd in her chamber, pinn'd down by her arms.

Anne. This is your idea of a prison, my love?

De Vere. To be sworn to a hot tub with you, love!

Anne. And me, as if I'm an iceberg melting
Into a sea of love and forgiveness.

De Vere. Melt on! And me a sheik with oil to spare;
It is I who is begging forgiveness.

Anne. Already we've spoken of this too much.

De Vere. Then down to business the rider did bear,

Anne. Her sleek steed rising to meet her mid-air.

De Vere. Thus away they rode o'er the countryside,

Anne. A landscape of dreams and tropical tides.

De Vere. And called she thus from her carnal carriage,

Anne. T'is time to consummate our remarriage!

   Steam. We hear witches cackle and then:

Witches. "Double, double, toil and trouble, Fire burn and cauldron bubble …"	*Macbeth IV, i, 10*
"All hail … [de Vere]! hail thee, [The Bard of Avon]!"	*Macbeth I, iii, 48*

   Act III, Scene XVI

   Time: Late 20th Century.
   Place: The Holy Trinity Church

   Another tour group enters Holy Trinity Church and begins to make its way across the stage. The bust of Shakspere turns red (lighting) with embarrassment and sheds tears on cue, but is unable to speak. De Vere is bathed in a greenish-yellow spotlight.

   Christ, visible in half-light, considers proceedings. Shakspere seethes.

De Vere.   RB
And here we have the famous bust of one William *Shakspere* who, in the absence of copyright law, and in a climate that encouraged aliases for aristocrats, pamphleteers, and playwrights alike, passed himself off as the author William Shake-speare, one of the pen names of Edward de Vere, 17th Earl of Oxford. Underneath this bust, in the words of one of the era's greatest satirists, Ben Jonson, we find the inscription in German, translated as "Look there [at] all that he hath writ," pointing across the way to the tomb upon which is what Mark Twain so eloquently identified as the entirety of Shakspere's only poem,

De Vere walks across to Shakspere's tomb.

"Good friend, for Jesus' sake forbear
To dig the dust enclosed here.
Blessed be ye man that spares these stones,
And cursed be he that moves my bones."

Hah! And there you have it, "The Complete Works of Wm. Shakspere Unabridged": [*He points to the statue.*] This pen and this paper, props added seven years after Shakspere's death, by my own family in need of a cover to publish the First Folio and assorted pamphlets, as fodder in the campaign to prevent England from returning to Catholicism. [*He laughs.*]

[I.] Tourist. Seriously? That's it?

De Vere. Yes, the monument upon which he rests his case [*Indicating the bust.*] is nothing but a cipher in the treasure hunt for an immortal buried at Westminster Abbey.

[II.] Tourist. A clever riddle! But once unraveled, what's the point? Don't the works stand on their own?

De Vere. And have you not suffered at the hands of those who butcher and bedraggle the canon of our master poet, clueless as to the subtext of the work?

[II.] Tourist. I see. Well, yes. The plays are rather long you know! And who can follow all those thees and thous, sirrahs and foresooths? Shorten it up I say! I've got a plane to catch!

[I.] Tourist. Too much like the Latin service, I say. Dumb it down for the masses. Aspire not to the syntax. The thoughts are too deep; the meaning too human! Let us have no insight into motive and madness!

[*All laugh.*]

De Vere: [*Segueing to the audience.*]
Then I, through my magical arts am, as Prospero
restored after a lifetime's absence to my rightful kingdom.
And you who once thought that my stories were

of pure invention wrought, what little you know
of the writer's temper and compulsion!
Great tragedies are from the heart deciphered
and only then by the mind's eye embellished.
Mine every story, from high seas piracies to imagined infidelities,
reflect a life long on adventure and short on thrift.
And now, my self in Christ identified,
I rest my case, desirous of heavenly passage.
[So] ... release me from my bands *The Tempest, Epilogue, 9-20*
With the help of your good hands.
Gentle breath of yours my sails
Must fill, or else my project fails,
Which was to please. Now I want
Spirits to enforce, art to enchant,
And my ending is despair,
Unless I be reliev'd by prayer,
Which pierces to that it assaults
Mercy itself and frees all faults.
  As you from crimes would pardon'd be.
  Let your indulgence set me free. [*Bows.*]

> *De Vere takes away Shakspere's pen and paper, leaving him with a sack of grain, and then moves off to the side to talk with group. They congratulate him. Shakspere pounds the sack in anger and oats pour forth. De Vere turns.*

De Vere. I'm surprised we didn't find used oats in that sack!   RB

> *Shakspere shakes a fist at de Vere, but his anger suddenly turns to fear as a loud cymbal is heard, followed by the witches cackling. Shakspere is consumed in flames and sulfuric smoke and descends into the Underworld [Appropriate music from* Don Giovanni*].*

EPILOGUE

> *The lights come up half in yellows and purples, like a Flemish master's palate. Christ dismounts from the cross approaches de Vere, and then addresses the audience. De Vere respectfully hands Christ the pen and paper he removed from the grip of Shakspere's bust.*

Jesus. While the seasons may argue against it,   *RB*
The words of this bard in time do entreat,
For as de Vere is "as Christ," so then I,
Like de Vere, shall be granted a new life
And redeemed. As his own play did for him,
So shall my own creative endeavor
Do for me, as He wisely shall see fit.

    Exeunt, Jesus with his arm around de Vere.

    The ghost light is rekindled and remains after all other lighting instruments have been extinguished.

                  Fini

Appendix 5

Chimera's Dream of Twelve Paintings

The following was transcribed verbatim from the tape recording of Chimera, with my commentary added. [RB]

"The dream begins with a voice from the darkness:

"The G-dhead is ever-present, though in most mortals it favors consciousness infrequently with its tale. Thus, we prepare ourselves for the rare infusions of omniscience as a gift from realms beyond ourselves, whence our spirit and perfection abide, in the hope of drawing our present world closer to its rightful destiny.

"Presently, this is a world into which children are born unwanted, unto adults that were unwanted themselves. To what can we attribute such unnaturalness? What peculiar inversion of the human form allows such behavior to take root? Does the newly-minted consciousness that accompanied our fall from grace separate us eternally from our nurturing instincts, or are we simply in exile from a more evolved state wherein we again shall have simultaneous knowledge, intuition, and instinct for right action?"

Chimera's posture relaxes slightly and her voice warms.

"The blackness begins to take abstract form and where a point of light had invisibly existed on the right side of the canvas there are now a few concentrated swirls of white—a life form—huddled and leaning away from a dangerous intrusion into what otherwise would be a nurturing womb. The danger, though crimson by nature, has, through a cubist transformation, morphed into bulbous protrusions of fetid violet, like cancerous sores, from whose essence emanate steely probes.

"'Am I not supposed to be here?' 'What did I do wrong this time?' 'Now I'm supposed to be punished.'

"Over and over again, whenever threatened, whenever spoken to in a raised voice, these same questions arise. The reflex of terror is never far from our present behavior, always waiting for the other shoe to drop.

"I escape the multiplying tumors of seething unhappiness only to be expelled from this warm, yet uncertain ocean into a cold, translucent atmosphere of shouting and slaps on the side of the head.

"The canvas is larger now, and objects come out of nowhere to strike me. The light changes constantly and I'm not sure where I am. Raised voices accompany looming shapes. The shapes become people—their faces, their hands. Later, I learn they are often arguing about me: 'You never wanted her!' 'I hate you!' 'You tried to abort her!'

"Darkness accompanies these assaults, slowing closing in on the painting from its edges. There's an escape. See here, this facet? When I'm old enough to walk, I go to my room and draw. I'm safe. Temporarily.

"Abstract expressionism changes to impressionism. I'm in my room. The bed, the paintings on the wall, the table and chairs, the rug and the pitcher are all distended, as if each were bright separate paintings hung in this space I inhabit.

"The voices are still with me. They no longer talk to each other, but instead address me directly: 'What makes you think you're supposed to be here?' 'You're not good enough.' 'You can't do that.' 'You don't deserve to be in a loving, mutually supportive relationship.'

"Only drinking can make the voices stop. Now I have a tool to keep them at bay. The patina on this canvass is a yellowish green.

"Suddenly we're at a ball. The colors and costumes are garish. My lipstick is smeared. Someone has taken liberties with me, but I don't care. It's what I wanted—I crave the touching. We're dancing. His eyes are glazed. The perimeter of the room is a blur. We go round and round. I pass out.

"I awake in a miniature canvass with someone I don't recognize. Nothing is familiar. My head aches. A neon sign flashes through the shades. The furnishings in the room are cheap, but there are a couple of unfinished bottles of wine. Half a glass later, I begin to feel better—until I see the wedding ring on my finger. Is the man I'm with my husband or a lover? My conscience reels from the uncertainty. Our faces are in darkness, except for the occasional neon-assisted glimpses of an ear, a nose, a bloodshot eye. This sequence is repeated over and over, with minor details changing each time: the face of the man, what we're drinking, the name of the hotel. It seems there's no way out of this looping motif. I can't tell whether I'm dreaming or awake. I wake up in another room with another man. This time, I don't take that drink. Immediately my situation changes.

"I'm on a long portico among lots of people. The canvass is very wide. It's a classical Roman setting, yet the characters are Semitic. Christ is speaking, and his radiance is reflected in the face of everyone present, each seeming to present a different aspect of the truth through their various selves. Christ is the very image of Michael.

"Instantly, I'm at his feet and he's pulling me up. The style of this new painting is similar, though the canvass is smaller and vertical. 'Of course I forgive you, Chimera, now you must forgive yourself,' Christ Michael says. I'm swooning. I don't deserve to be raised by Him, but He says, 'You are a beautiful soul who is as me. Spirit of darkness, let loose from this woman!' I'm unable to differentiate between Michael and myself. The sun is unrelenting, but I am not hot. The voices have stopped. I see myself standing in front of me. I'm standing in Michael's shoes. A strange but delightful feeling engulfs me. I am no longer a woman, nor a man. Conjoined with Michael's spirit, my soul is somehow completed. I am 'as Christ.' I am healed. I'm engulfed by white light that slowly dissipates by refracting into an infinity of multi-colored bright corpuscles within a new frame.

"I'm in a smock, pausing to reflect while I paint, facing the canvass in a self-portrait. I am older, but more serene. My eyes reflect a certain self-knowledge. The picture vibrates in an array of colors and strokes that blend and focus as one steps back from the painting. Clearly, this is my calling, my way to make sense out of a world that often seems senseless. My heart is reflected in my work and I am on my path, the path that is depicted on the canvass behind my image in the picture itself. The path beckons me to follow as it disappears into a magical forest where my future awaits me. I enter and am swallowed by a feeling of transcendental peace.

"I am being held in a passionate embrace, yet I am upright on a narrow, tall canvass. I am swathed in a regal wrap that holds both my lover and me. My head is thrown back in ecstasy. We are not standing at all, but on a bed of air. Underneath our golden blanket, my lover and I are naked in coital bliss. Our bodies are hidden because we are conjoined as one, a composite of beings, a Chimera, as it were. My lover's face is that of Rashan, but again we are lost in each other physically as I was with Michael spiritually.

"Later, we are separated and sitting at a table with eleven other people. The canvass is spread out horizontally as in the classical scene, but the characters are decidedly modern. Michael sits in the middle with his back to large windows that looks out upon alpine hills and towering snowcapped mountains crowned by a glorious sky at sunset. In front of Michael lie the sacraments of bread and wine. Michael is translucent. His light enraptures the twelve of us who gaze at him while he speaks.

Chimera's voice again takes a turn toward the distant narrative that began this session.

"Michael says, 'Behold, for I promised to return unto you so that you would know me as the Anomaly sent to deliver humankind from material space-time into spiritual eternity. Though you saw me not through this Age, truly, my spirit lived amongst you. Today, my voice is again my own, and a myriad of nations and races shall become one people in the face of timeless truth.

"'My recognition shall not come without trials, however. There are those Christians and Muslims that say they believe in me, yet practice not my teachings, and murder their brothers and sisters and despoil the Earth in my name and that of the One-Without-A-Name, the Great Anomaly. There are those Jews who recognized me not in my previous incarnation, and who today seek a Messiah that will reign from the City of David over Israel and the world as a ruler with armies and guns, and I say unto them, truly, I am of the House of David, yea its king, yet I seek not to enforce some ancient code from a temple mount or noble sanctuary despoiled by holy wars. Until that time when those who would kill others over this ground take up the cause of peace, love, and light, I cede Jerusalem. For my City of Peace, like the teachings from which I draw, has no bounds of time and place, and the One from whence I come has caused a comet to sanctify this vision to me.[1] So I say unto the Jews, Christians, Muslims, Hindus, Buddhists, Taoists, Bahá'í and the rest, whosoever shall murder or kill in my name is not of my flock.

---

[1] As the Hebrew prophets have repeatedly said, "The Land of Israel will in the future spread to incorporate all the lands of the earth." Metaphorically speaking, this is simply an extension of the peace of G-d the Great Anomaly to all realms.

"'Therefore, dwell in thy heart and know that none shall be excluded from eternal life save those that so choose to turn away from the transcendence of the soul, the preeminence of love, and the unnamable light-force from whence they come.'"

Appendix 6

The Proof

*Being the Dialectic of Matter and Spirit and the Convergence of Science and Spirituality—showing the congruency between physics (quanta), the philosophy of change (*I Ching*), incarnation (DNA), and history (space-time)—pointing beyond the Unified Field Theory and M-Theory to the Philosopher's Stone (the Perennial Philosophy), with Poincaré's Conjecture and String Theory as checks for the proof of the Quantum Torus Model and the Big Bang itself, and leading to: the appearance of the World Teacher, the unifying principle of all religions, and the next step in human evolution.*

The subtitle begins with a derivation from Georg Wilhelm Friedrich Hegel's and Karl Marx's quest to prove the logical connection and reconciliation of all knowledge as the result of dialectical processes inherent in reality itself.[1] It is a pursuit that Michael himself joined over 40 years ago as a student at Stanford University.[2]

The rest of subtitle reflects various longstanding questions that Michael addresses in the course of reconciling The Dialectic. In the current

---

[1] For Hegel, a philosophical idealist, the dialectic proceeded as it did for Plato, from 'Ideal Forms' to material specifics. For Marx, an historical materialist, the dialectic proceeded from the social reality to the idea. This conceptual inversion led Marx to remark of his teacher, "I have turned Hegel on his head." Michael's quip on this is that "I have turned Hegel and Marx inside out (with the Torus, Space-Time, and the Uncertainty Principle)."

[2] After morphing the idea of the dialectic to Einsteinian physics, Michael worked closely with "Herr" Paul Offenbacher (his "Engels" as he referred to him), to arrive at a preliminary outline for this effort. Over the next 38 years, Michael expanded this framework to include the present biological and spiritual components in the proof, "at last connecting the dotted lines," as he described it, synthesizing his toroidal-based model of quanta with The Dialectic and spirituality.

theoretical framework of physics and mathematics, M-theory is an umbrella "Theory of Everything" under which all operational models coexist.[3] M-theory is now being challenged by String Theory, which basically has formulated the mathematical equivalency between the four fundamental forces—the strong force, the weak force, the electromagnetic force, and gravity.[4]

To reconcile these contemporary scientific issues, Michael uses his concept of the Anomaly not only to account for the conditions under which the four fundamental forces are one and the same thing, as well as for the extra dimensions called for in String Theory, but also uses Poincaré's Conjecture and String Theory as checks for the Proof of his Quantum-Torus Model of light (as well as a proof of the Big Bang itself), thereby expanding dialectical materialism into "the dialectic of matter and spirit." Thus, Michael shows that physics, the philosophy of change (Δ, as delineated in the *I-Ching*), DNA, space-time, and spirituality all rest upon the same anomalistic principles defined in his Quantum-Torus Model.

Although pieces of the proof began to fall in place during Michael's childhood, including his introduction to the torus in 7th grade, by way of *The First Book of Topology* and to the concept of light as both a wave and particle, in his senior year high school physics class, the initial outline for these ideas was developed at Stanford in 1969, a couple of years before Michael began his study of Yoga. It began as *The Dialectic of Matter*, a framework for updating Hegel's and Marx's model by moving from the paradigms of Newtonian science and Euclidean geometry into a world of Einstein's relativity (non-Euclidean geometry) and Heisenberg's (acausal logic) uncertainty.

On the basis of that paper, Michael Solomon and Paul Offenbacher were accepted into the inaugural class at the California Institute of Arts, though due to political profiling by Roy Disney (It's a two-way street, David Horowitz!), their department, the School of Critical Studies, was abolished.

---

[3] See, Stephen Hawking, *The Universe in a Nutshell*, Bantam Books, New York, 2001, and *The Theory of Everything: The Origin and Fate of the Universe*, New Millennium Press, Beverly Hills, CA, 2002.

[4] See, Brian Greene, *The Elegant Universe: Superstrings, Hidden Dimensions, and the Quest for the Ultimate Theory*, W. W. Norton & Co., New York, 2003.

Michael's dialectical methodology continued to evolve, absorbing and fine-tuning as it went, integrating the entire spectrum of human knowledge into its framework—from the Singularity and Plasma Ball to Quantum Duality and Infinite Differentiation—manifesting in a myriad of analytical guises whose interrelationships it revealed.

The details of this evolution are chronicled throughout this book, including the development of the Quantum-Torus,[5] which brought Michael's scientific model to the point where it matched critical parameters of longstanding spiritual teachings, eventually culminating in *The Proof*, which uses Poincaré's Conjecture as a check for the model. Together, Poincaré's Conjecture and the model serve as a proof for the Big Bang theory itself, while the model leverages current empirical evidence to prove the existence of strings.

Finally, the proof not only shows how matter and spirit—science and spirituality—are intrinsically linked, but how their inherent anomalistic qualities prove that the Avatar (the human spiritual anomaly) necessarily will appear to explain these phenomena, including the significance of his own incarnation. Thus, the proof is toroidal in and of itself, begging the conclusion that Michael is indeed who he claims to be.

Solomon's Proof (www.SolomonsProof.com)

First posted: January 18, 2007
Last updated: December 24, 2008

The recent proof of Poincaré's Conjecture has the world of mathematics agog, but no one knows quite how to apply it. Likewise, the elegant mathematics of String Theory, which essentially solve Einstein's quest for the Unified Field Theory, harness the potential to revolutionize physics, but no one has come up with a proof for the existence of strings.

Now, in one elegant swoop, both these quandaries are solved in a scientific paper by Michael David Solomon (pseudonym), a late '60's Stanford anti-war activist turned yogi, who uses Poincaré's Conjecture to verify his Quantum-Torus Model of light and prove the convergence of science and spirituality, as well as prove the Big Bang Theory, the empirical evidence

---

[5] See *Appendix 2 - Prolegomena to Any Future Physics*.

for Strings, the appearance of the World Teacher, the unity of all religions, and the next step in human evolution.

While it may seem extraordinary that a sophisticated scientific proof would come from a spiritual source, it is exactly as predicted by Heisenberg, who said, "Perhaps it is not too rash to hope that new spiritual forces will again bring us nearer to the unity of a scientific concept of the universe,"[5] as we explain below.

THE PROOF OF THE QUANTUM-TORUS MODEL AND THE CONVERGENCE OF SCIENCE AND SPIRITUALITY, THE APPLICATION OF POINCARÉ'S CONJECTURE AS THE CHECK FOR THE PROOF, THE PROOF OF THE BIG BANG THEORY AND STRING THEORY, AND THE PROOF OF THE APPEARANCE OF THE WORLD TEACHER, THE UNIFYING PRINCIPLE OF ALL RELIGIONS, AND THE NEXT STEP IN HUMAN EVOLUTION.

MICHAEL DAVID SOLOMON

ABSTRACT: We describe our model of light, the Quantum-Torus Model, from which we derive the proof of the Convergence of Science and Spirituality. We check this proof with the recently verified Poincaré's Conjecture. We then apply Poincaré's Conjecture and our model to prove the Big Bang Theory. Next, we apply our model to show that the empirical evidence for Strings has already been discovered, thus verifying String Theory's mathematical framework for Einstein's Unified Field Theory, as well as providing a second check for the proof of the Big Bang Theory and the Quantum-Torus Model. Finally, we logically progress the model into the human genome and prove the appearance of the World Teacher, the Unity of All Religions, and the next step in Human Evolution.

1. INTRODUCTION

1.1. The Proof of the Convergence of Science and Spirituality. Scientists, philosophers, and spiritual teachers have long argued over the compatibility of scientific and spiritual principles, in most instances champions for one discipline trying to deny the validity of the other.

Whenever religion attempts to create an all-inclusive proof of the existence of G-d, it hides behind dogma at the expense of facts, thereby negating its inclusiveness. And whenever science attempts to create an all-inclusive proof of universal phenomena, it relies upon definitive mathematical equations at the expense of the indefinable, thereby negating its inclusiveness.

Yet as José Argüelles says in *Earth Ascending: An Illustrated Treatise on the Law Governing Whole Systems*, "The notion that there are different fields of knowledge that are unrelated to each other is fundamentally the result of a loss of sacred view."[1] In scientific terminology, this is much like saying, "Since everything is derived from a singularity (the Plasma Ball), then only the lack of information or the inadequacy of our analysis stand between our present fragmented world view and a unified version of creation.

And while there have been certain visionaries who have attempted to explain how these apparently opposite methodologies are linked, for example the Dalai Lama's recent book, *The Universe in a Single Atom: The Convergence of Science and Spirituality*,[2] these efforts fall into the category of persuasive opinions and arguments.

In this paper we will present a proof of the convergence of science and spirituality based on our Quantum-Torus Model, the development of which is covered in more detail in the soon to be published first volume of our memoir, wherein we also provide the outline for the cross-disciplinary synthesis and integration of human knowledge into one indivisible multi-dimensional database reflective of the universe that it describes, including the prescription for sustainable human evolution.

1.2. The Unified Field Theory, M-Theory, String Theory, and the Theory of Everything. Prior to the ascendancy of science and empirical methodology, it was the purveyance of philosophy and religion to explain all things under the Sun. In what evidence remains from the ancient world, the Chinese and the Greeks are prime examples of this impetus to categorize and cross-reference universal phenomena. Later, in the West, the Encyclopædists and Hegel further refined this integrative approach, incorporating contemporary scientific and social advances into their blueprint. As science matured, however, the unifying effort veered toward the construction of finite equations. Einstein's unfulfilled efforts to develop a Unified Field Theory gave way to a host of other such formulaic attempts—including M-Theory, the Theory of Everything, and String Theory—each with their own mathematical refinements. But even if String Theory's elegant equivalencies of the four fundamental forces are accepted as fact (in light of the empirical proof of strings described later in this paper), such a theory hardly qualifies as an all-encompassing framework, since it confines itself to a narrow realm of physics and mathematics. It is therefore the goal of our proof, in this paper and in our memoir, to offer a truly all-inclusive framework that, among other things, shows the logical progression of behavior from quanta to human consciousness and beyond.

1.3. Congruency in Scientific, Philosophic, and Spiritual Principles. We begin by employing analogous reasoning to establish the congruency between Taoism, Judaism, Platonism, and Quantum Theory, that is, between spirituality, philosophy, and science. Later, we will provide a check to this argument by deriving the same results from our Quantum-Torus Model.

The *Tao Tê Ching*[3] begins with the line, "The Tao that can be spoken is not the Tao." In other words, what Lao Tsu states is "That which is eternal cannot be described in words, because it is greater than anything that can be communicated or confined by a name." This is congruent to the stipulations of Judaism concerning the representation of the name of G-d. In Hebrew, the name of G-d is represented by four letters, which are Yod, Hé, Vau, Hé. Whenever a worshipper comes across these letters during reading or prayer, he or she is prohibited from pronouncing the letters as they are written, and must substitute the word "Adonai" instead. The de facto lesson in this practice is that there is no name that can be given to the Deity that would not be blasphemous, because the Deity cannot be confined to such limitations as are imposed by human speech, alphabet, or any other iconography or symbology. Therefore, both the Taoists and the Jews agree: The force that animates creation cannot be named. Carrying our analogous reasoning further, this Taoist and Hebraic principle is perfectly congruent to Plato's Allegory of the Cave, which says, essentially, that what we perceive as reality is only the shadow on the wall of our perceptual cave, and not the object nor the light source that casts it. Finally, science, too, has come to the same conclusion as these tenets of Judaism, Taoism, and Platonism, the expression of which is epitomized in Heisenberg's Uncertainty Principle, which posits that it is impossible to be certain of both the velocity and position of a sub-atomic particle.[4] As one applies Heisenberg's Uncertainty Principle to deeper levels of nuclear mysteries, the result is the same as the meaning behind the Hebrew symbols Yod, Hé, Vau, Hé , the *Tao Tê Ching*'s opening lines, or Plato's allegory, that is: There is a force at the core of the universe that we cannot accurately name or describe. In a nod to scientific parlance, we call this the Great Anomaly (see 2.5). In notation, it is the Greek letter Delta (Δ), meaning Change, since it does not conform to the logic of all that follows or precedes it. It is the G-d principle without religious dogma. All behaviors in this universe carry its indelible stamp and conform to its principles, as expressed in the behavior of the Quantum-Torus Model (see 2) and its infinity of derivatives.

1.4. Analogous Reasoning. This congruency between the principles of science, philosophy, and spirituality is the first step in the proof of the convergence of science and spirituality to the degree, as we have just noted, that proof or certainty exists. It is contingent upon accepting the idea that, based on an extrapolation of Heisenberg's Uncertainty Principle, these relationships are not expressed ultimately as an equation, but as a ratio (a : b :: c : d :: e : f :: g : h, etc., ad infinitum), that is, an analogous proof of the equivalencies between different emanations of the same force. Please note that the use of analogous reasoning for scientific derivations is common to both mathematics and logic; we therefore claim that our proof is scientific to the same degree as any other empirical endeavor. Indeed, science (in this case, physics and mathematics) are subsets of logic.

1.5. Heisenberg's Prediction of this Proof. Heisenberg himself foresaw this non-mathematical solution when he observed, "Perhaps it is not too rash to hope that new spiritual forces will again bring us nearer to the unity of a scientific concept of the universe ..."[5] and "The advance from the parts already completed to those newly discovered, or to be newly erected, demands each time an intellectual jump, which cannot be achieved through the simple development of already existing knowledge."[6] We hope that scientists who previously rejected such a possibility shall, for the purposes of this paper, follow Heisenberg's lead and consider our argument, for his prescient observation, with its inference of a holistic universe, is central to our point-of-view. We shall now apply the same analogous logic we used to establish the congruency of core scientific, philosophic, and spiritual principles to our Quantum-Torus Model and derive similar results.

2. THE QUANTUM-TORUS MODEL

2.1. The Torus. The torus is the fundamental figure of topology, the science of four-dimensional geometry. For the purposes of our model and proof, we have conceived of a torus as having the following properties:

- As the point is of one dimension, the circle of two, the sphere and the doughnut of three, so the torus is of four.
- The torus is a sphere changing in space-time.
- Three-dimensional circular motion along the circumference of a sphere becomes four-dimensional spiral motion on a torus as it expands and contracts in space-time.[7]

- The inside surface and the outside surface are experienced as the same surface on a torus in space-time. [8]
- Centrifugal and centripetal forces result from expansions and contractions of the torus in space-time. [9]
- The macrocosm and the microcosm conform to the laws of the torus. [10]
- The torus is a sphere that expands and contracts along a rotating spiral vector in space-time.
- During its cycles of expansion and contraction, the torus alternately experiences moments of movement (expansion and contraction) and non-movement (rest).

2.2. Quanta: Waves and Particles. Quanta have been observed as having the properties of both waves and particles. To understand the operational principles of quanta, and therefore to understand the operational principles of a universe manifesting as infinite differentiation of quanta, it is necessary to capture these two distinct qualities of quanta in a single model. This model would necessarily also show the equivalence of energy and mass ($E=mc^2$), with waves representing energy and particles representing mass. We do this by mapping quantum behavior directly to the torus as we have described it in 2.1. This juxtaposition immediately explains the apparently simultaneous quality of waves and particles as well as a variety of other properties.

2.3. Duality, Simultaneity, and the Fundamental Unit of Space-Time. Just as "God divided the light from the darkness," (*Genesis 1:4*),[11] so our model divides the behavior of quanta into two principles, light and dark, on and off, solid line and broken line, 1 and 0, sphere and doughnut, particle and wave, mass and energy. For the purposes of linguistic explanation, we ascribe quantum wave behaviors to the expansion and contraction phases (doughnut) of the toroidal model and quantum particle behaviors to the rest phases (sphere) of the toroidal model. The interval created by one cycle of these phases is the fundamental unit of space-time (see 6.3). It follows from Heisenberg's Uncertainty Principle that this unit is not subject to accurate observable measurement, and thus the illusory observation that quanta manifest in two places at once. This illusion is further explored in 6.4.

2.4. A Single 4-Manifold Model. The result of mapping the behaviors of quanta to our toroidal paradigm is a single 4-manifold model that essentially provides us with the Philosopher's Stone, that is, a fundamental key which unlocks the secrets of the universe, providing the requisite proof—including the check and application thereof—by which we may integrate human knowledge as we have previously described.

Specifically, the single 4-manifold model:

- Explains how light alternates between wave and particle
- Applies Perelman's proof of Poincaré's Conjecture as a check not only for our Quantum-Torus Model, but for the Big Bang itself (see 5 and 6)
- Applies key elements of Poincaré's Conjecture, the Big Bang, and the Quantum-Torus Model to debrief the empirical evidence for Strings, thus proving String Theory, the mathematical conclusions of which, in turn, serve as another check for the Big Bang Theory and the Quantum-Torus Model, i.e., all things come from the same source
- Applies the principles of our Quantum-Torus Model to the human genome (light manifesting as DNA) resulting in the proof of:
    - The appearance of the World Teacher
    - The unifying principle of all religions
    - The next step in human evolution

2.5. **The Great Anomaly or First Cause.** As we've noted, Heisenberg anticipated a model that escapes the gravity of contemporary scientific formulation. We attribute such foresight to his consummate understanding of the far-reaching implications of his Uncertainty Principle, that is, the recognition of the limits of scientific observation. It is through this ephemeral crack in the lockstep mathematics of science that the omnipresent factor in our Quantum-Torus Model comes to light. It is, as we have explained in 1.3, the part of the model that cannot be defined, spoken, or seen, yet is present in all phenomena, and indeed animates it; in other words, it is what we have termed the Great Anomaly, a neutral label for the G-d principle that we see subjectively colored in all religions; it represents one and the same idea previously identified in philosophic circles as the so-called "First Cause"—though in our proof, the assignment of a beginning and an end is purely arbitrary. This anomalistic behavior is present throughout the universe. It is evident in sub-atomic particles and galaxies and everything else in-between—quanta and nebula, white and black holes, protozoa and *Homo erectus*, shells and trees, movement and time, space and rest—just as the Great Anomaly at the heart of quantum-toroids is universally present. It is omnipresent, yet nowhere in particular; it

588   » The Proof

is part of the Quantum-Torus Model, yet is not assigned to any one part; it is invisible, yet infinitely manifest; it is the impetus behind the limitless fractal progression of reality.

2.6. Similar Models, both Conceived and Manifest. As a microcosmic phenomenon and as per Heisenberg's Uncertainty Principle, our Quantum-Torus Model necessarily has been synthesized from a list of behaviors and theoretical imperatives and not drawn from visual evidence. While its success at capturing these factors may qualify it as an operational model, we must invoke the previously referenced esoteric axiom, "As above, so below" (symbolized by the upward and downward triangles of the Star of David), to provide visual evidence of said toroidal paradigm. In doing so, however, we would like to note two other attempts at visualizing the microcosmic and macrocosmic model:

Babbitt's atom[12]

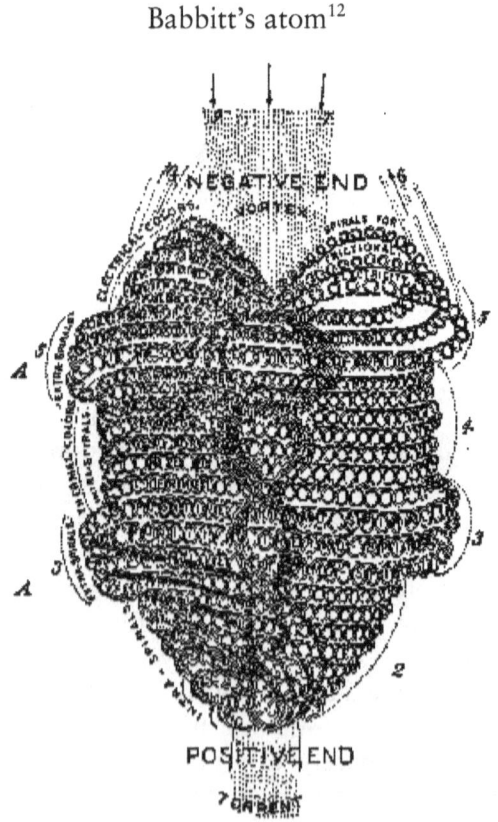

Compare this to the illustration of the Universe card and the image of the Cat's Eye Nebula that follow.

The Universe card from the Aleister Crowley tarot deck drawn by Frieda Harris. Note the similarity in the toroidal shapes of the background and foreground objects to the previous illustration of Babbitt's Atom and the image of the Cat's Eye Nebula that follows.

590 » The Proof

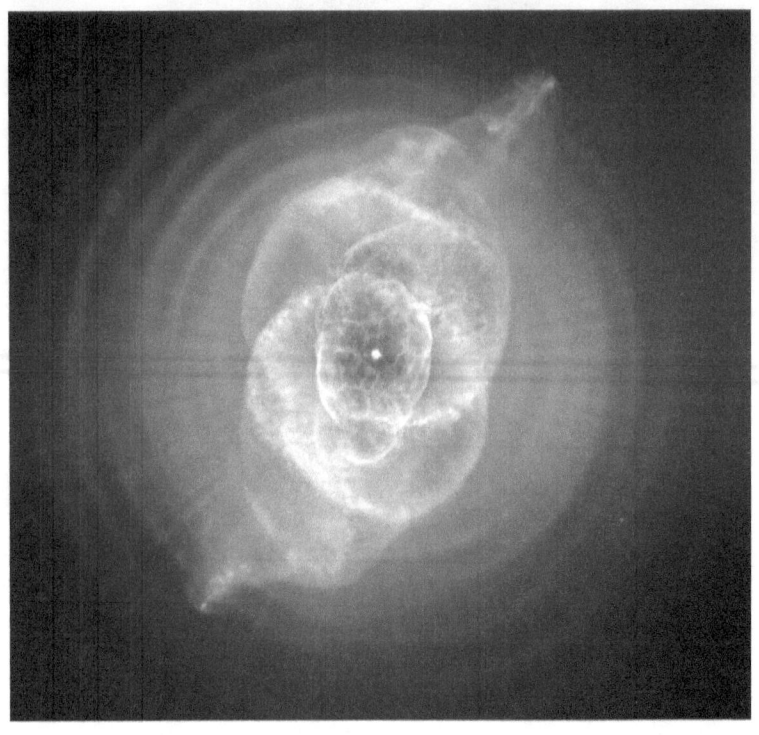

The Cat's Eye Nebula (NGC 6543), recreated from a Hubble image, replicates a near-perfect torus, the same geometry as that of quanta.

The principle difference between the toroidal behavior of the Cat's Eye Nebula and that of quanta is one of scale, not only in space but (of course) in time as well, the magnitude of which we contrast with one noteworthy example. Here we refer to our description of the torus (2.1) as "a sphere that expands and contracts along a rotating spiral vector in space-time."

Appendix 6 « 591

On a macrocosmic scale, as in this image, the rotational development of the toroidal surface and the vortices is relatively static from one observation to the next, while on a microcosmic scale, the expansion *and* contraction cycle of the toroidal surface (a tip of the hat to the prodigious powers of the strong force) and the rotational cycle of the vortices are also beyond also our observable capability, but for the opposite reason, that is, they are within one interval of a wave-particle phase of quanta, in other words, within the fundamental unit of Space-Time. Our inference that the vortices rotate along the entire toroidal surface supports both the spherical and doughnut moments of quanta (see 5).

2.7. Tangential Dimensions. Just as the normal states of matter break down at the limits of vibrational activity—e.g., the manifestation of the Einstein-Bose precipitate near zero degrees Kelvin (Absolute Zero) and the manifestation of the Plasma Ball near maximum degrees Kelvin (i.e., the singularity in the nanoseconds preceding the Big Bang)—so coincidentally and simultaneously at these limits do the restrictions of four-dimensional Space-Time dissolve into other states of Space-Time, as accounted for in the calculations of String Theory and other related formulations of multi-dimensional activity. These unitary states of matter that manifest at the extremes of vibration, in which infinity and zero are the same, are why String Theory derives additional dimensions. As so described, these additional dimensions and states are tangential to the Great Anomaly (First Cause or G-d principle).

3. BINARY CORRESPONDENCE

3.1. Quanta represented as Solid and Broken Lines. As previously noted in 2.3, the binary behavior of quanta may be represented by a variety of symbols, including light and dark, on and off, line and broken line, 1 and 0, sphere and doughnut, particle and wave, mass and energy, etc. Just as we employed the wave-particle duality of quanta to build our Quantum-Torus Model, now let us employ lines and broken lines to represent its behaviors, as we carry forward through analogous reasoning the Great Anomaly (First Cause) from the microcosm to the macrocosm, in this case from quanta to the human genome (3.4).

3.2. The *I Ching*. The oldest extant exploration of the implications of binary replication in Space-Time belongs to the *I Ching*, or *Book of Changes*, ascribed to Confucius and other scholars of his era. The premise of this work is to extrapolate forward six-fold (2^6)—from the anomalistic division of the First Cause (Great Anomaly) into binary phenomena (quanta)—to describe the subtleties of the variations or "changes" resulting from this progression. The fact that this mapping of the 64 basic phases of change against human behavior using poetic and philosophic symbolism was also used as a divinatory reference accessed through acausal selection (a methodology which we will not explore in this paper [notes are included in the memoir]) in no way prejudices our application of the 64 symbols (hexagrams or *kua*) and their linguistic representations to our analogous argument.

3.3. The Form of the Check for Our Proof of Congruency in Scientific, Philosophic, and Spiritual Principles. As described at the end of 1.5, we are now prepared to present a check for the proof of congruency in scientific, philosophic, and spiritual principles that we presented in 1.3. We define such a check as an analogous sequence taking an alternate, non-mirrored, route to the same conclusion as the theorem that it proves, i.e., science, philosophy, and spirituality are, in their most refined states, different methodologies and languages for describing the same universal phenomena.

3.4. The 64 Codons and the Human Genome. If the logical agreement and congruency between Heisenberg's Uncertainty Principle, Plato's Allegory of the Cave, and the Taoist and Hebrew prohibitions against representing the Deity is the first step (a : b, or "a is to b"), then Martin Schöenberger's discovery—directly correlating the binary patterns of the 64 hexagrams of the *I Ching* with humanity's biological building blocks, the 64 codons of the amino acids in DNA)—is the second step (:: c : d, or "as c is to d").[13]

3.5. The Anomalistic Hexagram and Genetic Anomalies. As we first described the Great Anomaly (1.3), it is essentially a state that "does not conform to the logic of all that follows or precedes it." Its equivalent representation in the otherwise binary-based *I Ching* is Hexagram 52, the anomalistic moment of rest in a seeming continuum of change. Given Schöenberger's mapping of the binary equivalence of the 64 hexagrams of the *I Ching* to codons essential to the replication of human DNA—and given that the anomaly present in the quantum-torus model is present in all things, since everything is derived from quanta (5.1 and 5.2)—it follows that we should find evidence of this anomaly in the human genome. And, indeed, as we shall see in 4.1, this is the case.

4. THE PROOF

4.1. Convergence of Scientific and Spiritual Prediction. For the purpose of exploring the parameters of the manifestation of the Great Anomaly in the human genome, let us preface our argument by citing the examples of Mozart and Einstein. Both exhibited properties in their work that exceeded what we would term "normal or incremental advances" relative to the other work in their fields. Rather, they created new, anomalistic paradigms that set the standard for generations to come, just as the quote Heisenberg explains in 1.5, "The advance from the parts already completed to those newly discovered, or to be newly erected, demands each time an intellectual jump, which cannot be achieved through the simple development of already existing knowledge," that is, the anomalistic nature of evolutionary change. Of course, expressions of such anomalistic singularity in the human genome occur in all fields, e.g., Abraham, Jesus, Buddha, Krishna, et al. in the spiritual realm, and in all humans, each as different as every proverbial snowflake. However, as Vedantic philosophy long-ago recognized in the hierarchy it assigned to spiritual incarnations based upon the periodicity of their occurrence, some anomalies are rarer than others. So, as is evident with Mozart, Einstein, Abraham, Jesus, Buddha, Krishna, et al., it follows that, though we may not be able to predict when such a genetic anomaly ("genius") occurs, we do know (according to the 2^6 binary progressions from our Quantum-Torus Model to the human genome) that it shall occur. This is essentially the same statement as "Therefore you also must be ready; for the Son of Man is coming at an hour you do not expect."[14] Ergo, scientific proof and spiritual prophesy converge on this specific point. And thus, as described in 3.3, we have presented a check for the proof of the congruency in scientific and spiritual principles that we posited "hypothetically" in 1.3.

4.2. The Separation of Dogma and Principles. One could expound on the nature of this manifestation of the human spiritual anomaly, the world teacher, who is predicted by our proof and various prophetic traditions, including Judaism, Christianity, Islam, Hinduism, Buddhism, et al., and we have done so at length in our memoir, but for the sake of brevity and consistency within the strictures of this form, we have distilled these descriptions in 7 and 8. The purpose of using this genre and this forum to present our proof is to parlay its empirical discipline and consequent lack of dogma into a universal discussion wherein the equivalencies between scientific, philosophic, and spiritual language are recognized. For example, where Adonai, G-d, and Allah, or Messiah, Christ, and Prophet have been used by particular religions to describe the G-d principle and its periodic anomalistic incarnations, we have substituted the terms Great Anomaly, "First Cause," and singularity or spiritual anomaly, avatar, and world teacher. In this manner, we hope to encourage a general cessation of hostilities between religious systems leveraging exclusive claims on the G-d principle and particular anomalistic incarnations to further the instinctive and egoistic objectives of their practitioners.

5. THE CHECK

5.1. The Proof of Poincaré's Conjecture. Grigory Perelman's recent solution to Poincaré's Conjecture, which concludes that all three-dimensional space is reducible to a combination of spheres and doughnuts, can be readily applied to four-dimensions, thus serving as a check for our foregoing proof of the Quantum-Torus model.

5.2. Application of Poincaré's Conjecture to Check our Quantum-Torus Model and the Big Bang Theory. As described in 2.1, "As the point is of one dimension, the circle of two, the sphere and the doughnut of three, so the torus is of four." Thus, proving that all three-dimensional space is reducible to spheres and doughnuts is congruent to proving that all four-dimensional space is reducible to a torus (specifically, our Quantum-Torus Model), which alternately contains the properties of both a doughnut (wave) and a sphere (particle) as it expands and contracts and rests. Therefore, Poincaré's Conjecture not only serves as a check for the Quantum-Torus Model (by showing the toroidal basis of four-dimensions [Space-Time]), but shows that our entire four-dimensional universe is derived from quanta (because quanta and the toroidal model are inseparable, that is, they are the fundamental unit of Space-Time) , and thus also serves as a check for the current cosmological model (the Big Bang theory), which postulates that our current universe first differentiated (from the singularity) as various forms of quanta and is therefore traceable back to this state.[15] The Big Bang (duality or "m" [matter]) is, then, the release of the potential energy ($E=mc^2$) of the singularity ("E" [Energy]) at the acceleration of light ("c^2").

6. APPLICATION OF THE PROOF

6.1. String Theory. Having checked our proof, we offer an application of key principles contained therein to solve another vexing scientific puzzle, that of strings and String Theory. As it stands today, String Theory has provided us with an elegant mathematical framework for solving the quest begun by Einstein, for a unified field theory, by mathematically expressing the equivalencies for the four fundamental forces—the strong force, the weak force, the electromagnetic force, and the gravitational force. But much like Einstein's Special Theory of Relativity awaited an empirical proof that came with Royal Society's and the Royal Astronomical Society's observations at Sobral (Brazil) and the island of Principe (West Africa) on May 29th, 1919, so String Theory awaits empirical proof for the existence of strings. Astonishingly, the experimental evidence has already been gathered, though it has not been recognized as such. As we shall see, this is in part due to the general lack of awareness that, like Poincaré's Conjecture, Strings are a subset of toroids.

6.2. White Holes, Black Holes, and the Great Anomaly. Before we debrief the experimental evidence for strings, it is necessary to revisit the implications we discussed in 2.7 concerning the breakdown of the general laws of the mass-energy-space-time continuum that occurs at the limits of vibrational activity (near absolute zero and near singularity [there's that zero and one again!]). For the purposes of this discussion we shall not delve into the progression of events that transpire during the final moments of a black hole leading to singularity, but rather on the initial moments after singularity, since the fingerprints that we seek from our current universal cycle begin there.

6.3. Artifacts of the Big Bang as Contrapositive Reflections of the Einstein-Bose Precipitate. Specifically, we describe the properties of the Plasma Ball as contrapositively related to the Einstein-Bose Precipitate, that is, the Plasma and the Precipitate arise under opposite conditions (maximum vibration v. minimum vibration) and exhibit congruent mirrored reflections of anomalistic behavior, i.e., abnormal states of matter in which the individuation of particles has ceased. In other words, much like the convergence of science and spirituality over a particular principle (4.1), the properties of the Plasma and the Precipitate converge over a specific quality—a unique form of unity in which the general laws of four-dimensions have been suspended, with Space-Time taking on new qualities (much as the tangential dimensions discussed in 2.7). The fractal progression of the Quantum-Torus is defined by these two states, which together contain a holograph of the entire universe of possibilities.

6.4. The Fundamental Unit of Space-Time at the Limits of Vibrational Activity. In addition, both these unique forms of matter (the Plasma and the Precipitate) exist entirely within "one interval of a wave-particle phase of quanta" (2.6), that is, they represent a fundamental unit of Space-Time at the limits of vibrational activity (2.7). As noted in 6.2, for the purposes of this discussion we are concentrating on events following the singularity, focusing on the remnants of the Big Bang as they proceed in Space-Time. And again, for the purposes of this discussion, we shall not concern ourselves with the general transformation of Plasma into a variety of quantum particles, but rather we shall focus on a particular class of artifacts of the Plasma that represent "one interval of a wave-particle phase of quanta." Regardless, as we have said, we shall see that, like Poincaré's Conjecture, String Theory, too, explores a subset of toroids.

6.5. Action at a Distance. As we noted in 6.1, String Theory awaits an empirical proof of the existence of the strings themselves and we propose that such experimental evidence has already been gathered, though it has not been recognized. We are referring to the "Action at a Distance"(so-called "Spooky Action") observations, in which two objects, apparently separated in space with no known connection, interact with each other as if they "know" the mass (in the case of gravity) or charge (in the case of electromagnetism) of the other distant object.

6.6. Empirical Evidence for Strings. Again, we go back (in the nanoseconds before the Big Bang) to the Plasma Ball (Singularity), when all of Space-Time was the very same substance—not atoms or particles of a homogeneous substance, but one indivisible entity, unmanifest within and of itself (represented by the Hebrew letter Aleph, א, which means, in this case, before the beginning).

The fact that Space-Time expanded and differentiated itself infinitely from this singularity doesn't mean that the original connection between everything that comprised the beginnings of this iteration of the universe was lost. Rather, this original "plasma" stretched, twisted, snapped, and evolved into other manifestations. Action at a distance, then, is simply the response of an artifact of creation, that is, different segments of a single string of quanta reacting to the same stimuli. The observation that the response is transmitted faster than the speed of light (which would violate Einstein's Special Theory of Relativity) is an illusion, because the stretched string is a remnant of the Plasma Ball, that is, a fundamental unit of Space-Time at the limits of vibrational activity (2.7). As per the Uncertainty Principle, our instrumentations and calculations are simply not now nor will they ever be capable of detecting an interval between the stimulus and the response, because the interval is less than the particle-wave periodicity of one quantum (the fundamental unit of space time)—thus it seemingly occurs instantaneously, in no Space-Time, that is, faster than would be possible if the two "ends" of this string were in fact separate quanta. So, as in the game of Jeopardy, the observations of spooky action are the answers to the question, "What are the indications that strings are not only present now, but have been present since the creation of this universe?" Note: Any variation between the "strings" described here and the strings in String Theory would be attributable to a variance in String Theory mathematics from the mathematics of toroids as manifested in the Quantum-Torus Model.

6.7. QED. From a metaphysical point of view, then, the infinite differentiation of the universe is the flip side of the unitary integration of the universe: the total connectedness present in the Plasma Ball (at the singularity) is still present, only masked by the countless permutations and combinations of the fractal progression of the Quantum-Torus. Matter is neither created nor destroyed and the laws of science (including logic and its subsets, physics, mathematics, etc.) and spirituality ("the mind of G-d") need only account for the Great Anomaly ("the G-d principle") and its infinite reflections to recognize their mutual consistency and convergence.

Hereafter, as Professor Igor Gamow (his father George being one of the principle theorists of the Big Bang) explained to me, the Quantum-Torus Model serves as the working model until it cannot explain key empirical evidence—allowing a generous amount of time to develop an explanation for such, while remaining consistent with its basic principles.

7. IMPLICATIONS OF THE PROOF

7.1. The Nature of the Spiritual Anomaly. Having thus presented our proof, its checks, and a few of its applications, let us now turn to its implications for human beings living in such a universe. As shown in 4.1 and 4.2, our proof concludes that a spiritual anomaly (like Abraham, Jesus, Buddha, Krishna, et al.) shall incarnate periodically, but that the time and place (and, for that matter, the details of such a manifestation) are unpredictable. Since the argument developed in this paper relies upon scientific protocol (unlike our memoir, which uses Socratic and Talmudic dialogue and journalistic observations) to expand upon the details of such a manifestation, let us continue in this empirical vein, albeit with a certain allowance for intuition and vision as notably employed by Newton and Einstein in deducing their famous formulations, and with a nod to Joseph Campbell in the use of mythological examples to inform our quest.

Like the Gospel of St. Thomas and (Thomas) Jefferson's Bible, we seek to strip away the mythological and fictional qualities attributed to a master teacher and lay bare the basic parameters that define a spiritual anomaly. Given, then, the perceived lack of Divine Revelation (in its narrowest sense) casting a spotlight on such a being, and given the lack of an inspired selection system such as that employed to identify each incarnation of the Dalai Lama, we are thrust into circumstances much like the times of King

David and King Arthur, both of whom were identified by the merits of their work and not by a genetic or spiritual pedigree.

7.2. The Philosopher's Stone. Synchronistically, it is worth noting that a stone plays a key role in both David's and Arthur's ascensions—for David as a projectile in slaying Goliath and for Arthur as a forge from which he alone extracts the sword, Excalibur—that is, the stone is a manifestation of the periodic Chosen One's power. Analogously, a stone is also the symbol we use to represent our predicted spiritual, philosophic, and scientific breakthrough—the so-called Philosopher's Stone, sometimes referred to as the Perennial Philosophy. Given the technology, information, and leisure afforded by our historical circumstances, the characteristics of this philosophy would be nothing less than "the outline for the cross-disciplinary synthesis and integration of human knowledge into one indivisible multi-dimensional database reflective of the universe that it describes, including the prescription for sustainable human evolution" as we refer to in 1.1 (and explore in detail in our memoir).

7.3. The Philosopher's Stone and the Spiritual Anomaly (as the Avatar or World Teacher). The relationship between the Spiritual Anomaly and the Philosopher's Stone is reflexive, that is, the proof of the Spiritual Anomaly's manifestation and the details thereof are derived from the Quantum-Torus Model (2.1 and 2.2) and the Proof of the Congruency of Science and Spirituality (1.4 and 4.1), key elements in the Philosopher's Stone itself. Contrapositively, if the time, place, and nature of the Spiritual Anomaly's manifestation are not predictable (as we have shown in 4.1 and as prophesized, "no man knoweth the Son, but the Father; neither knoweth any man the Father, save the Son ..." [Matthew 11:27]), it is only the Spiritual Anomaly that could derive and debrief such a proof (i.e., to the degree that the Great Anomaly [or G-d Principle] can be symbolized or made manifest in the flesh, the Spiritual Anomaly would be this event). Indeed, it is the Spiritual Anomaly's mission to present this proof as part of a larger effort at revealing the parameters necessary for the evolutionary progression and sustainable survival of the human race (detailed in our soon-to-be published memoir). To this end, the Spiritual Anomaly serves humanity periodically as the Avatar or World Teacher. However, it is important to note that just as idols misrepresent the anomalistic G-d principle, so do such singular-event notions as Christ or Messiah misrepresent the periodic nature of the Spiritual Anomaly, turning the recurring appearances of a once-in-an-age teacher into a divine form separate from its human (and thus dualistic) basis. In actuality, the appearance of the Spiritual Anomaly, the proof that he offers for his appearance, the availability of information, technology, and leisure that afforded him the opportunity to produce such a proof, and the space-time where and at which such events occur are inseparable and indivisible phenomena rooted in the singular origins of the universe in which they manifest.

7.4. The Analogous Method Extended to the Socio-Historical Paradigm. In addition to our proof of the convergence of science and spirituality and its check and application, we also observe that noted practitioners of both scientific and spiritual disciplines are issuing similarly dire warnings concerning the current and future state of humanity. Without going into a long list of evidence (as we do in our memoir), let us briefly note some of the key details that give rise to these warnings:

- Global warming/Climate change
- Pollution of the biosphere
- Geometric population growth
- Entrenched power of the war industry

Ironically, these threatening factors are a result of our success as a species when measured against the parameters of the Theory of Evolution and the Protestant Ethic as they are generally understood today. To a large degree, this so-called success has been economic, what we described in 7.2 as, "the technology, information, and leisure afforded by our historical circumstances."

Mapping the aforementioned positive and negative examples of contemporary human achievement to our Quantum-Torus Model, we can only deduce our position is on the cusp of a "phase shift" in organizational structure: We must evolve in order to survive, for the nature of Space-Time itself is evolutionary, regardless of whether the universe is expanding or contracting—i.e., the succession of quantum-torus intervals and the behaviors therein follow certain principles (except at the limits of vibrational activity). Going back to the various binary metaphors we have assigned to our model, e.g., "light and dark, on and off, line and broken line, 1 and 0, sphere and doughnut, particle and wave, mass and energy ..." (2.3), we observe that the self-conscious choice, or change, we face is one that resembles the transformation from darkness to light. Again, science and spirituality agree!

Indeed, this characterization matches the conclusion we reach by alternate analysis—mapping human consciousness to its consequence in human behavior, that is, deconstructing the two key evolutionary steps in human development and extrapolating their primary factors to describe our present circumstances. To wit,

The two key evolutionary steps in human development to which we refer are:

- Overcoming gravity and mastering physical tools (standing erect and prehensile thumbs)
- Overcoming communication barriers and mastering mental tools (developing language, music, mathematics, et al.)

Deconstructing these steps, we derive the following:

- Overcoming gravity and mastering physical tools = unconscious physical evolution
- Overcoming communication barriers and mastering mental tools = subconscious mental evolution

Extrapolating these characterizations leads to the following dialectical progression of *Homo sapiens*:

- Unconscious physical evolution (*Homo erectus*)
- Subconscious mental evolution (*Homo economus*)
- Conscious spiritual evolution (*Homo spiritus*)

Our scientific deduction and check proves to be the same as the spiritual teachings since time immemorial: we must overcome the tyranny of the instincts and the ego, by employing our spiritual tools, to evolve in a sustainable manner.

Another argument that we provide to support the choice of conscious spiritual evolution is derived from the nature of life itself, that is, light manifesting as DNA. Here, we find that just as the Great Anomaly (First Cause) animates creation with constant change (Δ, the Greek letter Delta), so the life-force (*prana*) exhibits the "will to live." Consider the tree that splits the stone of a mountain or the blade of grass that cracks the sidewalk, both to grow and evolve.

As we have noted, in human history, we have manifested the "will to live" at the instinctive physical level (standing erect) and at the egoistic mental level (mastering symbolic forms). Now we are at the crossroads of another major evolutionary choice, much like Hamlet as he ponders, "To be, or not to be."

Have we lost the will to live, or do we have what it takes as a species to survive? "That is the question." Our collective answers will determine whether we choose to survive (evolve) or not. As we discuss in 7.5, free will and determinism will mutually influence the outcome.

We now have shown four alternative arguments in 7 that point to the same conclusion concerning the present moment in human development: the appearance and role of the Spiritual Anomaly, overcoming the tyranny of the instincts and ego (conscious spiritual evolution), the mapping of our historical circumstances to the Quantum-Torus Model, and the self-conscious choice that the universe presently requires of earthlings for evolution.

7.5 Chaos Theory as Further Impetus for Conscious Spiritual Evolution. Chaos Theory equations show that even in a deterministic universe, outcomes remain unpredictable (quantifiable inputs produce unpredictable results). This means that Free Will and Determinism necessarily co-exist. The mathematics may be complex, but the meaning is simple: we must act as if we have free will, because as far as we can ever know, we have it. Before the mathematics of Chaos Theory were developed, the only way to prove the interdependence of free will and determinism was through the logic of letters (words and propositions). Now the letters and numbers agree: As the progression of the Quantum-Torus Model shows, "conscious spiritual evolution" is to be humanity's next step and it is to be accomplished one person at a time, through self-conscious action, arrived at through our own free will.

While it is not the focus of this paper to describe the specifics of this species-defining transformation (we do so at length in our memoir), we do believe it important to briefly note the range of individual actions with which the next stage of our evolution begins.

7.6. Individual Spiritual Practice as the Next Evolutionary Step. Essentially, what we have identified here is individual spiritual practice as the basis for progressive human development. The simplest form of such spiritual practice and the starting point for our work is nothing more than taking a deep breath and counting to ten. The purpose of this exercise—which, despite its apparent simplicity, is difficult to consistently employ—is to counter instinctive and egoistic reactions as they occur, for example, when we get cut off in traffic or are criticized by a significant other. By consciously and consistently choosing alternative behaviors to the instinctive reaction of responding in kind to such perceived offenses, we strengthen that part of ourselves which spiritual teachers identify as "the higher self" or Self. This is the same Self that Jung refers to in his essay, "Christ, the Symbol of Self,"[16] that is, an archetype within each of us (alternate descriptions of which, such as Messiah or Buddha or Krishna consciousness, are discussed at length in our memoir); in other words, a tangential point within each of us that reflects the Great Anomaly. These psycho-spiritual dynamics are the same for the Spiritual Anomaly (the Avatar or World Teacher), except for his/her periodic singular expressions synthesizing seemingly disparate elements and integrating them into a convergent framework for the current stage of the process.

Of course, in addition to the fundamental breathing exercise, there are other established practices that accomplish the same spiritual goal, a variety of which we discuss in detail in our memoir, in particular that of Yoga, through which we describe the (non-denominational) science of spiritual rebirth. However, we include within our scope here a mapping of the human body to our Quantum-Torus Model to explain the inside-out process by which Yoga catalyzes the coincidence of consciousness and the Great Anomaly and our experience of the Quantum-Torus through the heart (Love):

The Quantum Torus and Human Form
(Light Manifesting as DNA)
Original text and illustration:

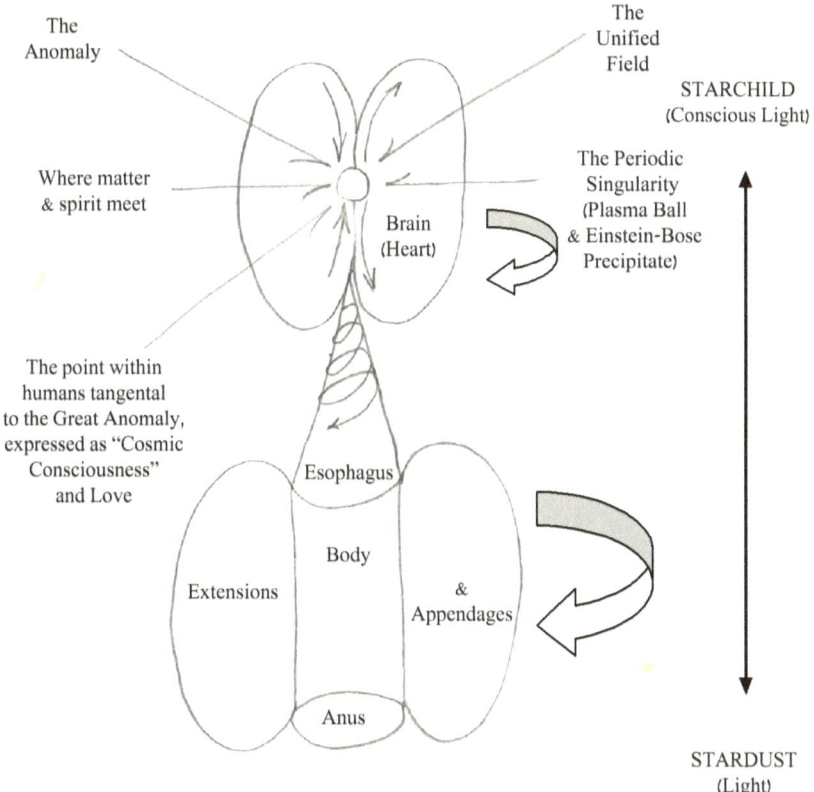

A conceptual representation of the relationship between the Torus, the Great Anomaly, Quanta, and the human mind-body-spirit. If we take the premise that Space-Time moves in a cycle from stardust to conscious light, then evolutionary growth is self-consciously achieved by employing the Quantum-Torus Model (Philosopher's Stone) to integrate the human paradigm with the Great Anomaly, i.e., the process of light becoming conscious of itself and experiencing the Quantum-Torus as Love (see the following illustration).

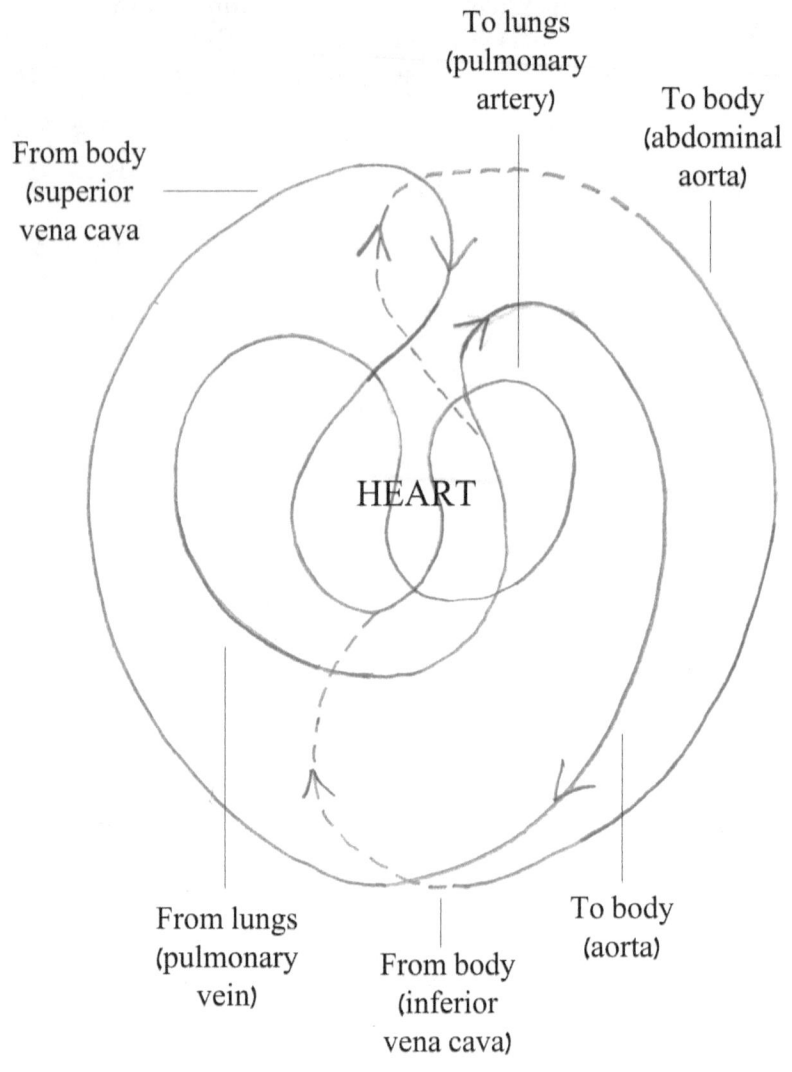

Blood circulation from the human heart as a Quantum-Torus. The heart is the first functional organ in a vertebrate embryo, signifying that Love is basis for our existence. Notice the similarity to the illustrations in 2.6 (Similar Models, both Conceived and Manifest).

Just as our physical bodies heal themselves through unconscious and subconscious processes (e.g., bleeding, coagulating, scabbing, etc.) in healing a physical wound, so our spiritual bodies heal spiritual wounds without the intervention of our egos. Yoga is simply a catalyst for accessing this life-force that, like the singularity from which it is brought forth, embodies certain indefinable anomalistic properties.

Through this scientific spiritual rebirthing process we rediscover our own connection with the Great Anomaly, and in so doing alter our consciousness and behavior—the primary result of which is in our willingness to share with others, a central objective of conscious spiritual evolution.

We fully expect to hear from cynics who posit that such a result is utopian, that is, beyond the capability of human beings and human nature to attain or sustain. We counter:

- Spiritual evolution may have been utopian at one time; it is now necessary.
- There is no such thing as fixed human nature; human beings are evolutionary, just as the light from which they are made.

Further, we have "the technology, information, and leisure afforded by our historical circumstances" (7.2) to make this work (for example, Buckminster Fuller's "World Game"), as well as any number of examples (take your pick—Abraham, Jesus, Buddha, Krishna, Mother Theresa, Gandhi, the Dalai Lama, et al.) from which to draw inspiration that such behavior is attainable. The parameters and outcomes for individual development certainly vary according to unique hereditary, environmental, and self-conscious factors, but, nevertheless, we each have a connection to the Great Anomaly—what Jung describes as the Christ (Messiah, Buddha, Krishna, et al.) archetype—that we are compelled to express.

8. MEMOIR

8.1. Publication. The means by which the Spiritual Anomaly (Avatar or World Teacher) presents the details of this mission takes the form of a memoir, the first volume of which is complete and soon to be published in the wake of this paper.

8.2. Public Reaction and Obstacles. The success of this mission will be determined by conscious individual choices. The primary obstacle to individual and group success is, as we have noted in 7.4, the tyranny of the instincts and the ego. On a global scale such behavior is currently exhibited in the priority to which we assign Capital over human evolution. Whether we interpret such behavior scientifically, by mathematically expressing it as and attributing it to the expansionary nature of Capital, both in terms of demand for resources and markets and thus the eventual commoditization of all things, or whether we interpret such behavior spiritually, as the worship of the Golden Calf and Mammon, the deduction is the same: Capital is an abstraction that rules our lives—that is, we now worship a false G-d.

The scope of this paper does not include a detailed analysis of the political, economic, and psychological dynamics that follow from this involuted behavior (such analysis is provided in detail in our memoir), but it is necessary to note here that those ascribing to such, by their own admission, worship at the altar of Capital and private gain at the expense of the spiritual evolution of the human race. However, it is also worth noting that those who exercise the greatest control over these now regressive forces individually profess in significant numbers to follow the tenets of the major religions, including Christianity, Judaism, Islam, Hinduism, et al. In presenting our proof of the congruency of science and spirituality and its applications, we sincerely hope that these individuals take heed that they "cannot serve G-d and Mammon,"[17] and stop professing to do both. We await their response, "for by thy works shall ye be judged."[18]

Secondary obstacles to the spiritual evolution of the human race include dogmatic religious bureaucracies and their subscribers, particularly those variants that claim to be privy to the truth to the exclusion of all other approaches. To counter the fallacy of such thinking, in addition to having heretofore proven the unifying principle of all religions (see "G-d principle" in 1.3, 2.5, 4.2, and 6.7), we employ the following cybernetic metaphor: We all have unique passwords to the same server; The Great Anomaly grants similar access rights to all users; There is no specific group that holds administrative rights to the exclusion of others. We call upon religious leaders to respond to our proof and to separate themselves and their followers from the temporal elements of their faith and those who seek to use spiritual trappings for material ends.

8.4. Contacting the Author and Receiving Notification of Publication.

The author of this paper wishes to retain his anonymity at this time. You may contact him by leaving your name, email address, and comments on the form below (see www.SolomonsProof.com). We shall not use any of your contact information for purposes other than contacting you concerning the publication of the aforementioned memoir, reporting progress following publication, or for replying to your inquiries. We shall not sell or otherwise share your contact information with other entities, corporate or personal.

8.5. The Ongoing Work. Finally, we urge everyone to "think globally and act locally." Identify and develop the unique gift that you have been given and share it with the world. In this way, we shall evolve one person at a time and together create a sustainable and enlightened world.

FOOTNOTES

[1] Argüelles, José A., *Earth Ascending: An Illustrated Treatise on the Law Governing Whole Systems*, Shambhala, Boulder & London, 1984.
[2] Dalai Lama, *The Universe in a Single Atom: The Convergence of Science and Spirituality*, Morgan Road Books, New York, 2005.
[3] *Tao Tê Ching* (*The Way of Life*), written by Lao Tsu in the 6th Century B.C., is the foundation of Taoism.
[4] "Heisenberg's uncertainty principle has frequently been misinterpreted by amateur philosophers. As Gilles Deleuze and F'elix Guattari (1994, 129-130) lucidly point out, in quantum physics, Heisenberg's demon does not express the impossibility of measuring both the speed and the position of a particle on the grounds of a subjective interference of the measure with the measured, but it measures exactly an objective state of affairs that leaves the respective position of two of its particles outside of the field of its actualization, the number of independent variables being reduced and the values of the coordinates having the same probability." (Sokal, Alan D., *Transgressing the Boundaries: Towards a Transformative Hermeneutics of Quantum Gravity*, http://www.sablesys.com/sokal.html)
[5] Heisenberg, Werner, *Philosophic Problems of Nuclear Science*, Fawcett Premier Books, New York, 1952, p. 28.
[6] Ibid., p. 27.
[7] A two-dimensional cutaway of this expression:

[8] This is much like Einstein's point that if you could travel faster than light you would come back to the same place that you started. Any slower speed would return you to a different place-time, i.e., the "inside" or "outside" of the point-of-origin, rather than the point-of-origin itself. In the drawing, Time is on the Z-axis that comes out of the page or goes through the page. The spiraled path (as noted by the broken line) experiences both the outside surface and inside surface of the Torus at the tangential "x" points (see drawing below, a 90-degree shift (rotated in and out of the plane of the page).

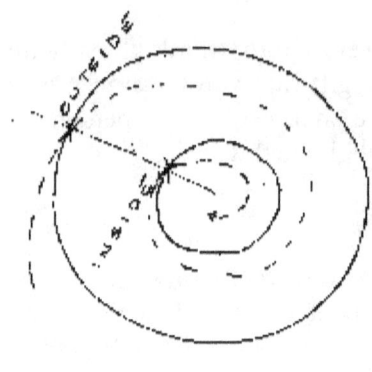

9

[10] As reflected in the esoteric maxim, "As above, so below," and the Star of David in its construction as an upright and an inverted equilateral triangle.

[11] For an in depth discussion of the parallels and compatibility of Genesis and the Big Bang (and evolution), see the works of Gerald L. Schroeder, particularly *Genesis and the Big Bang* and *The Science of God*.

[12] From Dr. Edwin D. Babbitt's *Principles of Light and Color*, 1878, as reprinted in Hall, Manly P., *The Secret Teachings of All Ages: An Encyclopedic Outline of Masonic, Hermetic, Qabbalistic and Rosicrucian Symbolical Philosophy*, The Philosophical Research Society, Inc., Los Angeles, 1968, XIII.

[13] Dr. Martin Schönberger, *The I Ching & the Genetic Code: The Hidden Key to Life*, Aurora Press, Santa Fe, 1992 (originally published in German as *Verborgener Schlüssel zum Leben*, Scherz Verlag, Bern and Munich, 1973).

[14] Matthew 24:44

[15] This also means that we could calculate, using Einstein's famous equation ($E = mc^2$), the original energy released by the Big Bang if we knew the mass of the universe, or, vice versa, we could calculate the mass of the universe if we knew the original energy released. The solution for this calculation, used in conjunction with the mathematics of toroids as an infinite fractal loop, would explain the illusion of our universe expanding faster than the speed of light and could be applied to the questions of inflation, the red shift, and whether our universe will continue to expand or eventually collapse.

[16] Jung, Carl, *Aion: Researches into the Phenomenology of the Self, Volume 9, Part II, The Collected Works of C.G. Jung*, Bollingen Series XX, Princeton University Press, 1959.

[17] Matthew 6:24 and Luke 16:13

[18] I Peter 1:17 and Revelations 20:12

Appendix 7

Michael's Notes

The following chapter is a directory of subjects of particular interest to Michael. For over thirty years, he's taken notes, clipped magazines and newspapers, and, lately, printed or saved articles off the Internet, to create a database from which he intends to draw in writing a daily commentary for a website to be started after the publication of this book. Additionally, he hopes to gather spiritual leaders and subject matter experts in world symposiums that shall consider these topics and work toward position papers that contribute toward human development and spiritual evolution. In its original form, this chapter is a Microsoft® Word file viewed in Document Map mode, where the user can click on any of the key subject words arranged alphabetically in the left margin window and be linked to commentary that appears in the main window. Space considerations in this edition allow us to print only a portion of Michael's notes.

Abortion—

In order to discuss this topic, it's important that everyone first understand their connectedness to each other and the implications of their every day actions. When Mick Jagger wrote in the lyrics for *Sympathy for the Devil*, "I shouted out who killed the Kennedys, when after all it was you and me," he was implying that our entire society and each of us within it are responsible for creating a climate within which such acts take place. The same is true for Love Canal, Birmingham Sunday, Vietnam, 9-11, and abortion. In America, driving a gas-guzzling car, eating meat at nearly every meal, wearing Nikes, or supporting Wal-Mart, etc., means contributing to imperialism, slave labor, and deaths elsewhere. Once we are able to admit this, self-righteousness begins to disappear. "We are as Gods and might as well get good at it," said Stewart Brand in *The Whole Earth Catalogue* in 1968. It is not so difficult to understand how abortion can be seen as taking a life, but do those who are opposed to abortion see—that by electing officials who send off young men to die in wars to further profit from militarism, oil consumption, and the interest on the borrowing for such purposes, or who use wars to generate election momentum, or who support the death penalty—they are also taking life? Do those who oppose abortion take an active role in encouraging healthy adoptions or encouraging honest and frank sex education as opposed to pseudo-religious indoctrination? If they oppose "murder," who is shooting abortion doctors?

In a perfect world, there would be no abortion or war, but this is not our current situation. Ending the need for abortion involves ending the need for over-consumption by one group of people and the starvation of others; it involves ending war, sexism, bigotry, capital punishment, and religious intolerance. For G-d's will to be done on earth as it is in heaven, we must lower birth rates, improve the feeding and educating of our brothers and sisters, and create a sustainable future. Then, truly, we will return to and abide in a garden where sentient beings may come to evolve. Until then, ending abortion but being opposed to aggressive action on global warming, or supporting abortion but continuing to live a consumptive life, both amount to the same sort of hypocrisy, that is, pro-death.

Recognize that, as Brand said, we are all as gods and make life and death decisions every day. Therefore, allow people to choose their level of involvement—abstinence, rhythm method, prophylactics, drugs (the pill or the morning after pill) or abortion—with the encouragement that we will strive to reduce the karma created by terminating strong life forces, not only during the procreation process, but also through militarism, capital punishment, and consumption patterns (driving, eating, etc.).

Agape—

The love of God or Christ for mankind. 2. the brotherly or spiritual love of one Christian for another. 3. unselfish, platonic love of one person for another; brotherly love. (*The Random House College Dictionary*, Laurence Urdang, Ed., Random House, Inc., New York, 1973.)

AIDS—

Nowhere is the lack of compassion by the government officials (masking as Christians), private industry (particularly the pharmaceutical companies) more evident than in the treatment of AIDS. In addition to the price gouging that has been practiced by the drug industry, the refusal of the poseurs who control the government apparatus to get involved in needle exchange programs or the distribution of prophylactics (on "moral" grounds no less!) is criminal. Is there any question what these "business people" worship? What's the "pro-life" position here, given that AIDS is contracted through both hetero- and homosexual interaction? Lost in the blindness of literal (fundamentalist) interpretations are love and compassion. Clearly those most adamant about their worthiness are lacking the most basic components of a Christian heart.

Alcoholics Anonymous/Twelve Step Programs/Addiction—

The perception that AA and other related programs are only for those with substance abuse problems is incorrect. The twelve steps work equally well for those suffering from addictions ranging from anger to sex to materialism. Given that the earth is being destroyed by materialism (which is, in itself, an outgrowth of our instinct and ego patterning), consider what would happen if we applied the program to our material compulsions:

- We admit we are powerless over our consumptive habits—that our environment has become unmanageable.
- We believe that a power greater than us can restore us to sanity and a balanced and sustainable life.
- We decide to subject our will and our lives to the care of G-d (The Great Anomaly) as we understand it.
- We make a searching and fearless inventory of ourselves.
- We admit to G-d, to ourselves, and to another human being the exact nature of our wrongs.
- We are entirely ready to have G-d (The Unknowable Mystery) remove all these defects of character.
- We humbly ask G-d (The One-Without-A-Name) to remove our shortcomings.
- We make a list of all persons we have harmed and become willing to make amends to them all.
- We make direct amends to such people wherever possible, except when to do so would injure them or others.
- We continue to take personal inventory and when we are wrong promptly admit it.
- We seek through prayer and meditation to improve our conscious contact with G-d (The Great Anomaly) as we understand it, praying only for knowledge of its will for us and the power to carry that out.
- Being awakened spiritually as a result of these steps, we seek to bring this message to others and to practice these principles in all our affairs.

Anomaly—

The "quantum jump" to which Heisenberg refers is Δ (the Greek letter Delta, meaning change), a dialectical leap or qualitative transformation. As such, it is indefinable—it is the flip between outer and inner—it occurs in no time, at all times, and is everywhere unpredictable. So, too, is the time for the Son of Man, the spiritual anomaly, unpredictable; yet it is an occurrence that is certain to occur.[1]

If I don't explain myself, who will explain me (much like Rabbi Hillel's famous question, "If I am not for myself, then who will be for me? And if I am only for myself, then what am I? And if not now, when?")? Given the nature of the spritual anomaly, who else but he could explain that which is peculiar unto himself? As Jesus says, "no man knoweth the Son, but the Father; neither knoweth any man the Father, save the Son ..." (Matthew 11:27)

The "invisible" value of the *I-Ching* is in its provision of a framework for hitherto unrealized thoughts—where subjective contents are projected onto the symbolism of the hexagrams (2^6 binary replications, that is, the unfolding of the Quantum-Torus Model); contrapositively, the changes represented by the hexagrams can be applied to daily life. In this way, the anomaly is the exoteric expression of esoteric truth contained in Hexagram 52, Keeping Still, Mountain—the moment of stillness, Yoga, the motionless union that takes place when one's consciousness is co-located with the point within us that is tangential to everything that ever was, is, and will be—the G-d principle, Christ-, Buddha-, Krishna- or Cosmic-Consciousness, the Great Anomaly.

"Fuller's life was a glorious anomaly. He made connections between things that no one else dared to link. And he was, in one of the bloodiest centuries in history, an unrepentant optimist." (*Chicago Tribune*, Arts, 3-11-01, re: Buckminster Fuller) So the Anomaly is able to focus on spiritual transformation and human evolution at a time when much of life on Earth is on the verge of extinction.

Antichrist—

"Every spirit that dissolveth Jesus ... is Antichrist ... of whom you have heard that he is cometh." (I John 4:3 [DV])

"If we see the traditional figure of Christ as a parallel to the psychic manifestations of the self, then the Antichrist would correspond to the shadow of the self, namely the dark half of the human totality, which ought not to be judged too optimistically." (Jung, C. G., *Christ: A Symbol of Self*

---

[1] See *Appendix 6 – The Proof*.

in *Psyche and Symbol*, Bollingen Series XX, Princeton University Press, 1958)

The Antichrist is us; it is our shadow. It is the unbridled instinctive nature and egocentricity that controls all persons without a spiritual practice to protect themselves. I would counsel those so adamant in pointing fingers at Antichrists external to themselves to look within and bear witness to the shadow that, if denied, rules over one's self and is truly the root of all Antichrist ("evil") activity. By our daily practice, the Antichrist shall be overcome and our higher selves—the Messiah, Christ, spiritual anomaly, et al.—shall rule.

And what of all the debate over specific persons representing the Antichrist? While there have been singular expressions of the Christ and Antichrist archetypes, they symbolize what is inherent in every individual. That is why the shadow, expressed through instinctive and ego-centric patterning as materialism and hate, is the real Antichrist. As Walt Kelly's famous swamp possum Pogo said, "... we have met the enemy and he is us."

Anti-Imperialism—

In the late '60's, the root of the movement against the Vietnam War wasn't simply "anti-war," as it was characterized in the corporate press, but "anti-imperialism," as an aspect of my beliefs may be characterized today. For example, the nation-states and city-states that I propose to be covered under spiritual protectorates—such as Tibet, Jerusalem, or Bali—are prime victims of various forms of imperialism—military, economic, cultural, and religious.

Imperialism is an outgrowth of capitalism, an affirmation that its nature is expansionary;[2] it has been perpetrated in one form or another by all races. Ultimately, it is an extension of our instincts and ego. And while it may be classified as "historical necessity" on the basis of being a natural part of the development of capitalism and humankind as we know it, it is not a tolerable behavior in advanced spiritual civilizations; it has brought us many gains in technology, information, and leisure, but on a worldwide scale it has outlived its usefulness; it cannot drive our economic system if we are to evolve. Spiritual goals and democracy shall decide how best to transform capitalistic tools to achieve our higher purposes, despite continued aggression and resistance from the "New World Order."

Astrology—

---

[2] This Marxian conclusion, derived in *Das Kapital*, is borne out daily in the *Wall Street Journal:* Grow or die!

Astrology, like the *I Ching*, is a system of self-analysis that emphasizes individualistic paths to Enlightenment based on the synchronicity of time and place, so-called acausal reasoning. Birth charts may be more or less propitious, but each represents its own unique way to salvation. Individuals may choose to use such a system to advance their self-discovery, or they may evolve using other tools, but they should not impugn astrological analysis just because some of its practitioners abuse it, or because they have been led to believe that there is no scientific basis for the influence of celestial bodies. Clearly, the menstrual cycle is a direct reflection of the moon's constant influence over our lives. And the sun's arc, is it not a trigger for nature's most basic circadian rhythms? What other influences of these central celestial bodies are unseen to us living in the cacophony and haze of industrial times? The point being, if a case can be made for the influence of the moon and the sun, why not for our proximate planetary neighbors: our solar system, like the rest of the universe, is still interconnected, just as it was during singularity; indeed the universe is holographic, meaning the original event is intrinsic to each part; thus even the lesser planets represent inalienable forces.

While Steven Weinberg,[3] in *Dreams of a Final Theory*, argues that the gravitational influence of the planets in our solar system on human consciousness and activity is insignificant, and therefore the astrological premise of ascribing events to these bodies is flawed (perhaps Weinberg forgets how much of current cosmological theory rests on small numbers, like Chaos Theory's butterfly that causes a hurricane), it should be noted that his logic is entirely causal, and does not account for synchronicity as an indication of significant influence and connectivity. For Weinberg and others to call synchronicity, and other such acausal phenomena, irrational, simply because such methods do not meet empirical (causal) standards, is to fall victim to what José Argüelles described as "... the loss of sacred view."[4] In our universe, even physicists would agree that everything is built from the same primordial matter (the Plasma Ball), and that the past and future are intrinsic to the present. Weinberg and other "logical" apologists are simply confusing irrational and acausal. This is why physicists are mystified by "Action at a Distance" (so-called "Spooky Action"), which we explain in our proof.[5] It is the nature of acausal reasoning that it be inexplicable just as the anomaly and Heisenberg's Uncertainty Principle are,

---

[3] Shared the 1979 Nobel Prize for Physics for a theory unifying electromagnetic interactions and the weak forces within the nucleus of an atom.

[4] "The notion that there are different fields of knowledge that are unrelated to each other is fundamentally the result of a loss of sacred view." Argüelles, José A., *Earth Ascending: An Illustrated Treatise on the Law Governing Whole Systems*, Shambhala, Boulder & London, 1984.

[5] See *Appendix 6 – The Proof*.

at a certain point, inexplicable. One can attempt to use metaphors to describe these processes, just as mathematics and musical notation can be used to describe music, or as letters and words are used to describe Samadhi and G-d, but these symbolic representations are only approximations of the event.[6]

This said, it also is true that Astrology is a much abused tool, confusing possible influences of the sun and the moon with psychic predictions and fate. The black and white astrological interpretation that certain aspects of the astral body, particularly squares and oppositions, are "negative" or "bad" is a good example of such hocus-pocus. It represents much the same misconception as medieval "humours" or our current mythology, "human nature." The astral body is akin to a circuit board. One way of testing it is to run more juice through it than for which it was designed. Under this stress, weaknesses show up. These are the areas to be worked on, improved, and fixed, not immutable flaws. All is subject to change, even our nature, else how would we have evolved from stardust to consciousness? These "lessons learned" are part of our development, which we must assume is necessary given the fact of our incarnation.

Whether you believe these arguments or not, Astrology's value as a means of introspection is undiminished by a lack of empirical proof for its "science." Like the *I Ching* and other acausal matrixes, Astrology's value is in the use of its framework for organizing our projections (shadows on the wall of the cave) at any designated point in time, not in the causal relationship of this matrix to our birth time or any other specific events for that matter. One can argue that there are better tools, but not against Astrology's value as a tool.

Atlantis—

Before the flood, in Atlantian cosmology, there was wide-scale acceptance of the unity of all things and the One-Without-A-Name, the Great Anomaly. Rather than the authoritarian and generally cynical (though at the time, necessary) view of humankind evidenced by Ten Commandments, Atlantian spiritual practice revolved around self-examination through 42 questions. After the flood, understanding of these principles became degraded as the human race and its history fragmented, leading to spiritual devolution. Now, we must retrieve that which is universal and eternal in each of the various belief systems that remain and recognize their original and singular source. (see Spiritual Unity)

Avatar—

---

[6] See *Appendix 6 – The Proof*, section 1.3, "Congruency in Scientific, Philosophic, and Spiritual Principles."

When J. Thomas Looney went looking for the likely author of the Shakespearean canon, he drew a profile of the suspect (à la Sir Arthur Conan Doyle's methodology) and found Edward de Vere, the 17th Earl of Oxford. Similarly, if G-d were advertising for an avatar, what would be included in the job description? Given the prophesies that call into account our current timeframe, and given the complex nature of human knowledge at this time, the likely qualifications include: Cross-cultural spiritual interests; vast interdisciplinary knowledge of the Arts, Humanities, and Sciences; extreme self-assuredness balanced with humility; the prophetic pedigree; self-sacrificing temperament; strength of convictions and a willingness to stand alone if necessary; extraordinary tolerance for sublimation; deep appreciation for the ancients and Paleolithic myth and culture; a poetic sense of metaphor and turn of phrase; familiarity with spiritual rebirthing processes; balanced masculine and feminine sensibilities; and prowess in various forms of physical culture. The *Übermensch* is not a fascist; he is the yogic millennial man.

"Revelation, according to Buddhism, is a continuous process, and another Buddha is due to be born on Earth in the not too distant future. Maitreya by name (Miroku in Japanese), he will be the embodiment of mercy, and will carry on the work of salvation begun by previous Buddhas."[7]

"The coming of a Teacher has always taken place whenever humanity had reached a certain point in its evolution; needed some new spiritual guidance; some new energy; an outline of a new way which would lead it into a new, higher experience of itself and its meaning and purpose ... We know Them historically as Hercules, Hermes, Mithra, Rama, Vyasa, Sankaracharya, Krishna, Buddha, as well as the Christ. There have been greater ones and lesser ones ... But never before, since Atlantean times, has there been the World Teacher, the Teacher for mankind, the Eldest Brother of the race, and at the same time, openly in the world, the Masters of the Hierarchy. This is the tremendous event which is now taking place."[8]

Bahá'í—

Bahá'ís believe in:

- One God.
- The oneness of humanity.

---

[7] Kakuzo Okakura, *The Book of Tea*, Dover Publications, Inc., New York, 1964 (reprinted from the original published by Fox, Duffield and Company, 1906), p. 70.
[8] Benjamin Creme, *The Reappearance of the Christ and the Masters of Wisdom*, The Tara Press, London, 1980, pp. 77-8.

- Independent investigation of truth.
- The common foundation of all religions.
- The essential harmony of science and religion.
- Equality of women and men.
- Elimination of prejudice of all kinds.
- Universal compulsory education.
- A spiritual solution to the economic problem.
- A universal auxiliary language.
- Universal peace.

Behaviorism—

An important aspect of personal growth, to use a business term, is "Research and Development." Here, progress can be invisible for long periods of time. Consider Einstein's observation, "Imagination is more important than knowledge." Like visions, the development of imagination is an internal product of time and individual work. It cannot be measured in any quantitative way because such change is qualitative and spiritual by nature. Behaviorists would do well to take note that the foundation for behavior begins with this process and that not only is it immeasurable, but that it is capable of transforming what they take to be immutable patterns of our personalities and turning them into creative and unique, i.e. unpredictable, beings. Such are the limitations of the so-called science of Behaviorism, for in an evolved world, behavior is thankfully less predictable than one in which everyone is subject to the same chain stores, curriculum, sitcoms, commercials, propaganda, and thought patterns.

Bill of Rights—

A study done on the 200th anniversary of the signing of the U.S. Constitution indicated that most Americans don't know what rights are guaranteed to them by the Constitution, with many even believing that some of these rights should be taken away. Such ignorance only aids those who readily undermine our rights to maintain their stranglehold over the state apparatus for the wealth and power that it enables, which manifests as obscene over-consumption and worship of the Golden Calf.

"The progress of science in furnishing the Government with means of espionage is not likely to stop with wire-tapping. Ways may some day be developed by which the Government, without removing papers from secret drawers, can reproduce them in court, and by which it will be enabled to expose to a jury the most intimate occurrences of the home. ... Can it be that the Constitution affords no protection against such invasions of individual security?" --Supreme Court Justice Louis Brandeis, 1928 dissent.

10-26-01, Susan Milligan, *The Boston Globe*, "Terrorism bill goes to Bush for signature," Washington – "Confronting a 'new world' of terrorist threats, the Senate voted nearly unanimously Thursday to grant sweeping new powers to federal law enforcement agencies, ushering in what analysts called a fundamental change in the relationship between the government and its citizens. ... The counter-terrorism bill, passed 98-1 and sent to President Bush for his signature, contains new wiretapping and surveillance authority, including the right to seek court-ordered searches of someone's home or property without prior notification, and to trace individual e-mail and internet use. ... 'I think it certainly fundamentally reorders the domestic role of the intelligence agencies, particularly the CIA,' said James Dempsey, deputy director for the Center for Democracy and Technology, a group that advocates Internet privacy. ... 'And in the name of fighting terrorism,' Dempsey added, 'gives the FBI a broad range of powers that really have no meaningful judicial constraints on them to collect information and probe individuals.' ... 'We have real concerns' about the package,' said Wayne LaPierre, of the National Rifle Association."

"Congress will fulfill its duty only when it protects both the American people *and* the freedoms at the foundation of American society. So let us preserve our heritage of basic rights. Let us practice as well as preach that liberty." --Sen. Russ Feingold (D-Wisconsin) before casting *the only dissenting vote* against the aforementioned "Anti-Terrorism" bill, H.R. 3162.

10-26-01, *Associated Press*, Washington – "Vice President Dick Cheney said Thursday that homeland security is not a temporary measure for the current crisis, but 'will become permanent in American life ... I think of it as the new normalcy,' Cheney said. The vice president spoke to a Republican Governors Association fund-raiser."

"It is fundamental that the great powers of Congress to conduct war and to regulate the Nation's foreign relations are subject to the constitutional requirements of due process. The imperative necessity for safeguarding these rights to procedural due process under the gravest of emergencies has existed throughout our constitutional history, for it is then, under the pressing exigencies of crisis, that there is the greatest temptation to dispense with fundamental constitutional guarantees which, it is feared, will inhibit governmental action ... The Constitution of the United States is a law for rulers and people, equally in war and peace, and covers with the shield of its protection all classes of men, at all times, and under all circumstances ... In no other way can we transmit to posterity unimpaired the blessings of liberty, consecrated by the sacrifices of the Revolution." --Supreme Court Justice Arthur Goldberg, Kennedy v. Mendoza-Martinez.

Blasphemy—

No matter what people say about the so-called sanctity of their religion, if they preach hatred or intolerance of others, they have nothing to do with G-d, Allah, Vishnu, or whatever they may call the spirit-force that animates the world. G-d (the Great Anomaly) on the human scale is love and compassion (the torus of the heart and mind), which, of course, is what his prophets preach. Anything less is politics disguised as religion and is not connected with the deity in any meaningful way.

The development of the canon of today's religions is much like a secret that is whispered around a campfire—by the time it gets back to the originator it bears little resemblance to the original teaching. Present day Judaism, Christianity, Islam, Buddhism, Hinduism, etc., are all much like this— vastly distorted from the unity they presume to represent.

All these G-ds that you have conjured are metaphors of my bounty, invented in the absence of there being a name by which you can call me, icons in which you see but a few of my infinite faces.

Don't do it "in the name of G-d," do it "in the name of compassion and love." You can't pronounce the name of G-d anyway, because there is no "name." Use a substitute name if you will, but "Love is the Law." Do unto others as you would have them do unto you.

Born again—

Don't think that by simply declaring that "Jesus Christ is my Lord and Savior" that you've fulfilled the requirements for being saved. On the contrary, "For the Son of man shall come in the glory of his Father with his angels; and then he shall reward every man according to his works." (Matthew 16:27) Most of the so-called devout and pious have little to stand on when it comes to spiritual works. Woe unto you hypocrites, for the One within you is not fooled!

So-called born-again Christians and fundamentalists of all stripes are long on talk and short on works, unless those works be to shame and confound their brothers and sisters. In fact most of their works involve proselytizing, denigrating, and even slaughtering those of other beliefs. They are not about love and compassion, but about self-righteousness.

Being born again in spirit is available to anyone and may be interpreted in an infinite variety of ways.

"In a stern message for the 21st century, the Dalai Lama said Wednesday that religious people must do more than offer prayers if the world is to become a better place to live ... 'Change only takes place through action,' said the exiled Buddhist spiritual leader of Tibet. 'Frankly speaking, not through prayer or meditation, but through action.'" (*Los Angeles Times*, 12/9/99)

Boulder, Colorado—

Many have speculated on the reasons behind Boulder's development as a spiritual center, from Michio Kushi's examination of Pi lines in *East West Journal*, to the Arapahoe tribes' Chief Niwot's prophesy surrounding the beauty of the valley itself. Indeed the town is a beehive of spiritual activity, as evidenced by the advertising in *Nexus*, the town's monthly alternative healing journal. This said, it suffers from the disease of materialism as all wealthy areas do: progressive restrictions on land-use have driven up real estate prices; up-scale restaurants and luxury cars crowd downtown streets, all populated mostly by Caucasians; and the police feel free to use the latest fascist tactics and technology against the residents with or without provocation.

Boulder became the first city in the United States to establish a tax for open space. It was the second city in the United States (after Petaluma, CA won a Supreme Court decision) to limit growth. It was also the first city in Colorado to establish campaign finance limits. Recently, Boulder became one of the few American cities party to the Kyoto Accord on global warming. The Boulder City Council also joined a number of other cities in passing a resolution expressing concern over the assault on civil liberties contained in the USA Patriot Act passed by Congress in October, 2001. While it is an easy target for those who wish to make fun of its new age earnestness and relatively homogenous culture, Boulder nonetheless addresses evolutionary issues that most other communities avoid.

"The city of Boulder has joined environmental groups in accusing the United States government of failing to study how some government-funded projects will affect the environment. ... The city, as well as Greenpeace and Friends of the Earth, plan to file a lawsuit in federal court today on behalf of Boulder citizens and members of the two organizations. ... They said the suit will charge that the Export Import Bank of the United States and the Overseas Investment Corp. have funded and insured oil fields, pipelines and coal-fired power plants without looking into the impact those projects would have on the environment. Marcos Mocine-McQueen, "Boulder takes on U.S. in lawsuit," *Denver Post*, 8/27/02.

According to a November, 2008, *Forbes* magazine article that mined data from the U.S. Census Bureau's American Community Survey, Boulder is the smartest town in the U.S., based on the proportion of people older than 25 with bachelor's, master's, professional, and doctoral degrees.

As radical as Boulder may seem to the rest of the state and the nation, so the town of Wayne seems to Boulderites.

Calvinism—

A survey by Yankelovich Partners conducted June 28 – July 8, 1999 showed that half of Americans believe money shouldn't be discussed in church, even though the Bible makes 2,340 references to money and material possessions. By ignoring their shadows, churchgoers have simply fueled the evils of materialism. By allowing this to happen, religions have abdicated their responsibility, sold their soul for gold, and relinquished any claim that they may once have had to represent the deity. Since Moses' parable on the subject of materialism wasn't enough—when he returned from Mount Sinai and drew a line in the sand between יהוה and the Golden Calf—I made it as simple as I could: "You cannot serve both G-d and mammon." However, in-between my last visit and the present one the scientific proof of this position has been established. This does not mean that we haven't received many valuable things from capitalism—technology, information, and leisure—but we now know it is a system that inherently must expand in order to survive.

The mathematics of this was proven long ago by Marx, in *Das Kapital*, just as the supporting details are published every day in the *Wall Street Journal*. But we are unsettled about how to self-consciously reorganize our economic affairs into a more spiritual and egalitarian state. Capitalists, liberals and conservatives alike, point to the so-called "failed experiments" of Russia and China, attempting to link socialism to the totalitarian nature of the regimes that claimed to be responsible for its so-called implementation. Of course, Russian and Chinese societies were totalitarian without Marx—the Commissars ruled as the Czars just as Mao ruled like a Ming. So, totalitarianism in these instances is a cultural phenomena not an economic one. After all, to blame Marx for Russian and Chinese totalitarianism would be like blaming Jesus for the bigotry and greed of so-called Christians.

That is why I'm suggesting the adoption of spiritual practice ("Taking a deep breath and counting to ten, *et al.*) as the first step in transforming the world, because evolving in this manner brings us to consciousness that embraces sharing. When we overcome the tyranny of our instinctive and ego-centric impulses through spiritual practice, we are uplifted by our higher selves to a state that makes sharing possible. What we call this state is irrelevant (Please, no "isms."), but it is nevertheless this state that makes it possible to realign our economic affairs with our spiritual goals.

Rightfully or wrongfully attributed, Calvinism has produced the so-called spiritual argument for the wedding of Christianity and Capitalism: "The wealthy are of the Elect," etc. This, in turn, serves as the pseudo-spiritual disguise for the denizens of the New World Order—the Rockefellers, the Bushes, *et al.*)—who, like Caesar and the Pope alike, justify their bloody rule as G-d-given. Clearly, the opposite is true: their behavior describes the very mammon worshipers that Moses and Jesus warned against; they are, at least metaphorically speaking, the Satanists among us.

Campaign financing—

In addition to the argument that the use of private monies in the electoral process unconstitutionally infringes upon the spirit of "one person, one vote" by giving more votes and influence to those with more dollars, the use of private monies would violate anti-trust laws if such laws were applied to the electoral process: A particular class of people (the rich) uses its prodigious market power (monopoly capital) to harm a competitor (any candidate they oppose) and stifle competition (alternative beliefs). Perhaps the Federal Election Commission ought to be sued for permitting Anti-trust violations. The Anti-trust arguments used by the government in the original Microsoft case should be applied to campaign financing. The rich and powerful can howl all they want about their right to spend as they wish as if this were a free speech issue, but the Supreme Court ruled that this argument doesn't hold up. Writing a concurring opinion for the majority in Nixon v. Shrink Missouri PAC (Jan. 24, 2000), Justice Stevens said, "Money is property; it is not speech. Speech has the power to inspire volunteers to perform a multitude of tasks on a campaign trail, on a battleground, or even on a football field. Money, meanwhile, has the power to pay hired laborers to perform the same tasks. It does not follow, however, that the First Amendment provides the same measure of protection to the use of money ... as it provides to the use of ideas to achieve the same results." It should be noted that this finding conflicts with the 1976 U.S. Supreme Court decision in Buckley vs. Valeo, which found that certain provisions of the Federal Election Campaign Administration "unconstitutionally interfere with the protected and valued right of each citizen to engage in the discussion of public issues and vigorously and tirelessly to advocate his own election." Which shall it be—the corporate-military-industrial state or the people's state? I suggest the first step in campaign finance reform is a constitutional amendment barring private monies from elections and making reasonable stipulations for alternative political parties.

We should be electing gifted people to office, not the whores of mammon who only pretend to have a spiritual practice. Through public campaign financing, and the supplanting of slaves and wage-slaves through technology and evolved social planning, the time for Plato's guardians has arrived. As surely as Jesus threw the money changers out of the temple, so shall we toss the influence-peddlers and bribe-takers from the temple of democracy.

The new bankruptcy laws are another perfect example of how campaign contributions directly bribed Congress into passing legislation favorable to those who control monopolistic proportions of capital. Within such legislation are the seeds of revolution, however, for during economic downturns a large underclass with no ability to pay its debts will sow its discontent, despite unconstitutional "anti-terrorist" laws. These laws are much like the reparations the Allies perpetrated on Germany after World War I. And what came out of that? Despite financial help from Rockefeller's Standard Oil and their allies and vassals, Hitler committed suicide in bunker.

On May 22, 2001, the Republican National Committee held a fundraiser featuring George W. Bush, several members of his cabinet, and most of the top GOP leaders in Congress. "Among the 121 names on the organizing-committee list for the dinner," reported *The New York Times*, "are lobbyists and executives from oil, gas and nuclear-energy companies that helped shape the White House energy plan, from manufacturing concerns delighted by Mr. Bush's early decision to overturn workplace ergonomic rules, from credit card companies grateful for Mr. Bush's support for a bill to make it harder for people to escape their debts in bankruptcy and from cigarette makers encouraged by reports that the government may drop a $100 billion racketeering lawsuit against the industry."

Cataclysm—

Biblical prophesies aside, the signs are everywhere that the earth's biosphere is being destroyed before our eyes: ice shelves are falling off at alarming rates; plant and animal species are being crowded out of habitats, eaten, or polluted to extinction; the ozone layer that protects us from harmful rays is being depleted; wars are prolific; and despite AIDS and other plagues, human populations are out of control. All of these events are directly related to over-consumption by too many people. Only by curbing our greed and cynicism—the dominance of our instincts, senses, and ego—through spiritual practice can we hope to evolve and thrive in a sustainable manner.

Censorship—

624   »   Michael's Notes

Americans like to think of themselves as the freest nation on earth, but scrutiny of the world press indicates that this is not so. The owners of America's media (a smaller and smaller group each year, now down to five or six) do an excellent job at suppressing major stories. For example, on the eve of the 2000 U.S. Presidential election the purging of tens of thousands of Florida voters, almost entirely blacks, Hispanics, and white Democrats, made headlines in London, but was totally ignored here. Every year *Project Censored*, a media watchdog group, publishes a list of major stories similarly suppressed. As footnoted in this book (*Appendix 8 - Anatomy of Treason*), J.P. Morgan and a small coterie of men bought out the editorial policies of the tone-setting newspapers in the United States. These same forces are at work today. Again, as we have quoted Teddy Roosevelt, "Behind the ostensible government sits enthroned an invisible government owing no allegiance and acknowledging no responsibility to the people." (see http://www.zeitgeistmovie.com/)

Charity / Welfare—

While G.W. Bush, who was largely appointed by corporate dollars, computer hacking, and five judges, remains hell-bent on redistributing middle and lower income tax dollars to the rich, America's safety net for those in need continues to shrink. The (privately) richest nation on earth refuses to consider improving its increasingly restrictive health care and social services systems for an ever-expanding underclass.[9] Instead, Bush suggests that private religious charities take care of these matters, so that more tax dollars can be freed up for tax breaks for the rich, military spending, and higher oil prices. In a spiritual country, Mr. Bush and his friends would be shunned as agents of the devil.

China—

Chinese greed and cynicism make them morally equivalent to every other destructive regime in the world. The denuding, rape, and genocide of Tibet is no less barbaric than the actions of the imperialists the Chinese were so fond of chanting about in the '60's and early '70's. While China may claim that the end vision of their philosophy of so-called "Marxism-Leninism-Maoism" somehow justifies the means, this is a travesty of the Dialectic and an insult to "scientific socialism." Their barbarism is a result of their lack of understanding of the philosophical implications of $E=mC^2$, the Big Bang, Poincaré's Conjecture, and the Quantum Torus model, namely, the transcendent and spiritual nature of the Great Anomaly.

---

[9] Jim Lobe, "Rich-Poor Divide Worst Among Rich Countries," Inter Press Service, 10/22/08.

An example of this limitation in current Chinese thinking is its adherence to the popular Marxist phrase that equates "Religion is the opiate of the people" to the absence of spiritual phenomena. On the contrary, science ends and begins where spirituality does—in the unnamable force that animates the world. The materialistic morass of "seeing is believing" represented by the present Chinese paradigm is just a few steps up from infantile solipsism, just as Chinese imperial aspirations are another insidious expression of what we've already seen from Babylon, Egypt, Rome, the Mongols, Europe, the Soviet Union, and the United States. Like Ozymandias,[10] civilizations such as these, based on hollow principles, shall be "relegated to the dustbin of history," as Marx put it, not because they were feudal, capitalistic, or perhaps even collectivist, but because the principles upon which they were built were short-sighted and temporal, and ignored their own dreams, unique truths, and the evolution of consciousness itself.

China's attempt to install its own Panchen Lama in place of the one that was identified by Tibetan Buddhist monks and rightfully represents this key lineage is an exact mirror of what Rome did with Christianity, by editing the teachings of Jesus, and with history itself, by burning the libraries at Alexandria: it is a blatant attempt by Chinese authorities to hijack Buddhist doctrine and use it for its own political purposes. It shall fail because it has no moral basis. Those driven by cynicism, power, and greed have consistently attempted to rob humanity of its spiritual legacy by replacing a history of evolution and spiritual development with a cynical view—"sinful human nature"—a concept totally lacking evidence. The continued Chinese attacks on Falun Gong show quite clearly that the Chinese government is not only devoid of spiritual intent, but weak in character and fearful of its claim to legitimacy.

The Chinese are worse than the Taliban—they destroyed far more holy sites in Tibet than the Taliban did in Afghanistan and elsewhere; and then the Chinese resurrected the Tibetan Church as a front for their political purposes—they are truly the Anti-Buddha (Antichrist) of the East. [Their executions, as well, far exceed the Taliban's in number and in contempt for the judicial process.] This strategy is exactly what Marx warned against, using religion as the opiate of the people. Their opposition to the Dalai Lama is not that he has a church, only that it is a church that does not support the purposes of the Chinese materialistic and imperialistic state: the religion of the Golden Calf.

---

[10] From the poem *Ozymandias* by Percy Bysshe Shelley. "Two vast and trunkless legs of stone/ Stand in the desert/... and on the pedestal these words appear:/ 'My name is Ozymandias, king of kings:/ Look on my works, ye Mighty, and despair!'/ Nothing beside remains. Round the decay/ Of that colossal wreck, boundless and bare/ The lone and level sands stretch far away."

I would expect the allure of capital to allay any reservations George Bush's superiors may have about Chinese intent, after all they see eye-to-eye when it comes to the ruthless exploitation of people and resources,[11] capital punishment, and the use of state force to suppress dissent. In fact, the Chinese lust for executions far exceeds Bush's own horrific record in Texas. And the lack of medical support for all except those who can pay is clearly indicative of a capitalistic, not socialistic, ethic—a far cry from the Chinese physicians of yore, who only got paid if they cured you, and paid you if they could not cure you. Clearly, the China and the U.S.A. are more alike in behavior than either would admit.

Christ Consciousness—

Christ consciousness is an integrated state of being that results from a combination of spiritual practice, Divine Syzygy,[12] dream awareness, personal empowerment, and study.

It is important to understand the distinction between this state of consciousness, which also may be called Messiah-, Buddha-, or Krishna-Consciousness, and the manifestation of spiritual anomalies that attain this state, namely Christ, Messiah, Buddha, Krishna, et al. As with any other field of human endeavor, spirituality has its anomalies that move the bar up to a qualitatively different standard. Cosmic consciousness is available to anyone, but teaching a new dispensation of such consciousness is a rare, periodic singularity, manifesting once an age or so.

Part of my reason for manifesting as a householder is to broaden the (artificially-limited) understanding of Messiah and Christ consciousness. Otherwise, why should the average person believe they can achieve the same state if the attainment had not already been shown? As the Dalai Lama explained, it's easy to behave purely when not saddled with the responsibilities of a householder: "If I went to work for a company ... I do not know how far I would be able to follow my own advice. I don't know—I might start stomping around, yelling and breaking things ... I might get fired!" (from *The Art of Happiness at Work*) Of course, there is ample evidence (some of which is secretly held by the Vatican) that Jesus was a householder.

For those who have a hard time believing in the divine nature of Jesus' or my or their own incarnation, such consciousness can be seen, alternatively, in purely psychological terms, as a repeatable achievement of the highest

---

[11] What ex-patriot Chinese novelist Dai Sijie calls "savage capitalism." Indeed, in July of 2001, the Chinese Communist Party invited capitalists to join.
[12] See in this index

form of human integration, *Christ, the Symbol of Self*, as Jung's essay describes.

Civilization—

Civilization is a thin veneer that tenuously covers our jungle heritage. Within it we stand on the shoulders of those that preceded us in building our "City of G-d" in a seemingly random and hostile environment. As we evolve, we come to see the perfection of the whole and the necessity of spiritual practice as a driving force in our work, overcoming the tyranny of the instincts and ego, embracing conscious spiritual evolution.

Civil liberties—

"They that give up essential liberty to obtain a little temporary safety deserve neither liberty nor safety." --Benjamin Franklin

Just as the powers of the Church and State are separated in theory, so shall Democracy and Capitalism be separated in fact. In this way, humanity shall be freed from the chains of an abstraction that converts value to the lowest common denominator; in this way, freedom shall be restored to the human spirit.

Conspiracy—

While many remain skeptical of CIA and FBI involvement in various assassinations, wars, coups d'états, and other such provocations, evidence continues to support this contention. Acoustic studies from London indicate that the shots that killed Kennedy came from more than one direction, just as the attending physician swore until the day he died.[13] Now we have FBI files showing that J. Edgar Hoover suppressed evidence that would have led to the prosecution of those responsible for the Birmingham church bombings 38 years before they were finally brought to Justice—not to mention Hoover's on-going harassment of Martin Luther King. (Who is it that supports Hoover's name remaining on the FBI building in Washington, D.C.?)

Remember, the mission of the CIA is conspiracy—i.e., committing acts and then denying complicity.

---

[13] As the original autopsy photos show and as the Zapruder film so graphically illustrates, Kennedy was hit first from the rear, and then from the front, when the right rear of his head was blown off. The stereographic prints of the autopsy photos, altered after various eyewitnesses had seen them, clearly reveal the forged patch.

The coup d'état of 2000, the cover-up of 9-11, and the lies that followed from the junta are, as we have detailed in Chapter 12 and Appendix 8, overwhelming proof of the real conspiracy behind the self-described New World Order:

> "We are grateful to *The Washington Post*, *The New York Times*, *Time Magazine* and other great publications whose directors have attended our meetings and respected their promises of discretion for almost forty years. It would have been impossible for us to develop our plan for the world if we had been subject to the bright lights of publicity during those years. But, the work is now much more sophisticated and prepared to march towards a world government. The supranational sovereignty of an intellectual elite and world bankers is surely preferable to the national auto-determination practiced in past centuries."
>
> --David Rockefeller, founder of the Trilateral Commission, in an address to a meeting of The Trilateral Commission, in June, 1991.

For a detailed examination of the consolidated financial interests behind world events, see http://www.zeitgeistmovie.com/.

Consumption—

Materialism is a disease worse than the Plague because those infected don't die; they continue to despoil the earth.

40% of all Nike shoes are made in China, where no independent unions have been allowed until at least until 2006. Other Nike manufacturing sites are similarly without human consideration. Of course, Nike is not alone in its medieval labor practices—these are standards across the world. Until those who pretend to follow a religious or spiritual teaching see the direct effect of their consumptive habits on others and take compensatory action, their faith is nothing more than hollow words.

In response to calls for energy conservation, President Bush's recent declaration that over-consumption is "the American way" is so preposterous as to defy believability. A recent *Los Angeles Times* poll (4/30/01) indicates that 50% of Americans believe that improving the environment should take priority over economic growth. In addition, an astounding 58% said that protecting plants and animals should trump protection of property rights.

"Drawing on research from a number of agencies and institutions, Worldwatch Institute, an independent research organization in Washington, said in its annual study 'State of the World 2000' that 1.2 billion people, the largest number ever recorded, are underfed and undernourished. But, the report adds, another 1.2 billion people are eating too much or too much of the wrong food and have become 'probably the fastest growing group of the malnourished.'" ("Obesity rivals hunger," Barbara Crossette, *The New York Times,* appearing in *The Denver Post,* 1/17/00)

The Reagan era deregulation of the savings and loan industry cost American taxpayers a half a trillion dollars to fix after our pockets had been picked by the likes of Neal Bush and other white collar rapists. Now we are being asked to ante up for the thefts under the guise of energy deregulation in the wake of the Enron debacle. Not only did George W. Bush campaign in Ken Lay's private jet, he and Dick Cheney invited the energy barons into the White House to set energy policy aimed at gouging consumers. Then they suggest that the answer to higher prices is to drill in wildlife refuges and build more power plants. The only real answer in the long run, however, is to consume less and develop alternative fuel sources.

Fuel Economy for New Cars Is at Lowest Level Since '80 (*The New York Times*, 5/18/01)

Corporate welfare—

In 1996, Congress passed a welfare reform bill aimed at reducing the number of people receiving public assistance. In theory, the idea was that people who received public assistance had no motivation to work and therefore needed to be forced to work by withdrawing government support for their "inactivity." Interestingly enough, the amount of tax dollars that go to supporting marginal or unnecessary corporate programs continues to increase. There are a couple of reasons for this morally upside-down state of affairs: Corporations control those who get elected; those who most vehemently claim to be followers of Christ are actually worshippers of mammon; and, pseudo-Christian moral self-righteousness loves to point fingers at the poor who are deemed undeserving when, in fact, prior to the industrial revolution, poverty was considered virtuous.

The very companies that asked for help in dealing with the energy crisis wrote the deregulation laws that led to their dilemma. Since they were unable to compete in the open market with cheap natural gas, and had wasted so much money on failed nuclear plants, bankruptcy and public welfare provided the easiest means for these companies to get paid for their failed policy-making.

Before that, Chrysler, Continental Illinois Bank, and the Penn Central railroad were bailed out by the public, just as the savings and loan industry, deregulated by Reagan and plundered by his buddies, was bailed out by the public.

Corporate tax shelters shift the tax burden of tens of billions of dollars a year onto individuals.

In 1995, the libertarian Cato Institute detailed 129 federal programs that channel $87 billion dollars into corporate subsidies.

The Agriculture Department spends hundreds of millions of dollars advertising products overseas for large corporations such as McDonalds and Pillsbury.

Tax loopholes for corporations and the wealthy amount to over $500 billion a year. In addition, the IRS has turned away from auditing large corporations ("The Light-Touch Tax Audit" editorial in *The New York Times*, January 15, 2007.

Former EPA Administrator Christie Todd Whitman limited the liability of Citigroup to clean up the Shattuck Super Fund site in Denver, while she and her husband hold hundreds of thousands of dollars in stock in the company. This is a small-time conflict of interest compared to the profit that the George Bush's family receives from his militaristic policies and the massive spending required to replenish weaponry and armaments every time we drop a bomb or lose a gun.

Crusades—

The devil is often disguised as G-d, which explains why more people have been slaughtered in the name of G-d than of the devil. While it is necessary to have compassion for those who, in their depravity, believe that it is their mission to convert others through proselytizing, Crusades, Inquisitions, Pogroms, and ethnic cleansings, it is important to recognize that their actions make them an instrument of the devil, not G-d. Such means have certainly spread the name of Jesus, Mohammed, and a host of others around the globe, but at what cost?

The missionary conversion process is hereby terminated. It is now our task to understand and have compassion for those who call the deity something other than what we are accustomed. It is now possible for most of the world to instantaneously recognize the unity of all spiritual practices, as I have proved to be the case.[14]

---

[14] See *Appendix – The Proof* or www.SolomonsProof.com.

Dalai Lama—

"During the early years of exile, when we were struggling to survive as a people and trying to preserve our identity and culture, the situation in Tibet was getting worse every year. The process of death and destruction, which had begun in the 1950s, escalated during the chaos of the Cultural Revolution. When it was all over, some 6,400 (99.9 percent) monasteries had been destroyed, and roughly 1,200,000 (out of a total of approximately 6 million) Tibetans had died prematurely - as a direct result of Chinese occupation policies." (http://www.gotaro2.homestead.com/)

"We Tibetans have an equal right to maintain our own distinctive culture as long as we do not harm others. Materially we are backward, but in spiritual matters—in terms of the development of the mind—we are quite rich." (From *Tibetan Portrait—The Power of Compassion*, photographs by Phil Borges, text by His Holiness the Dalai Lama, Rizzoli International Publications, Inc., New York, 1996.)

"Many times I am asked if I am angry at the Chinese for what has happened. Sometimes I lose some temper, but afterwards I get more concern, more compassion towards them. In my daily prayer, I take in their suffering, their anger, and ignorance ... and give back compassion. This kind of practice I continue." (*Ibid.*, Borges)

What is the difference between the Dalai Lama and a murderer? As the Dalai Lama indicates in the previous quote, it is not their instincts—they both have similar reactions to events. It is their spiritual practice. The murderer is controlled by his instinctive reactions and the Dalai Lama is not. So is the mass of humankind mostly controlled by its animal nature. The evolutionary path, from animals to spiritual beings, is long and seriously challenging. We have gone from the law of the jungle, survival of the fittest, fight or flight, where killing and rape were the rule, to the aspiration of morals and ethics, Logos and Eros. We are now at our crossroads: we must choose between the tyranny of our animal nature or individually developing a spiritual practice and conforming to the law of love.

"The reason why love and compassion bring the greatest happiness is simply that our nature cherishes them above all else. The need for love lies at the very foundation of human existence. It results from the profound interdependence we all share with one another." (*Ibid.*, Borges)

Death penalty—

So far, thanks to DNA testing, nearly 200 people who have been living on death row have been exonerated and freed for crimes they did not commit. How many persons have been executed for crimes they did not commit? Where are the so-called "pro-lifers" on this issue: voting for people who take glee in the number of state murders they expedite. Texas leads the nation and world in the ruthless pursuit of state murder.

Deforestation—

80% of the world's original forests are gone. The numbers are even worse in the United States, where 99% of the frontier forest has been destroyed or ruined. Between 1970 and 2001, 14% of the Amazon rain forest, the greatest source for oxygen replenishment on the planet, was destroyed. The argument against the regulation of these frightening activities is that human economic development is more important that protection of our biosphere. For excuses, these arguments quote *Genesis* as giving humankind dominion over all other life. While the *Torah* may offer apparently convenient and sympathetic support for our destructive practices, it is a gross miscarriage to believe that G-d condones the despoilment of paradise. Better were our numbers half of what they are today and the earth have a sustainable future, than one more acre of forest be destroyed. The majority of adult human beings agree with this, but, again, corporate dollars control governments.

Democracy—

Classical Greek democracy, as idealized by Plato in *The Republic*, depended upon a slave class. In *The Communist Manifesto*, Marx replaced these slaves with machines, theorizing that a proletarian democracy is possible. But in accounting for the soul, I insist that freedom goes beyond eliminating alienation of labor or increasing leisure; it must include love and compassion. Indeed, these are preconditions for eliminating the addiction to materialism, which stands between our present economic slavery and the creation of a free society.

The system of government in the United States is neither a democracy nor a republic. Jesus couldn't run for office under the current federal election laws and party rules that filter candidates. One must be a member of the capitalist party (Democrat or Republican, so-called left or right wing) to qualify. Variance from the aims of the so-called "New World Order" monopolists will disqualify a candidate, or get him or her shot.

Depression—

Sometimes even rigorous spiritual practice is unable to conquer depression. When this occurs, it is often worth considering if the depression—whether its origins are genetic, psychological, emotional, or spiritual—has become a chemically-induced state. If this is the case, depression then is like any other disease involving chemistry and warrants the investigation of medication. This does not necessarily mean the prescriptions of Big Pharma, but rather a course of vitamins, minerals, amino acids, and other natural substances based on what is missing from that person's body and preventing the instrument from functioning within a rational range. Pharmaceuticals are options of the last resort.

Descartes—

"I think, therefore I am." – René Descartes

The unnamable force that animates the world contains everything that ever was, is, or shall be: "it" (everything) is no (one) thing. As our proof reveals,[15] our universe came from one thing and remains whole simultaneous with its infinite differentiation. Therefore, that the Earth and everything upon it exists is certain because "it" is something that is possible, since, within the infinity of possibilities does, everything exists. So, "it" *is*, or to update Descartes, "I am therefore I am," which is much as יהוה put it."[16]

Deregulation—

The argument for deregulation by so-called conservatives in our country is nothing more than a smokescreen for the control of society by those who have the most capital, much as so-called "globalization" is used internationally to subject poorer states. In their inimitable cynical manner, corporate-monopolists (neo-fascists) use the term deregulation to mask their dictatorial goals. What they're aiming for is the privatization of capital—the concentration of money in the hands of the few (the Savings & Loan scandal, the accounting scandal [led by Enron, Anderson, and Worldcom], and the sub-prime mortgage crisis and bailout being the latest examples of the theft of the U.S. Treasury by deregulation). Economic statistics inarguably indicate that the gap between rich and poor is getting

---

[15] See *Appendix 6 – The Proof*.
[16] The outcome of Michael's thinking here is much the same as Robert Nozick's expression of the principle of fecundity in his book *Philosophical Explanations*, "that everything that is logically possible, exists. This is the only possibility which has the same beauty, simplicity, and symmetry as the state of absolute nothingness. It is the exact opposite of absolute nothingness: absolute being. ... There is not nothing because, everything that is possible, *must* exist. This statement goes far beyond what is described by the many worlds interpretation of quantum mechanics, yet, in a way, it's a logical extension of it."
(http://www.chrismaloney.com/projects/book/NotNothing.html)

wider. Amazingly, the fascists employ the name of Jesus to rally the ignorant to their cause. We must resist the hegemony of capital—metaphorically the Antichrist or Satan (our shadows)—and put the needs of human beings (our higher selves) above this.

De Vere, Edward ("William Shake-speare")—

"Edward de Vere, Earl of Oxford, is Hamlet in his essential character and circumstances alike ..." (Prof. Louis J. Halle, "Hamlet and the World," in *The Search for an Eternal Norm*, Washington, D.C., University Press of America, 1981, as quoted in Charlton Ogburn, *The Mysterious William Shakespeare—The Myth and the Reality*, Dodd, Mead & Company, New York, 1984, p. 366.)

Both Ogburn and Mark Anderson (*"Shakespeare" by Another Name*, Gotham Books, New York, 2005) make it clear that the everyday details of de Vere's entire life are contained in the Shakespearean canon. While there may be other candidates—writers for whom a few strands of circumstantial evidence present some intriguing questions—there is only one person whose biography is set forth, event for event, in the plays, sonnets, and epic poems.

As suggested in our play,[17] the hijacking of de Vere's work is similar to what happened to Jesus. The commercialized personality and teachings of the prophet sold by so-called Christian churches may be the popular conception of Jesus, but this is not the being whose teachings (more accurately represented by the *Gnostic Gospels* found at Nag Hammadi and the Essene Gospels [the *Dead Sea Scrolls*] found at Qumron) represent the spiritual metaphysic of the age, as revealed in our book.

> O good Horatio, what a wounded name
> Things standing thus unknown, shall live behind me!
> If thou didst ever hold me in thy heart,
> Absent thee from felicity awhile,
> And in this harsh world draw thy breath in pain,
> To tell my story. (*Hamlet*, V, ii, 355-360)

The Dialectic—

See the preface to *Appendix 6 – The Proof.*

Diet—

---

[17] See *Appendix 4 – The Bard's Ghost.*

In advanced industrial nations, where money, not wisdom, determines policy, dietary standards are set by food industry lobbyists. Interestingly enough, this appears to be one area where government policy has given some ground to pressures from evolved segments of the population, resulting in more accurate labeling of food products. However, this is only a small, tenuous step in the much greater process of creating a sane policy toward diet and the use of planetary resources.

But even those seeking to clean up the food chain lack an understanding of basic dietary tenets, as evidenced by the high incidence of "organic sugar" in food products sold in so-called natural food stores and supermarkets. Here again, self-described "new age" food stores determine their product line by profit, not health.

As discussed in this book, there are a number of factors—ecological (fertilizers, distance to market, waste products), physiological (pH, blood type, immune system and allergies), et al.—that must be considered when the world implements dietary standards that support a sustainable and spiritual future.

Divine Syzygy—

What I offer is not an exclusive path but one that works. By attaining Christ consciousness you become, in Jungian terms, your true self. This is what I meant when I was translated as saying, "... no man cometh unto the Father, but by me."[18] Not through me, Jesus, personally, but through that which I represent—the integration of the individual, the Divine Syzygy, Messiah, or Christ, the symbol of the self—shall you come unto your higher self. This is a basic esoteric teaching that is represented in the ancient Qabalistic symbol, the Tree of Life: that only through the Messenger (Mercury/Chokmah) can we approach the Father (Kether, the Crown).[19] Pardon the use of the male pronoun. The Hebrew letters used in the standard name of G-d, יהוה, are themselves balanced between masculine and feminine.

The Divine Syzygy—a union of anima and animus, feminine and masculine—provides the conditions for the infusion of the soul into the individual personality, a qualitatively different state of consciousness in which the higher self holds sway over the instincts and ego.

---

[18] John 14:6.
[19] Aleister Crowley, *The Book of Thoth*, Lancer Books, New York, trade paperback reprint circa 1974, p. 129.

Drugs/Addiction/12 Steps—

The government encourages drug use through its lack of support for treatment and its opposition to legalization. This policy bolsters crime and burdens society with the expense of extra police protection, military deployment, defoliation of the third world, and the burgeoning prison industry—ongoing profitable lobbies. One wonders if the price supports for drugs achieved by government policies aren't telling us who is getting money under the table from the drug cartels and their operations, since this is exactly the same process whereby big business gets politicians to support corporate welfare. The discovery of government involvement in drug trafficking during the Iran-Contra affair was no aberration. It still goes on. Witness the bumper crops and spike in distribution of heroin following the U.S. takeover of Afghanistan.

George W. Bush used and abused "drugs" in his young adulthood and he's President. If Bush weren't born into money and power and was, instead, subject to the same laws he seeks to enforce on others, he'd still be in prison for his drug use alone, not to mention his truly sinister crimes against humanity.

For Nixon or Nancy Reagan or the Feds to claim that smoking marijuana leads to heroin use is like saying that George W. Bush's abuse of cocaine and alcohol leads to fascism and hypocrisy. Sure, these actions may be shared by the same person, but there are many other factors that contribute to addictive behavior. Besides, others have cured their addictions and actually learned compassionate behavior. [While this argument could lead one to argue that perhaps there is hope for Bush, I believe his judgment day has long passed. It's why G-d has a recycle bin on his/her desktop. Matter is neither created nor destroyed within the interval of one universe (between white hole and black hole), but between black hole and white hole, all remnants and artifacts from usage during the interval are removed.]

The use of U.S. Armed Forces to create the appearance of fighting drugs in Columbia (and defoliate the countryside and poison its inhabitants in the process), rather than the use our resources to prevent the illegal destruction of the rain forest in Brazil, confirms that those controlling U.S. policy worship at the altar of Mammon.

What is it about the American psyche that stymies a rational policy on drugs? Clearly, a large part of this is a remnant of Puritanism and the hypocrisy and shallow nature of so-called Christian fundamentalism. These are thought systems based on fear, anger, and hate that ultimately become the shadow (Antichrist) by failing to come to terms with instincts and ego as well as other addictions—money and religion and such. This is why a twelve-step program for materialism and spiritual materialism is needed.

Ultimately, relying on anything but pure being is, to a degree, an addiction or attachment. So, the prescription is the same for us all: spiritual practice designed to overcome the tyranny of the instinct and ego.

Ecology—

Ecology is the study of the inter-relatedness of organisms and their environment. Much of the argument between those who support policies that protect the environment and those who don't stems from the differences in perception over how things are or aren't connected. If a so-called environmentalist goes on a cruise ship to admire Alaska's pristine Inside Passage and that ship discharges its waste into the ocean, what is the net effect on the environment? How is this different than those who gorge themselves at banquets on luxury cruise liners that discharge their waste into the Caribbean?

The food industry, which in America is pushing genetically modified crops because of their greater profitability, is in denial over the effects of these untested crops, to wit: in Canada, genetically modified canola has become a weed that can't be killed without using poisonous chemicals; in the U.S. and Mexico, pollen from genetically modified corn is killing monarch butterflies. This is just the beginning. Such is the arrogance of corporate culture that after a few years of experimentation changes are carelessly introduced to eco-systems that took hundreds of millions of years to evolve. This is an affront to G-d, the Great Anomaly, that is, our progenitor.

What will it take before captains of industry, and those addicted to the over-consumption that fuels our economic monstrosity, realize that their greed and out-of-control desires are ruining every aspect of our biosphere? Clearly, a change of heart is called for.

Economics—

Political rhetoric aside, the gap between the rich and poor, both in America and world-wide, is increasing and the policies of so-called Christian nations are exacerbating this trend. Through their ability to underwrite, and therefore control, political campaigns, the rich have successfully enacted laws that allow them to pay less income tax, less estate tax, less capital gains tax, less corporate tax, and shift the burden of taxation from the federal government to state governments and to the middle-class and the poor. On a world-wide level these policies of class war are known as "free trade" and "globalization," which serve as a smokescreen for economic imperialism by allowing monopoly capital to seize unprotected foreign markets.[20]

---

[20] See http://www.alternet.org/story.html?StoryID=12652.

Just as in the natural sciences, the social science of economics has principles that govern its operations. One of these principles, mathematically explicated by Marx, is that capitalism must continually expand in order to maintain its existence. This behavior has never been challenged by those who support this system; in fact, they regale at any indication that it is true, calling it "economic growth" and "earnings per share," as chronicled daily in business press (the *Wall Street Journal*, et al.). The earth is befouled and the so-called doctors are calling its cancer a tonic. Remember when cigarettes were touted as healthful?

U. S. Supreme Court Justice Antonin Scalia calls socialism "morally incompatible" with Christian virtues. (*The Associated Press*, reported in *The Denver Post*, 5/3/96) What is this man smoking? Surely, he is confusing Calvin with Jesus. Christianity, as taught by Jesus (not the Roman or Calvinistic versions), is socialistic. What other conclusion could one have to Jesus' admonitions to give away one's wealth, have compassion, and share with others? Yet, pundits have backed themselves into a corner by denigrating alternative forms of economic organization, painting the so-called socialism of the Russians and Chinese as evil. What is evil about their societies is the totalitarian political organization, for, as we have noted, the commissars ruled as the czars and Mao ruled as the Mings. Their so-called collectivism more closely resembled state capitalism than any form of socialism, for example, the kibbutzim in Israel. Regardless, we are forced to recognize the impressive economic results that these third-world systems produced in a relatively short time. It should also be noted that, contrary to Marxist theory, these results were achieved through the use of slave-labor: another indication of their capitalist framework.

Capital itself, like television or petroleum, is neither good nor bad—its moral value depends upon its use. Almost all societies, whether they are feudal, socialist, capitalist, or fascist, use capital. The manner in which capital is invested by these systems has a direct effect on the political system in which it operates, and can encourage democratic, republican, authoritarian, or totalitarian organization. In America, the hegemony of capital, over what was once a hybrid system of democratic and republican processes, has turned this country into a fascist state beholden to corporate interests above all.

Capitalism has provided us with technology, information, and leisure; it has also institutionalized the subjugation of the human race to profit. The nature of capital and its relationship to humans must change, from "an abstraction that rules our lives" (Marx), to a tool for human development. This shall be achieved by individuals transferring their shares (stock) to non-profit foundations and corporations that are focused on sustainability rather than growth.

"Thou hast taken usury and increase, and thou has greedily gained of they neighbor by extortion, and host forgotten me, saith the Lord God." -- Ezekiel 22:12.

"Ye cannot serve G-d and mammon." --Matthew 6:24; Luke 16:13.

The economic crisis of 2008 is a perfect opportunity to begin the transformative process. Obama's economic advisors should consider becoming a part-owner of GM, only they must make a better deal than Bush, a corporate servant, did with banks, where the U.S. Treasury purchased stock on behalf of the U.S., but with no voting rights. If the U.S. invests in G.M. it should have voting rights. This way it could have a say in transitioning the transportation industry to sustainable production and sustainable fuels. This is how the world economy will be changed from a growth dependent, earnings-per-share driven, war focus to a sustainable model.

Education—

"Today the child, swamped by information overload, desperately needs to be taught the means of pattern-recognition for the sake of psychic survival. Pattern-recognition is the role of the researcher and the explorer. Today's young children could recover high motivation in the learning process only if permitted to tackle their environment on a discovery basis." (McLuhan, *From Cliché to Archetype*, p. 201)

Our goal is to create an environment, much along the lines of Castilia (from Hesse's *Magister Ludi*), that provides discovery learning for the spiritually-centered individual.

Look for eLearning to mimic Google and provide pre-organized, media rich webs of curriculum covering the gamut of human endeavor.

Between beings, is not music the universal language? Indications are that melodic and rhythmic recognition is innate and that tonal communication with extraterrestrials, as was suggested by the film *Close Encounters of the Third Kind*, is not simply science fiction, but a logical first step in establishing common ground.

Evolution—

As we show in our proof,[21] space-time is evolutionary: it moves forward following certain principles. There are those that will hang on to their superstitious opinions and resist our logic that the next evolutionary step of humankind is to overcome the tyranny of our instincts and ego. Some of the resisters are fundamentalists who believe that humankind was deposited here "as is" in 4004 BC (as per Bishop Usher's calculations). They believe that human nature is fixed and sinful. To them I can only say that they have misread *Genesis*, for the Hebrew text clearly states that humankind is "incomplete" not "sinful." Others who resist evolution see Darwin's concept of "survival of the fittest" as the "law of the jungle"—eat or be eaten, kill or be killed—and have not noticed that our survival as a species depends upon conquering a new predator. No longer are we called upon to vanquish the likes of saber-toothed tigers or woolly mammoths or even other tribes to survive. Rather, *we have become our own worst enemy*. One of the best indications that our proof[22] is correct is that our behavior must overcome exactly what got us here. This aligns with the axiom that what is good and necessary at any one time in history will be detrimental at another ("What cures you kills you." Or, "Truth is Paradox."), for truly the unity of opposites (Hegelian [and later Marxian] dialectical reasoning in the West) and the Yin and Yang of the Tao (in the East) are agreed on this point. Those lacking the imagination to see the one-dimensional nature of a "dog eat dog" world are resisting the current of change and will eventually be swept away by the high tide of evolution, which evolves like everything else.

Humankind's evolutionary pattern is thus:[23]

- Unconscious physical evolution (*Homo erectus*)
- Subconscious mental evolution (*Homo economus*)
- Conscious spiritual evolution (*Homo spiritus*)

This is why the code among advanced extra-terrestrial cultures supports non-interference: each culture must necessarily go through specific developmental stages to evolve.

Despite the perceived lack of social evolution in comparison to our technological achievement, in truth, our cultural graces are, in general, quite an improvement over where we began in the jungle (rape for sex, killing for food and safety). The achievement of the World Wide Web and the changes in consciousness that it will eventually facilitate (when secured against corporate control) harbor the promise of a future both

---

[21] See *Appendix 6 – The Proof.*
[22] See *Appendix 6 – The Proof.*
[23] See *Appendix 6 – The Proof.*

technologically *and* socially innovative—one that reflects a unified inner and outer journey.

Creationists don't see that the unknowable force expresses itself in the logic and order of Darwinism; Darwinists don't see that the creationists' G-d principle (the Great Anomaly, or "First Cause," of the Quantum Torus model) is the force behind evolution.

A new movement called Intelligent Design, fed by politically-savvy fundamentalists seeking to disguise Creationism, has sought equal status with Evolution. However, if the "Intelligence" in Intelligent Design were redefined from "G-d" into scientifically explainable phenomena, then Intelligent Design would become Evolution (Darwinism) driven by an unnamable force (the Great Anomaly or G-d principle, above and beyond any particular religion) that, in and of itself, contains all possibilities. So much for the either/or of the bumper sticker war between Darwin's walking fish and Jesus' swimming fish. There is only one holographic universe, and any way we slice it (given the proper informational lenses) reflects an aspect of this unity.

"'Humanity has the option to be a success.' Just because we have the option doesn't mean we'll exercise it. It's 'utopia versus oblivion.'" (R. Buckminster Fuller, quoted by his grandson, *Chicago Tribune*, Arts section, 3-11-01.)

Think of your thoughts as your software and the new dispensation as a software upgrade. If you refuse the upgrade, future version upgrades, and patches, you will eventually end up with outdated software that not only has ceased to communicate with the rest of the world, but also reduces your ability to interpret and apply your data input. Today's evolution of the species is measured not in physical variation, but in cognitive and behavioral choices that further life on earth. For just as there are Neanderthal genes still among us, there is Neanderthal thinking as well.[24]

The point is: it's time to evolve past our mythologies and superstitions surrounding evolution. This is absolutely necessary for our survival as a species.

After a hiatus of a year and a half, the Kansas State Board of Education is allowing the teaching of evolution back into the public school curriculum. (John W. Fountain, "Kansas Puts Evolution Back Into Public Schools," *The New York Times*, 2/15/01.)

---

[24] See http://www.nytimes.com/2002/03/07/science/07ORIG.html and John Noble Wilford, "Neanderthals in Gene Pool, Study Suggests," *The New York Times*, November 9, 2006.

Extra-terrestrials—

To believe that there are not beings in the universe more evolved than ourselves is mathematically more absurd than believing that the earth is flat. In fact, there are approximately 40-50 million sites that would support extra-terrestrial life in our galaxy alone!

The government is reluctant to admit publicly that is has knowledge of extra-terrestrial visitations for the same reason that it would suppress information on the Second Coming: the ramifications of such awareness work against the interests of the so-called New World Order—that is, such knowledge would necessarily precipitate a change in the way human beings treated one another, resulting in more sharing and less demand on planetary resources (bad news for those who control the markets).

However, there are many government documents that clearly indicate contact has been made and, further, that these "visitors" have (up until the late 1970's) aided in research on the means they use to warp space-time for the purposes of intergalactic travel. The most frequent visitors to earth come from two different star systems, Zeta-Reticuli 1 & 2 and the Pleiades. One may wonder what these beings think of our "leaders," and why the cooperative nature of our interplanetary relationship was lost, though it figures that the greed and cynicism of those who control Earth is behind this falling out.

While scientific speculation concerning the propulsion systems of space-time travel has mostly centered on the technological specifications for approaching the speed of light, such an approach is unlikely to work due to a variety of mitigating factors.[25] The functioning systems that have actually been observed and tested by US government scientists are based on a different approach, which uses the amplification of gravity-a[26] waves to warp space-time. As astonishing as it may seem to us, the propulsion system that accomplishes this is not particularly complicated.

The key to developing vehicles (discs) that are capable of warping space-time is the use of Element 115, which is only synthesizeable on earth for less than $1/10,000^{th}$ of a second, but which exists in a stable form in other solar systems where greater gravitational and electromagnetic forces are present. Heavier elements, such as 115, possess gravity-a waves that extend

---

[25] Indeed, Stephen Hawking has a proof showing that it is impossible for such a scheme to work.
[26] There are two types of gravity waves, *a* and *b*. Gravity-a waves are generated by particles, such as atoms, and gravity-b waves are generated by large objects, such as planets and stars.

past the perimeter of the atom and are therefore accessible for amplification. When Element 115 is successfully targeted by a simple on-board particle accelerator, it briefly becomes Element 116 before decomposing instantly, giving off anti-matter. The anti-matter, in turn, is directed toward a gaseous matter target in a vacuum where the two types of particles collide and are annihilated, producing an explosion. The heat from this explosion is converted to energy at nearly 100% efficiency by a thermoelectric generator. The energy is then directed by gravity amplifiers toward the intended target. The effects of gravity amplification result in a stretching of the space-time continuum, with the location of the vehicle made coincident with its target location. Thus flying saucers move in a series of seemingly straight lines.

Fascism—

Remember that it was a former general, President Dwight David Eisenhower, who first warned of the dangers of "the military-industrial complex." How ironic that today's leaders celebrate the hegemony of monopoly capital and brute force over our former democratic and republican institutions.

America has only one established political party, the capitalist party, and the Democrats and the Republicans are simply the left and right wings of that party. Above and beyond their name references to the ideals of our founding fathers, and regardless of a few superficial crumbs thrown to the electorate (such as wilderness areas or voting rights acts), both these parties contribute to the on-going evolution of America into a fascist society: A state controlled by private corporate interests wherein serious dissent is ruthlessly terminated, the plundering and despoilment of the earth continues unabated, and the dollar is worshipped as the almighty and final justification for policy.

When the corporate-owned representatives known as Congress reduce government spending and services and argue that they are reducing "big government," they are simply shifting the control of government policy to the corporate sector. The government hasn't shrunk it's just been privatized, a classic example of fascism. Thus we have the foxes guarding the hen house: In the absence of a well-funded Environmental Protection Agency with teeth, the fascists have a self-policing Union Carbide and Monsanto. Welfare rolls been reduced, with millions of poor people being replaced by a few large corporations that will be paid billions to develop weapons and test them in adventurist wars in the Balkans, Middle East, Central Asia, Africa, South America, etc.

Heaven forbid if one of the multinational monopolists runs into some hard luck, for while individuals may not be able to declare true bankruptcy anymore, Uncle Sam would be more than happy to bail out Chrysler, Penn Central, Continental Illinois Bank, any saving and loan institution that has been looted by Reagan-era deregulation, energy companies that lobbied for deregulation and then declared bankruptcy to recover losses from failed investments in nuclear power, numerous brokerage houses, as well as Fannie Mae and Freddie Mac as well as almost any bank or investment bank. This redistribution and spreading of the wealth among corporations and their owners is the one form of socialism that is condoned by the monopolists, much like National Socialism (Nazism) which they admired and supported. Under fascism, social programs are shifted to the private sector where religious groups lean on the downtrodden to convert and support the pseudo-Christian agenda of the mammon worshippers. Perhaps the immoral majority on the Supreme Court that appointed George W. Bush will find a way to make this institutionalization of religion constitutional, or at least pretend it is not an issue. Clearly, such behavior is counter to the principles upon which this country was founded.[27]

Fatwa—

If Islam is, as Muslims claim, consistent with Judeo-Christian tradition, then the Ayatollah Ruhollah Khomeini would act out of love, not ignorance and hatred, for no lover of Jesus could condone killing. Instead, he issues a *fatwa*, charging Salmon Rushdie with blasphemy, as if the one G-d, which he calls Allah, is so weak that it is offended by the author's honesty. This is nothing more than self-centered politics disguised as religion: Islamism is not a religion, but a political movement.

Final Dispensation—

Updating ancient sacred texts, such as *The Pentateuch* (i.e., the *Torah* or the *Five Books of Moses*, the so-called *Old Testament* in Christianity), the *Christian Bible*, the *Koran*, the *Tao Te Ching*, the *Upanishads*, the *Bhagavad-Gita*, and such should be like updating software or like removing anachronisms (ethnic slurs or obscure references) from old plays and musicals. But the resistance to changes in religious teachings comes from fundamentalists unable to distinguish between temporal and eternal truths. No matter how inspired the scripture, it is always influenced to a degree by the speaker's historical specificity and, thus, subject to later refinement. That is why we update the old biblical metaphors of farmers, shepherds, and fisherman with computers, psychology, and physics. Eventually, this same sort of substitution will hold true for my work as well. Despite having been given the best of the best in all regards—parents, education, work, lovers, children, and inspiration—I am, to a certain

---

[27] See the final paragraph under "Fundamentalism" concerning Jefferson's views on this.

degree, a product of the 20th Century. One need look no further than the incidental details in our book to see the stamp of space-time.[28]

Flood—

The Chinese Annals, the Scandinavian Eddas, and the Torah all align on the details and dates of the Flood, yet current science has a very sketchy and incomplete understanding of this cataclysm. Throwing the baby out with the bathwater, theorists are loath to take the view proposed by Immanuel Velikovsky (the raised sea levels were attributable to a close pass or two by a large gravitation mass, probably Venus), while continuing to wallow in a bunch of irreconcilable suppositions.

Forgiveness—

I love you.
I'm sorry.
Forgive me.
Thank you.

Fundamentalism—

All fundamentalists (Christians, Muslims, Jews, Hindus, Sikhs, etc.) unknowingly empower the shadow, what they call Satan, so long as they are intolerant of other approaches to the G-d principle, the Great Anomaly. Their acceptance of killing in the name of their demon deity is a sure sign of this.

The lack of meditative practice in most religions facilitates hypocrisy by denying a dependable means to the higher self (spirit) that acts as a watchdog and sublimating influence over the lower self (instincts and ego).

The proof of the fundamentalist error in regards to the infallibility of the written word is shown precisely in their insistence at its veracity. To think that G-d could be captured in mere letters—even letters of fire![29]—is folly. The basic tenets of Taoism and Judaism are in agreement on this: The Tao that can be spoken is not the Tao, and יהוה cannot be captured in words. Remember, Jesus didn't worship Jesus and his G-d didn't have a name.

---

[28] Much as one of the significant pieces of evidence of Edward de Vere's authorship of the Shakespearean canon is the fact all topical references in the work, of which there are a multitude, end in 1604, when de Vere died.

[29] Letters of fire, i.e., the formal design of the Hebrew alphabet given by the priests who originally oversaw its development.

Those who prefer to use current religious metaphors as their reference points for spiritual practice would be well advised to become aware of the gaps between the universal tenets and the temporal prejudices of those that wrote and controlled these cosmologies.

Scientific advancement didn't occur because people believed the earth was flat. What makes us think that spiritual growth will be advanced by the time-bound mythologies to which most of the world ascribes?

Christian fundamentalists can't have it both ways, claiming that the bible is infallible and then using science and social science where it is convenient for them. If the bible is true, then fundamentalists, in the thrall of consumer consumption (cars, refrigerators, cell phones, lavish churches, extravagant preachers, etc.) are Mammon worshipers, and particularly dangerous ones at that, for they believe their support of capitalism and institutionalized greed is consistent with believing in G-d and Jesus.

Likewise, the Taliban are not at peace with the G-d they purportedly serve. Their destruction of Buddhist statues reveals the insecurity of rulers and their fear of other belief systems.

Billy Graham is soiled by his support for fascists and moneyed interests. He can shout about "Jesus!" all he wants, but he might as well be calling out "Mammon!" Besides, he's an anti-Semite. We can't take his recantations seriously; he's not changed his ways.

Fundamentalists are closer to the Antichrist than to anything else—they promulgate hatred toward minority groups and place a great deal of emphasis on shows of financial support to prove their faith. What their behavior really indicates is a lack of faith in the deity they purport to believe in. What kind of a G-d needs all this money and vitriol to prove itself? Not an omnipotent one. Only devils thrive on that kind of support.

"[When] the [Virginia] bill for establishing religious freedom ... was finally passed ... a singular proposition proved that its protection of opinion was meant to be universal. Where the preamble declares that coercion is a departure from the plan of the holy author of our religion, an amendment was proposed, by inserting the word 'Jesus Christ,' so that it should read 'a departure from the plan of Jesus Christ, the holy author of our religion.' The insertion was rejected by a great majority, in proof that they meant to comprehend within the mantle of its protection the Jew and the Gentile, the Christian and Mahometan, the Hindoo and infidel of every denomination."
–Thomas Jefferson: Autobiography, 1821. ME 1:67

Gay rights—

Opposition to equal rights for gays comes almost entirely from two sources: religious texts written by ignorant, fearful men charged with engendering progeny to keep their tribes stocked with fighters and/or men insecure with their own sexuality. Essentially, both these parties are saying, "Human sexuality has two forms: rabid testosterone poisoned animals and docile feminine counterparts." Those fearful of gay rights ignore the core teachings of Jesus and point to *Torah* prejudices that Jesus rejected. There is no conflict between the behaviors that Jesus taught—love and compassion toward fellow humans—and what science has recently proven: gays and straights are just at different points along a continuum of diversified genetic material, i.e., we are all brothers and sisters.

Genome—

Now that we are mapping human DNA, we are in a position to consciously alter our physical development. But if the few genetically modified crops that we have produced have caused such havoc, what would lie in store for us if we permit humans to tinker with genetic codes developed over billions of years? The philosophy that would permit such activity is based on a faulty belief that the ego can consciously foresee the complex repercussions of its actions—it cannot. When used properly, our ego is a subservient tool to our higher mind, including our sub- and unconscious faculties, within which the complexities of genetic reproduction are handled with aplomb. It's one thing to discourage breeding of those who carry debilitating genetic traits and quite another to change the code. Such intentions are doubly troubling when fascists control the state apparatus, harking back to "ethnic cleansing" and the perverted genocide experiments of the Nazis.

Ghandi—

"If socialism means befriending one's enemies, I should be treated as a true socialist." (D.G. Tendulkar, *Mahatma*, Vol. 8; 2nd Edition, 1960, Publications Division, p. 37.)

"Exploitation and domination of one nation over another can have no place in a world striving to put an end to all war." (D.G. Tendulkar, *Mahatma*, Vol. 7; 2nd Edition, 1960, Publications Division, p. 2.)

How Gandhi Defined the Seven Deadly Sins:
- Wealth without work
- Pleasure without conscience
- Knowledge without character
- Commerce without morality
- Science without humanity

- Religion without sacrifice
- Politics without principle

"Mahatma Gandhi said that seven things will destroy us. Notice that all of them have to do with social and political conditions. Note also that the antidote of each of these 'deadly sins' is an explicit external standard or something that is based on natural principles and laws, not on social values." (From Stephen R. Covey, *Principle Centered Leadership*, Simon & Schuster Ltd., West Garden Place, Kendal Street, London W2 2AQ, 1990, Chapter 7.)

Global Warming/Climate Change—

After years of corporate-led resistance to evidence that global warming is caused principally by pollution generated by human beings, public opinion has overwhelmingly embraced what science has shown for years. Despite this, American political leaders feign ignorance when it comes to the facts. Clearly, their obeisance to capital has hardened their hearts against G-d and life itself. While we may feel sorry for such lost souls and have compassion for their twisted condition, they must surely be displaced before the harm done to our life support system (Earth) is irreversible. Yet these whores of Mammon continue to use all means at their disposal to drain every last profit from fossil fuels and nuclear technology, arguing that environmentalists want the world to "freeze in the dark." Hardly. No one is calling for an end to energy production, just lower consumption, cleaner fuels, and redirected profits. Again, the interests of the super-rich are being placed above planetary survival. Worship of the "Almighty Dollar" is the same as worship of the Golden Calf—a metaphor for Satanism.

Golden Rule—

<u>Brahmanism</u>: This is the sum of duty: Do naught unto others which would cause you pain if done to you. (*Mahabharata* 5:1517)
<u>Buddhism</u>: Hurt not others in ways that you yourself would find hurtful. (*Udana-Varga* 5:18)
<u>Confucianism</u>: Surely it is the maxim of loving-kindness: Do not do unto others what you would not have them do unto you. (*Analects* 15:23)
<u>Taoism</u>: Regard your neighbor's gain as your own gain and your neighbor's loss as your own loss. (*T'ai Shang Kan Ying P'ien*)
<u>Zoroastrianism</u>: That nature alone is good which refrains from doing unto another whatsoever is not good for itself. (*Dadistan-I-dinik* 94:5)
<u>Judaism</u>: What is hateful to you, do not to your fellowman. That is the entire law; all the rest is commentary. (*Talmud*, Shabbat 31a)

Christianity: All things whatsoever ye would that man should do to you, do ye even so to them; for this is the law and the prophets. (*New Testament*, Matthew 7:12)

Islam: No one of you is a believer until he desires for his brother that which he desires for himself. (*Sunnah*)

--Source: *The 1999 Old Farmer's Almanac*

Guns—

How ironic the affinity between so-called Christians and the National Rifle Association. One would never have imagined that the teachings of Jesus could be aligned with those who cloak themselves in the flag and claim their fear and hatred is really freedom-loving patriotism. As always, the arguments promulgated for such positions are oversimplified: "If guns are outlawed, only outlaws will have guns." In the highest spiritual sense, only outlaws (from the spiritual truth) have guns now.

Gun proponents may argue that allowing indiscriminate arming of civilians will deter government forces from enslaving the citizenry, but the train's already left the station; the *coup d'etat* has already occurred—the Constitution has been shredded—and it isn't guns that will reverse this state of affairs.

The Great Invocation—

> From the point of Light within the Mind of God
> Let light stream forth into the minds of men.
> Let Light descend on earth.
>
> From the point of Love within the Heart of God
> Let Love stream forth into the hearts of men.
> May Christ* return to Earth.
>
> From the center where the Will of God is known
> Let purpose guide the little wills of men
> The purpose which the Masters know and serve.
>
> From the center which we call the race of men
> Let the Plan of Love and Light work out
> And may it seal the door where evil dwells.
>
> Let Light and Love and Power restore the Plan on Earth.

650 » Michael's Notes

*In the Buddhist, Hindu, Muslim, and Jewish translations of the Great Invocation, the name by which the Coming One is known in these religions is used—the Lord Maitreya, Krishna, the Imam Mahdi, and the Messiah. (http://www.lucistrust.org/en/service_activities/the_great_invocation__1)

Habitat/Extinction—

The Congo offers two contrasting examples of behavioral responses to the same facts. Recently, Congolaise Industrielle de Bois, a private timber company, announced the donation of the 100-square-mile Goualogo Triangle, a pristine Central African rain forest dense with gorillas, chimpanzees, and elephants, to the Republic of the Congo. In doing so, the company sacrifices an annual harvest of approximately $1.5 million in mahogany and other valuable hardwoods. In eastern Congo, however, mining for the mineral coltan, which is used in cell phones, microchips, and nuclear reactors, is damaging the Kahuzi-Biega National Park and the Okapi Wildlife Reserve and threatening lowland gorillas with extinction.

We must prioritize our needs. Species cannot be sacrificed for technology with the excuse that human beings need such resources for survival. The truth is, we do not need such resources; they are used for luxury playthings unnecessary for our spiritual evolution.

History—

The "proof" of the Christian *Bible*, including the blaming of the Jews and the exoneration of Pilate, is much like the "proof" that JFK, RFK, MLK, and Malcolm X were all killed by individual assassins unconnected to any CIA conspiracy—it's simply fiction used to maintain power by those in control, the very persons who perpetrated the crimes.

"I doubt if there is a thing in the world as wrong or unreliable as history. History ain't what it is. It's what some writer wanted it to be." --Will Rogers

Holocaust—

From day one, the Catholic Church has perpetrated policies that eventually led to the Holocaust—by blaming the Jews, rather than the Romans, for the crucifixion. This is what a real apology would have to address. Unfortunately, not one of the Popes has been willing to recognize this root cause, as it would bring to light the editing of the texts that comprise the Christian *Bible*. Nevertheless, the Church must address this painful truth in much the same manner that the Jews must address the basis for their rejection of their greatest prophet (due as it may be to the manner in which his truth was perverted, the blame for his death unrightfully pinned on them, and the threat of death for not believing) and as Islam must address its claim to be derived from this tradition and yet to embrace a violent religious doctrine that runs counter to Jesus' teachings.

Imperialism—

Not only does the world's most powerful nation exert its will through direct military and mercenary actions whenever it so desires, but in the name of globalization and free trade furthers the hegemony of monopoly capital over fledgling economies through the pandemic of multi-national corporations and the predatory policies of the International Monetary Fund (IMF), the World Bank, and the U.S. Treasury (see http://www.alternet.org/story.html?StoryID=12652).

Despite this transparent strategy of consolidation, American academics gleefully turn to such apologies as Michael Hardt's *Empire* to salve their consciences with the belief that power is actually decentralized under globalization. Not only is more power continually being concentrated in fewer hands, but the gap between rich and poor individuals and nations continue to grow. Again, the misinformation surrounding alternative economic systems and the sell out of major religions to the seduction of money has produced a rudderless mass schizophrenia that leaves society without any manner of judging the cogency of ideas economics and morality.

One of the ways in which United States is able to conduct military actions overseas without running into a hailstorm of criticism at home is to subcontract the work to U.S. military-trained private corporations and local police forces. Such is the case in Columbia, where contractors like Aviation Development Corporation of Montgomery, Alabama, and DynCorp of Reston, Virginia run surveillance and combat operations in concert with the Columbian National Police, in the U.S.'s stead. In addition, U.S.-backed defoliation of the Columbian landscape, supposedly aimed at coca production, continues unabated, poisoning the people and their environment, despite the opposition of the national government.

Instincts—

When we as a species were still living in the jungle, our instincts preserved us in very specific ways. To survive we had to be both aggressive, to protect ourselves from predators, whether other hominids or saber-toothed tigers and such, and we had to be nurturing, in order to raise our young. These functions are generally relegated by sex, although both sexes have elements of the other. Most of the aggressive instincts in humans manifest in the male sex. During the Paleolithic age, this was obviously a fruitful behavior, but as we move past the post-industrial to the cybernetic age and to the verge of the genetic age, such behavior becomes problematic, an obstacle to spiritual growth. When we marvel at the asymptotic curve of technological development that we are now riding, we can only bemoan the social stagnancy, violence, and object worship that accompanies it. The key to our becoming worthy of the potential we have unlocked with our technology lies not in a scientific solution, but in a psychological and spiritual adaptation: practices that help us to overcome the tyranny of our instincts and ego, and thus an antidote to all the self-preservative responses that feed materialism as well.

Internet—

The Internet, potentially representing as it does a democratic and unrestricted information exchange, is a threat to all governments that wish to control what people think, from the United States to China.[30] Our vigilance will be tested by those who claim that the Internet needs to be controlled because of pornography or terrorists. This is the same argument that is used to beef up police forces because of drug trafficking. Unfortunately, in their ignorance, many Americans have been willing to give up their constitutional rights to calm fears generated by their government's constant focus on and participation in domestic and foreign terrorism.

"They that give up essential liberty to obtain a little temporary safety deserve neither liberty nor safety." -- Benjamin Franklin

Islam—

As with Judaism and Christianity, the majority of Islam accepts war and killing as a matter of course. However, violence is not consistent with the true nature of any of these religions.

"The Nakshbandi order of Sufis, preaches an all-embracing form of Islam that abhors sectarianism and orthodoxy. For several centuries, it was the state religion in the area of Uzbekistan, and today has approximately 40 million adherents around the world.

---

[30] On September 29, 2006, the Senate adjourned without passing a House bill that would have killed Internet neutrality. The bill was a push by operators like AT&T, Verizon, and Comcast to gain corporate control over the functioning of the Internet. Unbelievable as it may be, Rep. Mark Udall, who represents a district in Colorado that includes the highest concentration of high-tech jobs in America, voted for this fascist bill.

"'Our movement is based on tolerance, cooperation and friendship,' Muhtor began. 'We respect all religions and beliefs. Evan an atheist can be a perfect human being. What matters is what you do in this world.'

"'Once the Prophet Mohammed was sitting with his students when a funeral procession passed,' the mullah continued. 'The prophet stood up in respect, and one of the students asked, 'Why are you standing? That funeral is for a Jewish person.' He replied, 'Nevertheless, he was a human being.'

"'The Koran tells us not to force people to accept any religion,' he added. 'Allah authorized the Prophet Mohammed to spread the holy word but not to put faith into people's souls. Only Allah himself can do that.'

"Such beliefs have placed the Nakshbandis at odds with Islamic fundamentalists (Islamists) in many countries, and in some places their adepts have even been forced underground.

"'There are people who have used Allah and the Muslim religion to pursue political goals,' Muhtor said, with gentle disapproval. 'Allah has never allowed such people to reach Paradise.'" (Stephen Kinzer, "Sufis shine light on tolerance," *The New York Times* reprinted in *The Denver Post*, 11/6/97, p. 32A.)

In the same way that Mohammed claims he was told that Judaism and Christianity had abandoned the teachings, so fundamentalist Islam has done the same. There is no basis for any spiritual belief that incorporates murder or racism into its philosophy. Whether the premise is Jihads, Crusades, Inquisitions, Pogroms, or Holy Wars, these are all works against the unity of G-d. Yet, the official position and teachings of the major Islamic sects and governments as well as their media embrace institutionalized racism against the Jews.

Anyone or any organization (Hamas, Hezbollah, The Party of G-d, The Taliban, etc.) that permit or encourage teaching their children that it is their duty to kill Jews and blow up synagogues are no different than the Nazis (and it is no coincidence that *Mein Kampf* has become a popular book among these groups); these people cannot rightfully call themselves Muslims because they do not worship an all-inclusive deity; rather, such a perspective is equivalent to 'satanic', that is, anti-Allah. The same can be said of any Jewish or Christian or Hindu sects that preach racist doctrines. Such belief systems are political, not religious, in nature and should be treated as such.

"If the worst, most reactionary, most medievalist strain in the Muslim world is treated as the authentic culture, so that the bombers and mullahs get all the headlines while progressive, modernizing voices are treated as minor, marginal, 'Westoxicated' as small news, then the fundamentalists are being allowed to set the agenda." --Salman Rushdie, *Step Across This Line: Collected Nonfiction, 1992-2002*, Random House, 2002.

Jerusalem—

Who shall rule Jerusalem? It is a city that has been ruled by Canaanites, Israelites, Persians, Greeks, Romans, Byzantines, the Caliphate, the Crusaders, Germany, the Mamluks, the Ottomans, Britain, Jordan, and finally Israelites again. During some of these reigns, religious pluralism was not respected.

There is no political solution in the Middle East unless it follows from a religious and spiritual agreement. All such proposed peace proposals (the Saudi plan, the Carter plan, the UN Resolutions, the Bush plan) are incomplete because they offer a political solution to a religious problem. What they fail to recognize is that: there is an element that hides under the banner of Islam that does not recognize the right of Israel and Jews and Christians to exist; there is an element that hides under the banner of Judaism that promulgates hatred toward Islam and Christianity; there is an element that hides under the banner of Christianity that seeks to convert Jews and Muslims to its beliefs. These three religions must repudiate these elements, for truly, those with such beliefs are not worshippers of the One-Without-A-Name—the G-d principle, the Great Anomaly—but are worshippers of a less-inclusive and less-empowered entity that seeks to compensate for its shortcomings by terrorizing others; in other words, a devil. Only in repudiating these elements will those committed to these three different ways of worshipping the same G-d be capable of a long-term agreement. Only ego holds them back from agreeing that they worship the same G-d.

"And it will be at the end of the days when the House of the Lord will be established at the top of the mountains ... and all of the nations will rush to it. And they will say let us go up to the mountain of the Lord, to the House of the G-d of Jacob; let us learn from their ways and let us walk in their paths for from Zion shall come forth Torah and the word of the Lord from Jerusalem. Nation shall not lift sword against nation and humanity will not learn war anymore." (Isaiah 2:1-4)

"The king in Israel was to be a representative of the Divine, a Mosaic 'rabbi-king' rather than a Platonic 'philosopher-king.' The primary task of the Davidic dynasty was not to establish its throne in Jerusalem but rather to establish G-d's throne in Jerusalem. G-d's throne means the acceptance of G-d's law, of ethical monotheism, of a divine ruler who demands justice and compassion, especially to the underprivileged. And when ethical monotheism and at least the seven Noahide laws of morality are accepted by the entire world, the messianic era of peace and redemption will be at hand." (Rabbi Shlomo Riskin [Orthodox], chief rabbi of Efrat, Israel, quoted in *Chicago Jewish News,* September 15-21, 2000)

"If there is ever to be a universal religion, it must be one which will have no location in place or time; which will be infinite, like the God it will preach, and whose sun will shine upon the followers of Krishna and of Christ, on saints and sinners, alike; which will not be Brāhminical or Buddhist, Christian or Mohammedan, but the sum total of all these, and still have infinite space for development; which in its catholicity will embrace in its infinite arms, and find a place for, every human being, from the lowest groveling savage, not far removed from the brute, to the highest man, towering by the virtues of his head and heart almost above humanity, making society stand in awe of him and doubt his human nature. It will be a religion which will have no place for persecution or intolerance in its polity, which will recognize divinity in every man and woman, and whose whole scope, whose whole force, will be centred in aiding humanity to realize its own true, divine nature." (Swami Vivekananda, in *The Yoga and Other Works*, edited by Swami Nikhilananda, Ramakrishna-Vivekananda Center, New York, 1953.)

Jesus (יהשוה)—

In the sacred Tetragrammaton (יהוה, the four letters, or Ha-Shem, i.e., The Name) and in the name of the Messiah (יהשוה) as well as in the *Torah* itself, Hebrew consonants are place holders for vowels whose specificity had been passed down through the generations by oral tradition. These vowels have been broken down into diacritical marks (Nekudim) for pronunciation and Masoretic (10th Century) accent marks that indicate the rise and fall of the voice when the prayers are sung. However, these representations are only approximations and vary according to local tradition and personal interpretation. This flexibility of dialect is akin to the diffused manner in which scripture represents both a combination of eternal *and* temporal truths, both The Living Word, spoken by G-d's representative (the Christ, the Messiah, the Avatar and World Teacher, etc.) in the flesh *and* the short-term conveniences of local politics and religion. The Latinized versions of the words for G-d and his agent, "Jehovah" and "Jesus," are as far from the original sounds as the English phonetic variations of Chinese have been from the actual indigenous pronunciations (notice how the English phonetic spellings of Chinese and Asian Indian names and places has changed in our lifetime).

How odd that so-called Christians, including Jerry Falwell and Billy Graham, believe that the Antichrist will be a Jewish male. I can only assume that they hold this position to prevent the real Christ from appearing—for where will they be, with all their hatred[31] and superiority when the Jewish radical for the downtrodden finally shows up? At least the equally dangerous distortion artist, Tim LaHeye (the apocalyptic "Left Behind" book series), believes that the Antichrist will be a European gentile who will kill lots of Jews during the seven-year tribulation. Come to think of it, didn't this already happen in the person of Hitler? Do these demagogues really believe that Jesus will show up as a "Christian" worshipping himself?

For Christians, accepting Jesus Christ as Lord and Savior is only the beginning of a spiritual path; it is hardly sufficient to be "saved." Everyone is responsible for the repercussions of his or her actions ("... he shall reward every man according to his works." Matthew 16:27). If your lifestyle is dependent on the exploitation of others or the earth, no religious declarations are going to save you, even if you are ignorant of the effects of your actions.

Jewish Christians—

"Catholics don't want to impose Christ on the Jews, but they are waiting for the moment when Israel too says yes to Christ." --Cardinal Joseph Ratzinger (now Pope Benedict XVI), oversser of Roman Catholic doctrine (9/10/00, *The Denver Post*, quoting an excerpt from his upcoming book). And they shall, but not to the Christ invented by the Roman Church, instead to the Messiah (Christ) from whom the early church and Romans stole and who has returned to reclaim his rightful kingdom. For he is as he always has been—a Jew born unto the House of David.

"The notion that the Jews were somehow responsible as a people for the death of Jesus had now become an accepted part of the Christian tradition. Time had obliterated the fact that the early Christians were Jews, that Jesus himself was a Jew. And time had obliterated any consciousness that the Crucifixion of Jesus by the Romans was the response of Rome to a defiance of its authority." (Abba Eban, *Heritage—Civilization and the Jews*, Summit Books, New York, 1984, p. 118.)

Had Jesus been accused of breaking Jewish law and found guilty, he would have been stoned to death.

Blaming the Jews for Jesus' death paved the way for Paul's success at controlling the spin of Jesus' legacy as a non-Judaic teaching, rather than as

---

[31] Graham spent a great deal of energy during the early months of 2002 trying to explain away the anti-Semitism remarks made in tape recorded conversations with then President Richard Nixon.

an outgrowth of Judaism, as James' (Jesus' brother) insisted. What followed was the greatest rip-off of intellectual property in history.

Since there is no copyright on the teachings, we are free to clear up ambiguities and make corrections.

Journalism—

Time was when journalism was a trade that sought out the truth. In our country, however, the combination of ownership of the press by a shrinking number of corporations (as facilitated by Congress in defiance of the intent of the 1934 Communications Act, in which the control of the airwaves was assigned to the people) and a contemporaneous reduction in the dialogue of ideas in our educational institutions has produced a generation of reporters that are incapable of asking the questions that would reveal the motives and facts behind the spoon-fed sound bites that have become mass touchstones.

Under the corporate-controlled Congress, the consolidation of media ownership is nearly complete. In the wake of Hitler using the centralization of the press in pre-war Germany to his advantage, the U.S. Agency for International Development (CIA) tried to decentralize the press in post-war Germany. Now the CIA and the power elite seek the same powers as the Nazis, knowing that such power makes nations susceptible to control and manipulation by those inclined toward totalitarianism and corporate fascism (see Bob Hoover, "A former right-wing golden boy—and, it turns out, gay man—recants," *Pittsburgh Post-Gazette*, 3/17/02, in the *Boulder Sunday Camera*).

Even those media outlets that have the theoretical capacity to serve as bulwarks against corporate centralization and control, namely public broadcasting, have fallen victim to the control of their funding agencies—Congress and corporate and foundation underwriters—and right-wing dollars. While "liberal" views may still be found in pockets on PBS, NPR, and other public networks, public broadcasting's analysis, particularly since 9-11 and the Kroc behest, rarely gets outside the box of information delineated by the very sources that need to be investigated. "Liberal bias of the media" is a myth (http://www.alternet.org/story.html?StoryID=12667).

Equally culpable in this critical shortfall of information is the American educational system that, subject to the same donors, has methodically eliminated courseware capable of providing the intellectual tools necessary to evaluate our changing political, social, and economic conditions.

"Next the statesmen will invent cheap lies, putting the blame upon the nation that is attacked, and every man will be glad of those conscience-soothing falsities, and will diligently study them, and refuse to examine any refutations of them; and thus he will by and by convince himself that the war is just, and will thank God for the better sleep he enjoys after this process of grotesque self-deception." --Mark Twain, *The Mysterious Stranger*, 1916, Chapter 9.

"In March, 1915, the J.P. Morgan interests, the steel, shipbuilding, and powder interests, and their subsidiary organizations, got together 12 men high up in the newspaper world and employed them to select the most influential newspapers in the United States and sufficient number of them to control generally the policy of the daily press. ... They found it was only necessary to purchase the control of 25 of the greatest papers.

"An agreement was reached; the policy of the papers was bought, to be paid for by the month; an editor was furnished for each paper to properly supervise and edit information regarding the questions of preparedness, militarism, financial policies, and other things of national and international nature considered vital to the interests of the purchasers." --U.S. Congressman Oscar Callaway, 1917

Freedom of the press—that is, the lack of government censorship, is no longer enough—not in a world where corporate ownership and centralization of the press accomplishes what the theoretically constitutionally-restricted government cannot: control of what is written and printed, said and seen. The mass media has become the public relations department of the corporate state—the voice of fascist America. Fascist propaganda represents the obliteration of memory, just as in Orwell's *1984*.

"This was a PR outfit that became President and took over the country." --former Reagan press aide Leslie Janka, as quoted by Mark Hertsgaard in "On Bended Knee: The Press and the Reagan Presidency." 8/21/88

King, Martin Luther—

"The ultimate measure of a man is not where he stands in moments of comfort and convenience, but where he stands at times of challenge and controversy." ("On Being a Good Neighbor," in *Strength to Love*, 1963.)

"I think the first reason that we should love our enemies, and I think this is at the very center of Jesus' thinking, is this: that hate for hate only intensifies the existence of hate and evil in the universe. If I hit you and you hit me and I hit you back and you hit me back and so on, you see, that goes on *ad infinitum*. It just never ends. Somewhere somebody must have a little sense, and that's the strong person. The strong person is the person who can cut off the chain of hate, the chain of evil. And that is the tragedy of hate, that it doesn't cut it off. It only intensifies the existence of hate and evil in the universe. Somebody must have religion enough and morality enough to cut it off, and inject within the very structure of the universe that strong and powerful element of love." (Excerpted from "Loving Your Enemies", a sermon delivered on 17 November 1957 at Dexter Avenue Baptist Church in Montgomery, Ala. From the Martin Luther King, Jr. Papers Project at Stanford University, http://www.stanford.edu/group/King/)

"A true revolution of values will lay hands on the world order and say of war: 'This way of settling differences is not just.' This business of burning human beings with napalm, of filling our nation's homes with orphans and widows, of injecting poisonous drugs of hate into the veins of peoples normally humane, of sending men home from dark and bloody battlefields physically handicapped and psychologically deranged, cannot be reconciled with wisdom, justice, and love. A nation that continues year after year to spend more money on military defense than on programs of social uplift is approaching spiritual death.

"I say to you today, my friends, that in spite of the difficulties and frustrations of the moment, I still have a dream. It is a dream deeply rooted in the American dream.

"I have a dream that one day this nation will rise up and live out the true meaning of its creed: 'We hold these truths to be self-evident: that all men are created equal.'

"I have a dream that one day on the red hills of Georgia the sons of former slaves and the sons of former slave owners will be able to sit down together at a table of brotherhood.

"I have a dream that one day even the state of Mississippi, a desert state, sweltering with the heat of injustice and oppression, will be transformed into an oasis of freedom and justice.

"I have a dream that my four children will one day live in a nation where they will not be judged by the color of their skin but by the content of their character." (Delivered on the steps at the Lincoln Memorial in Washington D.C. on August 28, 1963)

"Peace for Israel means security, and we must stand with all our might to protect its right to exist, its territorial integrity. I see Israel as one of the great outposts of democracy in the world, and a marvelous example of what can be done, how desert land can be transformed into an oasis of brotherhood and democracy. Peace for Israel means security and that security must be a reality." (March 25, 1968, less than two weeks before his death)

Mandela, Nelson (attributed, but actually from Marianne Williamson—

>Our deepest fear is not that we are inadequate.
>Our deepest fear is that we are powerful beyond measure.
>It is our light, not our darkness that most frightens us.
>We ask ourselves who am I to be brilliant, gorgeous, talented and fabulous?
>Actually, who are you not to be?
>You are a child of God.
>Your playing small does not serve the world.
>There is nothing enlightened about shrinking so that other people won't feel insecure around you.
>You were born to make manifest the glory of God that is within us.
>It's not just in some of us, it's in everyone.
>As we let our light shine, we unconsciously give others permission to do the same.
>As we are liberated from our own fear, our presence automatically liberates others.
>--1994 Inaugural Speech

Marx, Karl—

Marx may be known as the founder of Communism, a political theory, but his greatest work involved proving important truths about Capitalism, an economic theory. It was these truths that led him to search for a better form of organization. Unfortunately, those who claimed to be inspired by Marx's ideas took them entirely out of context. It's really a misnomer to call the Russian and Chinese models Marxism—their operations are better defined as state capitalism. This confusion is much the same as the appropriation of the term Christianity to justify murder and imperialism. In terms of practical action, Communism and Christianity (both theoretically based on sharing) begin and end with Jesus himself. Sharing must come from the heart. This is the objective of spiritual practice.

Medicine—

The medical profession has been sold down the river to the highest bidder. Once a practice in which conduct was based on the Hippocratic Oath that emphasized healing, medicine is now a bastion of corporate and individual greed where profit is placed above is health. In order to protect its control over public health, the American Medical Association has repeatedly opposed the use of any natural means that show promise in healing disease (since naturally occurring medicines can't be patented and sold for profit), while "new medicines" rarely contain anything new and are simply a means to protect patents and keep charging monopolistic prices.[32]

Less you think this behavior is something new, witch trials were used hundreds of years ago to eliminate natural healers who opposed the introduction of refined sugar (made available through colonialist wars) into the European diet. Now, natural herbs and compounds are converted into chemical formulas that can be patented, and are then priced beyond the reach of many who need them. Male domination over medicine (a continuation of Neolithic specialism and primogenitor property rights) is also evidenced in the diagnosis of "female hysteria," the Caesarian epidemic (treating pregnancy as a disease), and "Prozac nation" (the prescription of mood altering drugs to induce "normalcy").

"And it seems to me perfectly in the cards that there will be within the next generation or so a pharmacological method of making people love their servitude, and producing ... a kind of painless concentration camp for entire societies, so that people will in fact have their liberties taken away from them but will rather enjoy it, because they will be distracted from any desire to rebel by propaganda, brainwashing, or brainwashing enhanced by pharmacological methods." -- Aldous Huxley, 1959

"Years after three pharmaceutical companies agreed to offer medicines at no profit, only a tiny fraction of sufferers are receiving treatment." -- Theresa Agovino, *Associated Press*, 3/29/02, in *The Denver Post*.

Meditation—

Lost among the rabidity of so-called fundamentalist Christianity—and its belief that simply proclaiming Jesus Christ to be one's Lord and Savior is sufficient—is the paucity of its everyday practice. Those aspiring to walk in Christ's footsteps would do well to emulate the practice that he and other great spiritual teachers regularly performed as a means of attainment—meditation. Of course, part of the so-called Christian difficulty with meditation is that it is perceived as related to Buddhism and Yoga, which are characterized by these ignorant poseurs as G-dless religions. In fact, Buddhism and Yoga claim no such thing, only that perfection (call it what

---

[32] See Russell Mokhiber and Robert Weissman, "Stripping Away Big Pharma's Figleaf," @ http://www.alternet.org/story.html?StoryID=13398, June 24, 2002 and Melody Petersen, "New Medicines Seldom Contain Anything New, Study Finds, *The New York Times*, May 29, 2002.

you will) lies within. That this is also a principle taught by Jesus ("Neither shall they say, Lo here! Or, lo there! For, behold, the kingdom of God is within you." Luke 17:21) has been lost on those whose G-d is so far outside of themselves that they have lost any connection with it.

Millennium/Aquarian cusp—

The historical "speed up" that we are now experiencing—due to an increase in the information flow mostly attributable to electronic networks—is congruent to the effects of evolutionary currents on our nervous system. By increasing the amount of energy (or *prana*) that courses through our bodies, we are able to expedite our spiritual evolution. This is also reflected in the ebb and flow of cosmic energy that we receive from the center of the galaxy as our solar system follows its course around the Milky Way, with certain intervals of increased exposure to source energy engendering greater evolutionary progress than others intervals in which exposure to source energy is reduced.

Miracles—

As I predicted ("Greater works than I shall ye do." John 14:12), you have performed miracles beyond the imagination, and so also shall you, one by one, perform this greatest of miracles—conscious spiritual evolution and world peace.

Look toward the everyday details of life for your miracles, reducing your reliance on heroic measures to extricate yourself from difficulties that befall you as a result of not being present. You are the hero of your own novel in each instant of your life.

Miracles are signs from G-d showing that things are as they should be and that the synchronicity of the moment underscores the perfection. Spontaneous healings are based upon the strength of belief of the beholder. Thus, Jesus could facilitate healing in others without having the power to transform matter in ways that violate the laws of nature.

Monogamy—

Contrary to religious doctrine, monogamy has not been accorded any special status in the divine plan. Instead, it is a self-conscious choice made for spiritual and practical reasons.

As so eloquently described in an article on whales in *The New Yorker* magazine circa the 1980's, biologists can map the relative monogamy of mammals versus the ejaculatory power of the male of the species, so that the most monogamous mammals are represented by the weakest ejaculatory systems and the most polygamous mammals are represented by the strongest ejaculatory systems—the operational objective being the ability of the male of the species to wash out the sperm of previous coital incidents (i.e., strongest in polygamous mammals; weakest in monogamous mammals).

And where does humankind stand in such a scale?—exactly in the middle— a perfect representation of the historical ambivalence of our actions. The conclusion to be drawn from such evidence is plain to see: monogamy is a self-conscious choice that is compelled by the depth of the intimacy that can be developed from its practice. If there is spiritual weight on its side, it is based on this resultant state.

Monotheism—

"Every nation will walk each individual in the name of his god and we will walk in the name of the Lord our G-d forever." (Micah 4:5)

"... my house shall be a house of prayer for all peoples." (Yom Kippur liturgy)

One-Without-A-Name—

"The yogi teaches that the mind itself has a higher state of existence, beyond reason, a superconscious state, and that when the mind rises to that state, then this knowledge, which is beyond reason, comes—metaphysical and transcendental knowledge comes to that man. This state of going beyond reason, beyond ordinary human knowledge, may sometimes come by chance to a man who does not understand its science; he stumbles upon it, as it were. When he stumbles upon it, he generally interprets it as coming from the outside. So this explains why an inspiration, or transcendental knowledge, may be the same in different countries, but in one country it will seem to come through an angel, and in another through a deva, and in a third through God. What does this mean? It means that the mind brought out the knowledge from within itself and that the manner of finding it was interpreted according to the beliefs and education of the person through whom it came." (Swami Vivekananda, "Rāja-Yoga" in *Vivekananada: The Yogas and Other Works*, edited by Swami Nikhilananda, Ramakrishna-Vivekananda Center, New York, 1953, p. 614.)

As we have shown throughout this book and as summarized in *Appendix 2 – Prolegomena to Any Future Physics* and in *Appendix 6 – The Proof*, the Great Anomaly (or G-d) is reflected in every detail of the universe, and that the various differences from culture to culture in describing this transcendent reality is, as Vivekananda points out, due only to the limitation of symbolic expression on the part of the perceiver and not to the existence of multiple g-ds, which, as we have proven, would run counter to the laws of nature.

Original Sin—

The whole concept of sin and original sin is based on a misinterpretation of an ancient parable that we have come to know today as the story of Adam and Eve and the serpent. In the Far East, the serpent is a symbol of kundalini, the latent energy within us that is the key to our evolution (spiritual attainment). The raising of kundalini through the chakras is the process by which we become fully-realized beings. This interpretation of the serpent energy is echoed in the esoteric Hebrew doctrine that assigns mathematical equivalency to the spelling of, and moral interdependence to, the concepts of the serpent and Messiah.[33] The offering of the apple by the serpent is indeed an offering of knowledge, and, yes, "a little knowledge is a dangerous thing," but it is not a sin for human beings to seek or gain this knowledge. Certainly the journey began with a loss of innocence and put us at a loss as to why the world works as it does, but this is the price we must pay in moving from an existence based on instinctive reactions to one based on self-consciousness. So, we made up reasons for thunder (Thor) and reverberation (Echo) and whatever else we did not understand at the time. But today we know better. In fact, for the first time in our history on this planet, through the advancement of our inquiry, we have generated enough information to represent the perfection of the universe (the Great Anomaly or G-d) in scientific terms, thus arriving at a perspective from which spirituality and science represent the same reality.

The misunderstanding of the Garden of Eden parable has led to many regressive behaviors including male chauvinism and the use of the concept of sin to shame people. What most pseudo-religious folk call sin is nothing more than a carry-over of instinctive behaviors that are part of our genetic inheritance. Even the development of the Ego, frontal lobes, and the consequent ability to manipulate symbols is rooted in and complementary to self-preservative instincts. In the jungle, murder and rape are not sins; they are the natural behaviors of certain species. At some point in our evolutionary process, we began to develop notions of "civilized" behavior and began to reject these unbridled instinctive reactions. All of civilization, in fact, has been the process of aspiring to implement these higher, spiritualized motives. Today, we stand at the crossroads of our next evolutionary step, and can choose to continue along the instinctive path driven by fear, scarcity, hunger, sex, etc., or we can choose the path of spiritual growth, learning how to share and how to distinguish between

---

[33] MShICh (Messiah) and NChSh (the Serpent in Eden) = 358 (from Aleister Crowley, *The Book of Thoth*, Lancer Books, New York, (circa 1974), p. 100.

what we truly need and what our instincts want. This step will be achieved by individuals, one at a time, developing their own spiritual practice.

Pacifism—

Having declared themselves a nuclear free zone years ago, New Zealand has now eliminated its air defense and has reduced its navy. It's a small start, but far ahead of the rest of the industrialized world.

> "Nonviolence is the greatest force at the disposal of mankind. It is mightier than the mightiest weapon of destruction devised by the ingenuity of man."
> --Mohandas K. Gandhi

"... At the end of the talk someone from the audience asked the Dalai Lama, 'Why didn't you fight back against the Chinese?' The Dalai Lama looked down, swung his feet just a bit, then looked back up at us and said with a gentle smile, 'Well, war is obsolete, you know.'

"Then, after a few moments, his face grave, he said, 'Of course the mind can rationalize fighting back ... but the heart, the heart would never understand. Then you would be divided in yourself, the heart and the mind, and the war would be inside you.'"

Physics—

"The switch from the visual space of the Euclidean culture into the resonant space of quantum mechanics is completely misunderstood by the physicists who use the new paradigm of resonance. They are not aware that acoustic space has unique physical properties (a perfect sphere whose center is everywhere and whose margins are nowhere). The result is that quantum physicists continue to make efforts at visualizing the non-visual, constructing little iconic models of DNA particles and the like." (McLuhan, *From Cliché to Archetype*, The Viking Press, New York, 1970, p. 154)

What McLuhan speaks to is the unending attempts by scientists to split matter into smaller and different components. There is no end to this. Like mathematics itself, matter can be forever subdivided into different flavors, spins, harmonics, and other eccentricities. The mystery behind it (the anomaly) however, cannot be so divided; within it all forces (strong, weak, electromagnetic, and gravitational) are interrelated, as is postulated by the Unified Field Theory, expressed in the mathematics of String Theory, and evidenced by the Einstein-Bose precipitate and the Plasma Ball. As we have shown throughout this book and as summarized in *Appendix 2 - Prolegomena to Any Future Physics* and in *Appendix 6 - The Proof*, this anomaly is the key to proving the equivalency between scientific and spiritual models and for proving the Big Bang, the existence of Strings, the appearance of the World Teacher, the unity of all religions, and the next step in human evolution.

Pilate—

"Pilate is an extreme case: successive writers, intoxicated by what he represented and unhindered by knowing much about him, invented him almost from scratch.

"That process of 'invention' has taken some startling turns. For example, soon after Jesus' death, his followers gave a particular spin to the events. They initially saw Pilate as the villainous representative of Roman colonial power. Wroe's research supports this view, showing that Jesus may have been a local troublemaker, an affront to Roman authority. Here, Pilate's role would seem clear: He works to maintain the status quo of those in power, in Judea as well as Rome. Jesus must be dealt with, not merely swiftly and efficiently but made into an example for others to see.

"In a matter of decades, however, Christian believers began to paint Pilate in a more favorable manner in order to cozy up to Roman authority. In this scenario, Pilate, though still guilty of participating in Christ's crucifixion, is manipulated by the Jews into reluctantly condemning a man he's come to believe is truly holy. Wroe shows how this led to the scapegoating of the Jews and was undoubtedly a major contributing factor in the development of anti-Semitism." (from Davis, Duane, "Out of the Darkness," A review of Ann Wroe's *Pontius Pilate*, Random House, New York, 2000, as it appeared in *The Denver Rocky Mountain News*, Books section, 4/16/00, p. 1.)

Pollution—

The destruction of the natural world is ubiquitous. Not only is our air, water, and land contaminated with unhealthy and deadly substances, but our senses, too, are cut off from their natural environment. Light pollution prevents us from viewing the stars, chemical flavors hide natural tastes, and noise pollution prevents us from hearing the wind, the birds, or, heaven forbid, the silence. Our fears have led us to seek protection through artificial means and in doing so we have threatened our own existence. It is the conquering of our fears through spiritual practice (evolution) that will eliminate a system which of necessity pollutes as a function of its survival.

Population—

Ever since Thomas Malthus wrote his essay[34] in 1798, the issue of population growth has been controversial. Suffice it to say that the classic argument boils down to the disparity of the mathematics of human reproduction which, baring cataclysms, increases at a geometric rate, and the mathematics of agricultural production which, despite fertilizers, pesticides, and water diversions, all of which threaten our life-support systems, increases arithmetically at best. The upshot of this intersection of empirical calculations is simply that the earth cannot support in a sustainable manner the number of human beings that we have and continue to increase, *even if*, as Marx proposed, the means of production and distribution are aligned under equitable direction. The discussion is now centered on the question, "How can we compassionately reduce our numbers and alter our agricultural philosophy to evolve into a sustainable, spiritual society?"

In his curious Socratic manifesto, *Ishmael*,[35] Daniel Quinn posits that the current dilemma of humankind is a result of our agricultural methodology, whereby atmosphere replenishing forests are clear-cut and plowed under for crops and herds. Without disparaging or championing this compelling theory, at this point it is clear that we must stem the destruction of our forests and jungles to avert global catastrophe. To do this we must reduce the demand for agricultural products while at the same time improve the means by which we produce and distribute food. There are a number of means to accomplish this including, population reduction, dietary improvement (not dictated by multi-national conglomerates) including more eco-friendly forms of protein, and continued growth of organic, natural, sustainable agricultural methods.

Prophesy—

"It should be kept in mind that prophecy in the biblical sense does not mean to predict the future but to explain the will of God for the present, and therefore show the right path to take for the future." Cardinal Joseph Ratzinger (now Pope Benedict XVI), overseer of Roman Catholic Doctrine. (6/27/00, *The Boulder Daily Camera*, quoting 5/13/00 statement by the Vatican.

Roman Church—

The Church is indeed caught between a rock and a hard place. As the stone is about to be rolled away to reveal the "Second Coming," the oldest

---

[34] Malthus, Thomas, *An Essay on the Principle of Population*, London, printed for J. Johnson, St. Paul's Church-yard, 1798.
[35] Quinn, Daniel, *Ishmael*, Bantam Books, New York, 1988. Winner of the Turner Tomorrow award.

continual "Christian" institution is preparing to face the steely scrutiny of the Messiah, the Christ. In preparation for this cosmic event, the Church has been attempting to unburden its guilty conscience over a history of un-Christian actions that begin with the distortions surrounding Christ's death and lead inextricably through various inquisitions to the Holocaust itself. Since, in their estimation, Christ will reappear much as he was before, that is as a Jew descended from the House of David, the Church is rightfully nervous about His feelings concerning the treatment of his kinfolk at the hands of the self-proclaimed defender of the Faith. And rightfully so, since the being called Christ is more than just the fulfillment of Christian prophesy—he is the Messiah, the World Teacher, and Avatar as well—a fulfillment of many prophesies. The Church, therefore, needs to be concerned with more than just the lies it has promulgated regarding the role of the Jews in Christ's death, but its intolerance toward other religions as well, for this will not sit well with a lawgiver who recognizes "the truth is the whole" and offers proof of the unity of all religions.

Sexism—

In *The Origin of the Family, Private Property, and the State*, Frederick Engels proposes that patriarchic control over society began with the advent of specialization that was the Neolithic Age. He attributes this, in general, to the greater physical strength and stature of men and therefore their ability to exert control over valued objects. Before this, matriarchal societies were common among unspecialized Paleolithic hunter-gatherers. Today, societal rules have evolved and "physical strength" has no legal standing. Now anyone willing to pay the spiritual price for greed can amass material goods. As more and more women benefit from the breakdown of sexism in advanced industrial societies, they begin to suffer from the same life-shortening and life-force imperiling diseases as men, thus the gap in life expectancy between men and women narrows. It is a fallacy to believe that women, given the chance to rule, are any more benevolent than men. History has shown this to be untrue. They are subject to the tyranny of instinct and ego just as men.

The end of sexism is the marriage of masculine and feminine, anima and animus, creative and receptive, yin and yang, within each of us. Then, truly, will we have leaders that further peace and equality.

Social Contract—

Bodies corporate and politic are based on social contracts. In this country the social contract defined by the founding fathers has been abrogated. Large concentrations of capital control the legislative, judicial, and executive branches of the government as well as the military and intelligence apparatuses. The people must regain power over these governmental functions by real campaign financing reforms, auditable voting procedures, and regulation of media ownership.

Socialism—

It is not possible to objectively discuss socialism with Americans because they suffer from the very thing they attribute to others—brainwashing. Principally, Americans are unable to distinguish between political and economic forms of organization. They assume that their freedoms are a result of capitalism (an economic system) when, in fact, American freedoms (what few are left) are a result of the Constitution and the Bill of Rights (political documents). Perhaps this misperception is why Americans are willing to trade their rights for material goods or the perception of security. No doubt, many despicable acts have been committed in the name of socialism, but in general, these acts have little to do with socialism (a form of economic organization) and everything to do with authoritarianism and totalitarianism (forms of political organization). Life under Stalin was not much different for most Russians than life under the Czar, just as life under Mao was not much different for most Chinese than life under the Emperors. As far as socialism in Russia and China goes, one could question whether it ever happened, considering that Marx described socialism as a system that develops out of advanced industrial societies. Once one separates political and economic systems, it's easy to see that in America capitalism continues to thrive while democracy and republicanism are being swept away by corporatism, wherein concentrations of capital increasingly control the state apparatus. If this process is allowed to continue, then, truly, the American form of government will be indivisible from its economic system—the corporate state: fascism.

Lest we forget the money changers tossed from the temple, certainly no one who has ever lived by Christ's precepts would characterize his economic philosophy as capitalistic in nature!

Spiritual Unity—

Given the destruction of historical evidence by the Flood and the burning of the libraries at Alexandria, the debate over whether widespread spiritual unity existed in Atlantis may never be solved per se. However, there are more recent examples of such harmony. For example, during the eleventh and twelfth centuries in Moorish Spain, Jews, Christians, and Muslims lived together peacefully. The ruling Muslims considered Jews and Christians "peoples of the book," brothers who shared their monotheistic beliefs. This tolerant period was ended by the Inquisition, fomented by so-called "Christians." The same general scenario with different players occurred in Salonika (now Greece), following the Inquisition until the Holocaust.

Theatre—

The transformative process of theatre:
- Dramatic arc begins with the *sacred circle* of the players—a safe space for the exploration of emotions and spirit.
- The work created in this atmosphere is then conveyed to the audience through the players' performance, production crafts, and the *suspension of disbelief* by the audience.
- Through this gestalt, *identification* with the characters and *compassion* toward the human condition is achieved; the audience experiences the story as its own.
- As the dramatic arc is completed, identification and compassion bring *catharsis*.

Third eye—

Opening the third eye is simply the process of clearing an energy path for the kundalini to flow up the spine, through the brain, and out the frontal lobes. In the process, such a stream removes repressions, engrams, cathexes, et cetera—protein chain obstacles that stand in its way—and relocates them to less strategic areas of the brain associated with long-term memory (turning repressions into memory), thereby reducing their constant cycling and the energy dedicated to their preservation, clearing the mind for more evolved work. The void left becomes the path of pure being.

United Nations—

The U.N. organization holds great hope but, like the U.S. before it, exhibits a large gap between its creed and practice. Despite much good work, it is mired in ideologies that worship money, power, and isms, not brotherhood and sisterhood. When it consists of free and educated individuals from states with democratically-elected representatives, then it shall be ready to lead world healing and evolution.

Vegetarianism—

If those in the conservation movement kept a diet in consonance with the way they wish to preserve the earth, change would be hastened.

If it weren't so pitiful, I would laugh at the outrageousness of the State of Wyoming declaring that the notion of Jesus as a vegetarian is blasphemous. What are these fools thinking, that Jesus is pleased with the slaughter of animals for food? That he looks forward to a steak on his plate each evening? There is more evidence that he was a vegetarian than not. Once again, we have financial interests, the cattle industry, dictating spiritual standards. These are just so many money changers that should be tossed from the temple. My God, they're cutting down the rainforest in the interests of the most inefficient means of creating protein for humanity—cattle breeding. This is blasphemy.

Wealth—

I do not scorn the rich, I pity them. What was done to them that makes them so cynical about human possibilities? As I said before, little chance do those who worship and seek money for its own sake have of gaining heaven (Matthew 19:24, Mark 10:25, Luke 18:25). Yet they have invented a cosmology wrapped around Calvinism and Protestantism that is based on the temporal rewards of "survival of the fittest" and the accumulation of wealth. To the degree that you segment yourself by focusing on money is the degree to which you disconnect yourself from the whole and your spirit is diminished.

Yoga—

Yoga is a spiritual practice that is consciously aimed at self-awareness and overcoming of the instincts—i.e., the evolutionary path. Yoga stimulates the natural process of psycho-spiritual rebirth. It promotes self-awareness and healing through observance of the personality read-out that accompanies the emptying phase of this sacred act, thereby permitting the practitioner to consciously redesign his or her behavior. Through this process of male-female integration and the discovery of the archetype of the self (Messiah, Christ, Buddha, Krishna, et al.), one (eventually) achieves transcendence and mastership.

All techniques in Yoga are geared to help us free ourselves from limiting, life-denying thought patterns, and to identify with the channels of pure consciousness and unconditioned lovingness found within.

There are many different forms of Yoga, but for introductory purposes, the classical form of *Astanga* (eight limbs) Yoga is recommended. (See *Appendix 3 – Introduction to Yoga* and *Chapter 7 – Yoga*)

The eight limbs (steps) are:
- *Yama* (ethical principles, abstinences)
- *Niyama* (principles of self-restraint, observances)
- *Asana* (appropriate postures for meditative absorption)
- *Pranayama* (breathing techniques)

- *Pratyahara* (sense withdrawal)
- *Dharana* (concentration)
- *Dhyana* (meditative absorption)
- *Samadhi* (ecstasy)

The practice of Yoga begins with *Yama* and *Niyama,* where you define your relationship with Yoga by adopting general ethical principles and vows of self-restraint by which you are willing to define your practice.

In *Yama,* would-be yogins define their ethical considerations that involve their actions toward others and comprise the ethical foundations of the yogic life, while in *Niyama,* the practices involve oneself and organizing one's life. For example, *Yama* includes abstention from violence, lying, stealing, sex, and possessiveness (greed),[36] whereas *Niyama* includes purity, contentment, austerity (fast, silence, prayer, chanting), self-study (that supports spiritual practice) and self-surrender (immersion in the divine).

Once practitioners define the parameters of their work, the standards by which they've chosen to measure their thoughts and actions, the next limb of Yoga that is undertaken is *Asana.* *Asana* is the most visible and well known form of Yoga in the West; it consists of the postures (*asanas*) that have been incorporated into so many of the popular television shows, videotapes, and books on Yoga.

Aside from the general health benefits derived from stretching muscles, mobilizing joints, aligning the skeletal structure, and stimulating glandular and other systems, *Asana* prepares the body for the more rigorous disciplines associated with just-sitting and concentrating on the more subtle realms of being. Ultimately, a body capable of total relaxation facilitates the isolation of the mind in the next level of exercises, which will result in the mental relaxation and stillness that allows the soul to shine through.

There is confusion in the world over the role that *Asana* plays in Yoga. Many people are under the mistaken assumption that practicing postures is the be all and end all of Yoga. The extended practice of *Asana* engenders the development of the individual practitioner's ideal body form, much like the Greek golden section and golden mean, but there is a danger in overemphasizing this result. While *asanas* are designed to improve health by stimulating each and every physical system and, at the same time, bolster concentration and induce relaxation, they are not an end in themselves. There are schools of Yoga that seem to lose themselves in this aspect of the science, thus forming attachments to that which is, ultimately, transitory.

---

[36] These five ethical tenets are collectively known as The Great Vow among yogins within an order.

So, remember, the practice of *Asana* is a stepping stone to super-consciousness and transcendence, not toward the narcissism of physical perfection.

Pranayama, the next stage of Yoga, begins during the practice of *Asana,* with slow, full breaths that facilitate the stretching and accompany the stillness of and relaxation into the position. Here I must caution students that the practice of Yoga is best learned from an experienced teacher. It may be one thing to clarify goals and set parameters for oneself and begin to practice *Asana,* but very few individuals in the world are qualified to teach themselves *Pranayama,* even with the help of ethereal teachers. So take these guidelines as an elucidation of the nature and value of Yoga and not a guide to its daily practice, a roadmap for your vehicle and not hands-on driver's education.

Pranayama involves the expansion of *Prana,* the life-force. This practice can induce great changes to the student's physical, emotional, intellectual, and spiritual being. As long as these powerful gifts are received within the ethical context of *Yama* and *Niyama,* and in common sense—the middle path approach as put forth by teachers of this science—then you need not fear this practice.

Once the breathing techniques practiced in *Pranayama* have been internalized, your consciousness is ready to expand into states that are beyond the instinctive, physical, sub-conscious emotional and psychological desires of your lower self. You are then ready for the stage of Yoga called *Pratyahara,* where you move beyond identification with your senses.

Only when *Pratyahara* is accomplished, that is, when the first five stages of Yoga have been reasonably mastered, can we then leave the body and senses behind and turn inward to the mind to begin our transcendental work.

Dharana, Dhyana, and *Samadhi,* which roughly translate as concentration, contemplation, and transcendence of self-consciousness, are really different degrees of the same practice known as *Samyama,* in which the practitioner gradually frees herself or himself from mental distractions until these interruptions disappear altogether and the object of concentration and contemplation becomes one with the subject.

Like *Dharana* and *Dhyana, Samadhi* has subtle distinctions of degree as one approaches the Anomaly. Because this state is the holiest experience, it necessarily defies specific description except to say that it is the source of inspiration for what you are becoming.

The meditative practices and states of consciousness availed through this process are the most subtle in the entirety of the science of Yoga. There is no rushing this attainment. The message or assignment that we receive as a result of achieving 'enlightenment'—or fill-in-the-blank, Cosmic-, Messiah-, Christ-, Buddha-, or Krishna-Consciousness—differs from individual to individual. How this gift is to be shared is for each of us to discover for ourselves.

Yogajazz—

Yogajazz is a concept that signifies a non-dogmatic approach to spirituality. When practiced successfully, Yoga (as defined above) acts as a catalyst for soul-healing. Just as the body heals itself from, say, a scratch, by coagulating, clotting, scabbing, and regenerating without conscious intervention, so the soul has an innate power to heal itself. This power is often suppressed by the traumas life hands us. So, Yoga plays an important role in clearing the slate.

After that's accomplished, how do practitioners describe their experiences? Unfortunately, their new "truth" is usually described by some dogmatic philosophy that they have brought along as baggage, or by one to which they are in close proximity. But the truth is the whole, and while all philosophies and religions each contain some smaller truths that help explain certain questions, not one of them contains the whole truth. In order to maintain a state of "truthfulness" then, one must incorporate all these smaller truths in an eclectic, but progressive, fashion, much as jazz does with riffs and phrases, both original and borrowed. Thus, Yogajazz: Yoga as improvisational truth.

Also, Yogajazz is used by Michael as an overriding name for the confluence of Qabalah, Jnana Yoga, and the Glass-bead Game.

Youth Violence—

America is in denial over the causes of youth violence. What else could be expected of a society that feigns spiritual concern while maintaining its gluttonous consumption of world resources through military might and economic control? The violence of youth not only mimics that of their parents, but is a reaction against such blatant hypocrisy.

Appendix 8

The Anatomy of Treason:
Footnotes to Michael's remarks on
Coup d'État 2000, the 9-11 Reichstag,
the Junta, and American Fascism—

"There is no such thing, at this date of the world's history, in America, as an independent press. You know it and I know it. The business of the Journalist is to destroy truth; To lie outright; To pervert; To vilify; To fawn at the feet of mammon, and to sell his country and his race for his daily bread. You know it and I know it and what folly is this toasting an independent press? We are the tools and vassals for rich men behind the scenes. We are the jumping jacks, they pull the strings and we dance. Our talents, our possibilities and our lives are all the property of other men. We are intellectual prostitutes." --John Swinton, former Chief of Staff, *The New York Times*, circa 1880.

"Freedom of the press is guaranteed only to those who own one." -- A.J. Liebling

"Threatened as they may be from corporate takeover and monopoly capital, the Internet and print-on-demand publishing are the last bastion of the free press." --Michael David Solomon, 2008.

This appendix consists of footnotes to the arguments presented in Chapter 12 – Resurrection. *The number in brackets at the end of each footnote entry in* Chapter 12 – Resurrection *corresponds to the footnote number in this appendix.*

Accounting scandal: CPA firms and banks[1]

---

[1] At this point, KPMG, BDO Seidman, (David Cay Johnston, "U.S. Accuses 2 Audit Firms of Assisting Tax Violations," *The New York Times*, 7/10/02) and Ernst & Young (David Barboza, "Regulators Sue Ernst & Young in the Collapse of an S. & L.," *The New York Times*, 11/2/02) were under indictment by the government for their own accounting scandals, and Citigroup, J.P. Morgan Chase, and Merrill Lynch were being investigated for helping Enron peddle its shell deals

676   »   Anatomy of Treason

Accounting scandal: corporations[2]
Accounting scandal: government[3]
Accounting scandal: Bush and Cheney, Harken Energy and Halliburton[4]

(Richard A. Oppel Jr. and Kurt Eichenwald, "Inquiry Said to Examine Citigroup Role in Enron Deal," *The New York Times*, 12/9/02, "Citigroup, J.P. Morgan said to aid Enron deception," *Associated Press*, 12/10/02, and Richard A. Oppel Jr., "Senator Says Merrill Lynch Helped Enron 'Cook Books,'" *The New York Times*, 7/31/02). Eventually most of the nation's biggest brokerage houses agree to pay over $1 billion in fines for issuing misleading stock recommendations (Gretchen Morgenson and Patrick McGeehan, "Corporate Conduct: The Overview; Wall Street Firms Are Ready To Pay $1 Billion in Fines," *The New York Times*, 12/20/02).

[2] It's estimated that the 2002 "corporate fraud" scandals (to differentiate them from the 2008 "mortgage crisis" and other incidents in the ongoing fraud of the self-described "New World Order" [who control the privately owned Federal Reserve and direct its policy of forcing the government to borrow {for war and financial profiteering} to facilitate converting public tax monies into private profit]) have cost Americans $200 billion in lost investment savings, jobs, pension losses, and tax revenue (Marcy Gordon, "Report: $200 billion lost in corporate scandals," *Associated Press*, 10/18/02). This does not take into consideration the scandal's effects on the recession that they exacerbated. Given the Bush family's involvement in the Savings & Loan scandal in the '80's, as well as in numerous irregularities with HUD, the Bureau of Indian Affairs, and other government agencies, perhaps it's time to hold accountable those who have stolen trillions of dollars from U.S. taxpayers."

[3] As we shall see, it is the corporate-financed representatives serving in Congress that write the laws that permit massive "white-collar" crime, a particular class of criminals that control the economy, the state apparatus, the media, and the church.

[4] Michael writes in 2003: For a short time, while it was in vogue, the press began to take up an investigation of the sordid business dealings of the multi-asterisked President and Vice President of the United States. What they found was that Cheney cost Halliburton shareholders a bundle by buying an asbestos suit-plagued company and then covering up the losses by claiming (with the help of Arthur Andersen) $100 million in revenues that had not been received. Since then, Halliburton has lost 18,000 jobs and between $3 and $4 billion in value, and has stripped workers of much of their pensions. Bush, on the other hand (or is it the same hand?), had made a killing in Harken Oil company stock (that he had bought with $180,375 in unsecured loans that were later forgiven), selling it just before he knew it was about to experience a steep decline in price. Then he failed to report his sale on time. Since his daddy was President, the investigation was called off (though without exonerating Bush), and Bush used the proceeds to pay off a bank loan that helped him buy the Texas Rangers baseball team. Now, in the midst of the current (2002) corporate investigations, Bush goes on national television with his plan for corporate reform, calling for the return of any monies a company

Enron, 9-11, and the pipeline[5]
Enron, other energy companies, and the California energy crisis[6]
Other major bankruptcies[7]
Congressional laws perpetrate fraud and thievery[8]

---

executive receives for phony bookkeeping. The stock market dropped 178 points the following day. Both Bush and Cheney, "champions of small government," have also been recipients of large government loans, Cheney securing over $200 million in federal loan guarantees while at Halliburton, and Bush the recipient of over $150 million in public loans to build a baseball stadium for his team. Shortly thereafter, Bush ran for governor on the theme of self-reliance.

[5] See Ted Rall, "Bush Fuels Oil Conspiracy Theory, AlterNet (*http://www.alternet.org/story.html?StoryID=12205*), 1/10/02, Ron Callari, "The Enron-Cheney-Taliban Connection?," Albion Monitor, 2/28/02 (http://www.alternet.org/story.html?StoryID=12525), "Afghanistan plan gas pipeline," *BBC News*, 5/13/02 (http://news.bbc.co.uk/hi/english/business/newsid_1984000/1984459.stm), Bagila Bukharbayeva, "Pakistan, Turkmenistan, and Afghanistan sign $3.2 billion pipeline deal," *The Associated Press*, 12/27/02, "Asian states battle over Caspian wealth," *Power and Internet News Report*, 12/1/02 (http://www.yellowtimes.org/article.php?sid=900), and Gore Vidal, "The Enemy Within," *The Observer* (London), 10/27/02 (http://9-11congress.netfirms.com/Vidal.html).

[6] Michael writes in 2003: Indeed, power company trading irregularities are now epidemic: the Williams Companies, Duke Energy Corp., Southern California Gas Company, Sempra Energy, Mirant Corp., the Los Angeles Department of Water and Power, and Reliant Resources were all involved in manipulating markets in California; El Paso Corporation, American Electric Power Company, Dynegy Corporation, the Williams Companies, and CMS Energy Corporation were all involved in giving false trading information around the country. Given that California's "Gross National Product" makes it the fifth or six most developed "nation" in the world (alternating with France, depending on market values at any given time), one could consider these assaults an attack on national security if it weren't for the fact that the corporations that run the government are the ones profiting by the attack (Jonathan Peterson and Nancy Rivera Brooks, "Calif. Claims new proof in energy scam," *Los Angeles Times*, as reprinted in *The Denver Post*, 3/3/03). Later, Republicans will attempt to use the disastrous economic effects of these corporate attacks on California to impeach the Democratic governor, Gray Davis. As the *Los Angeles Times* pointed out in an editorial on 7/1/03, the blame belongs squarely on the shoulders of Bush and his fellow conspirators.

[7] WorldCom ($103.8 billion), Pacific Gas & Electric ($21.5 billion), Global Crossing ($25.5 billion), NTL ($16.8 billion), and Adelphia Communications ($24.4 billion). The price tag for Enron's bankruptcy was $63.4 billion.

Collusion of government and business to commit fraud[9]
9-11 Congressional investigation[10]
Assassination of Orlando Letelier[11]
The Big Lie[12]

---

[8] Two months after Xerox was ordered to pay $300 million to thousands of retirees, witness the Treasury Department's new rules allowing corporations to convert the manner in which they account for pension plans, thus slashing the pensions of older workers throughout the country ("Xerox Ordered to Pay $300 Million to Retirees," *The Associated Press*, 10/3/02, and Kathy Kristof, "Pension proposal assailed as cheating older workers," *The Denver Post*, 12/23/02).

[9] On 10/4/02, Bloomberg News reports that the Justice Department's antitrust chief, Charles James, stepped down to take a job with ChevronTexaco. A few weeks later, the amount of money that Bush sought for SEC investigations was severely cut back from what he had promised with great fanfare only months earlier (See, Stephen Labaton, "Bush Seeks to Cut Back on Raise for S.E.C.'s Corporate Cleanup," *The New York Times*, 10/19/02.) Following this, former FBI Director William Webster was appointed head of a new board formed to oversee audits, and then forced to resign (11/12/02) after it was revealed that he headed the audit committee of the near-bankrupt United Technologies. His successor, William Donaldson, helped hide accounting irregularities when he was chairman of Aetna.

[10] Michael writes in 2003: Consider the strategy implied in the scenario whereby the Homeland Security Department was approved and created long before any investigation into the causes of 9-11 was begun. Talk about foregone conclusions! The premise that we need to give up our liberties for greater protection against terrorists, who every couple of years manage to pull off an action because our rulers either allow or abet them, is ludicrous. As Benjamin Franklin said long ago, those who give up their liberties in order to increase their security deserve neither.

[11] Again, it was the CIA under the directorship of George H.W. Bush, and DINA (the Chilean secret intelligence organization), under the command of Augusto Pinochet (whom the CIA put in power by engineering a coup), that conspired to assassinate Orlando Letelier, the former Chilean ambassador to the United States for the popularly-elected government of Salvador Allende. (See, John Dinges and Saul Landau, *Assassination on Embassy Row*, Pantheon Books, New York, 1980.)

[12] "... The size of the lie is a definite factor in causing it to be believed, because the vast masses of a nation are in the depths of their hearts more easily deceived than they are consciously and intentionally bad.

"The primitive simplicity of their minds renders them more easy victims of a big lie than a small one, because they themselves often tell little lies but would be ashamed to tell big ones.

"Such a form of lying would never enter their heads. They would never credit others with the possibility of such great impudence as the complete reversal of facts. Even explanations would long leave them in doubt and hesitation, and any trifling reason would dispose them to accept a thing as true.

U.S. support for Nazism[13]
The Hostage Deal[14]
Corporate/government control of media[15]

"Something therefore always remains and sticks from the most imprudent of lies, a fact which all bodies and individuals concerned in the art of lying in this world know only too well, and therefore they stop at nothing to achieve this end."
--Adolph Hitler, Mein Kampf

[13] "What would have happened if millions of American and British people, struggling with coupons and lines at the gas stations, had learned that in 1942 Standard Oil of New Jersey [part of the Rockefeller empire] managers shipped the enemy's fuel through neutral Switzerland and that the enemy was shipping Allied fuel? Suppose the public had discovered that the Chase Bank in Nazi-occupied Paris after Pearl Harbor was doing millions of dollars' worth of business with the enemy with the full knowledge of the head office in Manhattan [the Rockefeller family among others]? Or that Ford trucks were being built for the German occupation troops in France with authorization from Dearborn, Michigan? Or that Colonel Sosthenes Behn, the head of the international American telephone conglomerate ITT, flew from New York to Madrid to Berne during the war to help improve Hitler's communications systems and improve the robot bombs that devastated London? Or that ITT built the FockeWulfs that dropped bombs on British and American troops? Or that crucial ball bearings were shipped to Nazi-associated customers in Latin America with the collusion of the vice-chairman of the U.S. War Production Board in partnership with Goering's cousin in Philadelphia when American forces were desperately short of them? Or that such arrangements were known about in Washington and either sanctioned or deliberately ignored?" --Charles Higham, researcher, about U.S.-Nazi collaboration during WWII

[14] I.e., the treason of interfering with the conduct of U.S. foreign policy while holding no governmental office. Known as the "October Surprise," the details are explored at http://www.webcom.com/~lpease/collections/denied/octsurprise.htm
http://www.consortiumnews.com/archive/xfile3.html,
http://www.consortiumnews.com/archive/xfile6.html,
http://www.consortiumnews.com/archive/xfile9.html,
http://www.consortiumnews.com/archive/xfile10.html.

[15] At the beginning of the war in Afghanistan (during the week of October 8, 2001), National Security Advisor Condoleezza Rice called the networks on the carpet for airing a videotape of bin Laden. Apparently, the pipeline for the tape had not been controlled by the overlords, as later (manufactured and "approved") bin Laden tapes were. This is just one small example of the control our shadow government has over U.S. mass media. On a daily basis, "[n]ot only do the so-called reporters have to get approval beforehand, including the quotes in an article, the White House can alter the original quotations." (Jim Romensko, http://www.poynter.org/. Romensko's site is well-known among journalists for its reporting and commentary on the media industry.

Speculative trading of stock in 9-11 targets[16]
Air Force stand-down[17]
U.S. Military deployment prior to the attack[18]

---

[16] See links to Michael C. Ruppert's "Criminal insider trading lead directly into the CIA's highest ranks" (http://www.ecologynews.com/cuenews43updates.html). The "official response" was that there was nothing out of the ordinary about the transactions, but the deviation in numbers from normal trading and the nature of "put options" belies this position. CNN also reported this story, but it was later removed from their website. The latest investigations of this trading have been expanded to include 38 stocks. On September 15, 2001, *The New York Times* reported that Mayo Shattuck III resigned, effective immediately, as head of the Alex (A.B.) Brown unit of Deutschebank, (http://www.fromthewilderness.com/free/ww3/02_11_02_lucy.html).

[17] See links at http://www.emperors-clothes.com , including the articles "Criminal Negligence or Treason", "Mr. Cheney's Cover Story", "Guilty for 9-11:Bush, Rumsfeld, Myers", "Scrambled Messages", and "Frequently Asked Questions about 9-11." This story also aired on Canadian television as "The Great Deception," on 1/28/02 on the Insight Mediafile at Vision TV (see http://emperors-clothes.com/indict/deception.htm. Plots concerning the hijacking and use of aircraft as suicidal bombs had been known to the U.S. intelligence community for some time. See Jim Gomez and John Solomon, *The Associated Press*, "U.S. warned about possible attacks in 1995," 3/6/02 in *Boulder Daily Camera* and numerous admissions by the FBI that such warnings were routinely ignored (David Johnston, "F.B.I. Says Pre-Sept. 11 Note Got Little Notice," http://www.nytimes.com/2002/05/09/national/09BURE.html?). One might note that in two separate news clips, Bush claimed to have seen the plane hit the first tower long before such footage had been aired by the networks. There has also been a detailed report written on the use of remote control devices and software to steer the planes. See http://www.flybynews.com/cgi-local/newspro/viewnews.cgi?newsid1014738186,11057, which would explain why such unskilled pilots were able to perform the intricate maneuvers needed to hit the targets. Eyewitnesses also report that Flight 93, which was brought down in Pennsylvania, exploded prior to its crashing. One must also say that the failure of the Air Force to respond according to standard procedures, given that "on Sept. 10, a group of top Pentagon officials suddenly cancelled travel plans for the next morning, apparently because of security concerns" (Source: *Newsweek*, Sept. 24, 2001 issue, story by Evan Thomas), refutes any argument that officials were surprised by the attacks.

[18] A friend of mine writes, "I was dating a Marine at the time and when I awoke and heard the news that fateful morning, I phoned him. And I phoned him and phoned him all day. Turns out he was in a briefing and couldn't be reached. The catch is that he was called for his briefing before the first plane hit—fifteen minutes prior, or something!—and was notified that there was a 'situation.' He

Implosion and explosion of WTC[19]

worked in the Antiterrorist unit, but had completed his service. He had served during the Bosnian War. So, he couldn't talk to me about it, and our relationship actually went down hill from there." Even if this soldier's call was only a precautionary action against possible terrorist actions, it shows that the government was, at certain levels, aware of the nature of the threat, contrary to what Bush, Cheney, and the rest of the junta has depicted. Clearly, this information contradicts any attempt to attribute the stand down of the Air Force to a lack of understanding about the intent of the hijackers. If fighter jets from Andrews Air Force Base in Washington had been instructed to carry out their squadron's mission, they could easily have intercepted the jet that was supposedly guided into the Pentagon. Instead, as we've already noted, Cheney lied to NBC News concerning the reasons why no jets intercepted the hijacked airliners. "Throughout the northeastern United States are many air bases. But that morning no interceptors respond in a timely fashion to the highest alert situation. This includes the Andrews squadrons which have the longest lead time and are 12 miles from the White House. Whatever the explanation for the huge failure, there have been no reports, to my knowledge, of reprimands. This further weakens the 'Incompetence Theory.' Incompetence usually earns reprimands." (http://emperors-clothes.com/indict/deception.htm)

[19] See Olivier Uyttebrouck's "Explosives Planted in Towers, New Mexico Tech Expert Says," *Albuquerque Journal*, September 21, 2001 (the on-line version of this story has "mysteriously" disappeared from the newspapers website), and Romero's apparently forced retraction in John Flaherty and Jared Israel's "In Curious Battle: An Expert Recants on Why WTC Collapsed" @ http://www.emperors-clothes.com/news/albu.htm
(Also, see http://home.comcast.net/~jeffrey.king2/Unanswered_Questions.htm). Additionally, seismic evidence indicates that explosives were detonated the moment before the towers imploded. This is also confirmed by a frame-by-frame analysis of the video of the collapse, wherein new plumes of smoke appeared immediately following the detonations. It might also be noted that the debris from the towers was scrapped and sold quickly to avoid any chemical analysis concerning the nature of the combustion. The removal of the debris destroyed evidence consistent with the detonation of thermite (which would explain the pools of melted steel, a byproduct of the thermite reaction), which melted the central columns triggering the collapse several seconds later. Many New York fire fighters agree with this analysis
(http://www.prisonplanet.com/analysis_lavello_050503_bombs.html) and, in fact, were ready to contain the fires when the detonations occurred. Note that for the buildings to come down the way they did, ALL of the load bearing supports on the ground floor would have had to fail at EXACTLY THE SAME TIME. So who put the explosives in the towers? Not surprisingly, there are witnesses who report that WTC workers who arrived early (5 AM) on 9-11 were told to leave the parking area by intelligence agents who were gathered around various vehicles. This, too, is consistent with the fact that molten steel was discovered where the 47 central

Seismic and eye-witness evidence for WTC implosion and explosion[20]

Executive branch collaboration in visas for hijackers[21]

---

support columns (of each building) were connected with the bedrock (*American Free Press*). Finally, in 2006, the key evidence in this thread showed up when Steven Jones, a retiring physics professor at Brigham Young University in Utah, was given samples from ground zero and found traces of thermite, a "high-powered, sulphur-laced explosive meant to 'cut through steel like it was butter.'" (John Aguilar, "Panelists raise doubts over 9/11," *Boulder Daily Camera*, 10/30/06) Finally, a third building, Building 7, which was not hit by any planes, was also imploded, falling perfectly in its footprint. Since then, an organization of licensed architects and engineers has verified the implosions (www.AE911truth.org), foreknowledge by the police and media, as well as numerous eyewitness accounts of the explosions that accompanied the collapse.

[20] Michael writes in 2003: On Thanksgiving, 2001, I am introduced, through a friend, to woman who works for a couple whose son worked at the World Trade Center. On the morning of September 11, 2001, he goes to work uncharacteristically early and is told in no uncertain terms by officials guarding a fleet of limousines to "get the hell out" of the parking garage. And let's not forget, the President's brother, Marvin Bush sat on the board of the company which had the contract for WTC security, as well as for Dulles Airport and United Airlines. (http://www.infowars.com/articles/sept11/marvin_bush_secrecy_surrounds_role_911.htm, http://www.infowars.com/print/Sept11/bush_security_link.htm, http://video.google.co.uk/videoplay?docid=3384141135554576594.)

As for the eyewitness evidence of the implosion and explosion, various films clearly show the occurrence of both. The foremost analysis of these films was produced by a group composed of over 1,000 professional architects and engineers (http://www.ae911truth.org/).

[21] The ease at which visas were issued from the U.S. embassy in Jeddah, Saudi Arabia links the hijackers and others "terrorists" to a joint training operation of the CIA and bin Laden in the U.S. See "CIA complicit on September 11?" at http://www.straightgoods.ca/ViewNote.cfm?REF=1267 and Daniel Hopsicker, "Mohamed Atta connected to the Saudi Royal family?" 3/8/02, @ http://www.madcowprod.com/index21.html. Why did high-ranking U.S. intelligence officers continually override Michael Springman, the former U.S. Visa Bureau chief in Saudi Arabia, when he wouldn't give visas out to suspicious characters who had no evident reason for wanting to enter the U.S.? "In Saudi Arabia I was repeatedly ordered by high-level State Department officials to issues visas to unqualified applicants." (Greg Palast, *The Best Democracy Money Can Buy*, Plume Books, New York, 2003, p. 102.) Another compelling fact that backs up the claim that the hijackers were let into the U.S. and abetted by the government in carrying out their plans is that, contrary to the FBI's "official" chronology of events, Mohammed Atta and Rudi Dekkers (the owner of Huffman Aviation, where a number of the hijackers were trained) were good friends,

The CIA's relationship with bin Laden[22]

maintained their public relationship up until August, 2001, and that the FBI was told this by witnesses three days after the attacks (http://www.fromthewilderness.com/free/ww3/031403_dekkers.html). Why has this been covered up?

[22] Michael writes in 2003: See Alexandra Richard's "CIA Agent Allegedly Met Bin Laden in July", from *Le Figaro*, 10/31/01, translated by Tiphaine Dickson, reprinted @ http://www.emperors-clothes.com/misc/lefigaro.htm, where bin Laden was being treated at the American Hospital in Dubai for kidney complications. Or perhaps bin Laden was set up in much the same way as Saddam Hussein was set up by U.S. Ambassador April Glaspie. On July 25th, 1990, eight days before the outbreak of fighting in Kuwait and Iraq that set off the First Gulf War, Glaspie told Hussein that any aggression on his part against Kuwait would be treated as an intra-Arab conflict (*The New York Times*, 9/22/90). Though capturing bin Laden was originally the main objective (at least for public consumption) of the undeclared war in Afghanistan, having served its purpose to create a climate of hate, it has been overtaken by much broader objectives. Bin Laden will never be caught, unless by mistake or a simulated version. Besides, his family and the Bushes are too intertwined financially. They both profit immeasurably from military construction and equipment purchases in Saudi Arabia. And contrary to public information, Osama is not estranged from his family (*Baltimore Sun*, 4/14/01, on Osama's relations with his mother, and *San Antonio Express-News*, 11/14/98, for Osama's relationships with his brothers, and the aforementioned article from *Le Figaro* on visits by his family when he was in the hospital). Thus, some al-Qaeda fighters escape each skirmish, and the CIA is in pursuit of DNA from the bin Laden family to be able to (you choose) prove or stage Osama's death ("U.S. Seeks Source for Some bin Laden DNA," http://www.nytimes.com/2002/02/28/international/asia/_28DNA.html and "U.S. Is Studying DNA of Dead Al Qaeda and Taliban Combatants," http://www.nytimes.com/2002/03/15/international/asia/15AFGH.html and "U.S. Concludes Bin Laden Escaped at Tora Bora Fight: Failure to Send Troops in Pursuit Termed Major Error," http://www.washingtonpost.com/wp-dyn/articles/A62618-2002Apr16.html). [Domestically as well, Attorney General John Ashcroft is seeking to expand the government's DNA database (*The Associated Press*, "Ashcroft seeks expansion of DNA samples database," 3/6/02, in *Boulder Daily Camera*).] The point is to further the Bush II administration's agenda of continual war, which serves armaments manufacturers (including many that benefit the former President [and daily advisor to the current President] George H. W. Bush-controlled Carlyle Group), expand U.S. control of worldwide oil production, and create a general climate of fear that excuses assaults on the Bill of Rights and the oppression and criminalization of anyone, foreign or domestic, opposed to such policies. See Jim Lobe, "The War on Dissent Widens," 3/12/02, @ http://www.alternet.org/story.html?StoryID=12612. Clearly, control over Osama bin Laden's identity and his whereabouts enables the "war on terrorism." All

investigations of Osama bin Laden and the bin Laden family were curtailed after George W. Bush stole the Presidency (*Agence France-Presse*, 11/4/01.) As far back as 1996, the Sudanese government offered to turn over Osama to the U.S. (*The Washington Post*, 10/3/01), and in October, 2001, much admired FBI agent John O'Neill complained in the *Irish Times*, "The US State Department – and behind it the oil lobby who make up President Bush's entourage – blocked attempts to prove bin Laden's guilt." This report is confirmed by the *Times of India* (11/7/01), and emphasizes the long-term "connections between the CIA and Saudi Arabia and the Bush men and bin Ladens." President Clinton, too, rejected opportunities to eliminate bin Laden at least three times: the first came from Sudanese officials, who offered to extradite him from Khartoum in 1996 ("Clinton's bin Laden gaff," *The Australian Sunday Times*, Jan. 7, 2002), the second came from the United Arab Emirates in July of 2000 ("FBI and US Spy Agents Say Bush Spiked bin Laden Probes before 11 September," by Greg Palast, *The Guardian*, Nov. 7, 2001), and the third came from Saudi Arabia, who offered to place a tracking device in the luggage of bin Laden's mother before she went to visit him in Afghanistan (http://www.freedom-force.org/hop.htm). In the end, "[o]n November 7, 2001, the London *Guardian* reported that they had obtained FBI documents showing that investigation of members of the bin Laden family in the U.S. had been stopped upon orders from the White House." (*Ibid.*, Palast)." This strategy has been confirmed by the military: "One defense official claimed a bin Laden escape could benefit the war on terrorism because popular support for continued military action in other regions would remain strong." ("Bombs halted; search continues," by Jonathan Weisman, *USA Today*, Dec. 19, 2001. p. 1A.) Who says Osama bin Laden still doesn't work for the CIA? This strategy, of encouraging terrorism and then using it to justify aggression, is clearly born out by U.S. underwriting of Islamic fundamentalist textbooks and extremist schools ("US aid cash for schools that teach terrorism," *Los Angeles Times* (*Sydney Morning Herald*), 4/16/03). Though we may generally question his opinions, when Syrian President Bashar Assad questions the existence of al-Qaeda ("Syrian leader doubts al-Qaida is real," *The Associated Press*, 5/25/03) we believe he may be on to something—this group of "terrorists" was organized by U.S. intelligence as a foil for their aggressive designs in the wake of the demise of the Soviet bloc. On December 12, 2007, Dan Froomkin, writing in the *Washington Post*, notes concerning the continuing CIA coverup of the actual events of 9-11 that "Robert Scheer writes in his San Francisco Chronicle opinion column: 'When the CIA destroyed those prisoner interrogation videotapes, were they also destroying the truth about Sept. 11, 2001? After all, according to the 9/11 Commission report, the basic narrative of what happened on that day - and the nature of the enemy in this war on terror that Bush launched in response to the tragedy - comes from the CIA's account of what those prisoners told their torturers. The commission was never allowed to interview the prisoners, or speak with those who did, and was forced to rely on what the CIA was willing to relay instead. 'On the matter of the existence of the tapes, we know the CIA deliberately lied, not only to the 9/11 commission, but to Congress as well. Given that the Bush administration has for six years refused those prisoners any sort of public legal exposure, why should we

Appendix 8   «   685

The Bush and bin Laden family ties[23]
U.S. totalitarianism[24]

---

believe what we've been told about what may turn out to be the most important transformative event in our nation's history? On the basis of what the CIA claimed the tortured prisoners said, President Bush launched a 'Global War on Terrorism,' (GWOT), an endless war that threatens to bankrupt our society both financially and morally.'" (http://www.washingtonpost.com/wp-dyn/content/blog/2007/12/12/BL2007121201438_pf.html)

[23] Michael writes in 2003: See "The Gang's All Here: Bush Sr. In Business With Bin Laden Family Conglomerate Through Carlyle Group," at http://www.globalcircle.net/1gnn1014kg.htm, Jared Israel's "Transcript of BBC Report: 'Has Someone Been Sitting on the FBI?'" [12 November 2001] at http://www.emperors-clothes.com/news/probetrans.htm, "BUSHLADEN" [8 October 2001] at http://www.emperors-clothes.com/news/bushladen.htm and "Gaping Holes in the 'CIA Vs. Bin Laden' Story," at http://www.emperors-clothes.com/news/probestop-i.htm . Also, see Jean-Charles Brisard and Guillaume Dasquie, *Bin Laden: The Forbidden Truth*, published in France (2002), which describes the U.S. State Department's interference in investigations of bin Laden.

[24] Michael writes in 2006: So far, what we've seen as a result of 9-11 is thousands of people arrested, detained, and abused without charges (for example, http://www.rense.com/general24/atroc.htm). Five years later, with only one of these detainees still in jail (Martha Endoza, "1 man still locked up from 9/11 sweeps," *Associated Press*, Oct 14, 2006), and only one conviction (Zacarias Moussaoui, see Neil A. Lewis, "Psychologist Says Moussaoui Is Schizophrenic," *The New York Times*, April 18, 2006), it's clear the arrests and detentions are a cover-up for the real perpetrators. As if what has already been done toward creating a police state were not bad enough, like some awful dream combining apartheid and Nazism, the government is now floating the idea of national ID cards. See http://www.almartinraw.com/column37.html and Jonathan Turley, "A National ID? Beware of what you wish for," *Los Angeles Times*, 1/13/02. It's worth noting that about 40 states already issue driver's licenses with bar codes or magnetic stripes that carry standardized data (http://www.nytimes.com/2002/03/21/technology/circuits/21DRIV.html?). Also see, Scott Lindlaw, *The Associated Press*, 1/25/02, "Bush wants an $38 billion for anti-terror programs," in *The Denver Post*, 1/25/02. A few days later, Vice President Cheney proposed that a military command be set up to coordinate the "defense" of North America (see "Cheney backs N. America Commander," *The Associated Press*, 1/28/02, in *The Denver Post*). Later, we are told that a "shadow" government has been created, without the consent of Congress, on the pretext that Washington, D.C. could be destroyed by a terrorist attack (*The Associated Press*, "Lawmakers briefed on 'shadow' government," 3/6/02, *Boulder Daily Camera*). The scariest part of all of this is that the shadow government, the CIA and its network of assassins, drug traffickers, gun-runners, and political operatives, has been around for years, the only change being that it is now firmly

U.S. fascist propaganda[25]

Control of Middle Eastern and Central Asian oil sources[26]

---

in control of the U.S. government and seeking a means to legitimize itself. (See http://www.fromthewilderness.com/free/ciadrugs/ssci.html)

[25] "An evil exists that threatens every man, woman and child of this great nation. We must take steps to insure our domestic security and protect our homeland." (--Adolph Hitler) Terrorism, like drugs, is a word that has been usurped by those in control of the state for their own nefarious purposes. In the U.S., the junta engages in the very same activities that they criticize in others, including bombings, drug-trafficking, gun-running, money-laundering through off-shore banks, election fraud, *coups d'état*, and assassination. (For an inside look at CIA drug operations, see http://www.fromthewilderness.com/free/ciadrugs/ssci.html. Yet, the administration attempts to link drug use and the support of terrorism [http://www.nytimes.com/2002/04/02/business/media/02ADCO.html?], pretending it does not engage in the same activities, all the while continuing to line the pockets of supporters [U.S. television networks] through an expensive anti-drug propaganda campaign.) The new anti-terror laws, pushed through after the state-sponsored events of 9-11 and the follow-up anthrax scam, are clearly being used for purposes outside those that were used to excuse the legislation in the first place (Dan Eggen, "Patriot Act used for more than anti-terror," *The Washington Post* [*San Francisco Chronicle*], 5/21/03).

[26] U.S. strategy to control foreign oil reserves is driven by Peak Oil, meaning that while worldwide oil consumption continues to increase, current levels of oil production coupled with known oil reserves places a specific timeline on the depletion of remaining supplies. Discovery of new oil has been declining since the '60's, worldwide consumption rate exceeded worldwide discovery rate in 1981, and worldwide production will peak between now and 2010. After that, at present consumption rates, oil will be depleted in thirty to forty years. Despite what may be promulgated in the mass media, U.S. foreign policy and military actions are directed at securing oil reserves (see: Graham Paterson, "Alan Greenspan claims Iraq war was really for oil," *Sunday Times*, 9/16/07; Chris Floyd, "Bush Surge Aimed at Securing Iraqi Oil," @ http://www.lewrockwell.com/floyd/floyd53.html; and *Democracy Now*, "New Iraq Oil Law To Open Iraq's Oil Reserves to Western Companies," http://www.democracynow.org/article.pl?sid=07/02/20/1523250), which in turn supports the overall consolidation of money and power by those who control such reserves (not to mention the private control of U.S. currency by the Federal Reserve and the state apparatus itself). Afghanistan and Iraq are only the beginning. "The Enron-Cheney-Taliban Connection?" (Ron Callair, *Albion Monitor*, 2/28/02, at http://www.alternet.org/story.html?StoryID=12525) is an exposé of how the mutual interests of the Bush II administration and Enron were at stake in India and the war in Afghanistan. Further details of this policy are available in "It's the Oil Pipeline, Stupid" (Peter Dale Scott, *Pacific News Service*, 3/5/02 at http://www.alternet.org/story.html?StoryID=12548). Other sources on Peak Oil, and the targets that follow Iraq (Saudi Arabia and Nigeria) include

Control over former Soviet Union territory[27]
Repeal of environmental protections[28]

---

http://www.fromthewilderness.com/free/ww3/051503_saudi_africa.html and http://www.peakoil.net/ASPOstatrew/ASPO-Stat-Rev-Intro.doc. As made clear in former Carter administration Secretary of State Zbigniew Brzezinski's *The Grand Chessboard – American Primacy and Its Geostrategic Imperatives* (Basic Books, 1997), the plan to grab Afghanistan and the surrounding oil fields had been around for at least four years by the time the ruse of attacks on the World Trade Center set the details in motion. Indeed, the Defense Planning Guidance document form 1992 argued that "the core assumption guiding U.S. foreign policy in the 21st century should be the need to establish permanent U.S. dominance of virtually all of Eurasia." (Jim Lobe, "The Anniversary of a Neo-Imperial Moment," AlterNet.org, 9/12/02) This same strategy was updated in "Rebuilding Americas' Defenses: Strategies, Forces And Resources For A New Century," by Bush, Cheney, Rumsfeld, Wolfowitz, et al, in September, 2000 (including the idea of a "new Pearl Harbor" to institute the program and a "Homeland Defense" for internal security), before the final details of the 2000 election theft had been worked out. The Bush team later followed up with the "National Security Strategy of the United States," in September, 2002, reiterating the same themes for public consumption. This strategy to control major oil producing sites is one of the reasons U.S. military spending is significantly greater than the next five highest nations combined. The partitioning of Iraq (see Katarina Kratovac, "Call for regional Iraq echoes U.S. plan," *Associated Press*, 10/13/07) and Saudi Arabia, should the dynasty topple, are part of the logistics of that plan.

[27] U.S. troops were first deployed in the Soviet republic of Georgia on 2/21/02. "[T]he personnel include Special Forces troops, who specialize in counterterrorism operations, and Air Force logistics personnel normally based at Incirlik, Turkey." (http://www.stratfor.com/products/premium/read_article.php?id=203242)

[28] Michael writes in 2003: The list of the Bush-Cheney junta's attacks on environmental protections is too long to fully detail, but here's a start: suspension of rules implemented during the Clinton administration to limit road building in the national forests, loosening of standards for arsenic in drinking water, the continued attempts to drill in the Arctic National Wildlife Refuge and other wilderness areas, withdrawal from the Kyoto Protocol on global warming, numerous appointments of industry operatives to environmental posts, a national energy plan (Cheney's infamous meetings, the minutes from which he successfully kept secreted from the Government Accounting Office and others) hatched by the very criminals in the energy industry who have been rigging energy prices in California and elsewhere, rule changes to put the timber industry's goals foremost in the management of the national forests, opening of 1.5 million acres of the Gulf of Mexico to oil drilling, weakening of the Clean Air Act (including a "Clear Skies" initiative that "actually enables industries to pollute more over a longer period of time, and avoids regulating carbon dioxide emissions." [Natural Resources Defense Council]), easing controls on genetically modified crops, attempting to limit the Environmental Policy Act of 1969 to permit military

688   »   Anatomy of Treason

Destruction of the social fabric[29]

Government infiltration by pseudo-religious fundamentalists[30]

---

destruction of marine habitat, slashing funding for cleanup at dozens of Superfund sites, weakening the rules protecting wetlands, protecting American corporations from overseas suits for industrial pollution, abandonment of family planning measures in the U.S. and around the world, destruction of marine mammal habitats for military sonar testing, and continued defoliation in the Amazon and related tropical basins (by American military controlled counterinsurgency forces) on the premise of fighting cocaine production.

[29] See: "Wealth distribution disparity growing: Richest 1 percent own 40 percent of global assets," *Associated Press* in the *Chicago Sun-Times*, December 6, 2006 (http://www.suntimes.com/business/161312,CST-FIN-fill06.article), Matt Crenson, "GAO chief warns economic disaster looms," *Associated Press*, Oct 28, 2006; Steven Greenhouse and David Leonhardt, "Real Wages Fail to Match a Rise in Productivity," *The New York Times*, August 28, 2006; Jonathan Tilove, "Minority Prison Inmates Skew Local Populations as States Redistrict," *Newhouse News Service*, Saturday, March 16 2002; *The Associated Press*, "Senate Advances Health Care Coverage Bill," in *The New York Times*, May 9, 2006; Greg Palast, "African-American Voters Scrubbed by Secret GOP Hit List," *Democracy Now!* and *BBC*, June 16, 2006; Steven Greenhouse and Michael Barbaro, "Wal-Mart to Add More Part-Timers and Wage Caps," *The New York Times*, October 2, 2006; Linda Greenhouse, "Women Suddenly Scarce Among Justices' Clerks," *The New York Times*, August 30, 2006; Brian Beutler, "Senate moves to give Bush more power to wiretap," http://www.rawstory.com/printstory.php?story=307; Linda Greenhouse, "A Supreme Court Setback for Whistle-Blowers; *The New York Times*, May 31, 2006; "Drug Company Profits Skyrocket $8 billion (27%) After New GOP Medicare Law Takes Effect," www.BuzzFlash.com, 09/20/2006; Pat Eaton-Robb, "Homeless Families on the Rise, with No End in Sight," *Associated Press*, 10/8/07; Brian Grow & Keith Epstein, "The Poverty Business: Inside U.S. companies' audacious drive to extract more profits from the nation's working poor," Business Week, 5/21/07, Tony Pugh, "U.S. economy leaving record numbers in severe poverty," *McClatchy Newspapers*, 2/23/07.

[30] Michael writes in 2002: The list begins with the President himself and Attorney General John Ashcroft, who, by any account, are too blood-thirsty, greedy, and unforgiving to even pretend to be Christians, and continues, most recently, with Dr. W. David Hager, Bush's appointee to head up the FDA. Dr. Hager is a practicing OB/GYN who describes himself as "pro-life" and refuses to prescribe contraceptives to unmarried women. Hager is the author of "As Jesus Cared for Women: Restoring Women Then and Now," which blends biblical accounts with case studies from Hager's practice. In another book Dr. Hager wrote with his wife, "Stress and the Woman's Body," he suggests that women who suffer from premenstrual syndrome should seek help from reading the bible and praying.

Massive military spending and corporate tax breaks[31]
Access to international drug trafficking sources[32]
Obstruction of potential investigations of the Bush family and others criminals[33]

---

[31] Ask yourself, "Qui bono?" (Who profits?) During the week of 2/3/02, Bush proposed to fund the largest military budget increase in history by severely cutting back on domestic programs including environmental initiatives and job training (not to mention cuts to Medicare and the gutting of its appeals process [http://www.nytimes.com/2003/03/16/politics/16HEAL.html, http://www.washingtonpost.com/ac2/wp-dyn/A13200-2002Feb2]). This is on top of the gigantic tax rebates that have been proposed for corporations that "overpaid" taxes going back to the 1980's and the bail-out of various industries, such as airlines and insurance (http://www.nytimes.com/2002/04/09/national/09INSU.html, http://www.nytimes.com/2002/04/30/business/30INSU.html?), adversely affected by imperial ruse of 9-11. (Tax cuts for wealthy individuals soon followed: $1.5 trillion over ten years. Not even billionaire investor Warren Buffett could stomach such greed [see "Buffett: Dividend tax cut is unfair," *The Denver Post*, National Briefing, 3/14/03, and "Buffett calls tax cut 'welfare' for the rich," *The Denver Post*, 5/21/03]. Nevertheless, by a vote of 51-50 [with Cheney breaking the tie], the Senate approved a $330 billion tax cut package.) By 3/22/02, the administration was back on capital hill asking for an additional $27 billion in emergency funds to strengthen domestic security, wage the war on terrorism, and expand the war beyond Afghanistan (see http://nytimes.com/2002/03/22/politics/22PENT.html?). Occasionally, the administration is able to wrap military buildup and anti-environmentalism into the same package (see http://www.nytimes.com/2002/03/30/politics/30ENVI.html?).

[32] On 1/4/02, the *Christian Science Monitor* reports on the explosion of drug trafficking in Florida following 9-11. On 2/18/02 the *Financial Times* reports that the estimated opium harvest in Afghanistan in the late-spring 2002 will reach a world record 4,500 metric tons. The *Far Eastern Economic Review* (4/18/02) and *The New York Times* (7/8/02) report on the assassination of Afghan Vice President Hajji Abdul Qadir, whose attempts to curtail the resurgence of opium ran counter to the CIA's sponsored programs. On 3/1/03, Agence France-Presse (via ClariNet via FromTheWilderness.com) report that Afghanistan has replaced Myanmar as the number one opium producing nation in the world. Finally, the CIA's and Bush/Cheney ties to the drug running (http://www.fromthewilderness.com/free/ciadrugs/index.html) can be tracked back to Iran-Contra and beyond. Cooperation between the CIA and Latin American drug cartels continues today ("Mexico Drug Plane Used For US 'Rendition' Flights: Report," Agence France Presse, September 5, 2008).

[33] "Afghanistan is a convenient war. All the previous congressional investigations of the Reagan and Bush regimes fraud have disappeared. These include

investigations into the $59 billion "missing" from HUD, the more than $10 billion "missing" from the Indian Affairs trust fund, and the $1.3 trillion procurement fraud from the Department of Defense. The investigation into illegal weapons trafficking in the Redstone Arsenal in Huntsville, Alabama has also been stopped." (From "Imperial America and the Homeland Colony: Return of the American Caesars" @ http://www.almartinraw.com/column41.html). One should also note the systematic means that the Bush II administration has used to hide its records from public scrutiny, including an Executive Order (No. 13,233) providing special protection for presidential papers, and the housing of Bush II's gubernatorial records in his father's presidential library. (See Mike Allen and George Lardner, Jr., "Former Presidents win more secrecy," from *The Washington Post*, as reprinted in *The Denver Post* on 11/2/01, and "New White House Order on Secrecy of Historical Presidential Records is Unlawful" @ http://www.citizen.org/pressroom/release.cfm?ID=896. In a defeat for Bush II, the Texas Attorney General has ruled the papers are subject to the state's open-records law. There was some movement in Congress to overturn Bush II's attempt to shield Reagan's and Bush I's papers (see http://www.nytimes.com/2002/04/13/arts/13ARCH.html?). On another front in the administration's assault on open records, in October, 2001, Attorney General John Ashcroft revised the rules under which federal agencies have to comply with the Freedom of Information Act saying, in part, "when you carefully consider FOIA requests and decide to withhold records ... you can be assured that the Department of Justice will defend your decisions." (Ellen Nakashima, "White House secrecy stirs frustration," *The Washington Post*, 3/3/02 in the *Boulder Sunday Camera*) Later, Ashcroft issued a gag order on lawyers in the Justice Department's Civil Rights Division curbing debate on the administration's retreat from enforcing employment discrimination laws. Then, on March 4, 2002, the White House said that Tom Ridge, the director of homeland security, would refuse to testify before the Senate concerning the president's request for $38 billion in domestic security programs (http://www.nytimes.com/2002/03/05/politics/05RIDG.html?). Following on the heels of a court order to turn over documents related to campaign contributors dictating energy policy, the administration has offered a compromise concerning Ridge's testimony (http://www.nytimes.com/2002/03/26/politics/26RIDG.html? and http://www.nytimes.com/2002/04/04/politics/04RIDG.html?), but the Senate has, so far not budged on the principle of accountability for funds and has refused to recognize the administration's attempt to establish a precedent of exemption (http://www.nytimes.com/2002/04/05/politics/05RIDG.html), even after Ridge testified behind closed doors with a House Appropriations subcommittee (http://www.nytimes.com/2002/04/11/poltics/11RIDG.html?). On 5/2/02, Ridge avoided testifying before the Senate Appropriations Committee by meeting with selected Republican senators. This effort at hiding documents, avoiding budget scrutiny, holding detainees incommunicado, and shielding witnesses, in addition to the suppression of facts concerning 9/11 air defenses, WTC explosions, Bush II's premature indication that he had seen video of the attacks, his failure to interrupt his schedule after he knew of the attacks, and former U.S. President George H.W.

Neo-cons call for another Pearl Harbor to further agenda[34]
Coup strategies for the New World Order[35]

Bush and Dick Cheney's "meeting" at the White House on the morning of 9-11, looks like the behavior of men who had foreknowledge of the events, have something to hide, and have contempt for the democratic process and the citizens to whom they remain morally accountable. The same behavior has apparently rubbed off on Pentagon officials who, on 2/11/02 "refused at its midday briefing to own up to any likelihood that U.S. troops beat 27 blameless Afghan civilians, helped the CIA kill three scrap-metal scavengers with a remote-control Hellfire rocket supposedly intended for bin Laden, or threatened the life of a Washington Post reporter looking into that incident." (Jim Hoagland, "Dead or alive?", *The Washington Post*, 2/15/02 in *The Denver Post*) No wonder the Bush administration has withdrawn from the world's first permanent war crimes tribunal (http://www.nytimes.com/2002/04/12/international/12COUR.html?)—they rightfully fear being prosecuted. Even members of Congress who are attempting to investigate how U.S. intelligence supposedly failed to anticipate the 9-11 attacks are finding the administration recalcitrant (see "Senator: DOJ, CIA hindering 9/11 probe," *The Associated Press*, 5/9/02, in the *Boulder Daily Camera*).

[34] "Further, the process of transformation, even if it brings revolutionary change, is likely to be a long one, absent some catastrophic and catalyzing event – like a new Pearl Harbor." in "Rebuilding America's Defenses—Strategy, Forces and Resources For a New Century," A Report of The Project for the New American Century, September, 2000, p. 63 (http://www.newamericancentury.org/RebuildingAmericasDefenses.pdf). Signatories to the project include Jeb Bush, Donald Rumsfeld, Dick Cheney, and Paul Wolfowitz. Also, see http://empireburlesquenow.blogspot.com/2005/03/dark-passage-pnacs-blueprint-for.html.

[35] Follow the bouncing ball ... In 1962, the Joint Chiefs of Staff developed the Operation Northwoods plan designed to stage phony attacks against U.S. targets to justify invading Cuba (See http://www.emperors-clothes.com/images/north-int.htm). In 1968, Edward Luttwak, a conservative scholar with a long career in the national security system, wrote *Coup d'Etat: A Practical Handbook*. (See http://www.lumpen.com/magazine/81/coup2k/). There is evidence to indicate that materiel was pre-positioned in Pakistan as early as May, 2001, in anticipation of the war in Afghanistan (see http://www.almartinraw.com/column37.html), and that the U.S. government had known for quite some time of airport training camps aimed at suicide plane attacks as well as the WTC as a prime target (see http://www.emperors-clothes.com/indict/coast.htm). Finally, and most damning of all, the intelligence organizations of a number of governments, including Germany, Russia, and Israel, had foreknowledge not only of the events of 9-11, while others, including Britain and Pakistan (and the Taliban itself) were told by U.S. intelligence months before of the war planned for Afghanistan in October, 2001 (http://www.copvcia.com/free/ww3/02_11_02_lucy.html and

http://www.whatreallyhappened.com/preplanned.html). These facts have been confirmed by a former Pakistani Foreign Secretary, Niaz Naik, who said on September 18, 2001, that the US had been planning the invasion of Afghanistan for some time. He said he was told this by US officials at a UN-sponsored international contact group on Afghanistan which took place in Berlin. (*BBC News*, September 18, 2001 @ http://news.bbc.co.uk/2/hi/south_asia/1550366.stm) In addition, on September 11, 2001, employees of Odigo, Inc. in Israel, one of the world's largest instant messaging companies with offices in New York, received warnings of an imminent attack on the WTC less than two hours before the first plane hits. Law enforcement authorities have gone silent about any investigation of this. (http://www.fromthewilderness.com/free/ww3/02_11_02_lucy.html). Later, they attempted to call this timing "a mistake." There is also formal evidence, part of the court record in Toronto, that former naval intelligence officer Delmart "Mike" Vreeland, in a document sealed by his Canadian jailers in early August, 2001, described the events planned for 9-11 and that stated that U.S. Intelligence was aware of these plans
(http://www.copvcia.com/free/ww3/03_15_02_vreeland_safehouse.html).
The same thing happened in Florida: "On January 6, 2002, the *Orlando Sentinel* (in Orlando, Florida) reported that a prisoner in the local county jail had tipped off the FBI a month before September 11 that he had information about a pending terrorist attack in New York City and other targets. Walid Arkeh was an American citizen who previously fled to England to avoid prosecution on charges of dealing in stolen goods and slapping his child. He had been arrested in Britain and sent back to the United States after spending ten months in prison there. During that time he became friendly with three Muslim inmates whom he identified as Khalid al-Fawwaz, Adel Abdel Bary, and Ibrahim Eidarous. They had been imprisoned because of their involvement in the 1998 bombing of the American embassies in Nairobi, Kenya, and Tanzania. Arkeh told the FBI that the terrorists confided to him that something big was about to happen in New York. He said he would provide additional details if they would help him reduce his jail sentence. He was not exactly a model citizen, to be sure, but he was trying to alert authorities to the planned attack. He said: 'I didn't want to be a terrorist. I wasn't working for them, but I became a part of them.' He thought the FBI would be eager to have this information, but such was not the case. As reported by the *Orlando Sentinel*: [Arkeh] said the FBI agents didn't appear impressed, and one stood with his hand in his pocket impatiently asking, 'Is that all that you have? That's old news.' Arkeh went on to explain that, after the attack on September 11, FBI agents returned to his cell and threatened that he could be charged with co-conspiracy if he told anyone that he knew about the attacks ahead of time. The impact this had on him is evident in the *Sentinel*'s report: When pressed by the *Sentinel* about whether he knew about the Sept. 11 hijacking and targets ahead of time, Arkeh, a compact and muscular man, paused a long time and looked down at the ground. Then he raised his head and smiled: 'No. If I did, that would make me a co-conspirator.' ("Inmate says he told FBI about danger to New York," by Doris Bloodsworth, Orlando Sentinel, Jan. 6, 2002,

Appendix 8 « 693

U.S. government complicity in anthrax scares[36]

---

http://www.orlandosentinel.com/news/local/seminole/orl-asecterror06010602jan06.story?coll=orl%sD.) Shortly after that, Arkeh was moved to an undisclosed location by the authorities, and his name, his photograph, and all traces of his presence in the system disappeared from the Department of Corrections web site. To the outside world, he ceased to exist. (In the book, *1984*, George Orwell described such individuals as 'unpersons.')" (http://www.freedom-force.org/hop.htm)

[36] Despite initial attempts by intelligence organizations to link the Anthrax scares to bin Laden's group or the Iraqi government, the evidence has always indicated that these were perpetrated entirely by domestic organizations operating within the U.S. (See Jack Dolan and Dave Altimari, *The Hartford Courant*, "Ebola, anthrax samples vanished from Army lab in '90's," reprinted in *The Denver Post*, 1/21/02). Perhaps these covert actions, including the late night experiments at these labs, were being done by U.S. intelligence agents? The CIA's latest ploy is to plant this activity at the feet of someone who is dead, i.e., a hijacker. (See William J. Broad and David Johnston, "Report Linking Anthrax and Hijackers Is Investigated," http://www.nytimes.com/2002/03/23/national/23ANTH.html, and *Reuters*, "No New Evidence Linking Hijackers with Anthrax—FBI," http://www.nytimes.com/reuters/news/news-attack-anthrax-doctor.html). On another front, the CIA attempted to plant the story that al-Qaida planned to develop biological weapons (http://www.nytimes.com/2002/03/23/international/asia/23STRA.html?). The point is not whether those fighting against the United States would use anthrax (Hey, what are WE doing with it?), but from whom they got it. In the summer of 2002, it was reported that "nearly a month before the first reported outbreak, White House officials start taking the powerful antibiotic Cipro to treat anthrax. By the end of the year it will be known that the Ames strain of anthrax used in the attacks against Sens. Leahy and Daschle was produced by CIA programs coordinated through Fort Detrick, the Batelle Memorial Institute, and the Dugway Proving Ground. [Source: NBC; CNN; www.tetrahedron.org, www.judicialwatch.org] (http://fromthewilderness.com/free/ww3/02_11_02_lucy.html). In an attempt to get to the bottom of this conspiracy, a family representing one of the victims of the attacks filed a $50 million wrongful death suit against the government. Peter Frances China, "Widow of anthrax victim still looking for answers," *South Florida Sun-Sentinel*, Posted on Fri., Sept. 15, 2006 @ http://www.bradenton.com/mld/bradenton/news/local/15521753.htm). After failing to generate credulity for blaming Al Qaeda for the distribution of anthrax (James Gordon Meek, "FBI was told to blame Anthrax scare on Al Qaeda by White House officials," NY Daily News, 8/2/08), and despite killing 14 world-class microbiologists, word still got out that the anthrax used was from a U.S. military laboratory, so the junta shifted focus to the U.S. First, they tried to blame Steven J. Hatfill, a biowarfare expert, but ended up paying him $5.8 million for defamation (*The New York Times* got their lawsuit dismissed when a federal judge

Failure to convict so-called suspects[37]

Pre-determined attack on Iraq[38]

---

said their columnist did not act with malice when writing about whether a Hatfill was responsible for the 2001 anthrax attacks.) Finally, the FBI found their shill, parlaying the instability of Bruce E. Ivins, into what they claim was a suicide. Their evidence is unconvincing, but it is currently the "official" solution to the case.

[37] Despite rendition flights to various torture sites in Europe and elsewhere, and despite the psychops and torture at Guantanamo, there have been only a couple of convictions of "suspected terrorists" associated with 9-11. Moreover, the convictions of underlings and those driven crazy include no conspiracy charges. No surprise here, since the real conspirators are the U.S. junta perpetrators.

[38] As a result of the first Gulf War, President George H. W. Bush secured a major portion of the huge Rumaila oil field in Southern Iraq, which became part of Kuwait following a border adjustment of 80 kilometers. This helped Kuwait, a former British protectorate, where U.S. and British oil companies have huge investments, to double its pre-war oil output (See Christopher Bollyn's "War on Terror Profitable—Same Old Names, Faces Primed to Make Big Bucks Off Tragedy" @ http://www.americanfreepress.net/10_01_01/War_on_Terror_Profitable/war_on_terror_profitable.html and http://www.greenleft.org.au/back/1993/84/84p13.htm). This time around, the junta under George W. Bush has manufactured more reasons for going after Saddam Hussein: Such an action acts as a deterrent to a variety of investigations of the administration's activities leading up to and following the 9-11 Reichstag; it prevents an examination of the failing U.S. economy (Paul Blustein, "Global dollar selloff continues," *The Washington Post*, 5/20/03, John Berthelsen, "Sliding greenback highlights trade deficit," *AsiaTimes.com*, 5/23/03, and Jeannine Aversa, "Fed prepared to steady prices, *The Associated Press*, 5/22/03), which continues to dive from the economic pillage that has followed 9-11; and it distracts from the systematic rape of the U.S. Treasury and the nation's natural resources by the "New World Order." Above all, the war in Iraq secured 11% of the world's oil reserves. It is for these reasons, and not any concern over weapons of mass destruction (WMD) or human rights or "democracy," that the junta wages war in Iraq.

Just before the invasion of Iraq, in a grand display of imperial arrogance, the junta ordered the covering of the Rockefeller-donated reproduction of Picasso's *Guernica* that hangs at the United Nations building (1/27/03), so that international representatives would not have to contemplate the horrors of war while considering U.S. demands (Why should this be a surprise? Remember, Ashcroft already covered the bare-breasted statue of Justice in his own lobby. [see Ian Williams, "Picasso Under Wraps; UN Under the Thumb," GVNews.Net, 3/15/03, @ http://www.gvnews.net/html/Crisis/gvabs023.html]), but worldwide protest reversed this act. Despite resistance from two members of the security council, France and Russia, the U.S. (where officials were denying protest permits and blocking march routes [Liaz Featherstone, "Report from New York," *Alternet.org*, 2/16/03]) and its lackeys, Britain (only 20% of Britons supported the war at its onset, with 1 million Londoners protesting on 2/15/03), and Spain (over 800,000 Spaniards demonstrated against the war on 3/15/03), proceeded with their war plans.

Leading up to the actual hostilities, Bush's supporters in the construction industry (Bechtel Group Inc., Fluor Corp., Halliburton Co. subsidiary Kellogg, Brown & Root, Louis Berger Group Inc., and Parsons Corp.) were already bidding on a $900 million contract to rebuild postwar Iraq, and more contracts were to follow. "... [I]f anybody were to suggest that the president or anybody on the Hill should be able to provide a cap or ceiling on the price of defending liberty and freedom, we don't know it," said press secretary Ari Fletcher. (Joey Bunch and Karen Crummy, "GOP-linked firms already lining up to rebuild Iraq," *Denver Post*, 3/16/03). As U.S. and "coalition" troops approached Baghdad, the cost to the U.S. for the war was put at $75 billion. (Since that time, with the chaos that has followed [Roland Watson, "Bush 'is on the brink of catastrophe,'" Times {London}, 5/23/03, "UNICEF fears 'major crisis' on way in Iraq," *The Associated Press*, 5/19/03, and "US post-war effort seen as on the brink of 'fiasco,'" *Agence-France Presse*, 5/19/03], the price-tag continues to escalate. "'When is the president going to tell the American people that we're likely to be in the country of Iraq for three, four, five, six, eight, 10 years, with thousands of forces and billions of dollars?' Biden said." [Ken Guggenheim, "Defense official defends postwar strategy," 5/23/03)

In addition to continued antiwar demonstrations in the United States and around the world, dissatisfaction with the administration continued to mount with conservatives as well, particularly over the manufactured evidence attempting to link Hussein to al-Qaeda and Iraq's supposed nuclear weapons program before the United Nations (http://www.fromthewilderness.com/cgi-bin/MasterPFP.cgi?doc=http://www.fromthewilderness.com/free/ww3/032503_perfect_storm_2.html, David Ensor, "Fake Iraq documents 'embarrassing' for the U.S.," *CNN* Washington bureau, 3/14/03, and Ken Guggenheim, "Bush deceived U.S., Byrd says," *The Associated Press*, 5/22/03). After Iraq fell to U.S. forces, no one produced any proof that Iraq ever had the WMD capability that the Bush Administration claimed (Barton Gellman, "Hunt for Iraqi Arms Erodes Assumptions," *The Washington Post*, 4/22/03, and Ron Fournier, "Bush: Iraq's WMD May Have Been Destroyed," *Yahoo! News* [*The Associated Press*], 4/24/03). This failure to produce evidence was particularly shocking considering that U.N. weapon inspectors were barred from re-entering Iraq (Steve Holland, "U.S. Balks at Return of U.N. Inspectors to Iraq," *The Washington Post* [*Reuters*], 4/22/03), which left the field wide open for to the Bush team to fabricate evidence. (Later, they did come up with a couple of mobile vehicles mocked-up as laboratories. At that point, independent inspection teams were invited back in [Dafna Linzer, "U.S. invites team of global experts to inspect 2 labs," The

Associated Press, 5/21/03, and John Hendren and Tyler Marshall, "Looters prey on nuke site in Iraq," *Los Angeles Times*, 5/22/03]. It is also worth noting that in the middle of the scramble to find Iraq's WMD's, the U.S. Energy Department announced it restarted production of plutonium parts for bombs (Ralph Vartabedian, "U.S. starts atomic bomb work," *The Denver Post* [*Los Angeles Times*], 4/23/03), and that American soldiers broke the seals which allowed looting of Iraqi radioactive burial sites (previously bombed by Israel in 1981 and the U.S. in 1991). When it became clear that their premises for invading Iraq were smokescreens, coalition leaders reluctantly admitted other motives (See James Kirkup, "U.S., U.K. Waged War on Iraq Because of Oil, Blair Advisor Says," *Bloomberg.com*, 5/1/03, and Neil Mackay, "US: 'Saddam had no weapons of mass destruction,'" *Glasgow Sunday Herald*, 5/4/03). Finally, the U.S. group investigating Iraqi WMDs left the country (Barton Gellman, "Frustrated, U.S. Arms Team to Leave Iraq: Task Force Unable To Find Any Weapons," *The Washington Post*, 5/11/03). So, the truth is out: What we are witnessing is imperial fascism: the systematic expansion of monopoly capital as it feeds its intrinsic need to consume ever-more resources. On 5/3/03, ChevronTexaco reported that its profit for the first quarter is triple that of the same time the previous year, "lifted by a dramatic rise in oil prices." (*Rocky Mountain News*, 5/3/03)

Conduct of U.S. troops during the occupation that followed the takeover was in the tradition of conquerors, as the invaders encouraged plundering of Iraqi antiquities ["Bush's top cultural adviser steps down over looting of Iraqi Museum," *Agence France Presse*, 4/17/03, and Amy Goodman, "Robert Fisk: Looking Beyond War," *Democracy Now!* (carried by *Alternet.org*), 4/23/03] and murdered those who demonstrated against them (Edmund Blair, "Iraqis Say U.S. Troops Kill at Least 13 Protesters," *Reuters*, 4/29/03). A coalition of lawyers and human-rights groups is gathering evidence to prosecute the U.S. government for war crimes before the International Criminal Court in The Hague, Netherlands, a court newly-formed by a treaty to which the U.S. has refused to be a signatory (Tosin Sulaiman, "Coalition may face war-crimes accusations," *Denver Post* (*Knight Ridder Newspapers*), 4/24/03). Yet the junta, regaling in its booty, treated its own soldiers as mercenaries, reducing veterans' benefits by $28 billion dollars in the midst of the war (Jan Schakowsky, "At a time of war, how dare we reduce veterans' benefits?" *Chicago Sun-Times*, 4/13/03).

Throughout the war, U.S. mass media outlets aided the administration in the manipulation of events. Clear Channel Communications, one of the major beneficiaries of the deregulation of media ownership that has evolved since the Reagan era (the company owns 1225 radio stations [half of all U.S. stations]), even sponsored its own pro-war rallies and stopped playing music by artists who criticized the war effort (Jacob Jordan, "Cheers, not jeers, greet Dixie Chicks," *The Associated Press*, 5/2/03 and "Springsteen Backs Dixie Chicks," http://www.wnd.com/news/article.asp?ARTICLE_ID=32265). The Pentagon further facilitated the integration of the press into its propaganda machine by inducting, training, and embedding "reporters" into its ranks. Only a few members of the press attacked this journalistic sell-out (Merissa Marr, "BBC Attacks U.S. Media War Coverage," *Reuters*, 4/24/03, and "MSNBC's Banfield Slams War Coverage," *Alternet.org*, 4/29/03). The Secretary of State's son, Michael Powell, who heads up the FCC, promises to ease the way for ever-greater media consolidation. Only such monopolies, Powell says, can afford to cover war like the one in Iraq (Danny Schechter, "War Coverage Rewrites History," *Globalvision News Network* [carried by *Alternet.org*], 4/22/03), and in limiting the coverage to this, we might add, suppress any opposing views: When Ed Gernon, executive producer of the CBS miniseries, "Hitler: The Rise of Evil," suggested that the suppression of dissent in the U.S. prior to the invasion of Iraq bore a resemblance to the conditions that gave rise to the Third Reich, he was fired (Joanne Ostrow, "Hollywood goes paranoid," *The Denver Post*, 5/18/03).

While corporate-controlled media gloated over U.S. military success in Iraq (Vernon Loeb, *The Denver Post* (*The Washington Post*), "Rumsfeld enters Iraq in triumph, 5/1/03), the easy victory itself proved that the junta's arguments for the war—that Americans were in imminent danger from Hussein's mighty weaponry—was a lie. Destroyed by American and British forces in 1991 and bombed continually since then, the Iraqi army was incapable of mounting anything more than token resistance. (Arianna Huffington, "Victory Aside, the Invasion Was a Bad Idea," *Los Angeles Times*, 4/16/03, and Firas Al-Atraqchi, "Before You Cheer," *YellowTimes.org*, 4/14/03)

Further examples of the Bush-Cheney junta's imperial aims in the invasion are evident in their hollow promises to rebuild a "democratic" Iraq. One only need look at Afghanistan to see that they have no such intention: "*The New York Times* reports that not a single house has been rebuilt, even in Kabul, and that not a single inch of roadway has been paved throughout the country. Sharia law, which keeps women in burqas, remains in full force, still enforced by the same old Taliban-era judges." (See Ted Rall, Illustrator, Columnist, Radio Commentator and Author of "Gas War: The Truth Behind the American Occupation of Afghanistan," @ http://www.buzzflash.com/interviews/03/03/11_rall.html, 3/11/03, and April Witt, "Afghans rip Bush for lack of help," *The Washington Post*, 5/7/03)

The American-led invasion of Iraq has also split Europe into two camps, much to the delight of the administration, which sees the continent as a potential rival to its economic and military hegemony (Rupert Cornwell, "Bush on a revenge mission," *The Independent*, 4/26/03, and "Will Europe and Russia Seek to Check U.S. Power?" *The Power and Interest News Report* [PINR], 5/12/03). It should be noted, however, that the French and Russians were quick to support the U.S. position on dropping sanctions against Iraq once a behind-the-scenes deal was reached for some of the Iraqi oil that had been under contract to them during the Hussein regime, and a piece of the rebuilding contracts was promised (John Leicester, "Chirac appeals for unity," *The Associated Press*, 5/22/03, Colum

False linkage of Iraq to 9-11[39]

Lynch, "Russia, France, Germany to OK lifting sanctions," *The Washington Post*, 5/22/03, and Matthew Riemer, "The sanctions game," *YellowTimes.org*, 5/19/03).

In Iraq, in addition to the privatization of the oil fields (According to Fadhil Chalabi, a former Iraqi oil minister who serves as a key advisor to the U.S. government, the Iraqi oil fields must be privatized to attract foreign investment following the war. [Oliver Morgan, "Iraq may have to quit OPEC," *The Observer*, 4/27/03]), big money stands to be made off U.S. taxpayers who will pay Bush's and Cheney's buddies at Bechtel, Halliburton subsidiary Brown & Root, Fluor, et al., to rebuild that part of the country's infrastructure which will best benefit the victorious warlords. One need look no further than the fact that Bechtel board member and former Secretary of State under Reagan, George Shultz, who is also chairman of the Committee for the Liberation of Iraq, to understand how the war lobby works: corporate-sponsored state terrorism keeps taxpayer-sponsored military contracts flowing.

While the U.S. made plans for taking control of Iraqi oil production (Colum Lynch, "Plan lets U.S. control Iraq oil," *The Washington Post*, 5/9/03, and "U.S. Plan for Iraqi Oil Worries Russia," *The Moscow Times.com*, 5/12/03), arguments were being made to convert Iraq to Islamic rule (Steve Schifferes, "US 'should back Islamic Iraq,'" *BBC News*, 4/25/03, Jared Israel, "Key US Official says US 'Goal' in Iraq is ... Islamic Rule," emperors-clothes.com, 5/7/03, Patrick E. Tyler, "In Reversal, Plan for Iraq Self-Rule Has Been Put Off," *The New York Times*, 5/17/03, and Susan Sachs, "U.S., Britain withdraw support for an Iraqi general assembly," *The New York Times*, 5/18/03).

This is why Cuban premier Fidel Castro, himself a target of the junta ("David Ruppe, "Friendly Fire: U.S. Military Drafted Plans to Terrorize U.S. Cities to Provoke War With Cuba," *ABC News.com*, 11/7/01) has called U.S. foreign policy "fascist." As stated earlier, it's worth noting that Operation Northwoods, designed to make it look like Castro had attacked the U.S. to justify invading Cuba, is the same tactic that was later used by the junta to abet the 9-11 attacks and use them to invade Afghanistan and Iraq for oil and geo-political strategic advantage.

[39] Patrick E. Tyler, "President invokes Sept. 11 to press argument for war," *The New York Times*, as run in *The Denver Post* on 3/7/03. No evidence has ever been presented that links Saddam Hussein with al-Qaeda despite U.S. government claims. In fact, it is clear that neither the U.S. nor Britain ever had such evidence (Sidney Blumenthal, "Bush knew Saddam had no weapons of mass destruction," *Salon.com*, 9/6/07; *Think Progress*, "Bush Now Says What He Wouldn't Say Before War: Iraq Had 'Nothing' To Do with 9/11," http://thinkprogress.org/2006/08/21/bush-on-911; Jim Abrams, "Senate finds no al-Qaida-Saddam link," *The Associated Press* in the Boston Globe, 9/9/06; and

Other oil-rich countries to become targets[40]
"It couldn't happen here" mentality[41]

Colin Brown and Andy McSmith, "Diplomat's suppressed document lays bare the lies behind Iraq war," *The Independent*, 12/15/06).

[40] As if on cue, as the invasion wound down in Iraq, and U.S. military bases had been shifted to Qatar and Kuwait, "terrorist" bombs went off in Saudi Arabia, signaling the next phase in the oil wars (Michael C. Ruppert, "Saudi Arabia, West Africa – Next Stops in the Infinite War for Oil," http://www.fromthewilderness.com/free/ww3/051503_saudi_africa.html, 5/15/03, and "U.S., Britain closing embassies in Saudi Arabia," *CNN*, 5/20/03). Even Mexico is feeling the pressure (John Rice, "Mexicans Outraged by Immigration/Oil Move," *The Miami Herald* [*Associated Press*], 5/10/03), and unrest in Liberia becomes a gateway to Nigerian oil fields. But the most likely candidate at this point (2007) is Iran. (Sarah Baxter, "Pentagon 'three-day blitz' plan for Iran," London *Times*, 9/2/07; Paul Krugman, "Scary Movie 2," 2/11/07, http://welcome-to-pottersville.blogspot.com/2007/02/paul-krugman-scary-movie-2.html; "Russia warns against Iraq-style 'proof' in Iran nuclear standoff," Pakistan Daily Times, 9/25/06; Sean Rayment, "Government in secret talks about strike against Iran," *Telegraph*, 4/3/06, http://www.telegraph.co.uk/news/main.jhtml?xml=/news/2006/04/02/wiran02.xml&sSheet=/portal/2006/04/02/ixportaltop.html). Whether the over-stretched U.S. armed foreces have the wherewithal to follow-up on these threats is another matter.

[41] Michael writes in 2003: Indeed, this is one of the arguments used by David Corn ("When 9/11 Conspiracy Theories Go Bad," 3/1/02, http://www.alternet.org/story.html?StoryID=12536), which is the only semi-serious attempt by an American journalist to refute the many facts that strongly indicate there was, at minimum, a foreknowledge in certain government quarters of the 9/11 attacks. Mr. Corn goes on to say that the CIA is not smart enough to pull off such a plan (though apparently he believes that al-Qaeda is) and that no one, particularly Mr. Bush, would risk such a plot (As we've said, this is much like what DINA [the Chilean secret police] and the CIA (with George H.W. Bush at the helm) argued about their involvement in killing Orlando Letelier [Dinges and Landau, *op. cit.*]. Such a bold strategy is exactly what Hitler meant by "the big lie." To believe otherwise, that is, in the stupidity and incompetence of the junta, can only be described as the "conspiracy of ignorance theory," a ploy at which U.S. intelligence agencies and their surrogates have become quite adept. In attempting to make his case, Mr. Corn ignores most of the evidence available—such as stock speculation, the stand down by the Air Force, the perfect implosion of the twin towers and Building 7, the actions of the President, the very specific early warnings from various foreign intelligence sources (Russia, Israel, et al.), attempts to discredit a witness whose claim (that he warned of 9/11 a month prior to the attacks, which is verified by the Canadian courts [http://www.straightgoods.ca/ViewFeature.cfm?REF=372],

and attempts to liquidate another witness in Florida—and argues that his exclusive interviews with CIA agents (so much for credible witnesses and Mr. Corn's own credibility) leads him to believe they would never commit such crimes on *American* soil (emphasis mine). In many cases, including the assassinations of JFK, RFK, MLK, Malcolm X, and Orlando Letelier, and at Pearl Harbor, American interests were served by letting other organizations do their dirty work. Even those who don't believe that the Bush Crime Family coordinated the WTC attack, or let it happen, or even ignored its own intelligence and reacted to the attacks after the fact must admit that the Bush II agenda has been fully served by sins of omission and commission. It should be noted that one congressperson, Rep. Cynthia McKinney, D-Ga., publicly implied that a conspiracy exists (Juliet Eilperin, "Democrat implies conspiracy surrounding Sept. 11 attacks," *The Washington Post*, 4/12/02, at http://www.washingtonpost.com/wp-dyn/articles/A34565-2002Apr11.html.) The reaction to her speech came hard and fast. As lawmakers lined up to indict her, the President called the Speaker of the House to dissuade him from any investigation. (Instead, Democrats and Republicans alike conspired against her re-election, allowing 40,000 Republicans to cross-over in the primary and vote for their Uncle Tom candidate.) Within a couple of weeks, however, the news broke that the CIA had informed Bush II in the summer of 2001 that radicals associated with al-Qaeda were planning on hijacking commercial aircraft. As a result, Democrats have called for an investigation of what the administration knew and when they knew it. Clearly, this is just another official cover-up, as illustrated by the attempt of the administration to have war criminal Henry Kissinger chair the panel, and after his resignation, thwart attempts to appoint worthy nominees. As the sham proceedings began, the junta resisted the panel's every effort to subpoena documents ("The Secrets of September 11," *MSNBC.com*, 5/1/03, Dana Priest, "9/11 probe triggers fight to declassify CIA secrets," *The Washington Post*, 5/1/03, Frank Davies, "White House refuses to release Sept. 11 info," *The Miami Herald*, 5/5/03, and Larry Lipman, "Lawmakers urge Bush to release Sept. 11 information," *The Atlanta Journal-Constitution*, 5/23/03). This strategy continued throughout the investigation, including baring the Kean Commission access to certain databases or to copy those they were allowed to see. In another legal counterattack to calls for investigations, a Houston law firm was engaged defend Saudi Arabia against a $1 trillion lawsuit brought by the victims of the attacks. To further thwart the inquiry, the Bush administration has cleverly managed to: 1) question the Democrats' patriotism; 2) drum up the vague specter of new terrorist attacks; and 3) make the FBI the scapegoat for the intelligence community's systematic refusal to respond to various warnings ("Missed 9/11 signs tied to the FBI," *The New York Times*, 5/27/02). Based on this supposed failure, the administration has created a super-spy organization (The Office of Homeland Security) and increased funding for domestic surveillance.

History of corporate manipulation of the press[42]
The fascist model for controlling the press[43]

---

[42] Michael inserts in 2003: "In March, 1915, the J.P. Morgan interests, the steel, shipbuilding, and powder interest, and their subsidiary organizations, got together 12 men high up in the newspaper world and employed them to select the most influential newspapers in the United States and sufficient number of them to control generally the policy of the daily press. ... They found it was only necessary to purchase the control of 25 of the greatest papers. ... An agreement was reached; the policy of the papers was bought, to be paid for by the month; an editor was furnished for each paper to properly supervise and edit information regarding the questions of preparedness, militarism, financial policies, and other things of national and international nature considered vital to the interests of the purchasers." -- U.S. Congressman Oscar Callaway, 1917. Now, consider how corporate control of the Congress has changed the laws concerning ownership of newspapers and radio and television stations. Editorial control of the mass media in America today is dictated by far fewer people than in 1917, to wit: "We are grateful to *The Washington Post*, *The New York Times*, *Time Magazine* and other great publications whose directors have attended our meetings and respected their promises of discretion for almost forty years. It would have been impossible for us to develop our plan for the world if we had been subject to the bright lights of publicity during those years. But, the work is now much more sophisticated and prepared to march towards a world government. The supranational sovereignty of an intellectual elite and world bankers is surely preferable to the national autodetermination practiced in past centuries." --David Rockefeller, founder of the Trilateral Commission, in an address to a meeting of The Trilateral Commission, in June, 1991.

[43] The Agency for International Development (AID) sponsored a film that was paraded throughout post-war West Germany, which featured the *Littleton Independent* (Colorado) newspaper, extolling the virtues of small, hometown newspapers and a decentralized press. In America, since the 1980's, consolidation of media ownership has accelerated as the Congress has come under greater control of corporations. From a rule limiting station ownership to 7 AM, 7 FM, and 7 TV stations and 35 percent of the U.S. market we now have conglomerates like Clear Channel Communications Inc. which owns 1,225 radio stations, covering all 50 states. Soon, it is likely for the market cap to move to 50 percent of U.S. homes. See
http://www.nytimes.com/2002/02/20/business/media/20IMPA.html,
http://www.nytimes.com/2002/02/20/business/media/20BROA.html,
http://www.nytimes.com/2002/02/25/business/media/25REGS.html, and Jeff Leeds, "Deregulation built an empire," *Los Angeles Times*, 2/3/02 in *Boulder Sunday Camera*. This strategy of media consolidation and control is being accelerated under the vehemently anti-public interest regime of FCC chair Michael Powell (http://www.alternet.org/story.html?StoryID=12696,
http://www.nytimes.com/2002/04/03/business/media/03VOIC.html?).

Anatomy of Treason

Fascist attitudes[44]

The Reichstag model for *casus belli* [45]

More Hitler parallels[46]

U.S. fabrication of *casus belli* [47]

(Michael writes in 2007: Under Powell's successor, Kevin J. Martin, the monopolization of the media continues unabated (see Stephen Labaton, "Plan Would Ease F.C.C. Restriction on Media Owners," *The New York Times*, October 18, 2007.) For examples of how the press distorts or lies about events, see http://www.alternet.org/print.html?StoryID=12941 and http://www.emperors-clothes.com/articles/jared/distort.htm. Indeed, the idea that we have a free press has been long recognized as a myth, even by insiders: "There is no such thing, at this date of the world's history, in America, as an independent press. You know it and I know it. The business of the Journalist is to destroy truth; To lie outright; To pervert; To vilify; To fawn at the feet of mammon, and to sell his country and his race for his daily bread. You know it and I know it and what folly is this toasting an independent press? We are the tools and vassals for rich men behind the scenes. We are the jumping jacks, they pull the strings and we dance. Our talents, our possibilities and or lives are all the property of other men. We are intellectual prostitutes." John Swinton, former Chief of Staff, *The New York Times*, circa 1880. A recent example of corporate reaction to critical journalism is ABC-TV's decision to cancel "Politically Incorrect." "The show's host, Bill Maher, has alienated some advertisers, ABC executives, and even the White House press secretary, Ari Fleischer, with a comment he made soon after the terrorist attacks of Sept. 11." (http://www.nytimes.com/2002/05/14/business/media/14ABC.html) All of which only proves A.J. Liebling's famous dictum – "Freedom of the press is guaranteed only to those who own one."

[44] While "Deutschland ueber Alles" has not replaced the "Star-Spangled Banner," the attitude that it engendered for the Nazis is not dissimilar to the "my country, right or wrong" mass hysteria currently drummed up by use of our own national anthem, the (modified) Pledge of Allegiance, and other forms of flag-waving and military presence at all major public events.

[45] Much like the Emperor Nero setting fire to Rome, evidence clearly indicates that Hitler's cabal burned the Reichstag, then conducted the investigation and used their "findings" to galvanize Germany against anyone they (the Nazis) considered enemies of the state. "[I]t is the leaders of the country who determine the policy and it is always a simple matter to drag the people along, whether it is a democracy, or a fascist dictatorship, or a parliament, or a communist dictatorship. Voice or no voice, the people can always be brought to the bidding of the leaders. That is easy. All you have to do is tell them they are being attacked, and denounce the peacemakers for lack of patriotism and exposing the country to danger. It works the same in any country." --Reichsmarschall Hermann Goering

[46] *Op. cit.*, Adolph Hitler, *Mein Kampf* (Also see *Appendix 8 – Anatomy of Treason*, footnote 12).

U.S. newspapers and the CIA[48]
Government control of the Internet[49]

---

[47] There is historical evidence indicating that the sinking of the U.S.S. Maine (which precipitated the Spanish-American War), the reporting of hostilities in the Gulf of Tonkin (which was used as an excuse to escalate the undeclared war in Vietnam), and the lack of preparedness at Pearl Harbor (which shook Americans out of isolationism and into WWII) were all inside jobs—the work of agents provocateurs or other intelligence conspiracies. How timely that on June 14, 2002, tapes were released from the LBJ Library that claim to confirm that U.S. naval vessels were indeed attacked on August 4, 1964. At this late date, it becomes increasing difficult to determine if suppressed documents and tape recordings have been tampered with, if the CIA attacked these ships to create an excuse, or if the North Vietnamese just got tired of having U.S. warships in their waters. However, Ben Bradlee, editor of *Newsweek* at the time of the supposed attack, insists that no such event ever occurred (See Ben Bradlee, "Deceit and dishonesty – the first James Cameron Memorial Lecture, *The Guardian* (London), 4/29/87 @ http://emperors-clothes.com/archive/bradlee.htm). The Joint Chiefs of Staff apparently took these "flag events" to heart when they drafted Operation Northwoods, a plan to stage attacks against the U.S. that would look like they had been perpetrated by Castro ("David Ruppe, "Friendly Fire: U.S. Military Drafted Plans to Terrorize U.S. Cities to Provoke War With Cuba," *ABC News.com*, 11/7/01). Further evidence on the Gulf of Tonkin hoax was recently detailed in Agence France Presse, "Report Reveals Vietnam War Hoaxes, Faked Attacks," January 9, 2008.

[48] A detailed rundown of the timeline of events leading up to and following 9-11 can be found at http://fromthewilderness.com/free/ww3/02_11_02_lucy.html . For the connections of the Sulzbergers (publishers of *The New York Times*) to the CIA see Ashley Overbeck's "A Report on CIA Infiltration and Manipulation of the Mass Media," @ http://www.geocities.com/cpa_blacktown/20000318mediaoverb.htm , and "Snow Job: Establishment Newspapers Do Damage Control for the CIA," @ http://www.thirdworldtraveler.com/Media/EstabPapersCIA_WMOZ.html . This manipulation of the media is a continuation of the same tactic used by J.P. Morgan in 1915, as referenced earlier in this chapter (footnote 42). It is also worth noting the hegemony of a few media conglomerates over the television networks and White House press corps, also referenced earlier in this chapter (footnote 43).

[49] See, "The Internet is being hijacked," Jeff Chester, Center for Digital Democracy (http://www.alternet.org/story.html?StoryID=12696) Also, consider that The Public Safety and Cyber Security Enhancement Act of 2001 automatically classifies any "cyber crime" as an act of "terrorism," and that the government's Carnivore system monitors all Internet traffic. Thankfully, this agenda was postponed on September 29, 2006, when, after passage by the House, the Senate narrowly defeated a bill that would have killed "Net Neutrality" and allowed corporate takeover of the Internet by AT&T and Verizon. "No thanks to our own local so-called Democratic congressman, Mark Udall," Michael notes.

Government disinformation[50]

Control over the 9-11 investigation[51]

Voting fraud in Florida: the actual coup d'état[52]

---

[50] In an effort to maintain its propaganda mill, the Bush administration sought to create an official agency of disinformation called the Office of Strategic Influence. The public outcry was too great for such a ploy at this time. But that hardly slows down the propaganda, given the snow job that the media conglomerates are doing with their daily dose of spoon-fed disinformation doled out to them by the administration. So, why would they need a new outlet? Perhaps to making lying legal and avoid any exposure when they're caught. See "Pentagon Readies Efforts to Sway Sentiment Abroad," http://www.nytimes.com/2002/02/19/international/19PENT.html, "Bush Will Keep Wartime Office Promoting U.S.," http://www.nytimes.com/2002/02/20/international/20INFO.html, and "A 'Damaged' Information Office Is Declared Closed by Rumsfeld," http://www.nytimes.com/2002/02/27/international/27MILI.html. For a perspective on how disinformation campaigns are conducted, see Maud S. Beelman, "The Dangers of Disinformation in the War on Terrorism," http://www.icij.org/about/beelman1.html and H. Michael Sweeney, "Twenty-Five Ways to Suppress Truth: The Rules of Disinformation," http://www.gwb.com.au/gwb/news/photo/truth.html.

[51] Despite calls by some Democrats for an independent inquiry of 9-11, the investigation is being conducted by appointees of the junta, who will decide which evidence warrants further scrutiny. In other words, it's another whitewash.

[52] As mentioned before, 57,000 voters were purged from the voting rolls. Katherine Harris, the Florida Secretary of State under Governor Jeb Bush, claimed these Democrats and minorities were felons (Bush and Harris managed to increase this amount to about 90,000 purged voters for Jeb Bush's re-election campaign in 2002. [In the South, where felony convictions prohibit future voting rights, a criminal justice system that charges and convicts blacks at a rate geometrically disproportionate to that of whites, is a convenient way of reducing minority registration. These laws remain in force throughout the Deep South, and in Florida alone prohibited 650,000 people from registering, including one in three African-American men.]) This story was ignored by the large American media conglomerates, though it made front page news in London. In addition to these purges, roadblocks were set up in minority precincts to keep voters from the polls, absentee ballots were tampered with, voter registrations were illegally executed, and voting machines were hacked. (See http://www.lumpen.com/magazine/81/coup2k/ and the definitive examination of actual voter roles in "The Great Florida Ex-con Game: How the 'felon' voter-purge was itself felonious," *Harper's Magazine*, March 1, 2002.) Rather than investigating these criminal acts, the Justice Department filed suit on 5/29/02 against three Florida counties. In a shameless attempt to limit damage to Bush and Harris, the Justice Department claimed that "it found no credible evidence that any Florida residents were intentionally denied their right to vote …" (Pete Yost,

Corporate control over the Supreme Court[53]
Other books presenting related evidence[54]
Assassination of witnesses[55]

"Inquiry: Polling problems minor," *Associated Press*, 5/29/02). To complete the crime, the *Associated Press* reported on 6/2/02 that Katherine Harris will be publishing a book to "debunk myths debated during the recount." In addition to this blatant attack on voting rights, the Republicans have control over the electronic voting machines and have apparently been using this access to steal a number of close elections, including those of Nebraska Senator Chuck Hagel (part-owner of the company that owns the company that installed, programmed, and largely ran the voting machines that were used by most of the citizens of Nebraska), Alabama Governor Bob Riley, and Georgia Senator Saxby Chambliss. Hagel's and Chambliss' "victories," along with the death of Democratic Senator Paul Wellstone in an airplane "accident," gave the Republicans control of the Senate following the November, 2002 elections. (See, "Was Paul Wellstone Murdered? •History Suggests It •Crash Inconsistencies Suggest It •Many, Including Some Members of Congress, Believe It. Democrats Twice As Likely To Die In Crashes," @ http://www.fromthewilderness.com/free/ww3/110102_wellstone.html, "If You Want To Win An Election, Just Control The Voting Machines," by Thom Hartmann, *Common Dreams News Center* @ http://commondreams.org/views03/0131-01.htm and "Computerized voting lack paper trail, scholar warns," and "Paper still needs to play a part in voting, computer scientist says," in *Stanford Report*, 2/4/03).

[53] That is, the five Republicans comprising the Supreme Court majority. For the whole sordid story, see http://www.angelfire.com/ca3/jphuck/Book4.html .

[54] Michael Moore, *Stupid White Men*, Regan Books, New York, 2002; Greg Palast, *The Best Democracy Money Can Buy*, Plume Press, New York, 2003; Noam Chomsky, *9-11*, Seven Stories Press, New York, 2001; Gore Vidal, *Perpetual War for Perpetual Peace* and *Dreaming War: Blood for Oil and the Cheney-Bush Junta*, Thunder's Mouth Press / Nation Books, 2002; and Michael C. Ruppert, *Crossing the Rubicon: The Decline of the American Empire at the End of the Age of Oil*, New Society Publishers, 2004.

[55] One known apparent murder of a witness related to the shenanigans behind 9-11 is that of a Tennessee drivers license examiner, who provided false IDs to a ring of Middle Eastern men that had access to the basement of the World Trade Center (see Bill Poovey, *The Associated Press*, "Burned car fuels intrigue over 9-11," *Rocky Mountain News*, 2/16/02). We await the fate of Delmart "Mike" Vreeland, a former U.S. Naval Intelligence officer who revealed the details of 9-11 to Canadian court authorities a month before it happened. He was, at last known contact, on the run in Canada. As we've mentioned a few retractions have been exacted as well, concerning the use of explosives at the WTC and the lack of military aircraft response. These figures, however, do not include the deaths of fifteen world class microbiologists (see

Corporate control over government regulators[56]

---

http://www.fromthewilderness.com/free/ww3/02_14_02_microbio.html, http://www.fromthewilderness.com/free/ww3/092402_biowarfare_cdc_plan.html, and Alanna Mitchell, Simon Cooper and Carolyn Abraham, "Scientists' deaths are under the microscope," http://www.globeandmail.workopolis.com/servlet/News/fasttrack/20020504/UMURDN?section=Science. (One can add Bruce Ivans, the FBI's so-called anthrax perpetrator, to this list.) We must also mention an article notable for its laughable statistical manipulation: *The New York Times* went to great lengths (7,800 words) to attribute these deaths to chance [See Lisa Belkin, "The Odds of That," *The New York Times Magazine*, Aug. 11, 2002, @ http://mba.tuck.dartmouth.edu/mdm/AlumniLearningLinks/TheOddsOfThat.html]. With the Enron scandal, there was one suspicious "suicide." More than this we don't know, since the "suicide note" has not been made public nor investigated. It's also worth noting that earlier in the energy deregulation wars, Jake Horton, a Vice President of Gulf Power, blew the whistle on sleazy accounting practices and days later was blown up in a company jet. After Enron, as widespread accounting scandals came under investigation, the treasurer of El Paso Corporation, one of several energy companies facing questions, also died of an apparent suicide (*Associated Press*, 6/4/02). This toll should also include Senators Mel Carnahan and Paul Wellstone (See, "Was Paul Wellstone Murdered? •History Suggests It •Crash Inconsistencies Suggest It •Many, Including Some Members of Congress, Believe It. Democrats Twice As Likely to Die In Crashes," @ http://www.fromthewilderness.com/free/ww3/110102_wellstone.html.), whose deaths were crucial to the Republicans gaining control of the Senate.

[56] The same goes for whether the Bushes and their fellow henchmen will be fingered as a result of the Enron scandal investigation. Between 1989 and 2002, Enron and company officials contributed approximately $6 million to Federal candidates and parties. Enron employees were the single largest funding source of George W. Bush's presidential campaign, and Bush used Enron Chairman Ken Lay's jet for his campaign transportation. Bush's cabinet and administration is filled with former Enron advisors and stockholders. 19 of the 21 members of the Senate Banking Committee, which held hearings on the matter, also received contributions. Enron officials (along with 17 other of the top 25 contributors to Bush II's presidential campaign), had numerous private meetings with Vice President Dick Cheney concerning the administration's energy policy (which, in many cases, was taken word-for-word from energy company proposals [http://www.washingtonpost.com/wp-dyn/articles/A28281-2002Mar27.html, http://www.nytimes.com/2002/03/27/business/27ENER.html?, http://www.nytimes.com/2002/03/28/politics/28ENER.html?, and http://www.nytimes.com/2002/04/04/politics/04ENER.html?]). Cheney, of course, refused to turn over records of these meetings. The General Accounting Office sued for access to these records and two different federal appeals courts ordered the administration to hand over the documents. When the documents were finally released, vast passages were blanked out or, in some cases, missing

(Bennett Roth, *Houston Chronicle*, "Energy Documents Released," 3/26/02, in the *Boulder Daily Camera*). Despite admitting to more extensive contacts with Enron that previously disclosed, the Bush administration dragged its feet in releasing any information. However, a federal judge refused to kill a variety of lawsuits seeking Cheney's energy task force notes ("Judge won't dismiss Cheney suits," 5/24/02, *Associated Press*). On another front, the Senate Governmental Affairs Committee was forced to subpoena the administration for all official documents ("White House staffers get Enron deadline, *Associated Press*, 5/25/02). In addition to its input on the Bush II administration's energy policy and for its contributions, Enron at its zenith was granted the ability to create a whole new unregulated business in energy derivatives (with the help of Sen. Phil Gramm, the number two recipient of Enron funds in the Senate, and his wife, Wendy. The Senate refused to close loopholes written into this law. See Richard Simon, "Senate rejects proposal on derivatives oversight," *Los Angeles Times*, 4/11/02.), had veto power over the appointment of federal energy regulators, had both Clinton and Bush II officials lobby the Indian government to protect an ill-conceived multi-billion dollar investment, and received a delay in government intervention that led to a share of the $12 to $30 billion in excessive charges during the California energy crisis that it helped create (See John Moyers, TomPaine.com, "Recuse Me! Congress Bought Off by Enron," 1/23/02 @ http://www.alternet.org/story.html?StoryID=12282 ; "Enron Total Contributions to Federal Candidates and Parties, 1989-2001," @ http://www.opensecrets.org/alerts/v6/enron_totals.asp; David Lazarus, *San Francisco Chronicle*, "Memo links Cheney to Enron," 1/30/02, *Boulder Daily Camera*; Dana Milbank; "Cheney won't release energy records," from *The Washington Post* as it appeared in *The Denver Post*, 1/25/02; Richard L. Berke; "Associates of Bush Aide Say he Helped Win Contract," *The New York Times*, 1/25/02; Molly Ivans, "Hands up! This is aggressive accounting!" *Creators Syndicate*, as it appeared in *Boulder Daily Camera* on 1/30/02; Michael Moore, "Enron Will Force Dubya's Resignation," @ http://www.alternet.org/story.html?StoryID=12330; Greg Palast, "Enron not the only bad apple," 2/1/02, @ http://www.gregpalast.com/detail.cfm?artid=114&row=0 ; Don Van Natta Jr. and Neela Banerjee, "Top G.O.P. Donors in Energy Industry Met Cheney Panel," http://www.nytimes.com/2002/03/01/business/01ENER.html; "Stop Lying About Enron!" http://www.howdarethey.org/whoppers.htm, which details much of the misinformation being spread by the administration and its supporters in Congress and in the media, or http://www.gregpalast.com/detail.cfm?artid=115&row=1, which shows that the British government and media were aware as early as 1995 of Enron's scam, while in America journalists were paid to shut up [see Richard Blow, "Enron Paid Off Top Journalists in Return for ... What?" at http://www.alternet.org/story.html?StoryID=12360 and "California Loses in Effort for More Power-Crisis Refunds" @ http://www.nytimes.com/2002/05/31/business/31ENER.html]). The Bush family ties to Enron began with George H. W., whose campaigns were also heavily financed by the company. In fact, the Bush I administration created the legal

Corporate tax evasion[57]
Government for sale[58]

---

exemption that allowed Enron to begin trading energy derivatives. (See Kevin Phillips, "The Bush family has been a prominent and well-rewarded collaborator in Enron's climb to national political influence," *The Los Angeles Times*, in *Boulder Sunday Camera*, 2/17/02). No wonder Bush and Cheney failed to curb Enron's fraud during the California Energy Crisis (Joseph Kahn, "Californians Call Enron Documents the Smoking Gun," Richard A. Oppel Jr., "How Enron Got California to Buy Power It Didn't Need," and Don Van Natta Jr., "Bush's California Energy Stance Faulted," all 5/8/02 in *The New York Times*). Michael writes in 2007: As we expected, the Enron investigations went no further than convictions for the company principals, who took the hit for the rest of the conspirators.

[57] Despite all the posturing about accounting controls, tax shelters, and offshore banking in the wake of the Enron scandal (David Cay Johnston, "Senators Assail Corporate Use of Bermuda as Tax Shelter," 3/22/02 [http://www.nytimes.com/2002/03/22/business/22TAX.html], wherein senior Senators from both parties called the use of tax shelters "greedy" and "unpatriotic" tax evasion), the laws protecting these practices continue unabated. On 4/26/02, by a vote of 334-90, the House approved an "accounting reform measure" that failed to address the revolving door between accountants and their clients. Those who voted for the bill received an average of $33,150 from Big Five accounting firms from 1989-2001 (http://www.howdarethey.org/news). Tax shelters and offshore banking were left untouched. In typical fashion, seeking to further transfer the tax burden from the rich to the poor, the Bush administration blamed the wave of offshore incorporations on an unfair tax code for American corporations. The same people who have no problem denying the U.S. Treasury revenues from their American profits and who encourage the citizenry to "buy American" and "Stand United" are the first to look for advantage in offshore headquarters and accounting. On 5/16/02, it was reported that House Republicans were "blocking an attempt by Democrats to force a vote on a measure that would prevent companies from avoiding income taxes by reincorporating in Bermuda and other offshore tax havens." (http://www.nytimes.com/2002/05/16/business/16STAN.html) Two days later, on 5/18/02, "Republicans led by Senator Phil Gramm of Texas and the accounting industry's trade group worked to kill a Democratic measure that would impose new rules on auditors, companies and investment banks in the wake of the Enron's collapse." (Stephen Labaton, "G.O.P. Fights Proposed Rules on Auditors," http://www.nytimes.com/2002/05/18/business/18ACCO.html)

[58] (The quote is attributed to John Emerich Edward Dalberg, 1st Baron Acton (1834–1902), British historian.) 43 major contributors to Bush's 2000 presidential campaign were rewarded with ambassadorships and other prestigious government positions. Anne Womack, a spokeswoman for the White House, said, "In every case, when we are seeking an individual to serve, their qualifications are scrutinized and they are chosen based on their merits." This is a perfect example of

Real campaign finance reform[59]

---

the derivative Calvinist misconception that Michael has repeatedly mentioned: Materialistic accumulation is taken as a sign of divine favor.

[59] Currently, the states of Massachusetts, Maine, Vermont, and Arizona are attempting to prove clean elections are possible. (See "Revitalizing Democracy" at http://www.neaction.org) As both Plato in *The Republic* and George Bernard Shaw in the introduction to *The Millionairess* argued, the rich have no business running the state, for the entrepreneurial skills required to create commerce run counter to spiritual values and the long-term evolutionary interests of society. Private monies must be eliminated from campaign finance, otherwise democracy will die at the hands of unbridled capitalism—i.e., the fascist state. The newest campaign finance law, passed by the Congress on 3/20/02 in response to pressures generated from the Enron scandal, is a small step in the right direction, but one that will not go unchallenged by those who equate unregulated capital to free speech (see
http://www.nytimes.com/2002/03/23/politics/23DONA.html?
and http://www.nytimes.com/2002/03/28/politics/28SUIT.html?).
On 5/31/02, the principal sponsors of the new law criticized the Federal Elections Commission's proposed rules for implementing the regulations (http://www.nytimes.com/2002/05/31/politics/31DONA.html).
This partisan control over election administration is why a constitutional amendment is necessary, which should (1) prohibit electronic voting machines and (2) institute independent oversight of elections along the lines of The Carter Center Democracy Program, though one not associated with a President (Carter) sponsored by David Rockefeller.

The body text of *Solomon's Proof* is set in 11-point Sabon LT. According to MyFonts (http://new.myfonts.com/fonts/linotype/sabon/), "In the early 1960s, the German masterprinters' association requested that a new typeface be designed and produced in identical form on both Linotype and Monotype machines so that text and technical composition would match. Walter Cunz at Stempel responded by commissioning Jan Tschichold to design the most faithful version of Claude Garamond's serene and classical roman yet to be cut. ... The name refers to Jacques Sabon, who introduced Garamond's romans to Frankfurt ..."

www.ingramcontent.com/pod-product-compliance
Lightning Source LLC
Chambersburg PA
CBHW021003230426
43666CB00005B/267